Elements of Banking

Elements of Banking

David Palfreman BA
Philip Ford BA ACIB

Pitman

PITMAN PUBLISHING
128 Long Acre, London WC2E 9AN

© David Palfreman and Philip Ford 1988

Second edition first published in Great Britain 1988

British Library Cataloguing in Publication Data
Ford, Philip
    Elements of banking.—2nd ed.
    1. Banks and banking—Great Britain
    I. Title   II. Palfreman, David   III. Ford,
    Philip. Elements of banking I and II
    332.1'0941   HG2988

ISBN 0 273 02952 5

Printed and bound in Great Britain

Contents

Preface   viii

Part one
1   Money   1
Origins of money   Coinage   Banknotes   Money today
Summary   Self-assessment questions   Assignments

2   Financial markets in the UK   42
The British banking system   The Bank of England
Money markets   Summary   Self-assessment questions
Assignments

3   The financial structure of a commercial bank   88
Introduction   The business of banking   The bank's
liabilities   The bank's assets   Controls on the banking
system   Summary   Self-assessment questions
Assignments

4   Savings and investment   122
Savings   National Savings   Banks and building societies
Other savings media   Capital market   Summary   Self-
assessment questions   Assignments

5   Interest rates   184
The nature of interest   Interest rate structure   Summary
Self-assessment questions   Assignments

6   Banks and their customers   215
Introduction   The banker-customer relationship   A
bank's legal rights and duties   Opening and operating an
account   Different types of accounts   The banking
ombudsman   Summary   Self-assessment questions
Assignments

7 Remittance of funds 254
Introduction Cheques The clearing system Other
clearing services Payments abroad Summary Self-
assessment questions Assignments

8 Banking instruments: an introduction 284
Negotiable instruments: what are they? Main types of
negotiable instruments Bills of exchange Cheques
Parties to a bill of exchange: their responsibilities and
rights Other negotiable instruments Summary Self-
assessment questions Assignments

Part two
9 Money supply and monetary policy 315
Introduction The money supply Monetary policy
Summary Self-assessment questions Assignments

10 Parallel money markets 348
The wholesale money markets Other financial markets
Summary Self-assessment questions Assignments

11 Personal services 375
Introduction Marketing financial services Personal
account services Investment services Financial
planning Travel services Summary Self-assessment
questions Assignments

12 Business services 420
Introduction Finance for business International
business Business support services Summary Self-
assessment questions Assignments

13 Lending 456
The principles of lending Banks and the Consumer
Credit Act 1974 Types of advance Types of borrower
Security Types of security Summary Self-assessment
questions Assignments

14 Financial statements 505
Introduction to financial statements Using financial
statements Financial statements and the lending banker
Summary Self-assessment questions Assignments

15 Property 547
Types of property   Ownership of land   Title to property
and its transfer   Taking property as security   Summary
Self-assessment questions   Assignments

16 Bills of exchange: the legal framework 607
Introduction   The legal characteristics of a negotiable
instrument   Types of holder   Liability of parties   The
progress of a bill of exchange   The collecting bank   The
paying bank   Summary   Self-assessment questions
Assignments

Index   650

Preface

The first edition was written for BTEC's modules *Elements of Banking 1 & 2* and because we saw no need for change we have retained its structure. Part One is self-contained but combines with Part Two to form a coherent whole. Nevertheless, we are conscious that our book is used extensively on other courses, in particular the Chartered Institute of Bankers' *Foundation Course* subject *Elements of Banking* and for parts of *General Principles of English Law*. In addition, it can be used for the Institute's new *Banking Certificate* subject *Banking: the Legal Environment* and covers much of the syllabuses for *Banking Operations 1* and *Banking Operations 2*. In short, we know that our book successfully satisfies a number of different markets.

Whatever the course, the principles and practices are similar. The classroom and the workplace are the best places to develop skills and the use of information and our primary aim in this book is to provide knowledge and explanations which can be used in student centred teaching. At the end of each chapter we have included a factual summary, self-assessment questions to test knowledge and understanding and ideas for assignments. The latter, suitably adapted and supplemented by background material perhaps, could form part of the assessment scheme for the BTEC modules.

In this second edition we have comprehensively updated the text in the light of developments in banking, legislation and the economy and endeavoured to make it even more 'user-friendly' and readable.

Our thanks must go to Wolsey Hall for allowing us to base some of the text on courses which we wrote for them, to John Beardshaw (co-author with David Palfreman of *The Organisation in its Environment*, Pitman Polytech) for use of material, and to our friends, colleagues and students for their helpful and kind (well usually!) comments and suggestions on the first edition. As usual, most thanks go to our wives—Hellen and

Shirley—and young families for their support and patience while we were otherwise occupied.

D P
P F

Part One

1 Money

Chapter objectives

After studying this chapter you should be able to:
- trace the evolution of money;
- outline the functions and attributes of money;
- list and define the forms that money takes in a modern economy;
- state the methods of measuring the money supply;
- explain the distinction between money and 'near money';
- state the shortcomings of money as an indicator of value.

The origins of money

We are all familiar with money. After all, we handle it every day of our lives and its use regulates many of our daily activities. Yet how often do we pause to consider just how artificial a device it is? Nevertheless, the invention of money was as crucial to the development of our modern commercial economy as the invention of the wheel was to the development of technology.

The need for money

Early man probably lived in small isolated communities where group efforts were pooled to satisfy group needs. There was no commerce with other groups. What the community could not provide for itself, it went without. Even today there exist simple human societies which retain this communal style of living in which individual skills are at a comparatively low level. Like a lone individual living in the wilderness and catering for his own needs without assistance, such societies have no need or use for money. As the control of environment develops, however, individuals begin to specialise in particular activities within the community as a whole and artisans and craftsmen of all types begin to appear. Beyond a certain point, the communal system of distribution of 'wealth' almost always seems to break down and another method has to be found to reward individuals fairly for their efforts. Usually, a commercial type of society develops in which individuals 'sell' the fruits of their labour (or just their labour) to the rest of society.

Barter

The problem for individuals is, quite simply, how to go about exchanging the things which they can produce for the things which they need but which are produced by others. The best carpenter in the world, for instance, cannot eat the things he makes; he has somehow to 'buy' his food with them. The obvious solution is barter: the direct exchange of one commodity for another. Thus, the carpenter may exchange a chair which he has made for a quantity of loaves produced by the baker. Unfortunately, this transaction depends on a 'double coincidence of wants': the carpenter wants bread and the baker wants a chair. What happens next time the carpenter wants bread if the baker decides that he has enough chairs for his needs?

The indirect exchange of goods may appear to offer a solution to this impasse but, in practice, it tends to create more problems than it solves. Suppose that the carpenter, having failed to persuade the baker to let him have any bread, discovers that the baker's wife needs a new set of kitchen pots but cannot find a potter who is prepared to take her husband's bread as payment. If a potter can be found who needs a chair, a three-way exchange might be arranged, with all three parties eventually obtaining the goods which they want. If a three-way exchange cannot be organised, a four-way trade would have to be sought, or five ways, or six ways. You can see how complicated such a system of trading could become.

The 'rate of exchange' between different articles, which is never simple to fix in a two-way barter, becomes a real source of difficulty in a multiparty trade. Clearly, both a chair and a set of cooking pots are each worth more than a single loaf but which of the two is worth more than the other? If the three parties cannot agree between themselves on the relative values of the three commodities, the whole deal may fall through. Furthermore, the problem of 'change' has to be overcome. If it is agreed that, say, the cooking pots are worth more than the chair, the potter will not hand over the pots until he receives some further item in addition to the chair to make up the balance. You might suggest that he should take a few loaves to even things up but then again we must remember that he did not want any bread in the first place, which is why this whole process was started!

A *medium of exchange*

What is needed is a medium of exchange on which all parties can agree and which can be used to express the *relative prices* of each of the goods which are to be exchanged. Once we have done this, we have invented money.

At this point it is fair to note that there have been societies which avoided the difficulties of barter by exploring different routes. The Peruvian Incas, for instance, are believed to have operated a system of total state control of the economy which provided for each individual's needs and which demanded from each individual an appropriate contribution to society's 'wealth'. In a very real sense, this is a development of the communal system of living, adapted to suit much larger units. Similarly, the medieval feudal system in Europe managed largely to dispense with the use of money by operating a very sophisticated form of barter economy. The lords provided for the needs of the people of the lower orders against payment in kind, either by way of direct labour in the lord's service or, in the case of freemen, by the contribution of a share of the individual's produce. Even so, money could intrude into this system, with people paying fees to be excused from their duty to work directly for their lord.

The functions of money

Once money has been invented, it soon comes to perform a number of different but related functions.

A *medium of exchange*

As we have seen, money was probably first devised to provide a medium for exchanging disparate commodities. It permits a simplified form of indirect exchange. The carpenter sells his chairs for an amount of money and then uses that money, or at least part of it, to buy his food. Likewise in a modern society, bank clerks sell their labour to banks for an agreed sum of money and then use that money to pay for the necessities of life: food, clothing, accommodation, and so on.

In the example which we have been considering, the three participants (and indeed their whole society) could have agreed to use bread as their money. In the early stages, items used as money would usually have an *intrinsic value* over and above their value as money. The holder would be reassured by the knowledge that he could use his 'money' either for its purchasing power or for its original purpose. Thus, the baker could have bought his pots for an agreed number of loaves and the potter could then likewise have purchased his chair using his 'money'. He would have some bread left over, which he could either eat or spend on something else. Significantly, the baker and the carpenter no longer need to meet to agree on the value of the goods which they are supplying.

A *unit of account*

The second function of money arises almost immediately: it comes to act as a unit of account by which the *prices of all commodities can be defined* and then *compared*. This, of course, simplifies the task of deciding how we wish to divide our income between widely disparate items. For this reason it is sometimes said that money acts as a 'measure of value'. And this is true if value is taken to mean both 'price' and 'worth', the latter being a much more subjective definition. Thus, we may say of an article at which we have been looking in a shop, 'It's not worth that price'. This could mean either that we believe that we could obtain the item elsewhere for less money, or that we are not prepared to pay so high a price for it, preferring to put our money to other uses which we think would be more rewarding. In either case we are using the money cost as our measuring rod.

A *store of value*

If we wish to purchase something very costly, we must first acquire sufficient 'wealth' to do so. Without money, this necessi- tates the stockpiling of other commodities pending their exchange for the desired item. This runs the risk that demand for the items held will diminish before the exchange can take place. It also causes problems for people who produce perishable items. Stockbreeders, for example, cannot indefinitely store meat; while trying to build up a store of wealth they would have to make an intermediate exchange of their meat for some more durable commodity.

In a similar fashion, the provident person will usually wish to build up a store of wealth out of which he can meet unexpected future needs. We often refer to this as a 'nest egg'. The use of money makes it relatively simple to accumulate just such an item, provided of course that the individual has a surplus of income over expenditure. By inventing money, we have now invented the concept of *saving*.

A *standard for deferred payments*

Finally, money can be used to set the level of a payment which is due to be made at some time *in the future*. Thus, our carpenter can enter into an agreement to produce a complete set of chairs and a table for completion next month in consideration for payment on delivery of an agreed sum of money. This is really an extension of the use of money as a unit of account. This function of money, of course, permits commercial *lending* to take place: a borrower can agree that if a lender supplies him with ten units of money today, he will pay back eleven units in three months' time. The *charging of interest* has become possible.

The attributes of money

Having established the need for money, society has to decide what article to use to fulfil the need. Of course, when money is first introduced, the decision is not usually taken consciously by holding a referendum or passing an Act of Parliament. It comes about by usage: people start to use a particular item as money and that article becomes, *de facto*, the currency of the society. At different times and in different locations throughout the world, many different items have been used as money. These include livestock, such as cows, sheep, camels, etc.; useful commodities, such as cigarettes, fish hooks, cocoa beans; things prized for their beauty, such as diamonds, cowrie shells; and the truly bizzare, such as pigs' teeth, discs of base metal, and oddly-inscribed pieces of paper!

Acceptability

The acceptability of a particular item as money is the first prerequisite for its use. In this respect, it really does not matter what we decide to use as money. If we cannot persuade most people to accept it, it will not work. As you saw when we were looking at the difficulties of the baker, the carpenter, and the potter, things would have been much easier to resolve if the loaves of bread produced by the baker could have been accepted as money. The potter did not want any bread *as bread*, but he might have been prepared to take it *as money* if he had known that everyone else with whom he dealt would also accept it as such.

Bread is a possible item to gain acceptance as money because it has an *intrinsic value* which does not depend on its use as a medium of exchange: it can also be eaten! Most items used as early forms of money had an intrinsic value, resulting either from their utility for other purposes or from the demand which there was for them because of their scarcity. Thus, for example, certain types of cowrie shells which have been used as money have an intrinsic value which does not arise because people wish to use them for a particular purpose but because they wish to possess them for their own sake.

Once people are used to the idea of money, they will usually be prepared to make use of items which have only an *exchange value*, acting solely on their faith in the item's continued acceptance by society as a whole. Even in a modern society, however, people will fall back on the use of valuable commodities as money if the delicate balance of the economic system is disturbed or somehow prevented from operating. For example, in the immediate post-Second World War period in Europe, many people lost faith in 'paper money' and would not accept it; cigarettes, nylon stockings, and chocolate (among other things) soon came to act as a substitute for money. They *became* money.

Uniformity

This is important as people will be less prepared to accept payment in units of currency which cannot be standardised, especially when the variations can affect their intrinsic value. This, of course, is where the use of livestock as money runs into difficulties. For instance, we could agree to pay you five horses a year for the rent of a farm which you own. When the time comes for payment to be made, you may be expecting to receive five young, healthy and well-fed yearlings. But we might try to give you five old, broken-down carthorses fit only for honourable retirement! Thus, the vital consideration is that each unit of currency should be *interchangeable* with each similar unit. If this can be achieved, people will not care which particular unit of currency they accept in payment of a debt. They will take any one, provided that it is of the correct face value. This attribute is sometimes called *fungibility* and it is, in fact, the reason why people do not check the serial numbers of £5 notes they are offered before deciding whether or not to accept them.

When money is not homogeneous, and different qualities of money are circulating, people will naturally try to hold on to as much of the 'good quality' money as they can, while disposing of the 'lower quality' money. For instance, where metal coins are in use, problems arise if the coins of a particular denomination do not all contain the same amount of precious metals. Thus, if some of our current £1 coins were made of gold while others were made of gold-coloured alloy (which in fact they all are), everyone would attempt to spend only the base metal coins, while holding on to any gold coins which they acquired. Sellers, of course, would try to avoid accepting payment in alloy coins. This is all because the gold coin would have a higher intrinsic value than the alloy coins.

There will always be differences in the intrinsic values of non-homogeneous forms of money, even if it is only the difference between a young horse and an old horse! Sir Thomas Gresham, a finance minister at the time of Queen Elizabeth I, was the first to notice the difficulties of using money of non-uniform quality, expressing his thoughts in a saying now known as 'Gresham's Law'. This maintains that 'bad money drives out good'.

Stability of value

Stability of value of the chosen form of money is an important factor in its acceptability. A form of money which is subject to constant depreciation could not function effectively as a store of value or as a standard for deferred payments. Potential savers, for instance, would be deterred by the anticipated loss of purchasing power of their funds and would decide either to spend all their money shortly after receiving it or to invest through some other medium.

Money which has only an exchange value depends for its stability largely on the *confidence of society* in its continued *purchasing power*. If that confidence is disturbed, the value of the money can be eroded by inflation. Money which has an intrinsic value is protected from the worst effects of inflation but is subject to the fluctuations of supply and demand for the item of which it is composed. If the price of the commodity falls, the purchasing power of the money will fall.

The supply of a particular form of money has a lot to do with its stability of value. For a thing to function as money, it *must be scarce*, although not so scarce that there is not enough to circulate and allow the economy to 'turn over'. This is why we could not use the leaves of trees as money: it would be far to easy to increase the supply by stripping the trees. When the Spanish *conquistadores* plundered the civilisations of South America, they flooded Spain with looted gold. The Spanish currency was based on gold which, of course, provided much of the motivation for going to the 'New World', and the sudden oversupply of this metal caused a rapid reduction of its purchasing power within Spain. The supply of money had outstripped the supply of goods on which to spend it. Another case can be found in the use of tobacco in prisons where, because of its scarcity, it acts as a substitute for the more normal forms of money which are denied to the inmates.

The supply of money can also be affected by the efforts of counterfeiters. If false money can be produced which cannot be distinguished from the real thing, it will be treated as real money and will for all practical purposes *become* real money. If it is large enough, the increase in supply will affect the value of money generally.

Divisibility

The divisibility of money into small units has already been mentioned. It is difficult to use large indivisible items to finance purchases which require only 'small change'. A problem experienced when using many items of intrinsic value as money is that their division into smaller pieces can reduce the value of the components to much less than their value as a complete whole. Some Iron Age societies are believed to have used axe-heads as a currency. Part of their value derived from their utility as potential tools; broken up into smaller pieces of metal, this utility was lost and their value reduced accordingly. In a similar fashion, livestock is difficult to divide into smaller units!

Durability

The durability of money also has an effect on its stability of value, where an item of intrinsic value is used. If the commodity is likely to wear away with use or deteriorate with age, it will naturally lose purchasing power. This would be the principal objection to the use of bread as money; constant handling would reduce it to crumbs very quickly. Even if it could be protected from this, it would go stale, become mouldy, and have to be thrown away within a short period of time.

Even if excessive wear does not reduce the purchasing power of money, it does cause practical problems and the early replacement of worn out currency is both costly and time-consuming. This, of course, was the reason for the introduction of the £1 coin in the UK in 1983. Paper £1 notes were circulating with such velocity that their useful life had been cut to less than a year and the continual need to recall old notes and issue new ones was causing a great deal of expense. The metal coins have a working life of many years.

Portability

The portability of money is the last of its important attributes. The item used must be capable of being easily carried about and it should therefore combine a high value with a low weight. It would not be very convenient to use coal as money as you would need a tonne of it to do the week's shopping!

Coinage

Of all the things which can be used as money, it soon became apparent that *metals* have great advantages. They most accurately fit the profile of attributes required of money. In a society which is incapable of mass production of metal, all useful metals have a high intrinsic value, so a considerable amount of purchasing power can be combined with small bulk and relatively low weight. Metals are durable and can be easily divided into small units or, where required, recombined into larger bars.

Precious metals

The early history of money saw the use of many metals including bronze, copper and iron. The so-called precious metals gold and silver, however, came to predominate principally because of their scarcity, which is just at the right level. Had they been any less commonly available, they would have been in too short supply to function properly as money and something else would have had to be found. On the other hand, if they had been more readily available, a situation would have arisen throughout the world similar to that which existed in pre-Columbian South America. There gold was so plentiful that it was viewed only as a pleasantly decorative metal which had the advantage of being easily worked. It was not very valuable.

An added advantage of precious metals is that they are especially resistant to corrosion, unlike iron which rusts or copper which oxidises. Gold, especially, is for all practical purposes impossible to destroy. It is reckoned that virtually all the gold which has ever been taken from the ground, apart from that which has been reburied either by accident or design, is still in circulation somewhere in the world. All the treasure of the Incas is still with us somewhere, whether it is incorporated into gold jewellery or in bars of gold bullion stored in the national treasuries of the world.

Coins

So it was that metals came to gain a wide circulation as money. Prices would be expressed in terms of a given weight of the chosen metal. From this it is but a short step to the production of *standard-sized* pieces of metal designed specifically to be used as money. This is clearly much more convenient than carrying a large bar of metal and having to saw off the appropriate amount each time a purchase is made. The weight of the standard piece of metal could easily be marked on it for ease of identification. Thus, the coin came into being.

The use of standard coins, however, immediately creates the danger that the unscrupulous will attempt to offer coins of slightly less than the expected weight. The practice of *clipping* became common. This involved paring shavings of metal from the edges of coins. If the doctored coins could be passed off at face value, the trickster would have as his reward the accumulated shavings of precious metal. Traders might therefore still wish to check that they were receiving the right amount of the metal in payment for goods sold; they would have to weigh the money which they had been offered. This is both safe and convenient; to this day banks find it easier to check large amounts of coin by weight rather than by counting.

A further problem affecting coins was related to the purity of the metal they were made of. In a society in which anyone may produce metal tokens which can circulate as coins, there will always be a temptation to pass off as pure coins which contain a proportion of base metal. Various tests could be applied to a coin to check the *fineness* of its metal. Its weight in relation to its size, the ease with which it can be bent, its resistance to scratching; these are all tests of the purity of the metal. However, they all add to the inconvenience. To overcome this problem and to promote the healthy functioning of a monetary system, the state began to play an active part in the issuing of coins.

The government could issue coins bearing its own symbol, often the effigy of the monarch of the country. Provided that the design of the coin was not too easy to counterfeit, it would act as the state's promise that the coin was what it purported to be and had its proper metal content. Over a period of time, the greater acceptability of the official coinage would discourage the use of other, less trustworthy coins.

Bimetallism is the term used to describe the situation which occurs when a state uses two different metals at once as the basis of its coinage, some coins being made, perhaps, of silver and others of gold. The arrangement has some advantages in international trade as it simplifies settlements with other countries which use either of the two metals as the sole basis of their currency. Within limits, it also helps the domestic value of the coinage by ironing out any minor fluctuations in the value of either of the two metals used. However, it is a difficult arrangement to pursue for any length of time as relative changes in the availability of the two metals will affect their relative worth. This will disturb the relationship between coins made of the different metals, thereby causing confusion. The people of 18th century England, for instance, needed to know that a golden guinea was always equivalent to 21 silver shillings, not that it could vary in value between 19 shillings and 23 shillings depending on the state of the bullion markets.

The *design* of coins and the form which they take is not vital to their ability to function as money. Early coins took many forms and throughout the world today coins of many different shapes are in use. There is, however, a principle of design that form should follow function; when the ideal shape is realised, it tends to resist change. It is for this reason, for instance, that the telephone handset has changed only marginally since the present basic design was introduced; it does its job better than any other design. So with coins, the optimum shape seems to be the disc, or a close approximation to it as in the UK 50p and 20p coins. We have already noted how the embossing of designs on coins came about. The *milled edge* which is seen on so many modern coins was invented in the 17th century as a means of protecting the coins against clipping.

Token coins

So far we have spoken of the development of coins which had an intrinsic value related to their metal content. You will be aware that modern coins, by and large, do not fall into this category; they are made of a hard-wearing alloy of base metals and cost much less than their face value to produce. How has this change come about?

The *debasement* of the coinage is always a temptation to the state when coins are expected to contain a certain amount of a particular precious metal. The process goes something like this. The people have come to accept particular coins as being genuine and good for their face value because they bear the government imprint. If the government calls in the coins, it can melt them down, mix some of the precious metal with a proportion of cheaper metals, and then reissue the coins to an unsuspecting populace who will continue to accept them at the same face value. The state keeps the surplus precious metal which it can use to pay its debts to other states (which will not perhaps be so trusting as its own subjects).

The process depends, of course, on the trust that the populace has in its rulers and their guarantees as to the value of the currency. While people have access to coins of the 'proper' content of metal, trust alone is never sufficient and the purchasing power of the debased currency will fall until it is more in line with its content of precious metals. Over a period, however, the populace will become more used to accepting and using coins which are not made entirely of precious metals. This prepares the way for the full acceptance of purely token money.

Fiat money is the technical term used to describe token money. It means that the coins are money solely because the government *says* that they are money. They owe their function to a government decree or 'fiat'. When people are confident of the stability and integrity of their state, they will be prepared to accept this money which has little or no intrinsic value. An important requirement is that the government must concentrate the issue of coins in its own hands and must maintain a close control of their supply. Oversupply of token coinage would have serious inflationary consequences, much like those resulting from the oversupply of gold that we noted in 'Golden Age' Spain. The effects, however, would be all the worse because, unlike the Spanish situation where the currency was based on gold, the purchasing power of the intrinsically valueless coinage would not be stabilised by its comparative value in relation to the currencies of other countries.

Because of the lack of any such stabilising influences, 'fiat money' is more subject to *fluctuations* in value than older forms of money. Its purchasing power will always be affected by the relationship between the supply of money and the supply of things to spend it on. (We will look at this relationship in more detail later.) Provided that confidence can be maintained in the state and its economic structure, confidence will be maintained in its currency which will thereby be able to function without having an intrinsic value.

The history of British coinage

The *silver penny* was the basis of the British coinage for a very long time. It is believed to be named after the Mercian king Penda and it was during Anglo-Saxon times that the *pound* came into existence when it was ruled that 240 silver pennies should together weigh one pound. The continued use of this unit of our currency is a living link with the days when money was measured directly by its weight.

The silver penny was retained after the Norman conquest when William the Conqueror established his mint at the Tower of London, producing pennies with a silver content of 2.5 grains troy. For the next 200 years this was the smallest coin in circulation in England. This was possible because, as we have already said, feudal society managed at least partly without money. If small change was needed, pennies were cut in half to provide halfpennies or in quarters to yield farthings (fourthings). Round coins of these denominations did not appear until the 13th century when increased monetary activity demanded their issue. Even so, for the following 300 years or more, shortage of smaller denomination coins caused problems. *Tradesmen's tokens* began to circulate as a form of substitute money, exemplifying the process which will always occur when the normally accepted form of money cannot be supplied. (By a similar process in Italy in the late 1970s, shopkeepers began to give change in the form of sweets or similar items because low denomination coins were not available.) To remedy the situation and to increase the supply of lower denomination currency, copper coins for lower values finally began to be circulated in England in the 17th century.

The *silver shilling*, equal to 12 pence, was introduced in 1494. It probably took its name from the weight which was used by traders to balance against a quantity of silver pennies when checking their value.

Gold was in comparatively short supply in medieval Europe. This meant that it was really too valuable to use as money. A *gold penny* was issued in 1257 during the reign of Henry III but, as its intrinsic value was higher than that of the silver penny, it was never circulated freely. This is an example of the operation of Gresham's Law. More successful was the *Rose Noble* of Edward III which was issued first in 1344 and had a value of 80 pence (a third of a pound). In 1489 Henry VII minted the first golden *sovereigns*. These had a value equivalent to one pound of silver and thus, although coins of this denomination did not come into regular circulation for some centuries, their introduction completed the basic components of the English currency as it remained until *decimalisation* in 1971. Twelve pennies made one shilling, and 20 shillings made one pound or sovereign.

The *gold standard* began to supplant the silver standard for English currency during the 17th century as gold became progressively easier to obtain and silver came into short supply. Very few silver coins were minted during the century. The *golden guinea* was first minted in 1664 during the reign of Charles II at the start of the period during which gold was coming into more ready supply. The worth of this coin in relation to the penny was not stabilised until 1717 when it was decreed that it would have a value equivalent to 21 shillings. Before that date, the 'exchange rate' between the two coins was determined by the relative supply and demand of gold and silver.

The *gold sovereign* took over from the golden guinea as a result of the Coinage Act of 1816 which formalised Britain's adherence to the gold standard. The British gold sovereign became recognised throughout the world as an acceptable currency for the settlement of international trade, thereby promoting the pound sterling as one of the major world currencies. The mint price of gold remained at £3 17s 10½d per standard ounce for most of the 200 years up to 1914. This formed the basis of the *international gold standard* which existed until then and was temporarily resumed as the *gold bullion standard* from 1925 until its final breakdown in 1931 (*see* below).

Modern token coinage

In the UK, this really followed the breakdown of the gold standard. We have already seen that base metal coins were introduced many centuries ago to represent very low denominations of money. At first these were made of copper, although in the 19th century their composition was changed to a more durable bronze alloy. Despite the alteration, many people continue to call small change 'coppers'. 'Silver' coins retained a significant silver content until quite recently, although the proportions of this to other metals in newly minted coins was subject to a series of alterations reflecting the changing market prices of silver. It was only after the Second World War that the decision was taken to substitute an alloy of copper and nickel in all newly minted coins. Older silver coins remained in circulation and the value of their metal content was by then significantly above their face value. The issue of the new composition coins enabled the government progressively to withdraw a large proportion of pre-war coins to extract their silver content. This was used to repay foreign debts which had been incurred meeting the cost of the war.

The general circulation of gold coins had ceased some time earlier than this. During the 19th century, the gold sovereign was gradually replaced in use by paper money. Bank of England notes were convertible into gold and apart from some periods of crisis such as the First World War, remained so up until 1931, when the Bank was released from its obligation to exchange its banknotes for gold on demand. From 1925 to 1931, single notes could not be exchanged for gold coins as these were no longer in circulation. Notes to the appropriate value could, however, be exchanged for bars of gold bullion. When the UK abandoned the gold standard in 1931, the convertibility of Bank of England notes was terminated altogether. Although a small number of gold sovereigns continue to be minted, their intrinsic value is far above £1 and they are solely used as an investment in gold. The gold-coloured £1 coins which were introduced in 1983 are, of course, made of an alloy which contains no gold at all.

Banknotes

Paper money in the form of banknotes is now so common and so universally accepted that you may be surprised to find that it has been in regular use in the UK only for a little over 300 years. Where did the idea come from?

Development of the banknote

The history of the banknote in the UK is closely intertwined with the history of commercial banking generally, both having their origins in the activities of the goldsmiths. (We look at the development of banking in greater detail in Chapter 2.)

Goldsmiths' receipts
You know that money is used as a *store of wealth*. From the holder's point of view, the one great disadvantage of using coins for this purpose is that they can be stolen by thieves. Their virtue of portability becomes a vice in this particular case. Many rich people began to deposit their surplus cash with the Royal

Mint which was securely housed in the Tower of London. This practice ceased rather abruptly in 1640 after Charles I appropriated for his own use £130 000 which was being held by the mint! The search was on for other locations where the wealthy could lodge their gold and silver coin for safe keeping.

Soon the goldsmiths were being asked to perform this service. The goldsmiths, of course, would have made their business premises secure so as to protect the stocks of gold and silver which they had to keep to carry on their trade. Holding a little more bullion on behalf of depositors would not therefore present goldsmiths with any special problems but it would save depositors the trouble and expense of making their own homes thief-proof. The goldsmiths made a charge for this service. They also found that they could make an extra profit by sorting through the many coins which came into their hands and extracting those which had a higher content of precious metals and therefore a higher intrinsic value. When clients requested repayment, they would be given coins of the lowest possible intrinsic value to the correct face value.

When coins were deposited, the goldsmith would issue a *receipt* for the appropriate sum. When the depositor wanted his money back, perhaps to pay a debt, he would return the receipt to the goldsmith and take the coins. In all probability, the coins would soon find their way back into the goldsmith's vaults because the recipient would want to protect his cash in just the same way. This process of taking coin out of the vaults only for it to be replaced a short time later is clearly something of an exercise in futility and it was soon realised that it would be much more convenient simply to pass on the receipt for the coins from debtor to creditor, leaving the coins where they were. This was possible because the good reputation of the goldsmiths ensured that people would have confidence in the receipts which they issued.

Promissory notes. At this time the goldsmiths' receipts took the form of a promissory note made out for the exact amount of coin deposited, naming as beneficiary the original depositor. It was not long before these notes began to circulate as money, although circulation would usually have been confined to the area within which the goldsmith was well known. Before the benefit of the note could be transferred to a third party, the depositor had to *indorse* it to show that he agreed to the transfer. If it was *indorsed in blank*, it became effectively a bearer document, payable to anyone who came into possession of it. In this condition it could circulate indefinitely, or until a holder decided to present it to the goldsmith and ask him to make good his promise to pay over the stated amount of coin. The notes were fully backed by coin, which meant that the gold-smiths always retained in their vaults enough coin to cover all the receipts which they had issued. Even if all the receipts had been presented for payment at the same time, they would have been met in full.

Fractionally backed notes. The goldsmiths soon realised that their receipts would not all be presented at the same time. In fact, only a small proportion of them would be brought in on any one day and even then it was probable that a proportion of the coin would find its way back to the goldsmith in a very short time. It was realised that this factor could profitably be made use of. The goldsmiths could make loans either by lending out some of the gold coins which they were holding or, more complicatedly, by issuing notes which promised to deliver amounts of coin which they had not in fact taken in on deposit. Goldsmiths found in practice that if they maintained in their vaults coin equal in value to some 10 to 15% of the notes which they had issued, they would always have enough on hand to meet normal day-to-day demands for repayment of coin. The relationship between coin held and liabilities to repay is known as the *cash ratio*. Table 1.1 shows how the balance sheet of a goldsmith would look if he were to take on deposit £2000 and use it to make loans up to a 10% cash ratio.

By issuing notes which were not fully backed by holdings of gold coins, the goldsmiths were in fact creating new money

Table 1.1. Goldsmith's balance sheet showing 10% cash ratio

Liabilities		Assets	
Notes issued	£20 000	Coin	£ 2 000
		Loans	£18 000
	£20 000		£20 000

which had not existed before, thereby increasing the money supply generally. (We shall be looking at this phenomenon in greater detail later.)

The business of lending was found to be *very profitable*. Most loans were made to the King or members of the nobility and very high rates of interest were charged. In order to expand this side of the business, goldsmiths encouraged the circulation of their 'paper' by issuing notes designed specifically for convenient use as money. These notes were payable to 'bearer' rather than to a named depositor and were made out for round amounts (£5, £10, etc.). Francis Childs was the first to print what were effectively *banknotes* in the 1680s. It is ironic to think that gold-smiths' receipts, which had at first been developed because of the need to protect money from theft, had now turned into money themselves and therefore subject to the same risk!

The private banks

By this time, the lending side of the goldsmiths' business had become their most important occupation. Many of them began to concentrate solely on this activity. They became *bankers*. Originally, almost all of the 'private banks', as they were known, were in London. With the coming of the Industrial Revolution, however, private banks sprang up throughout the provinces. By 1821 there were 781 'country' banks in England. Many of these were set up by prominent members of the local business community rather than by goldsmiths. All added to the supply of money by issuing their own fractionally backed or *fiduciary notes*, so called because they were supported principally by the faith of the public that the banks would be able to meet them.

Instead of charging a fee, banks began to offer *interest on deposits* as an inducement for savers to entrust their funds to them. The more deposits a bank could attract, the more it could lend. By now, of course, many of the deposits were being made in the form of banknotes rather than coin and depositors were receiving *credits to their accounts* rather than notes or receipts. This did not matter; provided that the bank maintained an adequate ratio between, on the one hand, the amounts owed to depositors and the value of any notes issued and, on the other hand, the total of cash held, all would be well. The process of *credit creation* had begun.

Reduced to its barest essentials, the balance sheet of one of the new private banks might be as shown in Table 1.2. You will see that a ratio of 10% has been maintained between coin and the total liabilities. If depositors requested repayment of any part of the £75 000 maintained in their accounts, the bank would normally issue notes to meet the request, thereby retaining the same ratio between coin and total liabilities. It would happen only rarely that a depositor would insist on receiving coin rather than banknotes.

Table 1.2. The balance sheet of a private bank

Liabilities		Assets	
Accounts in credit	£ 75 000	Coin in hand	£ 10 000
Notes issued	£ 25 000	Loans	£ 90 000
	£100 000		£100 000

Bank failures. Once a bank has issued fiduciary notes or created credit in this way, there is always the danger of a *run on the bank*. Depositors and holders of the bank's notes, becoming afraid that a bank might not be able to meet its commitments, descend upon the bank *en masse* demanding that they receive at once and in cash (*not* the bank's own notes) all the funds due to them. Clearly, if the bank is given time to call in its loans and if they all prove good, all the liabilities can be met. In a situation of panic, however, such indulgence is not likely to be granted. Much therefore depends on the financial backing which a bank has. This was a problem with the private banks, since they were constituted as partnerships having only the slenderest of financial backing. An Act of 1709 had prohibited joint stock companies from acting as banks in England and this was not repealed until well into the nineteenth century.

Many of the private banks invited disaster by operating with a cash ratio that was far too low, sometimes so low that they could not meet even normal demands for cash. In consequence, there were many bank failures. But, nevertheless, the banking system continued to grow and the fiduciary note issue became a regular feature of the economic scene.

Control of the fiduciary issue. It became apparent in the 19th century that the state needed to exercise closer control over the economy and that to do this it would have to regulate the supply of money to some degree. Furthermore, depositors and holders of banknotes needed protection against the growing rate of bank failures. As part of this process, a series of *Bank Acts*, particularly the Bank Charter Act of 1844, gradually brought an end to the private note issues. As the private banks merged with the newly emerging *joint stock banks*, so their note-issuing powers were taken away and transferred to the Bank of England. By this time, the Bank of England had emerged as the government's bank and was beginning to assume its role in executing government monetary policy. The loss of note-issuing powers did not, in fact, have the desired effect of restricting the activities of the commercial banks in so far as the growth of the money supply was concerned. Instead of creating *money* by issuing notes, the banks began to create more *credit* by granting more loan and overdraft facilities which, as you will see, are today just as much part of the money supply as are notes and coin. This change in bank practice promoted the development and use of the *cheque*.

Bank of England notes

The Bank of England had been set up in 1694 as England's first (and for a long time its only) joint stock bank. The Bank at first operated as a normal commercial bank but right from the outset it had close connections with the state. The government had permitted its incorporation in consideration of a loan of £1.2 million from the Bank to assist with the financing of a war with France. Over a period, the Bank assumed the role of a 'central bank' and gradually reduced its commercial operations. (We look at the history and role of the Bank of England in detail in Chapter 2.)

Immediately on its foundation, the Bank of England began to issue its own banknotes, just like the private banks. In the early years, its notes were handwritten and were always for £20 or more. By 1795 its smallest denomination was the £5 note; two years later £2 and £1 notes were being issued. The Bank Act of 1876, however, stipulated that the smallest denomination note that the Bank could issue would be the £5 note. It was this Act which also permitted the establishment of the first English joint stock banks (other than the Bank of England), although it stipulated that such banks had to be located not less than 65 miles (104 km) away from London.

Like the note issues of the private banks, Bank of England notes were at this time *fractionally backed*: enough gold was held to repay only a small proportion of the notes on issue. The remainder of the issue was *fiduciary*, owing its value only to the trust of the holders. You should not imagine from this that two different types of note were in circulation: any Bank of England note represented a claim for gold which was equally as good as that of any other note. Had all the notes been presented at once, however, they could not all have been paid in full.

Concentration of the note issue

The Bank Charter Act of 1844 placed certain restrictions on the fiduciary issues of both the private banks and the Bank of England. It was the first step in concentrating England's note issue in the hands of the Bank of England. At that time there were 72 private banks in England which issued their own notes. These were prohibited from increasing their note issues beyond the existing level. Any bank which amalgamated with another or, in the case of the 'country' banks which opened a branch in London, would lose its right to issue notes. No bank which had not previously issued notes was to be permitted to start doing so.

The 1844 Act allowed the Bank of England an unrestricted note issue overall but placed *limits* on the *fiduciary* element. The total value of its fiduciary issue was limited to £14 000 000, although this could be increased by two-thirds of the value of any note issue which had been lost by a private bank under the conditions set out above. All notes issued beyond this level had to be fully backed by gold or silver, with no more than 20% based on holdings of silver.

As the English commercial banking scene developed, more and more banks lost their right to a private note issue. Even so, it was not until 1921, when Fox, Fowler and Company was absorbed by Lloyds Bank, that the last of these issues was incorporated into the Bank of England issue. However, by the time this occurred, the private issues had long since ceased to be an important consideration in the operations of the banks.

Their place in the money supply had been taken by *cheques and overdraft facilities.*

In 1915, the *Treasury* began to issue £1 and 10s notes. These were to circulate instead of gold sovereigns and half-sovereigns which were withdrawn from circulation. At the same time, the convertibility of Bank of England notes to gold was suspended. These actions were taken to protect the country's bullion supplies during the First World War in order to ensure that purchases of war material abroad could be continued. In 1928 the Treasury note issue was taken over by the Bank of England.

Banks in Scotland and Northern Ireland were not subject to the same rules concerning note issues. To this day some of them continue to circulate their own notes. In 1987, for instance, the total outstanding note issues of the UK 'retail' banks totalled £769 million, the Scottish banks being responsible for the bulk of this sum. However, beyond £4.3 million, all Scottish and Northern Irish notes must be backed by holdings of Bank of England notes. Thus, the Bank of England note issue now represents for all practical purposes the whole of the UK note issue. In March 1987 the Bank of England note issue was more than £12.5 thousand million.

Development of the fiduciary issue

As the Bank of England took over the note issues of the other banks, the total value of its fiduciary issue grew. After this process was completed, the Currency and Bank Notes Act of 1928 restructured the position on a more modern basis. The rule restricting the Bank to the issue of notes with a value of £5 and over was removed, thereby allowing the takeover of the smaller denomination Treasury notes as we have already mentioned. The authorised amount of the fiduciary issue was set at £260 million, all of which had to be backed by holdings of either silver (up to a maximum of £5½ million) or of government securities— representing, in effect, loans made to the government. In this respect, therefore, the Bank of England fiduciary issue reflects the former fiduciary issues of the private banks which were backed by customers' promises to repay loans which had been granted to them. The Bank could, of course, continue to issue any amount of notes which were fully backed by gold holdings.

The 1928 Act brought the Bank of England's note-issuing

activities very much under the control of the Treasury. Any proposed changes to the level of the fiduciary issue (within the £260 million limit) had to be authorised by the Treasury before they could be put into effect. In addition, the Treasury could authorise temporary excesses of the fiduciary issue over the authorised limit; such excesses could not be permitted to last for periods of more than six months.

Between 1928 and 1954, a series of Acts of Parliament progressively increased the authorised limit of the fiduciary issue. In 1954, the Treasury was empowered to vary the level of the fiduciary issue at its discretion. By this time it had been realised that the note issue was only a small component of the money supply and that it has to be increased in proportion to increases in the money supply generally. If it were not, there would not be enough cash in circulation to meet the demands of the economy. This, however, would *not* reduce the growth of the money supply; it would simply compel people to use *other forms of money*, such as cheques. The reverse of this is not true; increasing the supply of notes beyond the necessary level does increase the money supply, usually by a *multiple* of the value of the notes issued. The issue of further notes should therefore be *closely related to the demands of the economy*. There are many economists who argue, for example, that there was an over-supply of notes in the mid-1970s which led to an unnecessary growth in the money supply, leading in turn to high rates of inflation.

Table 1.3 shows the growth of the fiduciary issue since 1928. The massive increase shown reflects the rise of price levels generally between the two dates 1928 and 1987.

Leaving the gold standard
We have already seen that from the 17th century until 1914 Britain was on the *gold standard*. That is to say, the basic unit of our currency was stated to be equal to a definite weight of gold of a definite quality (£1 sterling equalled $113\frac{1}{123}$ grains of pure gold). Gold coins had to contain an amount of gold at least equal to their value, although it could be alloyed with additional metals to produce a harder-wearing article. British sovereigns were 11/12 pure gold. Bank of England notes were freely convertible into gold on demand. The state, as represented by the Bank of England, had to hold reserves of gold to cover both

Table 1.3. Growth of the fiduciary issue since 1928

Year	£m
1928	260
1939	580
1946	1 450
1955	1 800
1960	2 250
1965	2 850
1970	3 500
1975	5 325
1981	10 256
1987	12 580

domestic demands for conversion of notes and settlement of international debts.

The system worked well enough, especially in regulating international finance, provided that all participating countries allowed gold to flow freely into and out of their economic systems in response to the ebb and flow of international trade. Unfortunately, the system tends to become inoperative in countries which earn much more in international trade than they spend, or which spend much more than they receive. In the former case there is a temptation to restrict the flow of gold into the internal economy so as to minimise its inflationary effects. (Remember what happened to Spain in the 'Golden Age'.) In the latter case, the outflow of gold reduces the amount of backing available for the internal money supply. If steps are then taken to reduce the money supply to an appropriate level, a downturn in economic activity is bound to ensue. (We shall be looking at the relationship between money supply and economic activity later on.)

In 1914, with the outbreak of the First World War, the British economy could not support continued adherence to the gold standard. In purchasing much-needed war supplies the country began to spend much more abroad than it could earn. The gold reserves had to be conserved to pay for these items. Gold coins were withdrawn from circulation to be replaced by the inconvertible *Treasury notes* which we have already mentioned and the convertibility of Bank of England notes was suspended.

In 1925 the convertibility of Bank of England notes was

restored when Britain adopted the gold bullion standard which represented an attempt to bring stability to international markets. The principal distinction from the old gold standard was that gold coins were not brought back into circulation. This meant that the convertibility of banknotes was convertibility into *bullion bars*. These bars weighed 400 ounces (11 340 grams) and were equivalent in value to some £1550! This system proved to be unworkable in the face of the great depression. In 1931 the gold bullion standard was abandoned and the convertibility of Bank of England notes was again terminated. It has never been restored.

In 1939, when the Second World War started, the Bank of England's gold reserves were transferred to the *Exchange Equalisation Account* which also contained the country's reserves of foreign currency. This arrangement continues to the present day. The account is used to support the value of sterling in the foreign exchange markets. When the pound is weak, reserves will be used to buy sterling so as to keep its value up. When the pound is strong, sterling can be sold to replenish the reserves. It follows that since all the country's gold reserves are now used for this purpose, there is no gold backing for Bank of England notes. Our currency is therefore *wholly fiduciary* in nature. The notes and coin which we use are *fiat money*; they are money only because the state says that they are money and we therefore accept them as such.

The issue of notes and coin

The Bank of England today is wholly responsible for the actual issue of notes in the UK. Notes are printed by specialist security printers under Bank instructions as the need arises. The Royal Mint is responsible for the issue of coin and is the sole organisation authorised to strike coins for use in the country.

As part of the process of maintaining the currency issue, damaged and worn notes are collected in by the Bank for destruction. In this, assistance is given by the commercial banks which play an important role in the distribution and circulation of cash. Notes and coin are made available to the public through the commercial banks which keep on hand reserves of currency needed to meet customers' demands. The banks regularly replenish these reserves by drawing new supplies of notes from the Bank of England and of coin from the Royal Mint. The Bank is thereby freed from the need either to keep large stocks of notes itself or to make complex arrangements for the distribution of new notes. The commercial banks will, of course, reissue used notes which have been paid into customers' accounts unless they have deteriorated too much, in which case they will be returned to the Bank of England and exchanged for new ones.

Money today

Bank deposits

We have already seen that money can consist of anything which people in general will accept in payment of a debt or for the purchase of goods or services. Soon after the wealthy began to deposit their coin with the early bankers, the receipts which they were given started to circulate as money; people were using the *document of title* to the money as if it were the money itself. These receipts, of course, eventually became banknotes. In the 18th century, bankers began to allow depositors to draw cheques on their deposits and this had an important effect on the story of money.

Use of cheques

From a practical point of view, a cheque is a *payment order* written by a depositor telling his banker to pay over to a named beneficiary a specified sum out of the money which the banker owes to the depositor. Allowing the customer to draw cheques on his deposits is clearly an alternative to giving him notes or receipts for them. A great advantage for the depositor is that whereas banknotes payable to bearer soon became as subject to the danger of theft as the coins which they had replaced, bank deposits as represented by cheques did not.

Soon cheques were being used to fulfil the function of money as a medium of exchange. Over the years, the acceptability of the cheque has grown to the extent that today many people make all but the smallest of payments by cheque or by way of some other more recently developed form of funds transfer offered by the banks. The acceptance of bank deposits as money was shown when people began to pay banknotes in to the banks for the credit of their accounts as well as paying in coin. They knew that the funds in the account could be drawn on when payments had to be made. You should note that, unlike the banknote, the cheque itself has not become money; the cheque is merely a *claim* to the money. It is the *bank deposit* which is the money. (You may wish to work out for yourself which of the attributes of money the cheque does not possess.) Today the bank deposit is the largest component of our money supply. How has this come about?

The creation of credit

You have already seen how banks could create money by the issue of banknotes which were only partly backed by their holdings of coin. Provided that a satisfactory cash ratio was maintained, the bank would always be able to meet the day-to-day payments demanded of it. Unfortunately, many banks did not maintain adequate cash ratios and bank failures ensued with unfortunate losses to both depositors and holders of notes. From the middle of the nineteenth century the issue of private banknotes became progressively more controlled; it was thought that this would put a stop to the uncontrolled creation of money by the banks. It did not work.

The holding of idle cash on deposit generates no profits and is anathema to bankers. If they could not use the funds as backing for notes, they could use them as backing for loans and overdrafts. So the banks turned from the creation of money to the *creation of credit*.

A single-bank system. To see how the creation of credit works, imagine that there is only one bank in the country and that this bank holds all the depositors' accounts. If the depositors had £100 000 in their accounts, the balance sheet of the bank would look like Table 1.4 (leaving out the fixed assets and the capital of the business).

The bank knows from experience that only a small proportion

Table 1.4. A simple bank balance sheet

Liabilities		Assets	
Deposits	£100 000	Cash	£100 000

of the cash deposited is required to cover demands for repayment; the rest can be lent out. Suppose that the bank decides that a cash ratio (deposits : cash) of 10% will provide adequate safety. This means that 90% of the cash held, i.e. £90 000, can be lent at interest. The people who borrow the money use it to pay for goods. The shopkeepers and so on who receive the money then pay it back into their accounts and the bank finds that the £90 000 which it lent out has been redeposited. We could describe this as *created deposit*, although you must realise that the bank cannot in fact distinguish between 'created deposits' of money that it has already lent and 'original deposits' of new money that have just been introduced into the system. Of the £90 000 just paid in, the bank needs to retain only 10% or £9000 to maintain its cash ratio; the remainder can be lent out again. The £81 000 which is lent out will soon find its way back to the bank and a proportion of it can be put out on loan, and so on. This process is known as the *multiplier effect* and it is illustrated in Table 1.5.

Table 1.5. The multiplier effect and the creation of credit

Liabilities		Assets	
Deposits		*Cash retained (10%)*	*Loans made (90%)*
Original deposit	£100 000	£10 000	£90 000
First redeposit	£90 000	£9 000	£81 000
Second redeposit	£81 000	£8 100	£72 900
Third redeposit	£72 900	£7 290	£65 210
Fourth redeposit	£65 210	£6 521	£58 689
"	"	"	"
"	"	"	"
"	"	"	"

The maximum possible creation of deposits occurs when:
Liabilities = £1 000 000   Cash = £100 000 + Loans = £900 000

Thus, at the end of the process, the whole of the £100 000 cash in the system has been retained in the bank. With a cash ratio of 10% this is adequate to cover total deposits of £1 000 000 and therefore loans of £900 000 can be made. The bank could have worked out the maximum amount of advances right at the outset but it would not be safe to allow advances up to this figure straight away. Time has to be allowed for the money to be redeposited to ensure that an adequate cash ratio is maintained at all times. Allowance also has to be made for losses from the banking system; some people will keep their cash in a cash box at home or under the mattress, rather than bring it into the bank.

In the example we have given, the bank's balance sheet at the end of the process will therefore look like Table 1.6.

Table 1.6 Balance sheet of a bank using a 10% cash ratio

Liabilities		Assets	
Deposits	£1 000 000	Cash	£100 000
(10% original)		Loans	£900 000
(90% created)			
	£1 000 000		£1 000 000

How does this differ from our example of a goldsmith creating money by the issue of fractionally backed notes? Apart from the fact that in the later case the figures are bigger, the answer is: very little. In both cases a 10% cash ratio is maintained between liabilities and cash. For the goldsmith the liabilities are notes issued; for the banker they are credits to customers' accounts. In the earlier case, cash represents gold coins held; in the later case the figure is made up both of coin and notes issued by the Bank of England as depositors will accept repayment of the sums due to them in either of these forms.

The limit of the credit creation process is determined by the cash ratio. If it were set at 5%, the maximum advance possible on £100 000 cash deposits would increase to £1 900 000; if it were set at 20% the maximum advance would reduce to £400 000. In fact, the English banks found that over a period spanning some hundreds of years a cash ratio of around 8% provided quite adequate holdings of coin and notes.

If all the banks in the country were to adopt a cash ratio of 12.5%, each £1 of cash held by the banks would support £8 of deposits consisting of £1 original deposit plus £7 created deposits. Looked at another way, this means that for every £1 introduced into the system, £7 will be lent out. Conversely, every time £1 is removed from the system, by people holding more cash under the mattress for instance, £7 in loans must be recovered! (Try to work out for yourself what the appropriate figures would be for some other cash ratios. The trick is to find what you have to multiply your ratio by to bring it up to 100%; that is the number of pounds deposit that £1 cash will support.)

A multi-bank system. If there is more than one bank, the system as a whole still operates in very much the same way, although there are some further considerations for each individual bank. Each bank has to be aware that money which it puts out on loan will not necessarily be redeposited with it; it could go to one of the other banks. At the same time, of course, money lent by the other banks could end up on deposit with this bank. On balance, gains and losses should even out but on a day-to-day basis the levels of inflow and outflow will fluctuate slightly. A somewhat higher cash ratio will be needed to allow for the uncertainty which this creates. Cashless transfers between accounts at different banks will occur, such as cheques paid in to accounts, credit transfers and so on. Again, these should cancel each other out over a period but cash transfers will have to be made between the banks if they do not. This is accomplished nowadays by making transfers through the accounts which the clearing banks maintain with the Bank of England.

Another factor for consideration is the relationship between the cash ratios of the different banks in the system. Imagine that one bank works to a 15% cash ratio while all the others work to a 20% ratio. The first bank will find over a period that it lends out more cash than it gets back on deposit. This is because it is giving out proportionately more of its deposits than the other banks but receiving only an equal share with them of the total redeposits. It is, therefore, losing cash to the other banks and will probably have to amend its ratio to recover the situation.

Modern banks consider more than just the cash ratio when deciding how much they have available for lending. In addition, the state, through the Bank of England, exercises certain quantitative controls on bank lending, both to guard against bank failures and, more importantly today, to control the growth of the money supply and minimise the volatility of changes. (We consider these aspects of control in Chapter 9.)

The money supply

As we have seen, the supply of money in the UK today consists of *notes, coin, and bank deposits*. Bank deposits are classed as money partly because they are available for the settlement of debts through the use of cheques and similar instruments. Does this mean that we can class as money only current accounts—termed 'sight deposits' because they are repayable on demand or 'at sight'—and that we must exclude ordinary deposit accounts, or 'term deposit', on which cheque books are not used and for which, at least technically, notice of withdrawal is required? What about overdraft facilities? If a bank grants a loan to a customer, entries appear on both sides of its balance sheet as both an asset (loan due from the customer) and as a liability (credit balance available to customer on his current account). When an overdraft facility is agreed, no change occurs in the bank's balance sheet until the customer draws on it by writing cheques. Should the amount of all undrawn overdraft limits be counted as part of the money supply?

Measurements of money stock
We shall examine how the money supply is both measured and controlled in Chapter 9 but at this point we should explain briefly some of the most commonly used measurements of money stock. The above questions have caused some controversy in recent years and because of the uncertainties three different measures of the money supply (or *money stock*) have been in simultaneous use in the compilation of official statistics. These are known as M1, M2, and M3. A very basic measurement (M0: essentially notes and coins) has also been used by recent governments.

M1. Notes and coin in circulation plus private sight deposits held on sterling current accounts with the UK 'monetary sector' together make up the M1 money stock. The word 'private' denotes the non-government sector of the economy. This includes the accounts of businesses as well as individuals but it excludes the accounts of all government and local government agencies and the nationalised industries. This is a narrow definition of the money stock but it can be useful in that it is closely related to the concept of money as a medium of exchange.

The monetary sector consists principally of the recognised banks and other licensed deposit takers (LDTs); we shall be returning to this in Chapter 3.

M2. This measure is not widely used these days. It consists of the non-interest bearing part of M1 plus UK sterling private 'time deposits' of less than one month, limited to balances of less than £100 000 with the monetary sector, including all deposit accounts with both banks and discount houses.

M3. This is a wider measure of money stocks. It includes *all* sterling deposits with the monetary sector for the private sector of the economy. In its broadest definition, it also includes the value of deposits denominated in foreign currencies but which are held in the UK for UK residents.

Near money
There are many assets which closely resemble money and which in some cases may be thought of as money by their holders; these are known as *near money*. While near money items do not form part of the money stock as we have just defined it, they have an effect on the overall levels of money stocks. A person holding a near money asset will usually be happy to reduce his holdings of 'true' money by an appropriate amount, thereby reducing the overall demand for 'true' money.

The identifying characteristics for near money are *liquidity* and the *need for conversion* into money before they are available for spending. Examples of near money assets include postal orders, money orders, premium savings bonds and national savings certificates.These items are all liquid, in that they can easily be converted into cash, but cannot be spent just as they are. Although somewhat less liquid than these, stocks and shares issued by limited companies and government bodies and even life assurance policies can also be classed as near money. It is worth while noting that with these items the holder often finds that conversion to true money involves *loss of value*, whereas true money will always exchange for its full value.

Building society deposits. These are somewhat anomalous. They are not included in the official definitions of M1, M2, or M3, and yet they are little different from bank deposit accounts. In recent years, the building societies have even introduced 'current account' types of facility on which cheque books can be used. Clearly holders of these accounts use their deposits just as if they were bank deposits. There is a strong argument that the building society deposits should now be counted as part of the money stocks of the country.

Private sector liquidity. This was the name given to a new measure of money and near money which was introduced in 1979. There are now two versions: M4 and M5. The calculation of M5 as at 31 March 1987 is shown in Table 1.8. Compare this with the calculation of M3 at the same date as shown in Table 1.7. You will see that this new measure of purchasing power in

Table 1.7. Money stock as at 31 March 1987

Money stock	£m	
Notes and coin in circulation	12 717	
UK private sector sterling sight deposits	67 053	
M1 money stock		79 770
UK private sector sterling time deposits	80 151	
M3 money stock (sterling)		159 921
UK residents' deposits in other currencies	28 502	
M3 money stock (total)		188 423

Table 1.8 Private sector liquidity at 31 March 1987

Money	£m
Notes and coin in circulation	12 717
Sterling bank deposits*	147 204
M3	159 921
Other money market instruments	4 265
Savings, deposits and securities †	110 656
National Savings Deposits	9 972
M5	284 814

* Includes certificates of deposit and excludes deposits with original maturity over two years.
† Mainly building society deposits or shares.
(*Source: Bank of England Quarterly Bulletin*)

the economy shows that liquidity is much more broadly based than the M3 definition would suggest.

The category of 'savings, deposits and securities' consists primarily of investments in building society share accounts and deposit accounts.

Legal tender

We must distinguish between money and legal tender. Money is anything which people generally *will accept* as settlement of a payment which is due; legal tender is what the law says they *must accept* if it is offered. Legal tender in the UK consists of Bank of England notes and coin, although there are limits to the amount of any one denomination that a creditor can be compelled to accept. Clearly you would not want to receive 500 pennies in settlement of a debt of £5. All legal tender is money; but not all money is legal tender. Thus, for instance, the law does not compel you to accept a cheque in payment of a debt; you may insist on payment in cash: notes or coin.

Changes in the value of money

While the country was on the gold standard, the value of money could not change unless the value of gold changed or the gold content of the standard unit of currency was changed—as, for instance, would happen if the currency was debased. Today money does not have the stability of value which would result from a relationship to gold; its value is determined solely by what it will buy. Changes in the value of money are usually categorised as *inflation* or *deflation*.

Inflation

Inflation is generally perceived as a rise in overall price levels, although in truth it is a *fall* in the value (the purchasing power) of money. There has been an almost permanent inflationary trend in the UK since the 1930s. There is no consensus of opinion about its causes. There are three principal theories, the truth probably being a combination of factors from all three.

According to the *monetarist* view of inflation, increases in the *supply of money* are automatically followed by decreases in the *value of money*. Although there is no obvious causal relationship between these two occurrences, the observable evidence of the last 40 years does seem to indicate that this effect occurs. *Demand-led inflation* occurs when people try to buy more goods and services than the economy is capable of producing. This *pulls up* the prices to levels at which the available money is matched by the prices of available commodities. Past governments have tried to control inflation by reducing demand through fiscal policies (tax) which reduce real income. *Cost push inflation* occurs when costs of production rise, leading to rises in the prices of goods sold. Among the factors which cause costs to rise are import prices, exchange rates, and wage settlements. The last of these, representing increases of income without corresponding increases in productivity, often tends to be discussed in political rather than economic terms, although it certainly has some connection with inflationary pressures.

Deflation
Deflation occurs when the purchasing power of money rises and the general level of prices falls. In inflationary times this situation may seem to be quite attractive but, in practice, the effects of severe deflation are as damaging, if not more so, than the effects of inflation. If prices are falling all the time, it is difficult for a manufacturer to recover the cost of goods he makes; wages and raw materials have to be paid for at today's higher prices, while sales will be made at tomorrow's lower prices. This situation increases the entrepreneurial risk with the result that industrialists become more cautious and reduce output. Production falls, unemployment increases, demand therefore decreases and production has to be further reduced; a vicious circle has developed.

Deflationary measures tended to be introduced as a part of the workings of the gold standard when a country was experiencing an outflow of gold resulting from a debit balance of payments. This occurs, of course, when imports and payments abroad exceed exports and earnings abroad.

Measuring changes in the value of money
The most commonly used measure of the value of money is the *Retail Prices Index* (RPI). In this the prices of some 3500 goods and services are sampled and their importance *weighted* in eleven major categories. The items sampled reflect the contents of a normal family's 'shopping basket'. The great difficulty is in

deciding what items should go to make up the contents of the 'basket'. Clearly more than just groceries must be included; among other items costs of clothing, fuel, and accommodation must be allowed for and the amounts spent on these will vary widely according to circumstances. The UK authorities construct two separate indices: the *General Index* convering the average family, and the *Single Pensioner Household Index* which takes account of the different spending priorities of retired people.

The prices of all the items selected for the 'basket' are added together to give one total which is then reduced to an *index number* having the value '100' on whatever date has been chosen for the starting point of our comparisons. Each time thereafter that the contents of the 'basket' are valued, the total cost is divided by the same factor which was needed to reduce the original cost to '100'. The RPIs currently in use in the UK take January 1974 as their base point. Let us demonstrate how the calculation is made by looking at the cost of one particular commodity. In 1974 the cost of one 'dialled unit' to a subscriber of the UK's telephone system was 1.68p. To convert this sum for use as our base of 100 all we have to do is to divide it by itself and multiply the result by 100, as follows:

$$\frac{1.68 \times 100}{1.68} = 100$$

By the end of 1983, when inflation rates began to fall the cost of such a unit had risen to 4.3p; dividing *this* amount by 1.68 and multiplying by 100 gives us the result, in round figures, of 256, as follows:

$$\frac{4.3 \times 100}{1.68} = 255.95$$

Thus, we know that for every £1 spent in 1974, a subscriber would have had to pay £2.56 in 1983 for the same number of units, an increase of 156%.

You will appreciate that different commodities will be subject to different price changes over the same period. For example, between 1974 and 1983 the price of natural gas for some domestic consumers rose from 5.98p per therm to 33.5p per therm. If we again express the 1974 price as base '100', the

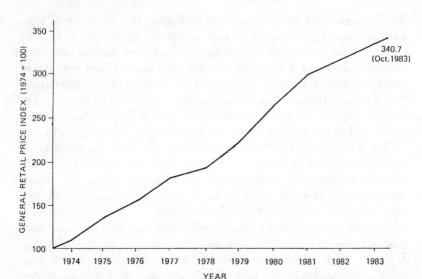

*Fig. 1.1 The General Retail Prices Index since January 1974
(Source: Annual Abstract of Statistics)*

equivalent expression of the 1983 price is '560'. This is, of course, a much greater level of increase than that affecting telephone charges.

The RPIs combine these varying levels of price changes for different commodities, reflecting *overall* changes in the cost of living. Fig. 1.1 shows the changes in the *General Index* between 1974 and 1983. You will see that over that period it had risen from the base level of 100 to 340.7 in October 1983. This means that on average prices had gone up by just over 240%. To put it another way, the pound was worth only 29% of its 1974 value.

Summary

1 The need for money arises with the growth of economic activity, when barter and indirect exchange of goods become unworkable.

2. Money has four functions:

(a) a medium of exchange;
(b) a unit of account;
(c) a store of value;
(d) a standard for deferred payments.

3 Any item used as money must have the following attributes:
(a) acceptability;
(b) uniformity;
(c) stability;
(d) divisibility;
(e) durability.

4 Coins developed out of the use of precious metals as money. Token coins were a later development and have a low intrinsic value.

5 Banknotes developed from goldsmiths' receipts. Goldsmiths found they could make advances by issuing fractionally backed notes.

6 Private banks subsequently continued the fiduciary issue of banknotes until their note issuing powers were concentrated into the hands of the Bank of England.

7 The Bank of England's note issue is now wholly fiduciary and its notes are no longer convertible into gold.

8 The development of the cheque and the overdraft allowed the commercial banks to continue the creation of money without issuing notes.

9 Today bank deposits are the largest component of the country's money supply, although there are several alternative measurements of the money stock.

10 The purchasing power of money can be affected by inflation and deflation.

Self-assessment questions

1 Define: (a) intrinsic value; (b) bimetallism; (c) promissory notes; (d) cash ratio; (e) near money.

2 List the functions of money.

3 True or false?

(a) Buyers and sellers of goods must always have a 'double coincidence of wants'.

(b) Anything can be used as money.

(c) The money supply today consists principally of fiduciary issue notes.

(d) There are practical limits on the extent to which a bank can create credit.

(e) Inflation and deflation can be equally damaging to the economy.

4 Why would it not be convenient to use the leaves of the trees as money?

5 In what circumstances might people in a modern society resort to barter?

6 How do cheques and banknotes differ from each other? Are they both forms of money?

7 Look at Table 1.5 (the multiplier effect). Draw up a similar table showing a 15% cash ratio. What would the bank's balance sheet look like at the end of the credit creation process, assuming that it started with the same deposit of £100 000?

Assignments

1 Memorandum to: Student
   From: Manager
   Subject: Notes at the counter

I have heard a number of complaints recently that the £5 notes which we are giving out to customers over the branch counter are becoming increasingly worn and dirty. I have checked with the Chief Cashier who tells me that this is because we cannot obtain as many new £5 notes as he would like from the Bullion Department. We are therefore issuing old notes which we have taken in. Would you please find out for me what is happening?

I don't know if this is connected, but when I sign the weekly bullion order, I notice that we hardly ever order any of the £1 coins but nevertheless our stocks do not diminish. Write a short report for me please.

2 Money
If confidence in our modern economy were to break down, it might mean that people would not accept our familiar notes and coin as money any longer.

What alternatives could you suggest and in what ways would these substitutes be better or worse than our present forms of money? What do you think would be the effect of such changes on the nation's commercial activities?

Make notes on these points for a class discussion.

2 Financial markets in the UK

Chapter objectives

After studying this chapter you should be able to:
- trace the origins and development of the UK banking system;
- understand the basis of the creation of credit;
- outline the development of the Bank of England and explain its role and functions;
- state the distinctions between the short-term money markets, the loan and savings markets, and the capital markets;
- identify the principal types of institutions which participate in the money markets and state their functions.

The British banking system

The development of a commercial society demands the development of an adequate financial infrastructure which incorporates the financial markets which we are going to examine in this chapter. The UK has both a well-developed industrial and commercial economy and a world-renowned financial system. London is the base both of England's national banking system and of a major international financial market. It was not always so. Even when British commerce began to develop in late medieval times, our financial systems tended to lag some way behind those in other parts of Europe.

Origins of banking

Banking as we know it today did not have its origins in the British Isles. This was because modern commercial development as a whole began in Mediterranean Europe, particularly Italy, some time before it spread to northern Europe. The activities of the bankers of Venice (12th century) and Genoa (15th century) predate any major banking activity in Britain. Indeed, the word 'bank' itself derives from the Italian *banco* which was the name given to a moneychanger's counter on which he laid out his piles of money. Nevertheless, as Britain's trade developed, so did the need for banking facilities, particularly money transfer and borrowing services. In the 13th century, some of the Italian (Lombard) moneylenders settled in London and offered their services to entrepreneurs. One of the main streets in the 'square mile' of the City of London's financial district is still called Lombard Street.

Some moneylenders had been active in the country before the arrival of the Lombards. Mostly these were Jews, some of whom had come from mainland Europe with William the Conqueror. The Jewish involvement with moneylending had come about in a rather strange way. The Christian population of medieval Europe believed that lending money for the purpose of earning a profit ('usury' as it was known) was sinful and had been proscribed by biblical testimony. They would not therefore engage in it. The Jewish faith contains no such prohibition and the Jews therefore felt free to take on the practice of usury. The Christian majority, although often professing hatred of the Jews for this 'sinful' activity, found it very convenient to have money-lending services available to them and, indeed, Jews were often forced into moneylending against their will by Christian prejudice. It is interesting to note that although most Christians now have a less extreme attitude to usury, the Islamic faith still regards it as sinful. Strict Muslims generally will not lend money at interest, even going so far as to refuse payment of interest due to them on an ordinary bank deposit account.

Moneylending must be distinguished from banking. A *money-lender* lends out his own capital. Thus, there is a rigid limit on the maximum amount which he can lend and this limit is unlikely to be particularly extensive. The identifying character-istic of the *banker* is that he lends out funds which he has obtained on deposit from others; he does not usually lend his own capital. A banker therefore has access to much more loan capital than a moneylender. The more he can induce people to deposit with him, the more he can lend.

Goldsmiths
As we have already seen, banking in England really began with the activities of the goldsmiths, many of whom were, in fact,

related to the Jewish or Italian moneylenders. To recap: in the early 17th century in London, goldsmiths began to accept deposits of gold coin to be held in safe keeping. The receipts or notes which they issued came to be used as money and from them the *banknote* was developed. When goldsmiths' notes began to be accepted as money in their own right, the gold-smiths found that they could increase their loanable funds by issuing notes promising to pay over amounts of coin which had not been deposited with them provided that they maintained a safe cash ratio between notes issued and coin actually held. By the time this stage had been reached (around the end of the 17th century), banking had taken over as the principal generator of profits and the trade of goldsmith declined. The lending of money had become the principal activity of the businesses; the *private bank* had arrived.

Private banks

The early banks were known as private banks. They were constituted as partnerships and by an Act of 1708 they were prohibited from having more than six partners. The only excep-tion to this rule was the Bank of England which had been estab-lished in 1694 as the nation's only joint stock bank. It was partly to protect the privileged position of the Bank of England that the private banks remained under these limitations for so long.

Most of the early private banks were located in London, which was already the principal commercial centre of England. In 1750 there were only twelve 'country banks' in the rest of the country. But you must appreciate that this was a very different England from the one we know today. At that time the population of London was around 675 000, which represented one-tenth of the whole population of the country. There were less than ten other towns with a population exceeding 10 000 and only about 30 towns had a population of 5000. Up to two-thirds of the people were engaged in some form of agricultural work, so it is not surprising that such country banks as there were had their origins not with the goldsmiths but with agricultural merchants in market towns. Nevertheless, the reasons for their establish-ment were very similar to those behind the growth of the 'city' banks.

Between about 1750 and 1850 (the era of *Industrial Revol-*

ution) everything changed. The population of the country grew explosively and new industries developed needing access to banking facilities. Many new private banks were set up outside London, often by local industrialists and entrepreneurs, to mobilise local capital. These banks were set up specifically to operate from the outset as banks, accepting deposits, issuing their own notes, and making loans. By 1821, the number of private banks in existence had grown to 781.

In the early part of the 19th century *bank failures* became, if not a regular occurrence, at least a significant danger to both depositors and holders of private banknotes. Many of the private banks which had so recently sprung up were imprudent either in the ratio maintained between notes issued and coin held or in the quality of their lending, or sometimes both. A 'run on the bank' might ensue if it became known that a particular bank could not meet its debts to depositors and note holders; bankruptcy usually ensued when creditors descended on the bank to ask for their money back. The fact that the banks were limited in their constitution to a maximum of six partners meant that often they did not have access to sufficient proprietors' capital to weather even the smallest financial storm.

At the end of the 18th century there was a period of comparatively high *inflation*. This was generally thought to be the result of the uncontrolled note issues of the private banks which were increasing the supply of money in the economy. As a consequence of this and the increasing incidence of bank failures, the government came under pressure to reform the law so as to allow the establishment of more soundly based commercial banks while restricting their powers to create money. This it attempted to do in a series of Acts beginning in 1826.

The joint stock banks

The joint stock banks were the forerunners of today's commercial banks. When joint stock *companies*, as opposed solely to partnerships, were allowed to operate as banks, the opportunity was created for wealthy industrialists and landowners to subscribe capital which would enable the small private banks to broaden their capital base and expand with safety.

The Bank Act 1826

This was the first Act to allow the formation of joint stock banks, other than the Bank of England of course. The new banks would have the power to issue notes but the Act included one vital restriction: no joint stock bank could be established within a radius of 65 miles (105 km) from London. This provision was incorporated to protect the Bank of England which, despite its growing involvement with the mechanisms of government, continued to act also as a commercial bank. It was thought that giving it a virtual monopoly in the London area was necessary to ensure that it would not be distracted from its role as the government's bank by increased competition in other activities. The effect of the restriction of joint stock banking in London was to depress the growth of the new-style banks. London was clearly the financial centre of the country and investors thought that any new bank had to be represented there if it was to thrive. Capital was not readily forthcoming for the new banks and there was therefore little development until this restriction was relaxed in 1833.

The Bank Charter Act 1833

Under the terms of this Act, joint stock banks were permitted to set up operations within the 65-mile radius around London but they were prohibited from issuing their own notes, a capacity which had been thought vital to the undertaking of banking business on any large scale. Despite the restriction, however, new banks were soon being established in large numbers. Many of the commercial banking networks as we know them today had their origins in this period as the new joint stock banks progressively absorbed the smaller private banks, building the foundations of their branch networks.

The attempt to restrict the rate of growth of the new banks by denying them a note issue failed because of the new phenomenon of *deposit banking* which we discussed in Chapter 1. The private banks had already found that it was not necessary to issue notes to expand the total funds available for lending; the same end could be achieved by *creating credit*, allowing customers to overdraw their current accounts. This had not been understood by the government of the day.

The Bank Charter Act 1844

This Act was an attempt to restrict the growth of the money supply. As we have seen, it put a stop to further increases in the note issues of the joint stock banks and the private banks. Furthermore, as existing banks amalgamated or were taken over, their note-issuing capacity would be forfeit. Newly established banks would never have a note issue. As a measure of monetary control it was a failure for the reasons already mentioned. It did nothing to slow down the growth of the money supply through the medium of deposit banking and it did not hinder the expansion of the commercial banks.

The Companies Act 1862

The concept of *limited liability* had been introduced to the British scene as long ago as 1662, although for a long time it was available to only a very small number of organisations. The advantage of the limited liability company is that investors' responsibility for company debts is limited to a set amount, usually the amount which they have subscribed by way of capital. The Companies Act of 1862 consolidated previous legislation and for the first time permitted *limited liability companies* to operate as banks. The last barrier to the establishment of very large banking units had been removed.

The 'High street banks'

Mergers and amalgamations

The branch banking networks of the commercial banks as we know them today are the product of a series of mergers and amalgamations which have taken place over the last 150 years.

The *advantages* of merging small banks into larger units are clear. The resulting organisations have larger supplies of capital and can better resist periods of difficulty. They can effect economies of scale. They have access to a broader customer base and are therefore less vulnerable both to individual bad debts and to loss of important depositors. They can diversify lending into different sectors of the economy. If they operate in diverse locations, they can transfer loanable funds around the country by taking deposits in one area and making loans in another. For example, the North of England, and Scotland even more so, is traditionally an area of saving, while the South is an area of borrowing. It is for this latter reason particularly that national banking networks have been built up, and links have developed between English and Scottish banks.

The process of amalgamation soon got under way after the 1833 Act. In 1841 there were 115 joint stock banks throughout England, some of which had been created through amalgamations of old 'private' banks. These banks expanded their networks by taking over the remaining private banks, by opening new branches and by amalgamating with one another. By 1914 most of the commercial banking activity in England and Wales was controlled by the (then) sixteen *clearing banks*. A Treasury committee was set up in 1918 to report on the amalgamations of banks. This recommended that further mergers should be controlled by legislation so as to avoid a situation in which the running of the banking system would be concentrated in too few hands. This could lead to excessive power and all the dangers of abuse of that power. In fact, legislation was not enacted but the Treasury received an assurance from the banks that no further mergers would be effected without prior consultation.

By 1920, through takeovers of some of the smaller banks, the number of clearing banks had been reduced to eleven, which were categorised as the 'big five' and the 'little six' (Table 2.1). There were no further mergers within these groups for almost 50 years, although it should be noted that Martins Bank was the only completely independent member of the little six.

Table 2.1 The clearing banks in 1920

Big five	Barclays
	Lloyds
	Midland
	National Provincial
	Westminster
Little six	Coutts
	District
	Glyn Mills
	Martins
	National
	Williams Deacons

Through the interwar period and in the postwar period until the end of the 1960s, the eleven clearing banks, especially the 'big five', concentrated on growth through opening new branches in areas where they were poorly represented. The 'little six' tended to be more localised in their distribution, Martins and Williams Deacons, for instance, being predominantly northern in their distribution. The 'big five' jointly controlled about 80% of clearing bank deposits.

High street banks today

The most recent round of amalgamations between the deposit banks occurred at the end of the 1960s in response to the changing economic scene. The banks felt that larger groupings were desirable to help them meet the challenges of computerisation, competition from overseas and 'fringe' banks, and the needs of the larger groupings of industry encountered in the modern economy.

In 1968 Barclays and Lloyds announced their intention to merge and to take over Martins. The government were concerned about the size of the resulting organisation and referred the proposals to the Monopolies Commission which ruled that the merger should not be allowed to proceed but that Martins could be absorbed by either of the other two banks. Martins subsequently became part of Barclays Bank. The same year the Westminster and the National Provincial proposed to amalgamate to form the National Westminster which would also absorb the branches of the District Bank, which was already controlled by the National Provincial. Although this would produce a bank of enormous size and power and would reduce the 'big five' to the 'big four', both objections, in fact, to the Barclays-Lloyds-Martins grouping, it was allowed to proceed.

In 1970 Williams and Glyn's Bank was formed out of a merger of Williams Deacons, Glyn Mills and the National, English branches of which had formerly been part of the National Bank of Ireland. All three component banks had for some time been in the control of the National and Commercial group which also owned the Royal Bank of Scotland, itself a product of several mergers of Scottish banks. These mergers reduced the English clearing banks from eleven to six: the 'big four', Coutts and Co. (controlled in any case by the National Westminster) and Williams and Glyn's.

In 1981 the Royal Bank of Scotland Group, which the former National and Commercial group was by then called, became the object of takeover bids by the Standard and Chartered Bank and the Hong Kong and Shanghai Bank. Both of these international banks, albeit with strong British connections, wished to acquire a 'retail' branch banking network in the United Kingdom. The government decided to prohibit both takeovers from going ahead, at least partly because of political pressure resulting from resistance among Scots to the idea of Scotland's largest bank coming under the control of a 'foreign' bank. The Royal Bank group has since merged the Royal Bank of Scotland and Williams and Glyn's to operate as a single bank in both countries. This was the first *operational* merger of two commercial banks on different sides of the border.

In recent years on the high streets, the ranks of the banks have been swollen by the emergence of three further competitors: the Yorkshire Bank, the Co-operative Bank, and the revamped Trustee Savings Bank. All are long-established institutions which have recently modernised themselves and changed direction to compete with the other high street banks. The latter two have gained seats in the English clearing house and have thereby become clearing banks.

The Yorkshire Bank. This has acquired a national standing although it retains a strong regional character, most of its 200+ branches being located in the North of England. Set up in 1859 as the 'Yorkshire Penny Savings Bank', it was very much a 'blue-collar' workers' savings institution for most of the first 100 years of its history. By 1959, however, it had shortened its name to 'Yorkshire Bank' and had set about converting itself into a modern commercial bank offering loan and overdraft facilities. It still specialises in catering for individuals and small businesses, much of its lending being undertaken on fixed interest terms over fixed periods, personal loan schemes for example. The capital of the Yorkshire Bank is jointly owned by four of the commercial banks—Barclays, Lloyds, National Westminster, and the Royal Bank of Scotland—which, however, do not participate in its day-to-day running. Yorkshire Bank cheques are cleared through the agency of the Royal Bank of Scotland, the bank having no seat of its own at the clearing house.

The Co-operative Bank. This is a part of the much wider cooperative movement and is wholly owned by CWS Ltd. It was incorporated as a separate bank in 1971, before which time it had been simply the banking department of CWS. It had been established originally to deal with the internal finances and banking needs of the various regional Co-operative Societies, which it continues to do. There are only some 70 full branches of the bank and these offer a wide range of personal services, including personal loan and credit card facilities. In addition, however, the bank operates over 4500 till extensions in Coop shops throughout the country, at which simple cash withdrawals and deposits can be made. These are known as *Handybanks*.

The Co-operative Bank has something of a 'down-market' image and tends still to draw much of its custom from people in the lower-income brackets of the private sector who require only basic banking facilities without needing access to many of more sophisticated services. Even so, business is being built up quite rapidly, including the acquisition of larger accounts, particularly those of some local authorities and trades unions which have been transferred to the Co-operative Bank at least partly for political reasons. It became a clearing bank in 1975 when it obtained a seat in the clearing house.

The Trustee Savings Bank. This became a clearing bank in 1978 when it too acquired a seat at the clearing house. This was an important milestone along the road bringing it into direct competition with the commercial banks. We shall be looking at the history of the TSB in greater detail in Chapter 14 when we examine the savings institutions but for the moment it is sufficient to note that for most of its history its services have been very limited and aimed solely at personal savers. In 1973, however, the Page Committee recommended that the TSB should become a third force in British banking. Since that date, the 72 independent local TSBs have been merged into a modern banking group which has started to offer a full range of banking services, including current accounts, cheque cards, credit cards and loan facilities.

The TSB had traditionally dealt with personal customers from the lower-income groups and the relationship with that market sector has been maintained. However, at the same time strenuous efforts have been made to create a more 'up-market' image which, together with a good range of services and low charges, has attracted much new business away from the other banks. Business accounts are operated and corporate borrowing facilities are available. As its experience has grown, the TSB has become a major competitor for the other clearing banks. In 1979 the TSBs began to be withdrawn from public sector ownership and investors may now buy shares in the TSB through the Stock Market.

Table 2.2 Members of the London clearing house

Bank of England
Bank of Scotland
Barclays
Co-operative
National Girobank
Lloyds
Midlands
National Westminster*
Royal Bank of Scotland
Trustee Savings Bank

* including Coutts and Co.

Functions of the high street banks

In the last few decades the various different types of banking institution have all broadened the basis of their operations and to some extent they have 'intruded' on one anothers' former preserves. In consequence, there is much overlap between the activities of the different types of bank and much confusion in the minds of the public over such terms as 'clearing bank' and 'deposit bank'. Perhaps the most widely used generic term today is 'high street bank'. This is used to describe all the institutions which operate 'retail' branch banking outlets offering traditional deposit, lending and money transfer services to the public at large. This category includes all the clearing banks plus a number of other institutions such as the Yorkshire Bank. The term 'deposit bank' denoted a former official classification of institutions used by the Bank of England in monitoring the monetary system. The Bank now prefers to group institutions according to the organisation with which they align themselves:

Committee of London and Scottish Clearing Banks, Discount Houses Association, Accepting Houses Committee and so on.

Deposit banking. This continues to be the 'bread and butter' of the high street banks, accepting deposits so that loans at interest can be made. The funds which the banks take in are largely due for repayment *on demand* (current accounts) or at *short notice* of a few days (deposit accounts) and, in consequence, the banks have traditionally seen themselves as short-term lenders. The dangers of *mismatching* assets and liabilities has been expressed in the saying: 'Do not borrow short and lend long'. However, the high street banks have a very stable deposit base and they have come to realise that the dangers of mismatching are not so great for them as for other smaller institutions. They can afford to use at least some proportion of the funds available for medium-term loans (up to ten years) and even long-term loans (over ten years) usually granted to industry. The process of using short-term deposits to fund the granting of long-term loans is known as *maturity transformation*. You will be aware that building societies traditionally generated funds for house purchases by a similar process and it is interesting to note that the banks entered the house purchase loan market once they were prepared to accept a degree of mismatching. As we shall see later, access to 'wholesale' money-market funds has also helped the banks to move towards the granting of longer term loans.

Funds transfer facilities. These are the second major activity of the high street banks, being one to which they devote some two-thirds of the efforts of their clerical staff. (We shall be examining these facilities in Chapter 7.) There is little direct profit to the banks from these services, despite the current account commission charges which they often levy. They are provided principally as an inducement for customers to maintain deposits with the banks. You should know that funds held on current account generally attract no interest and can therefore be lent out by the banks more profitably than deposit account funds which have to be paid for with credit interest. Since the early 1980s, several of the high street banks have encouraged customers to hold higher current account balances by agreeing not to levy a commission charge on current accounts if the balance during each charging period of three or six months has not fallen below a set level. At different times different banks have set this threshold at various levels, some even agreeing not to charge customers who simply do not overdraw their accounts.

Ancillary services. A wide range of personal and business services has been added to the banks' repertoires. Some of these are 'traditional', having grown organically out of the normal business of banking; examples would include *trustee services* and *payments abroad.* In more recent times other services have proliferated, often having no direct connection with banking as such, ranging from the provision of *travel insurances* to operations as *estate agents.* The objectives of providing such services are twofold. First, the service may generate profits in its own right. Second, and more importantly, the ability to cater for all a customer's financial needs is seen as a major factor in attracting new business through the concept of the 'one-stop' banking supermarket. It also helps in the retention of existing customers, if only because it results in each customer's financial affairs being so closely enmeshed that transferring the business elsewhere becomes more trouble than it is worth!

Other parts of the commercial banking system

National Girobank
The National Girobank was set up in 1968 (as the National Giro) by the Post Office. It is essentially a money transmission service based around a central computer to which all account holders' payment instructions are sent for processing. Provided that both remitter and recipient of payments maintain giro accounts it is a very efficient system. However, to attract accounts the Girobank was also compelled to offer current account cheque book facilities, enabling its customers to make payments to beneficiaries who do not maintain giro accounts. Facilities have been established for the banks to collect through their clearing system the proceeds of any girocheques paid in to customers' accounts. Giro account withdrawals and deposits can be effected through any one of the country's post offices.

The introduction of the National Giro and the threat of competition which it embodied encouraged the clearing banks to modernise their own money transmission services, and it was instrumental in hastening the introduction of bankers' automated clearing services. Because of the changes that they made, the banks were able to retain some 94% money transmission business, losing only 6% to the National Girobank. The same is true of personal accounts which have not been attracted to the Girobank in the numbers originally anticipated. In an attempt to attract more customers, the Girobank has since started to offer a broader range of banking services, including cheque guarantee cards and personal loans, applications for which are handled postally without an interview. Accounts are conducted without charge for customers who keep in credit.

The Girobank has been more successful in attracting business accounts, especially from businesses which collect large amounts of money from the public, such as the nationalised utilities (gas, electricity, etc.) and mail order businesses. However, the Girobank cannot put the funds so collected to profitable use since the businesses concerned make regular transfers out of their giro accounts, using the funds elsewhere themselves. The Girobank does not make business advances.

The Post Office, through the National Girobank, the National Savings Bank and its time-honoured postal orders and money orders, is thereby able to offer a reasonably complete, if somewhat fragmentary, banking and money transmission service. However, it is unlikely in the forseeable future to offer significant competition to the high street banks for the provision of either deposit banking or borrowing facilities.

Merchant banks

Many institutions today claim the title of 'merchant bank' and, indeed, some of the high street banks have set up their own merchant banking subsidiaries. What these organisations do is difficult to categorise; it varies greatly from one to another. Perhaps our best starting point is to recognise what they do *not* do. They do not undertake the normal high street banking activities of money transmission or deposit banking and lending for the public at large. (We shall examine in detail some of the things that the merchant banks do undertake in later sections of this chapter but for now a brief review will suffice.)

The origins of merchant banking were different from the origins of commercial banking. The first merchant banks arose out of the involvement of certain merchants in the finance of international trade, leading ultimately to the development of the *acceptance credit.* Under one of these facilities, a merchant with a 'good name' in a particular trade would arrange to *accept* on behalf of a little known British importer bills of exchange drawn on him by a foreign exporter in respect of goods shipped to this country. This type of business led to the establishment of specialist *accepting houses* and today it still forms the basis of the trade of many of the merchant banks.

Through their contacts with the money markets, the merchant banks came to act as intermediaries for other businesses wishing to raise both short-term and long-term capital. They began to act as *bankers* making loans to industry themselves and as *issuing houses* handling the issue of shares in new companies through the capital markets. They often act as *agents* in takeover bids and mergers and they handle *rights issues* of shares for existing public companies wishing to raise further capital. They act as general *financial advisers* to big businesses

Table 2.3 Assets and liabilities of the accepting houses 31 March 1987

Liabilities		£m
Capital and sundry liabilities		3 528
Deposits—sterling	15 814	
—currency	14 357	30 171
		33 699
Assets		
Coins, notes and balances with Bank of England		38
Bills discounted:		
UK Treasury bills		—
Other bills		316
Special deposits		—
Market loans		7 105
Certificates of deposit		1 327
British government stocks		538
Loans to UK local authorities		154
Advances		6 741
Currency assets		13 537
Other assets		3 943
		33 699

(*Source: Bank of England Quarterly Bulletin*)

and often take *equity shareholdings* in the companies which they advise, enabling them to share in the profits generated.

The breadth of interests which the merchant banks now have seems almost without limit. They operate unit trusts and manage investment portfolios for various classes of customer, including pension funds and charities. Some operate in the bullion market and the commodity markets. Some run insurance businesses. Some undertake merchanting transactions and so on. Each merchant bank has its own set of specialisations and no two are alike. However, all base their business around their knowledge of and contacts in the *London money markets* and *capital markets*. This variety of activities cannot be financed solely out of the merchant banks' own resources and they take deposits (of large sums) through the money market. A large proportion of their deposits still comes from overseas residents, keeping alive their original links with international trade.

British overseas banks

When Britain was a major colonial power, numerous banks were set up to offer a banking service for the colonies. Although the branches of these banks were located abroad (often spread throughout a number of countries), the head office remained in England. These banks came to specialise in two areas: the provision of retail banking facilities in the countries of operation and import/export finance for trade between those countries and the UK. While the overseas branches of these banks were established in the first instance for the benefit of the colonial administrators, they also served the needs of the developing local economies.

As independence was granted to Britain's possessions, the role of these banks changed. In many of the newly independent states the branches were 'hived off' to form the basis of an independent locally controlled bank, often involuntarily so through the process of nationalisation. In consequence, the banks to some extent turned their attention away from the provision of retail banking services abroad in favour of the provisions of more comprehensive international services between those countries and the UK. They now play an important role in the provision of finance and market intelligence for European businesses wishing to trade with or invest in the countries with which they are involved.

Following a series of mergers and takeovers, there are now two remaining independent banks in this category: Grindlays and the Standard Chartered Bank. Both still have branches throughout the world in countries which were formerly colonies—especially Africa and parts of Asia—and these still form the 'backbone' of the business. In addition, they are very active in the UK foreign exchange and money markets, particularly the *Eurocurrency Market* and the *Interbank Sterling Market*. None of the banks in this category provides a normal high street bank service within the UK, although it is interesting to note that the Standard Chartered Bank recently attempted to broaden its UK base by expanding into this area through its unsuccessful proposals to take over the Royal Bank of Scotland group. Later, the Standard Chartered Bank was itself the target of an unsuccessful takeover attempt by Lloyds Bank which would have achieved the same result from the other direction.

There are some 20 'Commonwealth' banks operating retail banking networks in Canada, Australia and New Zealand which also grew out of the need to provide banking services to British settlers. Although they maintain representative offices in London, their head offices have long been located in the principal country of operations. They still have close links with the UK however. The British Overseas and Commonwealth Bankers Association speaks for the interests of these types of bank.

Foreign banks

The UK, and London especially, has become a major attraction for foreign banks. Currently, over 400 foreign banks have some kind of direct representation in London. Nearly a quarter of these banks have their head offices in the United States. Less than ten of the world's 100 largest banks are not represented in London. What are the reasons for this state of affairs? It results principally from the simple fact that London is one of the world's major financial centres and access to its Foreign Exchange Market and its money markets is vital for any bank which wishes to operate a full international service. The Eurocurrency market is an especially important part of the money markets.

Many of these banks, especially the US contingent, have made major inroads into the UK *Corporate Finance* market. They often specialise in lending to particular sectors of the economy, such as commodity traders, shipping businesses and oil companies. It has been calculated that by 1983 the US banks alone accounted for around one-eighth of all lending to UK corporate borrowers. The funds which these banks lend are generated through money market or overseas operations, not through domestic deposit banking. The foreign banks generally do not offer a retail banking service in the UK, although a few have developed small branch networks serving the needs of particular ethnic groups in localised communities.

Consortium banks

Consortium banks are set up and jointly owned by a number of other banks (which could be merchant banks, commercial banks, etc.) including at least one overseas bank in their number. No one bank may have more than a 50% shareholding in the consortium bank. They developed to enable banks to put together adequate resources and knowledge to provide finance to meet the needs of major multinational companies and foreign governments. Their advantages are that through them small banks may participate in international lending and that they enable the interchange of expertise between participant banks. There are just over 20 consortium banks operating in the UK at the moment, many of them being set up in the early 1970s. Their importance seems to be declining as more banks set up their own international networks.

The Banking Act 1987

The Banking Act 1987 was passed as a result of the necessary 'rescue' of Johnson Matthey Bankers in 1984. It replaced the Banking Act 1979 which itself was a response to the secondary banking crisis of 1973–4, caused by a number of 'fringe banks' getting into difficulties by *borrowing short* and *lending long*. In doing so it abolishes the previous two-tier system of recognised banks and licensed deposit-takers, replacing it with the single designation of 'authorised institution'.

The main purpose of the Act is *prudential supervision*. It provides a statutory basis for the Bank of England's supervision of banks and other deposit-taking businesses and backs this up with a deposit protection scheme to cover any failures which may still occur. It does *not* directly regulate the way in which banks carry out their business.

Deposit taking

All deposit-taking institutions must be authorised by the Bank of England unless an institution falls within one of a number of specific exemptions. Building societies and local authorities, for example, are exempt.

The most important condition for authorisation is that the business must be conducted in a *prudent manner*. In particular, the institution must have adequate capital and liquidity, make adequate provision for depreciation and doubtful debts and maintain adequate accounting and other record and control systems. The Bank is not bound to follow rigid ratio requirements and is therefore able to make *qualitative* judgments as to whether a business is adequately capitalised and being prudently run. Any new institution, however, must have net assets of at least one million pounds at the time of authorisation.

The Act also regulates the issue, form and content of advertisement for deposits and requires overseas banks establishing offices in the UK to give notice to the Bank.

Use of the name 'bank'

This is restricted to larger institutions, those with a capital of five million pounds or more, although this test does not apply to overseas authorised institutions.

The deposit protection scheme

This provides a measure of protection to small depositors in the event of the failure of an authorised institution. All such institutions must contribute to a central fund, the resources of which would be used to pay any depositor who had lost money in a 'bank failure'. Payments to depositors are limited to 75% of the amount lost up to a maximum balance owed of £20 000. The 25% loss borne by the depositor is intended to promote prudence in selecting a home for his savings. The size of each institution's contribution to the central fund is proportional to the size of its deposit base, that is 0.3% of its deposit base up to a maximum of £300 000, with a minimum contribution of £20 000. The fund's assets total £5–6 million.

Changes in control

The Bank is empowered to block changes in the controlling shareholders of authorised institutions incorporated in the UK if it considers that the would–be controllers are not 'fit and proper'. Specifically, no shareholder may acquire a 15% or more stake without the Bank's prior consent nor an existing share-holder a majority shareholding.

The Bank of England

Main areas of responsibility

The Bank of England occupies a unique place in the story of the UK's banking system. Its role today is that of a *central bank*, which every modern economy must have. And yet it started out as a commercial bank in competition with all the other banks. The principal duty of a central bank is to exercise control of the monetary system on behalf of and under the control of the government. To discharge this duty it has four main areas of responsibility:

1   *Banker to the government* including, where appropriate, the raising of loans to finance government expenditure.
2   *Banker to the banking system* enabling banks to make settlements between each other, and acting as 'lender of last resort' to the other banks to provide a measure of stability to the system as a whole.
3   *Control of the money supply* including the issue of notes and coin.
4   *Control of the national debt.*

In some countries these duties have not all been delegated to one organisation. In the United States, for example, notes are issued by the US Treasury while the federal reserve banks together undertake the other duties of a central bank.

Today, the Bank of England is, in effect, a *major institution of government* and yet it remains a *public corporation* rather than having been transformed into a department of state. The special nature of the bank's role in bringing together government and commerce is emphasised by its location, isolated from the seat of government at Westminster, being two miles away in the heart of the City of London.

Development of the Bank of England

We have already outlined much of the history of the Bank of England in our examination of the growth of the British financial system generally. As you will remember, it was set up in 1694 as a private company and from the first it came to act as the government's bank. In 1718, for example, it began to manage the issuing of government securities and to arrange the collection of funds due from the purchasers.

Despite its close links with government, however, the Bank was also for the first 100 years or so a commercial bank. It accepted deposits, issued notes, discounted bills of exchange and made loans. It differed from all other banks of the period only in its constitution; it was a joint stock company which could seek the subscription of capital from any number of investors, while they were partnerships restricted to a maximum of six partners. This meant that the Bank of England had access to a much broader capital base, enabling it to grow much more rapidly than the private banks while remaining stable and safe. It soon became the largest bank in the country.

Growth of central bank duties

Development of the Bank's position as a central bank came about gradually over the years as it assumed or was given certain roles. As the largest bank in the country, the Bank of England found that the smaller private banks began to deposit their reserves with it for safe keeping; it became the *bankers' bank*. This later allowed the development of simple interbank settlement systems. In times of crisis the private banks would, of course, need to withdraw their reserves to meet depositors' demands for repayment. If their reserves were insufficient to prevent the development of a run on the bank, the private banks' last recourse was to ask the Bank of England for its support. This in turn could lead to problems for the Bank if it overextended itself. Although there were sometimes doubts as to whether the Bank would be able to meet all its obligations, it always managed to do so. It thus became the 'lender of last resort' to the banking system.

We have already seen that from the beginning of the nineteenth century the *note issue* came to be concentrated under the control of the Bank of England. The most important single piece of legislation was the Bank Charter Act of 1844 which laid the foundations of the Bank of England as we know it today. Under this Act the Bank was reorganised into two separate departments: the *issue department*, which would handle the note issue, and the *banking department*, which would look after all the other activities of the Bank. This was done because of the importance which was placed on bringing the note issue under proper control although, as we have seen, this proved to be a failure as a device to control the total money supply. The Bank was required to publish a weekly *bank return* showing the balance sheets of both departments. This is still published in the same format every Wednesday, although the work of the Bank is now so complex that it cannot be accomplished by two departments only.

Nationalisation

In 1946 the Bank of England was nationalised and its capital vested in the state. The *constitution* of the Bank, however, remained largely unchanged by nationalisation. Its management was entrusted, as it always had been, to a *court of directors*, consisting of the Governor, the Deputy Governor and 24 directors, all of whom are now appointed by the state. Perhaps the only really surprising thing about nationalisation is that the Bank had managed to function for so long prior to 1946 as an organ of government without the appointment of its officials being under the control of the state.

Functions of the Bank of England today

The functions of the Bank of England today reflect its role as the UK's central bank and are therefore quite different from the functions of the commercial banks. The role of a central bank is, in essence, to assist the government in *controlling the national economy* by regulating the monetary system. It is increasingly the case that this involves the implementation of specific monetary policies with the Bank having only limited freedom for independent action. It is worth noting that although the Bank has statutory power to enforce its instructions to the banking community, and has had since nationalisation in 1946, it has never been necessary to exercise it, operation of the system being achieved through co-operation rather than coercion.

Currency issue

As you know, the Bank of England is now responsible for practically the whole of the UK currency issue and is the only English bank with the power to issue banknotes. You will see from the recent bank return given in Table 2.4 that the modern currency issue is wholly fiduciary; the assets of the issue department held in support of the notes and coin consist of government and other securities. There is no longer any gold or silver backing for the currency. In managing the note issue the Bank follows instructions given to it by the Treasury, acting in effect as its agent. The Bank has no discretionary powers of its own to vary the level of the issue.

Table 2.4 The bank return as at 25 March 1987

Liabilities	£m	Assets	£m
	Issue department		
Notes in circulation	12 572	Government securities	2 517
Notes in banking		Other securities	10 063
department	8		
	12 580		12 580
	Banking department		
Capital	14	Government securities	458
Public deposits	90	Advances and other	
Special deposits	—	accounts	1 965
Bankers' deposits	1 011	Premises, equipment	
Reserves and other		and other securities	424
accounts	1 741	Notes and coins	9
	2 856		2 856

The government's bank

The Bank no longer generally maintains accounts for individuals and businesses in the private sector—there are some exceptions, such as the personal accounts of the staff—having given up the business of commercial banking. It does, however, maintain the accounts of government departments and these are shown in the bank return under the heading *public deposits*. If the balance shown seems small, this is because the government balances its revenue and expenditure through the use of *Treasury bills*, minimising the total of liquid funds held idle in its bank accounts. Short-term government borrowing is also effected by the use of Treasury bills, although occasionally the Bank will make direct short-term loans to the government; these are known as *ways and means advances*. The figure for public deposits also includes the dividend accounts of the *Commissioners of the National Debt*; managing the national debt is a part of the Bank of England's duties.

Managing the national debt

The *National Debt* represents *accumulated borrowing* undertaken by the government to finance its expenditure. Just like an individual, the state finances much of its normal activity out of its income—principally taxation in its many guises—but occasionally major projects or other items of expenditure arise, wars, capital projects and so on, requiring volumes of funds which cannot be met from this source. The government then borrows the money from investors, normally in this country but sometimes from abroad. The money required is usually readily available, it being unthinkable that the national government should be unable to repay its debts.

In October 1986, the total outstanding stood at £145 632 million, of which £2909 million was foreign currency debt. The sterling debt is made up of the following items.

Government stocks. These represent the long-term borrowing of the government; they are traded on the Stock Exchange where they are often known as *gilt-edged stocks*. When it needs to raise a long-term loan, the government will invite investors generally to subscribe to a new stock which it proposes to issue. The terms of the new stock will be announced in advance—in other words how much stock will be sold, the rate of interest that will be paid to investors and when they will be repaid.

Undated stocks have no fixed redemption date, the government having the option either to repay whenever it wishes or to allow the loan to run on indefinitely. It would be unusual now to issue a new undated stock (investors do not like them) but many of the modern government stocks quote a period during which repayment will be effected, the exact date being at the government's discretion, rather than specifying one fixed date from the outset.

The interest rate offered on the stock must, of course, be competitive with interest rates generally at the time of issue. Normally a *fixed rate* of interest will apply throughout the whole life of the stock, although recently some *variable* rate stocks have been issued. The name of a particular stock tells you much of the above information, as well as indicating the department of government which has arranged the loan, for example, Treasury stock 8¼% 1987–90.

The Bank of England handles the administration of these stocks, including the remittance of interest and redemption payments to holders of them. It also handles the issue of new stocks and advises on the timing of new issues, which may be made either to raise capital for additional government expenditure or simply to find the funds to finance repayment of an existing stock which is due for redemption. This latter purpose involves careful monitoring of the market levels of interest rates. When rates are high, new issues will be confined to *short-dated* stocks since the government will not wish to commit itself to paying unnecessarily high rates of interest for years into the future. Conversely, when rates are low, *long-dated* stocks will be preferred and, in addition, the Bank may advise the redemption of any high interest stocks which have entered the period within which repayment is permitted. The funds for such repayment will be found by making a new issue at the current (lower) interest rates and a cost saving can therefore be effected, although the administrative costs of the exercise must be offset against this.

Treasury bills. These represent the short-term borrowing of the government. A Treasury bill is a promise by the government to pay a specific sum of money (the minimum amount is £10 000) 91 days after the bill is issued. These bills are sold at a *discount* on their face value; a purchaser who holds a Treasury bill for 91 days will therefore get back more than he paid for it. This is, in effect, rather like receiving interest on the amount paid to the government when purchasing the bill. Treasury bills are sold each week by the Bank of England on behalf of the government and are used to raise the funds needed to bridge short-term gaps between the state's income and its expenditure. The *discount houses* always bid for the whole amount of each week's issue of Treasury bills under a gentleman's agreement and the government is thereby assured of raising the money which it needs.

Non-marketable debt. This comprises such items as national savings certificates, premium savings bonds, save-as-you-earn contracts and so on. All of these are aimed at the personal investor and form part of the *National Savings* movement. These items represent funds loaned to the government but they differ from gilt-edged stocks and Treasury bills in that they *cannot be on-sold* by the holder to a third party. The holder of a Treasury bill may sell it to someone else if he does not wish to hold it until maturity; the holder of a national savings certificate does not have this option, although he may ask for early repayment of it if he is prepared to suffer a loss of interest.

The role of the Bank in managing the national debt is, as you will appreciate, a very complex one. The work involved is not reflected to any great degree in the bank return.

Implementation of government monetary policy

Probably the most important single function of the Bank of England is its role as the government's agent in implementing its monetary policy in pursuit of overall national economic objectives. As part of this process, the Bank acts as a medium for the two-way transmission of information between government and the financial markets. Among other things, it collects a great deal of statistical information from all the financial institutions concerning the volume of their business, to what sectors of the economy they are lending, who is providing their deposits and so on. As a bank clerk, you might find yourself involved in compiling returns to your head office which will form part of your own bank's report to the Bank of England. A compilation of much of the data collected is published as the *Bank of England Quarterly Review*.

Through its influence on and its control over the other banks and financial institutions, the Bank is able to restrain or to increase the total money supply in the economy by affecting their ability to create credit. We shall examine these controls in some detail in Chapter 9 and until then a brief summary of the available techniques will be sufficient.

Open market operations. The Bank may undertake sales or purchases of Treasury bills and government stocks on the open market. This is done to influence the volume of money in circulation. Selling these securities 'mops up' excess purchasing power, thereby reducing the amount of money in circulation and pushing up interest rates. Buying securities has the opposite effect of releasing money into the economy.

Because of the *multiplier effect* of the credit creation process, the overall effect on the money supply of such manoeuvres is much greater than just the value of the securities bought or sold. When the Bank sells securities, for instance, the immediate result is a reduction in bank deposits as purchasers issue cheques in favour of the Bank. This puts pressure on the banks' *liquidity ratios* and they may have to call in some loans or overdrafts to maintain a safe relationship between assets and liabilities. In its turn, this action may again reduce deposits requiring a further contraction of credit and so on until equilibrium is regained. Because of this effect, open market operations are a particularly effective way of adjusting the availability of credit. In fact, today they are the principal tool of the Bank in its monetary operations.

Interest rates. The take-up of credit in the economy depends not only on its supply but also its price, as represented by the rate of interest which borrowers must pay. If interest rates rise, borrowing is discouraged and the credit creation process is slowed down. If rates fall, the reverse occurs. The Bank can influence the general level of interest rates by adjusting the rates which it charges when acting as the *lender of last resort* to the banking community as a whole. The rate charged is the foundation stone of the whole interest rate structure: other rates always tend to move in line with it. Until 1981 the Bank used to announce once a week the rate which it would charge; this was known as *bank rate* or, latterly, *minimum lending rate* (MLR). Now, however, the Bank works 'within a band of interest rates' which are not published, the Bank having stated its intention to follow interest rates rather than lead them. Even so, the availability of the Bank as lender of last resort remains the ultimate guarantee of the solvency of the financial system, and the banks continue to base their own interest rate structures on the rate at which the Bank of England is currently willing to lend.

Reserve ratios. You have already learnt that a deposit bank has to maintain an adequate cash (or liquidity) ratio between liquid assets and liabilities so as to ensure that it can meet day-to-day demands for payment. The level of this ratio will be determined by making a compromise between prudence and profits. The Bank of England may, however, *direct* that the ratio be maintained at a higher level than the deposit banks feel to be necessary. This has the effect of reducing the supply of credit because the higher the ratio becomes, the smaller the multiplier is in the credit creation process; the banks have to keep on hand a greater proportion of each deposit which they take.

From 1971 to 1981 the Bank of England required the banks to maintain a set level for their *reserve assets ratio*, specifying very exactly the types of asset and liability which had to be taken into account when making the calculation. This was not quite the same thing as a simple liquidity ratio since it did not include cash holdings. Since August 1981 there has been no direct management of liquidity ratios as a measure of control, although all banks and licensed deposit takers are required to keep $\frac{1}{2}\%$ of their *eligible liabilities* on special non-operational, non-interest bearing deposit accounts with the Bank. In addition, the banks are required to keep *prescribed averages* of liquid assets. (We shall be looking at this in Chapter 9.)

Special deposits. These represent an alternative method of affecting the banks' liquidity ratios. The banks may be instructed to deposit with the Bank of England cash equivalent to a stated percentage of their total eligible liabilities. These funds are not available for use by the banks and therefore cannot be incorporated in the calculation of their liquidity ratios, although the Bank may pay interest on the funds. Clearly, calling for special deposits is equivalent to establishing or increasing a reserve assets ratio and it has exactly the same effect.

Funding. This is the conversion of short-term government debt into longer-term debt. The Bank may be calling in securities which could be classed as liquid assets by the banks when they calculate their liquidity ratios, replacing them with securities which may not be included in this calculation. The effect is again to cause a contraction in the banks' ability to create credit, leading to the reduction in advances. This exercise is not particularly common because it can be costly to the government.

Supervision of the banking industry
Closely allied with its duty to control the money supply is the Bank of England's duty to supervise the banking industry in general. This area has grown in importance since the secondary banking crisis of 1973–74. The Banking Act 1987 puts this supervision on a statutory basis (*see* above).

Directives to the banks. During the Second World War, the Bank of England began to issue directives about their advances to the banks, indicating either how much they should be lending overall (*quantitative directives*) or which sections of the economy should be given priority in the queue for finance (*qualitative directives*). Although these directives could have been *enforced* if necessary, the Bank has never had recourse to this ability, having been able through 'moral suasion' (the Bank's term for friendly persuasion) to achieve its objectives. Quantitative directives have not been made since 1971 when the Bank began to use other methods to control the supply of credit but qualitative directives are still issued from time to time.

Lender of last resort
If the London money market is short of funds, the Bank of England will always come to its aid. This assistance will be used only as a last resort by the market since the interest rate charged by the bank will be higher than that charged for funds obtained from other sources. As we shall see, when money is short the banks will have to call in the short term loans they have made to the discount houses and it is they who will have to seek the Bank's help.

The bankers' bank
The commercial banks maintain accounts with the Bank of

England to enable them to settle transactions both among themselves and other financial institutions. The balances on these current accounts form part of their liquid assets, counting towards their liquidity ratios. These accounts are, of course, additional to any non-operational accounts, such as special deposits, which the Bank of England may require them to open.

International functions

The Bank of England has a number of international functions to perform on behalf of the British government, including representing the state in relations with foreign central banks and also in various institutions such as the Bank for International Settlements (BIS) and the International Monetary Fund (IMF).

Exchange control. Since 1946 the Bank has had the responsibility for 'disposing of the means of foreign payment in the national interest'. This means that it has the duty of enforcing any restrictions on payments abroad which the government may institute. For most of the period since the start of the Second World War all such payments were strictly controlled. However, since 1979 there have been no such restrictions in force and UK residents are free to make any foreign payment they require.

Exchange Equalisation Account. The Bank operates this account with the objective of stabilising the exchange rates between the pound sterling and the major foreign currencies. As we have said, the country's bullion reserves were transferred to this account in the 1930s when the note issue became wholly fiduciary. The fund's currency reserves are used to buy sterling when it is weak, bolstering demand and thereby stabilising its price. Currency reserves can be replenished by sales of sterling when the pound is strong and commands a favourable exchange rate.

The money markets

Introduction

London is the hub of the UK financial system. In consequence, it has become the centre of operations for a number of interlinked *finance markets* which extend their influence throughout our national economic activity. The three principal markets are the *money market*, the *capital market* and the *foreign exchange market*. You must not imagine that these three markets are entirely separate from one another; they are not. Events in one market influence events in the others. Many of the participating institutions operate in more than one section of these markets and are able to switch funds from one area to another. Furthermore, the dividing line between the activities of different markets is often blurred and difficult to define. For instance, between the two extremes of investing 'permanent' funds in a business (capital market) and making an overnight loan to the concern (money market) there lie an infinite number of inter-

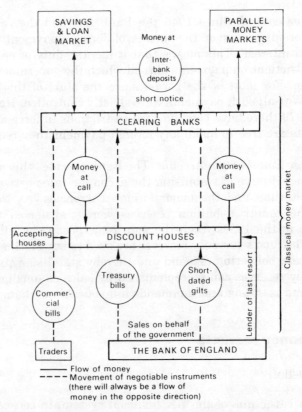

Fig. 2.1 The main participants in the London money markets

mediate arrangements which gradually shade into one another.

The main participants in the London money markets are shown in Fig. 2.1.

The 'classical money market'

The money market is concerned with the *short-term* borrowing and lending of money. Many of the loans arranged through it are in fact for very short terms, ranging right down to *call money* loans which are repayable on demand without a period of notice.

There are two complementary component parts to this market. First, the *discount market*, which provides short/medium-term finance both for government and for commerce by the discounting of Treasury bills and commercial bills of exchange. The discount houses do not use their own resources when discounting bills but raise the required funds by borrowing from the money market proper. Second, the *money market proper*, in which the main participants are the discount houses which use it to raise the funds which they use as their stock in trade and the commercial banks which provide the bulk of these funds. As well as lending to the discount houses, the banks will also lend short-term funds to one another through the *interbank sterling market*. The money market proper facilitates 'money trading' between different financial institutions and does not in itself involve any direct lending to or borrowing from people or organisations outside the financial community.

Banks acquire the funds which they use in their money market dealings through their activities in the *savings and loan market*, in other words their 'bread and butter' business of taking deposits from one set of customers and using them to make loans to another set of customers. As you know, some proportion of customers' deposits must be held in liquid form so as to be available to cover withdrawals. The banks have found that short notice loans in the money market make a profitable home for a significant part of their liquid holdings. The savings and loan market is a part of neither the money market nor the capital market, being to some extent an alternative to them. For example, a business requiring medium-term finance could obtain it either through the loan market by obtaining an over-draft from its bank or through the money market by discounting bills of exchange. (We discuss the *savings and loan market* in Chapter 4.)

Thus, the participants in the 'classical money market' are the banks, the discount houses, the accepting houses, which promote the availability of readily discountable bills, and the Bank of England which is the 'lender of last resort' to the system through the assistance which it can give to the discount houses.

The 'parallel money markets'

Since the Second World War, a set of parallel money markets has grown up alongside the classical market. These have arisen largely out of the desire of organisations other than the banks and the discount houses to have *direct access to the market* to deposit or borrow short-term funds without using financial intermediaries. The growth of these parallel markets has been assisted by the development of the interbank sterling deposit market and the *Eurocurrency market*. Principal participants in these parallel markets include the finance houses, local author-ities, commercial companies and even, on occasion, private individuals.

Discount houses

The discount houses are a group of financial institutions chiefly concerned with the processing of *short-term* money market funds. Together they make up the Discount Houses Association and, perhaps unexpectedly, they all developed as independent concerns not associated with, nor owned by, any of the other financial institutions. Their business is the collection of funds which the other major financial institutions have available as being surplus to their own needs in the immediate short-term. They on-lend these funds to other organisations which have a short-term borrowing requirement. Thus, they are an important part of what is known as the classical money market (Table 2.5).

Discounting bills of exchange

The original activity of the discount houses, and the one from which they take their name, was the discounting of commercial bills of exchange. Although less common than they were, term bills of exchange are still used to regulate the settlement of commercial transactions undertaken on short duration credit terms both in respect of inland trade and, more importantly, international trade. To explain: if, for example, a manufacturer agrees to supply goods to the value of £5000 on six-month credit terms, he may draw a bill of exchange on the purchaser ordering him to pay the appropriate amount at the expiry of the six-month period or, more commonly, after 180 days as this is a more specific measure of time. If the purchaser is happy with the arrangement, he will signify his agreement to pay the £5000 on the due date by marking (signing) the bill with his *acceptance* and returning it to the manufacturer who is known as the *drawer* of the bill. The drawer then holds the bill until the due date when he represents it for payment.

Table 2.5 The discount houses' sources and uses of funds as at 31 March 1987

	£m
Liabilities	
Money borrowed from:	
Bank of England	1492
Other UK banks	6795
Other UK sources	2480
Overseas: Sterling	5
Other currencies	229
Assets	
Money invested in:	
British government stocks	100
UK Treasury bills	313
Other sterling bills	6001
Local authority bills	117
Sterling certificates of deposit	3397
Other investments	1086
Currency assets	238
Cash ratio deposits	8

If the drawer finds that he cannot afford to wait until the maturity of the bills before receiving his money, he can try to sell the *accepted bill* to a third party. Clearly, he will not be able to sell the bill for its face value, as this offers no inducement to a prospective purchaser; he must be prepared to sell it at a *discount.* The amount of discount deducted by a purchaser from the face value will reflect both the length of time that he will have to wait to get his money back and the level of risk that the acceptor (the buyer of the goods) will not be able to pay up on the due date. The rate of discount is usually expressed as an annualised percentage and is, in effect, equivalent to an interest rate charged to the seller of the bill.

Many such bills are today discounted by the acceptor's bank but in the past banks were accustomed to leave this activity to the specialist discount houses. Discounting commercial bills is a comparatively risky business and the discount house will try to minimise the risk by looking for 'two good names' to each bill which it handles. In other words, both the drawer and the drawee (who becomes the acceptor when he signs for acceptance) should be good for the money represented by the bill. If the discount house cannot obtain payment from the drawee, it has the right of recourse to the drawer who then has to settle matters himself with the drawee! A bill bearing two good names is called a *first class bill.* Judging the creditworthiness of the drawee, especially in foreign transactions, is not easy and it was in this respect that the discount houses first built up their expertise. When the practice of discounting bills became common, specialist *accepting houses* sprang up which for a fee would add their good name to bills which might not otherwise have been discountable. Bills accepted by such a house are known as *bank bills* or *fine bills* and they can be discounted at a lower rate of discount.

Thus, the discounting of trade bills provides short-term finance for commerce; most of these bills are drawn for periods of six months or less. You will see from Table 2.5 that a large proportion of the funds available to the discount houses is channelled in this direction, classified as 'other sterling bills'.

Treasury bills

We have already outlined the procedure by which the Bank of England issues Treasury bills weekly, both to raise finance to cover temporary excesses of state expenditure over income and as part of its *open market operations* to mop up excess purchasing power in the economy. In this process the discount houses have come to act as *middlemen,* standing between the Bank of England and the financial markets generally. Every week, the discount houses bid for the whole of the Treasury bill issue in competition with one another and with any other institution wishing to purchase direct from the Bank. The share of the issue which each one obtains is determined by the competitiveness of its bid in relation to all the other bids. Since, as you will see, the discount houses are using borrowed funds to buy these bills, the amount tendered will be related to the prevailing rates of interest. If interest rates are falling, the discount houses will tender at a higher price—in other words they will deduct a *lower* discount from the face value of the bills in order to arrive at the tender price; if interest rates rise, the tender price will fall, reflecting the higher cost of money to the discount house.

The commercial banks invest some of their liquid funds in purchases of Treasury bills, arranging always to have on hand enough bills maturing each week in the immediate future to cover anticipated outgoings of funds. This helps them to plan their liquidity levels to ensure that they can always meet depositors' demands for payment while obtaining some return on their liquid funds. Liquid funds held in the form of cash would not generate any income. Since 1934 the banks have not tendered for newly issued bills in competition with the discount houses, preferring instead to buy all the bills which they need from the houses. This enables the banks to choose bills of the maturity they want so that money will become available just when they need it. This arrangement is also useful to the Bank of England as the discount houses provide a guaranteed market for all the Treasury bills which are issued, without the distraction of too much competition.

The discount houses will often hold Treasury bills for a month or more before on-selling them to the banks or other financial institutions. This, of course, affects the price at which they are sold; the closer a bill is to its maturity date, the closer its price will be to its *par value*.

Government stocks

The discount houses began to trade in government stocks during the 1920s and 1930s when other business was hard to find. They deal in *short-dated gilts* which usually have less than two years to run to maturity. Like Treasury bills, these can be bought at a discount and then held to maturity, when they are redeemable at *par value*. The amount of any discount will be adjusted to allow for any interest due to be paid to the holder of the stock during the intervening period. In fact, the discount houses do not usually hold the stocks which they buy to maturity, but make them up into 'packets' of convenient amounts, £100 000 and over in most cases maturing on the same day, and resell them to the commercial banks. As we have noted, the banks like to build up holdings of short-term assets maturing throughout the year to provide themselves with a steady inflow of liquid funds combined with a moderate rate of return.

Certificates of deposit

The use of certificates of deposit (CDs) has grown immensely in the last 20 years. A CD is a promise by a financial organisation other than a clearing bank to pay a fixed sum of money (denominated either in pounds sterling or, more recently, US dollars) on a specified day in the future. We shall examine the CD market later, but you should note now that a holder of a CD can sell it to someone else at a discount on its face value if the money is needed before the maturity date. The discount houses participate in this market which, after all, is very similar to their other areas of activity. The CDs which they acquire are again often resold to the banks to form part of their portfolios of maturity securities.

Sources of the discount houses' funds

Call money. As you will have seen in Table 2.5, the bulk of the funds used by the discount houses are obtained on loan from the UK banks. This money is usually borrowed at *call*. This means that the banks can ask for it back without giving any period of notice at all. Lending money on this basis is very useful to the banks because it allows them to lend money for one day at a time. If they need the money it is available almost immediately, so it is almost equivalent to holdings of cash in this respect. However, while the funds are out on loan they are earning interest, which is an advantage over cash holdings. The interest rate charged for call money is, of course, very low when compared with the rates for long-term money. The discount houses make their profits out of the difference between the interest which they pay on their borrowing and the discounts they deduct from the par value of the assets which they purchase with these funds.

Bank of England loans. If a bank calls in its money from a discount house, it is usually to settle an interbank debt. The discount house can often then reborrow the money from the recipient bank. If, however, the banks generally are *contracting their credit*, the discount house may be compelled to balance its books by borrowing from the Bank of England, acting in its capacity as the 'lender of last resort'. The Bank has guaranteed that it will always accede to such requests as a *quid pro quo* for the discount houses always taking up the whole of the Treasury bill issues. However, the interest rate on these loans will always be higher than the *Treasury bill discount rate*. This means that the discount houses will find themselves making a loss out of such a transaction. It is the fear of making losses which ensures that market rates of interest move in sympathy with the rates at which the Bank will lend to the discount houses.

In short, the discount houses act as a *buffer* between the commercial banks and the Bank of England. When the money market is short of funds, the banks withdraw their money from the discount houses who then have to turn to the Bank of England for support. If it wishes, the Bank can always inject funds into the money market by buying up eligible bills and gilt-edged stocks, that is open market operations avoiding the need to lend directly to the discount houses. Open market operations have become the Bank's preferred method of assisting the market since 1981.

Accepting houses

Merchant banking origins

In the 18th century the bill of exchange assumed great importance as the normal method for regulating payment in respect of international trade, especially for transactions undertaken on credit terms. Understandably, exporters in foreign countries were happier shipping goods to Britain if they knew that the purchaser (drawee) who was to accept their bills was of high repute and undoubted integrity. Certain merchants who had built up international reputations in handling specific types of goods thereby found that they had a significant advantage in the market place. Smaller importers, on the hand, found that exporters became less and less willing to trade with them and new businesses had the greatest difficulty breaking in to the chosen market.

To overcome these problems, the important merchants were often asked to 'lend their names' to transactions undertaken by lesser known importers. The exporter abroad would be asked to draw his bills on the 'good name' who would accept them and ultimately pay them on behalf of the true importer. The importer would have to pay the merchant both the amount which was due on the bill and a commission fee for the use of his name. Where a merchant entered into a regular arrangement for this to be done, he would set a limit for each importer and at any one time he would be prepared to have outstanding accepted bills up to this figure. The *acceptance credit* had arrived.

It was not long before similar facilities were being sought by foreign importers of British goods who wanted the well-known merchants to accept on their behalf bills drawn by the British exporters. This fostered in two ways the willingness of the British exporters to sell their goods to such buyers. First, they had an acceptable guarantee of payment from a known and trusted source. Second, while awaiting payment at the end of the credit period they would be holding an accepted bill which could be readily sold for cash through the discount market because of the reputation of the acceptor. In fact, it became possible for exporters to totally finance transactions by using the discount market to obtain, in effect, payment in advance. If they arrange with importers that they may draw bills on the accepting house as soon as the terms of the contracts have been agreed, they may immediately discount the bills. The proceeds of this action are then available to finance the purchase of any necessary materials and the costs of production.

The granting of acceptance credits became such a profitable part of many merchants' businesses that they gave up their own trade in commodities, becoming solely *merchant bankers*. From the 1930s onward, acceptance facilities came to be used increasingly to finance inland trade as well as international trade providing commerce with a competitive alternative to bank advances for the financing of day-to-day trade.

Accepting houses today

As we have already mentioned, the 'merchant banks' have a multiplicity of activities. Some have almost ceased to act as accepting houses, while some of the more recently established ones have never really built up this side of their business. Seventeen of the leading merchant banks, which continue to offer acceptance facilities as part of their business, together make up the *Accepting Houses Committee*. This acts as the representative body for the merchant banks generally in the UK as well as providing regulatory controls. Members include such well-known institutions as Hambros, Schroders, Lazards, and Rothschilds.

A bill that has been accepted by a London accepting house becomes a *bank bill* or a *first-class bill of exchange*. This makes it easier to sell on the discount market, usually at a fine (lower) rate of discount and may make it eligible for rediscount with the Bank of England. The list of eligible names now comprises over 50 'banks', including the English and Scottish clearing banks, the members of the Accepting Houses Committee and some other accepting houses, plus some overseas and 'commonwealth' banks. A bill accepted by any of these institutions is known as a *prime bank bill* or an *eligible bill*. Such bills are attractive to the discount houses as investments and they therefore command a particularly 'fine' discount rate.

In their guise as merchant banks, the accepting houses today undertake many other functions in addition to the granting of acceptance credits, particularly in respect of their operations in the *capital markets*. (We shall examine their role in these markets in Chapter 4.)

Parallel money markets

As we have already noted, in recent years new mechanisms have sprung up giving access to the money markets to institutions which previously had been unable to deal other than indirectly: these are known as the *parallel money markets*. Unlike the traditional markets, all borrowing on the parallel money markets is undertaken on an *unsecured* basis. As we said earlier, you should not imagine these markets as being truly separate from one another. They are simply alternative channels of access to the money market as a whole. Funds entering the market through any of the available channels may circulate for a time within the market—being passed from 'bank' to 'bank'—before being on-lent outside the market. (We shall examine the features of the parallel markets in detail in Chapter 10 and for the moment we will content ourselves with a brief review of the component markets.)

The interbank sterling market

Perhaps the most significant of the parallel markets, the interbank sterling market acts as a link between them all. It is a vehicle for the 'banking' institutions to lend to, or borrow from, one another according to their needs. The participants are the clearing banks, the merchant banks, discount houses and the foreign banks. Funds may enter the interbank market from any one of the parallel markets and move from one bank to another several times before being used or on-lent to another on the parallel markets. Deposits in the interbank market are for round amounts, usually of £100 000 or more, the term and rate of interest being fixed at the outset.

The local authority market

Like the national government, local government finances much of its activity, especially capital expenditure, by *borrowing*, using its income only to fund day-to-day expenses including payment of the interest on any loans obtained. As we shall see in Chapter 4, a great deal of this borrowing is *long-term* and is effected through the savings market and the capital market, by taking interest bearing deposits and by issuing various types of bonds and loan stocks. Since the 1950s local authorities have also raised short-term funds through the money market by the issue of *bills* and the taking of *short-term loans*.

The finance houses market

Finance houses are institutions which provide specialist finance to assist both private individuals and businesses with the purchase of capital assets such as vehicles and of other items. Their principal facilities are *hire purchase* loans and *leasing*. They raise funds by taking deposits from the general public or by borrowing from the money market. The latter course is particularly attractive to them for two reasons. First, it is much simpler to raise money by buying 'wholesale' in large amounts than it is to attract 'retail' deposits. Second, levels of finance house lending tend to be quite closely controlled by the government. In consequence, the finance houses need *flexibility* in their access to deposits, facilitating their increase or decrease at short notice.

The intercompany market

Developed since 1969, this market was originally the product of a period of tight credit. Businesses which could not raise finance from the banking system found that they could borrow direct from other companies which had surplus funds. Specialist brokers have now emerged to act as intermediaries in this market which consists of some 500 major companies. Loans are for £50 000 and over. Since these loans are made direct from one company to another, they have no negotiability; the lender cannot retrieve his funds by on-selling his rights to someone else. The intercompany market differs in this respect from the other money markets. A company which has surplus funds need not always dispose of them through the intercompany market. They could be profitably placed with a finance company, with a local authority, or through any one of the parallel markets. The options open to the company's finance director illustrate the interlinked nature of these markets.

Eurocurrency

Eurocurrency is the name given to deposits of the currency of one country held with a bank which is located in a different country. For example, US dollars held on an account with a bank in London would be called Eurocurrency deposits. Eurocurrency dealings began in the 1950s when holders of US dollars found that they could obtain better rates of interest if they deposited their funds with banks in Europe instead of in the United States.

The Eurocurrency market is no longer restricted to dealings in US dollars; several other currencies are traded in, including deutschmarks, Swiss francs, Dutch guilders, and sterling—held by banks outside the UK, of course. Neither is it now restricted to banks in Europe, although London remains the most important centre of the market. It is today an international market dealing in short-term, large amount currency loans. In recent years a *Eurobond* market has developed which deals in longer-term currency loans. The interest rates which borrowers pay for funds obtained through the Eurocurrency market are closely related to the prevailing rates in the country of the currency concerned. Thus, a borrower of Eurodollars will be paying a similar rate to borrowers in the United States.

Certificates of deposit

Dollar certificates of deposit. These were introduced in the mid-1960s to attract dollar deposits which were too small to be of interest to the Eurocurrency markets. The certificate acknowledges receipt of a dollar amount (minimum $25 000) by a bank, and is repayable on a stated date. This may be set at any time from one month to five years after the date of issue. The interest rate is fixed at the outset, having regard to prevailing interest rates and the period of the deposit. Usually, the longer there is to maturity, the higher the interest rate.

Sterling certificates of deposit. These were a later innovation. They operate in the same way as dollar certificates of deposit, being issued for deposits of £50 000 and over up to a maximum of £500 000. Both dollar and sterling CDs are *negotiable*. This means that holders can sell them to someone else if the money is needed before the repayment date. A *secondary market* for the resale of CDs is made by the discount houses. Thus, although the certificates may be issued for quite long terms, they are also suitable for short-term investment.

We said at the beginning of this section that the money markets are closely related to other UK financial markets, particularly the capital market and the savings market which are dealt with in Chapter 4. Many of the institutions which operate in the money markets are also active on the capital and savings markets and when you come to read Chapter 4 you will find much that will be familiar to you. Before we start to look at these markets in detail, however, we will examine in Chapter 3 the structures and workings of the *commercial banks* as they provide a vital link between these various markets.

Summary

1 British banking had its origins in the activities of the gold-smiths, out of which the private banks developed.

2 Joint stock banking began in 1826. At first these banks could not operate in London, but later this was permitted against the loss of their powers to issue notes.

3 In 1844 there were 114 commercial banks; by 1920 a series of amalgamations had reduced the number of clearing banks to eleven. By 1970 most of the country's banking activity was concentrated in the hands of the 'big four' clearing banks.

4 The commercial banks have three basic functions:
   (a) deposit-taking;
   (b) money transfer facilities;
   (c) lending.

5 Other components of the British banking system include:
   (a) the Trustee Savings Bank;
   (b) the National Girobank;
   (c) merchant banks;
   (d) British overseas banks;
   (e) foreign banks;
   (f) consortium banks.

6 Deposit-taking is regulated by the Banking Act 1987 which provides for the licensing of deposit-takers and for a deposit protection scheme.

7 The Bank of England is the country's central bank and has the following functions:
   (a) banker to the government;
   (b) banker to the banking system;
   (c) control of the money supply;
   (d) control of the currency issue;
   (e) control of the national debt;
   (f) supervision of the banking industry.

8 The money market comprises the 'classical' money market and the more recent 'parallel' money markets.

Self-assessment questions

1 List the functions of the Bank of England.
2 List the functions of the commercial banks.

3 Define: (a) the national debt; (b) the discount market; (c) acceptance credits; (d) clearing banks.

4 True or false?

(a) A certificate of deposit is a negotiable instrument.

(b) Only the 'big four' can properly be called clearing banks.

(c) The principal activity of a bank is the granting of loans.

(d) The Bank of England sets national monetary policy.

(e) The discount houses are a buffer in the money market between the Bank of England and the commercial banks.

5 Why do the commercial banks devote so much of their effort to the provision of money transfer facilities? Is there any profit in these services?

6 How has the growth of the parallel money markets affected the activities of the City? Have there been any repercussions on the activities of the commercial banks?

7 What would happen if the Bank of England was instructed by the government to cease exercising any control over the country's money supply?

Assignments

Memorandum to: Student
From: Branch Manager
Subject: Presentations at local school

We have been contacted by our local secondary school, the head-master of which has asked us to arrange for a member of staff to go along to speak to groups of 15–16-year-old pupils about banking. I have agreed, and two presentations will be required. I would like you to prepare the presentations and deliver them. The agreed subjects are:

The high street banks
What do they do, and why are they important to the general public? Please pay particular attention to the following points:

(a) The pupils seem to be confused about the differences between commercial banks/high street banks/clearing banks/etc.

(b) There have been some complaints in the local press about the number of banks in the shopping centre (and the lack of shops!).

(c) We ourselves have closed branches throughout the country in recent years, and this should be explained.

The City
How does it impinge on the lives of the general public?
This requires a brief résumé of the various institutions of the 'square mile', what they do, and how their activities affect our national commercial life.

I think you should bear in mind that the pupils would be unlikely to sit attentively through a 'speech'. Try to vary methods in your presentation, for example illustrations, charts, diagrams, handouts, etc.

(*NB:* This assignment would be suitable for group work, each individual group researching and presenting a particular topic within the overall presentation.)

3 The financial structure of a commercial bank

Chapter objectives

After studying this chapter you should be able to:
- recognise the structure of a commercial bank's balance sheet and be aware of its sources and uses of funds;
- identify the nature and significance of a bank's assets and liabilities;
- distinguish between a bank's liquid and other assets, and appreciate the security and profitability of each;
- outline the purposes of and the methods used for official control of bank credit;
- explain the main methods of protecting depositors' funds.

Introduction

You should already be familiar with the idea of a *balance sheet* and know that it tells us how the finances of a business are structured. A business produces its balance sheet annually, showing the value of its assets and the extent of its liabilities on the same day every year. Many of the figures shown would be quite different if the balance sheet were produced as little as one day later but, even so, one solitary balance sheet will tell us a great deal about the nature of the trade which the business is engaged in. We have said that a balance sheet shows the concern's assets and liabilities; looked at in a different way, these figures show us where the business gets its finance from and what uses it puts the money to.

A series of balance sheets can be even more enlightening as it shows us the general direction in which the business is going: whether it is expanding or contracting, whether one activity is becoming more important than another and so on. There is also the advantage that a series of balance sheets can reassure us that the position shown by one year's figures is not completely unrepresentative of the normal state of affairs. We shall examine the use of balance sheets in assessing the health of businesses generally in Chapter 14; in this chapter we concentrate on finding out what a bank's balance sheet can tell us about the business of banking.

The business of banking

Banks act as *financial intermediaries*, accepting money on deposit from one group of people who may want it back on demand or at very short notice and lending it out to other people for periods of time up to several years. The banks' function, then, is to convert short-run deposits into longer-run loans. On the one side stand people who have money which they would like to lend but who would also like to get it back whenever they wish. On the other side stand people who want to borrow but who may want to pay the money back over several years. They clearly cannot do business with one another directly. The bank acts as an intermediary, accepting deposits and paying interest on them and making loans and charging the borrowers interest at a higher rate. In doing so the bank relieves the depositor of the need to investigate whether a loan would be safe; the banks have built up considerable expertise in the granting of advances.

Profitability and liquidity

The banks' objective in providing services to borrowers and depositors is the generation of *profit*, like any other commercial organisation. The more money they can lend, the more profit banks can earn. However, a bank cannot lend out all the funds which it obtains on deposit as it must retain enough money in liquid form to be able to meet depositors' requests for repayment. In this we find the root cause of the *banker's dilemma* because, generally speaking, the more liquid the form in which funds are held, the less the rate of return. Cash holdings, for instance, being the most liquid form of asset, generate no profit at all.

The bank must therefore effect a careful balance between the maximisation of lending and the minimisation of liquidity to the lowest level consistent with safety. To some extent this task is taken out of the bank's hands by official controls but, nevertheless, there is still considerable room for manoeuvre. The conflicting requirements of profitability and liquidity can be viewed as resulting directly from the conflicting desires of the two groups who have provided the bank's financial resources: the shareholders and the depositors. The *shareholders* jointly own the bank and look to it to provide a return on their capital. The *depositors* have provided the vast bulk of the funds used by the bank and require safety and the ability to get their money out at short notice. A successful bank has to *reconcile the interests* of these groups or it would lose either its depositors or its shareholders.

Interest rates

We have already mentioned that banks pay interest on deposits and charge interest on loans. Before we move on to look at how these activities express themselves on the banks' balance sheets, we should ask ourselves what we understand by the term 'interest'. The simplest definition of interest is that it is a *payment made for the use of someone else's money.*

When we speak of a *rate of interest*, we should be aware that there are a multitude of different rates in operation at any one time. The particular rate of interest charged by a lender or paid to a depositor depends on a number of interrelated factors, the principal of which are the *risk element* and the *time factor.*

Perhaps the closest thing to a riskless investment is the purchase of UK government stocks; consequently these provide as low a rate of return as is likely to be found at any given time. Any other form of loan will carry an appreciably greater level of risk that the funds will not be recoverable and the rate of interest charged will increase accordingly. Eventually, the point will be reached where a proposed loan is so risky that a lender will not be found no matter how high the offered rate of return. Similarly, the longer the period over which the lender surrenders the liquidity of his funds, the higher he will expect the rate of return to be.

The *liquidity* of a loan can be defined in one of two ways; the loan can be granted for a *set period* of time, or it can become repayable only after the expiry of an agreed *period of notice.*

Table 3.1 The combined balance sheet of the London clearing banks at 19 October 1983

	£m	Per cent
Liabilities		
Sterling deposits:		
Deposits	79 986	
CDs	4 933	
Total sterling deposits	84 919	51.0
Other currency deposits:		
Deposits	57 465	
C/Ds	5 461	
Total other currency deposits	62 926	37.7
Other liabilities	18 826	11.3
Total liabilities	166 671	100.0
Assets		
Sterling assets:		
Cash and balances with Bank of England	1 330	0.8
Market loans:		
Discount market	4 018	
UK banks	13 889	
Local authority deposits	1 055	
CDs	1 757	
	20 719	12.4
Bills of exchange:		
Treasury bills	129	
Others	1 577	
	1 707	1.0
Bank of England special deposits	—	—
Investments	6 093	3.7
Advances	61 391	36.9
Miscellaneous assets	9 550	5.7
Total sterling assets	100 790	60.5
Other currency assets:		
Market loans	42 999	
Bills	93	
Advances	19 038	
Other	3 751	
Total other currency assets	65 881	39.5
Total assets	166 671	100.0

When we come to look through the banks' portfolios of loans, you will see that the risk element and the time factor often go hand in hand. The banks' loans to the money market, for instance, are both the safest and the shortest term advances they can make. On the other hand, loans to customers are the least liquid financial use to which funds are put, and they carry the greatest risk that repayment will not be obtained.

Table 3.1 shows the combined balance sheet of the London clearing banks as at 19 October 1983, reflecting the business being done by their branches in England and Wales. This has been put together by the Bank of England from information supplied to it by each bank and it concentrates principally on the financial uses to which depositors' funds are put. It does not give very much detail about such items as, for example, *shareholders' funds* or *capital assets*; these are incorporated into the sections headed respectively *other liabilities* and *miscellaneous assets*. Before we go on to look in detail at the items which are incorporated into a bank's balance sheet, it would be a good idea for you to lay your hands on an up-to-date copy of your own bank's balance sheet so that you can see how the organisation has responded to the general principles which all banks must follow.

(We have decided not to include a bank's balance sheet ourselves because this would inevitably be dated. The current balance sheets of all major banks are readily available. Obtain and use one as you read through the next section of this chapter.)

The bank's liabilities

The liabilities of the bank as shown in its balance sheet represent the *sources of the funds* which it uses in its business. Broadly speaking there are two main sources of funds: the *proprietors* (the shareholders) and the *depositors*. As we have said, it is the shareholders who control the bank, through the directors whom they elect, but the depositors who provide the bulk of the funds. Even so, the shareholders cannot ignore the needs of the depositors as to do so would result in the loss of the deposits to a more amenable organisation. Let us now look in detail at the funds which are at the bank's disposal. Following normal accounting conventions we shall begin with the proprietors' funds and progress to the more 'liquid' items later.

Shareholders' funds

This section of the balance sheet contains details of two items: the amounts of *capital subscribed* to the bank by shareholders when shares were first issued to investors, and any accumulations of funds due to the shareholders in respect of *retained profits* which have not been distributed by way of dividends. Looked at from another angle, this section shows how much cash would theoretically be left over to be divided up among the shareholders if the bank were to be closed down and liquidated. In such an event, the bank's assets would be realised—loans called in, buildings sold, etc.—and the proceeds used to pay off its liabilities to third parties: depositors, creditors and so on. Any remaining funds would be available to the shareholders, who take their money last. If the assets fail to reach their *balance sheet valuation*, any losses will fall on the shareholders simply because they are the last to be paid. You must remember that it is highly unlikely that any of the major UK commercial banks would be liquidated in this way; liquidation usually ensues only after a period of trading losses leading to *insolvency*.

The reason for buying shares in any business is the hope of *obtaining a return on the funds invested*. This return can come from two sources: dividend income and capital growth. Both depend in different ways on the *profitability* of the business. *Dividends* are a share in the profits distributed periodically, usually half yearly, among the shareholders. If no profits are made, there will be no dividends. *Capital growth* depends on a shareholder being able to sell his shares for more than he paid for them, this being determined by the demand for the shares. If a business is successful and makes regular profits, demand for its shares will increase and their market price will rise. If the business is unsuccessful, the shareholder may find that the value of his shares actually drops below the price he paid for them. Thus, dividends provide periodic income for the investor, while capital growth (or loss) is only realised when the shares are sold.

The value of a company's shares as shown in its balance sheet is known as the *par value* of the shares. This represents the amount that the company raised from the shares when it first sold them to investors. The par value is not directly related to the *market value*. The latter is the amount that a shareholder could currently obtain for the sale of his shares. (We shall be giving detailed consideration to the attributes of the different types of shares in Chapter 4, so for the moment a brief summary is sufficient.)

Preference shares

The holders of preference shares have the right to be paid dividends due to them before the other shareholders take any share of the profits. The annual dividend on preference shares is set at a stated percentage of their face value when they are issued, as in the case of Royal Bank of Scotland $5\frac{1}{2}$ per cent preference shares. For every £100 nominal of the above shares, the investor should receive £5.50 per year.

Ordinary shares

The bulk of proprietors' funds in the banks is provided by the ordinary shareholders. Dividends on ordinary shares are paid after dividends on any preference shares out of the remaining profits. Unless adequate profits are made, no dividend will be paid. Thus, there is less certainty of income with ordinary shares. However, the rate of dividend on ordinary shares is not fixed, which means that if the bank has a 'bumper year' for profits it can elect to pay the ordinary shareholders a 'bumper' dividend. The ordinary shareholders control the bank through the directors whom they elect at the *annual general meeting* of the company to direct the efforts of the bank and its staff on a day-to-day basis.

Reserves

Reserves consist of profits made in the past which have not been distributed in the way of dividends. The bank has instead retained the funds to 'plough back' into the business, enabling it to finance expansion. All well-run firms retain some of the profits in the business; a company which is 'milked' by the shareholders of all its profits tends to weaken and die. In most cases the bank's total reserves which have been accumulated over many years' trading now add up to much more than the nominal value of the share capital itself. Provided that a bank remains profitable, you would expect its reserves to carry on increasing year by year as a proportion of the annual profit is retained.

All the funds which make up the reserves belong to the shareholders. If there are no participating preference shares this means only the ordinary shareholders. If the bank were to be liquidated, they would therefore share out between themselves the nominal value of the shares on issue *plus* the whole of the reserves. Each shareholder would therefore receive much more than just the face value of his shares. This fact underpins the market value of the shares, although this is also affected by such considerations as the confidence of investors in *future* profitability and the health of the economy in general.

Medium and long-term liabilities

The 'shareholders' funds' section of the balance sheet shows the *theoretical value* of the bank to its proprietors; the value will never be realised unless the business is wound up. The remaining liabilities on the balance sheet comprise *debts* of one type or another due to outside parties. These must be paid at some stage. Some are due for payment on demand (*see below*) but in other cases the creditors have agreed to wait for a period of time before repayment falls due.

Loan capital

Under this heading are shown the total amounts of long-term and medium-term loans obtained by the bank from outside sources. Although these loans are most commonly denominated in sterling, some are denominated in foreign currencies to match commitments in these currencies.

Loan stocks. These are usually the longest term items when issued, representing an alternative to the issue of shares for raising capital on the investment market. The bank 'borrows' from the market against its promise to repay at the end of a stated period of time and, in the interim, to pay interest at a set rate on the amount it has borrowed. Loan stocks are therefore the commercial world's equivalent to gilt-edged stocks issued by the government. A typical example is Midland Bank 10¾% stock 1993–98. The holder of £100 nominal of this loan stock will therefore be entitled to receive £10.75 interest each year. You might think that in this the position is similar to the position of a holder of preference shares. There is, however, one vitally important difference, the interest on the loan stock *must be paid* each year even if the bank does not make a profit. Not all banks currently have loan stocks on issue.

The holder of a loan stock is a *creditor* of the company. This means that he is entitled to be repaid in full in a liquidation before any money is made available to the shareholders. This, of course, is an added advantage for the stockholder. Some companies make the position of a loan stockholder even safer by *securing* the loan with a mortgage over some of the company's assets. Bank loan stocks are generally unsecured, the stability of the bank being all the security that investors require. The drawback to the investor of putting money into loan stocks rather than into shares is that there is no participation in the growth of the business. No matter how successful the bank may be, loan stockholders will receive no more than the agreed rate of interest and the return of the original amount borrowed by the bank on the final repayment date.

Bonds. Bonds of various types and in various currencies may also be issued by the bank to obtain longer term finance. *Bearer bonds* are unusual in the UK but are quite common on foreign capital markets. Unlike loan stock certificates which are registered in the name of the holder, bearer bonds belong to whoever is *in possession* of them. This does away with the need to register the name of the new owner when bonds are sold but means that the bank does not have a record of who is entitled to the interest which is due on the bonds. To overcome this problem, each bond is accompanied by a set of numbered *coupons* and investors are periodically requested to submit the next coupon in the series to the issuing institution to claim the interest due. All the bonds in a particular issue are for a round amount, e.g. DM 10 000, so that the interest payment due is the same on each certificate.

Deferred taxation

This item represents a potential liability for taxation which probably will never fall due. The UK taxation system calculates a company's taxation liability—corporation tax—as a proportion of its profits. However, just as an individual is allowed to offset his personal tax allowances against his gross income to establish his taxable income, so a company may make certain deductions from its gross profits to find its *taxable profits*. Chief among these deductions are the allowances permitted in respect of new purchases of capital equipment. To encourage capital investment, companies are allowed to offset the cost of new equipment against their taxable profits although, if the equipment is subsequently sold the proceeds are taxable. The cost of a capital asset will be *written off* by the business over a number of years by offsetting a *depreciation provision* against annual profits. This reduction to profits is not *allowable* for tax purposes since the company will have had the advantage of the capital allowance instead.

Current liabilities

Depositors' funds

By far the largest component of the banks' liabilities is the money 'borrowed' from depositors, either 'retail' from businesses and the general public, or 'wholesale' through areas of the money market such as the interbank sterling deposit market. As you already know, the banks earn their profits by trading in money: taking it in on deposit and lending it out at interest. The bulk of bank profits comes from the difference between the cost of these funds to the bank and the cost of the loans to the customers. Remember that a bank cannot lend out all of its deposits. Some proportion has to be kept in liquid form, probably generating little income, and this means that the interest charged on loans has to be significantly higher than that paid on deposits. The term *deposits* is used in a general sense to mean all money lent to the bank on any type of account. You are aware that banks today take deposits in currencies other than sterling and the Bank of England's figures divide them into 'sterling deposits' and 'other currency deposits'.

Current accounts. These represent the cheapest way for banks to attract funds since generally speaking credit balances on customers' current accounts do not attract interest. Against this, however, we have to set the costs to the bank of operating a current account service with all the money transmission and other facilities which it implies. It is true that *commission charges* may be levied on current accounts but it is unlikely that such charges recoup anything like the whole of the costs incurred, especially where personal accounts are concerned. Since the end of the 1970s, all the major banks have offered a low cost, or even free, current account tariff for personal customers who keep credit balances permanently in excess of a stated level. Even where charges are levied, they are often reduced by a deduction of *notional interest* calculated on the credit balances maintained.

Customers are generally becoming more sophisticated in their financial dealings and are less inclined to leave funds idle on current account when they could be earning interest elsewhere. Current account balances consequently tend to be maintained at as low a level as is consistent with avoiding high commission charges. This process has been accelerated by the comparatively high level of interest rates in the UK since the mid-1970s.

Deposit accounts. These contain a large proportion of customers' funds held in bank accounts. On such balances the banks pay interest at *deposit rate* which is lower than base rate—usually between 2 to 4% below—and tends to fluctuate with it. Although the banks theoretically compete on interest rates, in practice their rates tend to follow one another quite closely. Cheque books and other money transmission services are not generally available on deposit accounts and this results in cost savings for the banks which can be offset against the interest payments.

Deposit accounts are a more stable source of funds than current accounts since they are used to build up and hold savings rather than to facilitate the day-to-day processing of income and expenditure. Technically, withdrawals from deposit accounts require seven days' notice although the banks rarely, if ever, insist on this. Withdrawals are normally permitted on demand against the customer forfeiting seven days' accrued interest on the sum withdrawn.

Investment deposit accounts. These are offered to customers who wish to make larger deposits; usually at least £10 000 is required, and on these better rates of interest are paid. The customer may be required to deposit the funds for a fixed term, which can be anything between one month and two years, the interest rate being fixed for the whole period of the loan.

Alternatively, the funds may be left with the bank indefinitely, subject to a stated period of notice before the customer may withdraw the funds or before the bank may vary the interest rate. In these cases the period of notice will be enforced by the bank. It may be set at anything between one day and several months.

All these types of account represent attempts to attract and to retain for longer periods substantial sums of money so as to *stabilise* the banks' deposit base and reduce its volatility. In general, the longer the period for which the bank can rely on holding the funds, the better the interest rate will be, although in a time of falling interest rates the rate for long-term money may nevertheless be lower than the rate for short-term money. Sometimes a particular bank may not be able to lend out all the funds which it already has at its disposal. In such a case it will not wish to attract further deposits and it will therefore quote uncompetitively low rates of interest for new deposits of this type.

Certificates of deposit

We have already discussed the use of certificates of deposit in Chapter 2. Issued either in sterling or foreign currency, specifically US dollars, they acknowledge receipt by the bank of substantial amounts of money deposited for a fixed term. Sterling certificates of deposit, for instance, are given for sums of between £50 000 and £500 000 deposited for at least three months and at most five years. Technically these longer-term certificates of deposits are not 'current liabilities' but it is convenient to group them with other customer deposits. The attraction of the fixed term certificate of deposit to depositors is that it enables them to 'have their cakes and eat it'. Because of the fixed term they obtain a better rate of return than for more liquid deposits, yet they can recover their money at any time by selling the certificate through the *secondary market* which exists to facilitate trade in them.

Other liabilities

Finally, we come to a number of commercial liabilities which we might find appearing on the balance sheet of any trading concern.

Table 3.2 Analysis by sector of retail bank deposits as at 31 March 1987

	Sterling deposits £m	Foreign currency deposits £m
UK monetary sector	11 377	6 856
UK private sector	102 675	6 079
UK public sector	3 774	
Overseas residents	12 496	29 088
Certificates of deposit	8 384	6 414
Total	138 706*	48 437
*Of which: Sight	69 089	
Time (including CDs)	69 617	

Creditors. This comprises sums due to suppliers of goods and services who trade with the bank on credit. The figure may include, for example, payments outstanding to the bank's stationery suppliers or to building contractors in respect of work done on one of the bank's branches.

Taxation. This shows the amounts accruing due to the Inland Revenue for current taxation. The workings of corporation tax are quite complex and beyond the scope of our discussions here. It is sufficient to note that at least a part of a company's annual tax assessment is paid in arrears, being shown for some months in the company's accounts as an outstanding liability.

Dividends. These are to be paid to shareholders out of profits and are always included on the balance sheet showing the bank's financial position at the end of its financial year. By the time the balance sheet has been compiled and published some little time after the year end, the payment of the dividend will have long ago been approved and the remittance made to each shareholder.

Subsidiary companies. These may be owed money by the parent company either in respect of goods and services provided, or in respect of loans made to the parent bank.

The bank's assets

The assets of a bank as shown in its balance sheet represent *what it has done* with the funds which it has obtained both from its proprietors (the shareholders) and from its creditors (the depositors). Remember what we have already said about the conflict between liquidity and profitability: funds tied up in long-term loans, for example, may be earning good profits but are not available at short notice to cover depositors' withdrawals. Some assets must be kept in liquid form. Some of a bank's financial assets will be denominated in foreign currencies, for example loans through the Eurocurrency market, and their sterling value is shown on the combined balance sheet (Table 3.1) in a separate section lower down than sterling items. Following normal accounting conventions, we shall rank the assets in order of liquidity, looking first at the most liquid items.

Liquid assets

The liquid assets of a business comprise those things which could readily be converted into *cash* in order to meet liabilities falling due. Except for the dictates of convention, there is no obvious dividing line between liquid and non-liquid assets; it is more a matter of steady progression. For example, investments in quoted companies' stocks and shares are readily realisable through the stock market. Even so, they are not classed as fully liquid assets, principally because forced liquidation in an emergency might entail having to sell at an unusually low price.

We have already seen that a prudent bank will maintain a satisfactory *liquidity ratio* between its liabilities to depositors and its liquid assets. Since August 1981 the Bank of England has given instructions that banks should maintain liquid assets in proportions which are related to the maturity dates of their liabilities. Thus, much greater cover is required for short-run liabilities than for long-run ones. (We shall return to this topic in greater detail later.)

Cash

This heading comprises two items: *notes and coin* held in the tills and strongrooms of the banks and their *balances with the Bank of England*. Assets held in either of these two forms are, of course, totally liquid but generate no income. The banks therefore keep the figure as low as is compatible with the need to be able to fulfil customers' requirements. Most UK banks maintain a *cash ratio* between the value of these assets and liabilities to depositors of around 4%. This is extremely low when compared with banks in the rest of the world. They are able to maintain such a low cash ratio with comparative safety because London has such a highly developed money market which enables them to convert other, less liquid assets into cash at very short notice. The growth of the interbank sterling market has had a major effect as it allows the banks to *buy in* any funds which they may need unexpectedly.

Notes and coin. Stocks of UK currency clearly have to be maintained by all the commercial banks in order to satisfy depositors' demands for cash withdrawals. Indeed, the Bank of England relies on the banks for the distribution of new notes and coin to the general public. So far as the banks are concerned, these items are merely their stock in trade on which no income is being earned and which therefore must be kept as low as possible. Most banks now operate quite sophisticated cash control systems intended to keep their stocks of cash down. The process is more complicated than you might imagine, as each branch has its own pattern of cash inflows and outflows. Much depends on the location of the branch, the time of the year, whether it has a cash-dispenser machine and so on. For example, during the summer months branches in seaside towns tend to take in much more cash than they pay out and arrangements have to be made to transfer that excess cash to other branches in the network where payments exceed receipts.

Balances with the Bank of England. The clearing system enables each of the commercial banks to collect payment of the cheques which are paid in to its customers' accounts but which are drawn on accounts maintained with other banks. Many thousands of cheques pass between the banks each day. At the end of each day the amount due from each of the *clearing banks* to each of the others is totalled. Since the process is reciprocal, the total amounts due between any two banks will tend largely to cancel each other out. Nevertheless, there will always be some small difference between the total amounts flowing in either direction.

This difference is settled daily by a transfer between the accounts which each bank maintains with the Bank of England specifically for this purpose. These accounts may be regarded as the banks' *current accounts*.

Since 1981 the banks have also been required to maintain *non-operational accounts* with the Bank of England. The balances on these accounts must be kept at a level equal to at least ½% of the banks' eligible liabilities. No interest is paid on these accounts and the balances are not available to be drawn on for the purpose of interbank settlements. They are required as a form of monetary control and to provide the Bank of England with funds. We shall look at these aspects later.

Market loans

This section shows the funds which the bank has lent through the London money markets. As we saw in Chapter 2, in the last 20 years these markets have expanded considerably as a result of the development of the *parallel money markets*. The basic principle remains unchanged, however: money placed through the money market is recoverable at very short notice and can therefore be converted into cash should the need arise.

The discount market. The discount houses borrow money from the commercial banks in order to purchase Treasury bills, gilt-edged stocks and so on. Repayment of these loans has to be made *at call* (on demand) or at *short notice* (up to a maximum of fourteen days but more usually seven days or less). The rates of interest charged on these loans vary according to the term or the length of notice, overnight loans attracting the lowest rate. Rates are also quite volatile from day to day depending on whether the market has a surplus or a shortage of funds. Since 1981 all banks have to maintain an average of 6% of their eligible liabilities in the form of secured loans to the discount market.

UK banks. The interbank sterling market has proved to be a very important vehicle for the borrowing and lending of funds between banks, enabling funds to flow throughout the whole of the money market. You will see that this is now by far the largest category of market loan made by the banks.

Local authority deposits. These are loans made through the money market to local authorities which raise a significant proportion of their finance by this method. They also raise money by issuing bills and bonds in a similar manner to central government.

Certificates of deposit. As you saw in Chapter 2, certificates of deposit were introduced to attract large sums of money (£50 000 to £500 000 or equivalent amounts in foreign currency) onto medium-term deposit of up to five years with the banks. Because of the term, these deposits attract quite high rates of interest. Even so, the depositor's funds are not 'locked in' for the whole term because the certificate of deposit itself is *negotiable*. If the depositor requires early access to his money, he can sell the certificate to someone else. The figure shown in this section of the balance sheet represents the total value of certificates of deposit held which have been issued by *other* banks; the bank's own certificates of deposit are shown as liabilities, of course.

Bills of exchange
This item consists of bills of exchange which have been *discounted* by the bank, in other words bills which it has bought for less than their face value. The UK banks arrange to have a portfolio of bills maturing and becoming due for payment at regular intervals, matching its known and anticipated levels of outgoings. Thus, if the bank knows that it will have a surplus of cash for the next two months, it may buy bills maturing in two months' time. In this way the bank is able to manage its liquidity to quite fine tolerances. By and large the commercial banks do not *trade* in bills; having been bought by a bank, a bill will usually be held to maturity rather than being on-sold. A bank which needs to increase its cash holdings at short notice will usually call in its money market loans rather than redis-count any of the bills which it is holding.

Treasury bills. These are bought by the banks from the discount houses. Under a gentleman's agreement the banks do not bid for newly issued Treasury bills in competition with the discount houses. As you know, Treasury bills are issued with a *tenor* of 91 days to maturity, but the banks do not usually acquire them until they are only some five or six weeks away from maturity.

The annualised *discount rate* applying to purchasers of Treasury bills is closely related to money market rates generally; it will be slightly higher than the *call money* rate since this is the rate at which the discount houses have borrowed the funds to buy in the stocks of Treasury bills from which they make sales to the banks.

Other bills. These comprise commercial bills of exchange discounted for bank customers as a method of providing finance and other first-class bills, including local authority bills, purchased from *bill brokers*. These bills carry a slightly higher level of risk of non-payment than Treasury bills which are, of course, government backed. In consequence the rate of discount on them will also be higher. The rate applying to bills discounted for customers will often be related specifically to the bank's *base rate*, being set at perhaps ½ to 1½% above base.

Cheques in course of collection

This very large item is made up principally of the total value of cheques drawn on other banks which are in the process of being collected through the clearing system. It also includes the balances of any accounts which the bank maintains for convenience with other banks. As you will see when we examine the clearing system in detail, it takes two working days before the collecting bank receives payment for cheques credited to its customers' accounts which are drawn on other banks. While the funds are awaited, they cannot be utilised and are, therefore, *dead money* earning no profits.

In this latter respect, the funds represented by cheques in the clearing system resemble fully liquid assets such as cash and, indeed, some banks group this item together with cash on the balance sheet. However, this money is not treated by the Bank of England as a liquid asset for the simple reason that the bank will never be able to realise the amount. There are two reasons for this. First, as fast as one day's cheques are collected, customers pay in some more, perpetuating the item on the bank's books. Second, even if the clearing process could be speeded up, each bank would still have to pay out to the other banks for the value of its own customers' cheques which were passing through the system: the inflow and outflow of funds should approximately balance each other out.

Special deposits

If the Bank of England wishes to restrain bank lending, it may call upon the banks to make *special deposits* with it. These deposits have to be regarded as *non-liquid* because they are repayable only when the Bank of England chooses; they therefore reduce the liquid reserves of the banks. The result of a call for special deposits is that the banks' ability to create credit will contract in the multiple manner described on page 68, thus restricting the growth of the money supply. The banks are usually able to absorb such pressures to reduce their advances by slowing down the rate at which new loans are granted. It is not normally necessary to call in existing loans. While special deposits are held by the Bank, interest is usually paid on them at a rate which is approximately equal to the prevailing Treasury bill rate. Some 'supplementary special deposits' in the past have not qualified for payment of interest, however.

When special deposits are called for, the amount required is expressed as a percentage (normally $\frac{1}{2}$ or 1%) of each bank's eligible liabilities. If the first call for special deposits does not slow down the creation of credit sufficiently, further deposits may be required. At the moment there are no special deposits. Since 1981 the Bank of England has relied on other forms of monetary control. However, this does not mean that their use as an instrument of control has been permanently discontinued; it is merely held in reserve and may be reactivated in the future if necessary.

Special deposits are not the same thing as the *non-operational accounts* that all recognised banks and licensed deposit takers are still required to maintain with the Bank of England. The balances of these latter accounts must represent $\frac{1}{2}$% of each organisation's eligible liabilities, the objective being to ensure that each one maintains an absolute minimum cash ratio, hence the fact that these accounts are sometimes called 'cash ratio deposits'. Consequently, they are not shown in this section but are grouped with the more genuinely liquid balances which the banks keep with the Bank of England, even though they are not available for the banks to draw on at will. You will understand why many bankers criticise these accounts on the basis that since the banks cannot draw on the funds they are not really part of their cash ratios; the banks have to keep adequate liquid funds in other forms to meet day-to-day commitments! Nevertheless, it would be unthinkable that the Bank would not agree to release the funds to a bank which was experiencing severe financial difficulties.

Investments

This section contains details of really only one type of asset: investment in *government stocks*. Commercial banks in the UK generally do not take *equity shareholdings* in companies to which they are providing financial assistance, restricting themselves to assistance by way of advances. In this they differ from their European counterparts whose balance sheets also include details of significant shareholdings in commercial concerns.

British government stocks

You have already seen in Chapter 2 how the government raises long-term loans by the issue of *gilt-edged stocks* on which interest is paid to holders, usually at a fixed rate. There are a small number of *undated* stocks which have no set redemption dates but most gilt-edged stocks are issued having a definite maturity, being repayable either on one particular date or, more commonly, at the Bank of England's discretion within a stated period. The banks always try to ensure that they have a maturing portfolio of these stocks so that a quantity of them mature each month to provide a steady inflow of liquid funds. The bank then has the option of holding the funds received in liquid form or reinvesting in further gilts. A bank's holdings of gilt-edged stocks are thus complementary to its holdings of Treasury bills.

The banks do not trade in gilt-edged securities; having bought them, they usually hold them to maturity. Generally they do not buy newly issued stocks but purchase older issues having only a few years to run to maturity. At any one time you would expect that over two-thirds of their holdings would have five years or less to run to the final redemption date. The discount houses are an important source of large value 'packets' of stocks all having the same maturity date.

Yield on stocks

Holders of gilt-edged stocks receive interest at a quoted (usually fixed) rate on the face value of the stock. This is known as the *coupon rate*. However, the actual *yield* to them depends on how much they paid for the stock; if they paid less than face value, the true rate of return will be higher than the coupon rate. For example, a certificate for a nominal £200 of *Treasury 10% Stock 1992* will earn £20 interest per year until redemption in 1992. If you were able to buy this certificate from the present holder for just £100, you would still receive the full £20 per year interest; the yield to you on your investment of cash is therefore 20%. Furthermore, by 1992 you will have the benefit of a *capital appreciation* as although you only paid £100 for the stock, the government will repay you £200. The market prices of gilt-edged stocks fluctuate considerably, reflecting a synthesis of each stock's coupon rate, the general levels of interest rates and how long the stock has to run to maturity. The important thing for you to remember is that the banks earn considerable income from their holdings of government securities at a rate of yield which is not directly related to the coupon rates of the stocks held.

Advances

The largest figure by far among the banks' assets represents the total of the advances which have been made to customers. This includes all forms of direct lending, both overdrafts and loans. Lending is the commercial banks' *raison d'être* and it can be one of their most profitable activities, provided that it is properly controlled and bad debts are not incurred to too high a level. The amount shown in the balance sheet for advances is a *net figure* after the deduction of the provisions (reserves) which the bank has set aside to cover potentially irrecoverable debts. Some banks show these provisions as a *liability* rather than as a reduction to the assets since these reserves will accrue to the proprietors, via the profit and loss account, if the debts prove good. It is generally accepted, however, that it gives a truer picture to show these provisions as a reduction to the assets.

Interest rates

The return on advances comes from the interest charged to

borrowers. In the case of all overdrafts and many loan facilities this is calculated as a percentage above base rate. The additional rate varies considerably, reflecting chiefly the bank's assessment of the *level of risk* that the advance will prove to be irrecoverable. Highly favoured and well-run industrial concerns may be able to negotiate rates as low as $\frac{1}{2}$% over base rate, while up to 7% over base may be levied on unsecured borrowing by personal customers who overdraw without making a prior arrangement. Most customers fall somewhere between these two extremes, the majority of 'good' customers—both small businesses and personal borrowers—paying between 2% and 4% over base rate.

The *effective rate* of interest on loans of the above types therefore fluctuates during the currency of the advance according to changes in base rate. Banks also operate a number of *fixed rate* loan schemes, particularly the *personal loan* types of facility, on which the rate of interest is set at the time the loan is granted and does not change thereafter. The interest rate on this type of loan is usually quoted as a *flat rate* on the original amount of the loan. Although this nominal rate of interest may be less than bank base rate, the *true rate*, or effective rate, of interest will usually be well above it because the interest is payable on the original amount of the loan throughout the whole of the borrowing period. Even though the amount outstanding gradually reduces with each instalment paid in, the regular interest payment remains constant. With more traditional types of loan the interest is calculated daily on the actual amount outstanding, although the interest is charged to the customer only quarterly or half yearly. Under the terms of the Consumer Credit Act 1974, a borrower must be informed of the 'true rate' of interest charged on personal loan type advances.

Illiquidity of advances

In theory, most bank advances are repayable on demand, reflecting the fact that customers' deposits are repayable on demand. In practice, the banks know that if their loans were called in only a very few could be paid off at once. Most customers would need time to repay their borrowing, unless they could raise a loan from another source! Advances are, therefore, an *illiquid asset* for all practical purposes. Provided that depositors do not suddenly lose confidence in the bank, their day-to-day demands for funds should remain broadly stable. Thus, if adequate liquidity is maintained through holdings of other assets, it should never be necessary to call in advances generally. In recognition of this fact and because of the general stability of the banks' large deposit bases, most banks are prepared to enter into some medium and long-term loans, using the short-term customers' deposits. This process is known as *maturity transformation*.

The lending ratio

The proportion of advances to deposits is determined by the proportion of deposits that the bank keeps in a liquid or partly liquid form. It used to be thought that the lending ratio of advances to deposits should not exceed 50%. Since, as you have seen, the percentage of liquid assets has declined in recent years, a greater proportion of deposits has become available for lending. In the balance sheet shown in Table 3.1, the sterling lending ratio is about 70% and it is unlikely that any bank would wish to increase this proportion any further. This does not mean that the *total* of advances will not rise; it can do so as deposits increase. It is the *proportion* of advances to deposits which will stay much the same.

The principles of lending

You should not suppose that the *rate of return* on a proposed loan is the bank's only concern when considering the application, or even that it is its first concern. The safety of the advance is much more important; there is no profit to be made from irrecoverable loans, no matter how high the interest rate. (In Chapter 13 we shall be looking at the specific 'tests' which are applied to each proposal for an advance to help the bank decide whether it is safe to lend.) Generally speaking, the banks like to ensure that loans are distributed through all sections of the economy: to the public sector, to the private sector, to private individuals and to industy. This diversification of the lending portfolio ensures that a bank is not vulnerable if one particular sector of the economy enters a period of difficulty. We have spoken already of the 'secondary banking crisis' of the mid 1970s; this was brought on by a slump in the property market in which the secondary banks had placed too great a proportion of their loanable funds.

Table 3.3 Analysis by sector of bank advances as at 31 March 1987

	Sterling advances £m	Foreign currency advances £m
UK private sector	91 682	6 559
UK public sector	462	149
Overseas residents	3 658	33 146
Total	95 802	39 854

From time to time, the Bank of England may try to direct funds into certain sectors of the economy by giving the banks *qualitative directives* about their lending policies. For instance, it may commend that the banks should give a more favourable response to loan applications from companies engaged in export trade. These directives could be enforced by the Bank if necessary but this power is never wielded since the commercial banks always comply voluntarily.

Fixed assets

Finally, we come to the most illiquid of all the assets of the commercial banks: their investment in subsidiary and associated companies and their investment in premises and equipment.

Trade investments

In the last 40 years or so the commercial banks have broadened their interests considerably and all have set up numerous *subsidiary companies* to operate in such related financial markets as leasing, hire purchase, insurance and so on. The value of each bank's holdings of shares in its subsidiary companies is shown in this section. In addition to their wholly owned subsidiaries, many banks have partial shareholdings in *associated companies*, sometimes jointly with other banks. These shareholdings are also reflected as 'trade investments'.

If for any reason the bank has any shareholdings in unrelated companies, these will also be shown in this section. The total amount of any such holdings is likely to be low since, as we have already noted, the banks do not usually take equity shareholdings in other businesses.

Premises and equipment

Clearly these items are almost totally illiquid: a bank could not sell off its branches or its adding machines to repay its depositors. Indeed, it should never need to do so as the *fixed assets* of the organisation will normally be more than balanced by the *fixed capital* representing the proprietors' (shareholders') stake in the business.

Premises. We saw in Chapter 2 that the 'big four' clearing banks each have upward of 2000 branches. Some of these are large buildings, some are small, but almost all are *undervalued* on the balance sheet. Remember that most of these branches are in prime commercial locations in the high streets and shopping centres of the country where property values show a permanent, if undulating, rate of rise.

You saw how the clearing banks were created out of mergers of a number of constituent banks, each of which already had a national branch network. One result of this process was that the new banks sometimes had a distorted distribution of branches with too many branches in some communities and not enough in others. Since the 1970s, the 'big four' have rationalised their branch networks, selling off their surplus branches. Many of these branches were bought by smaller banks seeking to expand their networks and by building societies which over the same period built up a major presence in the high streets.

Equipment. Banking is still a comparatively labour-intensive industry but much less so than it was twenty years ago. Starting in the late 1950s, the major commercial banks had computerised virtually the whole of their accounting procedures by the early 1970s using large *mainframe computers* located in centralised computer centres. These computer systems are continually updated and new equipment with greater work handling capacity is introduced at frequent intervals. This process has enabled the banks to keep down the growth of staffing levels to very low rates of increase despite servicing ever-increasing numbers of accounts. An indication of the continuing commitment of the banks to 'information technology' can be found in their holdings of related equipment. In 1975 the gross book value of all such assets owned by the London clearing banks was £257 million; in only six years this nearly tripled to £749 million. While the central computers and their in-branch terminals are the largest item in this balance sheet category, the banks also have significant investments in other items of equipment including cars, adding machines and alarm systems.

Controls on the banking system

You have seen that the government, through the Bank of England, exercises various controls on the banking sector. These controls serve two principal objectives. First, there is the duty of the Bank to implement government *monetary policy* formulated as part of its overall control of the UK economy. Second, there is the need to police the banking system to protect the public against the dangers of bank failure. We could call these two functions *prudential control* and *monetary control*. Generally, although not always, the requirements of these two areas tend to overlap and the major methods of control used work by affecting the banks' levels of *liquidity*.

Liquidity controls

Prudential control of liquidity

A bank must maintain an adequate level of liquidity to be able to meet normal levels of depositors' demands for repayment of funds due to them, whether in cash or through the money transfer systems. If adequate liquidity is not maintained, the bank may temporarily have to suspend payment while it realises some of its assets. This course of action will usually result in a panic among depositors who then all demand repayment of their balances. A 'run on the bank' ensues, probably resulting in the bank having to close down. We should perhaps point out that in today's highly interdependent financial market any bank or other financial institution which became the victim of a 'run' would undoubtedly be supported, or perhaps propped up, by the other banks to prevent the development of a run on the whole system.

The simplest way of determining the liquidity of a particular bank is to compare its *liquid assets* with its *total deposits*. This produces the *liquidity ratio* which is normally expressed as a percentage. For many years prior to 1971 the London and Scottish clearing banks had an agreement with the Bank of England that their liquidity ratio would not fall below 28%. For this purpose, liquid assets were defined as those items which could be converted into cash within three months, chiefly comprising holdings of notes and coin, balances on accounts held with the Bank of England, money at call with the London money market and holdings of Treasury bills.

Monetary control of liquidity

As you have already seen, the liquidity ratio which is adopted by a bank has a significant effect on its ability to create credit. The higher the liquidity ratio, the lower the total amount of loans which can be granted on a given value of deposits. Working through successive redeposits of advances made, the multiplier effect greatly magnifies any change in the level of the liquidity ratio, however small. (Look again at Table 1.5 to refresh your memory of exactly how the credit creation process works.)

The creation of credit is, of course, a vitally important contributor to the country's *money supply*, control of which is an integral part of the government's overall control of the economy. As the modern economy has become more complex, so the simple 'liquidity ratio' has become inadequate as a measure of control. Since 1971 there have been two systems used in succession by the Bank of England: the *reserve assets ratio* in use from 1971 to 1981 when it was superseded by the current *monetary control provisions*.

The reserve assets ratio

In 1971 the Bank of England issued a document entitled *Competition and Credit Control* which, among other things, introduced a new system of control over the money supply based around the concept of rationing credit by *price*. Thus, if the government wished to reduce the money supply, the Bank would reduce the *demand* for credit by forcing up interest rates, thereby increasing the 'price' of money. At the same time, however, the Bank retained its control over the *supply* of credit by requiring that a satisfactory reserve assets ratio be maintained by *all* institutions in the 'banking sector', and not just the London and Scottish clearing banks as before. The reserve assets ratio, which was originally set at 12½% although later other percentages were in force, compared the reserve assets of a bank with its eligible liabilities.

Eligible liabilities In this connection these comprise sterling deposit liabilities excluding any deposits having an original maturity of over two years plus any sterling resources obtained by switching foreign currencies into sterling. The banks were allowed to *offset* interbank transactions and sterling certificates of deposit, whether held or issued, in calculating their net liabilities. Adjustments were also made in respect of transit items.

Reserve assets. These comprised British government and Northern Ireland government Treasury bills, money at call with the London money market, government and nationalised industry stocks with twelve months or less to final maturity, local authority bills eligible for rediscount with the Bank of England and commercial bills eligible for rediscount at the Bank up to a maximum of 2% of the total eligible liabilities. In addition, balances kept with the Bank of England, other than on non-operational accounts such as 'special deposits', were also classed as reserve assets. The clearing banks, but not other banks, were required to maintain Bank of England balances equivalent to at least 1½% of their eligible liabilities on which they earned no interest and which, to their annoyance, were much greater than they needed to maintain for the purposes of interbank settlement and liquidity. You will no doubt have noticed that cash—holdings of notes and coin—was not classified as a reserve asset.

Thus, there are two essential criteria in defining whether an article may be classed as a reserve asset: it must be *liquid* and its supply must be *controlled* by the authorities in the form of the Treasury and the Bank of England. This latter criterion is the reason why commercial bills were subject to the 2% limitation—the banks may well have held much more in this form of asset—and why Bank of England balances had to be a minimum of 1½%; the banks would otherwise have held much less in this form.

By the end of the 1970s it had become apparent that the 12½% reserve assets ratio was both confusing and ineffective as a measure of monetary control. Moreover, the system had not changed to accommodate major developments in the money markets. A government Green Paper on this topic recommended that monetary control should be exercised specifically through the manipulation of market forces and that control of bank asset/liability structure should be directed more particularly toward satisfying the criteria of *prudential control*.

Monetary control provisions 1981

The latest monetary controls came into force in August 1981 and represent a move away from control of the 'global' liquidity ratios of the banks in favour of recommendations as to the *detailed composition* of that liquidity. The *monetary sector* as a whole is covered by the new regulations rather than just the old 'banking sector'. The monetary sector comprises:

1 All licensed deposit takers.
2 The National Girobank.
3 Banks in the Channel Isles and the Isle of Man.
4 The banking department of the Bank of England.

Eligible liabilities. These were slightly redefined in that there was a broadening of the definition of the items which may be offset against deposits in calculating the net total. All institutions in the 'monetary sector' are required to keep ½% of their eligible liabilities on non-operational, non-interest-bearing accounts with the Bank of England. Licensed deposit takers are further required to keep an *average* of 6% of their eligible liabilities on a secured basis with the discount market, such deposits not to fall below 4% on any one day.

Liquid Assets. These were also slightly redefined, now comprising:

1 Sums lent by one institution in the 'monetary sector' to any other, but not including any 'cash ratio' deposits or 'special deposits' with the Bank of England, and
2 Money at call with money brokers and gilt-edged market makers in the Stock Exchange and secured on gilt-edged stocks, Treasury bills, local authority bills and bills of exchange.

In place of the reserve assets ratio, the Bank of England has laid down *prescribed averages* of liquid assets which the banks and licensed deposit takers must hold. The asset cover varies with the different types of deposit which a bank may have accepted; greater cover is required for short-run liabilities than for long-run ones. For example, liabilities with a maturity of over a year might require only 5% liquid asset cover, while short-run money market liabilities might require 100%. The Bank continually monitors the monetary sector and adjusts its requirements as necessary. Thus, the liquid assets required by a bank depend on the type of deposits which it has accepted, the composition of which will vary from bank to bank and, indeed, from day to day. It is not possible to express this as a simple ratio. There are special rules for the discount houses and for banks with money trading departments.

Bank of England deposits

As you know, the banks maintain accounts with the Bank of England to enable them to settle debts due among themselves. In holding these accounts the Bank of England is fulfilling its role as the banker's bank. The balances maintained on these accounts and the levels to which they are kept are under the control of the banks themselves. The amounts in these accounts will therefore be kept as low as is consistent with the need to be able to make payments as they fall due. In addition, however, the Bank has at various times called on the financial institutions to make involuntary deposits with it. The making of such deposits affects the banks' liquidity and therefore their ability to lend.

Non-operational accounts
We have already mentioned that institutions in the monetary sector are required to keep ½% of their eligible liabilities on non-operational and non-interest bearing accounts with the Bank of England.

Special deposits
From time to time the Bank of England has called on the banks to make special deposits representing a percentage of their

eligible liabilities, interest at Treasury bill rate being payable on these balances. The objective of special deposits is, of course, to reduce bank liquidity and thereby put a brake on the creation of credit. If the first call for special deposits, usually at a rate of ½ or 1% of eligible liabilities, does not have the desired effect, a second call may be made, followed by as many subsequent calls as are required until the banking system does respond in the desired manner. Since 1981 there have been no special deposits held by the Bank of England.

Supplementary special deposits

Among other things, restricting the availability of credit generally results in forcing interest rates up in response to unsatisfied demand. In 1973 the government wished to restrict credit without raising interest rates since inflation was a particularly sensitive political issue at that time. The solution attempted was to restrict the growth of bank deposits rather than restricting lending as such. This was the supplementary special deposit scheme, or the *corset* as it became known. The system operated by penalising any bank whose interest bearing eligible liabilities (IBELs) rose at more than a stipulated target rate after a specified starting date. The penalties took the form of a requirement to make non-interest bearing supplementary special deposits with the Bank of England. The penal deposits for exceeding the target rate increased progressively with the degree of excess. The theory was that banks would be discouraged from attracting deposits and consequently would have to curtail lending.

Unfortunately for the operation of this scheme, it could be circumvented by the use of the *acceptance credit* under which a customer needing finance would draw a bill of exchange on the bank for the amount required. The bank would accept the bill of exchange and then *discount* it for the customer. The bank could then sell the accepted bill as a 'bank bill' through the money market. In this way the customer would have raised the necessary finance without an advance being created on the bank's books and, more importantly, without additional deposits having to be taken in. Supplementary special deposits were abandoned in 1981 when the new controls were introduced. It is unlikely that they will be reactivated in the future.

Summary

1 A bank's financial structure represents a compromise between profitability and liquidity.
2 The liabilities shown on the balance sheet represent the bank's sources of funds, of which there are two main categories: shareholders and depositors.
3 The shareholders control the bank through the directors whom they elect.
4 Holders of loan stocks are creditors of the company and do not participate in its management.
5 The bulk of the funds at the disposal of the banks is provided by way of deposits taken from customers or through the money market.
6 The assets shown on the balance sheet represent what the bank has done with the funds at its disposal.
7 A proportion of the assets must be kept in a liquid form, such as cash or bills of exchange, to meet depositors' demands for repayment.
8 Advances represent the bank's source of income but they are comparatively illiquid. The bank will seek to keep its *lending ratio* (advances as a percentage of deposits) as high as is consistent with overall liquidity requirements.
9 Banks have significant 'hidden reserves' in the difference between the balance sheet valuation of their premises and other fixed assets and their true market value. However, such assets are almost totally illiquid.
10 The Bank of England administers official controls of bank liquidity in pursuit of two objectives:
    (a) prudential control to protect depositors' funds;
    (b) monetary control to restrict the growth of the money supply.
11 Modern monetary controls concentrate on the detailed composition of a bank's liquid assets rather than on overall ratios.

Self-assessment questions

1 Define: (a) liquidity; (b) interest rates; (c) preference shares; (d) market loans; (e) eligible liabilities.

2 List the types of organisation which are included in the *monetary sector*.

3 True or false?

(a) Maturity transformation is the process of 'borrowing short and lending long'.

(b) Banks keep their lending ratios at a level of 75% or more.

(c) For the supply of loan funds, the banks are wholly reliant on deposits taken in by branches.

(d) UK banks do not normally take equity shareholdings in other businesses.

(e) The Bank of England controls bank lending by varying the reserve assets ratio.

4 If the shareholders ultimately control the activities of the banks, why are they unlikely to increase their dividends by ordering an expansion of lending activity regardless of the safety of the advances made? What would be the effect on deposits of such a course of action?

5 Explain why some people who invest in banks prefer to acquire shares while others prefer loan stocks. What are the relative advantages and disadvantages of each type of security?

6 State the reasons for the Bank of England's control of bank liquidity. Do you think that depositors' interests would be prejudiced if it abandoned these controls?

Assignments

1   Memorandum to: Student
    From: Area Manager
    Subject: Increasing branch lending

Your manager tells me what a good job you have been doing on the projects which you've been given, so here's a tough one for you.

You will be aware that I have been concerned in recent months to increase the lending at all the branches in our area. We have had some success but my managers now tell me that they cannot find any more borrowers who offer adequate certainty of repayment on demand. Furthermore, some branches are already lending out more money than they take in on deposit. Before I go back to the managers, would you prepare a report on the 'economics' of this, related particularly to the following points:

(a) Do we need to match the maturity of loans with deposits, i.e. can we lend for longer terms?

(b) Do we need to bother about repayment of advances *at all*? Provided that we are being paid the agreed interest, why can we not let loans run on indefinitely?

(c) Does it matter if a branch lends more than it has on deposit? Can the bank *as a whole* 'over-lend'?

2 (a) Calculate accurately from the combined bank balance sheets given in Table 3.1 the following ratios: (i) cash ratio; (ii) liquidity ratio; (ii) lending ratio.

(b) Write a brief report on the significance of each of these ratios, explaining what changes to them would denote.

4 Savings and investment

Chapter objectives

After studying this chapter you should be able to:
- outline the nature of savings and their role in the economy;
- specify the principal institutions which on-lend savings and state their role in the economy;
- identify and compare other major vehicles for saving and their relative attractions for savers;
- describe the workings and the functions of the capital markets;
- outline the role and workings of the Stock Market.

Savings

Definition

What do we mean by the term 'saving'? The simplest way of defining it is to say that saving is *refraining from spending*. This definition centres around what individuals or households do with their income. A certain amount must be spent on financing essential consumption; you have to pay for food, housing, heating, lighting and so on. It is possible that paying for such necessities will absorb the whole of the income but many households will have a *surplus*. The whole of this surplus can be spent on inessential items for consumption or a proportion may be retained as *savings*.

Money saved does not necessarily have to be put to work by being placed in a bank or a building society or by being *invested*. It could simply be *hoarded*. Some people keep their savings in cash hidden in the mattress or under the floor-boards for example. If a lot of hoarding takes place it can have a detrimental effect on the economy. Money hoarded is lost to the economy until it reappears and this disturbs the *circular flow of income*, which we shall examine later. By contrast, money saved via institutions such as banks is made available for other people to spend, thereby being returned to the flow of income. Fortunately, hoarding is not a problem in the UK, although it can be in third world countries.

Why do people save?

There are many reasons why people save their money rather than spend it. We have listed some of them below.

(a) *Precautionary motives:* money put by for a 'rainy day'.

(b) *Thrift:* some people or societies by habit or custom are more frugal in their consumption than others. People in the north of England and in Scotland are traditionally more thrifty than the people of the south-east of England.

(c) *Deferred purchase:* saving up to finance future consumption such as buying a car or going on holiday.

(d) *Contractual obligations:* money put by to meet mortgage or loan repayments, to pay insurance policy premiums and so on.

The principal determining factor in how much people save is the *level of their income*. As national income rises, so does the level of savings. The amount which people save is also influenced by taxation (which affects the level of people's *disposable incomes*), the government's policy towards saving, the availability of credit and the expectation of price changes. It used to be believed that savings were determined by the prevailing rates of interest. If interest rates went up, people would save more to gain the benefit of the higher rate; if interest rates fell, the incentive to save would be reduced. In practice, however, it appears that people will save whatever the rate of interest. During much of the 1970s and early 1980s, for example, interest rates in the UK were often lower than the rate of inflation with the result that the real value of the amounts saved, plus interest earned, suffered a steady decline. Nevertheless, saving still occurred. It seems that the motivation for saving is not primarily economic.

What do people do with their savings?

We have already seen that money not spent on consumption is, by definition, money saved. That money can be used to finance consumption in the future but in the meantime what can be done with it apart from simply hoarding it? The answer is that it can be put to work to earn the saver more money. Thus, for instance, money put into a bank deposit account will earn the depositor interest; money put into government securities will also earn the holder interest as well as providing in many cases a measure of *capital growth* over a period.

Although interest rates generally do not seem to be particularly important in determining the overall levels of saving, they can be important in influencing the *form* in which the savings are held. If banks are paying higher rates of interest than building societies, for example, you would expect the banks to attract a higher proportion of available savings.

Putting savings into a particular 'home' is often known as *investing* those savings. People talk about 'investing in a building society' or 'investing in a life policy'. You must be very careful about the word investment because it has two meanings. It can mean the deposit of one's savings in a particular form or it can be used to describe the acquisition of a new capital asset such as a factory or a machine. The latter is the sense in which an economist uses the word. Capital investment is vital to the community, providing the means whereby additional goods and services can be produced. Capital investment promotes the expansion of the *gross national product* (or GNP, our total national income), thereby improving our standard of living.

Savings media

The savings media comprise the different vehicles through which savings can be put to work for the saver. These media have a broader span than you may imagine. Bank deposits, building society share accounts, stock market securities and so on are fairly obvious examples of methods of investing your savings. But what about contributions to pension schemes and life policy premiums? These too are savings. Money used to keep up an insurance policy, for instance, is not being used to buy goods or services. It is paid to the insurance company which uses it to invest in stocks and shares or to lend out in some way to produce an income for the company. When the policy matures, either because of the occurrence of a specified event or because of the expiry of a stated period of time, the beneficiary receives a lump sum which can be spent. In the meantime it has been saved. In the same way, an employee's pension contributions are invested by the pension fund. The employee gets his money back as a pension when he retires. In the UK, each individual saves on average 8 per cent of his income when all these forms of saving are taken into account.

Attractions of different forms of saving

When choosing among the various different savings media which are available, the saver will pay regard to a number of different criteria. The relative importance placed on these criteria will vary according to the saver's circumstances and intentions.

Security. The principal requirement is generally the safety of the money put on one side. Savers will want to be able to get their money back at some stage in the future; an investment which carries a real risk of loss of capital will therefore be less attractive than one which offers security of capital.

There is, however, a qualification to this argument. This centres on the fact that the less risk a savings medium carries, the lower the rate of return will be. A high risk medium has to offer a high rate of return to attract funds. Of course, offering a high rate of return does not always mean that a high rate of return will actually be achieved!

Rate of return. While adequate security of capital is the principal requirement when selecting a savings medium, the rate of return provides the *principal motivation* for savers to look for a home for their money other than a hole in the back garden. The practical difference between hoarding and investing your savings is the return which accrues on properly invested funds. The security aspect can be a motive of course; money hoarded under the mattress can be stolen, while money held on a bank account cannot. The return on invested savings may come in the form of *income* such as interest on deposit accounts or dividends on shares, or a *capital appreciation,* that is, getting more back when the saving is realised than was originally put in. Often the total return is a combination of the two.

You have already learnt that there is an element of conflict between security and return. This savers will have to resolve to their own satisfaction. Of course, in times of high inflation such as the UK experienced in the 1970s and early 1980s, the rate of return becomes even more important. If the purchasing power of the money is to be protected, the saver must obtain a rate of return which at least equals the rate of inflation.

Liquidity. Another important consideration is the ease with which the savings can be converted back into cash, making the money available for spending. This aspect is also related to the rate of return. Generally, the longer the period over which the money is tied up, the better the offered rate of return will be. Savers may elect to keep some of their money in a comparatively liquid form to meet unexpected expenses but to invest the remainder on a longer-term basis. The amount to be kept in liquid form will vary with individual circumstances.

Importance of the savings media

The importance of the savings media in the national economy is that they convert savings into *investment capital*. For instance, funds put into a pension scheme are used by the pension fund to invest in, say, stock market securities. Although buying a share certificate on the stock market does not represent real investment in the company concerned, being merely a change in the ownership of existing shares, the existence of the stock market does allow companies to raise long-term capital. Similarly, savings put into a building society account are lent out to house buyers to provide the capital for the purchase of their home. It follows that savings and investment are closely related to one another. Without saving there could be no investment; the one is the corollary of the other.

Economists sometimes speak of the *paradox of thrift*. By this they mean that while saving is beneficial to the individual it can sometimes be detrimental to the economy as a whole. Money is removed from the circular flow of income and is unavailable for spending, leading to a reduction in demand for goods for consumption. Ultimately this can result in a general downturn in the economy. The limitation of this argument is that the paradox operates only when saving (not spending on consumption) is not used to finance investment (spending on capital assets). The savings media are therefore vital in returning savings to the flow of income by investing them.

The relationship between savings and investment

The flow of national income

We have already spoken of the circular flow of national income. Firms produce goods or services and households buy them. The individuals in the households provide the labour and the capital to enable production to be undertaken and the firms 'buy' these factors of production. Thus, money passes from firms to households and back to firms in one direction, while goods and services flow in the opposite direction. This is illustrated in Fig. 4.1.

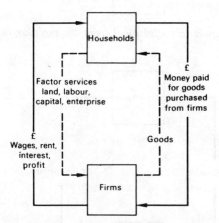

Fig. 4.1 The flow of money and goods between households and firms

If the value of consumption were equal to the value of income, the money flow would be in equilibrium and there would be no tendency for the level of income to change. Savings, however, represent a *leakage* from the system which leaves less money for consumption and therefore decreases the circular flow of income. In Fig. 4.2 savings are shown for simplicity as being carried out by households, although in reality firms are also capable of saving from their income.

Investment is an *injection* to the circular flow of income as shown in Fig. 4.3. Again for simplicity we show this only as investment through firms, although private investment is also possible. If these injections into the cash flow are greater than the withdrawals, then, other things being equal, national

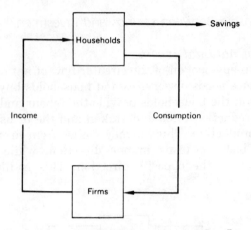

Fig. 4.2 Savings as a withdrawal from the circular flow of income

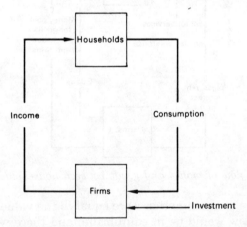

Fig. 4.3 Investments are an injection into the circular flow of income

income will rise. If, on the other hand, withdrawals are greater than injections, national income will fall. If injections are equal to withdrawals, then there is no tendency for the national income to change and it is in equilibrium.

Where do these injections of capital come from? Some amounts may come from outside the national economy, representing investment from abroad but these are comparatively small. Most of the money spent on investment comes from money saved within the economy. Obviously, both the saving and the investment can be carried out by the same person or firm but they need not be. A firm might well put money into reserve over a period of years, eventually utilising the funds to acquire a new factory building, in which case the saver and the investor are one and the same. On the other hand, an individual may put surplus cash into a bank account, enabling the bank to make an advance to a firm which uses the money to buy a new machine. Here the saver and the investor are different, although the investor is using the saver's money. The various savings media are a vital link in the chain passing funds from saver to investor, although sometimes this is done directly between the parties. This link is shown in Fig. 4.4.

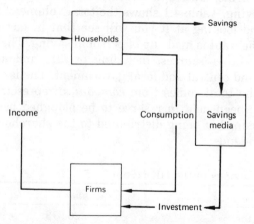

Fig. 4.4 The savings media as a link between saver and investor

Over a period, savings must equal investment. Bearing in mind that the level of savings is directly determined by the level of income, the *equilibrium* of national income can be explained in the following way.

(a) If investment were greater than savings then national income would rise.

(b) If national income rises, savings rise.

(c) This would continue until the increased savings equalled the original increased investment.

(d) The economy is returned to equilibrium at a higher level of income when once again savings equal investment.

The same is true in reverse if savings are not made available to fund investment.

(a) If savings were greater than investment then national income would fall.

(b) If national income falls, then savings fall.

(c) This would continue until savings were reduced to such a level that they once again equalled investment.

(d) The economy is returned to equilibrium at a lower level of income when once again, savings equal investment.

Sources of savings

We have said that savings can be undertaken by both households and firms, although so far we have concentrated on personal saving. Table 4.1 shows the total volume of UK saving in 1985, and looking at it you will see that in fact only about a third of the total is made up of personal saving. The remainder comes from other sources, including private and nationalised industries and central and local government. The largest contribution to the total comes from *companies*, representing profits which have been held in reserve to be ploughed back into the business instead of being distributed to the shareholders in the form of dividends.

Table 4.1   Savings in the UK (1985)

	£m
Personal sector	26 573
Companies	40 200
Public corporations	5 162
Central government	(−1 374)
Local authorities	(−3 276)
	67 285

Although smaller than industry's contribution, *personal sector* saving is still a very large figure. In this context, the personal sector embraces not only individuals but also all unincorporated businesses, including sole traders, partnerships, clubs and societies; and money saved through insurance policies, pension funds and similar schemes. The volume of personal saving can have an important impact on the national economy in that money not saved is largely spent on consumption. It follows, therefore, that if national income remains constant, increased saving must result in reduced demand for consumer goods and vice versa. In recent years, successive governments have attempted to manipulate this phenomenon to control inflation. By encouraging saving they have sought to reduce consumer spending, thereby containing price increases.

The figures shown in Table 4.1 contain an adjustment in respect of stock appreciation which is necessary because part of the profits of firms arises out of increases in the values of stock and work-in-progress. The difference in any particular year between real income generated and expenditure—in other words: savings—will be incorrectly assessed if no allowance is made for this appreciation.

Uses of savings

You know that savings provide the capital for investment and that over a period savings and investment must be equal to each other. Table 4.2 analyses investment of the funds saved in 1986 in two ways, showing both which sectors of the economy undertook the investment and the classes of assets invested in. Savings may be routed into these various uses either directly by the saver or, more commonly, indirectly through one of the several savings media which are available. All of these savings media are in competition with one another for savers' funds; the more they can attract, the more they can invest and the more profit they can earn.

National savings

The term 'national savings' is used to mean specifically that part of total savings which is deposited under one of the *national savings movement* schemes. These comprise principally national savings certificates, premium savings bonds, save-as-you-earn schemes, and accounts with the National Savings Bank. The various savings schemes which are offered are aimed predominantly at attracting personal savings, although a small amount of corporate savings are also held in this form. You will

Table 4.2 Capital investment in the UK (1986)

Types of investment:	£m
Aircraft, ships and vehicles	6 617
Plant and machinery	23 296
Dwellings	12 115
Other new buildings and works	14 985
Transfer costs of land and buildings	3 106
Investment by sectors:	
Personal sector	16 478
Companies	31 314
Public corporations	5 718
Central government	6 608
'Book value' increases affecting stocks and work-in-progress	3 565
	63 683
Net UK investment abroad	3 602
Net Capital Investment (equals total savings—see Table 4.1)	67 285

(*Source: National Income and Expenditure*)

appreciate that 'national savings' do not account for the whole of the savings of the community, nor anything like it.

The national savings movement generates a flow of funds from the private sector of the economy which can be channelled into the public sector to provide finance for government expenditure. Thus, money put into a national savings scheme can be looked on as money lent to the government. Through the national savings movement the government has sought to promote personal saving, both to raise finance and to reduce personal spending. Both aspects are important. If the government could not raise some of its finance in this way, it would have to place greater reliance on other methods, such as increased taxation! Reducing personal spending becomes very important at times when it is desirable to curtail personal *consumption*, such as during a war or in periods of high inflation.

The rates of return on some forms of national savings are currently very competitive, although in the past the movement has come under criticism for not keeping pace with other savings media. Saving by way of a national savings scheme offers savers absolute security of capital in monetary terms: they will always be able to get back as much money as they put in. This is attractive to small savers who often tend to be conservative in outlook and unsophisticated in their financial dealings, although you should not imagine that national savings are unattractive to the more sophisticated and well-off saver.

Although the average amount put into national savings by any one individual tends to be small, the total invested by the whole population adds up to a very large amount indeed, representing a significant proportion of the *national debt*. Table 4.3 shows the total of national savings at March 1986, broken down into the various types of saving available.

Table 4.3 National savings in the UK (March 1986)

	£m
National savings certificates	17 112
Deposit and income savings bonds	4 061
Premium bonds	1 831
Other stocks on the National Savings Stock Register	1 014
Save-as-you-earn	555
National savings stamps	1
National Savings Bank:	
ordinary account	1 709
investment account	5 624
	31 907

(*Source: Annual Abstract of Statistics*)

National savings certificates

National savings certificates represent a direct loan by the saver to the government, the certificate being the holder's receipt for the amount advanced. The terms under which national savings certificates are offered are periodically revised to keep them in line with market forces, for example, the rate of return must be neither too high nor too low. When a new issue of certificates is made available, the previous issue will be discontinued.

Certificates can generally be bought through post offices and banks. Each certificate represents a holding of a stated number of *units* of national savings certificates which are available in several denominations. In the current (33rd) issue the value of each unit is £25 and a certificate for ten units will therefore 'cost' the investor £250. For each issue there is a maximum number of units that any one investor may hold; for the current issue this is 40 units, or £1000 worth. This is in addition to any holdings of previous issues, of which the investor may hold up to the stated maximum number of units. The maximum holding differs from issue to issue.

The return on national savings certificates takes the form of a capital appreciation. This is realisable when the saver obtains repayment of his certificates. He will receive the original capital value plus the agreed accruals. The rate of return on each issue is fixed when it is launched, the return on the current issue being equivalent to a compound rate of 7% per annum for certificates held for a minimum of five years. A holder can cash national savings certificates at any time but if this is done within five years of issue, a lower rate of return is obtained than if they were held for the full term. (If 33rd issue certificates are cashed after being held for only 12 months, the return for the year will be a mere $5\frac{1}{2}\%$.) The return on national savings certificates peaks after five years, although interest will continue to accrue on certificates which are held for longer periods.

The great advantage of national savings certificates is that the return is completely free of UK taxes. This makes them an attractive investment for the taxpayer, especially one who pays tax at the higher rates. The return of 7% on the current issue, for example, is equivalent to a rate of 9.58% on a taxable investment for a saver who pays income tax at the basic rate. National savings are not therefore quite so attractive to investors who have no liability for tax. As an investment for the personal saver, they have the further advantages of *liquidity*, being realisable at any time, albeit subject to the interest penalty which we have mentioned, and of *simplicity*, requiring no monitoring during the five-year period to maturity.

Index-linked national savings certificates
In addition to the regular issues of national savings certificates, a number of index-linked issues of certificates are available. The first issue was available only to individuals of pensionable age, that is men over 65 and women over 60, hence its popular name of 'granny bonds'. The second issue which superseded it was

available at first to anyone aged 50 or over but since 1981 the issue has been available to anyone. It remains so for the current issue. The maximum holding for any one person in the current (4th) issue is £5000. Index-linked national savings certificates are not on sale in the banks and must be obtained through post offices.

Interest accrues over 5 years at a compound rate of just 4% but the repayment value of certificates held for more than a year is also adjusted to keep pace with changes in the *Retail Prices Index*. Thus, when a holder cashes them the amount which is received will have the same purchasing power that the funds originally invested had at the time that the certificates were purchased. Certificates encashed within the first year will realise only the face value without any accruals. They can be held for over five years and the capital value, including the terminal bonus, will continue indefinitely to be increased in line with the Retail Prices Index. Interest will also continue to accrue but at a variable rate.

The purpose of these certificates is to help the small saver to protect some proportion of his capital against erosion by inflation without having to take undue risks. In time of high inflation the rate of return will be correspondingly high and, indeed, no other low-risk investment will be able to provide a similar level of return. When inflation is low, however, these certificates are generally out-performed by numerous other investments.

Yearly plan national savings certificates
Both ordinary and index linked NSCs are intended for *lump sum* investment although regular savers can make use of them by buying a small number of certificates on a regular basis. The yearly plan, however, is specifically designed for the saver who wishes to put aside a set amount of income each month.

The saver may elect to invest any amount between £20 and £200 per month, to be paid into the plan by monthly standing order from a bank account. Payments can be continued indefinitely but the minimum period is 12 months.

The rate of return offered varies from time to time but for any particular investor it is fixed for the first five years at the rate on offer on the day that the application is received. The certificates can be cashed in early, i.e. before the five year period has been completed, but if this is done there will be interest penalties. As with other NSCs, the interest is tax free.

Premium savings bonds

Commonly known simply as 'premium bonds', these are in some ways very similar to national savings certificates, representing as they do a loan to the state. They can be purchased through banks and post offices and are available in several denominations. The smallest bond currently available is the £5 bond, the maximum holding which one person may have is £10 000 worth of bonds. Technically, the bonds are issued in *units of £1*, each unit having its own unique serial number. Thus, a £10 bond has ten serial numbers which are consecutive with one another.

Premium savings bonds may be encashed at any time and will always realise the full face value for which they were issued. However, no interest or other accrual is added to this amount. Hence, in inflationary times the real value of the capital invested is steadily eroded. In fact, interest is paid by the state on the value of the bonds which are on issue at any one time but it is not distributed to the bondholders in proportion to the numbers of bonds which they hold. The interest is instead paid into a *prize fund* from which periodic distributions are made to a few lucky bond-holders. Each week an electronic random number indicator (ERNIE) generates the serial numbers of the winning bonds. The current maximum prize is £250 000 (one each month), the lowest is £50 (some 45 000 each month) and a range of intermediate prizes is also paid. Bonds must be held for three months before they qualify for any prize distributions.

Premium bonds are not an investment for a saver in the commonly accepted sense of the word. They provide neither income nor capital growth for bondholders, except to those who win prizes. Prizewinners can benefit out of all proportion to the amount of bonds held. The scheme represents a sort of lottery but one which allows those who gamble on it to get their original stake back at any time. You should realise that the majority of bondholders either never win any prize at all or, if they do, they never realise as much money as they would have done by putting the same original amount into, say, a building society account!

Interest-bearing bonds

These are aimed at the saver who wishes to make a lump-sum investment. The two such bonds earn interest on the capital invested, the interest being calculated at a rate which varies from time to time in line with market rates. The rate will have to be kept competitive in order to attract new money and to retain the funds already invested. The interest paid is taxable but it is paid without deduction of tax. The investor has to account to the Inland Revenue for any tax liability. These bonds may be purchased through any post office.

Deposit bonds

Deposit bonds may be purchased in multiples of £50. The maximum holding for any one person is £100 000 and the minimum is £100. Interest accruing due on the bonds is added to their capital value, rather like national savings certificates, and the investor therefore realises the income only when he requests repayment of his bonds. Repayment can be requested at any time after purchase but three months' notice will be required before the payment is made. The rate of interest on a bond repaid before the first anniversary of purchase will be cut to half the published rate; thereafter there is no penalty for withdrawal. The Treasury reserves the right to redeem these bonds at its discretion at any time after they have been on issue for ten years.

Income bonds

These bonds are designed for investors who wish to receive regular monthly payments of interest on their savings. They may be purchased in multiples of £1000. The maximum holding is £100 000, and the minimum is £2000. Interest accruing on the bonds is paid direct to the bondholder on a monthly basis. Holders may obtain repayment by giving three months' notice of withdrawal, as with deposit bonds. There is a similar interest penalty if they are encashed within the first year.

Save-as-you-earn (SAYE) contracts

The SAYE scheme was designed to encourage regular saving by offering a mechanism for savers to set aside a set proportion of income each month. The amount to be saved would be paid over by way of a *standing order*. Alternatively, with the employer's co-operation, the amount to be saved could be deducted direct from the saver's wages and paid into the scheme without passing through the saver's hands.

Although several types of SAYE contract have been available in the past to which savers are still contributing, including an *index linked* scheme, there is only one type of contract currently available to new savers. This is the *Share Option Issue* and is for the use of individuals who are entitled to purchase shares in the company they work for under a share option scheme. The details of such schemes will vary slightly from company to company but, in principle, they work as follows. The employee agrees to pay a monthly sum into the SAYE contract for a stated number of years, generally three to five years. At the end of that period the funds saved will be repaid with a 'bonus' of some sort and the employee will have the option of buying shares in the company at a price agreed at the start. If the price of the shares is not attractive (if, say, their *market value* is lower than the agreed buying price) the money can be returned to the employee instead.

To make such schemes attractive to the employee, any *capital gains* received by the saver are free of income tax, provided that the scheme is one which has been approved by the Inland Revenue. Appropriate savings schemes are operated by some of the building societies as well as by the Department for National Savings.

National Savings Bank

The National Savings Bank has its origins in the Post Office Savings Bank founded in 1861 under the control of the Post Office. In 1969, when the Post Office ceased to be a government department and became a public corporation, the Post Office Savings Bank was 'hived off' to become the National Savings Bank. It is run by the civil servants of the Department of National Savings but it continues to operate through the country's post offices which are, in effect, its branches. This large network of branches is very much more extensive than the network of any of the commercial banks and gives it the advantage over some of them of being open to customers on Saturday mornings. However, it shares this network with the National Girobank, from which it is completely separate, and with the Post Office itself, which has its own range of customer services. Consequently, post office counters can be quite congested, sometimes resulting in delay and inconvenience for National Savings Bank customers.

The National Savings Bank has a very limited range of services for its customers offering just two types of account, suitable principally for depositors who do not require access to a full banking service. No borrowing facilities of any kind are available. Funds deposited with the National Savings Bank are managed by the Commissioners of the National Debt and are invested in government securities. Depositors' capital is therefore effectively guaranteed by the state. The income from these investments is used to meet interest payments to depositors and to finance operating costs.

Ordinary accounts

Ordinary National Savings Bank accounts may be opened by any person over seven years of age, with a maximum deposit at any one time of £10 000. Details of all deposits and withdrawals are recorded in a *passbook*, and withdrawals of up to £100 may be made on demand on production of the passbook at any post office or sub-post office operating NSB facilities. Larger amounts can be withdrawn at a few days' notice. After six months, the account can be converted into a *Regular Customer Account* on which withdrawals of up to £250 per day may be made at a chosen post office. A *paybill* facility allows customers to pay bills of up to £250 from their accounts without handling cash. It can be used for all bills usually payable at the post office, such as gas and electricity bills, television licence fees and rates demands. *Standing order* payments can be arranged, although payments cannot be made more frequently than monthly. Employers can remit wages direct to an employee's NSB account.

Interest is paid on ordinary account balances, being credited to the accounts annually on 31 December. The interest rate on these accounts varies according to the general levels of interest rates, the NSB being authorised to pay higher rates to attract deposits. In 1987, for example, the interest rate was set at 6% for accounts which maintained a balance of £500 or more and

3% on other accounts. Interest up to £70 in any one year, £140 on a joint account, is exempt from income tax.

Investment accounts

A depositor not wanting access at short notice may open an investment account in which the maximum deposit is £100 000. This is additional to the possible £10 000 on an ordinary account. The interest rate on an investment account is higher than the rate on ordinary accounts, being dependent on the income earned by the *investment account fund* in which the deposits are invested. Interest is paid gross and the account holder must account to the Inland Revenue for any tax liability. One month's notice is required for all withdrawals. These may be made in cash or by crossed warrant payable through a bank.

The National Savings Stock Register

Some personal investors may wish to purchase government securities (gilts) in preference to buying national savings certificates or premium savings bonds. Such investments are often effected through the services of a stockbroker but the investor may elect to buy, and later sell, gilts through the National Savings Stock Register. The necessary forms are available at any post office. The principal advantage of using the National Savings Stock Register is that the fees charged on the transaction are attractive on small or medium-sized 'bargains'. Up to £10 000 may be invested in any particular stock on any one day but there is no limit on the total amount which may be held at any one time. The prices at which stocks can be bought and sold reflect the current stock market prices of the stocks.

Banks and building societies

Commercial banks

We have already considered the functions of the commercial high street banks, so there is no need to look at them in detail again here. From a saver's viewpoint their importance is that they provide an alternative vehicle to accumulate and invest savings. The commercial banks accept deposits from their customers in much the same way as the savings banks but, unlike the savings banks, the bulk of the total sum deposited with them comes from commercial rather than personal customers. This does not mean that the majority of accounts held by the commercial banks are accounts of businesses, however, for millions of their accounts hold the funds of private individuals, Nevertheless, the sums of money deposited by firms can be much larger.

Types of accounts

Banks offer their customers two principal types of account: current accounts and deposit accounts.

Current accounts. Current account holders receive no interest on their deposits but have access to the full range of money transmission services. These include the drawing and collection of cheques, credit transfers, standing orders, direct debits and so on. Funds held on current account generally represent money set aside to cover current expenditure and to meet day-to-day needs, rather than being a permanent or semi-permanent cash surplus. Even so, current account balances are savings in the sense in which we defined the term at the beginning of this chapter. It is important to note that while the balance on any one current account may fluctuate over a wide range, the total of the balances on all current accounts provides the banks with quite a stable deposit base.

Deposit accounts. These give access only to a restricted range of money transfer facilities, but they pay interest to the account holders on their credit balances. The *deposit rate*, as banks term the rate of interest applicable to deposit accounts, is competitive with other interest rates, being slightly lower than bank base rate and fluctuating like it. Deposit accounts are intended as a home for longer-term savings, thereby providing the banks with a more stable source of loanable funds. To emphasise the longer term for which these funds are deposited, a period of notice, usually seven days, must be given before withdrawals may be made. In practice, this period is not normally enforced and depositors are allowed to make withdrawals on demand, provided that they are prepared to forgo seven days' accrued interest on the amount withdrawn.

Savings accounts. These are somewhat oldfashioned and were originally aimed at attracting small personal savers. They are usually based on the use of a *passbook* in which all deposits and withdrawals are recorded, instead of using the more modern statement system. Withdrawals up to a specified level may be permitted at any branch against production of the passbook. As with a deposit account, interest is allowed on the balance of the account, normally at deposit rate. Sometimes a home safe is issued to encourage the habit of regular saving. These accounts are costly and time-consuming to operate and the banks are not encouraging new customers to open them, although existing accounts will continue to be operated.

Most of the other types of account which are offered to bank customers are variations on the themes of deposit and/or current accounts. Thus, for example, many banks now offer a type of *budget account* to which the customer makes regular monthly contributions. These accounts provide automatic access to current account type overdrafts up to a specified multiple of the monthly contribution. When the account is in credit, however, interest is allowed on the balance as on a deposit account.

Tax on interest

The interest earned on bank deposits is paid net of tax to the private individual. This means that the bank has already deducted the tax and paid it over to the Inland Revenue. A standard rate tax payer incurs no further liability on the interest although a higher rate tax payer has to account for the extra tax which is due.

The amount of tax which the banks deduct is calculated at a *composite rate* which is intended to result in the collection of the same amount of tax as would have been collected from all the depositors if they were taxed individually. In practice, this results in a favourable rate of return for the tax payer because some of the tax due is being paid by the many depositors who would otherwise have no tax liability. Such depositors cannot claim back the composite rate tax which has been deducted from their interest.

Other savings facilities

In recent years the high street banks have introduced a number of schemes designed to encourage personal customers to make regular savings out of income. Such schemes generally offer a higher rate of interest than ordinary deposit accounts as an incentive. Several of the high street banks operate their own unit trusts for customers who wish to put their savings into stock market securities. For the customer who has adequate funds to invest directly in the purchase of stocks in his own name, stock market transactions can be arranged.

Other services

The commercial banks can offer an extraordinarily wide range of services, ranging from purely banking services such as money transmission, to non-banking facilities such as the operation of a travel agency. There are two principal motives for offering these services. Most obviously there is the simple profit motive. Many of the services do not operate at a profit, however; where, for instance, is the profit in money transmission facilities? The motive in offering such unprofitable services is simply to attract more depositors by providing a more complete banking service. The more depositors a bank can attract, the larger its deposit base will be and the more funds it will therefore have available to lend.

The National Girobank

The National Girobank is the second of the two banks which operate over the counters of the nation's post offices. As we saw in Chapter 2, the National Girobank was set up to provide an efficient money transfer service to operate in competition with clearing banks. *Current account* facilities for both personal and business customers consequently form the backbone of the organisation's operations. The current accounts of personal customers are conducted free of charge, provided that no over-drafts are created, and they operate in much the same way as bank current accounts. Cash may be paid in to the accounts at any post office and cheques can be sent direct to the Girobank's central office in Bootle from where they will be collected for the account holder.

A cheque book is provided to enable the account holder to make payments to third parties and to withdraw cash. Cash withdrawals of up to £50 may be made every other business day at either of two post offices nominated by the account holder when the account is opened. A Girobank '*postcheque card*' is available. This operates much like a bank cheque card, guaranteeing payment of cheques up to £50 each, and enables the account holder to cash cheques up to £100 at the 'first choice' post office, or up to £50 at any other. It also enables encashments to be made at banks throughout the UK and at post offices throughout Europe under reciprocal arrangements with other national post offices. A cash card enables the holder to draw up to £100 per day from any cash machine attached to the 'Link' network.

Deposit accounts are available to savers and these pay a competitive rate of interest. Transfers can be arranged between deposit and current accounts, the facility being free of charge. Budget account facilities are also offered and personal loan accounts are available in connection with consumer spending. All applications for loans are dealt with centrally, the customer applying by post for the required facilities. The Girobank also offers a credit card through its participation in the VISA network.

Building societies

To the small saver and, indeed, the private borrower the building societies are much like the banks, and are becoming more so. However, there are some important differences. A brief examination of the history of the building societies will help us to understand this.

The earliest building societies were just what their name implies: societies whose members jointly saved up enough capital to construct homes for themselves. All members would contribute an equal sum of money at regular intervals to the fund and when enough had been accumulated, a plot of land could be bought and houses built on it. Houses were built singly and allocated to members by drawing lots. All members would continue to contribute to the fund until a house had been built for everyone, at which time the society would be wound up. These *terminating societies* were a sort of self-help group owned and run by the members.

In the mid-19th century, societies began to be set up in which the members who contributed the funds to buy the houses were not necessarily the same people as the members who eventually lived in them. The depositing members had to be rewarded for the use of their money and this was done by paying them interest on it. The borrowing members were *charged* interest on the funds which were made available to them by the society. There is no reason why these *permanent societies* should ever be wound up while new depositors and borrowers can be found.

These permanent societies continued to grow and proliferate, offering a fairly narrow range of facilities to just two classes of customer: personal savers and house buyers looking for a mortgage.

For the saver, the societies could offer two principal types of facility, *share accounts* and *deposit accounts*.

Share accounts
In principle, the investing members of a permanent building society such as we have just described are among its *shareholders* and, like the shareholders of a limited company, it is they who run the greatest risk of losing their capital if the organisation has to be wound up at a time when assets are insufficient to cover liabilities. There are, however, some important differences. First, as we have seen, the return on a building society shareholder's investment is paid in the form of interest rather than as a dividend. Second, while a limited company has a fixed number of shares on issue at any one time, a building society's share capital can increase, and decrease, from day to day according to the deposits and withdrawals made by members. Finally, building society shares are not bought by one shareholder from another like company shares. They can be bought only from the society and are sold back to the society at face value (par) when the member wishes to realise some or all of the investment.

Deposit accounts
As well as allowing investors to become shareholders, many building societies also began to offer the alternative facility of taking money on deposit. Unlike shareholders, depositors are creditors of the society and, as such, have a prior claim for the return of their funds in the event of a liquidation. Because of this extra measure of security, the rate of interest paid on such deposits is generally a little lower (about a quarter to a half of one per cent less) than that paid on share accounts. In practice,

there is comparatively little difference between the operation of a deposit account and the operation of a share account and both provide the facility to make cash withdrawals of large amounts on demand. Neither type of account carries any appreciable risk and the majority of investors consequently prefer share accounts for the benefit of the higher rate of interest.

Savings schemes

Like the banks, the building societies find it very convenient if they can persuade customers to keep their money on deposit for a long time as this promotes stability of the deposit base and helps them to calculate how much they can lend at any one time. As a result, the building societies have introduced a number of savings schemes designed to induce savers to tie up their funds for longer periods. These schemes mostly fall into two categories: term savings and subscription schemes.

Term savings schemes. These require savers to leave their money with the society for a fixed term, agreed at the outset and anything from six months to several years. The attraction is that the interest rate offered is higher, sometimes considerably higher, than the rate available on ordinary accounts. Generally, the longer the agreed term, the higher the interest rate will be. The penalty which savers have to suffer is that they cannot normally recover their money until the end of the agreed term. Some schemes permit early withdrawals if savers are prepared to forgo all the interest which has been earned over and above the society's normal rates. Many building societies call their term savings schemes 'bonds', issuing the saver with a certificate as evidence of the amount paid in and showing the terms of repayment. Most of such schemes are share account schemes.

Subscription schemes. These invite savers to make regular, usually monthly, payments in to a building society account. Again, these are usually share accounts and a higher rate of interest is paid than on ordinary share accounts. The details of the schemes vary considerably but most offer some measure of withdrawal without penalty. Some, for instance, allow one withdrawal from the account per year. Withdrawals beyond the agreed limits may be permitted but they will invariably carry the penalty of loss of the extra interest.

Many of these accounts require subscriptions for a set period of time, commonly three to five years, although after this period the balance may be left in the account where it will continue to earn interest at the higher rate. If a saver ceases to make contributions to the account before the end of the set period, there will usually be some loss of interest. The flexibility of these accounts, combined with their comparatively high rate of return, has made them very attractive to personal savers.

Competition with the banks

By the end of the 1970s, the building societies had become the banks' principal competitors for personal deposits. In fact, they now attract more of these deposits than the banks and control more than half of the personal deposit market. This is not so disastrous to banks as you might think. They have found that they can 'buy in' on the interbank sterling market a larger proportion of the funds needed to grant loans. Nevertheless, the banks would like to recover some of the market share which they have lost.

In other areas, such as lending, the banks and the building societies hardly competed at all. Since the beginning of the 1980s, however, this has changed. Not only have the banks entered the house purchase loan market but the building societies have begun to widen their traditional range of services.

Current accounts

Most of the building societies have introduced a current account type of facility for personal depositors. The facilities offered on these accounts are limited when compared with bank current accounts. They are principally restricted to the ability to draw out cash on demand and the facility to issue 'cheques' on the account. The building societies, like the banks, are installing *automated teller machines* in many of their premises to permit 'out-of-hours' withdrawals. No overdrafts are permitted on these accounts but interest is paid on the credit balances which are maintained. The interest rate is somewhat lower than the rate applying on ordinary share accounts.

The interest on building society deposits is paid net of tax, in the same way as interest on bank deposits. A standard rate tax payer therefore incurs no further tax liability on the interest, although a higher rate tax payer has to account for the extra tax which is due.

Ease of access

Throughout the 1970s and 1980s the building societies have pursued a major branch opening programme. This has given them a presence in the nation's high streets which allows them to *compete* for retail deposits very much on an equal footing with the banks. Indeed, so far as the personal customer is concerned, the building societies have the advantage of being open on Saturdays, unlike some banks, allowing customers to make deposits and withdrawals six days a week. The banks of course have been installing automated teller machines partly to counter this threat to their business but then so have the building societies! It is interesting to note that just as certain groups of banks have negotiated agreements for the reciprocal use of each other's machines, so two groups of building societies have organised shared systems of building society automated teller machines.

Investors can be secure in the knowledge that their funds will be safe since the finances of the building societies are generally as stable as those of the banks. There have in the past been building society failures, particularly among the smaller societies, but in the event of such a failure occurring it could be expected that the other societies would bail out the insolvent society.

The Building Societies Act 1986

This Act has accelerated the development of the societies by freeing them from previous statutory restrictions on their activities. They are now permitted to offer a whole range of services in the banking, investment and housing fields. They are able, for instance, to improve their money transmission services, set up insurance schemes and so on. Most significantly, they are permitted to offer *unsecured loans*, so they are no longer tied almost exclusively to the house purchase loan market.

The Act nevertheless contains some restrictions which ensure that the societies will remain committed to their traditional lending and savings markets. Principally: in raising funds no more than 20% may be obtained from wholesale markets; only 5% may be lent out on an unsecured basis (so mortgages will continue to be their principal type of loan); and of their total assets, more than 80% must continue to be secured mortgage loans. One further restriction is that the capital backing for secured loans must not fall below 4.65%, thereby ensuring that the societies do not over extend their lending activities.

The response to this new freedom has been varied. The larger societies have begun to diversify, setting up estate agencies, bringing in private loan schemes and so on. The smaller societies have tended to stick closer to their traditional areas of activity, having neither the experience nor the resources to develop new services. A series of amalgamations and mergers has also begun to take place, and this can be expected to continue.

House purchase facilities

Many building society customers first open their accounts as a vehicle for building up enough capital to put down as a deposit on a home of their own. This has the added advantage of providing an introduction to a building society, thereby easing the process of raising a mortgage for the balance of the purchase price. Although it is not strictly necessary to have been a depositor with a particular building society before applying for a loan from it, the societies do give preferential consideration to established depositors when loan funds are scarce. In recent years, several societies have introduced special savings schemes, aimed particularly at young married couples, which give preferential access to home loan facilities when required.

The banks are, of course, also in competition with the building societies in the house purchase loans market and have achieved a substantial penetration of the market. Even so, in the public eye, the building societies continue to be the most apparent source of such finance.

Most building society loans continue to be granted for the purchase, or subsequent improvement, of owner-occupied domestic property. Repayment of the loan will normally be effected over a period of 25 years or until the borrower's retirement, whichever is the shorter period. The building society will be concerned to see that the borrower can afford to make the repayments out of income. In the case of a married couple, to which the majority of loans are given, account will be taken of income earned by both parties. As security for the loan, the society will require a *mortgage* over the house to be bought, and the advance will be limited, in most cases, to a maximum of 90% of its market value. The balance of the purchase price must be provided by the borrowers from their own resources. For certain types of property, such as houses over 100 years old, the societies limit their maximum advance to a smaller proportion of the valuation. The society will insist on adequate *fire insurance* being taken out on the premises.

Other savings media

Life assurance

Life assurance policies represent a means of guarding against and minimising the financial consequences of a person's death. Thus, for instance, a married man with young children may take out a policy on his own life to provide some financial comfort and support for his wife and family in the event of his early death.

There are three parties to a life policy in addition to the company which issues the policy:

(a) *the proposer* who takes out the policy and who pays the *premiums* at regular intervals (usually monthly);

(b) *the life assured* on whose life (or death) the policy is based;

(c) *the beneficiary* who ultimately collects any payment which the company makes under the terms of the policy.

These three roles can be filled by three separate people, or one person may be two or even all three.

When asked to issue a policy, the assurance company will first calculate when on average, given present age and state of health, the life assured might be expected to die. Using this as a basis, it will then calculate the level at which it has to set the premiums to ensure that it receives more money than it will have to pay out when the policy falls due. Each policy states the *capital sum assured*, this having been set at the time of issue. Of course, if the life assured dies early, the assurance company will incur a loss on the policy. If, on the other hand, the life assured lives longer than expected, the company will collect more than it has contracted to pay out. By issuing a large number of policies the assurance companies can ensure that overall their income exceeds their outgoings.

Money paid into an assurance policy by way of premiums is money saved, that is, money not spent in consumption, and many individuals look on assurance policies as a convenient and rewarding way of building up their savings and providing for the future. The premiums received by the companies are not allowed to lie idle pending payments to the beneficiaries of the policies; the money is put to work in profitable investments, notably through the *stock market*. The additional investment income which the assurance companies receive allows them to pitch their premiums at a lower level than would otherwise be the case.

Types of policy

There are several different types of life assurance policy, each designed to fit the needs of people in different circumstances.

Whole life policies. These are perhaps the simplest type of policy. It matures and the benefit becomes payable only when the life assured dies, however far in the future that event may be. The premiums on the policy therefore have to be paid for the whole of that person's life after the policy has been taken out. The amount of the premium will be determined chiefly by two factors: the *sum assured* and the *age* of the life assured when the policy is set up. A policy which pays out £10 000 on maturity will clearly require premiums which are twice as high as those due on a similar policy which is to pay out only £5000. Similarly, the older the life assured is at the time the policy is taken out, the higher the premiums will be for a given sum assured.

Temporary policies. These policies (often called 'term assurance') also become payable on the death of the life assured, but only if it occurs *before* a set date. If the life assured survives to that date, the policy becomes void and no payment is made to the beneficiary. A special version of this type of policy is the mortgage protection policy, designed to pay off a borrower's house mortgage if he dies before the end of the normal repayment period.

Endowment policies. These are the most popular form of life assurance. These policies pay out either on the death of the life assured or on his survival to a specified date, whichever is the sooner. The beneficiary is therefore certain to receive the proceeds by a *known date* in the future. These policies can be set up for any desired term but most fall within the range of 10 to 25 years. They provide both protection against the death of the life assured and a simple-to-use form of personal investment which can be used as an alternative to the regular savings schemes offered by the banks and building societies. An individual wishing, for example, to set aside £10 per month for the next ten years may set up an endowment policy on his own life maturing in ten years' time, naming himself as beneficiary. The assurance company will calculate the value of the cover which can be offered for that premium, this being the sum which will be paid out on maturity. If the policyholder dies before ten years have elapsed, his estate will receive the full capital value to be passed on to his next of kin.

Attractions to investors

The annual premium income of the British assurance companies is enormous and their investment experts handle huge sums of money every day. All of this money comes from the premiums collected from thousands of individual households, each one of which may have decided to take out assurance policies for any one of a number of reasons. First, and most obviously, there is the *precautionary motive*. It is, for instance, very reassuring to know that a policy-holder's family will receive a lump sum of money if the household's breadwinner happened to die unexpectedly. This is why many husbands take out assurance policies on their own lives. It can, of course, be just as important to arrange cover on the life of a wife; in many households today she can be the principal wage earner. Even if she is not, the value of her services to the family should not be underestimated. It can be very costly to hire the services of someone to take on the work performed by a traditional housewife. Assurance can help to cushion the family against these costs if she were to die prematurely.

Second, there is the attraction of endowment assurance as a *medium for investment*. The return on an endowment policy can be comparable with the return on other forms of saving. This is as it should be. If you look at assurance from a different angle, you will see that by issuing an endowment policy the company is undertaking to collect regular contributions from the policyholder, to invest the money in a variety of areas and then eventually to pay back the money subscribed plus some accruals of income from the investments. Policyholders thereby receive professional investment management on their money, even though they may not be aware of it.

The essential objective of an assurance company's investment managers will be, of course, to make a profit on the money at their disposal. This has to be combined with the need to preserve the value of the capital against loss and the need to ensure adequate liquidity to be able to make payments to beneficiaries as they fall due. To this end, the money is spread over a number of investments including stock exchange and government securities and property. The more successful that the investment managers are, the more profits the company will make. Policyholders can share in these profits if they take out their policies on a *with profits* basis. In return for a slightly higher premium, the company will each year add on to the capital sum assured a *bonus* representing a share of the year's profits on the investments. In the case of a policy which is set up with a lengthy term, say 15 years or more, the accumulated bonuses can often add up to more than the basic sum assured by the time the policy matures. Of course, such policies run the risk that if no income is generated in any one year, no bonuses will be added on. Some companies now offer special 'equity linked' policies, the capital value of which is directly linked to the market value of the investments into which the premiums have been directed.

Until 1984 the *rate of return* on an assurance policy was effectively increased by the tax concessions which were offset against the premiums payable. The proposer paying the premiums could claim *tax relief*, that is, pay no income tax on a sum equal to half the annual premium. An individual paying tax at the standard rate of 27% who puts £200 a year into life assurance policies could claim relief on £100 of these premiums, thus saving £27 which would otherwise go to the taxman. These provisions were changed in the 1984 Budget. Life policies taken out after April 1984 do *not* qualify for any tax relief, although *existing policies* continue to be eligible as before. The premiums on qualifying policies are paid *net of tax* to the assurance company which claims the remainder from the Inland Revenue.

If the policy-holder needs ready cash before the maturity of the policy, it is often possible to *surrender* the policy to the issuing company for a lump sum cash payment. If this is done, the policy is cancelled and no further premiums are payable. The *surrender value* of the policy will reflect the total amounts that have been paid in by way of premiums and it will therefore usually be very much less than the capital value which would have been payable on maturity. Similarly, in the case of a with profits policy, only a proportion of the accumulated bonuses will be added to the surrender value, the rest being forfeited.

As an alternative to surrendering a life policy, a proposer who needs cash may wish to raise a *loan against the policy*, either from a bank or from the issuing company. Any such loan will of course be restricted to the amount of the surrender value since the lender will be relying on the possibility of surrendering the policy to obtain repayment if all else fails. Although interest will have to be paid on the loan, borrowing does have the advantage of keeping the policy in force and maintaining the value of any bonuses. The lender will require the policy to be deposited and, usually, execution of a form of *assignment* giving the right to surrender the policy and collect the proceeds if the need arises. As you will see when we come to look at bank lending in Chapter 13, life policies are a most acceptable form of security for all types of bank advance.

Annuities

Most assurance companies will also issue annuities, which are a little like life policies in reverse! Instead of paying regular premiums and receiving a lump sum at death, or on survival to a set date, with an annuity the customer deposits a lump sum with the company which then pays the customer a regular income. The amount of the payments to be made by the company is fixed at the outset and in inflationary times this is a drawback since the purchasing power of a given sum can soon be dramatically eroded.

There are several different forms of annuity. With an *immediate annuity* the payments to the annuitant begin to be made straight away, continuing until some specified time. Payments often cease only on the death of the annuitant.

Clearly, the younger the annuitant, the greater the lump sum deposit will be to obtain a given level of income. Under a *deferred annuity*, in consideration of a lump sum deposited now, the company will pay a regular income to the annuitant as from some specified date in the future. Again, payments will usually cease on death. Until payments commence, the company has the use of the funds paid in to the annuity and it can invest these as it wishes. The agreed level of payments on a given sum invested in a deferred annuity will be higher than those paid on a similar sum invested in an immediate annuity. A *reversionary annuity* provides a regular income to the survivor of two people who have set up the annuity together, the parties to this type of arrangement usually being husband and wife. An *annuity certain* scheme provides for a set number of payments to be made even if the annuitant dies before all payments have been made. If this occurs, the remaining income will go to the annuitant's estate.

Why do people put money into annuities? Clearly the objective is to provide additional income for themselves, the commonest purpose being to boost pension income after retirement from work. The tax treatment of annuity income has an important effect in this respect. Part of each payment is classified as a return of the original capital investment and therefore is not taxable. The remainder, however, is classed as investment income and is therefore taxable as being unearned income. The younger the annuitant is when payments start, the greater the number of payments that he can expect to receive in his lifetime and, therefore, the smaller the return of capital with each payment. This means that for a young person most of each payment will be treated as taxable. With an older individual, the position is reversed and the larger part of each payment will be tax free, thereby increasing the yield to the annuitant.

Since annuities involve the deposit of a lump sum, they are not suitable for funding out of regular income. Pension schemes (which we shall be looking at shortly) are a better method of providing extra income after retirement for the normal wage-earner. The lump sum put into an annuity can be acquired in a number of ways, perhaps the commonest being by way of inheritance or the maturity of an assurance policy. In recent years *severance payments* to redundant employees have also provided an important source of funds.

Friendly societies

Most policies of life assurances are issued by the country's insurance companies or, less commonly, through the under-writers of Lloyds of London. Some of the insurance companies are *mutual organisations* operated expressly for the benefit of the policyholders, while others are normal commercial *joint stock* companies which also have to earn a profit for their share-holders. A small, and comparatively minor, amount of assurance continues to be provided by the *friendly societies* which had their origin in self-help societies of previous centuries. These societies exist to provide help for members and their families when in need, whether through sickness, unemployment, retirement, or death of a member. They take voluntary subscriptions from members and are controlled by the Friendly Societies Acts and the Industrial Assurance Acts.

Societies which operate under the provisions of the Industrial Assurance Acts are empowered to issue *industrial assurance policies*. These policies, which can also be issued by the commercial insurance companies, typically have very small capital values and premiums paid to collectors who visit the policyholders personally at frequent intervals. For this latter reason, the friendly societies which engage in this kind of busi-ness are often known as 'collecting societies'. The policies may take the form of either whole life or endowment assurance. They were very popular with the 'working classes' of the industrial areas of the country in the late nineteenth and early twentieth centuries—hence the name—as they provided money to meet needs which could be covered in no other way. Many people still refer to industrial whole life policies as 'burial policies' because the death benefit would provide enough money to pay for a funeral for the life assured and very little else.

The friendly societies are less important today since their functions have been taken on by other sections of society, especially the state itself. The social security system, for instance, provides a national safety net against unemployment and other cases of financial hardship and has superseded the role of the societies in this area. Similarly, the need for small assurance policies to provide for such items as funerals has been removed by changes in the fabric of our society as a whole.

Pension funds

A very large component of the saving undertaken by the nation is represented by money set aside in pension schemes to provide individuals with an income after retirement from work. Much of this money is tied up in the state pension scheme which provides an income for all of the nation's retired people aged over 65 for men or 60 for women. In addition, many working people contribute to supplementary schemes to provide for additional income in their old age.

The state pension

The state provides two complementary pension schemes comprising a basic (flat rate) pension and an additional earnings related pension scheme. The *basic state pension scheme* makes available a minimum level of income for all the nation's elderly. As we have said, men become entitled to receive their pension at 65 and women at 60, provided that they have ceased full-time employment. The levels of payment are regularly reviewed by the government and periodically increased so as to ensure that the purchasing power of the pension is not too far eroded by the rising cost of living. Nevertheless, many pensioners who have no other resources often cannot manage to meet all their outgoings on such low levels of income and have to have recourse to the state's *supplementary benefits* scheme.

The funds needed to finance the operation of the state pension scheme are provided largely by *national insurance contributions* collected from all in employment. These contributions are compulsory and, in most cases, are deducted direct from employee's wages by the employer, rather like PAYE taxation, who then remits the appropriate amounts to the state. Part of the financing comes from taxation and is provided in the way of a direct subsidy from the Treasury.

The *earnings-related scheme* was introduced in 1978 to provide a second state pension for retired workers which would be additional to the basic pension and which would enable them to maintain their standard of living into retirement. The principle on which the scheme operates is that the more an employee earns, the more the employee will pay into the scheme as contributions and the higher the ultimate pension will be. For each year's contributions to the scheme—up to a maximum of 20 years—the individual will receive a pension equal to $1\frac{1}{4}\%$ of salary. Someone who is in the scheme for 20 years, or more, will therefore receive a pension equivalent to 25% of salary, plus the basic pension of course. In computing the salary level on which the pension will be based, account is taken of the employee's twenty 'best', or highest paid, years' earnings during the contribution period, revalued in line with inflation. A person who contributes for less than twenty years will obviously receive a reduced pension. Contributions to the scheme are taken from both the employee and employer. An employer can elect to contract out of the scheme (not join it), as long as employees have access to an earnings-related pension scheme which offers benefits that are as good as, or better than, the benefits of the state scheme. These latter schemes are known as *occupational pension schemes* and where they are set up, both the employer's and the employee's compulsory contributions to the state schemes are reduced accordingly.

Occupational pension schemes

Occupational pension schemes provided by employers were traditionally viewed as a benefit of managerial and clerical jobs. Today, however, they are available to a much broader spectrum of employees. The provision for employers to contract out of the state scheme has had an important effect in this regard. Schemes may be operated on either a contributory or non-contributory basis. In a *contributory pension scheme* the fund is built up by contributions from both the employer and the employee. Employees' contributions are deducted from wages and no income tax is payable on this proportion of salaries. In a *non-contributory scheme*, the whole of the fund is built up by contributions from the employer in respect of each employee.

The details of the benefits will vary but, as we have already noted, the minimum benefit permissible is the equivalent of that provided by the state scheme. The *maximum* pension entitlement under current government regulations is the equivalent of one-sixtieth of the employee's final salary for each year's contributions to the scheme, up to a total of 40 years. Thus, the highest possible pension, for an employee of 40 year's standing or more, is equal to two-thirds of his final salary. Many schemes include provision for employees to commute a part of their pension entitlement and obtain a lump sum cash payment on retirement. This facility has enabled pension schemes to act as an important vehicle for capital accumulation. Today's workforce is very mobile, with people changing employment much more frequently than in the past, and the ability to transfer accumulated benefits from one scheme to another is therefore another important consideration.

Large employers frequently operate and manage their own occupational pension schemes without outside assistance, employing specialist staff to invest the money which is at the fund's disposal. Smaller businesses generally cannot afford to do this and turn to outside advisers, predominantly insurance companies. The insurance companies can effect economies of scale in respect of administration and management costs by offering the same pension fund services to large numbers of smaller businesses. Pension fund monies account for a large proportion of the money handled by insurance companies and it is interesting to note that the institutional investors, of which the pension funds are the largest section, provide more than half the money which is invested through the UK stock market.

Personal pension plans

The pension schemes we have outlined so far are aimed at employees but there also provisions for the *self-employed* to contribute to a personal pension plan. Up to $17\frac{1}{2}\%$ of the individual's income may be put into such a scheme and this amount can be claimed as a tax allowance against liability for income tax. Pension drawings may begin at any time after the age of 60 provided that the 'pensioner' has ceased work. Part of the funds accumulated may be taken out in a lump sum on retirement although this will, of course, reduce subsequent pension income.

Personal pension plans are operated, among others, by insurance companies and banks. They are very attractive to the self-employed, especially those with substantial incomes, as they offer a very *tax-efficient* way of dealing with income for the individual's personal benefit. They are available to people who are *partly self-employed*, such as employees who do extra work in their own time like writing textbooks or part-time lecturing at evening classes. A proportion of their 'extra' income can be put into a pension scheme. Similarly, participants in the state earnings-related scheme can put aside an extra slice of their income to provide extra pension benefits for themselves.

Unit trusts and investment trusts

The personal saver may wish to put his accumulations of capital to work by buying *shares* on the stock market. Since we shall be looking at the operation of the stock market in detail later in this chapter, it is sufficient for us to note here that the principal watch-words for those investing in company shares are *diversification* and *vigilance*.

Diversification means not putting all your money into buying one company's shares, as if that company were to fail the shares would become unsaleable and the capital would be lost. Funds should therefore be used to buy shares in a number of companies, preferably ones operating in different sectors of the economy, so that failure of any one company will not be totally disastrous. With any luck, capital losses in any one investment will be counter-balanced by increases in the values of others. The problem for the small investor is that a small amount of money can be spread only so far. Furthermore, the costs of dealing in a large number of shares can become prohibitive where small holdings are concerned.

Constant vigilance is necessary after the shares have been purchased to ensure that their value and capacity to generate income remain adequate. If shares begin to perform poorly, a decision has to be taken whether to hold on to them in the hope of recovery or whether to cut one's losses and dispose of them. It is obviously better if potential problems can be spotted *before* the value of the shares is affected. This is, of course, a technical and a time-consuming process and most investors have neither the time nor the expertise to carry it out properly. The wealthy can afford to pay for the services of a professional investment adviser but, once again, the costs are not proportionate to the benefits for the small saver.

The way out of the dilemma is for the small saver somehow to pool his funds with others and to arrange for those funds to be invested *professionally* on their behalf. We have already seen that this can be accomplished, albeit somewhat indirectly, by putting the money into an assurance policy. The assurance companies put a large proportion of their available funds to work in stock market investments. Unit trusts and investment trusts provide somewhat more direct methods of achieving this objective.

Unit trusts

A number of financial institutions, including several of the banks, operate unit trusts. Savers are invited to subscribe money to the trust fund, that money then being invested in a range of stock exchange securities. Early unit trusts were 'fixed funds' which collected a fixed amount of money from savers and invested it for a set period in a chosen range of investments. The managers of such funds had very restricted powers to vary the holdings after the fund had been set up. Modern funds are much more flexible than this, the managers having wide powers to change the investments subject to certain *legal constraints*, the principal of which are the requirements that at least twenty different stocks must be held at one time and that no more than $7\frac{1}{2}\%$ of the fund's capital may ever be put into any single stock in any circumstances.

Modern funds will continue indefinitely to accept the subscription of further funds from the public, all receipts being used to purchase more of the chosen range of securities. Subscribers of the money do not personally own a proportion of the portfolio of investments. They receive instead a number of 'units' in the trust entitling them to receive a proportionate share of the trust's distributions of income. The value of the units is determined by the value of the underlying securities, rising and falling according to stock market prices. The purchase price of new units (the *offer price*) is calculated on the basis that subscriptions will increase the value of the fund and therefore new securities will have to be purchased. The offer price per unit is therefore based on the lowest price at which the managers could buy the securities backing any one existing unit.

Unit holders can realise their investments by selling units back to the managers who are obliged to repurchase them. The *bid price* at which the repurchase would be effected is calculated on the basis that underlying investments would have to be sold. It therefore represents the best price which could be obtained in the market for the stocks less the costs of dealing. In practice, the managers may be able to effect repayments out of new funds subscribed by purchasers of units.

Types of unit trust fund
Before a unit trust can solicit subscriptions from the general public, it must be *authorised* to do so by the Department of Trade. The Department will first ensure that its operations will conform to the various legal requirements and that subscribers' funds will be adequately protected. There are several hundred such authorised unit trusts available for investors, some managed by banks, some by specialist managers. All follow their own investment strategies so every investor should be able to find at least one fund which is following a strategy appropriate to his needs.

There are two major components in setting the overall investment strategy of a unit trust. The first of these concerns the type of investments which are to be sought. *General funds* will spread their available money throughout all sectors of the economy. *Specialist funds* concentrate on particular areas. Some, for instance, place their money in fixed interest and government stocks—these are often known as 'bond funds'—while others invest exclusively in foreign shares. The second consideration is whether to invest for *income* or for *capital growth* or for some point in the spectrum in between. Trust managers will generally make their overall strategy quite plain in their advertising literature.

Types of unit
Many trusts offer two different types of unit which differ in the way in which the trust income is dealt with. With *accumulation units* the income from the underlying securities is reinvested in the trust. In the case of *income units* this income is distributed periodically to the unit holders as a regular 'dividend' on their investment. If the fund's holdings perform poorly, there may be no income either to distribute or to reinvest. If an investor requires a reliable flow of income from his holdings, he may select a *withdrawal fund*, which will guarantee a stated level of annual income. Payments will be paid out of investment income so far as is possible. If this is insufficient, some of the underlying holdings will be sold to realise the required funds. Over a period this can seriously deplete the value of the capital investment, which in turn reduces the investment income in future years.

Attractions to investors
The principal advantages of unit trusts are the diversification
of investment and the professional investment management
which they provide. Like all forms of stock market investment,
unit trusts also provide the possibility of *capital growth*, although
this is balanced by the corresponding risk of capital losses if the
chosen investments perform poorly. As a vehicle for saving, unit
trusts are reasonably liquid in so far as the managers are bound
to repurchase the units on demand. Of course, the saver has to
recognise that if the stock market values of the underlying
securities are depressed, so the bid price will also be low. A
forced realisation in an emergency may therefore bring in less
money than was originally put into the investment.

Investment trusts
Investment trusts developed before unit trusts. They are similar
in that they provide a vehicle for indirect investment on the
stock market but they differ in their financial structure. Investment trusts are limited companies which use their shareholders'
funds, as well as money borrowed by way of loans and loan
stocks, to invest in stocks and shares. Unlike a unit trust, an
investment trust is *not a trust* in the legal sense of the term.

A saver wishing to put money into an investment trust may
buy its shares through the stock market just as he would buy
shares in any other company. The shareholders receive dividends on their shares which are paid out of the dividends
received by the company from its investments. The value of the
shares will reflect the value of the company's investments.
Shareholders tend to have larger holdings than those investors
in unit trusts and the investment trusts are not in the business
of attracting small savings in the way that unit trusts are.

The directors of an investment trust perform a similar function to the managers of a unit trust in monitoring the investments and making changes as appropriate. However, they often
pursue a more entrepreneurial investment strategy. If the
management needs more and more money to broaden the range
of investments, it has the option of either borrowing the
required funds or of increasing the equity capital by floating a
new issue of shares in the company. This latter course would be
attempted only if the directors were confident that the whole of
the new issue would be taken up by investors.

Local authorities

We saw in Chapter 2 how the local authorities finance much of their expenditure by borrowing, using their income (from rates, government grants, etc.) only to fund day-to-day expenditure, including payment of interest on any loans obtained. Much of this borrowing is undertaken through the money market on a short term basis but a significant proportion of the funds required is raised from the general public by the issue of various types of bond and loan stocks. The attractions to the personal investor of such schemes is that they offer highly competitive rates of return combined with good security of capital. It is almost unthinkable that a local authority should ever find itself unable to meet its debts. Smaller authorities tend to offer slightly higher rates to overcome the preference of the public for the larger authorities.

Local authority loans

For many years the traditional type of local authority loan was the *mortgage loan* which attracted a fixed rate of interest payable half-yearly. In recent years the very similar but more flexible local authority *bond* has become popular. These bonds are issued for fixed periods, usually of between one to seven years, and there is generally no provision for early withdrawal of capital, although some authorities may agree to early repayment in cases of emergency. Furthermore, the bonds are not negotiable and cannot therefore be sold to a third party to realise the funds tied up in them. *Yearling bonds* have become very popular because they offer a good rate of return combined with a comparatively short term to maturity. Subscriptions for new issues of bonds are solicited through advertising in the national press.

The interest rate on these loans and bonds is fixed at the outset for the whole of the term. If interest rates rise after the bond has been purchased, investors are unable to get their money out until maturity and cannot therefore reinvest it at will in higher yielding investments. This accounts in part for the popularity of yearling bonds, since savers cannot be locked in to a low yielding stock for a very long time. In times of falling interest rates, of course, these factors work in reverse. Savers know that when their bonds mature they will be able to reinvest only at lower interest rates. The minimum investment in this type of loan is generally £100.

Local authority stocks

Just as the central government issues gilt-edged stocks, so the local authorities issue very similar *negotiable stocks* which can be dealt in on the Stock Exchange. These are issued offering a slightly higher rate of return because the security of repayment is in theory slightly less. As we have already noted, in practice it is highly unlikely that a local authority would be allowed to become totally insolvent. Stocks are issued with a fixed repayment date and a fixed rate of return which is expressed as a percentage of the face value. They are redeemed *at par* by the local authority on the maturity date.

The advantage to investors of stocks over bonds is that stocks can be sold to a third party through the medium of the Stock Exchange if funds have to be realised at short notice. However, investors have to be aware that a forced sale before maturity may realise much less than the face value of the stocks. This is because the market price is affected by changes to prevailing rates of interest. If interest rates rise, the price of a stock will fall since purchasers will wish to obtain more of the stock for their money in order to increase the effective rate of return to a competitive level. This process works in reverse of course: if interest rates fall the value of a stock rises, which is to the investor's advantage.

Hire purchase finance companies

Finance companies are institutions which exist to provide specialist finance to assist both private individuals and businesses with the acquisition of capital assets such as vehicles, machines and consumer durables. Their principal facilities are *hire purchase* loans and, in some cases, *leasing*. The majority of such finance in the UK is provided through the 30 or so larger companies which are members of the *Finance Houses Association*. Many of the finance companies operating in the UK are either wholly owned subsidiaries of a bank or jointly owned by a number of banks.

In many ways the basic operation of a finance company closely resembles that of a bank. Money is 'borrowed', or taken in on deposit, and as large a proportion of it as possible is then re-lent at higher interest rates. These finance houses have three principal sources of funds: bank loans, money market operations—including the discounting of bills—and the taking of deposits from the general public and from commercial concerns. As with the banks, the ability to buy in funds wholesale on the parallel money markets is very important to the finance companies, the higher interest rates which are demanded being compensated for by the large volume of funds which can be acquired in any one transaction. Nevertheless, deposits from the general public continue to be an important source of funds. Finance houses which accept such deposits are registered as licensed deposit takers (LDTs) under the Banking Act 1986.

The finance houses compete against the other financial institutions for their deposits and they offer highly competitive interest rates. By and large they are not interested in small deposits and the larger houses set a fairly high minimum deposit. Most deposits are taken for fixed terms or are withdrawable only after long periods of notice, three to six months' notice commonly being required. They are not generally suitable for the smaller saver who will normally require more ready access to his funds.

Capital market

The final part of the country's financial structure which we are going to examine is the capital market. It is complementary to the loan and savings markets. You should realise that the separation between these markets is a rather artificial one, each of the three combining with the others to form an interdependent whole. The capital market consists of the various media through which business concerns, particularly companies, can attract long-term investment funds. You will appreciate that money 'invested' in a business is money that has been 'saved' by the investor and money that could have been 'deposited' with a bank or other institution.

The stock market

The principal component of the capital market is the *stock market* which, from an economist's point of view, is the market which exists between buyers and sellers of shares in limited companies and other stocks. The operations of this market have been institutionalised in the Stock Exchange through which such buyers and sellers meet and which sets rules as to how they must deal with each other. The stock markets of the UK and of Ireland operate as one; the principal exchange is located in London, although there are *local exchanges* in Dublin, Birmingham, Manchester and Glasgow. These locations are nowadays closely linked by telecommunications networks and this means that traders on any one exchange are always kept up to date with what is happening at the other exchanges.

Functions of the Stock Exchange

Raising investment capital. The Stock Exchange had its origins in the London coffee houses where merchants involved in importing and exporting would congregate. Anyone wishing to find investors who might be prepared to put money into a business venture could go along to these places and put the proposal to the merchants there. If the proposals were attractive enough, some of the merchants might be persuaded to put up the required funds against the promise of a proportionate share in the profits and, not unreasonably, a say in the management of the venture.

This type of investment has found its ultimte expression in the form of the *joint stock company* which today is the dominant form of business organisation. Most of them are limited companies, the principal form of which is the company limited by shares. When such a company is floated, the required capital is divided up into shares which are then issued to would-be investors. Suppose a new company wishes to raise £500 000. It could issue 500 000 shares at £1 each, or 1 000 000 50p shares, or 2 000 000 25p shares. It does not matter what value is chosen provided that all the shares can be sold. The face value of each share is called the *nominal value* or the *par value*. The company is called a 'limited company' because the liability of each investor to contribute to the assets of the company should it go into insolvent liquidation is limited to the nominal value of the shares he has agreed to take up.

It is possible to float small companies by selling shares to business acquaintances or within a family group. However, if large amounts of capital are required, a wider spread of investors must be contacted, and this is where the Stock Exchange finds its role. In the modern world it would be technically possible to reach potential investors without involving the Stock Exchange; a television advertisement, for instance, could be very effective. However, issues of new shares to the general public are still effected with the help of the Stock Exchange because of its second function.

Market for the sale of existing stocks. Most of the work of the Stock Exchange today revolves around the provision of a market in which holders of existing quoted shares wishing to sell them can contact people who might wish to buy them. This is a very important function. Someone wishing to buy some ICI shares, for example, cannot simply buy them from the company because all its issued shares are already in the hands of its shareholders. The prospective purchaser has to find someone who holds some of these shares and who is prepared to sell them. The buyer can do this simply by letting his intentions be known at the Stock Exchange; if a seller appears, the transfer can be effected. In practice, buyers and sellers of stocks do not have to be so specifically matched with one another. You will appreciate that transactions of this nature, unlike a new issue of shares, generate no funds for the company concerned. All that happens is that a share in the ownership of the company is passed from one person to another. Even so, the purchaser of such shares will normally refer to the transaction as 'investing in ICI' because, so far as the purchaser is concerned, that is what has happened.

This function of the Stock Exchange is vital to its role as a vehicle for the issue of new shares. It would be much more difficult to sell new shares in a fresh business venture if potential investors believed that they were locking-up their funds for a number of years. Investors in a company which is quoted on the Stock Exchange know that they can easily sell their shares to someone else through the Exchange if they need to liquidate their investment for cash at short notice. Remember, however, that sellers may obtain less than the par value of the shares if the company concerned has been performing poorly. On the other hand, the market price of shares in a successful company will tend to rise.

It is this *secondary market* in shares which has promoted the acceptability of investment in the *equity share capital* of public companies. This in turn has fuelled the growth of the UK economy over the last 200 years or so. An added advantage to individual investors is that by referring to the current market prices of particular shares they can establish the up-to-date value of their portfolio of investments.

Stock Exchange securities

A number of different types of security are dealt with on the modern stock market, but the principal items continue to be stocks and shares issued by limited companies.

Stocks and shares

There are three main types of shares, which differ from one another in respect of the rights of their holders in three areas: control of the company, receipt of dividends, and return of capital if the company is liquidated.

Preference shares. These confer the right to receive a dividend out of company profits in priority to other shareholders, usually at a fixed rate. In the absence of any statement to the contrary, they are *cumulative*. This means that if the company does not generate enough profit to pay the dividend due in any one year, the shortfall must be paid with next year's dividend before other shareholders may receive any payment. If the company makes a loss in two successive years, the preference shareholders should receive a triple dividend the following year, and so on. *Participating preference* shares pay a fixed preference dividend and also allow the holder to share in the company's surplus profits with the ordinary shareholders.

The holders of preference shares do not normally have a vote at the meetings of the company's shareholders. They therefore do not participate in the management of the business. Furthermore, the preferential aspect of these shares does not necessarily extend to the return of capital invested if the business is liquidated, although the company may so provide in its constitution. If no such provision is made, the preference shareholders take an equal chance with the ordinary shareholders of not being able to get their money back. Some *participating* preference shares also give the holders the right in a liquidation to share with the ordinary shareholders in the amount of any reserves of undistributed profits or other surplus assets.

Ordinary shares. The precise rights of ordinary shareholders vary according to the terms of the articles of the company but in general they receive a dividend out of surplus profits. This fluctuates according to the level of profits generated. If the company does well, ordinary shareholders may receive much more dividend income than preference shareholders; if it does badly, they may receive nothing at all.

The ordinary shareholders exercise ultimate control of the company by being entitled to attend and vote at meetings of company members. Among other things, this gives them the right to elect the directors who will direct the efforts of the company and its staff on a day-to-day basis. Few of the shareholders actually attend the annual general meetings of the company at which such appointments are made, appointing instead a company official as their *proxy* to cast their vote for the preferred candidate. A large proportion of the shares in most public companies today is held by the *institutional investors* such as insurance companies and pension funds. This means that the voice of the private investor is, in fact, of minor importance in the management of the company.

If the company is liquidated, the ordinary shareholders are entitled to share out between themselves the residual value of the assets after all debts have been discharged and shareholders repaid. Thus, they own the *equity* of the company, hence the expression 'equity shareholders'. It follows that ordinary shares are the *risk-bearing* shares—there might be no equity left after all other calls have been satisfied—and they carry the greatest potential for either profit or loss.

Deferred shares. These are rare today but they are still sometimes issued to the promoters or employees of a company. No dividends are paid to the holders of deferred shares until adequate dividends have been paid to both preferential and ordinary shareholders. Thereafter, however, all the surplus profits may be distributed as dividends to the deferred shareholders. This means that if the company is very successful, it is the deferred shareholders who reap the major benefit.

Common stock. Fully paid up shares may be converted by the company into stock. There is, however, no advantage in doing this today and the holder's investment in the company remains the same, merely being expressed in different terms. For example, 1000 £1 shares can be converted into £1000 worth of stock. The essential difference between stock and shares is that stock is expressed in terms of money and can be transferred in fractional amounts, for example £89.75 worth, although a company's articles will usually restrict transfers to round amounts. Shares, on the other hand, are units, for example 10, 50, or 500 shares, and can only be transferred as such.

Company loan stocks

Many companies raise some part of their long-term capital through the issue of *loan stocks* and *debentures*. These are very different from shares in that they represent a *debt* due from the company to the holders. They do not confer ownership of any part of the company's undertaking. The income which a holder receives on these types of security represents *interest* on the amount which the company has borrowed. The debenture holder has the right to receive this interest whether or not the company makes a profit.

Loan stocks may be redeemable or irredeemable. *Redeemable stocks* will be repaid by the company on a set date or within a given period. *Irredeemable stocks* remain on issue indefinitely or until the company is wound up. In a liquidation, the loan stock holders are *creditors* of the company and have the right to the return of their money in full before any distribution can be made to the shareholders. Many loan stocks are *secured* by a charge over some of the company's assets. This further reduces the risk of the holder losing his money.

Holders of loan stocks therefore enjoy greater security of both capital and income than the shareholders. Against this, however, it must be remembered that they will obtain no extra benefit no matter how successful the company is. All the surplus profits and the increased value of the business belong to the shareholders, who are the owners of the company.

Gilt-edged securities

We saw in Chapter 2 that the government raises much of its long-term finance through the issue of loan stocks. The money which it borrows in this way is used to complete long-term projects such as the building of roads, hospitals, and so on. These government loan stocks are usually called gilt-edged securities (or simply gilts) because in the past the certificates which were issued to investors had a gilt edge.

From the investor's viewpoint, government loan stocks are very similar to company loan stocks. Most are *redeemable*, falling due for repayment by the government at some time in the future, either on one particular date or between two specified dates. Some are *undated*, which means that no specific date is set for their repayment, the government having discretion when to redeem or even whether to redeem at all. Again, like company loan stocks, most gilts bear a fixed rate of interest on the par value although in recent years some *variable rate* stocks have been introduced.

When a new stock is floated by the government—through the Treasury—subscriptions will be solicited from the general public. An investor who subsequently wished to dispose of his holding, or some part of it, may sell it to someone else through the Stock Exchange, just as with company securities. The *market price* of a gilt-edged stock will vary according to the interaction of two factors: how long the stock has to run to maturity and how prevailing rates of interest compare with the rate of interest, known as the *coupon rate*, applying on the stock itself. If interest rates in general rise, the market price of a stock will fall so as to afford a purchaser a competitive rate of return on his outlay. The reverse is true if interest rates fall. However, if a stock is close to maturity, when it will be redeemed at par, a holder will not be prepared to sell at too low a price, preferring to retain his investment until the due date.

New issues

When the promoters of a company wish to raise finance by issuing shares to the general public, they must first publish a *prospectus*. This will set out the objectives of the company, its past performance as a private concern, if applicable, extracts from past balance sheets and so on. The objective is to give prospective investors adequate information to form a balanced judgment of the company's prospects for success, thereby preventing them from being misled. A copy of the prospectus must be delivered to the Registrar of Companies before it is issued.

The Stock Exchange does not itself participate in the issuing of the new stock, being concerned only with the transfer of 'second-hand' shares. Its existence is, as you have seen, vitally important to the new issue market, however, since the ease with which quoted shares can be sold encourages people to invest as they know that they can easily turn their investment back into cash. Before the shares of any enterprise can be dealt in on the Stock Exchange, permission must be obtained from the Council which governs it. The Council will check that the company complies with all the Stock Exchange regulations before adding its name to the list of companies whose shares can be traded on the floor of the Exchange. This is known as a *listing*, and the shares themselves are known as *listed securities*.

In 1980 the Stock Exchange opened an *unlisted securities market* followed later by the *Third Market*. These are subsidiaries of the main exchange in which dealings can be undertaken in the shares of approved public companies which would not qualify for a full listing. Generally, these are smaller concerns which do not meet the minimum criteria laid down for the amount of issued capital. Investment in unlisted shares is somewhat more risky than investment in listed securities but it does offer the possibility of quite spectacular capital growth.

The issue of a new stock can be handled by the company itself and this sometimes happens. It is more usual, however, for the flotation to be handled by an *issuing house* such as a merchant bank or a firm of stockbrokers. To guard against the possibility that some of the shares will remain unsold, the issuing house may engage *underwriters*, for example, banks and stockbrokers, who agree to buy any shares that the public do not take up. This is important as shares cannot be allotted if the minimum subscription is not received. The issue itself can be handled in a number of ways.

Offers for sale

The whole of the new issue is purchased by the issuing house which then resells the shares at a higher price direct to the public. The price at which the securities are to be sold is fixed, often being considerably higher than the par or nominal value. Advertisements are placed in the 'quality press' and copies of the prospectus are made available to prospective investors.

Offer for sale by tender
This method is becoming more popular. Instead of the shares being offered at a fixed price, investors are asked to put in bids for the number of shares they want, specifying the maximum price they are prepared to pay. If the issue is *oversubscribed*, the shares are of course allotted to the highest bidders.

Placing
This is a procedure in which the issuing house subscribes for the whole of the issue itself and then invites its clients, for example, insurance companies and pension funds, to purchase them at a higher price. Alternatively, without subscribing they may act as the company's agents in placing the securities offered, receiving a commission called brokerage for their services. Placing is a popular method of raising finance for a small public company where the amount is too small to warrant either direct invitation to the public or an offer for sale.

A company which already has a listing will sometimes issue further shares in itself to rank on a par with the existing shares. These subsequent issues will take one of two forms.

Rights issues
These occur when the company wishes to raise further finance. New shares are offered for sale, the rules of the Stock Exchange requiring that the existing shareholders be offered first refusal for their purchase. If existing shareholders do not wish to exercise their right to subscribe for some of the new shares, they can pass it on, or sell it to someone else.

Bonus issues
These raise no further finance for the company. New shares are *given* to existing shareholders *pro rata* their existing holdings, for example, one new share for every two already held. Bonus issues are usually undertaken as a special method of dealing with undistributed profits.

Stock Exchange procedures

Through the Stock Exchange an investor can buy or sell shares and loan stocks issued by both listed and unlisted companies and deal in government securities. Before October 1986, the actual trading on the Exchange was undertaken by *jobbers*. Each jobber specialised in a particular type of security in a particular sector of the economy. A member of the public could not approach a jobber direct but had to use the services of a *broker* to act as an intermediary between the investor and the floor of the Stock Exchange.

In 1986 there was a major change to the way in which the Stock Exchange operated and the old *single capacity* system was swept away. This change is often referred to as 'The Big Bang'. Under the new system, the market consists of two principal types of trader.

Market makers

Market makers are similar in many ways to the former jobbers, except that they can trade directly with the public. They buy and sell securities on the market, specialising in particular areas. They trade as *principals*, which means that they keep the securities on their own books.

Broker dealers

These are similar to the brokers in the old system, except that they can buy and sell securities on their own behalf as well as placing orders with the market makers behalf of clients. Thus, when a client places a sale, for example, the broker dealer may either buy the shares himself or arrange the deal with a market maker. In the first case he would be acting as *principal* and in the second as *agent*. In either case, he is under a duty to obtain the best price available at the time the deal is put through and he must inform his client in which capacity he deals.

Stock Exchange Automated Quotations

The market price of a security is, of course, defined by the prices quoted by the market makers who deal in it. Prior to the 'Big Bang', it was necessary to contact a jobber on the actual floor of the Stock Exchange (or, preferably, several jobbers) to arrange a deal at the best price. Now, however, deals can be done through the *Stock Exchange Automated Quotations* system, usually referred to as SEAQ. This is a computer based system run by the Stock Exchange into which the market makers input their buying and selling prices for each security, Stock Exchange members, including broker dealers, have their own terminals and screens from which they can read the current prices. By this system, they can establish the best price for a deal. Since deals can be completed over their own computer terminals, there is no real need to visit the actual floor of the Stock Exchange, although it continues to operate.

Contract notes
Investors generally continue to refer to both market makers and broker dealers as *stockbrokers* (or just brokers). Having arranged a deal for his client, the 'broker' will send him a *contract note* which sets out the details of the transactions and whether he was acting as principal or agent. It shows how many shares have been purchased or sold, the agreed price and the total amount to be paid or received. A seller will also receive with the contract note a *stock transfer form* for signature. This allows the transfer of the stock out of the name of the seller so that it can be registered ultimately into the name of the purchaser. The shares will not normally be transferred directly to the purchaser but will first pass through an intermediate nominee company called *Sepon Limited* (Sepon stands for Stock Exchange Pool Nominees) which is operated by the Stock Exchange. Sales of a company's shares are transferred into the 'pool' and purchases are drawn out of it. This procedure was first introduced in 1979 when the Stock Exchange set up a computerised system for the settlement of sales and purchases of shares. This is called *Talisman* (Transfer Account Lodgement for Investers, Stock Management for Jobbers), and the particular type of stock transfer form used is known as a *Talisman transfer*. Most transactions in UK stocks and shares are now settled on the Talisman system using the form illustrated in Fig. 4.5.

The contract note also shows the date on which the contract is to be completed. Deals in gilts are always done on a *cash basis*. In other words a purchaser has to pay up as soon as he receives his contract note. All other deals are settled at the end of the *account period* in which they were set up. The Stock Exchange divides the year into a number of account periods of

TALISMAN SOLD TRANSFER

This transfer is pursuant to a Stock Exchange transaction, and is exempt from Transfer Stamp Duty.

Above this line for Registrar's use only

Bargain Reference No:

Name of Undertaking

Certificate lodged with Registrar

Description of Security

(for completion by the Registrars/ Stock Exchange)

Amount of Stock or number of Stock units or shares or other security in words | Figures

In the name(s) of

Account Designation (if any)

Name(s) of registered holder(s) should be given in full; the address should be given where there is only one holder.

If the transfer is not made by the registered holder(s) insert also the name(s) and capacity (e.g. Executor(s)) of the person(s) making the transfer.

PLEASE SIGN HERE

I/We hereby transfer the above security out of the name(s) aforesaid into the name of SEPON LIMITED and request the necessary entries to be made in the register.

Balance Certificate Required for (amount or number in figures)

Bodies corporate should affix their common seal and each signatory should state his/her representative capacity (e.g. 'Company Secretary' 'Director') against his/her signature.

Stamp and Firm Code of Selling Broker

1 _____
2 _____
3 _____
4 _____

Date

SEPON LIMITED is lodging this Transfer at the direction and on behalf of the Member Firm whose stamp appears herein ('the Original Lodging Agent') and does not in any manner or to any extent warrant or represent the validity or genuineness of the transfer instructions contained herein or the genuineness of the Transferor's signature. The Original Lodging Agent by delivering this Transfer to SEPON LIMITED authorises SEPON LIMITED to lodge this Transfer for registration and agrees to be deemed for all purposes to be the person(s) actually lodging this Transfer for registration.

Form 124

Stock Exchange Operating Account Number (if applicable)

TAL 112/1

Fig. 4.5   A 'Talisman transfer' form (Courtesy: E Couchman & Co. Ltd)

either two or three weeks' duration and all deals entered into in any one period are all settled at the same time. *Settlement day* is always the second Monday following the end of the account. The accounting period is a useful device which allows brokers time to complete all the necessary paperwork and it has the advantage that jobbers do not have to balance sales and purchases every single day. Unfortunately, it also facilitates two types of speculation in shares by people who are referred to as bulls and bears.

When asked to quote for a particular stock, a market maker does not ask whether he is being asked to buy or sell and he will quote a price for both possibilities. This ensures that he keeps his prices competitive. The price at which he would be prepared to buy the stock will be lower than the price at which he would sell. The difference between the two prices is known as a *turn* and represents his source of profit; he does not charge any commission for his services. A market maker who contracts to sell a stock may already have arranged to purchase the necessary shares from someone else. If not, he must 'balance his books' by arranging such a purchase. If he has miscalculated his prices, he may find himself paying more for the shares than he will receive for them.

Bulls are optimists. They expect the market price of a particular stock to rise. Early in the account period they therefore place an order to buy some of the shares, in the hope of reselling at a profit. If both purchase and sale are effected within the same account, bulls will not have to put up any money themselves, they will simply collect the difference between the buying and selling prices, less broker's commission and so on. Of course, if the price falls bulls will make a loss on the deals. In stock market jargon, 'bullish' is used generally to mean optimistic.

Bears, on the other hand, are pessimists. They expect the market price of a stock to fall. They can place an order at the start of the account to sell an amount of stock which they do not hold. Provided that this is reversed by a purchase order later in the same account, all is well. If the price *has* fallen in the interim, bears will make a profit because they will pay less for the purchase than they will receive on the sale. They are, of course, vulnerable to price rises.

Investors

It would be wrong to see the Stock Exchange primarily as a vehicle for speculation. Most of the deals done represent genuine investments for the purpose of generating income or long-term capital growth. Who then are these investors? Figures produced some years ago by the Royal Commission on the Distribution of Wealth, headed by Lord Diamond, suggested that just over two million people in the UK owned shares directly and another one million invested through unit trusts and investment trusts. These figures, however, are tiny when compared with the number of people on whose behalf the institutional investors hold stocks and shares.

The *institutional investors* consist principally of the life assurance companies and the pension funds. Some fourteen million people invest in life assurance, and over eleven million participate in pension funds. In addition to this latter category, many trades unions run benevolent funds to provide for their members in retirement or during illness. These institutions therefore have enormous volumes of money at their disposal. A large proportion of this money is invested through the stock market so as to provide capital growth and income. The pension funds, for instance, depend on the income which they receive from their holdings of stocks and shares to provide the pensions when their contributors retire. The institutional investors have no interest in speculation and they bring a great degree of stability to the capital markets.

Regulation

The move away from single capacity (brokers and jobbers) in the Stock Exchange created more opportunity for dishonest dealing, such as quoting prices to a buyer much higher than the market rates. To ensure that this does not happen, a *Securities and Investment Board* (*SIB*) oversees the operation of all investment business, including the Stock Market.

Under the overall control of the SIB, the Stock Market has been granted the status of a *Self-Regulating Body* which means that the Stock Exchange itself is responsible for the day-to-day policing of its members' activities. Members must adhere to the Exchange's *Code of Conduct* which contains provisions designed to protect the investor. For example, firms dealing in securities will often become party to private information about their clients. Such information may enable other members of the same firm to anticipate changes in share prices which they could use to their own advantage. This is known as 'insider dealing'. To prevent this happening, these firms are required to set up internal 'barriers', known as *Chinese Walls*, to prevent the passing of privileged information.

All firms dealing in securities are required to appoint *compliance officers* to ensure that the provisions of the Code of Conduct are followed.

Summary

1 Savings result from the act of refraining from spending the whole of income; they may be hoarded or put to work generating more income via the savings media.
2 Factors influencing the choice between different savings media include:
  (a) security;
  (b) rate of return;
  (c) liquidity.
3 Savings represent a withdrawal from the circular flow of national income; investment represents an injection into it. Over a period, savings must equal investment.
4 The national savings movement is promoted by the state to encourage personal saving. Its principal schemes are:
  (a) premium savings bonds;
  (b) national savings certificates;
  (c) deposit bonds and income bonds;
  (d) save-as-you-earn contracts;
  (e) National Savings Bank;
  (f) National Savings Stock Register.
5 The banks (including the Trustee Savings Bank and the National Girobank) and the building societies compete with each other to attract deposits from savers. Other organisations such as finance companies and local authorities also compete for deposits.
6 Life assurance policies are a very important form of saving. The assurance companies invest their premium income pending payments under the policies which they have issued.

7 In a similar way, the pension funds control huge sums of money saved out of contributors' incomes.

8 Unit trusts and investment trusts represent relatively safe and convenient ways for personal savers to invest in stock market securities.

9 The Stock Exchange exists primarily to provide a market in second-hand company shares and government stocks, but its existence is vital to the flotation of new public companies.

10 New issues of shares can be brought to the market in a number of ways including:

(a) offer for sale;

(b) offer for sale by tender;

(c) placing.

11 Existing companies may undertake:

(a) rights issues, which raise further funds for the company;

(b) bonus issues, which do not.

12 Stock exchange transactions are effected through broker dealers and market makers.

Self-assessment questions

1 List:

(a) The means by which a share issue in a new venture can be floated

(b) The various national savings schemes

(c) The attractions of saving with a building society

(d) The functions of the Stock Exchange

(e) The parties to a life policy

2 Describe the attributes and attractions of premium savings bonds and national savings certificates.

3 Define the paradox of thrift.

4 True or false?

(a) Bonus issues raise further capital for an existing limited company.

(b) Building society savers gain preferential consideration when applying for a house purchase loan.

(c) More people save through life assurance and pension schemes than through all other savings media.

(d) Unit trusts are an investment medium for the wealthy.

5 Analyse and explain how saving differs from investment.

6 Distinguish between broker dealers and market makers.

7 Explain the circular flow of national income.

8 Explain why savings must equal investment in the long term.

9 In recent years the banks have experienced increasing difficulty in attracting on to deposit the savings of individuals. Why has this situation occurred?

10 A personal customer has just inherited £2000 which he wishes to invest on the stock market. What advice would you give him as his banker?

Assignments

Memorandum from: Manager
To: Student
Subject: In-branch savings promotion

The Area Manager has been on to us again about getting new business. This time she wants us to attract into the branch more new money from personal customers by drawing attention to our savings schemes. I shall have to call on you to do some research for me. There are two things I would like you to do.

1 Prepare a table comparing all the various schemes for regular savings which are available both from ourselves and our competitors, such as other banks, building societies, national savings, etc. (You can ignore any schemes aimed particularly at attracting larger lump sum deposits.) I expect that your best source of information will be the promotional leaflets which everyone displays these days, so I recommend you to undertake a tour of the local branches of the banks and so on to see what you can find (in your lunch-hour of course).

I would like your table to show the attributes and, particularly, the benefits of each scheme in such a way that we can easily find whether the bank offers an acceptable alternative to any non-bank scheme which a customer may be considering.

2 I expect that some of the 'prospects' whom we approach will raise the question of saving through the purchase of Stock Exchange securities. I find that I have to spend a long time with such first-time investors explaining how the stock market works

so I would like you to prepare a 'briefing sheet' that we can give out to such people to save my time (and my voice). I would like the briefing to provide:

(a) A note of the principles of investment that the customer will have to bear in mind before taking the plunge.

(b) A brief rundown of how Stock Exchange sales and purchases can be effected through the bank.

(c) An analysis of any alternatives to direct investment in Stock Exchange securities.

(d) A glossary of Stock Exchange terms—for example bulls, bears, stags, bonus issues and so on.

5 Interest rates

Chapter objectives

After studying this chapter you should be able to:
- define the meaning and role of the rate of interest;
- identify the factors which influence interest rates;
- describe the structure of interest rates in the UK;
- identify the principal rates of interest in the UK economy and explain their interrelationships;
- explain the effects of interest rate changes.

Interest rates are at the heart of the UK financial system and, as a banker, the more you know about them the better. The charging of interest still represents the banks' most important source of income despite the recent proliferation of ancillary services. Similarly, the payment of interest on funds deposited with them represents, together with staff costs, the banks' most important item of expenditure. What then do we mean by the term 'interest'?

The nature of interest

What is interest?

Interest is most simply defined as the cost of using someone else's money or, viewed from the other end, as the price to be charged for allowing someone else to use your money. (Clearly, one person's *cost* is someone else's *income*.) Just as it is possible to hire a car for a period, paying the car hire company a *rental* which varies with the length of the period of hire, so it is possible to 'hire' a sum of money in return for payment of an agreed interest charge. Thus, although interest is often referred to as 'the price of money', it would really be more accurate to call it the price of the *use* of money.

Lenders and investors

It is important at this stage to remind ourselves of the differences between *lending* and *investing* money. Both lenders and investors will expect to receive some sort of return on their capital, but their attitudes to this return will be different because of differences in the treatment of this capital. Money lent is repayable at some stage in the future, while money invested is not. Thus, funds put into a bank account, that is, lent to a bank, or used to buy a newly issued 'gilt-edged' (government) loan stock will ultimately be repayable at face value. Although in the former case repayment is available on demand while in the latter it is available only at term, in both cases lenders have the comfort of knowing that they should eventually get back what they put in. In the interim they will expect to receive an adequate payment of interest on 'their' money. If an inadequate level of interest payment is offered, potential lenders may prefer to put their money somewhere else, or even simply to hold on to it.

Investors, on the other hand, do not have the right to expect repayment of their money in full. Thus, for example, people who purchase shares in a limited company would not normally expect to be able to get their money back from the company itself except in a liquidation. Even then they would get only a fair share of the *equity* of the company after all debts to third parties had been paid off: this could be more or less than they had originally invested. They could, of course, realise their investment by selling the shares to someone else but again the amount which they would receive is not certain. It is therefore in this uncertainty of the return of their capital that investors differ principally from lenders and this affects their attitudes to the anticipated income.

In practice, however, the distinction between lending and investment may not be as clear as in the examples which we have given. The uses to which investment funds can be put vary across a broad spectrum, over which lending merges into investment. Take the example of building society savings; savers have the option with most societies of putting their money into a deposit account or a share account. The former is a loan to the society while the latter is not but, in general, the terms and conditions of both types of account are very much the same. A deposit account might pay a very slightly lower rate of interest, because the saver's capital is slightly safer, but in reality funds in a share account are unlikely to be lost.

Rates of return

Interest rates are expressed as a *percentage* per annum of the amount borrowed or lent. Hence, if an interest rate of 15% per annum were to be quoted for house purchase loans, borrowers would know that they would have to pay the lender £15 each year for every £100 borrowed. In the same way, a published rate of 10% per annum on bank deposit accounts would indicate to savers that that they could expect to receive £10 per year on each £100 kept on deposit. The simplicity of this formula enables both borrowers and lenders to compare the relative merits of different facilities or of different organisations.

Although it is common to talk of *the* rate of interest, there are many different rates of interest in force at any one time. The rates of interest available for, say, bank deposits can be compared between banks *and* with the rate of return since this can also be expressed as a percentage on other investments. The *yield* on any investment can be easily calculated by expressing the amount of the annual income received as a percentage of the original amount of the investment. Consider an individual who five years ago purchased 1000 shares in a limited company at 50p per share and who last year received total dividends of £75, that is 7½p per share, on the holding. This represents a yield of 15% on the original investment as shown in Table 5.1

Table 5.1 Calculation of the rate of yield on an investment

$$\text{Yield per cent} = \frac{\text{Annual return} \times 100}{\text{Amount of investment}}$$

$$\frac{£75 \times 100}{£500} = 15\%$$

A prospective new investor may not be able to buy shares in the company for the same price, of course. In this case the yield would be determined by the *current market price*. Suppose that the market price of the shares now stands at 75p each. This would mean that the cost of 1000 shares would have risen to £750. Assuming that dividend payments will stay at the same level as last year, the yield for a new investor would be only 10%, as established by the following calculation:

$$\frac{£75 \times 100}{£750} = 10\%$$

You will see that the change in price of the shares has increased the current capital value of our first investor's shareholding from £500 to £750 and this is not reflected in the yield which we have calculated. The calculation which we have used produces what is known as a flat or *running* yield. If the investor was to realise his shareholding it would be possible to calculate a *redemption yield* allowing also for the capital growth which has occurred. However, it is not normal to do so for most investments since such a calculation would be *retrospective*, showing only what has happened in the past, while investors are really interested in what will happen in the future.

Investors generally will accept a lower running yield on equities (shares) than savers will accept as an interest rate on their deposits. This is because they hope to enjoy the benefits of capital growth. Capital growth is extremely important in times of high inflation, such as the UK experienced in the last 30 years, since it can help to maintain the real purchasing power of the original investment. Remember, however, that the possibility of capital growth with investments is inevitably accompanied by the alternative possibility of capital losses.

Why is interest charged?

We shall be looking later on at the theories of what determines the specific levels of interest rates at any one time. Before doing so, however, we can consider the underlying factors that borrowers and lenders consider before accepting a particular interest rate. These factors account for the differentials between interest rates rather than for the general level of rates. Generally speaking, the wishes of lenders carry more weight since without lenders there could be no borrowers; there will always be those who are prepared to borrow at any price.

Productivity of capital
We saw in Chapter 2 that in medieval times the Church castigated for the sin of usury anyone who charged interest for

moneylending. In a similar way, Marxism condemns capitalists who profit from the investment of their money at the 'expense' of workers who have only their labour to contribute to the economy. Both notions seem to take as their starting point the idea that it is immoral to earn 'something' for 'doing nothing'. In fact, it can be argued there is no justification for such an attitude towards interest; both capital and labour, or the two together, can be used to produce something that was not there before. Just as the 'worker' deserves payment for the use of his labour, so, you might feel, the 'capitalist' deserves payment for the use of his money.

Suppose you had saved £10 000 out of your income and wanted to do something useful with it. You might decide, for example, to set up a small market garden, using the funds to rent a small plot of land for twelve months and to buy a year's supply of seed and fertiliser. At the end of the year you harvest your crops and sell them for £11 000. An income of £1000, or 10%, has been generated by the use of the capital of £10 000: would others begrudge you this income? This sort of income is referred to as the *net productivity of capital* and it raises two important points.

First, our project depended entirely on the *availability* of capital. Anyone who has not saved the £10 000 would have to borrow it and would presumably be prepared to pay for it provided that the net productivity was greater than the cost of the borrowing, as represented by the interest charge. Ultimately, of course, the payment of all interest rests on the net productivity of capital. Second, a holder of capital would have to be *induced to lend it out* by the promise of some return on it. If no interest is offered, the capitalist will clearly find it more attractive to go into the horticulture business personally. It follows, therefore, that the rate of interest will reflect a compromise somewhere between the rate at which the borrower cannot make a net profit and the rate at which the lender will be tempted to take the work on personally.

It is worth noting that the payment of interest also encourages people to forgo current consumption to build up capital which can be 'invested'. In the long run it would be highly detrimental to the economy if no-one was to 'save' in this way. As we shall see later, interest rates are not the only reason why people save, but they are an important factor.

Liquidity

The lender is giving up some measure of liquidity by handing over funds to the borrower and the interest charge can, to some extent, be seen as a payment for this. Some forms of lending, however, are so liquid that this payment is minimal, if it exists at all. Bank deposits are an example of this. Current accounts being the most liquid type of deposit generally pay no interest at all. Deposit accounts do not give access to such sophisticated money transfer facilities and theoretically require a short period of notice for withdrawals, although in practice this is usually waived; the rate of interest which is allowed is therefore largely determined by the lower level of liquidity.

You would expect, therefore, that the longer the period of the loan, if for a fixed term, or the longer the period of notice required before repayment, the higher the interest rate will be. In general this is true, especially as regards loans or deposits made under differing periods of notice. Thus, money placed at 'call or short notice' through the money market will attract a lower interest rate than money put into Treasury bills which have a maturity of 91 days.

When money is lent for a fixed period, however, it is not always true that the rate will increase with longer terms. If it is thought that interest rates in general will fall in the foreseeable future, borrowers will be unwilling to take on long-term loans at high fixed rates. Unless lenders reduce their rates for longer-term money, therefore, borrowers will prefer to borrow short term in the hope of refinancing their needs at a later stage at lower interest rates. Thus, at such a time the interest rates for fixed period long-term loans or deposits will represent a compromise between the upward pull of lenders giving up liquidity and the downward push of future interest rates.

The risk factor

The lending of money presupposes that ultimately repayment will be forthcoming. Every loan carries the risk, however small, that repayment will not be made. Clearly, the greater the risk that the loan carries, the higher the offered reward will have to be before lenders will part with their money. Some propositions are so risky their lenders will not support them at any price. Theoretically, therefore, we should be able to separate every interest charge into *pure interest*, that is, the cost of 'hire' of the money, and payment as reward for the risk being taken.

In practice, bank deposits and purchases of government loan stocks (gilts) are treated by savers as riskless loans, it being unthinkable that the major banks or the government should ever find themselves unable to pay their debts. If they ever did so, the whole of the country's monetary system would be in ruins anyway! It therefore follows that prevailing rates of return on such items as these are as close to pure interest as we are likely ever to see. Any deposit-taking institution other than a major bank has to offer higher rates than the banks in order to attract deposits. This is because depositors perceive a marginal but real element of risk that they might not get their money back. The extra interest which they demand is the measure of their estimate of that risk.

Closely allied to the question of reimbursement for risk-taking is that of the cost of *risk assessment* which is also often absorbed into and covered by the interest rate charge. Thus, bank *personal loan schemes* involve higher interest rates than many other forms of bank lending, covering both the higher risks accruing from the types of lending undertaken and the costs of administering the schemes. It is interesting to note that when looked at individually some personal loans will obviously carry a higher level of risk than others. Even so, all loans granted through the scheme will be made on the same terms, thereby averaging out from the bank's viewpoint both the risk and the return.

The rate of interest

We have already noted that rates of interest are related to the *net productivity of capital* but that they are not identical with each other. There are, of course, many different rates operating within the economy at any one time. Examples include bank base rate, Treasury bill rate, personal loan rate and so on. These differ from each other for the reasons which we have already examined but, when changes of rate occur, all the rates tend to fluctuate together, or at least very closely, so that the differentials are maintained. What is it that causes these general fluctuations? There is a certain amount of disagreement among economists on this point and we discuss some of the more important theories next.

The loanable funds theory

Different people, as well as firms and other organisations, have different *time preferences* as far as their use of money is concerned. Some people would prefer to have the use of a larger sum of money now, even if that means that they will have less money available to them in the future. These are the potential borrowers who are quite happy to *pay* interest on top of the necessary capital repayments, although this means that for the term of the loan their disposable income is reduced. By contrast, other people are potential lenders, or savers, who will put their money aside for future use, happy in the knowledge that in the interim it will be increased by the *accruals* of interest. Thus, for example, the purchase of an article costing £120 could be effected immediately by borrowing the money and repaying at £10 per month plus interest over a period of a year. Alternatively, the purchaser could save £10 per month and buy the article at the end of the year, in which case he would also have the benefit of the interest that his money had earned during the year. The individual has to decide whether the benefit of having the article now outweighs the penalty of paying the interest, or whether the benefit of earning interest outweighs the penalty of having to wait a year before obtaining the desired article. Clearly, the level of interest rates will have an important effect on this decision.

Put at its simplest, the *loanable funds* theory of interest states that the prevailing rates of interest at any one time represent an *equilibrium price* at which the demand for credit, from those who prefer to have the goods now, will equal the supply of loanable funds, from those who prefer to have the interest. This is the 'classical'—some might say oldfashioned—view of how the general level of interest rates is determined. Figure 5.1 shows how this would work at a given level of supply and demand for loanable funds at which the equilibrium price of borrowed money is 7%. Demand is shown by the curve D–D, and supply by the curve S–S.

If interest rates are at 5% there would be excess demand and the interest rate would rise, encouraging more people to save, until at 7% demand and supply come into equilibrium.

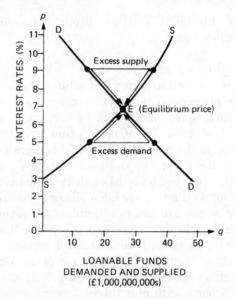

Fig. 5.1 Loanable funds theory: determination of equilibrium price

Conversely, if interest rates were at 9% there would be excess supply and lenders would have to reduce their rates, thereby encouraging an increase in borrowing. At the same time, the reduction of rates would induce some people to *liquidate* their savings with the financial intermediaries such as the banks, thereby reducing the supply of loanable funds. Of course, these occurrences are generalisations which are not true for everyone. Some people may be encouraged by a *rise* in interest rates to *reduce* their savings because they can earn the same level of return on a smaller capital sum. What matters is that the majority of people will not take this view but will be attracted by the idea of increasing their savings when rates go up.

Unfortunately, the interest rate is not the only thing which determines the levels of supply and demand of loanable funds; others factors intrude. When one of these other factors leads to a change in either supply or demand, a new demand curve or a new supply curve would have to be drawn on our diagram, as shown in Fig. 5.2.

Here the underlying demand for loan funds has been stimulated by other factors in the economy and has risen from its original level (curve D–D) to a higher level (curve D^1–D^1). This

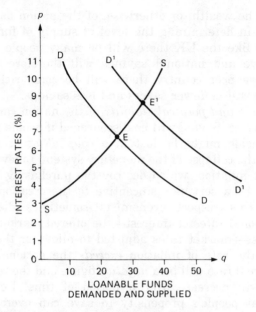

Fig. 5.2 Loanable funds theory: shifts in demand

has had the effect of raising the equilibrium rate of interest from point E to point E^1. The question we must now ask is what factors other than interest rates might cause a change in the level of supply or demand for funds? The answers are often difficult to reconcile with the loanable funds theory.

The supply of funds. It is *saving* which provides loan capital, whether lent out directly by the saver or agglomerated into larger amounts through the savings institutions. As we noted in Chapter 2, people's *propensity to save* is not wholly, or even chiefly, determined by the available rate of return on the savings. There will be a certain level of saving *whatever* the rate of interest.

It would appear that the chief determinant of the propensity to save is *the individual's level of income.* Below a certain level of income people cannot afford to save since all their funds have to be spent on necessary consumption. On the other hand, once they achieve a surplus of income over expenditure people will want to save for the various reasons which we have already considered. The wealth, or otherwise, of the nation as a whole is important in determining the level of supply of funds. In a 'rich' society like the UK there will be many people who can afford to save and national savings will therefore be high. Although in a poor country there will be some rich people, overall there will be fewer savers and less savings.

The *economic and political stability* of the nation can also be important factors. Saving will be discouraged if people fear that money put aside might be lost in a *coup d'état* or rendered valueless by the collapse of the monetary system. Likewise, very high rates of inflation, which destroy the purchasing power of savings, can be a serious disincentive to the creation of loan capital. In this respect economists sometimes distinguish between notional rates of interest—the offered market rates—and real rates—market rates adjusted to allow for the rate of inflation. If the rate of inflation *exceeds* the notional rate of interest the real rate will be a *negative* figure and the real value of savings will decrease over a period of time. Remember, however, that people's propensity to save can overcome the disincentive even of a negative real rate provided it is not too great. This occurred in the UK in the late 1970s, when people continued to save despite the fact that the true value of their savings was being continually eroded.

We can draw a number of conclusions from the above considerations. First, the willingness to save is much greater in the well-off and highly developed western world, being lower in the poor, and less stable, third world countries. This explains why interest rates are much higher in these latter countries. Second, in drawing up Fig. 5.1 for countries like the UK we should really have shown the supply curve as being much *flatter*—not rising so steeply from right to left. This is because it takes quite major changes of interest rates to encourage savers to modify their level of saving.

You should not assume that what we have said above indicates that interest rates are completely unimportant to savers and that the loanable funds theory is wholly wrong. That is far from the truth. It is true, however, that interest rate *differentials* are usually more important to people than the general levels of rates. Thus, while savers are unlikely to say, 'Interest rates have gone up, I must double the amount of money I have set aside', they are quite likely to say, 'Building society deposit rate has gone up, so I must switch some money out of my bank deposit account where rates are less attractive'.

The demand for funds. Like the supply of funds, demand does fluctuate according to changes in the interest rate but it does so to a much lesser extent than you might imagine. Let us examine why this is so. Suppose that interest rates were to rise; this would affect the demand for loans in two ways. Existing borrowers at variable rates might wish to reduce their commitments, while potential new borrowers could be deterred from taking on loan commitments. In practice the first of these is unlikely to occur since most existing borrowers are not usually in a position to pay off their loans at short notice, having accepted the risk when they obtained the loan that interest charges might rise. You will be aware of course, that some types of consumer borrowing, such as bank personal loans, can be granted at *fixed rates* which do not fluctuate with the general levels of interest. However, these types of loans represent only a small proportion of the nation's total borrowing.

What of the deterrent effect on potential new borrowers? In the first place most loans are granted at *variable rates* of interest. In consequence borrowers tend to take a longer-term view of the commitment which they propose to take on. Thus, although the currently quoted rate may be high, borrowers may anticipate, or just hope, that it will reduce to a more acceptable level during the term of the loan. In the second place, the decision to borrow, like the decision to save, is not necessarily taken having regard only to the cost of the borrowing. To understand this we must briefly examine the sources of the demand for advances and the reasons why borrowing is undertaken.

Personal borrowing is sometimes undertaken to finance normal living expenses. More often it represents the source of funds needed either for the purchase of a consumer durable, or some other item of consumer spending, or in connection with the purchase of a house. Borrowing for the purpose of consumer spending does not seem to be particularly responsive to interest rates. People generally seem to be more concerned with the availability of the finance rather than its relative cost. Evidence for this can be found in the way that borrowers hardly ever 'shop around' for competitive quotes for consumer finance. It is a constant source of frustration for the banks that purchasers of cars, for example, will borrow on a hire purchase basis from finance companies which have links with the motor dealers when a visit to the bank would often enable them to borrow the money more cheaply through the personal loan facility.

House purchase loans, obtained from building societies or banks, are generally granted for quite long terms. The normal repayment period is 20 to 25 years or until the borrower retires from full-time employment, whichever period is the shorter. These loans are invariably granted at fluctuating rates of interest. Clearly, if interest rates rise a little, home buyers in general are unlikely to put their houses back on the market so as to pay off their mortgages; it would require a massive rise for such an effect to be produced. They will usually prefer to hold on until rates fall again. The demand for new mortgages may be temporarily depressed by high rates but, given the long terms of the existing loans, it would take a long time for such a slow-down to have an appreciable effect on the total volume of home loans. In any case, the desire for home ownership is deeply rooted in the UK. In consequence, the cost of the finance tends to be important only in so far as it impinges on the size of the loan that the borrower can afford to take on. It does not have a dramatic effect on the desire to borrow.

Business advances may be sought to finance day-to-day trading (working capital advances) or to complete a capital purchase. It is this latter type of borrowing which is most responsive to interest rate changes. As we have already said, the proprietors of a business will generally be concerned with the *net productivity* of capital borrowed. It would not make much sense to borrow at 15% per annum if it was known that the funds would generate annual profits of only 10%. Nevertheless, good businessmen try to take a long-term view of the prospects for their trade. If, as the result of such an analysis, they think that in future profits will rise and/or the levels of interest rates will fall, borrowing might still go ahead. You should also realise that if, on the other hand, potential profits far exceed the cost of borrowing, as is often the case, it would take a huge rise in interest rates before capital investment was curtailed.

Working capital advances are less affected by rate changes. This type of advance is sought to enable a business to even out temporary imbalances between income and expenditure. The amount of the borrowing will fluctuate from day to day according to the levels of receipts and payments. Provided that in the long term payments do not exceed receipts, the advance should not prove too troublesome to the bank and the limit on the account may well be renewed each year over a period of many years. Often, the only way in which such a business *could* reduce its overdraft limit would be to reduce *turnover*, in other words, reduce the volume of business being undertaken. While it can sometimes make 'economic' sense to do this, it may not make 'commercial' sense, as trade lost is hard to recover later.

Government borrowing, as we have seen, is both a major component of the national demand for loan funds and an influence on the general cost of borrowing. The government will always seek to issue its fixed gilt-edged loan stocks when interest rates are at as low a level as they can reasonably be expected to reach. Even so, its ability to delay its borrowing is strictly limited. Loan stocks are generally issued for one of two reasons: to finance a new project or to refinance an existing loan stock which is due for repayment. In either case the government has no real choice about whether or not to raise the funds; its choice is merely as to when, within a fairly short timespan, it would be most appropriate to float a new loan stock. In anything other than the short term, therefore, this type of borrowing is little affected by the level of interest rates.

The *loanable funds* theory is sometimes called the theory of 'true' interest rates because it contains the assumption that interest rates are determined by 'real' factors, the decision whether to lend or borrow being a wholly rational one. As we now know, this is not always the case. The biggest weakness of the theory is that it requires too direct and simple a link between the levels of saving and investment in the economy; it takes no account of the other things that people might do with their money. Even so, the theory is far from being wholly misleading. It does offer a simple and effective way of explaining the short-term fluctuations of rates in a particular market over a specified period. Thus, for example, the rates quoted in the London money market fluctuate from minute to minute in response to the pressures of supply and demand.

The liquidity preference theory

In many ways this theory is a simpler one than the loanable funds theory. It approaches the problem from a different viewpoint, seeking to explain the levels of interest by reference to the interaction of two principal factors: the *supply of money* and the desire of savers to hold their savings in cash or near-cash: their *liquidity preference*. The argument starts with the idea that if no interest was payable, savers would keep all of their savings in cash, there being no encouragement to do anything else with them. You would think, therefore, that the higher interest rates were to go, the more people would be prepared to forgo liquidity and the more loanable funds there would be. There is nothing basically wrong with this conclusion but we need to modify it because people will always want to hold some cash, irrespective of how high interest rates climb. John Maynard Keynes, who first formulated this theory, considered that interest was 'the reward for parting with liquidity for a period', and he identified three motives for the desire to maintain cash holdings: the transaction motive; the precautionary motive; and the speculative motive.

The transaction motive. We all have to keep some of our assets in a liquid form, either in cash or in a bank current account, to meet our day-to-day living expenses. We have to strike a balance between income and expenditure which ensures that we have adequate funds on hand to cover outgoings until next payday. The amount which each person requires for this purpose is covered by three factors:

(a) *the frequency of income:* most people are paid either weekly or monthly, although some people receive their incomes less frequently. The longer the period between payments, the higher the average cash holding will have to be to provide an adequate 'float';

(b) *the level of income*: while the poor may have to hold a higher *proportion* of their incomes to cover outgoings, the actual *amounts* held by the wealthy are likely to be greater;

(c) *the standard of living*: a great deal depends on the extent to which people live up to their incomes. A household with an annual income of £30 000 but a frugal lifestyle may actually need to hold less cash than a household with an income of £20 000 which is all committed to current expenditure.

Although we have spoken so far only of persons, it is clear that businesses too will have to maintain adequate liquid funds to cover anticipated transactions. The general level of cash held for this purpose by both households and firms will be quite stable over the short term.

The precautionary motive. Over and above the minimum amount of money needed to meet anticipated outgoings, people like to keep a further reserve of cash in case of *unforeseen* expenses arising. After all, your car, hifi set, etc. could break down unexpectedly and it would be embarrassing to have to sell part of your record collection, or even to borrow, *every* time such a problem occurred just so as to be able to pay for the repairs. Furthermore, price rises can increase costs which have been budgeted for. In reality, the extra amount of cash which people and firms hold in respect of these eventualities are quite difficult to distinguish from the cash held as a result of the transaction motive. It is not unreasonable to treat the two motives as if they were one.

The speculative motive. We saw in Chapter 4 that the prices of fixed interest securities such as government stocks and market rates of interest vary *inversely* with one another. To take a typical gilt as an example, Treasury stock (undated) has a coupon rate of $2\frac{1}{2}\%$ meaning that for every £100 *nominal* of stock held an investor will receive £2.50 in interest each year. If interest rates were generally at 10% per annum, this would discourage people from buying the stock at par since they would be able to obtain a better return elsewhere. Consequently, the price of the stock would fall to around 25p in the £1. At this level an investment of £100 would purchase £400 *nominal* of stock, on which the annual interest would be more attractive. The reverse process occurs, of course, when interest rates fall.

This phenomenon affects liquidity preference by encouraging the amassing of speculative cash holdings by those who can afford to when interest rates are low. At such a time, bond and stock prices will be high and people who anticipate a rise in interest rates will prefer to hold cash in the hope of acquiring more bonds for their money when the consequent fall in prices occurs. Provided that the anticipated fall in prices exceeds the interest that could be earned over the same period, the purchase will be postponed. Conversely, when interest rates are high and bond prices are low, cash holdings will be reduced as people buy stocks both for the immediate benefit of the interest paid on them and for the possible benefit of being able to sell later at a profit when interest rates fall.

We have already said that the demand for money for the precautionary and transaction motives remains generally stable in the short term. It therefore follows that the *principal variable* in the liquidity preference of the population is the speculative motive. Putting all these factors together, we can construct a *liquidity preference curve*, as in Fig. 5.3, showing that the higher interest rates are the smaller liquid holdings will be and that the lower rates are the greater the liquid holdings become. The curve does not touch the sides of the graph since, for the reasons we have discussed, money holdings will never reduce to zero no matter how high the interest rate, while lending will reduce to nil some time before a zero rate of interest is achieved.

Note that any liquidity preference curve which we may construct is valid only for one society at a given time. Changes in the economic scene in general may cause changes in people's desire for liquidity and this will result in a *shift* in the curve. Factors which might have such an effect include changes in consumers' tastes, altered expectations of what the future may hold, or simply altered levels of income.

We must not forget, however, the importance of the overall level of the supply of money in the economy. In general terms it is fair to assume that the *richer* people are, the *greater* their

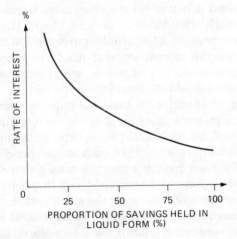

Fig. 5.3 The liquidity preference curve

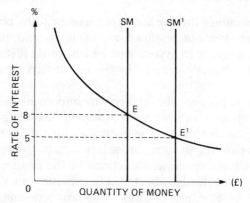

Fig. 5.4   Liquidity preference curve and the money supply.

savings will be and the *smaller* the inducement required for
them to give up liquidity on a proportion of their savings. This
applies to societies as a whole as much as to people individually.
In other words, the greater the money supply, the lower interest
rates are likely to be. We can demonstrate this by drawing a
graph on which the money supply is plotted against the liquidity
preference curve, as shown in Fig. 5.4.

Here the liquidity preference curve is intersected by the lines
SM and SM¹. You can see that when the money supply is at a
lower level (SM), interest rates are at 8%. If the supply of money
increases to SM¹ this has the effect of decreasing interest rates
to 5%. Thus, for a given level of money supply and at an established level of liquidity preference it is a simple matter to determine the equilibrium rate of interest. The liquidity preference
theory of interest is therefore in essence a *monetary theory.*

An integrated view of interest rates

Since we have demonstrated flaws in both the *loanable funds
theory* of interest and in the *liquidity preference theory*, it would
not be surprising if you were feeling a little confused as to where
the truth does lie. In fact it almost certainly lies somewhere
between the two theories. It is clear that the rate of interest and
the volume of saving and investment are not related to one
another in any simple or direct manner but neither are they
completely independent. In the long term they *must* interact to
bring about change. If, for example, the interest rate remained
high for a long period it would eventually depress consumption

by making consumer finance too expensive for some people. This would in turn lead to a slowdown of industrial production, followed by a cutback in investment which would further reduce the demand for loanable funds. In the end interest rates would have to fall.

The money supply is also clearly an important determining factor and changes in the money supply are largely under government control through the controls which it exercises over the country's banking system. Indeed, it is hard to overstate the importance of the government's actions in the determination of interest rates since it also affects them through its own massive demands for loan capital. Thus, we can conclude that the prevailing rates of interest result from the interaction of several forces which often conflict with each other. These forces include: government borrowing, state manipulation of the money supply, liquidity preference, business expectations and inflation rates.

As well as being influenced *by* the economy, however, interest rates are also a major influence *on* the economy, affecting the development of and expansion of economic activity. In the example just quoted you saw how an inordinately high interest rate would result in a reduction of consumer spending and a downturn of production. Furthermore, high rates of interest have other depressing effects on the economic scene; wholesalers reduce their holdings of stock reducing demand on manufacturers even further and capital investment is deferred both because of the high cost and because the lower levels of consumer demand do not justify it.

Interest rate structure

We have already seen in our studies of the money and capital markets that the UK has a complex and highly developed infrastructure devoted to the processing of loan and investment funds. The *rates of yield* which are available in these various markets are clearly influences on each other and they tend towards the same level although adjustments have to be made to allow for factors such as liquidity and safety. As in all free markets, speculators will attempt to take advantage of yield rate differentials between different sections of the markets by liquidating investments, or borrowing, in one area and reinvesting at a higher rate of return in another. Their operations are part of the mechanism which irons out such differentials. In this section we are going to explore the links between these various rates.

Short-term and long-term rates

The most basic distinction between interest rates is that between short-term and long-term rates. You already know that the long-term rates will normally be higher than short-term rates because the lender is giving up more liquidity and taking a greater risk that he will not get his money back. Nevertheless, this relationship can be upset if people expect that short-term interest rates are going to rise dramatically in the future: the long-term rate will fall below the short-term rate. It can be argued, in fact, that a long-term rate is composed of a series of short-term interest rates.

The general level of short-term interest rates is demonstrated by the yield on Treasury bills and on Stock Exchange securities that are nearing maturity and have twelve months or less to run. The level of long-term rates is demonstrated by the yield

Table 5.2 London money market rates at 11 September 1987

	Over-night	7 days notice	Month	Three Months	Six Months	One Year
Interbank	$9\frac{3}{4}$–7	$9\frac{1}{2}$–$9\frac{1}{8}$	$9\frac{3}{4}$–$9\frac{9}{16}$	$10\frac{1}{4}$–$10\frac{1}{16}$	$10\frac{9}{16}$–$10\frac{3}{8}$	$10\frac{3}{4}$–$10\frac{5}{8}$
Sterling CDs.	–	–	$9\frac{11}{16}$–$9\frac{9}{16}$	$10\frac{1}{8}$–10	$10\frac{7}{16}$–$10\frac{5}{16}$	$10\frac{1}{2}$–$10\frac{3}{8}$
Local Authority Deps.	$8\frac{3}{4}$	$9\frac{1}{8}$	$9\frac{5}{8}$	$10\frac{1}{8}$	$10\frac{3}{8}$	$10\frac{1}{2}$
Local Authority Bonds	–	–	10	$10\frac{1}{4}$	$10\frac{1}{2}$	$10\frac{11}{16}$
Discount Mkt Deps.	$8\frac{1}{2}$–7	$9\frac{7}{16}$–9	$9\frac{7}{16}$	$9\frac{3}{4}$	–	–
Company Deposits	$9\frac{1}{2}$–$8\frac{1}{2}$	–	$9\frac{3}{4}$	$10\frac{1}{4}$	$10\frac{5}{8}$	$10\frac{3}{4}$
Finance House Deposits	–	$9\frac{5}{8}$	$9\frac{11}{16}$	$10\frac{3}{16}$	$10\frac{1}{2}$	–
Treasury Bills (Buy)	–	–	$9\frac{17}{32}$	$9\frac{7}{8}$	–	–
Bank Bills (Buy)	–	–	$9\frac{9}{16}$	$9\frac{27}{32}$	$9\frac{31}{32}$	–
Fine Trade Bills (Buy)	–	–	$10\frac{3}{16}$	$10\frac{15}{32}$	$10\frac{19}{32}$	–
Dollar CDs	–	–	7.40–7.35	7.60–7.55	8.00–7.95	8.50–8.45

Source: The Financial Times)

on government securities which are 'long dated', that is, having no fixed redemption date. Table 5.2 shows the London money market interest rates on 11 September 1987 as published in *The Financial Times*. You will see that the terms quoted there vary from *overnight* up to *one year* but the actual range of rates is quite small showing how closely related all these rates are. *Bank base rate* was at 10% and *deposit rate* stood at 6%.

Money market rates

Treasury bill rate

We saw in Chapter 2 how Treasury bills are sold every week by the Bank of England on behalf of the government as a way of raising state finance. Each bill is a promise by the government to pay a specific sum (minimum £10 000) 91 days after it is issued. They are sold at a discount on their face value, the principal bidders for each issue being the *discount* houses, although other interested parties may also submit competing bids. Bills will be sold to the highest bidders, that is, those who offer the *lowest rate of discount* by being prepared to pay the closest to 100% of face value. In September 1987 successful bids for Treasury bills were averaging approximately £9757 per £10 000 bill. This represents a discount of £243 on the face value of the bill over its 91-day term. We can re-express this as an *annualised rate of discount* by using the following formula:

$$\left(\frac{243}{10\ 000} \times \frac{100}{1} \times \frac{365}{91} \right) = 9.75\% \text{ per annum discount rate}$$

The discount rate which we have just calculated is not quite the same thing as an interest rate however. This is because it is based on the difference between the *face value* of the bill and the amount of discount deducted from it to produce the purchase price. An *interest rate* would compare the purchase price, that is, the actual amount invested, with the yield to maturity, this latter amount being in fact the same as the amount of the discount. To show this as an annualised percentage we would make the following calculation:

$$\left(\frac{243}{9757} \times \frac{100}{1} \right) \times \frac{365}{91} = 9.99\% \text{ per annum rate of yield}$$

The difference between the discount rate and its representation as the equivalent interest rate is slight but it can be vital because the money market works to very fine differentials.

Some investors in Treasury bills prefer to buy them 'second-hand' from the discount houses, often after a significant part of the 91-day period has elapsed. This is how the commercial banks acquire their holdings of these bills. The rates at which such secondary sales of bills can be arranged is reflected in Table 5.2 under the column headed 'Treasury Bills (Buy)'. You will see that different rates are shown for one month and three month bills; these are, of course, annualised percentage representations of the rate of discount. Clearly the actual amount of discount to be deducted from the face value will reduce with each passing day as a bill comes closer to the date on which it will be redeemed at par.

The Treasury bill discount rate can be seen as a *key rate* in the structure of short-term money rates; it is the rate which other borrowers must match if they are to attract money away from the discount market. At the same time, discount rates are themselves determined by market forces since the discount houses *borrow* at call from the banks the funds which they use to purchase their holdings of bills. Clearly, therefore, if interest rates are likely to rise the discount houses will bid a lower price for bills to compensate for the extra cost of their finance. Conversely, if interest rates are likely to fall, the discount rate will also fall as bidders offer higher prices to ensure that they obtain the bills which they require.

The Bank of England guarantees the liquidity of the discount market by acting as its *lender of last resort*. Thus, if the discount houses find that bank funds are withdrawn, they will always be able to borrow from the Bank of England. This is, however, very much a last resort because the Bank of England's rate will always be pitched higher than Treasury bill rate. This means that when using this source of finance the discount houses pay a higher rate of interest on their borrowing than they are earning on their investments. Since August 1981 the Bank of England has ceased to publish the rate at which it would be prepared to lend; instead it operates within a 'band of interest rates', generally seeking to follow market rates rather than to lead them.

Other money market rates

As we saw in Chapter 2, the 'classical' and the 'parallel' money markets have developed into very sophisticated mechanisms for routeing wholesale supplies of money from lender to borrower. They include such subsidiary markets as those for sterling certificates of deposit, local authority deposits, intercompany deposits and so on. All sections of these markets offer rates of return which fluctuate in line with one another but differ slightly according to the safety and liquidity of capital which they offer. These rates are also shown in Table 5.3.

The development of the interbank sterling market in particular has been very important for the commercial banks as it has freed them from their heavy dependence on the retail deposit market. You will see from Table 5.3 that in September 1987 the interbank rates showed a moderate increase according to *term*: overnight loans would earn a minimum of 7% per annum return, while one-year money might earn nearly 11% per annum.

The banks could, of course, earn more from the funds at their disposal if they lent them all out for as long a period as possible but, as we have already seen, this would conflict with the need to maintain adequate liquidity. The relationship between the banks and the discount houses, for instance, helps with this liquidity management. Instead of bidding for Treasury bills themselves, the banks lend to the discount houses at *call* and *short notice* at rates of interest that are lower than discount rate. They obtain a slightly lower rate of return on their funds by this course of action but they find it easier to recover their cash at short notice than they would if they had purchased the bills themselves.

It is interesting to note that while the bank's advances to the discount market are all nominally at very short notice and can be quickly recovered in time of need, in reality many of the arrangements tend to run on for quite long periods. The banks categorise their loans to the discount houses as either 'regular money', that is, loans which are allowed to run on unless the lending bank needs the money back, or 'floating money', that is, loans which must be renewed or recovered on a daily basis. Regular money is cheaper for the discount houses, the cost being determined by the lower figure for 'overnight' interbank money shown in Table 5.3. Floating money is a more costly source of finance.

Eurocurrency rates

The growth of the Eurocurrency market since the 1950s has been quite phenomenal. Eurocurrency can be most simply defined as deposits in the currency of one country which are domiciled with a bank in a different country. Thus, for example, US dollars deposited with a bank in the UK would be Eurocurrency. This market began in fact with dealings in US dollars, but it now comprises several other major world currencies. The interest rates prevailing on Eurocurrency transactions are related to the current rates of interest in the country of the currency rather than those in the country where the account is maintained. These rates are also published in *The Financial Times*. Table 5.4 shows the rates for 11 September 1987. You will see that, as with sterling money market rates, different rates are quoted for different terms.

In the case of the Eurocurrency rates, two rates are quoted for each term. The lower of the two is the rate at which banks were taking deposits at the close of business on the day shown; the higher figure is the rate at which banks were making Eurocurrency available. The difference between the two rates represents the banks' potential for profits. The principal users of the Eurocurrency markets are multinational companies which have operations in many countries and importers and exporters who have dealings in foreign currencies.

Table 5.4 Eurocurrency interest rates as at 11 September 1987

	Short term	7 Days notice	One Month	Three Months	Six Months	One Year
Sterling	$9\frac{1}{4}-9$	$9\frac{5}{8}-9\frac{3}{8}$	$9\frac{13}{16}-9\frac{11}{16}$	$10\frac{3}{16}-10\frac{1}{16}$	$10\frac{9}{16}-10\frac{7}{16}$	$10\frac{3}{4}-10\frac{5}{8}$
U.S. Dollar	–	$7\frac{1}{4}-7\frac{1}{8}$	$7\frac{9}{16}-7\frac{7}{16}$	$7\frac{5}{8}-7\frac{1}{2}$	$8\frac{1}{16}-7\frac{15}{16}$	$8\frac{5}{8}-8\frac{1}{2}$
Can. Dollar	$9-8\frac{3}{4}$	$9-8\frac{3}{4}$	$9-8\frac{3}{4}$	$9\frac{3}{8}-9\frac{1}{8}$	$9\frac{15}{16}-9\frac{11}{16}$	$10\frac{7}{16}-10\frac{3}{16}$
D. Guilder	$5\frac{3}{16}-5\frac{1}{16}$	$5\frac{1}{4}-5\frac{1}{8}$	$5\frac{3}{8}-5\frac{1}{4}$	$5\frac{9}{16}-5\frac{7}{16}$	$5\frac{11}{16}-5\frac{9}{16}$	$5\frac{3}{8}-5\frac{1}{4}$
Sw. Franc	$1\frac{1}{8}-\frac{7}{8}$	$1\frac{1}{4}-1$	$3\frac{11}{16}-3\frac{9}{16}$	$3\frac{3}{4}-3\frac{5}{8}$	$4\frac{3}{16}-4\frac{1}{16}$	$4\frac{1}{4}-4\frac{1}{8}$
Deutschmark	$3\frac{13}{16}-3\frac{11}{16}$	$3\frac{7}{8}-3\frac{3}{4}$	$4\frac{1}{16}-3\frac{15}{16}$	$4\frac{1}{8}-4$	$4\frac{1}{2}-4\frac{3}{8}$	$4\frac{5}{8}-4\frac{1}{2}$
Fr. France	$7\frac{3}{16}-7\frac{1}{16}$	$7\frac{5}{8}-7\frac{3}{8}$	$7\frac{7}{8}-7\frac{3}{4}$	$8\frac{1}{4}-8\frac{1}{8}$	$8\frac{7}{8}-8\frac{3}{4}$	$9\frac{7}{16}-9\frac{5}{16}$
Italian Lire	$12-10$	$17-15$	$14\frac{5}{8}-13\frac{7}{8}$	$13\frac{1}{2}-13$	$13\frac{7}{8}-12\frac{7}{8}$	$13\frac{1}{4}-13$
B. Fr. (Fin.)	$6\frac{1}{8}-6$	$6\frac{3}{8}-6\frac{1}{8}$	$6\frac{1}{2}-6\frac{7}{16}$	$6\frac{3}{4}-6\frac{5}{8}$	$6\frac{7}{16}-6\frac{3}{16}$	$7\frac{7}{8}-7\frac{5}{8}$
B. Fr. (Con.)	$6\frac{1}{4}-5\frac{3}{4}$	$6\frac{1}{4}-5\frac{3}{4}$	$6\frac{5}{8}-6\frac{1}{4}$	$6\frac{7}{8}-6\frac{1}{2}$	$7\frac{1}{4}-6\frac{7}{8}$	$7\frac{1}{2}-7\frac{1}{8}$
Yen	$3\frac{5}{16}-3\frac{3}{16}$	$3\frac{9}{16}-3\frac{1}{2}$	$4\frac{1}{8}-4\frac{1}{16}$	$4\frac{3}{16}-4\frac{1}{8}$	$4\frac{7}{16}-4\frac{5}{16}$	$4\frac{9}{16}-4\frac{1}{2}$
D. Krone	$9\frac{3}{8}-9$	$10-9\frac{7}{8}$	$10\frac{1}{8}-9\frac{3}{4}$	$10\frac{1}{2}-10\frac{7}{8}$	$10\frac{3}{4}-10\frac{3}{8}$	$11\frac{1}{4}-10\frac{7}{8}$
Asian \$Sing.	$7-6\frac{7}{8}$	$7\frac{3}{8}-7\frac{1}{4}$	$7\frac{9}{16}-7\frac{7}{16}$	$7\frac{9}{16}-7\frac{7}{16}$	$8\frac{1}{16}-7\frac{15}{16}$	$8\frac{5}{8}-8\frac{1}{2}$

(*Source: The Financial Times*)

Domestic banking interest rates

As well as dealing on the wholesale money markets, the commercial banks also deal in retail deposits and loans through their branch networks. Indeed, for many years this constituted the whole of their business. Even today it remains the backbone of their operations. The interest rates which they apply on these transactions are, of course, slightly different from the rates which we have already discussed in relation to money market transactions.

Base rate

Base rate forms the underlying foundation for most of the domestic interest rates, each bank setting its own base from which it derives most of the rates which are actually applied to customers' accounts. In the past it was the practice for all banks to relate their interest rates to the *bank rate* which was set by the Bank of England. They converted to the present system in 1971 when bank rate was discontinued in favour of minimum lending rate, which in turn was discontinued in 1981. In theory, the banks do not operate a joint *cartel* to fix their rates at the same level. In practice, they are all bound by the same market forces and it is unusual for their base rates to differ by more than a fraction of a per cent for more than a few days. In mid September 1987 the base rates of all the major clearing banks stood at 10%. The rate is subject to change periodically in response to market forces.

Base rate is not an operational rate in that it is not normally applied 'raw' to any customer's account. Its principal use is as the basis for quoting the interest rates which will apply on most overdrafts and loans which the bank grants. On a personal overdraft, for instance, the customer may be asked to pay 4% *over* base rate; with base rate at 10% this would mean that the actual cost of the borrowing would be 14% per annum. If base rate changes while the customer is still overdrawn, the rate charged will also change, of course, maintaining the same differential over base rate.

The additional percentage charged on a particular loan will depend largely on the level of risk which the bank sees in the proposition. Large commercial concerns, which often also provide the bank with high commission income, may be able to borrow at between 2 to 2½% over base rate. Such rates are as low as a bank is ever likely to charge on normal commercial propositions. They are known as *blue chip* rates. (Blue chip is an expression borrowed from the stock market where it is used to denote a well-run and respected company.) Secured loans to smaller businesses and to personal customers may be charged at around 3% over base rate. Unsecured loans will attract rates of 4% or more above base. Up to 7% over base might be charged for unauthorised overdrafts created by the presentation of cheques without the bank's prior permission.

When interest is quoted on such terms, it is calculated daily on the balance actually due to the bank rather than on the agreed limit on the account. Thus, if a customer reduces his borrowing he reduces his interest charges; this is very important in the case of an overdraft since the balance may fluctuate greatly from day to day. This 'daily calculation' is also the basis on which the interest credited to a deposit account is worked out.

Deposit rate

The rate at which the bank pays interest on deposit accounts is not specifically related to base rate but is advertised as a separate rate. Nevertheless, it responds to the same market forces as base rate and it tends to fluctuate in much the same way. Deposit rate is always lower than base rate, usually by 2 to 4%, the difference between it and the lending rates representing the bank's source of profits. In September the banks had set their deposit rates at 6%.

We can see something of the links in the interest rate structure in the way that deposit rate changes. Individuals and firms with funds of £10 000 or more to invest for a short term have the choice, among other alternatives, of putting the funds on deposit with the bank or of purchasing a Treasury bill. A bank deposit is more convenient and easier to arrange but even so the existence of the alternative means that the banks cannot allow their deposit rates to get too far out of line with Treasury bill rate.

House purchase loan rate

This is a more recent addition to the banks' array of interest charges, being introduced following the banks' entry into the home loan market in the early 1980s. It too fluctuates in line with market forces and the rate in force at any one time applies to all bank mortgages, including existing ones as well as newly granted ones. The banks attempt to keep the home loan rate more stable and less volatile than other rates and they therefore attempt to implement changes less frequently than they do in respect of base and deposit rates.

The banks are, of course, in competition with the building societies in granting home loans and the cost of their loans has to be comparable. Until 1983 the major building societies, unlike the banks, did operate a rate-fixing *cartel* which ensured that they all charged and allowed the same rates as one another. A much less formal arrangement now exists between societies. The building societies operate like the banks, of course, in so far as they attract deposits by the offering of one (lower) interest rate, lending out the funds which they acquire at another (higher) rate, the difference between the two rates respresenting their source of income.

Personal loan rates

The banks' personal loan schemes were introduced in the 1960s as a way of competing with the hire purchase companies for a share of the growing market in consumer finance. They are, therefore, designed to be particularly suitable to finance the purchase of consumer durables such as cars and domestic appliances. With these schemes the borrower pays off the amount due for both capital and interest by a series of equal and regular (monthly) instalments over a preset period. This payment method gives us a clue as to the major difference between this type of borrowing and the traditional bank loan: the *way the interest is calculated*.

On a traditional type of loan, the amount of interest due is applied to the account only at the end of each charging period, usually of three or six months, rather than monthly. Furthermore, the amount of interest due each time declines throughout the term of the loan, being calculated on the *decreasing* debit balance of the account. With a personal loan the amount of interest to be paid each month remains constant, being calculated at a *flat rate* on the original amount of the loan. An example will demonstrate how this works. In September 1987 the major banks were quoting a flat rate of 9½% per annum for personal loans. Supposing that you, as a customer, had arranged to borrow £3000 so that you could buy a car, the bank would require you to pay interest of 9½% cent of £3000, £285 for each full year that the loan is outstanding. This will have to be paid by monthly instalments of £23.75. As well as the interest, of course, capital repayment would have to be made; if the loan is to be·paid off over three years, a monthly repayment of £83.33 will be required. The total monthly cost of the loan will therefore amount to £107.08.

You might think that 9½% per annum is a very attractive rate of interest. After all, we said that 'blue chip' lending would cost perhaps 2% over base rate, which would have produced a rate of 12% in September 1987. However, the two rates are not directly comparable, the one being applied to the reducing balance while the other is worked on the original (maximum) amount of the loan. The total of the interest to be charged on your £3000 personal loan over the three-year term would be £855. If the bank were to calculate the interest on the reducing balance of the loan, it would have to use a rate of 18.4% per annum to produce the same level of charge. This is considerably above 'blue chip' rate. Rates which are to be applied to a reducing balance are known as *true rates* of interest. The Consumer Credit Act 1974 requires that borrowers must be informed of the equivalent true rate as well as the flat rate to be applied to a proposed loan, thereby giving them the opportunity to make valid comparisons between facilities offered by different lenders.

The true rate of interest which the lender must quote is known as the Annual Percentage Rate of Charge (APR). The formula for calculating it is very complicated and to save time and mistakes the banks supply their branches with printed tables from which the APR can be read. In some cases, the bank's computer can be used to make individual calculations.

One more difference between personal loans and other forms of bank lending is that once the loan has been taken out, the interest rate applying remains *fixed* throughout the whole term, irrespective of changes to base rate or any other rate. This can be to the customer's advantage if rates in general rise, or to the bank's advantage if they fall.

The range of interest rates

By now you will appreciate that the principle on which banks and all financial intermediaries operate their interest rate structures is 'buy cheap and sell dear'. Each percentage point difference between the rates at which funds can be obtained represents an opportunity for someone to make a profit. The commercial banks can make much of this profit available to themselves, as is shown by the spread of $12\frac{1}{2}\%$ between a deposit rate of 6% and a true personal loan rate of almost $18\frac{1}{2}\%$. In this respect, however, the banks incur higher levels of cost than many other institutions because they are dealing in the 'retail' markets for money.

In the 'wholesale' money markets, costs per £1 borrowed are much lower because the participants are dealing in much larger amounts. The *margin* between borrowing and lending rates can therefore be much finer. Table 5.5 shows the broad spread of short-term rates as at 11 September 1987.

Table 5.5 The spread of short-term interest rates as at 11 September 1987

Type of deposit/loan rate	Per cent		
Bank deposit rate	6		
Average 'overnight' money market rate	$8\frac{1}{2}$	Profit gap for discount houses	Profit gap for banks
Yield on Treasury bills	$9\frac{3}{4}$		
'Blue chip' lending rate	12		
True personal loan rate	$18\frac{1}{2}$		

Summary

1 Interest is the price to be paid for the use of someone else's money.
2 Interest is charged by lenders to ensure the productivity of their capital. The actual rate will vary according to:
    (a) the level of liquidity which they are giving up;
    (b) the element of risk in the loan.

3 There are opposing theories about the background level of interest rates.

4 The loanable funds theory stresses the interaction of the supply and demand for loanable funds with the rate of interest.

5 The liquidity preference theory concentrates on the extent to which lenders have to be persuaded to forgo liquidity. Three motives are identified for the desire for liquid holdings:

(a) the transaction motive;

(b) the precautionary motive;

(c) the speculative motive.

6 The UK has a well-developed money market with a complex structure of interrelated interest rates.

(a) The key short-term rate is the yield on Treasury bills;

(b) The key long-term rate is the yield on long-dated gilts.

7 Domestic banks set a base rate in terms of which most of their operational rates are expressed.

8 Personal loan interest is normally charged at a flat rate on the capital amount borrowed. The true rate calculated on the reducing balance is much higher.

Self-assessment questions

1 Define: (a) liquidity preference; (b) base rate; (c) net productivity of capital; (d) Treasury bill rate; (e) the propensity to save.

2 List the motives for holding surplus funds in liquid form.

3 List the components of the demand for loanable funds.

4 True or false?

(a) Interest is the price of money.

(b) A flat rate is one that has been adjusted to allow for inflation.

(c) Borrowing on personal loan is cheaper than borrowing on overdraft.

(d) The demand for consumer advances is highly responsive to changes in the interest rate.

(e) If interest rates were increased, this would cause a fall in the price of Treasury bills.

5 What would be the effect of a decreased liquidity preference on the rate of interest?

6 Explain why a zero rate of interest will never occur.

7   Calculate the monthly payments required to cover capital repayment and interest on a personal loan of £2500 taken out over eighteen months at a flat rate of $9\frac{1}{2}\%$ per annum.

Assignments

1   Draw up a table comparing the various different interest rates which are in force today through the banks and the money markets. You will need to refer to today's *Financial Times* or the business section of another 'quality' newspaper.

Prepare a brief report explaining the links between the rates which you have discovered.

2   Memorandum to: Student
    From: Branch Manager
    Subject: Personal loan accounts

I think it is time that we tried to boost our branch's contribution to the bank's interest income. As our customer base is mostly made up of personal accounts, it would seem logical that personal loan accounts would be the most productive area to go for. I would like you to do two things for me:

(a) Identify methods which will enable us to pinpoint the customers to whom it would be appropriate to mention our personal loan facilities.

(b) Draft out a letter that we can send to such customers explaining how the scheme operates, how much loans will cost, what they can be used for and so on.

6 Banks and their customers

Chapter objectives

After studying this chapter you should be able to:
- define the terms banker and customer;
- explain the nature of the banker–customer relationship;
- state and fully appreciate a banker's rights and duties arising from this relationship;
- distinguish between different types of bank accounts;
- explain the procedures for opening and operating such bank accounts.

Introduction

So far as we have discussed banks from commercial, historical and administrative points of view; we must now begin to consider them, and their relationship with their customers, from a more formal legal perspective. Remember, however, that it would be wrong to consider this as a separate subject—the legal framework is part and parcel of the business of banking. It is just that the legal framework is particularly evident, as it must be, in this topic.

Definitions

We must start by defining the terms 'banker' and 'customer'. You may, at first, consider this rather unnecessary—after all everyone knows what a bank is, and presumably a banker is someone who works in one. Similarly, a customer is clearly someone who uses the services of a bank. Well, we must be rather more precise because your relationship with your customers gives rise to important legal rights and duties quite apart from any commercial considerations. So, we must ask some preliminary questions.

Who is a banker?

If you look for an answer in the Banking Act 1987, you will be disappointed! As you saw in Chapter 2, the Act's purpose is the regulation of deposit-taking and it only deals specifically with 'banks' in so far as the use of the name 'bank' is restricted by the Bank of England to larger authorised institutions. Even then, overseas banks are exempt from this restriction. The Act tells us very little about the role and characteristics of a banker. Unfortunately, the same is true of other relevant statutes. For example, according to the Bills of Exchange Act 1882, s.2, the term 'Includes a body of persons whether incorporated or not who carry on the business of banking'.

Our most profitable line of enquiry is to consider the phrase *business of banking*, for here we will see that the common law (the judge-made law) has considered the activities inherent in this business as being the criteria for determining who is and who is not a banker. In *United Dominions Trust* v. *Kirkwood* (1966), it had to be decided whether UDT were moneylenders within the Moneylenders Act 1900 or, as they maintained, bankers and therefore exempt from registration under the Act. The Court of Appeal identified the performance of three activities as definitive characteristics of bankers: (a) they accept money from, and collect cheques for their customers and place them to their credit; (b) they honour cheques or orders drawn on them by their customers when presented for payment and debit their customers accordingly; (c) they keep current accounts, or something of that nature, in their books in which the credits and debits are entered. In addition, the court stressed that the definition was not static and would always depend on current practice. Indeed, the majority of the court accepted a secondary test of the reputation of the organisation in question with other bankers as a means of determining whether the organisation could be regarded at law as a bank. On the facts, UDT, while not a conventional bank, were held to satisfy both tests.

Who is a customer?

If you thought that statute would define a customer, you would be mistaken. Once more we must look to the common law. Decided cases show that a customer of a bank is a person who has entered into a contract with the banker for the opening of an account in his or her name.

It is not essential for a course of dealings to be maintained over a period of time; the relationship is contractual and therefore arises when the customer's offer is accepted by the bank. The existence of an account is essential, however, and no matter how many transactions have taken place between a bank and an individual, such as cashing cheques payable to him, he will not be a customer unless and until his application to open an account has been made and accepted, i.e. a contractual relationship established.

Nevertheless, a banker may owe duties to another person before an account is opened, and even if an account is never opened. In *Woods* v. *Martins Bank Ltd.* (1959), a bank manager who gave financial advice to a person who intended to become a customer, and who did so shortly afterwards, was held to owe him the same contractual duty of care as if he were already a customer.

The banker–customer relationship

The relationship between you and your customers is basically *contractual*. It is fundamentally the relationship of debtor (the banker) and creditor (the customer) with the position reversed where the banker makes a loan to the customer. Various categories of rules govern the workings of this relationship.

General rules of contract

No doubt you will already have covered some contract law in your other studies, or soon will. The rules relating to offer and acceptance, consideration, etc., while seldom being the cause of dispute in banking are directly relevant to the creation and operation of the relationship. For instance, the opening of an account is a practical example of 'offer and acceptance', the customer's application being the offer with the bank being at liberty to accept or reject that offer. Again, 'consideration'—the exchange of value—is represented by the facilities and services offered by the bank in return for the customer's payment of bank charges and permission to dispose of his money as the bank pleases, provided valid cheques are honoured.

One rule established in contract law which is particularly important to banks comes from the decision in *Devaynes* v. *Noble* (1816), always referred to as the *Rule in Clayton's Case* (1816). You will immediately see why. The *Rule* states that in a current account payments in are appropriated to the debit items in order of date, unless the customer or bank has taken steps to appropriate particular credits against particular debits. An example will show you how the *Rule* works.

X, Y and Z were in partnership. At the date of X's retirement, the firm's overdraft was £5000, for which he was of course liable. If the account had been continued unbroken and credits of £5000 had been paid in and payments of £5000 had been made, the debit balance for which X was liable would have been completely extinguished, through the operation of the *Rule*, although the overdraft itself would have remained at £5000. However, only Y and Z would now be liable on it. Thus, banks will invariably take steps to avoid the *Rule* operating to their disadvantage wherever possible.

Perhaps the most remarkable fact about the nature of the banker–customer contract is its informality. It is made without written agreements but instead governed by oral discussion, largely administrative forms, brief letters and banking custom and practice. How many customers are aware (or made aware) of the rights and duties which are implied into the contract (*see* below)? However, the position may possibly change. Some banks already produce customer leaflets explaining in everyday language the main terms of the banker–customer contract. Credit card agreements already detail the terms of issue and the responsibilities of the cardholder and the increasing use of electronic banking is likely to continue this trend, particularly in relation to limits on a bank's liability for loss.

Rules of agency

In important respects a banker acts as his customer's agent, particularly in collecting cheques paid in by the customer for the credit of his account. As such there exists what is usually referred to as a more complex *implied contract* between banker and customer which imposes many duties on a banker similar to those imposed on an ordinary agent. These duties, together with reciprocal rights, are well established by banking practice and supported by many judicial decisions. We discuss them below.

Rules of bailment

A bailment arises where one person (the *bailor*) deposits goods with another (the *bailee*) for a specific purpose on terms that the goods will ultimately be redelivered to the bailor or otherwise dealt with according to his instructions. The bailor retains ownership of the goods. The use of banker's safe deposit facilities by his customer gives rise to a bailment agreement.

The law draws a distinction between a gratuitous (unpaid) bailee and a bailee for reward (a paid bailee). Both may be liable in *tort* for loss or damage to the property bailed but the former is only expected to take the same care of the property as a reasonably careful person would take of similar property of his own. The latter, however, owes an additional *contractual duty* to the bailor under which he is judged against the highest professional standards.

A tort can be said to be a legal wrong against an individual which gives a right at civil law for damages. Not a particularly helpful definition perhaps but there are a number of specific torts, each of which can be defined more precisely in terms of legal duties protecting individual rights and, to a lesser extent, by the manner of their commission. We will see this below in relation to the tort of conversion.

Modern safe custody facilities and procedures mean that a banker is unlikely to be liable for the tort of *negligence* in relation to safe custody deposits although this is always a possibility should property held in safe custody be destroyed by fire or otherwise lost or stolen. Remember too that the Unfair Contract Terms Act 1977 subjects any term or notice excluding or limiting possible liability, in this case as bailee, to a test of reasonableness.

A banker is more likely to incur liability in relation to a safe custody deposit in the tort of *conversion*. This can be committed in many ways but most commonly by wrongfully taking possession of goods, wrongfully damaging or destroying them, wrongfully disposing of them or by refusing to part with them when possession is demanded by someone entitled to possession. The essence of the tort is that the defendant's conduct amounts to a denial of the plaintiff's *right to possession and control* of the property. You can see that the last two examples are relevant to you as a banker in relation to safe custody deposits. A banker would, for example, commit conversion by refusing to hand over the property bailed to the bailee when he demands it or by delivering the property to an unauthorised person. Liability in conversion is *strict*, that is the breach of the legal duty resulting in the infringement of the individual's right is enough, proof of intention or negligence is unnecessary. This means that a banker would still be liable in conversion even if he should wrongfully deliver property held in safe custody by pure mistake or against the most skilfully forged authority; in both instances he would still have infringed the bailor's rights in the property bailed.

The distinction between a paid and a gratuitous bailee is, in theory, relevant in banking in so far as some customers are offered safe custody facilities without specific payment for them, an apparently gratuitous bailment, while a specific charge is made in other cases, a bailment for reward. The better view today, however, is that a banker who accepts property for safe custody can nearly always be regarded as a bailee for reward; in other words, the bailment is considered to be part and parcel of the wider contract with his customer, whether or not specific payment is made for the facility. In any case, the same high standard of care is always taken of property deposited for safe custody whatever the exact nature of the bailment agreement.

You should note that *night safe* agreements expressly provide that the bailment which arises is gratuitous until the wallet is opened and the contents deposited.

Rules of banking practice

Such rules may have evolved over a considerable period of time and often reflect the commercial environment of which banking is itself part. The rules contained in the Bills of Exchange Act 1882, and the judicial interpretation of them, for example, are largely the codified practices of merchants developed over the previous 100 years or so. Even where such rules have not been incorporated in statute, they are largely recognised and enforced by the courts and may acquire the force of mercantile custom if they are universally accepted.

A full survey of the rules of banking practice is out of place in this book—you would study them in professional banking examinations—but one example will illustrate the relationship between banking practice and the law. In *Baines* v. *National Provincial Bank Ltd.* (1927), it was held that a bank is allowed a reasonable period of time to complete its business after its advertised closing time. Thus, in the case the bank was allowed to debit its customer's account with a cheque (for £200) cashed five minutes after closing time and a countermand the following morning was ineffective. The decision is important in itself but let us consider it in relation to s.60 of the Bills of Exchange Act 1882. This section protects a banker against liability to the true owner (the holder) of a cheque which bears a forged or unauthorised indorsement provided the banker pays it in good faith and in the *ordinary course of business*. Relying on the decision in *Baines* which, remember, is a judicial recognition of banking practice, we can safely say that cheques paid in a busy branch within ten minutes or so of the advertised closing time would still be considered as paid in the ordinary course of business. It follows that the protection of s.60 would still apply, if required.

A special relationship

The law recognises a series of *fiduciary relationships* where one person is presumed to be in a position of trust and influence in relation to another. Examples include: solicitor and client; teacher and pupil; parent and child. In such relationships the law demands that those in the superior position act in complete good faith with regard to the other; in particular, such people must not let their own interests influence the relationship. The banker–customer relationship is *not* a fiduciary relationship as such, but decided cases show that a *special relationship*, imposing a very similar fiduciary duty (that is, a very strict duty of good faith) can arise with particular customers who have come to *trust and rely upon the banker for advice*. This duty is independent of the contractual relationship between them.

The leading case is *Lloyds Banks* v. *Bundy* (1975), where the defendant, an elderly farmer of little business acumen, twice mortgaged his home to the plaintiff bank to secure an overdraft to his son's company. The bank sought to exercise its right to sell the defendant's property under the mortgage when it became clear that the son's company was not going to be able to make repayment. The Court of Appeal held that it should not be allowed to do so. The defendant had come to rely on the bank for advice and, on the facts, the bank owed a fiduciary duty towards him. They had broken this duty by not ensuring that he had had independent advice before mortgaging his home. While such a situation is unlikely to arise frequently in practice, you as a banker must always be aware of the possibility of such a special relationship arising and act accordingly.

Nevertheless, in a decision welcome to banks the House of Lords in *National Westminster Bank plc* v. *Morgan* (1985) held that a contract will not be set aside for undue influence merely because a confidential relationship is proved to exist. It must be shown that the contract is to the clear disadvantage of the party seeking relief. The principle of undue influence is based on the prevention of 'victimisation' of one party by the other, not merely their relationship.

A bank's legal rights and duties

Arising from the banker–customer relationship are a number of rights and duties. These, as you will see, underlie the practical operation of the relationship.

Rights

1 To *charge its customers reasonable commission* for services rendered to them, and to *charge interest* on loans made to them.
2 To *repayment on demand* from its customers of any overdrawn balance which has been permitted on a current account. In *Williams and Glyn's Bank* v. *Barnes* (1980), however, it was held that a reasonable period of notice must be given where the terms and circumstances of the contract of lending clearly *imply* such notice.
3 To be *indemnified* by its customers for expenses and liabilities incurred while acting for them.
4 To *exercise a lien* over any of its customers' securities that

are in its possession, other than those deposited for safe custody, for any money owing to it. (A lien, pronounced le-en, is a right to retain possession of the property of another in lieu of payment due from that person.)

5 To *dispose of its customers' money as it pleases* provided it honours its customers' valid cheques.

6 To *expect its customers to exercise due care in drawing cheques*. This right was established in *London Joint Stock Bank Ltd.* v. *Macmillan and Arthur* (1918), where a partner in the defendant firm signed a cheque payable to the payee or to bearer made out by a clerk for the sum of £2. The amount payable was shown in figures only. The clerk fraudulently altered the figures to read £120, wrote this amount on the cheque and obtained payment from the plaintiff, the firm's bank. The court held that the bank was entitled to debit the firm's account with the value of the cheque as altered.

Clearly, it is good banking practice to advise a customer, who is making out cheques in a way which facilitates their fraudulent alteration, to make them out properly.

7 To *set-off* or combine accounts. In other words, where a customer has more than one account with a bank, the bank is entitled to settle an overdrawn balance on one account by transferring money from the credit balance on another.

Duties

1 To *abide by any express mandate from its customer*, such as a standing order.

2 To *honour its customer's cheques*. This duty is subject to a number of provisos, for example:

(a) the cheques must be properly drawn, not stale nor overdue—a cheque is *stale* when it has been in circulation for a considerable period of time, usually more than six months; a cheque is *overdue* when it has been in circulation for an unreasonable length of time, a question of fact but possibly where it is not presented within ten days of its issue;

(b) a credit balance or an agreed overdraft facility exists;

(c) there is no legal bar to payment, such as a garnishee order or an injunction;

(d) the customer has not countermanded payment;

(e) the bank has no notice that its customer has died, become mentally incapable of managing his affairs or had a bankruptcy petition presented against him;

(f) there has not been a bankruptcy order or winding-up order made against him.

By analogy this duty also applies to the payment of standing orders.

3 *Not to disclose information about its customer's affairs.* In *Tournier* v. *National Bank of England* (1924), it was held that this duty of secrecy is not absolute but *qualified* and disclosure is justified in four situations. These are where:

(a) compelled by law to do so, for example, by a court order under the Bankers' Book Evidence Act 1879, the Companies Act 1985, the Drug Trafficking Offences Act 1986 (*see* Chapter 2) and income tax legislation;

(b) it has a duty to the public to do so, for example where it acquires knowledge of terrorist activity involving a customer;

(c) its own interests require disclosure, for example, where legal proceedings are required to enforce payment of an overdraft, or where a surety asks to be told the extent to which his guarantee is being relied upon by the bank;

(d) it has the express or implied consent of its customer to do so, for example, where it supplies a reference for its customer.

4 To *render statements of account* to its customer periodically or upon request.

5 To *collect cheques and other normal banking instruments* for its customer and to credit the amounts collected to his account.

6 To *exercise proper care and skill* in carrying out any business it has agreed to transact for its customer. This duty is evident in relation to any activity or transaction carried out or entered into on behalf of a customer, including safe deposit facilities (*see* above), but it is of most practical importance in relation to the collection and payment of cheques. Every day, banks pay and collect many thousands of cheques on behalf of their customers. Each payment and collection must be properly made in accordance with legal rules and banking practice if a bank is to enjoy the necessary protection afforded by the Bills of Exchange Act 1882 and the decisions of judges. Before we leave this particular duty, it is worth noting that the duty of care and skill can

extend beyond the scope of traditional branch banking; it can for example, cover investment advice: *Woods* v. *Martins Bank Ltd.* (1959) (*see* above).

7 To *give reasonable notice before closing a credit account.* There are two reasons behind this duty. First, it gives the customer time to make other arrangements. Second, it means that the bank does not have to return cheques already issued by the customer. This saves administrative effort and prevents an allegation that the bank damaged the customer's reputation by returning the cheques unpaid.

Opening and operating a bank account

Introduction

Banks largely make their profits by lending out the money which customers have deposited with them. Therefore they compete for customers. The various inducements to open accounts offered to students are excellent examples—the student of today being, at least in theory, the worthwhile customer of the future. However, the legal framework governing banking operations requires that they take certain precautions before opening an account. A particularly important case in point is the protection afforded to a collecting bank by s.4 of the Cheques Act 1957. The section provides that a bank which acts in good faith and *without negligence* incurs no liability to the true owner of a cheque collected by the bank for its customer where its customer was not entitled to the cheque. Clearly, if payment of a cheque is received by a bank in such circumstances and the bank did not take up its customer's references before opening the account, the protection of s.4 would not be available; the bank would not have acted 'without negligence' as required. This, however, is the strict *legal* position. Banking practice varies, as we explain below.

Opening an account

Before opening either a current or a deposit account a banker must be satisfied as to the character and standing of the applicant and know his employer's name and nature of his employment. This information can be obtained either (a) by a *personal introduction* from an existing customer or another branch or bank; or (b) by *taking references*, usually two, one of which should be from the applicant's employer. In the latter case, if the referee is unknown to the banker, the authenticity of the reference should be checked, for example, through the referee's own banker.

Taking references should avoid opening what may become an unsatisfactory account and usually secures the protection of s.4 (*see* above). Although some banks have now again begun to insist on references in certain high risk geographical areas, the trend has been for few references to be taken and fewer to be checked. At law this is clearly a dangerous practice but commercially it has made good sense on the basis that the time and expense involved in taking and checking references outweighs the risk of not doing so. In addition, a fiercely competitive environment demands that opening an account should be as easy as possible. The situation perhaps nicely illustrates the possible conflict between traditional banking virtues and attitudes and the more market oriented approach dictated by change in the financial services industry.

Opening formalities

Banks differ as to the exact procedures and formalities involved in opening an account. You should obtain your own bank's account application form and ensure that you are familiar with the specific opening formalities. However, the following are the standard opening formalities.

1 *Specimen signatures* of all parties to the account must be obtained.
2 A *mandate covering all operations* on the account must be obtained if it is other than a sole account.
3 A *cheque book* should only be issued when a satisfactory introduction or references have been obtained and checked and any cheque opening the account cleared.
4 A *cheque guarantee card* should only be issued after the bank has established that the account will be run in a regular and

responsible manner, or where there is no doubt about the person's integrity and responsibility as an account holder.

5 If possible, *commission and interest charges should be agreed* when the account is opened in order to avoid having to rely on a banker's implied right to recover reasonable charges and commission. Most banks do, in fact, have standard tariffs for charges and commission.

Operation of an account by an agent

First, who is an agent? An *agent* is a person who acts on another's behalf, the other person being known as his *principal*. The essential feature of the relationship created is that the agent is able to alter his principal's legal position in relation to third parties by making contracts with them. Since an agent contracts on his principal's behalf, it follows that the agent generally incurs neither rights nor liabilities on any contract that he makes.

A bank will often have to deal with people who are agents, such as directors of companies, partners in firms and occasionally a person who holds a power of attorney, and it is therefore important for a banker to ascertain and understand the scope and extent of the agent's authority before dealing with him. Remember also that an important aspect of the banker–customer relationship is a bank's role as its customer's agent in collecting cheques paid in by its customer. In addition, a bank may also act as an agent in dealing with securities on its customer's behalf, and in connection with the numerous other services that a bank can provide or arrange for its customers.

You should note the following points about a customer delegating his authority to an agent in connection with a bank account.

1 Delegation by the principal is not always permitted by law; for example, trustees may have power to delegate only in certain circumstances.

2 If there are two or more parties to the account, all must authorise the delegation; for example, where A and B operate a joint account, both must authorise C to sign cheques in place of B.

3   Since agents act on behalf of their principals, agents need not themselves have contractual capacity; for example, a minor can act as agent.

4   The power to sign on an account does not include the power to draw, accept or indorse bills of exchange, or to overdraw or charge the principal's property as security unless such powers are expressed in the mandate.

5   A written mandate must be taken from the customer; standard mandate forms exist for this purpose. The mandate will stipulate that the bank has authority to act on the agent's signature and that the bank will continue to act on the agent's instructions until a written revocation of authority is received from the account holder.

6   A specimen of the agent's signature is required.

7   The agent must sign on the account in a way that avoids personal liability. The usual way is to sign 'Per pro' of 'For and on behalf of' followed by the signature.

What is the position where an agent acts in excess of his authority? The agent is personally liable because by his actions he has warranted that he has authority which in truth he has not. The agent is, therefore, liable for *breach of warranty of authority*. This, however, may be of little use to a bank who has acted on the agent's instructions, for the sums involved may be great while the personal resources of the agent may be small. A bank, in these circumstances, would wish to make the principal liable if at all possible. Leaving aside the possibility that the principal may accept liability to preserve his reputation and banking facilities—technically he is said to *ratify* the agent's unauthorised act—in what circumstances can the principal be made liable at law?

Most agency situations arise as a result of a contract in which the express terms of the agency are spelt out. If a bank has knowledge of them it must, of course, adhere to them. However, in addition to the express authority given by contract, agents will also at law have *implied authority* to undertake acts which are reasonably necessary for the completion of their authorised tasks. For example, an agent employed to sell land has implied authority to sign a memorandum in writing of the contract as required by the law of Property Act 1925, s.40.

Agency can also be created by *estoppel* where one person

allows another to appear to be his agent to third parties. Where a third party relies on this appearance and deals with that person as an agent, the 'principal' is *estopped* (prevented) from denying that person's authority. Such agency results from the principal's words or conduct, not from an agreement between the agent and principal. A simple banking example of agency by estoppel would be where a customer has regularly sent an employee to collect bank statements. If the employee was dismissed but still came to collect a statement as usual, but for his own purposes, and the bank gave it to him, estoppel would arise because the customer would be prevented from denying to the bank that the ex-employee was still his agent for that specific purpose. Once notice to the contrary was given, estoppel would cease to operate.

The problem of an agent's unauthorised acts affecting a bank arises mainly in two areas: first, unauthorised *borrowing* and second, wrongfully *handling cheques*. If an agent borrows money from a bank without authority, the debt cannot be enforced against the principal unless the principal either ratifies the loan or is estopped from denying the agent's lack of authority. The problem is potentially most important in relation to borrowing by a director of a company which is *ultra vires* the company. The company cannot ratify the contract, because it is legally incapable of making it in the first place, and the bank cannot rely on the Companies Act 1985, s.35. However, when we consider this important question of *ultra vires* borrowing by a director, or indeed by the company itself, fully in Chapter 13, you will see that the bank is not entirely without effective remedies.

Whenever an agent handles cheques for his principal, the possibility that he may be exceeding his authority arises. For example, he may draw cheques on his principal's account payable to himself without authority or he may indorse cheques payable to his principal and pay them into his own account. A bank would be liable to the true owner of the cheque if its negligence allowed the agent to act in this way. In *Midland Bank Ltd* v. *Reckitt* (1933), for example, the bank was held to have acted negligently, and was therefore liable to its customer, when it collected for the personal account of a solicitor cheques drawn by him on the account of the customer for whom he held power of attorney. The power of attorney did not remove the need to make enquiries before paying the cheques.

Termination of a banker's authority to pay

A bank's authority to make payments from its customer's account ends in the following main situations.

1 Where a *countermand of payment* is received. Only the drawer can countermand payment and he must do so in writing in unequivocal terms to the branch on which the cheque was drawn. The drawer must also give complete details of the cheque, in particular: (a) the payee's name; (b) the amount of the cheque; and (c) its number. The number of the cheque to be countermanded is the most important detail to communicate. If the wrong number is given, a bank incurs no liability if it pays the cheque that its customer intended to stop.

The countermand is ineffective unless and until it comes to the actual attention of the bank. For example, in *Curtice* v. *London City and Midland Bank Ltd.* (1908), a telegram countermanding payment of a cheque was delivered after banking hours and left in the bank's letter box. The next day the countermand was accidently overlooked. It was found the following day but by this time the cheque had been paid. It was held that since the bank had no actual knowledge of the telegram, the countermand was ineffective and the bank was entitled to debit the plaintiff's account with the amount of the cheque. It is worth noting that while the decision against Curtice might seem to be somewhat harsh, it is practical and there is little doubt that he would have succeeded had he brought an action for negligence rather than for money had and received.

What is the position when the drawer attempts to countermand by telephone? Here the bank is entitled to postpone payment or dishonour (non-payment) pending the drawer's written confirmation. If the cheque is returned in the meantime, you must indicate that confirmation of a countermand is awaited.

Two final points to note. First, it is not possible to countermand a cheque properly issued against a cheque guarantee card. Second, if a bank mistakenly pays a 'stopped' cheque, it is entitled to recover payment from the payee unless the payee changes his position in good faith, for example, by entering into a transaction purely because he had received the payment and without knowledge that the payment was mistaken.

2   Where *notice of the customer's death or mental incapacity* is received.

3   Where *notice of a bankruptcy petition against the customer* is received. After notice is received, the Insolvency Act 1986 protects payments made to the debtor from his account, if it is in credit, but not cheques payable to third parties, that is, payments from the account to persons other than the customer.

4   Where a *bankruptcy order or winding-up order is made against the customer.* (A winding-up order applies to a customer which is a registered company.) It is the making of the order, not notice of it, which terminates your authority to pay.

5   Where *a legal bar to payment exists.* This may be either a garnishee order or an injunction. A *garnishee order* may be obtained by a creditor who has obtained judgment against a credit balance in the debtor's account. An *injunction* may be issued by the court when, for example, the ownership of certain funds is disputed, thereby preventing them from being disposed of before ownership is determined by the court.

6   Where the bank has *knowledge of a defect in the presenter's title to the cheque.* Such knowledge is unlikely to exist but the bank may know, for example, that the presenter is an undischarged bankrupt and the cheque should not be paid in this case because the proceeds may belong to the presenter's trustee in bankruptcy.

Closing an account

As you have already seen, a bank must give reasonable notice before closing a *credit account.* What is reasonable is a question of fact in the circumstances. A bank will usually close an unsatisfactory account by requesting the customer to withdraw the balance and return any unused cheques. A formal notice in writing is necessary if the customer does not comply with the request. A credit account would be regarded as unsatisfactory where cheques exceeding the available balance in the account are frequently drawn or where the customer otherwise inconveniences the bank.

Since an overdraft is normally repayable on demand, a bank has no difficulty in closing an unsatisfactory *debit account* which has been operated beyond the agreed limit. Where an agreed limit is not exceeded, a threat to close the account should be made unless the way the account is conducted improves. In the case of a *loan account*, there must be a breach of the loan agreement, for example, failure to make repayments as prescribed, before the account can be closed.

Bank statements

A bank owes a duty to its customers to keep accurate records of transactions on their accounts. Customers have no obligation to check bank statements and inform the bank of an inaccuracy in them. Furthermore, if a customer does check the statements, the customer is not estopped (prevented) from subsequently challenging their accuracy.

Overcrediting the account

If you overcredit a customer's account, the excess credit may not be recoverable. However, to defeat a claim for repayment, the customer must fulfil the three conditions laid down in *United Overseas Bank* v. *Jiwani* (1976):

(a) the state of the account must have been misrepresented to the customer by the bank;

(b) the customer must have been misled by the misrepresentation; and

(c) as a result of the reliance, the customer must have changed his position in a way which would make it inequitable (unfair) to require him to repay the money.

Let us consider the case itself. $11 000 were credited by telex to the defendant's Swiss bank account making a total balance in the account of $21 000. The defendant issued a cheque for $20 000 in connection with the purchase of a hotel. Subsequently, written confirmation of the telex was received but the bank mistakenly treated this as a second credit and advised the defendant accordingly. The defendant then issued a second cheque, for $11 000, towards the hotel purchase. The bank sought to recover this amount from him. The court allowed the claim. On the facts the defendant had alternative funds which he would have used for the purchase, irrespective of the mistaken credit. Thus, while the first two conditions were satisfied, the defendant failed to satisfy the third.

Incorrectly debiting the account

Whatever the reason for the incorrect debit, a bank is obliged to refund the amount. Quite simply, it has no mandate for the debit. If, as a result of incorrect debits, cheques are dishonoured for apparent lack of funds, a bank is liable for the wrongful dishonour of the cheques and must compensate the customer for the injury to the customer's credit and reputation. This may even result in an action in tort for defamation.

Power of attorney

Definition

A power of attorney is a *deed* giving a person(s) (the donee or attorney) power to act on behalf of the person giving the power (the donor). The power of attorney may be either *specific*—for a particular purpose; or *general*—general authority for a particular period of time. It is usually encountered where the donor is going abroad or ill, or where a trustee or personal representative wishes to delegate this power for up to one year.

A power granted in the form prescribed by the Powers of Attorney Act 1971 and expressed to be made under the Act gives the donee authority to do on behalf of the donor anything that he can lawfully do by an attorney. However, since it is uncertain whether even this general (unlimited) power gives an attorney authority to borrow or charge assets as security, a bank will prefer to have specific clauses inserted dealing with these acts.

Banking practice in relation to powers of attorney

You must examine the power of attorney carefully to ascertain its exact nature and extent. It is usual for the donor's bank account to be specifically mentioned and authority given to the attorney to operate the account. Since a general power to operate a bank account does not usually include authority to do so, specific clauses must be included if the attorney is to collect, draw and indorse bills of exchange; borrow money; charge the donor's property as security and withdraw safe custody items. Despite its wording, the omnibus or general clause merely gives the attorney power to do acts which are ancillary to those stated in the specific clauses. More generally, a bank must also ensure that:

(a) the attorney's identity is verified;
(b) the power is still in force;
(c) it is under seal; and
(d) the power is operated strictly according to its terms.

You will see later (Chapter 16) that banks are sometimes given power of attorney when they take an equitable mortgage of land, for this enables them to realise the security far more easily if repayment of the advance is not made.

Revocation of a power of attorney

There are five ways in which a power of attorney may be revoked.

1 By the donor *expressly revoking* the power. However, some powers are expressed to be *irrevocable* and are given to secure a proprietary interest of the donee, for example, a bank holding an equitable mortgage of land. In those cases the power cannot be revoked without the donee's consent while the proprietary interest remains.

2 By the *death, mental incapacity or bankruptcy* of the donor or donee, that is by operation of law. However, under the Enduring Powers of Attorney Act 1985, a power of attorney can be created which is not automatically revoked when the donor becomes mentally incapacitated. Such a power facilitates the administration of the donor's affairs without interruption just when the ability to do so is probably most needed.

3 When the *purpose for which it was given is fulfilled.*

4 When the *period for which it was given expires.*

5 By *implication*, for example, where a new power is executed or where the donor again begins to operate the account himself. Good banking practice demands that such implied revocation be checked and confirmed with the donor.

Standing orders and direct debits

A *standing order* is a standing instruction given by a customer to make a regular periodic payment from his account to the account of a customer of the same or other bank. Each order must be signed by the customer in accordance with the mandate for the account and it can only be cancelled on the written instructions of the customer.

The purpose of a *direct debit* is the same as a standing order. It differs in that the beneficiary's (the person receiving payment) bank raises the entries receiving the debits through the clearing system or by computer entries. Written authority must be given by the payer to his bank enabling it to debit the account, and the beneficiary must agree to *indemnify* the paying bank against all claims which may arise before he can operate the system.

Both standing orders and direct debits are used to make regular payments from an account, such as mortgage, insurance, rates and subscription payments. As you will learn in the next chapter, the greater flexibility of the direct debit has resulted in an increase in its use and a corresponding decrease in the use of the standing order.

Different types of accounts

While you may provide a very similar range of services and facilities for the vast majority of your customers, they are far from being an homogeneous body. Different groups exist and different legal rules may apply to them. It follows that different banking considerations may also apply.

Minors

Contractual capacity

A minor is a person under 18 years of age and has only limited contractual capacity. This is the most important thing for you to remember. At common law a minor can only be bound by contracts for 'necessaries' (basically food, clothing, lodging and other things without which it would be unreasonable to expect the minor to live) and advantageous contracts of employment, for example, those containing an element of education and training such as articles of apprenticeship or other training schemes. Contracts involving continuing rights and duties, for example, a partnership agreement or a lease, may be *avoided* during minority or within a reasonable time afterwards. Contracts of loan made with a minor are *unenforceable* but after the age of 18 the minor can ratify the loan. (Until it was repealed by the Minors' Contracts Act 1987, the Infants Relief Act 1874 rendered a loan to a minor absolutely void.) A cheque, or other bill of exchange, is also unenforceable against a minor.

Minors' bank accounts

Up to the age of seven, a minor's credit account will be treated as a *trust* account (*see* below), the parent(s) being the trustee(s). After this age the minor is usually allowed to operate the account personally. If 'unusually' frequent or large withdrawals are made, a bank would probably inform the parent(s) although technically, at least, this constitutes a breach of the bank's duty of secrecy.

A minor should generally not be permitted to overdraw an account because the debt created is unenforceable against and can be repudiated by the minor. However, under the Minors' Contracts Act 1987, a guarantee of a loan to a minor is enforceable even though the loan itself is not. In addition, the court can order the minor to repay any money lent or hand over any property bought with it. Thus, whether to make a loan to a minor is more a question of policy and judgment than law since the bank can adequately protect its position.

The practice of allowing minors' cheque guarantee cards is clearly a risk because of the unenforceability of any overdraft created. Although, in theory, the bank could seek recovery of property bought with the money under the Minors' Contracts Act 1987, in practice the bank's only remedies are procedural, taking back the card or closing the account. However, the risk is calculated to be small and more than justified in terms of marketing and customer goodwill.

Married women

At law, a married woman is in exactly the same position and has exactly the same powers as a single woman or a man. Thus, special considerations will only apply if she is also a minor. As you will surely know, the Sex Discrimination Act 1975 makes it illegal to discriminate on grounds of sex alone.

When a married woman opens an account the usual procedure is followed, save that some banks still require the name of her husband and details of his employer and employment. Technically, at least, this is contrary to the 1975 Act but may still be required because it has been held that if a bank does not obtain this information it loses the protection of s.4 of the Cheques Act 1957 should a husband use his wife's account to obtain payment of cheques drawn by his employer and to which he is not entitled. The relevant knowledge should enable an efficient banker to spot and prevent the fraud. Most banks, however, prefer to avoid the possibility of offending new women customers and accept the (slight) risk involved in not asking for this information. Of course, it would be perfectly correct under the 1975 Act to ask every married person, of *either* sex, for such details when an account application is made but banks have in the main not adopted this approach on the grounds of cost and customer goodwill.

When a married woman deposits security for the account of another person, frequently her husband or a company with which her husband is closely associated, a bank may sometimes still require that she receives independent advice, from her own solicitor for example. This avoids any possibility of her subsequently seeking to set aside the charge on the grounds that she was unduly influenced by the third party/husband or, conceivably, by the bank. The usual 'free will' and attestation clauses, the latter usually signed by her own solicitor, in bank guarantees are particularly good examples of this. However, the bank's action must, since the Sex Discrimination Act 1975, be based upon her lack of understanding or appreciation of the transaction and not upon the grounds of sex or married status. It goes without saying that you should adopt exactly the same approach if there is doubt about a single woman's or a man's understanding or appreciation in a similar situation.

Joint accounts

A joint account is any account opened in the names of two or more persons, other than an account of a partnership, personal representatives or trustees. The typical joint account is that of a husband and wife.

The mandate, signed by all the parties to the account, must

include the following: a clear indication as to *who can make withdrawals* from the account, e.g. 'either to sign' or 'all to sign'; admission of *joint and several liability* for any overdraft (*see below*); and (usually) a statement that the survivor(s) can give a satisfactory discharge to the bank. This last term enables a credit account to be continued on the death of one of the parties, the bank only requiring the instructions of all the other parties to deal with the balance.

You should note four further points about joint accounts. First, the death, bankruptcy or mental incapacity of any one party *cancels the mandate*. Second, any one party can *countermand* payment of a cheque. Third, if an agent is to sign on the account, all the parties must sign the authority for the agent to do so. Fourth, if one party opens an account in the joint names of himself and another *without the latter's authority*, the authority of both parties is still necessary to authorise a release of funds.

Joint and joint and several liability

The distinction between these two forms of liability is important to a bank. If you study the consequences of the distinction carefully you will see why a bank will always insist upon joint and several liability being admitted on all joint accounts as well as on the accounts of partnerships, executors and trustees.

The main disadvantage of joint liability has now, in effect, become part of history. *Joint liability* gave the bank, or any other creditor, only one right of action. This could be exercised by suing one debtor, a combination of them or all of them. However, obtaining judgment prevented any further action against any remaining debtors, even if the judgment remained unsatisfied. This might mean, for example, that a wealthy joint debtor who was previously unknown but who could repay the debt received complete immunity from legal action. This rule was abolished by the Civil Liability (Contribution) Act 1978 and it is now possible, under joint liability, to sue a party who was omitted from the original legal action.

Joint and several liability has always given a right of action against the debtors severally (individually) and successively until the whole debt is recovered. This gives greater flexibility of action to the creditor.

An important facility for a banker is to be able to *set-off* the credit balance on one of a customer's accounts against the debit balance on another. Joint and several liability gives a *right of set-off* between private accounts in credit and an overdrawn joint account when the mandate on the joint account is determined or as otherwise agreed. No such right of set-off exists where joint liability is admitted.

Another important disadvantage of joint liability is that the death of one joint account holder completely releases the estate from liability for debts on the account; this is not so with joint and several liability.

Finally, joint and several liability enables a bank to claim for money owing on the joint account against the estate of a bankrupt joint account holder while retaining its rights against the solvent parties. This is probably not so where only joint liability is admitted.

You will recall that earlier in this chapter we explained and stressed the importance of the *Rule in Clayton's Case* (1816). While joint and several liability strengthens a banker's position where a joint-account holder dies or becomes bankrupt, in both cases the joint account must be *stopped* and a new account opened (to prevent the *Rule* operating), thereby preserving the liability of the deceased or bankrupt joint-account holder for any debit balance. In fact, the mandate may expressly exclude the operation of the *Rule*, in which case such action is not technically necessary.

Personal representatives

When somebody dies, the persons appointed to wind up and distribute the estate are called personal representatives. If appointed by a will they are known as *executors*; if appointed by the court they are known as *administrators*, for example, where the deceased dies intestate (without leaving a will).

Before an executor can deal with the deceased's account and securities his appointment and authority must be confirmed by *probate.* This is a process where the will is exhibited and proved in court, the original being deposited in the court registry and a copy, called the *probate copy*, made out under the court's seal and delivered to the executor, together with a certificate of its having been proved. *Letters of administration* is the official document from the court empowering the administrator to administer the deceased's estate.

The deceased's account

The probate certificate or letters of administration must be presented to the bank and recorded before the balance on any credit account can be withdrawn. The same applies to securities and safe custody items deposited by the deceased. The personal representatives will be informed of the liability on any account, the account having been stopped on notice of the death. If securities are held for the overdraft, the personal representatives must decide whether to pay off the amount and thereby obtain the release of the securities, or have them sold to realise and pay off the amount owed.

Any credits received after the death can be credited to the account or held in suspense until the personal representatives obtain authority to act, provided that you do not have notice that the payments have ceased to be due on the death. This would be the position, for example, in relation to an annuity payable during life.

The personal representative's account

An *executor's account* can be opened immediately on the death of the testator (the person making the will). An *administrator's account* is not usually opened until letters of administration are produced. In either case, references should be sought if the individuals are unknown to the bank.

The *mandate* for the account will normally provide that any one representative can sign for and bind all in connection with estate affairs and that all admit *joint and several liability*. The latter gives a right to set-off credit balances in the personal representative's personal accounts against a debit balance in the executor's/administrator's account. Any one representative can countermand a cheque drawn on the personal representative's account.

Executors/trustees

When the estate is wound up, an executor automatically becomes a trustee in relation to any property remaining which the will directs must be held in trust for beneficiaries. An administrator may be placed in the same position by the court. When this position is reached, the account must be operated as a trust account (*see below*).

Trustees

A trust is basically an arrangement whereby legal title to property is given by one person to another (trustee), with the latter promising to use the property for the benefit of a third person (the beneficiary).

A trust account is not necessarily opened as such, in fact it is any account which to the bank's direct or indirect knowledge is being operated by trustees, or persons acting in some other fiduciary capacity. Sometimes the account may be opened as 'Trustee of . . .' in which case the bank has direct notice that it is a trust account, and sometimes as, say, 'A.N. Other, Squash Club Account', in which case the bank has indirect notice. Alternatively the trust account may arise by operation of law, for example where personal representatives become trustees if a trust arises out of the deceased's estate (*see above*).

To open a trust account a mandate signed by all the trustees must be obtained. Since trustees cannot normally delegate their authority among themselves, *all* trustees are required to sign on an account unless the trust instrument or law permits delegation. The Trustee Act 1925, as amended by the Powers of Attorney Act 1971, for example, allows a trustee to delegate his or her duties by power of attorney for a period of up to one year.

A very strict duty of good faith is imposed on trustees and if they, even innocently, misapply trust property they commit a breach of trust for which they are liable to the beneficiary. What is more, the law also allows an action against a bank that intentionally or, more likely, negligently facilitates any such breach. Whether or not a bank is liable when a breach of trust occurs is always a question of fact in the circumstances. Mere suspicion, or an accusation by a beneficiary, of trust funds being misapplied would not of itself justify dishonouring a trust cheque but allowing a trustee to draw a cheque on the trust account to reduce a personal overdraft, particularly if the bank had been pressing for repayment, would almost certainly mean that the bank had knowledge of the breach of trust and intentionally or negligently facilitated it.

Clubs and societies

The first point for you to remember here is that unincorporated clubs and societies have no legal existence separate from their members and therefore cannot be sued in their own name. Furthermore, members are not liable for borrowing on the association's behalf by its officers unless they have individually assented to it although appointed officers are probably liable for borrowing authorised by the management committee. You can see, therefore, that such account holders present, at least in theory, rather more problems than you might imagine.

The mandate must be in accordance with the rules and constitution of the association, a copy of which may be lodged with the bank, and confirm that at a meeting of the association it was resolved to open the account and to authorise the persons named to operate the account. The chairman and secretary should certify the mandate.

Partnerships

Introduction
'Partnership is the relation which subsists between persons carrying on a business in common with a view of profit': Partnership Act 1890, s.1. A full discussion of partnership law is outside the scope of this book but we can usefully add a few important points relevant to banking to what you will probably have already learnt about partnerships in your other studies.

Partners as agents
Agency is the foundation of partnership law relating to a firm's dealings with outsiders. Each *general partner* has actual authority and implied or usual authority (authority as it appears to others) to bind his fellow partners when acting in the usual course of the firm's business, unless the outsider either knew that the partner had no authority in the matter, or knew or believed that he was not a partner. Thus, an outsider dealing with a general partner is not affected by any secret limitation on his authority. (This is a basic principle of agency.)

For example, in *Mercantile Credit Ltd* v. *Garrod* (1962), A and B had entered into partnership to let garages and to repair motor cars. The partnership deed expressly excluded the buying and selling of cars. A, without B's knowledge, purported to sell a car, to which he had no title, to the plaintiff. The proceeds were paid into the partnership bank account. It was held that B was accountable for the proceeds since the buying and selling of cars *appeared* to be within the firm's normal course of business. The limitation in the partnership deed was no defence.

A partner in any type of partnership has implied authority to bind the firm by:

(a) buying and selling goods in the course of the firm's business;

(b) receiving payment of debts due to the firm, and giving receipts for such payment;

(c) engaging employees for the firm; and

(d) drawing cheques.

In a *trading partnership* (one whose business consists mainly of buying and selling) a partner's implied authority also includes:

(f) borrowing money on the firm's credit;

(g) pledging the firm's goods or giving an equitable mortgage over the firm's premises by deposit of title deeds or land certificate to secure such borrowing; and

(h) signing bills of exchange on the firm's behalf.

Liability of partners

For debts and other obligations, the liability of the partners is *joint*; for torts authorised by the firm or committed in the ordinary course of the firm's business liability is *joint and several*.

You have already seen the differences between joint and joint and several liability and the importance of the Civil Liability (Contribution) Act 1978 on them. Two points, however, deserve to be mentioned regarding partnerships. First, the Rules of the Supreme Court largely avoided possible complications with joint liability by allowing an action to be brought against a partnership in the firm's name (the business name of the partnership). In this case, judgment operated against the firm and therefore each partner individually. Second, it has always been standard banking practice to insist on joint and several liability being accepted by each partner in dealings between a bank and a partnership.

The partnership account

Rarely, if ever, will a bank have to verify the existence of the firm but it must ensure that the names of all the partners are known. Under the Business Names Act 1985, the names of persons using a business name must be legibly stated on all business letters and written demands for payment. These must give an address where court documents can be served and accepted. In addition, a notice giving the names and addresses of the persons or partners using the business name must be displayed prominently in any place where business is carried on and to which customers have access.

The importance of *verifying the names* of all the partners lies, once again, in the statutory protection of s.4 of the Cheques Act 1957. We can illustrate this with an example. In *Smith and Baldwin* v. *Barclays Bank Ltd.* (1944), the defendant bank collected cheques payable to a firm for the private account of its customer after he had produced a certificate of registration (under the Registration of Business Names Act 1916—now no longer in force) showing him to be its registered proprietor. The customer, however, was a partner in the firm and had been able to obtain the certificate because the partners collectively had not registered the firm name. On these facts, the bank was held not to have collected the cheques negligently; it was entitled to rely on the certificate produced by its dishonest customer. Clearly, the case is no longer of direct relevance but presumably, and by analogy, a bank which relies on the statutory requirements under the Business Names Act 1985 would be considered to have acted without negligence unless there are circumstances which a reasonable bank (not a detective) would consider warranted further investigation.

References should be taken to ensure the firm's suitability as a customer, although this requirement may be waived where one or more of the partners is already known to the bank. The account must be operated in the names of *all* the partners and the mandate, showing how and by whom the account is to be operated, must be signed by all the partners. However, the mandate may be cancelled by any one partner and any one partner can countermand payment of a cheque, irrespective of whether or not he signed it.

You have seen above that the partners will be required to

admit joint and several liability in the mandate. There are three specific reasons for this:

(a) a credit balance on a partner's private account may be set-off against a debit balance on the firm account;

(b) the bank will rank equally with separate creditors should a partner die or become bankrupt (normally, separate estate pays separate creditors and joint estate joint creditors, any balance remaining on one going to augment the other);

(c) should the partnership itself become bankrupt, the bank has a double right of proof: it may prove against both the joint estate of the firm and the separate estate of each partner.

If a partner *retires* or dies and the firm continues in business, new mandate forms must be signed by the remaining partners and any incoming partner. New security forms must also be completed unless those held remain effective despite changes in the constitution of the firm. If the firm's account is in *credit*, it may be continued unbroken, although cheques drawn by the retiring partner should be confirmed by the remaining partners. A retiring partner or a deceased partner's estate remains liable for the firm's *debts* but the account must be broken, and further entries passed through a new account, in order to preserve his liability and the bank's rights over any security deposited by him to secure the account. This procedure is dictated by the *Rule in Clayton's Case* (1816), which we have already explained. If a firm is dissolved on a partner's *death*, the surviving partner(s) may continue the account in order to wind up the firm's business. Cheques previously drawn by the deceased partner and presented after his death should be confirmed by the surviving members.

Limited companies

Introduction

As with partnerships, a thorough discussion of the legal framework relating to companies is outside the scope of this book. Most likely, however, you will have covered, or will cover, companies as organisations in your other studies. Bear this in mind when you read this section. Here we will just remind you of a few particularly important points and then concentrate on limited companies from the banker–customer perspective.

A company can be defined as an organisation of individuals who contribute finance to a common stock which is to be used for business activities and who share the profit or loss arising. The common stock is the company's financial capital and the contributors of it are its members, the shareholders. A *limited company* is one where the liability of its members to contribute towards the payment of its debts is limited to either their investment in the company, that is, a company limited by shares, or to the amount that they have undertaken to contribute should the company be wound up through insolvency, that is, a company limited by guarantee. Most limited companies are limited by shares and companies limited by guarantee are usually non-profitmaking organisations—for example, BTEC. Under the Companies Act 1985, a newly registered *public* company must be limited by shares.

A company is a *corporation*, in other words, an artificial legal person recognised by the law as having an existence, rights and duties quite separate and distinct from the individuals who are its members. This concept is fundamental to the relationship between a bank and its company customers, as it is to the framework of company law generally.

The vast majority of companies are incorporated by registering certain documents with the Registrar of Companies in accordance with the Companies Acts. These documents are:

(a) the memorandum of association;

(b) the articles of association;

(c) a statement of the names of the intended first director(s) and the first secretary, together with their written consents to act as such, and the intended address of the company's registered office;

(d) a statutory declaration of compliance with the Companies Act 1985 regarding registration; and

(e) a statement of the company's capital, unless it is to have no share capital.

Of these documents, the memorandum of association and the articles of association are the most important. The *memorandum of association* governs the external activities of the company, while the *articles of association* regulate its internal administration, the relationship between the company and its members and the relationship among the members themselves.

Of particular importance is the *objects clause* in the memorandum of association. This states the purposes for which the company was formed. The clause is subject to the *ultra vires* rule which provides that any transaction entered into by a registered company which is not authorised by its object clause, or which is not reasonably incidental to its objects, is *ultra vires* (beyond the powers of) the company and void.

In addition to the objects of the company, the memorandum will normally list a number of powers which are reasonably incidental to its objects. Such powers would be implied if they were not listed, for example, the power to acquire similar businesses and the power to issue bills of exchange. The power to borrow money for the purposes of the business is implied in the case of a trading company but it must be expressly given to a non-trading company. Borrowing money is *not* an independent activity, even if the memorandum states that it is an independent object of the company. Thus, a company's borrowing must only be for the purposes consistent with its objects clause. An interesting example of this occurred in *Introductions Ltd.* v. *National Provincial Bank Ltd.* (1970), where the company's main object was to provide entertainment and services for overseas visitors, but the objects clause also gave the company power to raise money as it saw fit. It provided that each of its objects was an independent object. The company changed to the sole activity of pig-breeding and the bank, who had been given a copy of the memorandum of association, lent money for this purpose and took debentures as security. On the company's liquidation both the loan and the debentures were held to be void.

The *ultra vires* rule is subject to s.35 of the Companies Act 1985 which provides that persons dealing with a company can enforce an *ultra vires* contract against it provided (a) they dealt with the company in good faith, and (b) that the transaction was sanctioned by the directors. Under the section third parties may assume that the powers of the directors to bind the company are free of any limitation under the memorandum or articles, they have no obligation to make enquiries, and they are presumed to have acted in good faith unless the contrary is proved. It follows that s.35 does not protect persons dealing with the company who have actual knowledge of its objects. They are not considered to have acted in good faith unless they can show that they honestly and reasonably failed to appreciate that the transaction was *ultra vires* the company.

How does this affect a bank? Since a bank will receive, or at least inspect, a copy of the memorandum of association and articles of association before opening an account for a company, it is highly improbable that it could ever rely on s.35 in such a situation. If the facts of *Introductions Ltd.* v. *National Provincial Bank* (1970), were to recur today, s.35 would probably protect, say, the company's suppliers but almost certainly not its bank. (At the time of writing plans exist to abolish the *ultra vires* rule. If this is done, s.35 will become redundant. The problems of *ultra vires* borrowing by companies, which we discuss in Chapter 13, will also be removed.)

Company bank accounts

A company can pursue its business activities in much the same way as a sole trader or partnership and this includes operating a bank account. Nevertheless, as a consequence of a company's corporate status and the very comprehensive legal framework regulating the operation of companies, special care must be taken before opening a company bank account. Before doing so, a bank must ensure that:

(a) the company has been properly incorporated, for which sight of the certificate of incorporation is required;

(b) in the case of a public company, that a trading certificate has been received from the Registrar;

(c) it obtains or inspects a copy of the company's memorandum and articles of association and makes sure that they are up to date, if need be by making a search at Companies House;

(d) it receives a certified copy of the resolution appointing the first directors, if they are not named in the articles (and afterwards that it is notified when a director retires or a new director joins the board); and

(e) the bank's mandate form is signed by the chairman and secretary of the company after the resolutions that they contain have been passed by a meeting of the board of directors.

The account must be conducted in strict accordance with the memorandum and articles of association, and you should check that the company's activities in general are within its stated objects because you cannot, as you have seen earlier, rely on the protection of s.35 of the Companies Act 1985. The mandate must also be strictly adhered to; for example, each cheque must bear the required signatures.

A person signing, accepting or indorsing a cheque or other bill of exchange on behalf of a company must clearly indicate that he signs as agent of the company. He can do this by using words such as 'per pro', or 'for and on behalf of', followed by the full name of the company, his signature and his capacity within the company, for example, director or secretary. If he does not make his representative capacity quite clear, he incurs personal liability on the bill. Furthermore, failure to state the company's name accurately and in full means that the person signing the bill incurs personal liability if the bill is not paid by the company: Companies Act 1985, s.349. This provision is applied strictly. In *British Airways Board* v. *Parish* (1979), omission of the word 'Ltd.' was held to be a breach of s.349 and sufficient to render the person who had signed a cheque personally liable on it. Another example: in *Maxform S.p.A.* v. *Mariani and Goodville Ltd.* (1979), Goodville Ltd. traded under its business name of 'Italdesign' and its sole director accepted bills drawn on the company in that name. Three bills were dishonoured by the company when they were presented for payment. The court held that the director was personally liable on them, use of the business name (even though it was registered in the now defunct Registry of Business Names) was insufficient; the director should have accepted in the form in which the company's cheques were signed—'Goodville Ltd. trading as Italdesign'. Such decisions are clearly to a bank's advantage.

In operating a company's account you must always be aware of the possibility that one or more of the directors could be using the account for his own purposes. This is most likely to occur, perhaps innocently through ignorance of a director's duties and the requirements of company legislation, in the case of small companies and 'one-man' companies in particular. If such misuse occurs and a reasonably aware businessman would have realised that it was happening, a bank will be liable to the company for the loss incurred.

The Banking Ombudsman

Disputes will invariably arise between banks and their customers. When they do it is normally in the interests of both sides to settle them amicably between themselves. For example, a missing credit transfer can usually be found and an apology is usually sufficient. If a dispute cannot be resolved in this way, then resort to legal action has always been possible. However, this takes time, costs money and can cause bad publicity and distress. Indeed, in relation to the amounts involved and the increasing competitiveness of the financial marketplace, it is often commercially far better for a bank to stand a small loss than fight—*if* the customer has the resources and determination to pursue the claim.

Nevertheless, the vast numbers of cheques and automated payments processed each day and the increasing use of ATMs and electronic funds transfer creates ever greater opportunity for fraud and greater risk of error. Mistakes will happen and disputes will ensue. Against this background the Banking Ombudsman was set up in January 1986 to resolve disputes between banks and customers and investigate customer complaints.

The Banking Ombudsman is funded by the major banks—the services are free—but is independent of them, being responsible to an independent council. Personal customers, i.e. individuals, sole traders, partnerships, clubs, trade unions and charities ('individuals' as defined by the Consumer Credit Act 1974) may take a dispute to the Ombudsman but corporate customers, e.g. companies, cannot. However, a referral is very much the last resort. Customers must first try to resolve the dispute at branch level, asking the branch staff to refer it to a higher level if they are still dissatisfied. Only after the bank's own complaints procedures have been exhausted can the Banking Ombudsman be involved.

Only alleged *mistakes* involving less than £50 000 can be dealt with. Complaints involving the commercial judgment of the bank, e.g. the rejection of a loan application, or involving the use of its discretion under a will or a trust, are outside the terms of reference, as are the activities of finance house, travel agent and estate agent subsidiaries, and banking services provided abroad. The Ombudsman can order a bank to rectify a mistake and can make an award to a maximum of £50 000. Banks participating in the scheme are bound to abide by decisions and awards of the Ombudsman but customers are not, they can still take the dispute to court. The Office of Fair Trading recommended in 1987 that all banks offering retail services should become part of the scheme and that the claims limit should be set higher.

So far, the most common complaints are disputed withdrawals from ATMs, closely followed by 'irregular conduct' of an account, for example, not supplying statements or not paying standing orders, and disputes about bank charges.

Both banks and customers stand to gain from the existence of the Banking Ombudsman. The office helps to maintain and improve public confidence in banks' operations while to customers the office offers a way to effectively pursue complaints without having to take on the might of wealthy and powerful organisations in court.

Summary

1 A bank is basically a business organisation that accepts money and collects cheques for its customers, honours their cheques and keeps current accounts.
2 A customer is a person who has entered into a contract with a bank for the opening of an account in his or her name.
3 The banker–customer relationship is essentially a debtor–creditor contractual relationship.
4 Other rules clarify the relationship, that is, those of agency, bailment, banking practice, and, in some cases, particular requirements of good faith.
5 Although the banker–customer contract is usually made very informally, implied into it are a number of well established rights and duties.
6 When an account is opened, certain formalities must be observed, in particular, references should be taken and checked. An agent's operation of an account requires particular care.
7 A bank's authority to pay its customer's cheques can be terminated in one of six ways, most commonly by the customer countermanding payment, that is stopping a cheque.

8 A bank is usually able to recover an incorrect *credit* to an account but is always obliged to refund an incorrect *debit*.

9 Different legal rules apply to different types of accounts—banking practice must reflect these. For example, a minor is not liable for any overdraft and joint account holders must always accept joint and several liability, as do partners on a firm account.

10 A company's bank accounts must be operated in strict accordance with its memorandum and articles of association and the mandates strictly adhered to.

11 The Banking Ombudsman exists to investigate complaints against banks when the banks' own complaints procedures have been exhausted.

Self-asssessment questions

1 Define the following terms: (a) banker; (b) customer.

2 List the duties of a bank.

3 What are the usual formalities involved in opening an account?

4 Distinguish between joint and joint and several liability.

5 Define a trustee.

6 What is meant by corporate status?

7 True or false?

(a) A course of dealings is essential before the banker–customer relationship can arise.

(b) A fiduciary relationship exists between a bank and its customer.

(c) A bank's duty of secrecy is absolute.

(d) A cheque can only be countermanded by its drawer.

(e) Notice of a bankruptcy petition against a customer prevents the payment of third party cheques.

(f) A company can refer a dispute with its bank to the Banking Ombudsman.

(g) Repayment of an overdraft can never be enforced against a minor.

(h) Probate is a necessary legal process when a person dies intestate.

(i) A partnership can only arise when two or more persons are in business together in order to make a profit.

8 Explain why references may be taken before opening an account.

9 What is the difference between a standing order and a direct debit.

10 Explain the *Rule in Clayton's Case* (1816), and its importance to a banker.

Assignments

1 The account of Tom Smith, a 19-year-old student possessed of little financial understanding, was accidentally overcredited by £20. He realised that he had more money than he thought on receiving his bank statement but put this down to his own bad record-keeping. As a result he went out and bought two LPs he had been wanting to buy for some time.

You receive the following memo from your manager.

To: Student
From: Manager

Re: A/c 1234567 Tom Smith

We've overcredited the above account—Miss Jones has all the details—a little exercise for you as part of your training.

Please send me a memo explaining whether we are entitled to recover the money overcredited and what other factors, if any, we might take into account before we seek to do so. In any case, attach a suitable draft letter for my signature to T. Smith requesting the return of the £20.

2 A director of the St John's Bus Co., a well-established coach operator, approaches your deputy manager for a loan to purchase two articulated lorries, offering a mortgage on its premises as security. Resolutions of the full board authorising the purchase and the application for the loan are sent. The proposition appears to be financially sound.

The deputy manager is due to meet the directors next week and he has asked you to prepare some notes for his use explaining whether or not the loan should be granted and supporting your conclusion by references to relevant legal rules.

7 Remittance of funds

Chapter objectives

After studying this chapter you should be able to:
- state the different methods for making inland payments and explain their workings and attributes;
- explain the operation of the bank clearing systems;
- outline the methods of making international payments.

Introduction

In this chapter we are going to examine the various methods available through the banks for the remittance of funds from one person to another. Together with the taking of deposits and the granting of loans, money transmission services form part of the 'trinity' of traditional bank services. The mundane function of handling customers' payments is often the least regarded, even by bank staff, and it is overshadowed in the public consciousness by the many ancillary services which have proliferated in recent years. A true measure of the continued importance of this area of activity to the banks is perhaps to be found in the effort which they devote to it. It has been calculated that, even today, money transmission and related activities absorb some two-thirds of the clerical efforts of the staffs of the UK clearing banks, despite the impact of computerisation and automation!

The greatest force for change in the commercial world is the rapid, almost explosive, growth in processing information by computer, often referred to as the 'information technology' revolution. The transfer of funds from remitter to beneficiary (to use the technical term) is, in the final analysis, no more than the processing of a piece of information, whether that piece of information is represented by a £5 note, by a cheque drawn on a bank account, by an international money transfer or by any of the other methods of payment which are available. It is not surprising, therefore, that in recent times money transmission services have been subject to enormous changes resulting from the impact of modern technology. This process is certain to continue for some time to come.

Cheques

Using cheques

The cheque is the single most important item in the banks' repertoire of methods for transferring funds. The increasing acceptability and use of cheques since the middle of the eighteenth century has been an important factor in the growth of the commercial banks.

What is a cheque?

We shall be looking in detail at the legal aspects of cheques in Chapter 8; for the moment it is sufficient to note that a cheque is a specialised form of a bill of exchange which is drawn on a banker and is payable on demand. From the practical viewpoint, it is a payment instruction addressed by a customer to his bank, telling the bank to pay a specified sum of money to the named payee or order. The words 'or order' mean that the payee may indorse the cheque and thereby authorise the bank to pay the funds to another person.

Standard cheque forms

A cheque may be drawn up by a customer on any blank piece of paper or, indeed, on any other object which he may wish to use. For the convenience of both the customer and of the bank, however, customers are provided with standard printed cheques to use. A typical example is shown in Fig. 7.1.

The *bank and branch* on which the cheque is drawn is shown at the top of the cheque. Each branch of the UK clearing banks is allocated a unique six-digit sorting code number which is shown in the top right-hand corner of the cheque. As we shall see, this is used to simplify the clearing process if the cheque is collected for the payee by another bank.

The cheque should be *dated* by the customer when it is issued and, as we have seen, a cheque will usually be paid on demand. Sometimes customers 'post-date' cheques by entering a date

Fig. 7.1 A typical cheque

which is some time in the future and in such cases the bank must not pay the cheque until that date arrives. We can perhaps add here that in *R* v. *Gilmartin* (1983), the Court of Appeal held that by giving a post-dated cheque (indeed any cheque) in payment for goods the drawer implies that at that time the state of his affairs is such that in the ordinary course of business the cheque will be paid when presented for payment on or after the date specified. If otherwise the offence of dishonestly obtaining property by deception under s.15 of the Theft Act 1968 is committed. Hence, over-optimism in customers should be discouraged!

The cheque must, of course, be *signed by the customer* before it can become valid. The signature space is nowadays usually personalised with the name of the customer. The details shown will correspond with the account number shown in the bottom line of magnetic characters. This and other information is printed in special *magnetic ink* and can be machine read. The details which are recorded in this line are, from left to right: *cheque number*, cheques are issued in books, usually containing 30 cheques, each cheque being numbered consecutively, *sorting code number*, repeating the number shown at top right, and finally *customer's account number*. The right-hand end of the line is left blank to allow the bank handling the cheque to encode it with the amount for which it is drawn. Magnetic characters are used to enable the relevant accounting information to be captured electronically by the paying bank, thereby avoiding the need for each cheque to be 'posted' manually to the appropriate account.

Obtaining payment of a cheque
When he has accepted a cheque in settlement of a debt due to him, what can the payee do with it? If the payee presents the cheque personally to the bank on which it is drawn, he may be able to *obtain cash* for it, provided that the drawer has sufficient funds in his account. Only 'open' cheques may be cashed in this way, and the drawer may prevent this by 'crossing' the cheque. A crossed cheque is one which has two parallel lines drawn across its face. Unless a customer specifically asks for uncrossed cheques, banks issue cheques which have a preprinted crossing. A crossed cheque can be paid by the bank on which it is drawn only for the credit of an account either at the same branch or at another branch of a bank. Crossing a cheque provides a safeguard against the misuse of lost or stolen cheques by making it possible to trace the person who receives the payment.

If the cheque is crossed or if the payee does not wish to cash it, the payee may take it to his own bank for *credit to his account*. It is possible that his own account may be maintained at the same branch as the account on which the cheque is drawn. Normally, however, the two accounts will be at different branches and the payee's bank will therefore have to collect the proceeds of the cheque on his behalf. To do this, the cheque must be presented to the drawer's bank, usually via the clearing system.

If the payee has no bank account, he may pass the cheque on to a third party, either in settlement of a debt or simply to obtain payment through the third party's bank account. As we have already said, before a cheque can be *negotiated* or *transferred to a third party*, the payee must indorse it by signing it on the back. This is his authority for the funds to be paid to someone other than himself.

The clearing system

In order to collect payment of cheques drawn on other branches, the banks need a method of remitting these items to one another. While cheques were uncommon it was possible to do this directly between the branches concerned but, as the usage of cheques increased, this system soon became inadequate. The Bankers' Clearing House in London was established in 1833 to facilitate the central daily exchange of cheques between banks and to provide a mechanism for daily settlement. At first, the Clearing House dealt only with the work of the private bankers but the scale of its operations increased rapidly in the late 19th century as the joint stock banks built up their branch networks.

As well as clearing their own cheques through the system, the modern day clearing banks also provide agency arrangements for the clearing of cheques drawn on numerous other banks which do not have direct access to the Clearing House.

The general clearing

The vast majority of cheques to be handled are processed through the general clearing. The scale of the operation can be judged by the fact that in 1987 the number of cheques passed through the general clearing in a year was 1962 million with a total value of approximately £766 000 million. The path of a single cheque through the system is shown in Fig. 7.2; look carefully at this now and refer to it as you read the text below.

Day one
At the end of each business day, branch banks sort into bank order all the cheques drawn on other banks which have been paid in by their customers. Once sorted, the cheques are stamped with the details of the bank and branch at which they were paid in. The stamp used is called a crossing stamp and the details are required in case of a future query or if the cheque has to be returned unpaid for any reason. Each cheque is then encoded on the bottom line with the amount in magnetic ink.

All of the cheques drawn on the branches of each of the other banks are then bundled together, each bundle being accompanied by a list giving the total value, as well as the amount of each individual cheque. A similar bundle is produced of all the

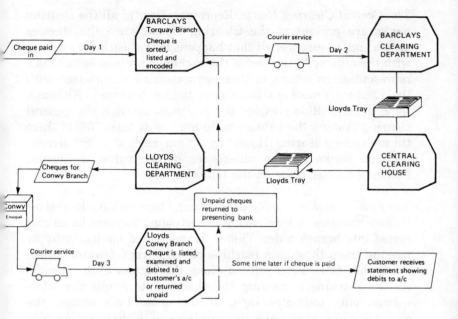

Fig. 7.2 Path of a cheque through the clearing system

cheques drawn on the other branches of the remitting bank. The cheques are then sent off to the remitting bank's clearing department in London to arrive the next morning. To ensure prompt delivery, the banks use a courier service.

Day two

The remitting bank's clearing department. The clearing department of each bank will receive daily from every branch a parcel containing bundles of cheques drawn on each of the other clearing banks and on its own branches. The total of each bundle is checked and the bundles are amalgamated, all the cheques drawn on any one bank being placed together on a trolley ready for despatch to the Central Clearing House. Each trolley is accompanied by the listing slips for all the bundles and a summary of them giving the total value of the cheques on the trolley. Cheques drawn on the remitting bank's own branches are retained at the clearing department to be forwarded to the branches on which they are drawn.

The Central Clearing House. Representatives of all the clearing banks are present at the Clearing House when the cheques arrive and, in essence, all that happens is that each does a swap with the others. At the end of the exchange process, each bank's representatives return to their own clearing department with the cheques drawn on their own bank's branches. Although some eight million cheques per day pass through the general clearing system, the banks aim to process at least 75% of them through the Clearing House by 11 am each day. Settlement between banks for the differences in the value of cheques exchanged takes place on the following day.

The paying bank's clearing department. Once each bank receives its own cheques at its clearing department, they are listed and sorted into branch order. This is accomplished mechanically by passing them through a machine called a 'reader/sorter' which scans the information printed along the bottom of the cheque. As the machine is reading the cheques, it records the information onto computer tape, at the same time sorting the cheques into branch order in accordance with their sorting code numbers. Each machine has the capacity to process 2000 cheques per minute.

The computer tape is then transferred to a printer which prints the information onto a paper printout. A separate printout is produced for each branch, giving details of cheque number, account number and amount of each cheque addressed to that particular branch. At the same time, the information is input into the bank's computerised accounting system. The cheques drawn on each branch are then bundled up together with the relevant printout, and sent off to the branch to arrive in time for the start of business on the next day.

Day three

After the cheques arrive at the branch they are checked against the computer listing. The bank's computer system will automatically charge the amount of each cheque to the appropriate customer's account at the end of the day, using the information extracted by the 'reader/sorter' machines the day before. If the branch wishes to return the cheque unpaid, the computer system must be advised not to debit that particular cheque to the customer's account. This is accomplished via the branch's computer terminal and the cheque itself is returned direct to the remitting branch as shown on the stamped crossing. A few cheques which cannot be read by the 'reader/sorter', for whatever reason, have to be processed through the system manually.

Unpaid cheques

A bank has a duty to honour its customers' cheques if at all possible, but if a cheque cannot be paid it should be sent back to the presenting bank at the end of the day on which it is received. There are several factors which the branch must consider when deciding whether to honour a particular cheque. We covered these generally in Chapter 6, and we will be looking at them again more fully in Chapter 16, so we need only mention here those which have more specific relevance to general clearing.

First and foremost the customer must have *sufficient funds* in his account to meet the cheque, unless the branch is prepared to extend overdraft facilities to him. The clearing banks have agreed that if a cheque which should have been returned for lack of funds is inadvertently paid, it may be returned on the day after receipt, provided that the presenting branch is informed of the action before 12 noon. This provision may not be used for cheques which should have been returned for any other reason. Second, the cheque must be complete and regular on the face of it, that is, *technically correct*, so far as the bank can tell. In other words, it must be signed by the customer in accordance with any mandate held, the amount shown in words must be the same as the amount shown in figures, it must not be post-dated and so on. Third, at any time before payment is made by the bank, a customer can *countermand* a particular cheque and a careful record is kept of such instructions.

When a cheque is returned unpaid for *technical reasons*, the drawee bank will mark on it a message for the presenting bank and its customer, indicating the reason for the return of the item. The standard messages used include 'drawer deceased', 'words and figures differ' and 'payment countermanded by order of drawer'.

Where a cheque is returned for *lack of funds*, it will usually be marked 'refer to drawer'. This avoids direct disclosure by the bank of the information that the customer is issuing cheques which cannot be met. The beneficiary of the cheque is, in effect, told to ask the drawer why the bank has returned the cheque, although he will normally draw his own conclusion from this phrase. If the bank believes that in the near future funds may be credited to the account to cover the cheque, it may extend the answer given to read: 'refer to drawer, please represent', which tells the collecting bank that the cheque may be passed through the clearing system again. This effectively allows the drawer a further three days to come up with the funds but it does not in any way *guarantee* that the cheque will be paid on representation. Banks will not normally allow a cheque to be represented more than twice. If a cheque cannot be paid at that point, the words 'please represent' will be deleted from the message on the cheque and the payee will be left to take matters up with the drawer.

Claims for unpaids. When a cheque is presented through the clearing system, the branch on which it is drawn is debited with the amount for which it is made out. If the cheque is returned unpaid, this amount cannot be applied to the customer's account and must therefore be reclaimed from the presenting bank. This is accomplished by completing a 'Claim for unpaid' form addressed to the presenting bank. Most of the clearing banks use this form as a basis to debit the presenting bank through the computerised 'automated debit clearing' which we shall be examining in greater detail later when we look at the facilities available from BACS (Bankers' Automated Clearing Services).

Direct presentation of cheques

The general clearing system is very efficient and effective. It does, however, suffer from the defect that it provides no positive indication that a particular cheque has been paid. It is normally assumed that a cheque has been paid if it is not received back unpaid on the third day after it was paid in (this would be day four of the clearing cycle), although this does not make allowance for any postal delays. There are times when this assumption is not adequate. For instance, the payee may wish to establish for certain that a cheque has been paid before releasing goods to the drawer, or the payee's bank may not be prepared to allow him to draw against cheques paid in until they have been 'cleared'. An added complication is the time delay of three days for the general clearing process. This may not always be acceptable to the parties concerned.

To overcome these difficulties, a small number of cheques are *directly presented*. The collecting bank will forward the cheque direct to the drawer's bank with a covering letter asking for the proceeds of the cheque, if paid, to be remitted back by credit transfer. This is usually followed up by a telephone call the next day, to establish the fate of the cheque, thereby discovering within the space of a day whether it has been paid. Where cheques are specially presented in this way at the customer's request, a fee is usually charged, to which the costs of postage and telephone calls will be added.

The town clearing

As well as the *general clearing*, the Clearing House also deals with the *town clearing* which processes cheques for large amounts (£10 000 and over) cleared between branches within the City of London. The town clearing is intended to serve the needs of the institutions which make up the London money markets and of large companies such as those concerned with insurance and shipping. These institutions deal in very large amounts and must have a speedy system for clearance. There is an understanding that any cheque dealt with through the town clearing will be cleared the same day. If a cheque is unpaid, it will be received back by the presenting bank on the same day.

Same-day settlement
Approximately 90 branches of 12 banks participate in the town clearing, all of them within walking distance of the Clearing House. These branches close for business at 3.00 pm each day, half an hour earlier than other branch banks, and a customer who wishes to obtain same-day settlement of a town clearing cheque must pay it in before this time. Messengers take each branch's remittances to the Clearing House, where the latest time for cheques to be accepted is 3.45 pm. After this time, the cheques are taken to the drawee branches and any which are to be returned unpaid are sent back to the presenting bank via the Clearing House, where they must be received before 4.30 pm.

The advantage of using the town clearing is that the beneficiary will be allowed to draw against the funds on the following day. Perhaps more importantly, his bank will treat the funds as being cleared for interest purposes immediately and the beneficiary will not lose any interest on them. This contrasts markedly with the general clearing where, in making the interest calculation, the credit will be deferred for three working days, representing the period during which the bank is waiting for the funds to come into its hands. The saving on interest amounts to millions of pounds each day and, as well as the financial institutions, many larger commercial concerns take advantage of the system by maintaining their accounts with town clearing branches.

Volume of town clearings

Comparatively few branches participate in the town clearing and the vast majority (in number) of cheques processed each day pass through the general clearing. In terms of value, however, the position is completely reversed. Table 7.1 shows the comparison between the volumes of cheques passing through the two clearing systems. You will see that the average value of each cheque passing through the town clearing exceeds £2 million!

Table 7.1 Cheques passing through the clearings (12 months to 3 December 1986)

	Number of items (million)	Total value (£000 million)
General clearing	1.962	766
Town clearing	4	8.173

(*Source: Banking Information Service*)

Other clearing services

The credit clearing

The last 30 years have seen the development of a credit clearing system. This is a counterpart to the cheque clearing system and enables credits to be remitted to accounts at any of the branches of the clearing banks. A clearing service based on the transmission of credit vouchers has been available from the Bankers' Clearing House since 1960. These vouchers are variously called credit transfers or bank giro credits, the latter term being introduced in the early 1970s, underlining the system's competition with the money transmission facilities available through the Post Office (latterly National) Giro service.

As well as enabling bank customers to pay in for the credit of their own accounts at any bank branch throughout the UK, the credit clearing system allows both customers and noncustomers to remit credits for the accounts of third parties. They must, of course, know the necessary details of where the beneficiary's account is maintained. Many people, for instance, now pay their gas, electricity, and telephone bills by this method, using the preprinted credit transfer which is attached to the quarterly bill.

Operation of credit clearing

The workings of the credit clearing are very similar to the workings of the cheque clearing system. At the close of every working day, each branch sorts and lists all the credits which it has accepted for accounts maintained elsewhere and remits them to the bank's own clearing department for onward transmission via the Bankers' Clearing House. The credits are 'exchanged' at the Clearing House and arrive at the recipient branch on the second day after the day they were taken in.

The credit clearing process has not yet reached quite the same level of automation as the debit clearing, largely because the fewer items involved did not justify the necessary expenditure. In addition, the variety of different items passing through the credit clearing has presented special problems.

Although the volume of credits being processed through the system is still very much lower than the current volume of cheques, numbers are continuing to grow each year, despite the introduction of the paperless electronic transfer systems which we shall look at later. In 1987, the number of credits handled was in excess of one million per day. As a result of this growth, efforts have been made to *automate* the process as fully as the debit clearing and to make all credit transfer vouchers machine readable in the same way as cheques. The format of credit transfer slips (Fig. 7.3) has been standardised and magnetic

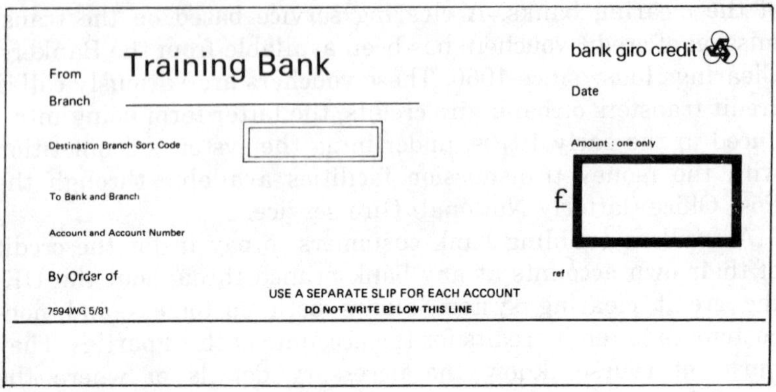
bank giro credit

From Training Bank

Branch

Date

Destination Branch Sort Code

Amount : one only

To Bank and Branch

£

Account and Account Number

By Order of

ref

USE A SEPARATE SLIP FOR EACH ACCOUNT

7594WG 5/81

DO NOT WRITE BELOW THIS LINE

Fig. 7.3 A typical bank giro credit

sorting and accounting information is now appended to the credits which are supplied to customers. Since 1982 the remitting branch has been encoding each credit with the amount for which it is made out, just as with cheques. The quality of the paper on which the credits are printed has had to be improved to permit machine handling and sorting.

Bankers' Automated Clearing Services

One of the most significant developments in the field of remittances was the setting up of Bankers' Automated Clearing Services (known as BACS) in the late 1960s. Its objective is to promote the move into *electronic funds transfer* which will remove the need for banks to transmit paper vouchers between themselves; instead, the necessary data will be reduced to electronic messages passed between computers. Participants in BACS include the English and Scottish clearing banks, as you would expect. In addition, the larger building societies, including the Halifax and the Abbey National, have started to become members.

BACS can process both instructions to credit accounts with funds due and instructions to debit accounts with funds owing. It is, therefore, a competitor for many of the functions performed by both cheques and credit transfers. Indeed, where the use of BACS has been shown to be particularly appropriate, for the payment of monthly salaries for example, it has already largely superseded the more traditional methods of payment.

Operation of BACS

The system is based on the daily passing of computer information in the form of magnetic tapes to participating banks, informing them of the amounts which are to be debited or credited to specified customers' accounts at specified branches. This information is fed directly from the tapes into each bank's own computerised accounting system. The output from BACS which goes to each of the banks is compiled from input data provided to BACS by the banks themselves and by their customers as to the amounts which are to be paid or collected. The output therefore represents an amalgamation of the daily input from a large number of sources. To add to the flexibility of the system, BACS is able to accept input data in a number of forms; it may be presented on magnetic tape, on cassette, on floppy disk or, the most recent innovation, via telecommunications links direct to the BACS computer centre.

Credit payments was the first application of BACS to gain widespread acceptance, making direct payments to beneficiaries' accounts. The most common use is that of making *salary payments* to employees. It is estimated that up to two-thirds of all UK monthly salaried personnel are now paid via direct BACS credit to their bank account. An examination of the procedures involved illustrates the working of BACS. The first step is for the employer to prepare details of the salary payments which are to be made. Details of the bank accounts of both the employee and the employer must be recorded so that the appropriate debit and credit entries can be raised. The second step is sending the information to BACS, either by physically sending a computer record in one of the several forms available, or by transmitting the data to BACS via a telecommunications link. BACS will normally process the data immediately on receipt, and details of the payments to be made will be incorporated into the tapes sent out on the following day to participating banks. The funds will be available in the beneficiaries' accounts at the start of the third day following the input of information into the system. In appropriate cases, it is quite acceptable for an employer to send the data in advance once it has been prepared, with the request that transmission be deferred until the due date.

Thirdly, and simultaneously with the processing of the credits, a single debit will be transmitted direct to the employer's account representing payment for the total value of the salaries paid over. Thus, the payment cycle is completed with synchronised debiting and crediting of the appropriate accounts.

Use of the BACS direct credit system is not restricted to salary payments. It can be used to effect many other similar remittances such as monthly or weekly payments to the trade creditors of a business (Fig. 7.4).

There are several *advantages* to the use of BACS direct

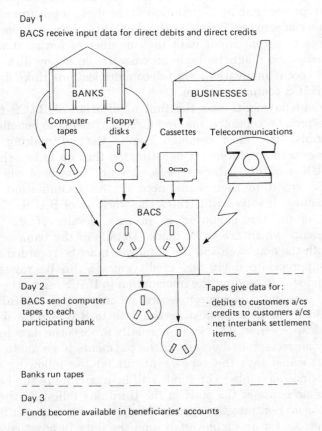

Day 1
BACS receive input data for direct debits and direct credits

BANKS

BUSINESSES

Computer tapes   Floppy disks   Cassettes   Telecommunications

BACS

Day 2
BACS send computer tapes to each participating bank

Tapes give data for:
- debits to customers a/cs
- credits to customers a/cs
- net interbank settlement items.

Banks run tapes

Day 3
Funds become available in beneficiaries' accounts

Fig. 7.4   The BACS system

credits. First, there is a significant *cost saving* over the transmission of a paper voucher which can cost £1 or more each to prepare and remit. The use of a computer to compile the data can result in spin-off cost savings. For instance, a program which is used to prepare salary payments will usually automatically calculate items such as tax and pension deductions; furthermore, less staff time will be required than for manual payroll calculations.

Second, the remitter's *cash-flow control* is improved by the use of BACS in so far as his account will be debited on the same day that the accounts of the beneficiaries will be credited. Compare this with the use of credit transfers which, to allow time for the clearing process, would have to be taken in to his branch at least two days before the due date, accompanied by a cheque for the total amount which would be debited to the remitter's account immediately.

Debit transmission

You have already seen that BACS can charge debits direct to the accounts from which they are due. The most immediately identifiable use of this facility is the transmission of the debits which represent payment for direct credits transferred on behalf of users of the system. Much more significant in the long term is the possibility which it creates for creditors to claim payment of sums due to them *direct* from the debtors' accounts without the use of cheques or similar instruments. This facility of direct debiting is a very important step in the direction of electronic funds transfer and we shall return to consider it in greater detail later on.

Standing orders

The standing order service offered by the banks predates the setting up of BACS but it has been so greatly modified by it that today it is generally looked on as part of the BACS system. The principle of the standing order is very simple: a customer who has a recurring payment to make can instruct his bank to record the details of the payment and to remit it on his behalf each time it falls due, debiting his account accordingly.

Standing orders provide a convenient and reliable method of ensuring that regular payments are made on time, encompassing such items as loan repayments, mortgage or rent payments, annual subscriptions and insurance premiums. If the amount of a particular payment has to be changed, this can be done by a simple instruction to the bank. Clearly, however, standing orders are not suitable for payments which, although they fall due at regular intervals, vary each time as to amount. The customer would have to inform his branch each time of the appropriate amount to pay.

Manual standing orders

The standing order service grew up with, and was a product of, the credit transfer system. For each payment to be made, the branch would prepare a credit transfer voucher to be remitted through the credit clearing, balancing it with a manually applied debit to the customer's account. Today, however, most standing orders are processed via BACS, although manual payments are still encountered, usually where payment details are complicated or where there is doubt that the customer will always be able to meet the payment when it falls due and the branch wishes to keep close control of the situation.

Automated standing orders

With the introduction of computerised accounting systems, banks took the opportunity to load most standing order records onto computer. This has the benefit that a properly recorded instruction can never be overlooked. More importantly, details of payments to be made each day can be produced by the bank's central computer in a form capable of being input direct into BACS, thereby avoiding the need for any clerical operations at the time that the payment is made.

We can best explain how the system works by examining the cycle of operations which are involved. On *day one*, at the computer centre of each bank, the master file containing records of all automated standing orders will be run to identify all the payments which are due for processing the following day. Details of all the credits which are to be remitted are collated and recorded on a tape which is sent to BACS. At the same time, a record is produced of the account debits which correspond to these credits. Since the debits are all to be placed to accounts which are maintained at branches of the remitting bank, details of them do not have to be submitted to BACS but can be input direct into the bank's computerised accounting system.

On *day two*, customers' accounts are debited with the amounts of the payments made on their behalf. Each branch will receive a listing of the payments which are to be made and this must be examined to ensure that the customers' authorities are still held and that they have sufficient funds in their accounts to meet the payments. BACS processes the details of the credits and transfers the data to the tapes which are sent to each of the recipient banks.

On *day three* recipient banks receive tapes from BACS. These are processed and the data input into the accounting system. On *day four* the beneficiaries' accounts are credited, and they will be able to draw against the funds immediately.

Recall of automated standing orders

The one practical difficulty associated with the automated standing order system is that of cancelling a payment for lack of funds or for technical reasons. As we have seen, the payment is in course of transmission before the account-holding branch is made aware of it. The *solution* to this problem has been provided by allowing the remitting branch to instruct the recipient branch that when a particular payment is received it is to be returned and not to be credited to the beneficiary. This is termed the 'recall' of an automated standing order. The recall instruction is normally in the form of a standard letter which must be in the hands of the recipient branch on or before the day the credit is received. To ensure that recall instructions are received by day four of the payment cycle, the remitting branch should send them off by the close of business on day two. Telephone recall requests will be acted on only if they are for payments of £100 or more and they must be made before noon on day four.

When a payment which has been recalled reaches the recipient branch, it is recredited to the remitting branch via the credit clearing using a credit transfer voucher. Thus, the payment never appears on the account of the beneficiary. The banks have agreed that standing orders for less than £20 will not be recalled for lack of funds, although they may be recalled for other reasons such as the remitter cancelling his authority to pay at too late a stage for the details to be removed from the computer system. There is no provision for the recall of a manual standing order since the paying branch is in a position to withhold the remittance if necessary.

Direct debits

An alternative method of automating regular payments is the direct debit system. This enables a creditor to originate a debit for the sum due which is applied direct to the debtor's account. The paying branch will, of course, require the authority of its customer to meet the payments when they are presented.

Originators of direct debits
Most originators of direct debits are major commercial concerns or large clubs and associations to which the service is useful because of the volume of payments, often for small amounts, which they have to collect. All originators must be *sponsored by their bankers* for entry into the scheme. This ensures that only reputable concerns are allowed to participate. This is important to protect against misuse of the facility and to ensure public confidence in the scheme. Further protection for the public is afforded by the *indemnity* which each originator is required to provide before any claims for payment will be processed. The indemnity is intended to guarantee the repayment of any debits which are incorrectly claimed. Thus, if payments are processed for amounts which exceed the debtor's mandate to his bank, or are presented after the customer's authority has been rescinded, their refund is assured.

Variable amount direct debits
The customer's authorisation for his branch to meet direct debit claims will specify the name of the creditor who will be making the claim and will usually quote the periods at which claims will be presented. It may also be specific as to the amount which may be claimed. However, variable amount direct debits (VADD) are now more usual. In these, customers authorise their banks to accept and charge to their accounts claims for any amounts which originators may submit, frequently permitting them to make claims whenever they wish as well. Although the dangers

of giving such an authorisation are obvious, they are minimised by the conditions which originators must satisfy and the VADD has gained wide public acceptance.

The VADD is useful in cases where payment is collected regularly from a debtor, the amount of which of which may vary. Thus, for instance, many societies and associations collect annual subscriptions from members using VADDs. If the level of subscription changes, the VADD system enables the association to vary the amount to be claimed from each member without further formality and without having to rely on the member to implement the change.

The system is at its most valuable when the same amount is to be collected from a large number of debtors, as occurs with membership subscriptions for clubs and associations. If the amount of the subscription is amended, one central change is all that is required to ensure that all members pay the revised subscription. Compare this with the consequences of such a change if subscriptions were paid by standing order; subscribers would each have to instruct their branches to amend the amount to be paid, resulting in thousands of separate amendments being made.

The advantages of direct debits over standing orders have resulted in a massive growth in use of the former. Table 7.2 shows the volumes of standing orders and direct debits. From the originator's point of view, perhaps the chief advantage of direct debiting is that it knows which payments have been made. *It* has originated the payments and it knows which ones have been met and which refused. Bookkeeping and reconciliations are therefore greatly simplified.

Table 7.2 Credit transfer and direct debit payments (12 months to 31 December 1986)

	Number of items (*million*)	Total value (*£000 million*)
Standing orders and credit transfers	532	150
Direct debits	412	106

(*Source: Banking Information Service*)

Daily settlement

At the end of each working day, the banks must summarise all transactions which have passed between them as a result of the town clearing, the general clearing of the previous day, the credit clearing and the Bankers' Automated Clearing Services. On a daily statement the balances due from the other banks are shown as debits and balances due to other banks are shown as credits. The difference between the two sides of the statement represents the net balance due to or from the other banks collectively.

Settlement of the amount due from one bank to another is effected by way of the accounts which they both maintain with the Bank of England. Clearly, the end result must be that the total of debits to clearing bank accounts with the Bank of England must equal the credits. Thus, although millions of debit and credit items are passed through the various clearings each day, final settlement consists of a mere handful of payments between the clearing banks.

Clearing House Automated Payments System

The most recent development in the field of electronic funds transfer is the introduction in 1984 of the Clearing House Automated Payments System (CHAPS). This is an automated computer-based network linking the member banks which enables them to make transfers between themselves without the generation of any paper vouchers. Its use is limited to remittances of £10 000 and over. Payments can be fed into the system at any branch of the participating banks for the credit of an account at any other branch of the banks. The transfer will be effected on the same day it is input and funds will be treated by the receiving branch as being cleared, thereby enabling the beneficiary to draw on them immediately.

Initially, the system's major use was to be found in the processing of interbank payments, especially those made between banks acting as agents for international banks and other financial institutions which do not have direct access to the system. Payments can also be made on behalf of branch customers, however, and as awareness of the system has increased so the volume of customer remittances has grown, especially where security of payment or speed of settlement is required. In the long term CHAPS will supplant the town clearing as the preferred medium for the same-day transmission of large payments between customers.

Large corporate customers may arrange direct access to the CHAPS system through a 'gateway' provided by their bankers. Through their own computer terminals they can themselves generate payments between their accounts and those of their trading partners.

EFTPOS

Electronic Funds Transfer at Point of Sale (EFTPOS for short) is another possible development in the computerisation of banking, and is the one which has been exciting comment for some years. The basic idea is simple. If retailers and other traders could be equipped with a card reader and keyboard which was connected into each of the clearing bank's computer systems, a customer could pay for goods and services using the same card that operates the Automated Teller Machines (ATMs), including credit cards. The retailer would 'read' the details from the card into the terminal and key in the amount due; the customer would key in his personal identity number (PIN) and the account would be debited immediately. In fact, the process would be just like using a cash machine but without cash being dispensed!

Unfortunately there are snags which have yet to be overcome and no proper network has been set up, although there have been some pilot schemes. The main problem has been in deciding who should pay for the equipment and the computer systems; neither the banks nor the retailers wishing to suffer the enormous capital outlay unless compelled to do so! Interestingly, the delay on the part of the banks resulted in 1986 in one of the country's first substantial schemes being set up by a building society—the Anglia.

In 1986, however, the financial institutions and the retailers at last began to concentrate jointly on setting up a national scheme, with the first trial installations going live in 1988. By the end of the decade therefore, it is anticipated that EFTPOS will have become an everyday feature of shopping.

Electronic banking and the law

There is little directly relevant law on electronic banking; the present legal framework was designed to regulate a paper-based payments system. However, it is clear that electronic banking (essentially automated payment by computer) will increase in importance and volume at the expense of payment by cheque. Change in the industry, particularly the application of technology, has outpaced the law's ability to evolve in parallel. And yet electronic banking is very different. An example will illustrate. A cheque commits the paying bank *only* when it decides to pay, the payee's right of action is against the drawer. On-line electronic payments, e.g. CHAPS, ATMs, EFTPOS, involve immediate payment, are irrevocable and only involve the immediate parties—a cheque can be negotiated remember. Failure to complete a payment is a straightforward contractual matter between the customer and the bank. To cite a very specific issue, is an electronic code (PIN) the equivalent of a signature? The law, at present, provides no clear answer although it would seem reasonable to us that it is the 'electronic equivalent'.

Perhaps what is most appropriate for us to do here is to cite a series of unresolved issues identified by the National Consumer Council in 1983 in relation to debit cards.

- What is the legal status of a debit card, the sort you use in an ATM or EFTPOS terminal? In practice the card performs many of the functions of a cheque.
- Should there be safeguards against unsolicited cards? If the card enables the holder to obtain credit, it is presumably already covered by the Consumer Credit Act 1974.
- Should there be documentary evidence of every electronic transaction?
- What should be the position if a card is misused after it is lost or stolen? Should there, for example, be a statutory limit to liability on the card? What should be the position if an apparently responsible teenage son or daughter misuses the family debit card after being told the PIN?
- How are mistakes and incorrect records to be resolved and rectified?
- The issuers of a credit card are liable for the default of suppliers, e.g. unmerchantable goods. Should this liability be

extended to the issuer of a debit card when the user of a card is allowed to create or increase an overdraft by its use, i.e. obtain credit?

- What special steps, if any, need to be taken to ensure secrecy in connection with customers' affairs is maintained? Access to information on accounts is now more easily obtained.

Payments abroad

So far we have considered only the question of remittances made within the UK. We must remember that the banks also offer their customers special facilities for making payments abroad. Customers are generally discouraged from using personal cheques for this purpose, especially where payments are to be made in the currency of the beneficiary. Currency cheques can cause problems if they inadvertently find their way into the sterling clearings, as they sometimes do.

International funds transfer

The most commonly used method of payment abroad is the international funds transfer. This makes use of the correspondent arrangements that have been set up between banks in different countries. Under this system, a bank which has been asked to pay a sum of money to a beneficiary abroad will simply pass on the request for payment to its correspondent bank in the country concerned. Payments on behalf of UK customers may be made in sterling or in the currency of the beneficiary.

Settlement of international funds transfers
Banks which have a correspondent relationship will maintain accounts with each other, out of which reimbursement for such payments will be effcted. Thus, an English bank will maintain a US dollar account in the United States with an American bank, while the American bank will maintain a pound sterling account in the UK with an English bank. From the UK bank's point of view, the currency account which it maintains abroad is known as a *nostro account*, while a sterling account operated in the UK for the foreign bank is termed a *vostro account*. If the UK bank asks the American bank to make a sterling payment

on its behalf, it will credit covering funds to the sterling vostro account which it operates for its correspondent. If the payment is to be effected in US dollars, however, the American bank will be instructed to deduct the amount from the balance of the US dollar account which the UK bank maintains in the United States.

In some countries a UK bank may have correspondent relationships with more than one bank; on the other hand there may be some countries in which a particular UK bank has no agency arrangement. In the latter case, payments to the country concerned must be routed through another bank which acts as correspondent for both the remitting bank and the bank in the country of receipt.

Methods of payment

A customer who wishes to make an international funds transfer will inform his branch of the amount to be paid and the identity and address of the beneficiary. He must also specify the method by which the funds are to be made available to the beneficiary in the country of receipt. Under the *credit to account* system, funds can be credited direct using local credit clearing systems if the bank and branch at which the beneficiary has his account is known. Under the *notify and pay* system, the correspondent bank will send a payment direct to the beneficiary at the address quoted, accompanied by a covering letter indicating the source of the payment. Under the *payment on application and identification* system, the beneficiary will be asked to present himself at the bank holding the funds. These will be paid over to him on production of satisfactory proof of identity. The remitter can instruct that the funds be held at a particular branch of a specified bank in the destination country.

Methods of advice

The remitting bank must send a payment instruction to the paying bank advising how the payment is to be effected. This can be transmitted in several ways. The simplest method is by *airmail letter*. This is both speedy and cheap. The instruction letter must be in a form which the correspondent bank can authenticate and recognise as genuine. If the payment is urgent, instructions can be sent by *cable or telex* as appropriate. This method is significantly more costly than airmail, the extra cost being passed on to the customer.

Wherever possible, however, instructions will be sent over the *SWIFT network*. This is an international interbank computer linkup. SWIFT stands for Society for Worldwide Interbank Telecommunications and is a method of sending messages between participating banks. Set up in 1977, it now links banks in over 30 countries, not only in Europe but also in North and South America, Japan and Hong Kong. All the 'high street' English banks have access to SWIFT.

SWIFT messages are keyed in on a computer terminal at the sending bank. After checking and authorisation they are transmitted through one of the system's three computer centres (located in Belgium, Holland and the United States), arriving at the recipient branch within minutes of despatch. The great advantages of the system are its speed and its security. Messages can be transmitted only if the sender inputs a valid authorisation; the recipient is thereby assured that any messages received are genuine. When dealing with a correspondent bank which can be reached via the SWIFT network, the remitting bank will always use this method for transmitting payment advices rather than by airmail or cable. If a payment is extremely urgent, the remitter can still be offered the choice of sending it 'express' in which case his instructions are given priority treatment; an extra charge is levied for this service.

SWIFT is not confined to use for advising payments abroad but can be used to pass any message between participating banks. It is used, for instance, to confirm foreign exchange deals and to notify details of letters of credit which are to be set up.

Bankers' drafts

Sometimes customers will wish to send the remittance themselves. They may, for instance, wish the payment to be accompanied by a covering letter explaining how the amount being sent has been calculated. In these circumstances the bank can provide a draft in favour of the beneficiary which the remitter then sends out to the foreign country. The draft, which may be expressed either in sterling or in a foreign currency, will be drawn on an account which the bank has with the appropriate correspondent bank. It is, in effect, analogous to a cheque issued not by a customer but by the bank; it has the advantage to the payee that unlike a personal cheque it is unthinkable that it would be returned for lack of funds in the account! The recipient of the draft will pay it in to his bank account or, if he wishes, negotiate it to a third party. If the draft has been drawn in sterling, the bank will convert it into local currency before crediting the account. A slightly better rate is usually obtained for a draft in comparison to personal cheques as a result of the greater certainty that it will be met on presentation.

Bankers' drafts are sometimes called for when making payments *within the UK*. This normally occurs when the recipient of the funds is not prepared to take a personal cheque from the remitter unless the remitter is prepared to wait while the beneficiary obtains clearance of the item; it is usual for the amount concerned to be quite large. (We discuss bankers' drafts in more detail in Chapter 8.)

Summary

1 Money transmission services absorb up to two-thirds of the clerical efforts of the clearing banks' staff.

2 The cheque represents the single most important method of funds transfer.

3 The clearing system enables the participating banks to collect the proceeds of cheques drawn on one another efficiently and effectively.

4 The majority of cheques pass through the general clearing. The town clearing is restricted to cheques of £10 000 and over cleared between branches within the City of London.

5 The credit clearing system permits the remittance of credits between participating banks. Like the cheque clearing systems, it is now partially automated although it still depends on the transmission of pieces of paper between the banks.

6 The objective of BACS (Bankers' Automated Clearing Services) is to promote the move towards electronic funds transfer. Its principal services are:

(a) direct credits, e.g. salary payments;
(b) direct debits;
(c) automated standing orders.

7 Payments abroad can be effected through the banks in two principal ways:

(a) international funds transfers;
(b) foreign drafts.

Self-assessment questions

1 Define: (a) a credit transfer; (b) direct debits; (c) town clearing; (d) standing order payments; (e) the Clearing House.
2 List the ways in which money remitted abroad by international funds transfer can be made available to the beneficiary.
3 True or false?
(a) The SWIFT system is a computerised interbank communications network.
(b) BACS is concerned solely with the processing of direct debits.
(c) A crossed cheque may not be cashed over a bank counter.
(d) An unpaid cheque must be sent back to the remitting branch at the end of the day on which it is presented to the branch on which it is drawn.
(e) The CHAPS system will eventually replace the town clearing.
4 A customer wishes to send £20 as a birthday present to her teenage grandson in Australia. What advice could you offer as to how the payment should be made?
5 How would you reassure a customer who has expressed concern at being asked to sign a VADD authority in favour of an insurance company? The payments are in respect of a fire policy which he has taken out covering his home and its contents.
6 Explain why banks will usually insist on waiting three days before allowing customers to draw against cheques which they have paid into their accounts.

Assignments

Memorandum from: Area Manager
To: Student
Subject: Employee accounts

First let me congratulate you on how well the recent 'small savers' and 'personal loans' promotions have gone at your branch. I am sure that the briefings which you produced had a lot to do with it.

This month in our 'business drive' we are going to change direction slightly and go for employee accounts. As I'm sure you know, a significant proportion of the UK workforce, particularly those paid weekly, continues to receive wages in cash. Large numbers of these people consequently never open bank accounts. This gives us in the bank two problems: (1) counter staff are very busy on Thursday and Friday preparing the cash for business customers' wages withdrawals; (2) the cash paid out is lost to the bank until it is redeposited, usually some time later when it has been spent. To reduce these problems, we are going to try to induce some of these employees to open bank accounts and to transfer to a system of cashless pay.

I have asked all my managers to draw up a list of local businesses which continue to pay wages in cash. If we can persuade the management of these businesses that it will be to their advantage to encourage their workforce to accept cashless pay, we will then arrange a series of presentations to the employees. As a starting point I would like you to prepare two briefings.

1   *For meetings with management*
I require an analysis of the various non-cash methods by which we can help businesses to pay wages (I can think of at least three). You might wish to draw up a chart comparing their attributes and benefits with the use of cash. Please pay particular attention to the following points.

(a) *Cost.* We should emphasise any cost savings which these systems have over cash. Are there any prerequisites (such as access to a computer) and will they lead to any possibilities of cost saving?

(b) *Cashflow.* I am sure employers will not want wages payments to come out of their accounts any earlier than they already do, so we must be clear on exactly when payments will be debited to the account.

2   *For presentations to the workforce*
Please prepare a résumé of the benefits of a bank account. Don't be defensive; we are offering the workforce an alternative which is better in every way than cash, so let's say so. You needn't

bother with references to our ancillary services (including loans) at this stage, as we are dealing with people whose financial needs are relatively unsophisticated. I think the main points to concentrate on are:

(a) *Methods of payment.* What alternatives to cash do we offer as a means of paying bills etc. and in what ways are they superior? Don't forget that everyone needs to have some cash on hand, so you will need to refer to methods of making cash withdrawals.

(b) *Convenience.* Set out the general advantages of keeping money in a bank account rather than in cash around the house or in one's pockets. I'm sure we shall hear the old chestnut: 'You know how much money you've got with cash', so we will have to be prepared to counter it.

8 Banking instruments: an introduction

Chapter objectives

After studying this chapter you should be able to:
- identify the main types of negotiable instruments and their characteristics;
- explain the nature of a bill of exchange and outline the responsibilities and rights of parties to it;
- define a cheque and outline its development as a method of payment;
- explain the origins and current meanings of crossings on cheques;
- explain the rights and liabilities involved in the use and misuse of cheque cards.

Negotiable instruments: what are they?

Let us begin with something with which you are familiar: a cheque. A *cheque* is a negotiable instrument, today by far the most common and important type, and we can discuss the nature of negotiable instruments by reference to cheques.

First, let us look at negotiable instruments from a functional perspective. Here we can say that they are *documents used in commerce to secure the payment of money*. Consider the cheque; despite the growth in direct transfers of funds between accounts, the cheque remains a very common method of settling both commercial and personal debts. Paying large sums of money in cash is both inconvenient and risky despite the boost to one's ego which might result!

This functional definition, while perfectly accurate, is very general and fails in all but one respect to provide a basis for a framework of rules to regulate their use. The one respect in which it is sufficient is the reference to 'commerce'. Negotiable instruments are the creation of commerce and the rules regulating their use essentially the creation of businessmen. You will see this clearly as we discuss this framework in this chapter and, in more detail, in Chapter 16.

The exact legal definition of a negotiable instrument is rather complex, relying as it does on references to its legal characteristics. For this reason, we are going to content ourselves for the present with a definition which categorises negotiable instruments by type of property. Study Fig. 8.1.

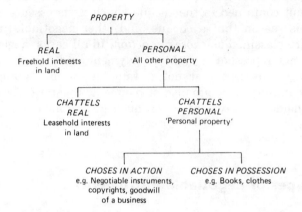

Fig. 8.1 Types of property

Negotiable instruments come into the category of *choses in action*, that is property which has no physical existence. Consequently, they cannot be physically possessed or protected and the right to them can only be enforced by legal action. Think about our copyright in this book, it is not something which we can pick up and hold; it is an idea, a concept. Nevertheless it is very real in that it is (we hope) valuable and will give us a return on our invested time. If anyone infringes that right, for example, by photocopying the pages and selling them, the only way we can protect our proprietary interest is by court action, although a suitable warning letter may prevent a recurrence of the infringement. Compare a *chose in possession*, the actual book you are reading for example. You can pick it up, protect it and retake it if someone takes it from you, altogether a much simpler form of property to deal with.

Consider the cheque once again. You are probably thinking that it is possible to pick up a cheque and physically protect it.

Indeed, if someone takes it from you they commit the tort of conversion, and since conversion protects a person's right to possess and control property a cheque must have physical existence. An understandable misconception; we can in fact draw a distinction between the paper on which the cheque is written and the promise of payment which it contains. It is possible to commit conversion against the former and, of course, the piece of paper is a *chose in possession*. However, it is the promise of payment contained in the cheque which is its essence and it is for this reason that a cheque, and other negotiable instruments, are classified as *choses in action*. In all cases, negotiable instruments represent a right to payment and a right is, by definition, a concept and not a tangible piece of property. Even a banknote is a promise of payment, theoretically entitling its holder to payment in so much gold from the Bank of England.

Main types of negotiable instruments

Since the whole concept and practice of negotiability is based on mercantile custom, the categories of negotiable instruments are similarly determined by universal commercial recognition. Hence, the categories are theoretically never closed, although the legal recognition of a new category is very rare. For example, bearer debentures were recognised as negotiable instruments by the courts in 1898 (*Bechuanaland Exploration Co.* v. *London Trading Bank*) and negotiable certificates of deposit, issued in sterling, dollars and Eurodollars, are accepted as negotiable by the usage of the London money markets.

The types we shall consider here are bills of exchange, including cheques; promissiory notes, including banknotes; Treasury bills; certificates of deposit; dividend warrants; and various bearer securities.

For any document to be a negotiable instrument it must be in a 'deliverable state'. Some are payable to *bearer* but others, such as bills of exchange and cheques, are drawn in favour of a specified person. In this case, they will need to be *indorsed* by that person to put them into a deliverable state. (We discuss this in Chapter 16.)

Bills of exchange

Introduction

A bill of exchange constitutes a legally binding written promise by the drawer that the person who takes it in payment will be paid in cash when the bill is presented for payment to the drawee at the proper time and place. (We will analyse the statutory definition of a bill a little later in this section.)

Initially three parties to the transaction are involved; the *drawer*—the person who makes the order; the *drawee*—the person to whom the order is addressed, and who becomes a *acceptor* and incurs liability on the bill by signing (accepting) it; and the *payee*—the person to whom the bill is made payable. If the bill is transferred (*negotiated*), another person becomes a party to the transaction. The acceptor is the party primarily liable on the bill, the drawer and other persons who have signed (indorsed) it are sureties for the acceptor's payment. In other words, the person entitled to payment (the *holder*) must look first to the acceptor for that payment but if the acceptor does not pay it the holder may then look for payment to the drawer (after all, the drawer was the person who drew the bill to pay a debt) or any person who subsequently incurred liability on it by signing it.

In some bills, for example those used in overseas trade, the drawer and the payee are the same person. Look at Fig. 8.2. Continuing the example in Fig. 8.2, if David Palfreman owed £5000 to Graham Bell, a bill could be drawn involving all three persons and settling both debts. Look at Fig. 8.3.

```
£5,000                          Manchester
                                30 June 1984

Pay to me or to my order on presentation the sum of
£5,000 for value received.

To Philip Ford       David Palfreman
```

Fig. 8.2 A bill of exchange in which the drawer and the payee are the same person

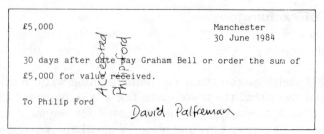

Fig. 8.3 A bill of exchange to which there are three parties
Note that the drawee has accepted the bill by signing it

Apart from cheques, bills of exchange are seldom used in commercial transactions in the UK outside the City of London. Even in international trade their importance has greatly diminished with the introduction of more efficient forms of international payment, such as bankers' commercial credits and bank transfers. When used, however, bills have two important advantages: (a) as a method of payment, they avoid the need to transfer large sums of cash, particularly from one country to another; and (b) the conflicting demands of buyer and seller can be reconciled. The buyer obtains a useful period of credit if he draws the bills payable at a future date; he hopes that in that time he can resell the goods and pay the bill out of the proceeds of that sale. On the other hand, the seller has secured a sale and has the choice of retaining the bill until it matures, negotiating (transferring) it to one of his own creditors who is willing to take it in payment or *discounting* (selling) the bill for a little less than its face value, thereby obtaining immediate payment. Thus, bills both *provide credit* and *settle debts*.

The legal definition

Now that we have seen what a bill of exchange is and does, we are in a better position to consider its statutory definition. The Bills of Exchange Act 1882, s.3(1), defines a bill of exchange as '. . . an unconditional order in writing, addressed by one person to another, signed by the person giving it, requiring the person to whom it is addressed to pay on demand or at a fixed or determinable future time a sum certain in money to or to the order of a specified person, or to bearer'. Let us consider each part of this rather long definition.

An unconditional order
This is a question of construction. Virtually all bills state 'Pay', so few problems arise here, but the bill must also be unconditional between the drawer and drawee. Thus, a requirement that payment is only to be made provided that something is done, for example that the payee has signed a receipt attached to the bill, would render the bill invalid. The same would be true if payment was made conditional upon the happening of a future uncertain event—a contigency. An example of this would be payment made dependent upon the arrival of a particular ship. Even the subsequent happening of the event does not make the bill valid. Another example of a conditional order would be a proviso to pay only if the goods supplied are up to standard.

In writing
A bill may be written in any language and on any substance (except metal) capable of delivery. Every banker has a story of an unusual cheque; classic examples range from A. P. Herbert's 'negotiable cow' to the 'shirt cheques' sent to the Inland Revenue in settlement of a tax bill.

Addressed by one person to another
If the drawer and the drawee are the same person, the holder (the owner) can choose to treat the instrument as a bill of exchange or a promissory note.

Signed by the person giving it
The signature must be that of the drawer or his agent. A signature in the form of a trade name is acceptable and a corporation's seal is equivalent to a signature. Many cheques are today signed with a facsimile signature, often a form of security printing, and these probably satisfy the section provided that there is oral evidence that it was applied by the drawer or his agent.

It is a basic principle that a signature is required before liability is incurred on a bill of exchange. A forged signature is completely ineffective. Applied to a cheque, this means that a bank has no authority to debit a customer's account if the customer's signature is forged.

On demand, or at a fixed or determinable future time

A bill is *payable on demand* (immediately) when it is expressed to be so payable, or payable at sight (by the drawee) or on presentation (for payment), or when no time for payment is given.

Many bills are expressed to be payable 'X days after sight', that is sight by the drawee of the bills when they are presented for acceptance. In these cases it is unnecessary for the date to be determinable when they are drawn. Other bills are payable so many days after the date they bear. Still others are payable on the happening of a future but certain event, such as the death of a prominent person. In these cases the date of payment is not determinable even when they are accepted. However, it must be possible *at some stage* to fix or to determine the date of payment in order to (a) establish the liability of the parties; (b) present the bill for payment; and (c) if necessary, give notice of dishonour. (We will be covering these important aspects in Chapter 16.)

Fig. 8.2 is of a bill payable on demand and Fig. 8.3 of a bill payable at a fixed future time. Look back at these now.

A sum certain in money

A sum of money is still certain within the meaning of the Act although it is paid (a) with interest; (b) by stated instalments; or (c) according to an indicated rate of exchange to be determined as directed by the bill. If there is a discrepancy between the amount of the bill as it appears in figures and as it is written in words, the words take priority.

To or to the order of a specified person, or to bearer

A bill is *payable to order* if it is expressed to be payable to a particular person or to somebody indicated by him, that is 'Pay X' or 'Pay X or order'.

A bill is *payable to bearer* if it is:

(a) drawn payable to bearer;

(b) indorsed in blank, that is, the payee or a subsequent holder of the bill signs it on the reverse without designating an indorsee; or

(c) drawn payable to a fictitious or non-existing payee.

This last category needs some further explanation. The phrase does not mean a person who literally does not exist, such as Father Christmas or Superman, it means a person to whom the drawer never intended to make payment. Thus, it may appear to be an order bill but actually it is not. Before we look at a well-known case to illustrate this rather strange position, one important fact: a bearer bill is negotiated merely by *delivery* (physical transfer), it does not need to be indorsed. It follows, therefore, that any indorsement on a bearer bill, even if the indorsement is fraudulent, can be ignored. In *Bank of England* v. *Vagliano Brothers* (1891), for example, a clerk employed by the defendant merchant bank forged a number of bills drawn on his employers using an existing client for the drawer and the name of a real company as the payee. He then used the defendant's usual office routine to get the bills accepted by his employer, forged the payee's indorsement on them and subsequently obtained payment in cash from the defendant's account at the Bank of England. The House of Lords held that on the facts the plaintiff had not been negligent in paying the bills and that because the defendant's clerk—the drawer of the bills—intended that he and not the named payee should receive payment, the payee was a 'fictitious person' within the meaning of the Act. Thus, the forged indorsements could be ignored and the Bank of England was entitled to debit the defendant's account with the amount of the bills.

Cheques

Definition

A cheque is a bill of exchange drawn on a banker payable on demand: Bills of Exchange Act 1882, s.73. As such, it must satisfy the requirements of s.3(1) which we have discussed above. In more general terms it amounts to a written promise by the drawer that the banker on which it is drawn will pay to the payee on demand the amount stipulated.

In addition to being a negotiable instrument, a cheque is also a mandate from the customer authorising and directing his bank to pay the holder, and a piece of property, a *chose in action*. A cheque as a mandate accounts for the fairly common practice whereby customers draw 'cheques' on their own banks payable to 'cash' or to 'wages'. Since they are not drawn payable to a specified person or to bearer they do not satisfy s.3 and are therefore *not* cheques. They are, however, valid orders to the bank to pay the stated amount from the customer's account. Needless to say, such instruments are not negotiable.

Distinguished from other bills

By s.73 of the 1882 Act, the provisions of the Act applicable to bills payable on demand apply equally to cheques unless otherwise stated. So, what are the distinctions?

Acceptance·
A cheque is never accepted by the bank on which it is drawn. Hence, the rules relating to acceptance of bills do not apply to cheques. This means that a bank is never liable to the holder (owner) of a cheque if it does not pay, for example where the drawer has countermanded payment. The payee's only course of action is to sue the drawer and any indorsers.

Negotiation
Relative to the number drawn, few cheques are ever negotiated—one estimate is less than 3%—the vast majority being paid straight into the payee's account. In practice, therefore, the rules relating to negotiation are of very limited relevance to cheques.

Indeed, there is a school of thought that says that cheques should cease to be negotiable instruments altogether. The argument is that because so few are ever issued to be later negotiated the attribute is completely unnecessary. It could even lead to unforeseen and awkward consequences. For example, you pay for an article by cheque, the article will not work, you stop the cheque and think that is that. But you do not know that the trader has negotiated the cheque to a supplier in payment of a debt. Title to the cheque has passed to the supplier and he can enforce the cheque against you; stopping the cheque is irrelevant to his claim. Granted, this is unlikely to happen in practice and crossing a cheque 'Not negotiable' prevents the situation arising in the first place. This is because the supplier would then take the cheque subject to any defect in the trader's title to it or subject to any counterclaim you had against him—in this case the fact that you were sold a duff article! In other words a cheque can be deprived of its negotiability very simply in any case. All the more reason, it is argued, why they should cease to be negotiable. (We explain crossings fully below.)

Delay in presenting for payment

A drawer of a bill payable on demand is discharged from liability by delay in presenting the bill for payment, since any delay increases the chances of the bill being fraudulently indorsed, altered or stolen. This is not the case with the drawer of a cheque; he is only discharged to the extent of any actual damage he suffers by the delay. In effect this means the bank on which the cheque was drawn failing when there would have been sufficient funds in the account to meet the cheque if its presentment had not been delayed. Since the failure of a UK bank is most unlikely to happen today, for all practical purposes the drawer of a cheque remains liable on it for six years from its date or its date of issue, whichever is the later: Limitation Act 1980.

Crossings

The rules relating to crossings are confined to cheques (and certain other instruments); other bills cannot be crossed.

Forged and unauthorised indorsements

In certain circumstances, an order cheque bearing a forged or an unauthorised indorsement is discharged by the bank on which it is drawn making payment: s.60, Bills of Exchange Act 1882. Payment by the acceptor of a bill under similar conditions does not discharge it, rights and liabilities still exist on it. (Section 60 is discussed in Chapter 16.)

Banker–customer relationship

The contractual obligations which exist between a bank and its customer are most unlikely to exist between the drawer and drawee of a bill of exchange.

Banker's drafts

In the previous chapter we discussed bankers' drafts as a method of making payments overseas and mentioned that they are also used within the UK. We must now consider their legal form more fully.

Bankers' drafts are negotiable instruments drawn payable to order by a bank as drawer on the *same bank* as drawee. Legally, they are both bills of exchange and promissory notes—whichever the holder wishes—because the drawer and drawee are the same person. This is so even though the draft may be drawn, as is usual, by a branch on the head office; the bank is considered as one entity for this purpose. The protection afforded to paying and collecting banks by the Cheques Act also extends to bankers' drafts however.

It goes without saying that a banker's draft is as good as cash for many commercial purposes, dishonour of it being unheard of unless the bank knows that the presenter is not entitled to it. Common examples of their use are in house purchase or in payment for a car. In both cases the amount concerned is likely to be relatively large and using a draft avoids the delay involved in having a personal cheque specially cleared. Fig. 8.4 is a typical form of banker's draft.

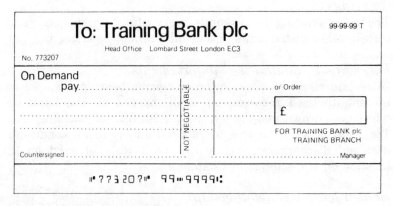

Fig. 8.4   A typical banker's draft

Cheques as a means of payment

You saw in Chapter 2 how the modern UK banking system began with goldsmiths accepting deposits of gold and silver for safekeeping which in turn led to the emergence of private banks. Where does the use of cheques fit into this evolution?

Customers of these early banks soon realised that it was often inconvenient and sometimes dangerous to go personally to their bank to withdraw money each time they needed cash. Thus, the practice developed of customers giving written instructions to their bank to pay the bearer (a messenger) of the note the sum of money specified in it by withdrawal from their account. These written instructions or notes were the first cheques. Once this practice became generally recognised and accepted, it evolved further and such notes began to be used to make payments in settlement of debts. This was done by making the notes out to whoever required payment, instead of to bearer, and this person paid the note or order (the cheque) into his own account. Alternatively, the payee could indorse the bill and thereby make it payable to someone to whom he in turn owed money and that person could then either indorse it again or pay it into his account. If you consider the modern use of cheques, it is in essence still the same, although indorsement of cheques is comparatively rare.

The early banks were keen to promote the use of cheques and they began to provide special cheque forms to assist their customers. The use of cheques was to their advantage because withdrawals by cheque which were then paid into the payee's account meant that notes and coins did not change hands, merely the ownership of bank deposits. The position was the same if the payee banked with another bank provided the banks kept accounts with each other or at the central bank and had some means of clearing the cheques.

This process meant that only a small part of each fresh deposit needed to be kept in cash and also that any loan to a customer could be made through an overdraft, against which cheques could be drawn, instead of handing over actual cash. Thus, what began as practice for the convenience of customers became central to building the pyramid of credit which we discussed on page 28.

Crossings

Virtually all cheques bear two bold parallel lines across their face. This is the crossing. But why is it there, what is its origin, and what variants are possible on the basic or general crossing? First of all, a general statement of its legal meaning and effect.

A crossing is a direction to the *paying bank* that the money proceeds of the cheque should be paid only to another bank as agent of the payee and not directly to the payee himself. A crossing therefore restricts payment of a cheque.

You may be thinking that there is one common situation where this rule is not applied. Banks will allow their own customers, or their known agents, to cash crossed cheques over the counter. Sometimes the customer is required to open the crossing by writing 'Please pay cash' and signing (not initialling) the opening, but more usually an opening is not requested. The practice, although technically incorrect at law, is convenient and promotes goodwill, while the risk involved is slight. The problem is avoided altogether if the customer makes out the 'cheque' to cash when withdrawing money. The 'cheque' is then not really a cheque at all because it is not made out to the order of a 'specified person, or to bearer' as required by the Bills of Exchange Act 1882, s.3(1). Legally it operates as a demand for repayment which the bank is contractually bound to honour provided sufficient funds or an agreed overdraft facility exist. The crossing which the 'cheque' bears is therefore irrelevant.

Origin of crossings

Crossings are the result of banking practice, specifically the practice of the Clearing House in the 18th century. Clerks of different banks would meet to exchange cheques drawn on their respective banks, settling any outstanding balance in cash. In time the cheques were left in each bank's 'drawer' in the Clearing House instead of being given personally to the bank's clerk. So that each could make their accounts up properly and to enable them to return any cheque for lack of funds, the clerk of, say, bank X would write bank X's name between parallel lines on cheques which were left in, say, bank Y's drawer.

As this internal practice became known outside, customers themselves began adding crossings to their cheques since making cheques payable only through another bank account reduced the chance of a third party fraudulently obtaining payment. Customers crossed cheques adding the words 'and Company' (or 'and Co') between the parallel lines or the name of the payee's bank when they knew it. The latter crossing meant that if any person other than the payee tried to obtain payment of the cheque he would have to do so at the payee's own bank and any attempted fraud would most likely come to light.

In the second half of the 19th century crossings were legally recognised as a material (integral) part of a cheque. By s.78 of the Bills of Exchange Act 1882, any unauthorised alteration of a crossing will discharge (end) the liabilities of the parties to the cheque.

The purpose of crossings today

More efficient methods of clearing (*see* Chapter 7) have long since taken over the original purpose of crossings and today they are used to minimise the chances of persons fraudulently obtaining payment of a cheque.

The best way to appreciate this is to consider the position with an uncrossed, or 'open', cheque. An uncrossed cheque does not have to be paid through a bank account, payment can be made over the counter. Thus, a person finding or stealing an uncrossed cheque would be able to obtain payment over the counter at the drawee bank provided that he had reasonable identification as the payee and provided the payee was not personally known to the bank. The first proviso certainly would not be difficult for a determined rogue to satisfy, and the second is most unlikely to apply.

Contrast the position with a crossed cheque. This, as you know, can be paid only through another bank account and therefore assumes that the rogue has one or can persuade someone with a bank account to pay in the cheque suitably endorsed by the rogue and obtain the proceeds on his behalf. In itself, although a deterrent to a would-be rogue, it is not that great a protection against fraud because a determined attempt to open an account in a fictitious name using bogus referees if need be will often succeed. Taken with other factors, however, it without doubt makes it considerably more difficult for a fraudulent person to obtain the proceeds of a cheque. In particular, the consequences of a crossing increase the time available for discovering the fraudulent activity and gives the drawer more time to stop payment of any stolen cheque.

Furthermore, even if payment has been made before the loss or fraud is discovered, it can almost always be recovered from the person for whom it was collected since he would have to have an account at the collecting bank. The exceptions would be where the rogue had opened an account in a fictitious name and could not be traced, or where a bearer cheque had been lost or stolen and the customer for whom it was collected had given value (something in return) for it to the finder or thief without knowledge of the circumstances. The customer would then be its true owner (its *holder in due course*) and entitled to the proceeds.

Having considered the purpose of crossings we must now look at the various types. The two primary categories of crossings are 'general' and 'special'.

General crossings

A general crossing consists of two transverse parallel lines across the face of the cheque, with or without the words 'and Company' between the lines (unusual today), and with or without the words 'not negotiable'.

Where the words 'not negotiable' are added to the crossing they deprive the cheque of its negotiability. This means that the person taking the cheque does not receive and cannot give a better title than that of the person transferring it. (The ability to do so is, as you will see, the very essence of negotiability.) The words do not mean that the cheque cannot be *transferred*, however; a crossed cheque is just as transferable bearing these words as without them, the person to whom it is transferred is just in a far weaker position if the transferor's title proves to be defective. The effect of the words on an uncrossed cheque is uncertain; they may merely deprive it of its negotiability, as on a crossed cheque, or prevent its transfer altogether, as they do on bills of exchange other than cheques. However, the point is relatively academic since uncrossed cheques are very unusual and uncrossed cheques bearing these words extremely unusual.

Sometimes the words 'account payee' appear within the crossing. These words are, strictly speaking, not part of any crossing since they are a direction to the *collecting* bank as to how the money must be dealt with after its receipt. While they have no statutory significance, the courts recognise them as a warning to the collecting bank that collection of the cheque for a person other than the named payee without enquiry and sufficient explanation is *prima facie* proof of negligence. The words do *not* affect the negotiability of the cheque.

From what we have said, you have probably worked out that

Fig. 8.5 Types of general crossing

unless you are absolutely certain that a cheque you draw is going to be paid straight into the payee's account, crossing it 'Not negotiable, account payee' should guarantee that you will not have an unknown third party seeking to enforce the cheque against you if the cheque is lost or stolen, or later stopped by you. Fig. 8.5 shows the possible forms of general crossings.

Special crossings
A special crossing consists of the name of a *particular bank* and often a *particular branch* to which payment must be made. The name itself is the crossing, and while they often appear, two transverse parallel lines (the essence of a general crossing) are unnecessary. The words 'not negotiable' and 'account payee' can be added to the crossing, and they then have the same effect as on a cheque crossed generally. Fig. 8.6 shows the forms of special crossings.

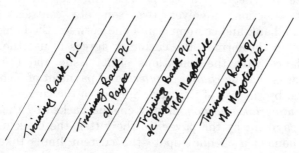

Fig. 8.6 Types of special crossing

Cheque cards

First of all we must distinguish between *cheque cards* and *credit cards*. While the latter, such as Access and Visa, play an ever more important role in retail purchasing they are outside mainstream banking and we are therefore only concerned with the former at this point. Remember, however, that a Visa card is both a credit card and a cheque guarantee card for someone with an account at either Barclays or the TSB. As the name suggests, credit cards allow their holders 'to buy now and pay later' and they are used quite independently of a cheque book and bank account; the position is the reverse with a cheque card. For our present purposes, this is sufficient distinction.

How are cheque cards used?

The use of cheque cards is now very common. In ordinary retail sales a cheque will frequently not be accepted in payment unless it is 'backed' by a valid cheque card. The main advantage of the cheque card system is that it avoids the need to carry cash and is therefore a safer method of payment. Essentially cheque cards are a means of identification which

(a) enable customers to *cash cheques* up to a prescribed limit (at present £50) at branches of banks other than the one at which they have an account; and

(b) *guarantee* that a cheque taken in payment 'backed' by a card will be honoured, whatever the state of the customer's account, subject to a prescribed limit per cheque (at present £50) and provided that the card is properly used.

The use of cheque cards to 'back' cheques, their more important function, involves two separate contracts: one between the bank and customer, and one between the bank and the payee. In the former, the customer agrees to use the card in accordance with the conditions of its issue and use and acknowledges that he *cannot countermand* payment of a cheque guaranteed by the use of the card. Subject to the current limit, the bank *undertakes to honour* any cheque backed by the card taken in payment by the payee. In the latter, the bank undertakes to honour a cheque (up to the current limit) taken in payment provided the payee takes it relying on the card and according to the instructions printed on it.

If you look on the back of a cheque card you will find the following instructions:

(a) the cheque must be signed in the presence of the payee and the signature must agree with that on the card, or actually be that of the cardholder;

(b) the card must not be out of date;

(c) the cheque form must be written on the bank's standard printed cheque and bear the sorting-code number on the card;

(d) the cheque card number must be written by the *payee* on the reverse of the card; and

(e) the cheque must not exceed the stated guaranteed amount.

Remember that the £50 limit (at present) is a limit per *single transaction*. If, for example, the amount involved is £75 and two cheques are made out in payment, one for £50 and one for £25, the guarantee will only cover *one* of them. However, it could be argued that drawing two cheques in this way is a breach of the conditions of use which nullifies the guarantee on *both*. If a cheque card is used to back a cheque for more than £50, the guarantee is also nullified, in other words, it does not even apply to the first £50.

Above we have outlined a couple of possible problem situations involving cheque cards and you may be able to suggest others. The legal position is uncertain in some of them because, in practice, a bank will only question payment of cheques backed by cheque cards when either insufficient funds are in the account or where unauthorised or irregular use is made of the card. In the latter case, the problem is simply solved by taking back the card or, ultimately, by closing the account. (*See also* pages 386–9.)

Fraudulent use of cheque cards

Cheque cards offer great potential for fraud, both by the customer to whom a card is issued and by a thief or finder of a cheque book with the relevant cheque card. Thus, cheque cards are not normally issued until customers have proved to be responsible in the operation of their accounts, or their integrity and responsibility is undoubted or they are willing to provide the bank with acceptable security beyond the potential risk, in other words in a book of 30 cheques—£1500. Students are, however, frequently issued with cheque cards without these requirements being fulfilled, but this is a calculated risk by the bank in the hope of securing their loyalty in future years.

Furthermore, the terms of issue printed on the card will specify that it remains the property of the bank, that it does not entitle the customer to overdraw the account without prior agreement and that the card should be carried separately from the cheque book in order to prevent fraud if one or the other is lost. These terms put the bank in a strong position as against its customer should the card be misused, although whether action is taken is essentially a practical rather than a legal decision.

We must consider the position of three parties in relation to the fraudulent use of cheque cards: the payee, the customer and the bank. The payee's position is secure provided that the instructions on the card have been followed; the bank guarantees that the cheque will be paid. The most likely situation where the bank can refuse payment is where the signature on the cheque does not agree with that on the card, for here the possibility of fraud arises and the payee would be wrong to accept the cheque without further enquiry or proof of identity. This, however, does not give the bank a great deal of protection against the determined and professional rogue. Indeed, because of rising losses through fraudulent use of cheque cards, banks have begun to take a stricter view of their obligations. In such a case they may refuse to pay a cheque because the *signature is not that of the customer*, despite the forgery being indistinguishable from the real thing. Needless to say, retailers are not happy about this change of policy but the evidence is that in the past they have frequently not exercised reasonable care in accepting cheque cards.

The customer's position is also secure where a cheque book and cheque card have been fraudulently used, for without the customer's signature on the cheque the bank has no authority to debit his account. Where, however, the customer's own negligence, for example, in the care of his cheque book and cheque card, was responsible for the fraud being perpetrated the bank, while still having no right to debit the account, would have a claim against him for the amounts of the cheques which they had to honour.

The misuse of a cheque card by the customer to obtain an

unauthorised overdraft is the *criminal offence* of dishonestly obtaining a pecuniary advantage by deception under the Theft Act 1968, s.16. This was so decided by the House of Lords in *Metropolitan Police Commissioner* v. *Charles* (1976), where the defendant, who had been granted an overdraft limit of £100, issued 25 cheques each for £30 with each properly backed by a cheque card during the course of one evening at a gambling club. The bank was obliged to honour all 25 cheques, even though the defendant's overdraft now stood at £750. It was held that the issue of a cheque combined with the production of a cheque card constitutes a representation by the drawer that he has authority between himself and the bank to use the card in order to oblige the bank to honour the cheque. If the representation should be false, an offence is committed. (In *R* .v. *Lambie* (1981), the House of Lords held that it is similarly an offence under s.16 of the Theft Act 1968 to use a credit card after the credit card company has asked for its return. Such use again implies a representation by the user that actual authority exists to make a contract with the retailer on behalf of the company to the effect that the company will honour the credit card voucher signed by the user.) On facts similar to those in *Metropolitan Police Commissioner* v. *Charles* (1976), the Court of Appeal in *R* v. *Navvabi* (1986) held that theft under s.1 of the Theft Act 1968 was *not* committed. Theft requires the misappropriation of another's property and since there was no debt before payment of the cheques (i.e. no unauthorised overdraft existed before they were paid) the defendant could not have misappropriated the bank's property.

Finally, the bank's position. We have seen that the bank is obliged to pay if the payee has followed the instructions on the cheque card. Thus, the bank's interest is in recovering some or all of the money if this is possible. Clearly, it would not be in a bank's interest to try to recover a small sum from its customer when a cheque book and a cheque card have been either lost or stolen with no blame attaching to the customer. This would hardly be conducive to good customer relations. However, where the customer has been grossly negligent in the care of his cheque book and cheque card, or has been unnecessarily slow in reporting a loss or theft, the customer has broken his duty of care to the bank and it would be possible to commence a civil action to recover the monies. This would probably be the course of action followed by a bank if the customer has fraudulently used the cheque card and there appears to be a reasonably cost-effective prospect of the customer being able to repay the overdraft.

Parties to a bill of exchange: their responsibilities and rights

Since a cheque is a bill of exchange, we are going to consider bills and cheques together in this section unless we state otherwise. Remember, however, the *differences* between cheques and other types of bills; in particular that a cheque is never accepted by the bank on which it is drawn and that comparatively few cheques are negotiated by the payee, most being paid straight into his or her own bank account.

We have already seen that there are three primary parties to the transaction: the drawer, the drawee and the payee. Be sure that you can distinguish them before reading any further. We must now define and explain another party: the *holder*.

The holder

The Bills of Exchange Act 1882, s.2, defines a holder as: 'The payee or indorsee of a bill who is in possession of it, or the bearer thereof'. What does the terminology of the section mean?

Indorsee

We know the meaning of 'payee' so let us consider the term 'indorsee'. If a person wishes to negotiate (transfer) a bill which is made out to him by name, for example 'Pay J. Smith' or 'Pay J. Smith or order', the bill is an *order* bill and can only be negotiated by J. Smith first signing the bill on the back. This is known as *indorsing* the bill. J. Smith may wish to negotiate the bill to a specific person, say, P. Brown, in which case the indorsement must read 'Pay P. Brown' followed by J. Smith's signature. P. Brown is now the *indorsee* and, therefore, the holder of the bill. Note that to be the holder the indorsee must be in possession of the bill. If J. Smith merely signs the back of the bill and does not specify to whom he intends to negotiate it, the indorsement is an *indorsement in blank* and the bill becomes payable to *bearer*, that is, payable to whoever has possession of it at any particular time.

Bearer bill
Lastly, you need to be sure that you remember the meaning of the term 'bearer bill'. You have seen what an order bill is: a bearer bill is essentially the opposite. It is payable to anyone in physical possession of it. Specifically, a bill is payable to bearer if it is: (a) drawn payable to bearer, (b) indorsed in blank, or (c) drawn payable to a fictitious or non-existing payee. A bearer bill is negotiated by delivery alone.

The holder: some further points
It is worth exploring the term 'holder' a little more fully at this point because it will be useful for your later studies. You should note the following three points:

(1) The term includes an *unlawful* holder, that is someone to whom the bill is expressed to be payable but whose possession of it is unlawful. Examples include the finder or thief of a bearer bill and a person who obtained the bill's transfer to himself by fraud.

(2) It follows from (1) above that anyone in possession of a bearer bill is a holder. This includes a finder or a thief, although such a holder obtains *no rights* against the parties to the bill and a claim brought by him on the bill will fail on proof of his defective title.

(3) The term does *not* include a *mere wrongful possessor*, for example, a person who has stolen an order bill or a person holding under a forged indorsement—a forged signature is, as you will see later, entirely inoperative.

These points are important (a) when a question of liability on the bill arises, for instance the acceptor does not pay and an action is taken against the drawer or an indorser—only a holder can bring such an action; and (b) when the bill is paid, the liability of the parties to the bill will generally only be discharged if payment is made to the holder of the bill. (We examine these important aspects in Chapter 16.)

Indorser

We have explained what *indorsing* a bill is; remember it can either be a special indorsement or an indorsement in blank. The indorsee becomes the holder of the bill and able to negotiate it to another party by delivery, in the case of a bearer bill, or by indorsement and delivery in the case of an order bill. To negotiate an order bill he must sign it and by so doing he becomes an *indorser* and a party to the bill, acquiring both responsibilities and rights. Thus, we find that in addition to the primary parties to the transaction—drawer, drawee (who becomes the acceptor when he signs for acceptance) and payee—we also have the concept of a holder and possibly one or more indorsers. Let us now look briefly at their respective responsibilities and rights as an introduction to a more detailed study in Chapter 16.

Responsibilities and rights

Drawer
Basically the drawer's *responsibilities* are in the form of two promises. First, by drawing the bill he promises to any holder that it will be accepted by the drawee and paid by him when presented for payment. The second promise is really a corollary of the first: that he will compensate the payee if the drawee does not accept the bill or, if once accepted, he dishonours the bill by refusing payment.

This second promise extends to any indorser who has to pay the bill since, as you will see below, an indorser guarantees the acceptor's payment.

The drawer's basic *rights* are twofold. First, he has a contractual right to expect the acceptor to pay the bill and hence to compensation from him if he does not. Second, if the bill is dishonoured he has the right to have the correct procedure for dishonour followed. (This is explained in Chapter 16.)

The above rights and responsibilities apply to any bank that draws a bill on, usually, another bank or other organisation but it is unlikely that the bank as drawer would ever to have to pay since a bill should only ever be drawn on a reputable organisation and not issued to the payee until the drawee has accepted it.

Drawee/acceptor

Until a drawee has signed a bill, and thereby indicated acceptance of it, he is not a party to it. It follows that a drawee has
neither rights nor responsibilities. Thus, a bank that wrongfully
dishonours its customer's cheque will not be liable to the holder,
although it will, of course, be liable for breach of contract to its
customer.

An acceptor's primary *responsibility* is of the essence to any
bill; he promises that he will pay the bill and, clearly, an action
for the amount of the bill can be brought against him by its
holder if he does not. This, of course, is the position of any bank
which has accepted a bill (not a cheque—for these are never
accepted) drawn on it.

An acceptor's main *right* is to have the procedure for acceptance properly followed. (This again we consider in Chapter 16.)

Holder

The holder's *responsibilities* are to ensure that the bill is properly accepted, if it has not already been, and that the correct
procedures for presenting the bill for payment and/or giving
notice of dishonour (if acceptance or payment is refused) are
followed.

The holder's main *right* is really the reciprocal of the
acceptor's main responsibility, that is, the holder has the right
to enforce payment of the bill against any prior party to it. Thus,
while he must first seek payment from the acceptor, he can sue
either the drawer or any indorser if the acceptor does not pay
for they have guaranteed that he will. For this reason, a bank
will normally insist on the drawer or at least one indorser being
a reputable person or organisation of financial soundness before
taking a commercial bill as holder.

Indorser

The indorser's main *responsibilities* are similar to those of the
drawer in that he promises first that the bill will be accepted
and paid when presented; and second to compensate any party
to the bill who has had to pay as a result of the bill being dishonoured. In return he is entitled to have the proper procedure
for dishonour followed.

Sometimes a bank will sign a bill to give it greater

acceptability: the holder knows the bank can and will pay. While the bank is not an indorser in the sense that it has taken the bill as a holder, it incurs the liabilities of an indorser by signing it. Another example would be a director of a company personally indorsing a bill to which the company is a party.

Other negotiable instruments

So far in this chapter we have concentrated on bills of exchange which, of course, include cheques. This is perfectly proper in this book because as a practising banker it is with these that you will be primarily concerned. Indeed, unless you work in the City of London or spend time in a department concerned with foreign business you may seldom deal with an ordinary bill of exchange, only with cheques. However, at the start of the chapter we identified certain other main types and we deal with these now.

Promissory notes

The Bills of Exchange Act 1882, s.83, defines a promissory note as '. . . an unconditional promise in writing made by one person to another signed by the maker, engaging to pay, on demand or at a fixed or determinable future time, a sum of money, to, or to the order of, a specified person or to bearer'. If you compare this definition with that of a bill in s.3(1) you will find that the definitions are very similar. Now look at Fig. 8.7 which reproduces typical promissory notes.

You should be able to notice the following points from a comparison of the definitions and from Fig. 8.7. First, while a bill is in the form of an order, a promissory note is a *promise to pay*. Second, the *drawer and drawee* are the same person, which means that there are only ever two original parties to the transaction in the case of a promissory note, and, following from this, third that a promissory note is *never accepted*. This means, fourth, that its *maker* is always the party primarily liable for payment. Should the payee negotiate the note by indorsement he then becomes liable as surety for the maker's payment. Promissory notes are uncommon.

Banknotes are promissory notes issued by a bank. They differ from other promissory notes in being issued for certain fixed

```
£5,000                        Manchester
                              1 July 1988


Two months after date I promise to pay to Philip Ford
or order the sum of £5,000 for value received.

To Philip Ford

   Edinburgh            David Palfreman
```

```
£5,000                        Manchester
                              1 July 1988


I David Palfreman promise to pay to Philip Ford or Order
the sum of Five Thousand Pounds for value received by equal
monthly instalments of £500 commencing on the first day
of September 1984 together with interest on the amount for
the time being unpaid of the said Five Thousand Pounds
at the rate of nine pounds per cent per annum by way of
addition to the said monthly instalments but so that if
any of the said instalments together with the interest
added thereto shall not be fully paid on the day when the
same falls due the balance outstanding of the said Five
Thousand Pounds shall immediately become due and payable.


   To Philip Ford

                         David Palfreman
   Edinburgh
```

Fig. 8.7   Typical forms of promissory notes

amounts, always payable to bearer and on demand. They are, of course, also legal tender.

Treasury bills

As you have already seen Treasury bills are short-term securities drawn on the Consolidated Fund and issued weekly by the

Fig. 8.8   A treasury bill

Treasury (see Fig. 8.8). They are, therefore, receipts for cash lent to the government, incorporating a promise to repay the loan in 91 days. They are promissory notes, rather than bills, made payable to bearer and fully negotiable. Their negotiability allows them to be bought and sold on the discount market.

Certificates of deposit

A sterling certificate of deposit is a document issued in the UK by a British or foreign bank certifying that a deposit has been made with the bank. Certificates are usually issued at par for periods of three months to five years and for sums of £50 000 rising by multiples of £10 000 to a normal maximum of £500 000 per certificate. They are payable to bearer and fully negotiable.

Dividend warrants

A dividend warrant is a form of cheque drawn by a company in favour of a shareholder for the payment of dividends. An interest warrant is similar but used for the payment of interest on other securities. Dividend warrants consist of two parts: an advice informing the member of the particulars of payment, and the warrant proper which is in the form of a cheque directing the company's bank to pay the sum due to a member. The advice part of the warrant also contains the required information concerning deduction of income tax, which must be deducted at source. This should be retained by the shareholder and produced to the Inland Revenue authorities in support of any claim for the recovery of income tax.

Bearer securities

Bearer securities include *bearer bonds,* issued by governments; *scrip certificates* or *letters of allotment,* issued by the government or by a company until all instalments due on the government stock or the company's shares or debentures have been paid; *share warrants to bearer* issued by public companies in respect of fully paid-up shares or stock; and *bearer debentures,* issued by companies.

As fully negotiable instruments payable to bearer, title to such bearer securities passes by *mere delivery.* It is not practical for the issuing body to maintain records of the actual owners and numbered coupons are attached to share warrants or bonds so that dividends falling due may be claimed. Since title to them passes by mere delivery, bearer securities provide excellent security for a bank loan. Bearer bonds of foreign governments are the most common bearer security deposited with banks for this purpose.

Summary

1 Negotiable instruments are documents used in commerce to secure the payment of money. Legally, they are choses in action.
2 The main types of negotiable instruments are: bills of exchange, including cheques; promissory notes; Treasury bills; certificates of deposit; dividend warrants; and various bearer securities.
3 A bill of exchange is a legally binding written promise by the drawer that the person who took it in payment will be paid in cash when he presents the bill for payment at the proper time and place.
4 A cheque is a bill of exchange drawn on a banker payable on demand.
5 A crossing on a cheque is a direction to the paying banker to pay the proceeds to another banker as agent of the payee and not to the payee directly. Crossings may be either general or special.

6   A cheque card is used to guarantee payment of a cheque up to a prescribed limit, at present £50. Fraudulent use of a cheque card is a criminal offence under the Theft Act 1968, s.16.

7   The holder of a bill of exchange is the payee or indorsee of a bill who is in possession of it, or the bearer of a bearer bill.

8   An indorser is a person who transfers a bill by signing and delivering it to another person.

9   A promissory note is a written promise to pay in which the drawer and drawee are the same person.

10   Bearer securities are excellent security for a bank loan or overdraft because title to them passes by mere delivery.

Self-assessment questions

1   List the main types of negotiable instruments.

2   In what circumstances is a bill of exchange payable to bearer?

3   How does a cheque differ from other bills of exchange?

4   What is the difference between a general and a special crossing on a cheque.

5   What is the main function of a cheque card?

6   Define a holder of a bill of exchange.

7   True or false:

(a)   A bill which specifies that it is to be paid in four instalments is still within the meaning of '. . . a sum certain in money . . .' under the 1882 Act.

(b)   A bill drawn 'Pay J. Smith or bearer' is an order bill.

(c)   A forged signature on a bill of exchange is entirely inoperative.

(d)   Banking practice dictates that a crossed cheque will only ever be paid through a bank account.

(e)   The words 'not negotiable' and 'account payee' when written on a cheque both affect its transferability.

(f)   A bank will always pay a cheque on which its customer's signature is forged if it is backed by a cheque card.

(g)   If X impersonates Y and thereby persuades Z to transfer an order bill to him, X becomes the holder of it.

(h)   An indorsee is not a party to a bill of exchange.

8   Explain the responsibilities of a drawer and acceptor of a bill of exchange.

9   Explain how a promissory note differs from other bills of exchange.

10 Why are bearer securities excellent security for a banker's advance?

Assignments

1   Explain whether or not each of the following clauses in a document purporting to be a bill of exchange will affect its legal validity as a bill of exchange:

(a) Pay A or order £5000 on or before 30 June 1988.

(b) Pay B or order £5000 on 30 June 1988 with interest at 10% per annum.

(c) Pay C or order £5000 in three equal instalments due 30 April 1988, 31 May 1988 and 30 June 1988.

(d) Pay D or order £5000 on arrival of SS *Peerless* at Liverpool.

(e) Pay E or order £5000 on 30 June 1988 and charge the same to proceeds of sale of 1000 tonnes of wheat shipped per SS *Peerless*.

2   Jones draws a cheque for £50 payable to Green or bearer. Green indorses it 'Pay to Brown, (signed) Green' and transfers it to Brown. Brown transfers the cheque to Smith without indorsing it. Explain whether or not Smith has a good title to the cheque.

Part Two

9 Money supply and monetary policy

Chapter objectives

After studying this chapter you should be able to:
- outline the link between the money supply and the level of bank and economic activity;
- list the various money aggregates and analyse the differences between them;
- state the factors which bring about changes in the money supply;
- identify the broad objectives of government economic policy and explain the role of monetary policy;
- describe the different techniques for implementing monetary policy and their effects on the banks.

Introduction

You should already know a great deal about money and the money supply since we considered these topics in the very first chapter of this book. In this chapter we are going to examine the money supply in greater detail and see how the control of it fits in as a major component of the government's *overall economic policy*. This can be generally said to pursue three basic objectives.

(a) *Full employment*, or at least the minimisation of unemployment.

(b) *Control of inflation*, which has been a constant part of the economic scene since the Second World War.

(c) *Balance of payments surpluses*, to ensure that the country does not constantly spend more than it earns.

As we shall see later, these objectives conflict with each other to some extent. Full employment, for instance, promotes the growth of consumer demand which in turn may lead to both demand-led inflation and higher volumes of imports which can upset the balance of payments. Depressing demand—by whatever means the government chooses—may alleviate these problems but it will also result in unemployment! Economic policy therefore has to follow a fine line between these problems and yet promote overall growth.

Control of the money supply is a vital part of this policy. As you will appreciate, money in a modern society is much more than just a *medium of exchange*; it has become a dynamic factor which directly affects the level of national economic activity. An increase in the volume of purchasing power, all other things being equal, will stimulate consumer demand and investment, promoting increases of output and reducing unemployment. A reduction in purchasing power would have the reverse results.

Money can be controlled in two ways: by *price*—the manipulation of interest rates, and by *quantity*—the manipulation of the volume of money in the economy. It is a general economic principle that it is not possible to control both the price and the supply of a commodity at the same time: the supplier must fix one variable and let market forces determine the other. However, before we begin to delve too deeply into how monetary controls work, we must first examine the economics of money a little more closely.

The money supply

The quantity theory of money

You will recall that in Chapter 1 we discussed the problems that developed in Spain in the sixteenth century when the country was flooded with precious metals—gold and silver—brought from South America. Since these metals were the basis of Spanish coinage, an oversupply of money developed and too much money was soon chasing too few goods. The inevitable result was *inflation*, causing a fall in the value of money which eventually brought the money supply and the supply of goods back into equilibrium. The basis of what happened can be found in the fact that over a period the total amount of money spent must equal the total monetary value of the items purchased. On the face of it this may seem a facile statement but it is the starting point of an important equation between money and consumption. There are four principal variables in this equation: the quantity of money; the velocity of circulation; the general level of prices; and the volume of trade.

The quantity of money

If the quantity of money is increased without a corresponding increase in the number of goods which can be bought, the value of each unit of money will fall owing to an excess of consumer demand over supply of goods. Imagine that in our society there are only one million units of money and one million things to spend it on. Selling and spending would be in equilibrium with purchases having an average value of one unit. If the number of money units was suddenly doubled, people would find that they had nothing on which to spend half their money. Their response to this would be to compete with each other for a larger share of the goods that were available for purchase. They would do this by offering more money for the goods they wanted and this would, of course, force up the general level of prices. Eventually the average price of all purchases would be two money units rather than one as it had previously been.

For the purposes of our equation let us call the money available in a society at any particular time M.

The velocity of circulation

Money once spent is not destroyed: it is put back into circulation sooner or later when the recipient spends it in turn. Consider how long—or how short—a time 'change' stays in our pocket. Think again about our hypothetical society in which there are now two million units of currency. If we knew that over a period of a month the total cost of all items purchased had come to six million units, we would be able to calculate that each unit had been used on average three times during the month. This is the *velocity of circulation* which we shall call V. In any given period, therefore, M—the amount of money—multiplied by V must be equivalent to the total amount of money spent.

Looking at this from another angle, we can see that a change in the velocity of circulation of money will have a very similar effect to a change in the amount of money. Suppose that instead of circulating three times in a month the currency in our example came to circulate four times. This would raise monthly spending power to eight million units. Unless it was matched by an increase in the supply of goods and services, this change would again result in a fall in the value of one unit.

Changes in the velocity of circulation can be brought about by developments in methods of money transmission. There is clearly a finite limit on the speed with which cash—such as a £5 note—can circulate, although in practice this limit is unlikely to be reached. However, as you know, the bulk of the money in our society consists of bank deposits and similar items. Technical developments in the financial institutions' money transmission systems have steadily increased the speed at which deposit money can circulate. Even so, the principal determinant of the velocity of circulation is the *liquidity preference* of the population, in other words, whether people like to spend their money or to save it.

As we noted in Chapter 5, the three motives which determine a person's propensity to hold cash are the transaction motive, the precautionary motive, and the speculative motive. The amounts of money held in response to the first two of these motives will remain broadly stable while the supply of money remains stable. If the supply of money increases, this usually indicates that society as a whole is becoming richer, in which case people will generally increase their liquid holdings. Increased liquidity preference results, of course, in a *decreased* velocity of circulation since more money is being held out of circulation for longer periods. Thus, in our calculation of $M \times V$, we might expect an increase in M to be counterbalanced to some extent by a decrease in V.

Money held for speculative reasons, on the other hand, is likely to be much less stable since its level is determined by the differentials between current and anticipated rates of interest. Overall, therefore, liquidity preference is likely to be quite volatile and hence the velocity of circulation will also be subject to change, although this will not be wholly unpredictable. It is worth noting that in inflationary times liquidity preference is lowered because people do not trust money to hold its value and therefore they prefer to spend as much of it as they safely can, reducing cash holdings to a minimum.

The general level of prices
We have said that, all other things being equal, if the supply of money or the velocity of circulation increase, so must the

general level of prices. (The reverse is also true.) Clearly in a complex economy such as our own there are many thousands of commodities being bought and sold each day. The prices of these commodities will vary at different rates since each one will be subject to different forces of supply and demand. For example, the 10 years from 1974 were a period of particularly high inflation in the UK. During this period, although in general prices rose by approximately 240%, some prices rose much more sharply, some much less so. Measures such as the Retail Prices Index are used to show how price levels in general change from one period to another.

In our equation the general level of prices is known as P.

The volume of trade

Just as the supply of money has to be related to the velocity of circulation so as to establish how much money is being *spent* by buyers, so the level of prices has to be related to the number of purchases to establish how much is being *received* by sellers. So, for instance, if an increase in the supply of money *is* matched by an increase in the volume of goods and services available for purchase, the number of transactions should increase while prices remain stable.

If we call the volume of trade T, we will be able to express the amount of money paid to suppliers in a given period as P—the level of prices—multiplied by T. Since the money value of commodities sold must be the same as the amount of money spent, we are finally in a position to express the relationship as the simple equation:

$$MV = PT$$

Clearly, the figure for T must include all transactions on which money is spent including, for example, sales of second-hand goods. In reality such a figure would be extremely difficult to establish, so economists usually substitute for it the figure for *net national income* (NNI) (Table 9.1). The NNI is calculated by adjusting the gross national product (GNP) for that part of the nation's output which has to be used to replace items of the country's capital stock—roads, railways, factories, etc.—which wears out. This is known as *capital consumption*.

The net national income is commonly denoted by the letter Y and if we include this in our equation instead of T, it becomes:

Table 9.1 Net national income by category of industry 1985

	£m
Agriculture, forestry and fishing	5 485
Manufacturing	76 800
Construction	18 651
Energy and water	34 335
Transport	12 913
Communication	8 044
Distributive trades, hotels and catering	40 304
Insurance, banking, finance and business services	42 473
Ownership of dwellings	17 775
Education and health	26 187
Miscellaneous services	17 998
Public administration, defence and social security	21 599
Total	322 624
Adjustment for financial services	−16 883
Gross domestic product (GDP)	305 741

(*Source: National Income and Expenditure*)

$$MV = PY$$

Although Y is not quite the same thing as T, it is comparable and it is fair to assume that changes in one would be reflected in changes in the other.

Monetary control

The equation which we have produced shows the relationship which exists between the various factors outlined and it demonstrates quite clearly that the money supply is directly related to the gross national product. What it does not do is to show, or even to suggest, any particular causal relationship between the factors. It does not for instance signify that increases in the money supply are *caused* by increases in the general levels of prices or vice versa. However, it does suggest that manipulation of any one of the four factors must result in a change in at least one of the others and this can be used as a basis for structuring the government's control of the economy.

Our equation can be re-expressed in a number of ways. If $MV = PY$, then:

$$M = \frac{PY}{V}, \text{ and } V = \frac{PY}{M}, \text{ and } P = \frac{MV}{Y}, \text{ and } Y = \frac{MV}{P}$$

If we wished to manipulate the general level of prices, for example, we would look at the third of these expressions. This indicates that we may attempt to achieve the desired effect by adjusting either Y, M, or V. If we wished to *reduce* the level of prices, and thus inflation, we could attempt to do so by decreasing the supply of money or the velocity of circulation, or by increasing national income. Whichever one we chose to adjust, we would have to hold the other two stable at the same time so as to produce the desired effect. If we chose to reduce the money supply, perhaps by restricting the availability of notes and coin, we might find an increase in the velocity of circulation of the reduced amount of available currency. This would nullify the effect of the reduced level of money supply and leave the level of prices unchanged.

Attempts to stabilise or reduce the velocity of circulation would normally be directed at shifting the *liquidity preference curve*. In inflationary times, liquidity preference is reduced because people fear for the future purchasing power of their money holdings. If confidence can be boosted on the future stability of monetary values people will be less affected by this fear and will increase their money holdings.

From the above considerations you will understand why successive governments have found control of the country's money supply to be such a tempting target in their battle to control the economy. It offers such broad-ranging possibilities of effect, whether the desired result is reducing inflation, boosting national income, or whatever. The first step is, of course, to decide just what the money supply consists of and it is to this topic that we now turn our attention.

Measuring the money supply

We saw in Chapter 1 that money consists of anything that society will accept as money, provided that it can adequately perform the required functions. In a modern society most money is in the form of 'book entry' money held in bank accounts rather than the actual cash which is in circulation. You might think that it would be a comparatively simple task to find out how much money there is in the economy: all we have to do is to total up all the money held in bank accounts and add on the value of notes and coin in circulation. Unfortunately it is not quite as simple as that to produce a useful *money aggregate*, since the dividing line between what is money and what is not can sometimes be difficult to define. For example, is an overdraft facility, that is, permission to draw more out of your bank account than you have in it, part of the money supply and, if so, how would you measure the value of all the overdraft facilities that have been agreed but not yet fully utilised? Furthermore, some *near money* assets such as building society deposits are increasingly treated by the public as direct substitutes for money, so we must decide whether to include these in our calculations.

As a result of these difficulties, several different aggregate measures of the money supply are in simultaneous use, each one incorporating a slightly different range of monetary items. The variety is useful because each one tells us something slightly different about how the economy is operating. Although the most common of these measures have consecutively numbered titles—*M*0–*M*5—we are going to examine them out of order for reasons that should become apparent as we progress.

*M*1

The *M*1 money stock consists of notes and coin in circulation plus private sector 'sight' deposits held on sterling accounts with the UK 'monetary sector'. Several parts of this definition deserve further explanation.

Notes and coin in circulation is exclusive of any currency held in the tills of the banks or by the Bank of England since this is not actually in circulation. *Sight deposits* are funds which can be withdrawn without the need for any notice being given to the bank and therefore they essentially represent the deposits held on current accounts. Deposit accounts are excluded even though the banks do not generally insist on the appropriate period of notice being observed. The *private sector* is the non-governmental area of the economy. *M*1 therefore includes the current accounts of businesses as well as individuals but it excludes the accounts of all government and local government agencies and of the nationalised industries. The *monetary sector* consists primarily of the recognised banks and other deposit takers which together are classed as 'authorised institutions'.

*M*1 is a narrow definition of the money stock but it can be useful in that it is closely related to the function of money as a *medium of exchange*. It comprises the private sector's holdings of fully liquid monetary items. Until recently it was generally considered that *M*1 demonstrated how the level of interest rates and the population's liquidity preference interacted with one another. Since *M*1 assets were largely non-interest bearing, it was to be expected that an attractive rise in interest rates would induce people to switch some of their liquid assets out of *M*1 holdings and into something else, possibly accounts with building societies. Unfortunately, this movement has now been disturbed by the growth of interest bearing current accounts. Clearly, if depositors are receiving interest on their sight deposits, it is going to be more difficult to persuade them to transfer their funds into something less liquid.

This phenomenon is doubly unfortunate since one of the main weapons in the government's arsenal for control of the money supply is the manipulation of interest rates. *M*1 is becoming progressively less responsive to minor changes of rate. As a result of this, some economists are now referring to a narrower measurement of *M*1 which consists only of notes and coin in circulation and non-interest-bearing private sector sterling sight deposits. This measurement is known as *Nib M*1 (Table 9.2).

Table 9.2 Nib *M*1 and *M*1 as at 31 March 1987

	£m
Notes and coin in circulation	12 717
UK private sector non-interest bearing sterling sight deposits	28 438
Nib *M*1	41 155
UK private sector interest bearing sterling sight deposits	38 615
Total *M*1	79 770

(*Source: Bank of England Quarterly Bulletin*)

M3

M3 is a wider measure of money stocks in that it includes *all* sterling deposits with the monetary sector from the private sector of the economy.

The difference from M1 consists of the addition of the UK private sector's *time deposits*. Time deposits are, of course, either deposits on which notice of withdrawal is required, or deposits which have been made for a fixed period of time. In its broadest definition M3 also includes the value of deposits denominated in foreign currencies but which are held in the UK for UK residents. This is known as M3c.

Table 9.3 Sterling M3 and total M3c as at 31 March 1987

	£m
M 1 (*see* Table 9.2)	79 770
UK private sector sterling time deposits	80 151
M3 money stock (sterling)	159 921
UK residents' deposits in other currencies	28 502
M3 money stock (total)	188 423

(*Source: Bank of England Quarterly Bulletin*)

M3 gives a clearer measure than M1 of the total purchasing power available to the country and for this reason it is the measure most commonly referred to by the government and used by it as a target for regulating the money supply. Even so, there are still some major omissions from it, particularly the amounts of building society deposits and the value of any undrawn overdraft facilities. The first of these is included in M2, M4 and M5 (all of which we shall be examining later), but the latter does not find its way into any of the official calculations.

In 1980 the government published a *Green Paper* which recommended that M3 should continue to be used as the basis for controlling the growth of the money supply and that the government should continue to express its monetary targets as M3 levels rather than using any other measure. It was recognised that no single monetary aggregate told the whole story but that M3 gave the best overall picture. Since that time, however, there has been an increasing swing towards the placing of a greater proportion of private sector funds in building society accounts at the expense of bank accounts. As a result, the rate of growth of M3 has become somewhat misleading, and two further aggregates—M4 and M5—have been introduced.

M4

M4 consists essentially of sterling M3 plus the private sector's balances with building societies in both deposit accounts and share accounts. There is one complication, however. Since some of the money held on deposit with the building societies is redeposited by them with the banks, it is already included in M3. That amount, which represents the societies' liquid assets, therefore has to be deducted from M4 or it would be counted twice!

Table 9.4 M4 as at 31 March 1987

		£m
M3 money stock (sterling)		159 921
Building society deposits	121 895	
Less liquid assets	11 239	
M4		110 656
		270 577

(*Source: Bank of England Quarterly Bulletin*)

M5

To arrive at M5, the total of M4 is again augmented by adding on the private sector's holdings of money market instruments and its investments in national savings deposits and securities. 'Money market instruments' comprise such items as Treasury bills, bank bills, and local authority deposits.

This is the broadest definition of 'money' currently in use. Although it incorporates 'wholesale' as well as 'retail' deposits, the assets which it comprises are all comparatively liquid, and therefore it can be taken to indicate the overall purchasing power in the community. In this connection, however, don't forget that the private sector does not consist only of private individuals; it includes public and private companies as well as

Table 9.5 $M5$ as at 31 March 1987

	£m
$M4$	270 577
UK private sector holdings of money market instruments	4 265
National savings deposits (and certain securities)	9 972
	284 814

(*Source: Bank of England Quarterly Bulletin*)

organisations such as building societies. By the way, the additions to $M4$ once again have to be adjusted for the building societies' holdings of the relevant items since not to do so would result in 'double counting' of the amounts involved.

$M0$

We have already said that $M3$ has been the major target used by the government in its monetary controls. However, use of $M3$ targets is never fully satisfactory simply because the main weapon used to affect the money supply is the management of interest rates. $M3$ is not particularly sensitive to small changes in interest rates because it consists largely of deposits which already bear interest and on which the marginal value of such changes would be minimal. For these reasons, the government started to use a much more narrowly based monetary base called $M0$ as an indicator of monetary conditions and it also redefined $M2$ to provide a broader measure of overall private sector purchasing power.

$M0$ (usually pronounced 'M nought') consists of notes and coin in circulation plus the money in the banks' tills and their deposits with the Bank of England other than cash ratio deposits (Table 9.6). You should note that the latter two items were not included in any of the aggregates which we have considered so far. $M0$ is, quite simply, the *monetary base* of the economy and it can be directly controlled by the government. At the moment, notes and coin are issued largely in response to demand by banks. There is, however, an argument that if the government maintained specific limits on the issue of currency, this, together with existing requirements for banks to keep set proportions of their assets on deposit with the Bank of England,

Table 9.6 $M0$ as at 31 March 1987

	£m
Notes and coin in circulation	12 717
Banks' till money	1 860
Banks' operational deposits with the Bank of England	232
	14 809

(*Source: Bank of England Quarterly Bulletin*)

would control the whole process of *money creation*. The theory is that if the monetary base were to be tightly controlled, tight constraints would be placed on the banks' ability to create deposits. Quite simply, the funds would not be available to permit any major increases. The problem with such a strategy is that it is likely to disrupt the pattern of interest rates which in turn would disturb the workings of the money market and other financial markets. Thus, changes in $M0$ are used as a measure of what is happening to the money supply rather than being used as *targets* for the purposes of monetary control.

Since $M0$ contains no interest-bearing items, it is assumed that it should respond positively to changes in interest rates, thereby showing whether control measures are taking effect. However, there is some doubt about whether this assumption is wholly correct. In the first place, the measurement is very narrow, as it excludes current account balances which in our society are almost indistinguishable from cash. If notes and coin were to come into very short supply, people would largely be able to overcome the problem by issuing more cheques. Indeed while cash represents over 90% of $M0$, in the real world it is becoming less and less important. In this respect it is interesting to note that a growing proportion of the UK's workforce receives its pay by bank transfer rather than in cash. This move away from cash may mean that $M0$ will become progressively less relevant to the realities of economic life. In the second place, the other component of $M0$—the banks' deposits with the Bank of England—is wholly unresponsive in itself to changes in interest rates since the level of deposits is determined solely by the need to ensure the liquidity of the interbank settlement systems. It is precisely because they are so unresponsive to interest rate controls that bankers' deposits are excluded from the other aggregates.

M2

The M2 measure of money stock is intended to provide an indication of the volume of 'retail' deposits in the UK and it therefore excludes all 'wholesale' money market deposits. To achieve this objective, the calculation includes only the components of Nib M1 plus interest-bearing deposits with a maturity of less than one month and limited to those having a balance of less than £100 000. There are two component parts of M2: retail deposits with the monetary sector and retail deposits outside the monetary sector. The principal items in this latter category are balances on building society share accounts and deposit accounts.

Table 9.7 Composition of M2 as at 31 March 1987

	£m
Notes and coin in circulation	12 717
UK private sector non-interest bearing sight deposits	28 438
(Nib M1)	41 155
Other UK private sector 'retail' deposits with the monetary sector	43 943
UK private sector 'retail' deposits with building societies	84 115
NSB ordinary accounts	1 666
	170 879

(Source: Bank of England Quarterly Bulletin)

You will see from Table 9.7 that the total of M2 as at 31 March 1987 was very close to the total of M3 on the same date. However, the way in which the two totals are made up is very different! M2 in effect represents the balances which are available to the private sector immediately or in the near future to finance transactions. It therefore reflects quite well the *short-term* spending power of the nation.

Domestic credit expansion

The money aggregates which we have discussed so far can be

used to demonstrate changes in the level of money supply by comparing the totals calculated at the start and at the end of any given period. However, they all suffer from one major drawback in that they concentrate solely on the domestic money supply. This would not matter if the UK was a closed economy

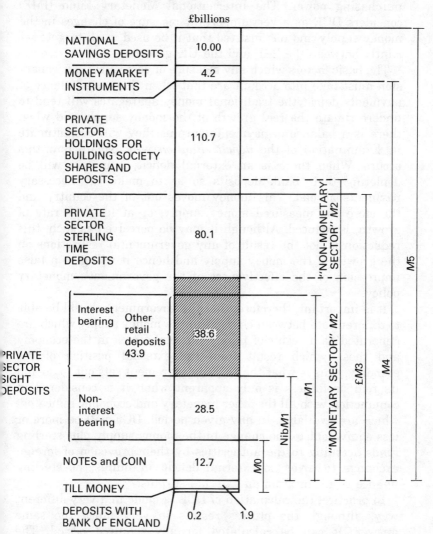

Fig. 9.1   Components of the money aggregates: 31 March 1987 (Source: BEQB)

which had little or no dealings with other communities as there would be no inflows and outflows of purchasing power resulting from foreign trade. However, the UK has an open economy. That is why the measure of *domestic credit expansion* was adopted in 1969 as an indicator of the broader changes in national purchasing power. The International Monetary Fund (IMF) considers DCE as a very important measure of changes in the money supply and has insisted that it be used in all targets set jointly between the IMF and the UK government.

The basic factors which any measure of domestic credit expansion must take into account are that when there is a balance of payments deficit the traditional money aggregates will tend to underestimate the real growth of the money supply and when there is a balance of payments surplus they will overestimate it. Examination of the *deficit situation* will explain how this occurs. When there is an external deficit, importers will be depleting their bank deposits so as to make the necessary payments abroad. This money moves out of the country and therefore the measured money supply, or at least its rate of growth, is reduced. Although it may be perceived as such, this reduction is not the result of any governmental restrictions on the growth of the money supply and hence it will give a false impression of the effectiveness of the government's monetary policy.

It is important, therefore, that the government should be able to differentiate between changes in the money supply which are generated as a result of purely internal forces in the economy and those which result from the external position of the economy. This is what the DCE measurement sets out to do and its real usefulness is only apparent when it is considered in conjunction with all the other monetary and economic indicators which are available. In any given period, DCE will be more or less equivalent to the change in the money supply plus sterling funds accruing to the authorities by their provision of foreign exchange to cover an external deficit, or minus the sterling finance resulting from an external surplus.

In practice, the calculation of DCE is made in a very different way, although the process results in very much the same answer. It can be calculated for any required period. The formula used is to add together:

(a) The *public sector borrowing requirement* (PSBR) over the period in question, less purchases of public sector debt by the private sector other than the banks.

(b) Sterling lending to the private sector.

(c) Bank lending overseas in sterling.

DCE demonstrates clearly the links between the public sector borrowing requirement and changes in the money supply. The PSBR is quite simply the amount that the state needs to borrow to finance any deficit between its income and its expenditure over the period in question.

Monetary policy

Economic controls

As we said at the start of this chapter, management of the money supply is just one of the tasks undertaken by the government as part of its overall duty of directing national economic activity in pursuit of the four principal objectives which we identified. Even within one political party there is often disagreement about the specific policies to be followed but underlying all economic policies is the need to promote *economic growth* to provide for an increase in the real national income of the country. If this can be achieved, everyone will enjoy a better standard of living and other objectives, such as full employment and control of inflation, may also be achieved.

In the eighteenth century Adam Smith believed that the economy would run itself without government interference if the 'invisible hand' of self-interest was allowed to guide it. Indeed government influence was held to be the one thing that would be most disruptive to such a system. We no longer accept this theory and place the principal responsibility for the health of the economy squarely on the shoulders of the government. In fact, the actions of the government generally now have such an impact on every aspect of our daily personal and commercial lives that it cannot possibly escape responsibility for exercising economic control as well. The direction of the economy is, of course, an economic process rather than a legal one: the government cannot pass a law controlling inflation or abolishing unemployment! There are three main ways in which it can control the economy.

Fiscal policy

This is the direction of the economy through taxation and government expenditure. In the UK the way in which the government spends its money is an important factor in the regulation of the economy since it is responsible for disposing of over 40% of the gross domestic product (GDP). Even more important, however, is the relationship between taxation and government spending, in other words, whether the government is running a budget deficit or surplus. If there is a *deficit*—expenditure being greater than taxation—national income will tend to rise and aggregate consumer demand for consumption will increase. If there is a *surplus* the reverse will occur. This means that from year to year the government must decide whether or not to balance the budget, having regard to background economic conditions. Table 9.8 shows the sources of government income for 1985.

Table 9.8 Financing of central government expenditure in 1985

	£m
Direct taxes	
Income tax	35 448
Corporation tax	9 128
Indirect taxes	
Motor vehicle duty	2 389
Customs and excise duty:	
Alcohol	4 147
Tobacco	4 342
Hydrocarbon oils	6 260
Other (import duties)	1 422
VAT	20 962
Other (including car tax and excise)	1 629
Petroleum revenue tax	7 369
National insurance and NHI contributions	24 068
National insurance surcharge	45
Other taxes and levies	1 000
Other income	12 788
Total	130 997

(*Source: National Income and Expenditure*)

Monetary policy

Monetary policy involves the direction of economic activity through control of the supply and price of money. The government can attempt to influence the economy by varying the quantity of money available to the country or by raising and lowering interest rates. Generally, it is assumed that increasing the supply of money will stimulate the economy while restricting it will depress the economy. In a modern society, however, *liquidity*—in the form of money and near-money substitutes such as building society deposits—has become more important to people than simply access to money proper. This has reduced the effectiveness of quantitative controls on the money supply.

Monetary control through management of the interest rate is based on the premise that *raising* the rate, and thereby also the price of money, will reduce the level of *aggregate monetary demand* (AMD), thereby depressing demand in the economy in general. *Lowering* interest rates will increase the AMD and stimulate the economy. The basic options as to monetary policy are summarised in Table 9.9.

There are four types of monetary strategy available to the government:

(a) *Inflation:* allowing uncontrolled expansion of the money supply.

(b) *Deflation:* rapid contraction of the money supply.

(c) *Reflation:* allowing a mild form of inflation designed to gently stimulate the economy.

(d) *Disinflation:* a mild form of deflation designed to slow down economic activity without causing a severe depression.

Figure 9.2 shows the effects of these four options on a hypothetical *prices index*. Since 1945, successive governments have each followed alternating policies of reflation and disinflation,

Table 9.9 Monetary policies: action, effect and result

Action	Effect	Result	
Restrict money supply	tight money ⎫	deflation	
Raise interest rates	dear money ⎰		disinflation
Expand money supply	easy money ⎫	inflation	
Lower interest rates	cheap money ⎰		reflation

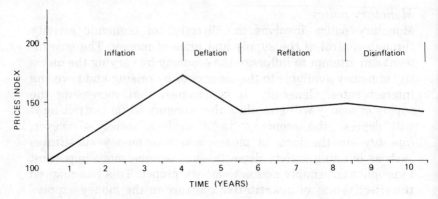

Fig. 9.2 The four types of monetary policy

earning government economic planning the derisive description: 'stop/go'. This situation has arisen because of the opposing government economic objectives which we noted earlier. Thus, while reflation promotes full employment, it also reduces the value of money and while disinflation stabilises the value of money it brings about a reduction in output and in employment. When unemployment becomes too big a problem governments tend to reflate; when inflation becomes too big a problem, they deflate.

Direct intervention

Both monetary and fiscal policy aim to *induce* the economy to move in a particular direction. Sometimes, however, the government may intervene directly to see that its wishes are carried out. Perhaps the most obvious example of this is a *prices and incomes* policy designed to control inflation by blocking price rises and wage rises. No UK government which has attempted it has yet managed to operate a wholly successful prices and incomes policy. This underlines the point we made earlier about the distinction between law and economics. Economic forces cannot be effectively controlled by legal provisions alone.

Rationing is another form of direct intervention in the economy: arranging for the distribution of commodities throughout the community according to need rather than according to the ability to pay for them. Such a procedure clearly disrupts the operation of the price mechanism and has a far-reaching impact on the economic scene. Often, however, a *black market* develops for illicit transactions in supposedly controlled commodities and in this the price mechanism reigns supreme. There has been no general rationing of goods in the UK since the early 1950s; it had been introduced during the Second World War when all commodities had to be strictly controlled in pursuit of the war effort.

Instruments of monetary policy

Although monetary policy is decided by the government, it is implemented principally by the Bank of England. The Bank has a variety of instruments which it can use to enforce a particular policy and which are often referred to as the *weapons* of monetary policy. As you have seen, these weapons are mainly aimed at affecting either the volumes of money, principally in the form of bank deposits, or the rate of interest. Some of the available measures are in disuse at the moment although this does not mean that they may not be reactivated at a later date. Cynical commentators are apt to remark that there are fashions in economic controls just as much as there are in clothing and that everything will 'come round again' in time. These instruments of policy do not necessarily have to be used in isolation. In fact, it is common for two or more of them to be in use at any one time, the effect of one reinforcing the effects of the other or others. Combined monetary policies of this sort are often referred to as *package deals*.

The fiduciary issue
We have already noted that the government could attempt to control the money supply by placing strict restrictions on the issue of notes. This should ultimately result in a reduction in the banks' ability to create new deposits. However, the penalties of such a strategy, particularly the disruption of the pattern of interest rates, have deterred governments from implementing it. In practice, it would not be very easy for the Bank to refuse to supply the notes which the banks need in order to satisfy customers' demands. This does not mean, however, that the supply of notes is not subject to any restriction. Printing too much money can expand the money supply unnecessarily, leading to high levels of inflation. There is some evidence to suggest that this is what occurred in the mid 1970s when a

massive rise in the fiduciary issue was paralleled by an excessive rate of inflation, although there were certainly other contributing factors as well.

Open market operations

This method involves the sale or purchase of government securities or eligible bills by the Bank on the open market with the intention of influencing the liquidity of the banking system (the amount of money in circulation) and the rate of interest. Sales of such bills or bonds should reduce the volume of money and decrease interest rates; purchases should have the opposite effect. Since 1981, this has been the principal method of controlling the money supply, centring chiefly on the purchase or sale of *eligible bills*. So that the market in Treasury bills and commercial bills is large enough to ensure that interest rates are affected, the Bank has admitted more than 50 banks to the list of 'first-class names' whose bills it is prepared to rediscount for the discount market.

Suppose that the Bank wishes to reduce the money supply and instructs the government broker to sell £1000 of securities on the open market at a time when the balance sheet of X bank looks like this:

Bank X before open market sales

Liabilities		Assets	
Deposits	100 000	Liquid assets	25 000
		Securities	25 000
		Advances	50 000
	100 000		100 000

The public will pay for the securities which have been sold by issuing cheques drawn on their accounts with X bank. The government broker pays the cheques in to the Bank of England which of course collects the proceeds from X bank by deducting the funds from its account with the Bank. Provided that the government does not thereafter spend the money and reinject it into the economy, the money supply will thus have been reduced by £1000 and the balance sheet of X bank will look like this:

Bank X after open market sales

Liabilities		Assets	
Deposits	99 000	Liquid assets	24 000
		Securities	25 000
		Advances	50 000
	99 000		99 000

However, this is not the end of the story because X bank now has a liquidity problem of its own. Although there are no longer any official requirements as to *reserve assets ratios*, a prudent bank will still seek to maintain a safe *liquidity ratio* between liquid assets and deposits. At the start of our example, X bank was maintaining a ratio of 25% but this has now been reduced to 24.2% (£24 000 expressed as a percentage of £99 000). To restore its ratio to a safe level, X bank must now either reduce deposits, sell securities or call in advances. Whatever it does, the supply of money will be reduced still further. Suppose that at the end of the process X bank's balance sheet looks like this:

Final position of Bank X

Liabilities		Assets	
Deposits	96 000	Liquid assets	24 000
		Securities	24 000
		Advances	48 000
	96 000		96 000

You will see that, over all, £1000 of money market operations have resulted in a total reduction in the money supply of £4000. The actual amount of the reduction is, of course, dependent on the liquidity ratios being maintained by the banks. Furthermore, in all some £2000 (£1000 by the Bank of England and £1000 by Bank X) worth of securities have been sold in the open market which will have depressed security prices. As you know, a fall in security prices results in an increase in *yields* and this will tend to push interest rates up. All these effects would work in reverse if the Bank was to *buy* on the open market.

There are some drawbacks to open market operations. First, when securities are sold by the Bank a great deal depends on whether they are bought by the public or by the banks. If bought by the banks there will be little effect on their liquidity ratios since most of the securities are classed as liquid assets. Second, there is the question of how closely the banks are working to their minimum liquidity ratios. If they are close to the limit they will have to reduce deposits or loans as we have demonstrated. If they are not close to the limit, it would take a massive sale of securities to affect them. Indeed there have been times when the banks have held unusually high levels of liquid assets with the deliberate intention of deterring the government from employing this weapon. The Bank can counter such a tactic by calling for *special deposits* (which we shall be looking at later) to absorb and freeze part of the banks' liquid holdings.

Liquidity ratios

As we have just seen, all banks must maintain some minimum proportion of deposits in liquid form so as to be able to meet customers' demands for repayment. The appropriate sum does not all need to be held in cash. Indeed, it would be wrong for this to happen; some of it should be held in other forms. The assets which the Bank of England recognises as being liquid comprise:

(a) Balances with the Bank of England.
(b) Money at call with the London money market.
(c) UK Treasury bills.
(d) Local authority and other eligible bills.
(e) Gilt-edged securities with less than a year to run to maturity.

The important point to note about liquidity ratios is that the greater the proportion of liabilities covered by liquid assets, the smaller will be the banks' ability to create money from a given initial level of deposits. This results from the operation of the *multiplier effect* which we explained in Chapter 1 when we were discussing the creation of credit. (Turn back to page 29 and refresh your memory if you are not sure how this operates.) The Bank of England can use this effect to restrict the supply of money by setting *mandatory* liquidity ratios which the banks must observe. If the ratio set is higher than the ratio that the banks would observe for prudential reasons, their ability to create credit will be curtailed. In consequence the money supply will be reduced.

From 1971 to 1981, for example, the Bank operated just such a system of monetary control which was known as the *reserve assets ratio.* (We considered this in detail in Chapter 3.) Under this system, all institutions in the banking sector had to hold reserve assets equivalent to a stated proportion of their eligible liabilities. For most of the period the requirement was set at $12\frac{1}{2}$%. Eligible liabiltites comprised principally sterling deposit liabilities except any deposits having an original maturity exceeding two years. Reserve assets consisted of those liquid assets which were listed above, although no more than 2% out of the required $12\frac{1}{2}$% could be in the form of eligible commercial bills. The basic criterion for a liquid asset to qualify as a reserve asset was that its supply had to be under the control of the authorities.

The principal criticism of the reserve assets ratio was that it was solely a measure of control which did not assist the banks with their need to maintain liquidity for reasons of prudence. Further liquid resources had to be maintained for this purpose. By the end of the 1970s it had become apparent that the ratio had become both confusing and ineffective as a measure of monetary control. It was finally abandoned, together with special deposits (*see below*) in August 1981. As you know, this does not mean that there are now no liquidity controls on the banks; there are, but they exist chiefly to ensure adequate prudential control of liquidity and not primarily to control the creation of credit.

Special deposits

An alternative method of affecting the banks' liquidity is to call on them to make 'special deposits' with the Bank of England equal to a set proportion of their eligible liabilities. This money is frozen and the banks cannot draw on it like their ordinary deposits. A call for special deposits has exactly the same effect as instituting or increasing a reserve assets ratio. In fact, special deposits had to be used in the 1970s when it was found that the introduction of the $12\frac{1}{2}$% reserve assets ratio had actually allowed the banks to *reduce* their liquidity levels, thus fuelling a massive growth of the money supply! At times in the 1970s the clearing banks had to make special deposits equivalent to 3% of eligible liabilities as well as maintaining a reserve assets ratio of $12\frac{1}{2}$%. Thus, $15\frac{1}{2}$% of eligible liabilities were tied up and not capable of being used to finance the granting of credit.

Special deposits, like the reserve assets ratio, have some advantages. They are simple and cheap to implement and they are both effective and quick-acting. They do, however, have the major disadvantage that they can annoy the banks whose co-operation is vital for the smooth running of any system of monetary control. Use of special deposits was abandoned in 1981 when the government decided that it would no longer seek to control the money supply through liquidity controls on the banks.

Supplementary special deposits

While special deposits seek to control the banks' ability to create credit out of any given level of deposits, supplementary special deposits attack the creation of credit at source by controlling the banks' ability to attract deposits in the first place. In other words, they act on the other side of the banks' balance sheets. As an instrument of control they were in use in the UK in the mid-1970s. During this period, if a bank allowed its interest-bearing eligible liabilities (IBELs), that is, interest bearing deposits, to grow beyond a certain target level a proportion of the excess had to be deposited with the Bank of England on an account on which no interest was paid. However, the system could be circumvented by the use of *acceptance facilities*.

Funding

Apart from foreign liabilities, the National Debt can be divided into two broad categories: floating debt and funded debt. *Floating debt* consists of short-term government borrowing via such instruments as Treasury bills and 'ways and means' loans from the Bank of England. It used to be thought that floating debt should be kept to as low a level as was consistent with the need to balance short-term flows of income and expenditure. In fact, the proportion of floating debt has grown in recent years as a result of the ease and comparative cheapness with which such finance can be raised. Long-term borrowing, through gilt-edged securities for example, is known as *funded debt*. It accounts for about three-quarters of the total debt.

Funding is the process of converting some of the floating debt into funded debt by the issue of a new long-term loan stock. It has two effects on the money supply. First, it will reduce the supply of liquid investments which the banks could hold as part of their 'reserve assets' and this may mean that they would have to reduce their deposits as described above. Second, the purchase of these longer-term securities would clearly absorb some of the short-term liquidity (purchasing power) of the nation, thereby reducing the money supply. The principal difficulty with funding is that it is costly for the government since the rate of interest payable on long-term loans will usually be much higher than that applying to short-term borrowing.

Interest rates

The measures which we have discussed so far affect the *supply* of money by controlling in some way the banks' ability to create credit. It is also possible to approach the problem from the other end, affecting the *demand* for money by controlling its price, that is the rate of interest. It is true that the controls on supply will also have an effect on interest rates; reducing the availability of credit, for example, will tend to force interest rates upward. Although such results are incidental to the operation of the measure, they do reinforce the effectiveness of the controls.

The 'traditional' method for the Bank of England to directly affect interest rates was through changes in *bank rate*. Bank rate was the name which used to be given to the rate at which the Bank would rediscount Treasury bills or other eligible bills of exchange from the discount houses when acting in its capacity of lender of last resort. To avoid potentially serious losses if their liquidity came under pressure, the discount houses, when buying bills, had to keep their interest rates close to bank rate and this would have a knock-on effect throughout the interest rate structure. Indeed, the banks used to relate many of their interest rates directly to bank rate. Thus, by raising bank rate the Bank of England could increase interest rates generally and could bring about a reduction by lowering it.

In practice, raising or lowering the Bank of England's interest rates would not on its own bring about general changes of interest rates. The participants in the money markets generally need to be 'reminded' about the possibility of having to borrow from the Bank before falling in line behind bank rate. Thus, changes in bank rate were usually accompanied by other measures, particularly open market operations, designed to affect the liquidity of the markets. Even so, the market occasionally chose to ignore changes of bank rate, being convinced that in the short term there would be enough liquid funds available. Generally speaking this was not the case and bank rate changes did lead to changes in market rates.

You would think that raising interest rates would discourage investment and consumption, thereby depressing the demand for money and slowing down the growth of the money supply. However, as we saw in Chapter 5, the actual effect on spending and borrowing is quite small unless the changes are massive. Furthermore, where interest rate rises do affect investment plans, they are much more likely to affect long-term ones than short-term ones. This is because the longer the period over which the financing of a project is spread, the greater the proportion of interest in the total cost. This is the reverse of what the government wants to happen; it would usually prefer to depress consumer spending rather than investment which is vital for the long-term prosperity of the country. Furthermore, interest rate changes do not affect all sectors of the economy with equal force. Booming industries may be able to cope with massive rises in the cost of money while depressed industries might be driven under by very small changes.

In consequence, recent governments have moved away from the practice of controlling the supply of money through price. The first milestone was in 1972, when bank rate was abandoned in favour of *minimum lending rate* (MLR). This was still the rate at which the Bank of England would assist the money market but instead of leading market rates it was led by them. MLR was related to, and derived from, Treasury bill rate, being set at a small percentage, usually between $\frac{1}{2}$ to $\frac{1}{4}$%, above. MLR was therefore a penalty rate for the discount houses as they could not borrow from the Bank of England to reinvest in Treasury bills other than at a loss. Occasionally changes to MLR moved it further away from Treasury bill rate, usually as a signal that the Bank wished to see changes in market rates.

In 1981 the Bank ceased publication of minimum lending rate, thereby moving further away from day-to-day control of interest rates. It will still act as 'lender of last resort', of course, but it now operates within an unpublished band of interest rates rather than at one published rate. However, it still retains the right to announce the rate at which it will operate if it thinks that to be necessary to influence rates in a particular direction.

Of a different order are the direct controls which have sometimes been imposed on the rates of interest which the banks may pay to attract deposits. If deposit rates are held down, people will not find saving so attractive and may reduce their bank balances through increased spending. As a result, the banks' ability to create advances will be curtailed. As you will realise, the effect of such a policy is likely to be minimal in the overall level of saving. It is more likely to divert available funds into other, more rewarding, media such as building society accounts. Indeed, this latter result has sometimes been the objective of bringing in deposit rate controls, ensuring that the housing loan market has not been starved of funds.

Treasury directives

As we saw in Chapter 2, the Treasury, through the Bank of England, used to issue directives to the banks concerning their lending. *Quantitative directives* concerned the amounts which the banks were permitted to lend, restricting the overall volume of advances for whatever purpose. *Qualitative directives* sought to restrict the granting of loans for specified purposes, thereby directing funds into areas which it was in the national interest to promote. You will appreciate that only quantitative directives would have an important effect on the total money supply. They were discontinued in 1971 and the Bank now makes only qualitative directives.

Both types of directive are very unpopular with the banks which do not like to be told how much they can lend or to whom they may or may not lend. The Bank reinforces the directives which it gives with *moral suasion*, which really means 'leaning on' the banks to accept them. Everyone concerned knows that the Bank has the statutory power to enforce its rulings if it wished to, so the banks' capacity to refuse is strictly limited.

Adjuncts to monetary policy

In pursuing its monetary objectives the government can employ some further techniques that do not have a direct effect on the supply of money but can help to create the economic conditions in which specific monetary policies will be most effective. We have already seen that monetary policy is just a part of the government's overall economic policy.

The Regulator

As you saw in Table 9.8, a significant proportion of the government's income is raised through indirect taxes, which are principally taxes on expenditure, such as VAT and duties on tobacco and petrol. Amending the levels of these taxes will therefore effectively reduce or increase the spending power of the population and this will have its effect on demand and the money supply. Increasing VAT or other taxes on expenditure will check demand, acting as a deflationary measure. Reducing VAT will stimulate demand for goods and services, having a reflationary effect on the economy.

The government can vary the levels of indirect taxes by a significant proportion (up to 25%) by making an Order in Council. No complex legislative procedure is required. Furthermore, such tax changes will start to bite almost immediately. This means that they can be used to fine-tune the working of the economy. Hence the term 'Regulator' which is applied to them.

Consumer finance regulations

Consumer spending, particularly in respect of consumer durables, can be controlled by the imposition of restrictions on the availability of consumer finance. There are two major ways in which these controls can be applied.

(a) Altering the minimum permissible period of repayment for any loan.

(b) Setting minimum levels of deposit in respect of certain classes of purchase.

By shortening the repayment period or increasing the proportion of the cost that the borrower must fund from his own resources, the authorities can depress consumer demand. On the other hand, reflation can be encouraged by the relaxation or abolition of consumer finance regulations. Their principal shortcoming is that they affect spending on only a limited range of goods, particularly the more costly consumer durables. As a result, certain industries are disproportionately affected by the introduction of restrictions. In 1971, the Crowther Report recommended that they should no longer be regarded as an instrument of monetary policy. Although since that date such regulations have been imposed from time to time, their place has largely been filled by more general fiscal policies.

Monetary controls today

Most governments of the last fifteen years have pursued policies of attempting to control inflation through, among other things, restriction on the growth of the money supply and containment of public sector spending. This is especially true of the Conservative government which first came to power in 1979 with the intention of following a more strictly monetarist line than previous administrations. Central to its policies was the belief that if the money supply could be properly brought under control, ultimately many other problems in the economy, particularly inflation, would also be resolved. Proceeding on this basis, the government pursued a policy of stringent cuts in public expenditure and in 1981 introduced a new set of provisions for monetary control which still apply.

Under the new controls, the government planned to regulate the money supply solely through open market operations centred principally on the sale and purchase of eligible bills. In order to provide for an adequate supply of eligible bills large enough for the purpose, it was necessary to increase to about 50 the number of eligible names, that is, financial institutions whose indorsement or acceptance of a bill turns it into an eligible bill. The Bank ceased lending directly to the discount houses, preferring to make funds available to the market when necessary through open market purchases. As we have noted, the publication of MLR was discontinued. The Bank's objective is to keep very short-term interest rates inside a band which is thought to be consistent with targets set by the government for the growth of the money supply.

The reserve asset ratio which had been mandatory on all banks ceased to apply but all institutions in the newly defined and wider monetary sector came under a requirement to maintain adequate levels of liquid assets. In this connection, eligible liabilities have been redefined. The new provisions are designed more for the purpose of prudential control of all 'banking' institutions, rather than as a way of controlling the money supply. They are much fairer than the previous arrangements which compelled the banks to operate under restrictions which did not apply to their competitors. The ability to call for special deposits is retained although, as yet, no such deposits have been required.

Summary

1 Control of the money supply is part of the government's overall control of the economy, the chief objectives of which are:
  (a) Full employment
  (b) Control of inflation
  (c) Balance of payments surpluses.
2 The quantity theory of money equates four factors:
  (a) Quantity of money—M
  (b) Velocity of circulation—V
  (c) General level of prices—P
  (d) Volume of trade—T
in the equation $MV = PT$.
3 There are several measures of the money supply:
  (a) $M0$ = the monetary base
  (b) $M1$ = 'current' account
  (c) $M2$ = 'retail' deposits including building society items
  (d) $M3$ = all monetary sector deposits
  (e) $M4$ = all monetary sector and building society deposits
  (f) $M5$ = overall purchasing power
4 Other forms of economic policy include fiscal policies and direct intervention.
5 Monetary policy will aim for disinflation or reflation. The conflicting needs in the economy often result in a 'stop/go' cycle which alternates between the two.
6 The principal instruments of monetary policy are:
  (a) Open market operations
  (b) Mandatory liquidity ratios
  (c) Special deposits and supplementary special deposits
  (d) Funding
  (e) Management of interest rates
  (f) Lending directives
These may be reinforced by:
  (a) The 'Regulator'—varying indirect taxation
  (b) Consumer finance regulations.
7 Current government policies concentrate on managing the money supply principally through open market operations.

Self-assessment questions

1 Define: (a) fiscal policy; (b) the quantity theory of money; (c) 'retail' deposits; (d) direct intervention; (e) special deposits.
2 List the components of (a) $M0$, (b) $M3$ and (c) $M5$.
3 List the instruments of monetary policy.
4 True or false:
  (a) If the velocity of circulation increases, the total amount of money spent in a week will increase.
  (b) $M1$ is a better measure of private purchasing power than $M2$.
  (c) Reflation is an extreme form of inflation.
  (d) Special deposits enable banks to increase their lending.
  (e) Raising interest rates encourages long-term investment.
5 List the alternative strategies of monetary policy which can be followed and explain their effects.
6 Explain why monetary policies tend to follow a 'stop/go' cycle.
7 Define 'open market operations' and explain how they affect the money supply.
8 Why did the Bank of England abandon the use of supplementary special deposits?

Assignments

1 Update figures for $M0$, $M1$, $M2$ and $M3$ given in Tables 9.6, 9.2, 9.7 and 9.3 respectively.
  Write a report on the significance of the differences between your results and the levels of these aggregates in March 1987.
2 Obtain the up-to-date balance sheet of your own bank and from it calculate the liquidity ratio using the definitions of 'liquid assets' and 'eligible liabilities' given on page 338.
  Write a report explaining what would happen if the Bank of England introduced a mandatory reserve assets ratio which was set 5% higher than the one your bank is maintaining. Explain what effects this might have on the balance sheet.

10 Parallel money markets

Chapter objectives

After studying this chapter you should be able to:
- list the component parts of the wholesale money markets;
- describe the origins and functions of these markets;
- evaluate their role in the economy;
- describe the components and functions of the foreign exchange market.

In Chapter 2 we looked at the interlinked finance markets of the UK and examined in detail the workings of the 'classical' money market. We also mentioned, albeit briefly, the functions both of the *parallel money markets* which have arisen in the last 30 years and of the related *foreign exchange market*. In this chapter we are going to examine these latter markets in greater depth.

The wholesale money markets

Introduction

The money market as a whole is concerned with the short-term lending and borrowing of money, providing a pool of liquid funds on which the banking system can draw. The 'classical' money market consists of two parts: the *discount market* and the *money market* proper. The principal participants in these markets are the banks, the discount houses and the Bank of England. The classical money market can trace its history back to the 1830s when bill brokers began to buy commercial bills of exchange in the North of England in order to sell them to London bankers. Over the years this market has developed into a very efficient market in liquid deposits which enables the banking system to reduce its cash ratios to a bare minimum. Borrowing in this market is invariably on a secured basis.

Since 1945 a set of *parallel money markets* has grown up alongside the classical market. These have arisen largely out of the desire of organisations other than banks and discount houses to have access to markets for short-term borrowing or lending of large amounts of money. Because of the relatively large volumes of money involved, these markets have become known as 'wholesale' money markets to distinguish them from the 'retail' markets in which the banks compete for smaller individual deposits. The participants in these parallel money markets include the finance houses, local authorities, commercial companies and even, very occasionally, private individuals.

Until around 1970, the parallel markets were quite distinct from the classical markets. The latter satisfied the liquidity needs of the commercial banking system, while the former were a vehicle through which the secondary financial sector could regulate its liquidity. In recent years, however, the two markets have become very much more closely bound together and today all the separate markets can be considered as component parts of one unified whole. Their relationship is illustrated in Fig. 10.1. This intertwining of the separate markets was promoted in the 1970s when the Bank of England encouraged the secondary banks to place funds with the discount houses by allowing them to count such loans as 'eligible assets' for the purposes of liquidity control. Furthermore, at the same time the clearing banks found that they could use the developing *sterling interbank market* to earn a useful return on their excess liquid funds.

The development of these parallel markets has encouraged the growth of specialist *money brokers* whose role is to bring borrowers and lenders of money together. In the early days of the parallel markets these brokers specialised in one particular area. Today most broking firms have expertise in several of the component markets.

The local authority market

Like the national government, local government in the UK finances much of its activity, especially capital expenditure, by borrowing. Local authorities use their income—from local property taxes (rates) and the sale of services such as public transport—only to cover day-to-day expenses, including payment of the interest on any loans obtained. As we saw in Chapter 4, a great deal of this borrowing is long term and is effected through the *savings market* and the *capital market* by taking interest-bearing deposits and issuing various types of bonds and loan stocks. These are very popular with personal investors. In addition, since the 1950s local authorities have raised an increasing proportion of their finance on a short-term basis through money market operations.

Development of the local authority market

Until about 30 years ago, local authorities were expected to satisfy their borrowing requirements by obtaining advances from the *Public Works Loan Board* and the existence of this body meant that they were under no pressure to explore other sources of finance. In 1955, however, the Treasury ruled that in future local authorities would have to meet their financial requirements by borrowing 'commercially' in the open market. Loans from the Public Works Loans Board would still be available but only after all other sources of finance had been tried without success. This change of policy was because the government believed that the high level of the public sector borrowing requirement (PSBR), including the funds needed to make loans to local authorities, was contributing to increasing rates of inflation. Compelling the local authorities to borrow commercially was expected to reduce their willingness to borrow, thereby reducing overall public sector deficits.

It was anticipated that most local authority borrowing undertaken would be *long-term* through the investment market. At first this was the case. As we saw in Chapter 9, however, it can be very attractive to cover long-term financial requirements through continued short-term borrowing by rolling-over the loans on a regular basis. The major advantage of doing this is reduced cost to the borrower. Generally speaking, as you know, short-term interest rates are lower than long-term interest rates. Moreover, when interest rates in general are high there is an added attraction to borrowing short; it affords the possibility of refinancing the loan at lower cost at a later date when interest rates have fallen. Thus, just as central government came to rely on floating debt rather than funded debt for much of its finance, so local government increased the proportions of its short-term borrowing.

The overall proportion of temporary local authority debt is

strictly controlled by the Bank of England at about 15% of total borrowing. The highest proportion which it ever reached was some 25% in the 1960s. Even at about one-sixth of the total, however, the volumes of funds raised through money market operations are enormous. The development of this market for loan funds attracted many lenders who were prepared to make funds available at rates only slightly higher than those applying in the discount market and brokers made a business of bringing together borrowers and lenders. Money brokers have now become a major feature of the London money markets, charging a fee which is additional to the interest that the borrower must pay to the lender. These brokers continue to be the principal route through which funds move into this market.

Funds were attracted into the local authority market from a number of sources, particularly from the secondary (non-clearing) banks. Its development promoted the growth of the other parallel money markets such as the *sterling interbank market* and the *Eurocurrency market*, all of which we shall be examining later. Both of the markets which we have just mentioned developed originally, at least in part, as vehicles by which funds were made available for on-lending to local authorities. Thus, for example, the Eurocurrency market would facilitate the swapping of a US dollar deposit into sterling which could then be lent to be a local authority.

Methods of borrowing

There are two principal means by which the local authorities borrow from the money market; these are the *issue of bills* and the raising of *direct loans*.

Local authority bills. These are very similar to Treasury bills and operate in much the same way. They are sold at a discount and mature at par after a set period of time. Their issue is confined principally to the larger municipalities. They are negotiable instruments which means that the holder of a bill can liquidate his investment prior to maturity date by selling the bill to someone else. The rate of discount at which bills are bought and sold is, of course, a reflection of current short-term market rates of interest.

Like Treasury bills, local authority bills are eligible for re-discount at the Bank of England or for use as security for loans from the Bank. Consequently they have become an important component in the portfolios of liquid assets maintained by the banks and discount houses and there is an active market in them. You may recall from Chapter 3 that the London clearing banks' holdings of local authority bills are now much greater than their holdings of Treasury bills.

Local authority loans from the money market. These are usually repayable at short notice: usually from 2 to 7 days' notice of repayment must be given. This means that there is no set repayment date and, although in theory these loans are short term, in practice many of them are allowed to roll-over for quite long periods without either the lender of the funds or the local authority giving notice of repayment. Rates of interest paid on these loans may be varied by the local authority following the appropriate period of notice. Fixed-term loans, generally up to a maximum of one year, are also available. On these the interest rate is fixed at the outset and cannot be varied by either side. Interest rates in general will respond to the pressure of competition for funds from other markets.

Local authority loans are usually for amounts of £50 000 or multiples thereof. Amounts of £250 000 and over are quite common. Some of the smaller authorities may float smaller loans, down to as little as £1000. These smaller loans are generally taken for a fixed term. The local authority will issue a *deposit receipt* to the lender, a proof of the sum due to him. This is not a negotiable instrument and in the case of fixed-term loans there is no provision for early recovery of the capital sum invested.

The sterling interbank market

Perhaps the most significant of the parallel markets, the sterling interbank market, acts as a link between them all. It is a vehicle for the banking institutions to lend to or borrow from one another according to their needs. (Of course, we are using the term 'bank' in its wider sense here, incorporating a much broader range of institutions than just the clearing banks.)

Development of the market
The interbank market was at first a market for the borrowing and lending of short-term funds between secondary (non-

clearing) banks through which they would adjust their liquidity positions. It developed as an alternative to the traditional methods of liquidity management, as practised by the clearing banks, by way of holdings of Treasury bills and commercial bills bought and sold on the discount market. As we have seen, it received a major boost following the growth of the local authority market when the secondary banks found that they could often make a profit by borrowing surplus liquid funds from other institutions and lending them to local authorities. In particular, during the 1960s, foreign banks operating in the UK found that this market offered a useful method of utilising surplus liquidity. They wished to keep their liquid holdings of sterling low because at that time it was becoming a weak currency subject to continuing depreciation of its international value.

The funds which flow through this market may be looked on as a pool of *wholesale money* which the participants can draw on to increase their own lending. It was not long before the clearing banks saw this potential and began to trade in this market on their own account. This has had a significant impact on the domestic banking scene. Although deposits obtained through retail branch banking operations are still a vitally important source of loanable funds, they are no longer the only one. A significant proportion of deposits is now bought-in on the interbank market. We saw in Chapter 3 that in October 1983 the total sterling deposits (other than certificates of deposits) of the London clearing banks was almost £80 billion; of this total, some 18% (£16 billion) came from money market operations. By 1987 the overall total was £130bn, with a similar proportion coming in via the money market.

Access to this source of funds permitted the clearing banks to expand greatly the volume of domestic credit which they granted but it did bring some new techniques to be learned, particularly in the area of liquidity management. Traditional retail bank deposits are almost all theoretically short term but the banks know that over any given period the demands for repayment would come to only a small, and largely predictable, proportion of the total held. Most of the deposits are for comparatively small sums, so no one depositor would be able to bring about a major change in bank liquidity. There will be seasonal fluctuations in the pattern of demand for repayment but these can be allowed for.

While borrowing on the interbank market allows the banks to obtain much larger amounts in single sums, it also brings the potential need to be able to repay these large sums at short notice. In practice, however, the incidence of repayment of individual money market loans is much more predictable than is the case with retail deposits. This meant that once the banks became accustomed to the system, they were able to forecast their borrowing/refinancing requirements much more accurately. It is largely as a result of this that they have expanded their operations in this area to such a great extent. The clearing banks now permit a measure of controlled *mismatching* between the short-term 'wholesale' deposits which they take and the longer term 'retail' advances which they grant.

Operation of the market

As we have noted, the principal participants in the sterling interbank market are the clearing banks and the other banking institutions, including foreign banks, merchant banks and the discount houses. In addition, there are many non-banking organisations which lend funds to the banking system via this market. These include pension funds, insurance companies, savings institutions (including building societies) and large commercial companies, all of which will have spare liquid resources from time to time which they wish to invest to obtain a return. The advantage of the interbank market is that it offers their lenders the opportunity of a competitive rate of return on their funds combined with minimal loss of liquidity. This means that the funds will be available for their use when they need them.

Deposits in the interbank market are for round amounts, usually of £100 000 or more, the term and the rate of interest being fixed at the outset. Prevailing rates of interest fluctuate in line with other market rates and the previous day's rates are published daily in *The Financial Times*. The increased volume of wholesale money used by the clearing banks has meant that their interest rate structures have become more closely linked than ever to market rates. In particular, their *base rates* are determined at least in part by the interbank rate, known as LIBOR (London Interbank Offered Rate), for three-month money. In late September 1987 for example, three month LIBOR was around 10% and bank base rate was 9%. Clearly, base rate

is not adjusted daily or weekly to follow LIBOR; periodic adjustments are made when the two rates vary too greatly from one
another.

At the same time as bank interest rates became more closely
related to money market rates, they also drifted away somewhat
from the retail rates being offered by other deposit-taking institutions. This came about because the banks did not feel the
same pressures as before to compete with institutions such as
the building societies for small deposits. One result of this was
that bank deposit rates in the early 1980s became progressively
less attractive to personal savers than those offered by building
societies. In consequence, more and more of these deposits found
a home with the building societies rather than with the banks.
To an extent, the banks have countered this problem by introducing special types of accounts, such as 'High Interest
Accounts' to attract the larger depositor.

Deposits in the interbank market are almost all for short
terms, ranging from *call* and *overnight* arrangements up to fixed
deposits of one year, although these latter items are in a
minority. The majority of deals done are for overnight money.
A number of specialist money brokers have emerged, taking a
commission for bringing lenders and borrowers into contact with
one another. All the participants in the market normally use
brokers to place or obtain their funds, although occasionally
deals will be done directly between borrower and lender. The
great advantage of the broker is that he is in contact with all
parts of the market and can usually find a lender or borrower
much more quickly than his principal. Speed is important
because of the volatility of the market rates offered; a change
of as little as $\frac{1}{16}\%$ can represent a significant difference in the
actual amount of the interest to be applied in respect of such
large deposits or loans. Furthermore, if it becomes known that,
for example, a bank is trying to raise a large loan through the
market, interest rates will tend to rise in response to the excess
of demand for funds over their supply. If the loan can be raised
speedily through the services of a broker, the bank will escape
the worst effects of this increase.

We have already said that the interbank market acts as a link
between all the parallel money markets. Funds may enter the
interbank market from any one of the parallel markets and
move from one banking institution to another several times

before being used or on-lent to another of the parallel markets. Perhaps the most significant point to note about the inter-relationships of these markets is that the discount houses have now become full participants in the interbank market. In contrast with the situation in the 1950s and 1960s when the 'classical' and the 'parallel' money markets were almost entirely separate from each other, today they are simply different facets of one integrated market which provides a pool of liquidity for the banking system as a whole.

The Eurocurrency market

Eurocurrency is the name given to deposits of the currency of one country held with a bank which is located in a different country. For example, US dollars held on an account with a bank in London would be called a Eurocurrency deposit.

Development of the market

Eurocurrency dealings began in the 1950s when holders of US dollars found that they could obtain better rates of interest if they deposited their funds in Europe, particularly London (hence the name 'Eurocurrency'), rather than in the United States. At that time interest rates were being held down in the United States by the federal reserve banks. Furthermore, the US balance of payments deficit meant that people in other countries were building up holdings of US dollars which they wished to place on deposit to earn an adequate level of interest. Included in this situation was the USSR which made more dollar deposits available when it began to place its US currency earnings with European banks in preference to American banks; in this case the motivation was political. Because these deposits were all of US dollars with European-based banks, the market was originally known as the *Eurodollar* market.

The development of the market was greatly encouraged by the move to *external convertibility* in western Europe in 1958. This was part of the general relaxation of exchange control regulations which took place as the continent gradually recovered from the effects of the Second World War. The granting of external convertibility meant, for example, that a US dollar deposit owned by a *non-resident* of the UK could be freely transferred into or out of the UK according to the wishes of the owner without being subject to any restriction. Furthermore, the funds could be converted into any other currency which meant that dollars borrowed in the market could be freely exchanged for, say, French francs for use in France. You should note that at that time (and indeed until 1979) UK residents could not transfer UK resident funds out of the country or convert them into a foreign currency without the permission, either general or specific, of the Bank of England. As a result of the intro-duction of external convertibility, holders of 'non-resident' foreign currencies were encouraged to deposit the funds in London, where they could be on-lent via the Eurocurrency market, in the knowledge that they could recover their capital and re-export it at a later date if required. We have already seen how there was a flow of funds from abroad into the UK's local authority market for loan funds.

The demand for Eurodollar loans came originally from two sources: UK importers and US businesses. In 1957 there had been a sterling crisis that led to the introduction of particularly severe exchange control regulations restricting the availability of sterling to finance foreign trade. In consequence, many UK traders turned to the Eurodollar markets to raise the funds they needed to pay for goods which they wished to import into the UK. At the same time in the United States domestic credit was becoming tighter and more difficult to obtain. Many US com-panies therefore turned to borrowing from the European Euro-dollar markets to raise the dollars which they needed to finance their operations in the United States.

The granting of external convertibility led in time to the growth of the more generalised Eurocurrency markets which take deposits and grant loans in currencies other than just US dollars. Most of the major European currencies are now represented in these markets, including: sterling (held by non-residents of course!), Dutch guilders, Deutschmarks, French, Belgian, and Swiss francs, Danish krøner and Italian lire. In addition, certain other non-European currencies are now dealt in, particularly Canadian dollars and Japanese yen. The main 'home' of the Eurocurrency market is in London where the active encouragement of the Bank of England promoted its development. Eurocurrency dealings are also carried on in other major financial centres throughout the world and these several markets are closely linked in their operations despite their geographical separation.

The market today

The Eurocurrency market today provides a valuable source of additional liquid funds which can be borrowed to finance international trade or investment in any part of the world. It is an international market dealing in short-term, large-amount currency loans. Generally speaking, the minimum amount of any transaction on the Eurocurrency market will be for 1 million US dollars or its equivalent in another currency. As we saw in Chapter 5, the interest rates which borrowers pay for funds obtained through the Eurocurrency market are closely related to the prevailing rates in the country of the currency concerned. Thus, a borrower of Eurodollars will be paying a similar rate to that being paid by domestic borrowers in the United States. Among the principal users of the Eurocurrency markets are multinational companies and importers and exporters who have dealings in foreign currencies.

A bank which receives a deposit of Eurocurrency may on-lend it immediately or may *swap* it into a different currency before lending it if interest rate differentials between the two currencies make this worth while. Of course, the bank will still have a liability to repay the deposit in the original currency when the depositor wants his money back or just at the expiry of the agreed term of the deposit. There is the danger that exchange rates will have changed dramatically during the term of the deposit. However, this can be guarded against by setting up a *forward exchange contract* to fix the exchange rate at which the currency will be obtained on the foreign exchange market when repayment is due. (We shall be examining the foreign exchange market later in this chapter.)

The forward exchange rate offered will differ from current or 'spot' rate by an amount which reflects the interest rate differential between the two countries. This means that, in theory, the costs of borrowing £1 million sterling for a period of three months are exactly the same as the costs of borrowing the equivalent in US dollars through the Eurocurrency market and arranging a forward contract to cover repayment. It is for this reason that there is no advantage for a trader who has no currency income to borrow in a foreign currency, even though interest rates may be lower than sterling rates. In practice, there will occasionally be very small rate differentials between two Eurocurrencies and these can be exploited by the banks.

Eurobonds

In recent years a *Eurobond* market has developed which deals in longer-term loans, usually over periods of ten to fifteen years. An interesting development related to the issue of these bonds is the novel practice of denominating some of them in units of *special drawing rights* (SDRs) rather than in any particular currency. SDRs are the unit of 'currency' used by the International Monetary Fund; their value is calculated from the value of a basket of five real currencies. The practice of issuing such bonds grew out of the market's reluctance in the late 1970s to issue bonds denominated in particular currencies, especially US dollars, because of the fluctuations in value that were affecting the foreign exchanges. If the currency in which a bond was expressed was to fall in value, lenders of the funds would receive back much less in terms of 'international purchasing power' than they had originally parted with.

Certificates of deposit

The certificate of deposit market grew out of the Eurocurrency market in the 1960s as a vehicle for the processing of sums of money which were too small to be of interest to the parent market.

Dollar certificates of deposit

The first certificates of deposit were issued in the United States in the early 1960s and were introduced into London via the American banks in 1966 to attract the smaller dollar deposits, although the UK and continental banks were quick to follow suit when the popularity of CDs became apparent. The certificate acknowledges receipt of a dollar amount (minimum $25 000) by a 'bank' and is repayable on a stated date which may be set at any time from one month to five years after the date of issue. The issuing bank has the use of the funds for the period to maturity and can on-lend them through any of the money markets, perhaps after 'swapping' them into another currency. The longer term of some of these certificates assists the banks with their long-term liquidity planning.

Sterling certificates of deposit

These were a later development, although they operate in just the same way as dollar CDs, being issued in respect of deposits of £50 000 and over up to a maximum of £500 000.

The interest rates applying on CDs are of course linked to the appropriate Eurocurrency rates and, in general, you will find that the rate rises with the length of the term of the deposit. One particular advantage to the bank is that purchasers of CDs will accept a slightly lower rate of return than investors in other fixed-term deposits. This is because CDs are *negotiable instruments* which can be sold to someone else if the holder needs to recover his capital at short notice instead of waiting for the certificate to mature.

A *secondary market* in 'second-hand' CDs issued in the UK is operated by the discount houses and this provides a mechanism by which the holder of a CD can dispose of his holding at any time. The price obtainable for the certificate will depend on current rates of *yield* at the time the sale is made. As we saw in Chapter 2, when interest rates rise, the price of existing fixed interest securities will fall; when interest rates fall, prices will rise. This ensures that the purchaser of such stocks will always obtain the going rate of return on his investments. It also means, of course, that a forced sale at short notice can result in a capital loss for the seller if he has to sell at a high rate of *discount*. Nevertheless, a limit is placed on these fluctuations of value by the fact that a CD will eventually be redeemed at par by the issuing bank. The existence of this additional touch of liquidity in the investment has made CDs very popular, particularly with the non-bank investor.

The finance houses market

We saw in Chapter 4 that finance houses are institutions which provide specialist finance to assist both private individuals and businesses in the acquisition of capital assets such as vehicles and machines. They are often called 'hire purchase finance companies', although this term tends to understate the broader range of facilities which they offer. Their principal facilities are *hire purchase loans* and *leasing*. Like the 'banks', they operate principally on borrowed money, using funds taken on deposit to fund loans and credit facilities. As you know, they raise some of these funds by taking deposits from the general public in competition with the banks and other savings institutions. However, a significant proportion is raised through the money markets.

Money market operations are particularly attractive to the finance houses for two reasons. First, it is much simpler to raise money by buying in 'wholesale' in large amounts than it is to attract 'retail' deposits. Second, levels of finance house lending tend to be quite closely controlled by the government through the operation of the Regulator (which we discussed in Chapter 9) in its attempts to control the economy. Their volumes of lending may therefore vary considerably over very short terms in response to applications of the Regulator. The finance houses consequently need flexibility in their access to deposits, facilitating their increase or decrease at short notice. This is much more easily achieved in the wholesale market than in the retail market.

The finance houses cannot acquire all their deposits through the money market as this would leave them with too unstable a deposit base. Just as they can reduce at short notice the level of deposits which they take from the market, so the market can reduce at short notice the level of deposits which it makes available to them. This can cause severe liquidity problems. Just such a situation has arisen on a number of occasions when foreign exchange fluctuations have encouraged foreign investors to remove their funds from the London money market to prevent them from being eroded by devaluation of the international purchasing power of sterling. For this reason, most finance companies as a matter of policy obtain some proportion of their funds from the retail market.

The intercompany market

Developed since 1969, this market was originally the product of a period of tight credit. Businesses which could not raise finance from the banking system found that they could sometimes borrow direct from other companies which had surplus funds. Specialist brokers have now emerged to act as intermediaries in this market which consists of some 500 major companies. Loans are for £50 000 and over. Since these loans are made direct from one company to another, they have no negotiability; the lender cannot retrieve his funds by on-selling his rights to someone else. The intercompany market differs in this respect from other sections of the money market.

A company which has surplus funds need not always dispose of them through the intercompany market. They could be profitably placed with a finance company, with a local authority or through any one of the parallel markets. The options open to the company's finance director exemplify the interlinked nature of these markets.

Since 1986, a *sterling commercial paper* market has developed in competition for company funds. Through this market, companies wishing to raise funds can issue 'paper' which can then be bought or sold by the lenders. This 'paper' is in effect an IOU, similar to Treasury bills or certificates of deposit. The banks participate in the issuing of the paper and make a market in it, guaranteeing to buy and sell it at the market price. By doing so, they have made themselves intermediaries in a part of the money market from which they were previously excluded.

Other financial markets

The foreign exchange market

A further market with which the banking sector is heavily involved is the foreign exchange market in which foreign currencies are bought and sold. Although not directly related to the money markets which we have been discussing, the foreign exchange market does have an effect on these markets and is in turn affected by them.

Functions of the foreign exchange market
The UK is primarily a trading country which makes its living out of doing business with other countries. Raw materials are imported and manufactured into finished goods, some of which are then re-exported to earn the funds to purchase more raw materials. The services of UK businesses, including banking services, are also sold to foreign customers, thereby earning

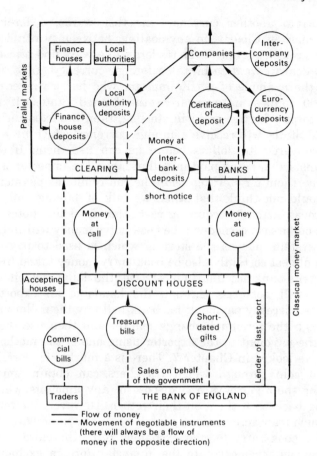

Fig. 10.1 The relationship between the 'parallel' and the 'classical' money markets

further funds from abroad. Some of the country's foreign earnings have to be spent abroad to purchase foodstuffs since the country cannot meet all its requirements out of domestic production. If the country as a whole is trading at a profit, that is, it is earning more abroad than it spends, there will be a *balance of payments surplus*. If it is trading at a loss there will be a *deficit*.

Foreign trade of this nature creates the need for a medium by which amounts of money denominated in one currency can be converted into another currency, in other words, a foreign exchange market. Clearly, in any dealings between two traders in different countries, one of the traders will always find himself having to deal in what to him is a foreign currency. Take, for instance, the example of a UK importer who has arranged to buy 10 000 tonnes of grain from the United States. If he arranges to pay for the grain in sterling, then the exporter in the United States will receive a 'foreign currency' which he will have to convert into dollars before he can use them. If the exporter insists on being paid in dollars, then the importer will have to buy them for sterling before he can remit the payment.

You should not think that when we talk of 'buying dollars' that we mean actually acquiring cash, that is, dollar notes or coins; the dollars concerned will be book-entry money within the financial system, just as the sterling which is used to pay for them will almost certainly also be book-entry money taken from the importer's bank account. In most cases the dollars which are purchased will not pass through the hands of an exporter making the currency payment; his bank will buy the dollars for him through the foreign exchange market and then use them to make the payment to the exporter using one of the methods at which we looked in Chapter 7. There is a market for foreign notes and coin through which travellers can obtain 'small change' for their journeys and dispose of any amounts which they bring back with them on their return. However, the total value of such transactions is very small when compared with the market for book-entry foreign exchange. It is, therefore, very much a subsidiary market to the 'financial' foreign exchange market.

The existence of an active foreign exchange market servicing the needs of importers and exporters creates the opportunity for funds to be converted from one currency to another for reasons other than the needs of traders. We have already noted, for example, that it is common practice in the Eurocurrency markets to take deposits in one currency and then 'swap' them into another currency before on-lending them. *Currency speculators* may use the market to acquire or dispose of holdings of a currency in anticipation of it fluctuating in value relative to other currencies. For example, if you believe that over the next few weeks dollars are going to become dearer relative to sterling, you may decide to convert your sterling holdings into dollars straight away. After the price variation has taken place, you can convert them back, obtaining more sterling than you had to start with! Of course, you run the risk that the value of dollars will not rise relative to sterling, or even that it may fall resulting in a net loss. The value of one currency expressed in terms of another is called an *exchange rate*. In some countries, exchange control regulations restrict people's ability to hold currency or even to purchase it for the purpose of making payments abroad. This is not the case in the UK.

Exchange rates

An exchange rate expresses the value of one currency in terms of another currency. In other words, it tells you how much of one currency you will be able to buy for a given amount of another. In the UK it is usual to quote what are known as currency rates which indicate how much of a foreign currency a buyer may expect to receive for £1 or how much a seller would have to give to get £1. Thus, for example, a US dollar rate of 1.40 means that £1 sterling can be traded for US 1 dollar 40 cents. In other countries the local currency will be used as the base for the exchange rate, instead of sterling. Thus, in the United States the dollar:sterling rate will express how much sterling will be traded for one dollar. If the sterling:dollar rate is 1.40 as above, the dollar:sterling rate will be 0.71½.

You will recall how in Chapter 1 we explained that when a country was on the *gold standard* the value of its currency in the international market remained stable, being determined by the amount of gold in the coinage or, latterly, the amount of gold that a standard unit of currency was stated to be worth. The UK finally left the gold standard in 1931, since when the exchange rate of the pound sterling has been allowed to *float*. This means that the exchange rate prevailing between the pound and any other currency will not remain the same for any great length of time; it will fluctuate according to the relative levels of supply and demand for the two currencies. If the UK spends more abroad than it earns, there will be a greater demand for foreign currencies (to pay the bills) than for sterling and the price of sterling will fall. Such changes of value may be either long term or short term. On the one hand, sterling exchange rates will rise and fall marginally within each day, often from minute to minute. On the other hand, over the longer term of months or years there may be a general rising or falling trend in the value of sterling.

Between 1945 and 1971 there was a system of *fixed exchange rates* under which countries could allow the exchange rates for their currencies to fluctuate only within 1% on either side of an agreed *par value*. If the sterling exchange rate moved outside this range, the authorities had to intervene directly in the foreign exchange market, either to prop up the rate by buying sterling (and thereby reducing currency reserves), or to reduce the value of the pound by selling sterling (and increasing the currency reserves). Since 1971, exchange rates have been *freely floating*, their level being determined by market forces alone. Although the Bank of England still occasionally intervenes in the market to damp down violent fluctuations in the exchange rate, it is no longer required to do so by international agreement.

The UK's balance of payments is the principal determinant of change in the exchange rates between sterling and other currencies but there are a number of additional factors which influence the international value of the pound. These include:

1 *Interest rates:* high rates of interest in the UK as compared to other countries will attract investment funds into the country, increasing the demand for sterling. Low rates of interest will reduce the international value of the pound.

2 *Confidence in the economy:* if it is believed that a country's economy is in decline and that there are poor prospects for the future, traders and investors will be deterred from entering into dealings with that country. This will depress the exchange rate for its currency. Confidence in a booming economy will have the opposite effect.

3 *'Leads and lags':* traders who anticipate significant changes in the exchange rate may attempt to manipulate these changes to their own advantage by bringing forward or postponing currency payments due to them or from them in respect of their foreign trade. A UK exporter who expects the value of the pound to *fall* will therefore *bring forward* the payments due to suppliers abroad so as to obtain the maximum amount of currency for each £1. If he expects the value of sterling to *rise*, he will *postpone* payments as long as possible. These operations themselves effect the exchange rates by increasing or reducing

demand in the short term; in the longer term they do not affect the overall balance of payments situation.

4 *Speculation:* people with no commercial need to trade in a currency may nevertheless do so as a speculation. If a holder of a foreign currency believes, for example, that at the moment the pound is too cheap, he may convert his funds into sterling. Similarly, if holders of sterling believe that its international value is about to fall, they may convert their holdings into other currencies. Speculation is often denounced as a bad thing which tends to destabilise the foreign exchange markets by introducing unpredictable flows into and out of particular currencies. On the other hand, however, it can also be seen as a useful influence because the efforts of speculators will help to iron out any marginal price differentials between different sections of the markets.

The nature of the foreign exchange market

The London foreign exchange market is made up of dealers and brokers. Although there are some specialist currency dealers who pursue no other business, most of the dealers are in fact employed by the banks, all of which run their own *dealing sections* to buy and sell foreign currencies for the bank. Bank currency dealers operate sometimes as agents for customers who wish to trade for large amounts of a particular currency. More commonly, however, they are operating to adjust the bank's own stocks of currency. Purchases of smaller amounts of currency from customers or sales to them are usually made through these stocks rather than being placed directly on the market. This enables the currency dealers to trade only in the larger amounts which the market expects, usually the equivalent of at least 1 million US dollars.

Unlike the stock market, the London foreign exchange market never had a central market place at which dealers could meet and trade with each other. All dealing is done over the telephone and there is a network of private lines which has connections to all the major dealers. Dealers make their profits (or their losses!) out of the difference between the rate at which they can buy currency and the rate at which they can sell it. Their maxim is 'buy high and sell low'. This is known as *arbitrage dealing*. If you think about it, you will see that it is really no different from what a shopkeeper does: buying-in supplies at one price and selling them at another (higher) price.

There are also a number of foreign exchange brokers operating in the London market. They do not actually trade in currencies themselves; their function is to bring buyers and sellers of a currency into contact with each other. They make their profits out of a commission fee which is payable by both the buyer and the seller. This fee, often called brokerage, is calculated as an agreed percentage of the value of the deal which the broker has helped to arrange.

The London market now thinks in terms of a US dollar base instead of a sterling base for the exchange rates which the dealers quote to each other. This is because the US dollar is now the major commercial currency of the world and to do so eases communication with foreign exchange markets in other parts of the world. Although many of the currency deals done by the London dealers are done with other London dealers, there clearly has to be contact with foreign exchange markets in other parts of the world. The London market cannot be a closed system which trades only with itself.

The international foreign exchange market brings together buyers and sellers of currency located in different countries from each other. It is made up of a number of local foreign exchange markets, such as the London market, that are linked together through modern telecommunications media: telephone, telex, etc. The market hardly ever closes because at any time of the day somewhere in the world, foreign exchange dealers will be at work and in contact with dealers in other countries. Because of these permanent operations, the international market operates as a single integrated unit with, in effect, a single set of prices. If it was discovered, for example, that currency dealers in Hong Kong were selling sterling at cheaper rates than elsewhere, buyers would flock to buy from these dealers. This would increase demand in that particular market, pushing the price of the pound up and bringing the Hong Kong exchange rate back into equilibrium with the rest of the market.

Spot and forward currency dealing

Foreign exchange deals may be categorised as either spot deals or forward deals. Spot deals are for amounts of currency which will be delivered from seller to buyer straight away. Forward deals are for currency which is to be delivered at some time in the future. Dealers negotiating a forward deal with a client will offer the alternatives of a *fixed contract* which specifies the particular day on which the contract will be completed, or an *option contract* which allows the client the choice of when within a given period he wishes to complete the contract.

Spot rates are the basis of the exchange rates which prevail in the exchange market. Dealers always quote two rates for any given currency; the price at which they will buy and the price at which they will sell. As we have seen, the difference between the two prices represents their source of profit. The forward rate is based on the spot rate adjusted to allow for interest rate differentials between the two countries, as we discovered when looking at the Eurocurrency market. If the interest rate in the foreign country is higher than in the UK, the forward rate will make the currency cheaper *vis-à-vis* sterling than the spot rate. The currency is therefore said to be at a *discount*. If the foreign interest rate is lower, the forward currency will be dearer. It is said to be at a *premium*. These differences simply reflect the different potential income to be earned by depositing covering funds at interest in the two countries concerned.

The London International Financial Futures Exchange

In September 1982 a completely new financial market opened in London: the London International Financial Futures Exchange (LIFFE). This market is very similar in many ways to the markets in commodities futures which have existed for many years. A commodity futures contract is an agreement for the supply of a certain amount of a particular *commodity*, such as wheat, potatoes, ore, etc., at a fixed price on a particular date in the future. A financial futures contract is an agreement to provide a certain amount of *finance* at a fixed price on a particular date in the future. The market therefore exists to provide a mechanism for hedging against changes in the cost of finance for those who will need finance at some time in the foreseeable future and for those who will have funds to invest. In order to facilitate the working of the market, LIFFE trades in standardised financial contracts. This enables finer—more exact—prices to be quoted and makes it easier to trade the contracts. Two distinct types of contract are offered: *interest rate* contracts and *exchange rate* contracts.

Interest rate contracts

These are contracts to supply or take deposits of money at a specified rate of interest at some time in the future. Clearly, for any particular contract to be agreed there has to be someone who is prepared to make the deposit and someone who is prepared to take it on the same terms on the same date. Three types of interest rate contract are currently available through the market.

Three-month sterling time deposits. The depositor agrees to deposit sterling funds for a fixed period of three months on a particular date in the future. The minimum deposit amount is £250 000.

Three-month Eurodollar deposits. A deposit in Eurodollars must be provided on the agreed date. The minimum contract size is £1 million. In both this and the previous case, the person receiving the funds must provide an instrument evidencing deposit of the appropriate amount in one of a number of specified banks—essentially a certificate of deposit.

Twenty-year gilts. Intended for the long-term hedge, this type of contract must be for a minimum of £50 000. When the depositor provides the funds, the receiver must provide an appropriate amount of a government stock with fifteen to twenty years to maturity.

The value of these contracts, especially the first two, will be principally to company finance directors. Consider the case of a company which knows that in three months' time it is going to have £500 000 available for deposit as a result of the completion of a major project. If the finance director believes that interest rates are going to fall before the funds come into his hands, he can attempt through LIFFE to arrange a contract to put the funds on deposit when available at a rate fixed now. This removes a major element of uncertainty from the company's financial planning, just as arranging a forward exchange contract removes the uncertainty from dealing abroad in foreign currency.

Exchange rate contracts

Exchange rate futures are in effect a standardised form of forward exchange contract, the minimum amount of any contract being £25 000 or its equivalent. The market deals with several currency rates including sterling, US$, Deutschmarks, Swiss francs and Japanese yen. When the contract is set up, the two parties agree to deliver to each other agreed amounts of the specified currencies on a fixed date in the future; clearly in such a transaction the exchange rate is also fixed. Through this market and the interest rate market, LIFFE provides a further bridge between the money market and the foreign exchange market.

Summary

1 The money market is concerned with the short-term lending of money. It can be divided into:
(a) The classical money market.
(b) The parallel money market.

2 The parallel money market comprises six interlinked markets:
(a) The local authority market
(b) The sterling interbank market
(c) The Eurocurrency market
(d) The certificate of deposit market
(e) The finance houses market
(f) The intercompany market.

3 Local authorities finance much of their expenditure by borrowing from the capital market and from the money market. Their principal money market instruments are:
(a) Local authority bills
(b) Local authority loans.

4 The sterling interbank market developed as a means for secondary banks to lend to or borrow from each other. The clearing banks now raise a significant proportion of their deposits through this market which acts as a link between all the wholesale money markets.

5   Eurocurrency is the name given to currency deposits with a bank in another country. The market provides a valuable source of additional liquid funds.

6   Eurobonds provide a vehicle for longer-term deposits of currency amounts.

7   Certificates of deposit are negotiable instruments which allow purchasers to liquidate their funds before maturity if required. Both sterling and dollar CDs are available.

8   Finance houses, like banks, lend money taken in on deposit and it is convenient for them to raise a proportion of their funds through the money markets.

9   The intercompany market exists to allow major companies to make direct loans of liquid funds to each other.

10 The foreign exchange market is an international market with one set of prices throughout.

11 The London foreign exchange market is made up of brokers and dealers through whom exporters, importers, investors and speculators can acquire or dispose of foreign currency holdings.

12 An exchange rate is an expression of the value of one currency in terms of another.

(a) A spot rate is for currency which is to be delivered immediately

(b) A forward rate is for currency to be delivered at an agreed future date.

13 The London International Financial Futures Exchange deals in futures contracts for the supply of money. It treats money as a commodity.

14 There are two types of financial futures contract:

(a) An interest rate contract

(b) An exchange rate contract.

Self-assessment questions

1   Define (a) exchange rates; (b) certificates of deposit; (c) Eurocurrency; (d) futures contracts; (e) forward exchange contracts.

2   List the components of the parallel money markets.

3   List the types of financial futures contract.

4   Describe the workings of the local authority market.

5   True or false?

(a) The classical money market is entirely separate from the parallel money markets.

(b) Banks now hold more local authority bills than Treasury bills.

(c) The Eurocurrency market is a market for dollar deposits held outside the United States.

(d) Currency speculation is a bad thing as it disrupts the pattern of exchange rates.

(e) Forward currency exchange rates represent what the dealer expects the spot rate to be on the maturity date of the contract.

6   Explain the ways in which an importer might find it to his advantage to introduce 'leads and lags' into his currency payments.

7   Analyse the reasons why the clearing banks become involved in the sterling interbank market. What effect has this had on their operations?

8   Explain why currency rates of exchange continually fluctuate. What are the determining factors?

Assignments

1   Obtain a recent copy of *The Financial Times* and find the page which gives details of foreign exchanges and money markets (usually both are on the same page).

Find the sections which give details of Eurocurrency interest rates and the pound Spot and Forward.

(a) Select any three Eurocurrencies and calculate the average interest rate differential between each of these currencies and sterling for *three-month money*.

(b) Draw up a table comparing these differentials with the amount of *discount* or *premium*, expressed as an annualised percentage, by which the three-month rate for each currency differs from spot rate against sterling.

2   Obtain an up-to-date copy of your own bank's balance sheet. (You may have one on hand which you used when reading Chapter 3.)

(a) Calculate as percentages of total deposits the funds that have been raised through each of the money market vehicles which we have discussed.

(b) Prepare a brief talk for a meeting of your local Institute of Bankers on the significance of these proportions.

11 Personal services

Chapter objectives

After studying this chapter you should be able to:

- describe the range of personal services available to bank customers;
- identify the main personal services available and state their attributes;
- relate the attributes of these services to the needs of specific personal customers;
- evaluate the methods adopted by the banks for marketing their personal services.

Introduction

Traditionally, the operations performed by the UK banks centred on only three areas of activity: the taking of deposits, making advances, and operating a money transfer service. Clearly, these are all closely related to one another, the objective being to *lend money* which is the profitable activity of the three. Taking deposits generates funds for lending and money transfer services are necessary for the attraction of deposits. Since the 1950s, the banks have introduced progressively more sophisticated versions of these services and have diversified into innumerable areas of activity not directly related to this traditional 'trinity'. The UK bank of today has turned itself into something of a 'financial department store', capable of meeting all the financial needs of each customer from the cradle to the grave, hardly ever needing to refer the customer to outside specialists. The objective of this transformation is, of course, the pursuit of profit. It has assisted this in two principal ways. First, the services available themselves may generate profit; second, and more importantly, the provision of a full range of services promotes *customer loyalty* and encourages customers to obtain *all* their financial requirements from the bank rather than shopping around.

Marketing financial services

The range of services to personal customers is breath-taking, the majority of the new services having been introduced within the last twenty years. You can imagine what a major change has occurred in branch banking as a result of these introductions. Branch staff have had to become familiar with a large number of services and branch managers have ceased to be purely lenders and have become more general financial advisers. The most striking change, however, is the acceptance by the banks that their services have to be *marketed effectively* and that customers have to be attracted to use them against competition from other financial organisations and from each other.

Business development programmes

Marketing the products is an essential, one might say *the* essential, activity of any business. If at the end of the day no-one buys the goods or services produced, the business will fail. Marketing may be said to comprise four principal activities:

(a) *identifying* the most profitable markets, both now and in the future;

(b) *assessing* the present and future needs of customers in these markets;

(c) *designing and producing* products to meet these needs;

(d) *promoting and managing* the products to achieve pre-set business development goals.

In a bank, these activities are performed at both Head Office and branch level. Clearly, Head Office staff set the bank's overall marketing strategies and design the new services. Nevertheless, branch managers have a great deal of autonomy in pursuing their responsibility for business development at local level; it is usually they who decide which of the bank's portfolio of services best merit promotion in the *market segment* which the branch serves.

Benefits of services
The principal requirement of a successful service is that it *must meet customers' needs*; the principal objective of the selling

process is to show customers how well a particular product will satisfy their needs. Consumers do not buy goods or services for what they are but for what they can do for them. They purchase the *benefits* of the services rather than the *attributes*. Thus, for instance, you would not purchase a television set simply because it contained 74 transistors, 152 resistors, and came in an attractive walnut effect cabinet; you would buy it principally for the benefit of watching television programmes. It is just the same with bank services.

The selling process, then, involves the matching of *needs* and *benefits*. Staff who are involved at branch bank level must be able to identify a customer's needs, select the appropriate service and show the customer how that service satisfies the need. This involves much more than just knowing how the service operates. When the large-scale introduction of ancillary services began in the 1960s, there was some considerable resistance from bank staff to the idea that they would have to assume the role of salesperson. This stemmed largely from the mistaken notion that selling involves persuading people to buy something they do not want. Certainly the first step may be to show the customer that he has a requirement which has not previously been recognised but if there is no true underlying need for the product its sale should not be attempted. 'High-pressure' selling tactics may result in sales being made but they do not generally produce satisfied customers. The banks are very dependent on repeat business and, therefore, satisfied customers are very important to them.

Target markets

The benefits of a particular service are appropriate to the needs of a particular group of customers. This is known as the *target market* for the service. The target market for some services will be extensive, for others it can be quite restricted but the market for each service will be *unique* as no two services meet the needs of identical groups of customers. Any one bank customer will, of course, be part of several target markets for several different services. Knowing the specific identifying characteristics of customers who go to make up the target market for a particular service is very important to the branch banker because it helps in identifying which services are appropriate to which customers.

There are two alternative strategies which can be adopted as a basis for identifying the 'prospects' among existing customers to whom bank services can be promoted. First, there is the option of selecting a particular service and then deciding, on the basis of information extracted from branch records, which customers may have an *unsatisfied need* for the service. The question being asked is, 'Which among the branch customers make up the target market for the service?' One of the great advantages enjoyed by the banks is their captive market of account holders, about whose affairs they have a considerable depth of knowledge. The second option is *cross-selling* to particular customers. This approaches the problem from the other end. It involves concentrating on existing customers and, after analysing their probable needs for financial services, approaching them with details of appropriate facilities which they are not already using. It can often be used at a time when a customer is making use of one service which combines well with other services. Thus, for instance, a customer who requests the supply of travellers cheques and foreign currency should always be asked whether he or she has arranged travel insurance. The question being asked here is, 'What *other* target markets does the customer belong to?'

Advertising and promotion

The promotion of bank services may be done on a national basis or on a local basis through a particular branch and usually both types of promotional effort will take place at the same time. It is each branch manager's responsibility to build up the business of his branch and this involves a constant drive for new business by *all* branch staff. When a national advertising campaign is undertaken by a bank, local efforts are usually designed to be complementary to it so as to gain the maximum benefit from the raised public consciousness which should result from the national campaign. When there is no national campaign, branches are usually free to follow their own sales programmes.

In-branch promotions
The commonest methods of reaching existing customers with messages about services they are not using are in-branch displays and 'statement stuffers'. This latter method involves

including advertising material with the regular statements of account sent to all customers. The material used may be nothing more than the bank's current advertising leaflet about a particular service or it may be a quite elaborate personal letter to the customer explaining why the branch manager feels that the customer could benefit from the service concerned. In either case the system is quite cheap, since postage costs will be incurred anyway on the statement sent out. Unfortunately, the material sent out is all too easy to ignore, often being consigned straight to the customer's wastepaper bin.

New customers are, of course, vital to the long-term growth of a bank but attracting them presents branch staff with a completely different set of problems. Perhaps the most important source of new contacts is the network of personal relationships which branch staff can build up in the local community. Active fostering of local connections with solicitors, accountants, and other professional people is vital if the bank's name is to be remembered when new financial arrangements are being sought.

National advertising

The 'big four' clearing banks all undertake national advertising campaigns, as do many of their smaller competitors. There are several different possible objectives for such campaigns. *Organisational advertising* is designed to keep the name of the bank in the public mind and to foster a particular 'brand image' for the bank calculated to appeal to the market segments which the bank sees as its major source of business. It does not seek to promote particular services. *Product awareness* advertising is designed to make the public aware of the broad range of services available from a particular bank, again without concentrating on the details of any particular service. Many people do not have direct access to a bank account and there is still a great deal of ignorance about even the basic banking services. *Product advertising* in respect of specific services is also undertaken, often either to counter competition from other sources or to promote new services.

The message communicated will normally be about the *benefits* which the customer may expect to gain as a result either of bringing his or her business to the bank or of using the particular service being promoted. The advertising will generally also seek to differentiate between the service offered by the advertiser and that available from its competitors. The points of distinction accentuated may be very slight; in reality the services of all the commercial banks are very similar.

The media for advertising varies from nationally broadcast television commercials to small inserts in local newspapers. In general, a bank has to balance the cost of the advertising against the number of people that it will reach. Television reaches the largest audience but it is very costly; newspaper advertising is cheaper but reaches a smaller number of people; it is also less immediate and therefore easier to ignore. The advertising medium chosen must also be appropriate to the target market. It is, for instance, unlikely that a bank would advertise an investment management service on a commercial 'pop' radio station since only a very small proportion of the audience would be potential users of the service.

Personal account services

Types of account

You will certainly be familiar by this stage in your studies with the various types of account which are available to bank customers. Indeed, we have discussed many of their attributes individually elsewhere in this book. Nevertheless, before proceeding to examine some of the more recently introduced services, it is important that we briefly re-examine collectively these most basic of banking facilities.

Current accounts
The current account is the archetypal bank account, being available in its complete form from no other type of organisation. The balance of a current account is withdrawable on demand either by way of cash withdrawals or through the use of cheques which are the principal identifying feature of the current account. Standing orders and direct debit facilities are also available for making payments out of a current account.

Overdrafts. These become available through the use of the current account, the customer being permitted to draw cheques or other orders for the payment of funds in excess of the balance standing to the account. Interest is charged on a day-to-day basis on the outstanding overdrawn balance. Interest rates range from a minimum of 2% over base rate for well secured overdrafts agreed with the bank in advance, up to 7% (or more) over base rate for unauthorised advances created by the unarranged presentation of cheques in excess of the balance. There is no *right* to an overdraft on a current account and when cheques are presented which create an overdraft without prior arrangement the bank has the option of returning them unpaid.

Commission charges. These may be levied quarterly or half yearly on current accounts to compensate the bank for the work undertaken in operating the clearing system and other necessary parts of the service. Each of the high street banks publishes a standard tariff showing how it calculates its commission charges. In recent years these have become quite complex. Generally, the arrangement is for a charge to be levied for each item passing through the account with different levels of charge for different items. Processing cheques, for instance, involves more work than processing automated standing orders and, therefore, the charge for cheques is higher. Against the total of charges accrued in the charging period, the bank may offset *notinal interest* (at a very low rate) on any credit balances maintained on the account. No credit interest as such is paid on current account balances. In recent years many banks have waived all charges on current accounts provided that during the charging period the balance has not fallen below a set limit. The level of this limit has varied from bank to bank with £100 credit being quite common; some banks do not charge customers who simply stay in credit. This can still be profitable because of the use the banks can make of these credit balances to finance their lending activities. Customers whose balances fall below any such limit find that their accounts attract charges at the published tariff for the whole of the relevant charging period, not just the period they are below the limit.

Statements of the account. These are sent to the customer at regular intervals; the commonest frequency is quarterly, although many customers prefer to receive them monthly to help them control their finances. This is important in view of the large number of transactions which pass through the average customer's account. Today, just over half the working population of the UK is paid by funds transferred into a bank account, usually a current account, rather than in cash. The banks are seeking to extend this to a greater proportion of the workforce and it is anticipated that the proportion will be at least 80% by 1990. Twenty-four-hour access to banking facilities via *automated teller machines* is expected to be an important factor in wooing the 'unbanked' portion of the workforce, who are predominantly manual and 'blue-collar' workers, towards the idea of *cashless pay*. A recent change in the law will undoubtedly help. Until 1986, employees had rights to demand payment of wages in cash and this was a significant hindrance in persuading certain sections of the public to accept payment into a bank account. The Wages Act 1986 provides that payment by bank transfer is a legally acceptable alternative to cash, thereby removing that difficulty.

Deposit accounts

While current acounts are designed to facilitate the processing of short-term funds flows, deposit accounts are for the holding of medium-term and long-term surpluses of funds. Cheques are not available for use with deposit accounts which therefore provide the banks with a much less volatile source of funds for use in lending. Payments into a deposit account may be made in cash, by credit transfer, by transfer from a current account or by cheque.

Credit interest. This is paid on the balances standing to the credit of a deposit account. Deposit rate generally follows the fluctuations of base rate, being between $1\frac{1}{2}$% to 3% below it at any one time. In theory, the banks compete for deposits through the interests rates but in practice these tend to conform very closely to one another.

Withdrawals from deposit accounts are subject to seven days' notice, although it is usual to permit withdrawals on demand in consideration of the depositor losing 7 days' accrued interest on the amount withdrawn. Credit interest is paid net of tax. Tax at the *composite rate* is deducted from the amounts due to all personal customers.

High interest accounts. Most banks offer accounts with higher interests for customers who can keep their deposits above a minimum level, commonly £2000. These accounts, sometimes also called 'Gold Deposit' accounts, may also permit withdrawals on demand and without penalty. The drawback is that if the balance falls below the minimum level, the interest rate also falls, probably to well below the standard deposit rate.

Investment accounts. Different banks have different investment account schemes but they all revolve around the idea of paying more attractive rates of interest for more stable deposits from small savers. Some are regular subscription schemes which involve a monthly deposit of an agreed small amount; these are sometimes called *bonus savings* schemes. Others involve the deposit of a lump sum, usually £1000 or more, for a fixed term of up to 2 years at fixed rates of interest. The dividing line between these latter accounts and *money market* type deposits is very hard to define. Money market accounts usually pay slightly better rates of interest but are limited to amounts of £10 000 or more.

Savings accounts. These are similar to 'ordinary' deposit accounts in that interest is paid at only a moderate rate on credit balances and the use of chequebooks is not permitted. The principal difference is that savings account deposits and withdrawals continue to be recorded manually in a *passbook* which the account holder must produce at every transaction. Deposit accounts have now almost all been transferred onto the more modern statement system, under which statements of account are produced periodically through the bank's computer system and forwarded to the account holder as a record of all transactions since the last statement. Use of the passbook, however, enables the bank to allow savings account customers to make withdrawals at other branches of the bank, although these withdrawal facilities are very limited, commonly a maximum of £10 per day, because of the possibilities of fraud should the passbook be lost or stolen. In the absence of any special arrangements, deposit account holders may make withdrawals only at the branch at which their accounts are maintained.

Credit interest is paid on savings accounts, usually at a rate which is the same as or slightly below deposit rate. Many banks' savings account schemes provide for regular saving through various different schemes such as the provision of money boxes ('home safes') for the accumulation of deposits. These accounts are something of an anachronism in the modern world and they are not now actively promoted by the banks. They make up only a very small proportion of total bank deposits.

Premium accounts. In recent years, banks have introduced various hybrid accounts combining some of the features of both current and deposit accounts. Perhaps the most common is the Premium or 'Gold' account. This offers use of a cheque book while paying interest on the credit balance provided that it does not drop below a prescribed amount. The amount varies from bank to bank but it is always several thousand pounds.

These accounts are targeted at customers who maintain high credit balances which they would otherwise be tempted to transfer into investment accounts, on which the bank would have to pay even higher interest.

Loan accounts

This is the other traditional method of lending and it differs quite significantly in operation from the overdraft. When a loan account facility is granted, a separate loan account is opened in the borrower's name; the full amount of the loan is debited to the account and the funds credited to the current account for use. Repayment of the loan is by regular uniform *instalments* over a period of time, most commonly between one and three years although medium-term and even long-term loans are now granted to businesses. As with an overdraft, interest is charged periodically at an agreed percentage above base rate, being calculated daily on the outstanding balance of the account. Loan accounts are intended to finance lump sum capital expenditure, while overdrafts finance short-term excesses of expenditure over income.

Personal loan accounts. These have largely superseded the traditional loan so far as the private customer is concerned. The principal difference between the two types of loan account is in the method by which interest is calculated and applied. On a personal loan, the interest is calculated at a *flat rate* percentage on the original amount of the loan multiplied by the number of years over which the loan is granted. The total amount of the interest is then added at the outset to the capital amount borrowed for repayment with the capital by regular instalments over the agreed period. The *true rate* of interest on personal loans, calculated on the reducing balance, is much higher than the quoted flat rate. The Consumer Credit Act 1974 requires the bank to inform borrowers of both rates so that there is no confusion. Most personal loan schemes are restricted to advances of £500 to £5000 over periods of up to three years.

Budget accounts

Budget accounts are a modern, formalised version of the overdraft. They are designed to help customers plan for and meet their regular expenses by ironing out temporary excesses of expenditure over income. There are two variants: traditional and cashflow accounts.

'Traditional' budget accounts. These require the customer to complete an analysis of all regular payments (gas and electricity bills, mortgage payments, insurance policies and so on) which are to be made out of the budget account over the next 12 months. The customer agrees to credit the account each month with one-twelfth of the total of these payments. Payments are made as they fall due. It does not matter whether the budget account is in credit or overdrawn at any particular time; at the end of twelve months the account should in theory return to a nil balance, payments in having balanced with the payments out. In fact, estimated payments for the year never prove be the entirely correct and some residual balance remains at the year end. This is extinguished by a transfer to or from the current account. The process is then started all over again with an estimate of the following year's expenditure. No interest is paid on credit balances and no interest is charged on debit balances but an annual *management fee* is charged, calculated as a percentage of the total annual payments made out of the account. (We cover budget accounts in greater detail in Chapter 13.)

Cashflow accounts. These are a more modern variant of the budget account. Under this arrangement the customer agrees to make a regular monthly payment, usually a minimum of £20, to a special account which is marked with a borrowing limit of thirty times the monthly contribution. The account is then used for making regular payments by utilising a specially prepared chequebook. There are two practical differences between this type of account and the 'traditional' budget account. First, *unbudgeted* payments may be made out of the account provided that the limit is not exceeded; it may therefore be used to pay for unexpected car repairs or for impulse purchases of goods and so on. Second, the account does not have to be cleared once a year. Provided that the monthly contribution is continued, the borrowing limit will continue to apply. Thus, the account provides a *revolving credit* facility. This is much more convenient than the previous annual arrangement although some customers feel that the ready access to credit is too much of a temptation. Interest is charged at a set percentage above base rate on any overdrawn balance and a small fixed rate of credit interest is paid when the account is in credit. A *commission charge* is also levied based on the number of items passing through the account.

Cheque cards

Probably the most striking development in the banking world in the last twenty years has been the proliferation of different types of plastic cards which are offered to the customers of the banks and other financial institutions. Generally these cards relate to one or both of the traditional bank services of money transfer or borrowing facilities. Approximately one in four adults in the UK now hold one or more of these cards. Probably the most familiar of these cards is the cheque guarantee card, commonly known as the *cheque card* or the *banker's card*. Cheque cards are issued by all the commercial high street banks, including the Trustee Savings Bank, with the exception of Barclays, as their Barclaycard fulfils the dual role of cheque guarantee card and credit card (see below).

Purpose of the scheme
We have already explained that use of a cheque card *guarantees* payment of the holder's cheques up to a certain level, provided that certain conditions are complied with. A person taking a

cheque backed by a cheque card therefore no longer relies on the implied warranty of the drawer that he has sufficient credit available in his account to meet the cheque; reliance is placed instead on the promise of *the bank* that the cheque will not be returned unpaid irrespective of the state of the drawer's account.

The cheque card scheme was first introduced in the mid 1960s with the specific intention of promoting *current account banking* which, as you know, is attractive to the banks because of the 'free balances' which it generates, enabling them to increase the profitability of their lending. As a greater number of 'ordinary' people were persuaded to open current accounts, the use of cheques ceased to be a prerogative of the 'monied' classes. Unfortunately, this reduced the general acceptability of the cheque as traders felt that there were increased dangers of losses through dishonoured cheques. The cheque card restored the balance, but only at the cost of the banks taking on to themselves the responsibility for any bad debts created through their use.

It is certain that the cheque card was a vital factor in the phenomenal growth of current account business in the 1960s and 1970s, but a situation has now been created in which personal cheques are virtually unacceptable without the backing of a cheque card. Consequently, access to cheque card facilities is requested by almost all current account customers, many of whom may not meet the strict criteria of creditworthiness which the banks would wish to apply. You will appreciate that giving a customer a cheque card and, perhaps, two books of thirty cheques each creates for the bank a very real credit risk. The bank may be called on to substantiate its guarantee to pay all sixty of the cheques, even if the customer has disappeared leaving no funds in his account to meet the cheques as they are presented. In 1986 losses to the banks in respect of cardholders' bad debts and fraudulent misuse of stolen cheque cards exceeded £26 million. It is clear, therefore, that the character and reliability of an applicant for a cheque card will be very important considerations for the bank.

The cheque cards issued by the commercial banks are all in the same format, and the same conditions must be observed if the beneficiary of the cheque hopes to obtain the protection of the guarantee (*see* page 300).

Operation of the cheque card scheme

Cardholders. Cheque cards are aimed at all creditworthy current account customers. Since use of the card may result in the creation of overdrafts, it is normal to restrict their issue to customers aged 18 and above who are therefore legally liable for their own debts. Cards can be supplied to the parties to a joint account provided that an 'either to sign' arrangement applies; shopkeepers and others accepting cheques drawn on the account could not be expected to know the signing arrangements on the account! In fact, 'both to sign' joint accounts are becoming much less common.

Before a cheque card is issued, the customer will be required to sign a standard form of agreement which sets out the terms and conditions for the use of the card. The customer's acknowledgement that he or she will not *countermand payment* of any cheque issued with the backing of the card is particularly important. Clearly, since the bank guarantees payment of such cheques, it cannot accept orders not to debit them to the customer's account. In signing the agreement, the customer also acknowledges that the cheque card remains the property of the bank and that it will be returned on demand. This provision enables the bank to recover a cheque card which is being misused by the customer to create unauthorised overdrafts.

Reciprocal encashment facilities. The participating banks, together with Barclays, have agreed that they will cash cheques backed by cheque cards for each other's customers. The encashment limit is £50 in any one day. To ensure that this is observed, each personal cheque book issued by the banks contains at the back a *frequency marking page*. The cashier who cashes a cheque under the scheme must mark this page to show the date that the transaction took place. If a further withdrawal is attempted elsewhere on the same day, the second cashier is thereby alerted to the previous transaction. Before allowing the second transaction, permission must be obtained from the account-holding branch.

With a few minor exceptions, a customer of any one of the participating banks who cashes a cheque at a branch of any of the other banks will have to pay a fee of 50p. This benefits the banks with a wide distribution of branches and gives them a competitive edge over banks with small or localised networks.

Electronic funds transfer. Current issue cheque cards include on the reverse a *magnetic stripe* which can be encoded with details of the cardholder's branch, account number and so on. This enables the cards to be available for use in electronic funds transfer systems such as automated teller machines and point-of-sale terminals through which a shop can debit a customer's account directly with the cost of goods purchased. As yet, there is no large-scale operational system for electronic funds transfer at the point of sale (EFTPOS), although a few pilot schemes are in operation. The cheque card might form the basis around which such a system could operate, although as yet its electronic capacity is unused.

Credit cards

Use of credit cards in the UK has developed over the same period as the use of cheque cards but there are some vitally important differences between the two services. While cheque cards are specifically a *bank service* related to the operation of current accounts, a credit card scheme may be offered by a non-banking organisation. As it happens, the two major UK credit cards are operated by banks and of the cards in use in 1987 over 20 million were bank-issued cards.

The major national credit card operators are Access (10.7 million cards on issue), Barclaycard (8.9 million cards) and Trustcard (2.5 million cards). Access is run by the Joint Credit Card Company run jointly by a number of high street banks including Midland, National Westminster, Lloyds, Royal Bank of Scotland, Clydesdale, Ulster Bank and Northern Bank; it is affiliated to the world-wide MasterCard network. Barclaycard and Trustcard are linked to the international Visa organisation, and operated by Barclays and the Trustee Savings Bank respectively. Barclaycard is also offered to customers of the Co-operative Bank who require a credit card.

Use of a credit card

A credit card can be used to purchase goods and services from suppliers, known as 'outlets', who participate in the system. It can also be used to obtain cash at branches of participating banks and recent developments have enabled these cards to be used in bank automated teller machines. For each transaction a *charge voucher* is prepared showing the nature of the transaction, the amount due and the details of the cardholder's account with the credit card company. These latter details are impressed on the voucher direct from the card using a special *imprinter* machine with which each outlet is supplied. An account is maintained centrally for each cardholder; this account is separate from the cardholder's bank accounts and, indeed, some cardholders do not have bank accounts at all. At the end of each day, the supplier totals all the charge vouchers which he has collected from the holders of a particular credit card and arranges for them to be remitted to the appropriate operating company. This can be done by handing them in at a branch of a participating bank together with a *bank giro credit* for the supplier's own bank account.

When the charge vouchers are received centrally they are debited to the cardholders' accounts. Once a month each cardholder receives a statement showing all the items received since the last statement and the balance owed. When the card is issued, the account is marked with a borrowing limit appropriate to the cardholder's circumstances and the cardholder is advised accordingly. If the cardholder uses his card to make payments which exceed his limit, the credit card company may terminate the arrangement and request the return of the card.

On receipt of his monthly statement the cardholder may pay off the whole of the balance due or just a portion of if. Government restrictions require a minimum monthly repayment (at present of £5 or 5%) of the balance outstanding, whichever is the higher. The cardholder has a period of twenty-five days from the date the statement was issued to make his payment; thereafter interest is calculated on the outstanding balance. You can see that if a cardholder buys goods with his card immediately after receiving a statement, it will be a month before he receives a statement showing the purchase and a further twenty-five days before he has to make a payment. Thus, he has the benefit of an interest-free credit period of almost two months. The interest calculation on cash withdrawals ('cash advances' as they are often termed) may be somewhat different: some companies charge interest from the date the cash is drawn, while others levy an extra service charge for each withdrawal.

The credit card offers the holder permanent access to credit facilities up to the limit on the account. As soon as some of the borrowing has been repaid, further purchases may be made.

This is known as *revolving credit*. The interest on the borrowing is calculated monthly on the outstanding balance, as we have seen, and the rate charged is comparatively high. In January 1988, for instance, the interest rate on credit card borrowing was 1¾% per month, which is equivalent to a true annual rate of 23.1%. (This is slightly higher than you might have expected, i.e. 20%, because over the year interest is charged in later months on interest paid in earlier months.) In the same month, the overdraft interest rate was between 12% and 15% for most personal customers. Generally, cardholders are prepared to pay the higher rates for short-term borrowing because of the convenience of the revolving credit facility and because of its informality; there are no interviews before a loan is taken, for instance. The cost of credit card borrowing makes it relatively unattractive for long-term borrowing.

Charge cards

Charge cards comprise items such as Diners' Club cards (260 000 UK cards) and American Express cards (750 000 UK cards). In use they are very similar to credit cards, the cardholder presenting the card when paying for goods or services which have been supplied. The essential difference is that the cardholder must repay in one lump sum the whole amount due on receipt of each month's statement; there is no credit period allowed. Unlike the credit cards which are issued free of charge, the operating companies relying on interest payments for their income from cardholders, the charge cards are subject to commission charges. The operating companies levy an *enrolment fee* when the card is issued and an *annual membership fee* thereafter. Both credit card and charge card companies also levy a commission charge on the 'outlets' which accept their cards. This charge is calculated as a percentage of the amount of each payment accepted; the level varies from outlet to outlet but never exceeds 5%.

Gold Cards. These are a development of the charge card. They are intended for use by people earning £20 000 or more per year and, as well as the normal charge card facilities, they offer extensive cash withdrawal facilities and 'automatic overdraft' services. The banks have participated with the charge card companies in finding potential users of these cards.

Automated teller machines

These machines are in effect online computer terminals operated by the customers. To gain access to the service he requires, the customer inserts his ATM card and keys in his Personal Identification Number (PIN). At the end of the transaction the card will be returned to him by the machine.

Cash dispensing facilities are the most important service offered, and the customer may select the amount required. Most banks restrict the amount of withdrawals to a maximum of £100 in any one day. More importantly, before the cash is paid out, the customer's balance is vetted, taking account of any overdraft limit marked on the account; the transaction will be refused if the account contains insufficient funds. At the bank's discretion the ATM cards themselves may be encoded with a small over-draft limit to permit 'emergency' withdrawals.

Other facilities available capitalise on the connection between these machines and the bank's central computer, although not all of the following services have been introduced by all the banks which operate automated teller machines. The customer will usually be able to request the machine to display his balance and he may even be able to obtain a ministatement showing the last few entries to his account. Requests can be made for a new chequebook or an up-to-date statement, and these will be dispatched direct to the customer by the appro-priate branch. The machines are capable of allowing the customer to make transfers between accounts, to make payments to third parties through the credit transfer system, and even to set up standing orders. Depending on where they are located, some machines also accept deposits for customers' accounts; this is in the nature of a simple *night safe depository* facility and is not automated. Branch staff clear the deposits from the machine once a day and remit the credits to the appro-priate accounts after checking the deposit manually.

Interbank reciprocity. This is the latest stage in broadening the use of automated teller machines. Until recently, the customers of one bank could use only the machines installed by that bank but now two interbank cash withdrawal networks have been set up. The Midland and National Westminster banks were the first to announce a link-up, later being followed by the TSB. A second network links the machines of Barclays, Lloyds, Royal Bank of Scotland and Bank of Scotland. Furthermore, although all the banks which operate automated teller machines provide customers with ATM cards, it is possible to arrange for these machines to accept appropriate credit cards.

There are two further ATM networks available on today's high streets. The 'Matrix' network has been set up by a group of building societies, including the Leeds, Woolwich, Anglia and Alliance & Leicester societies. Of even more interest is the 'Link' network for this links both banks, including Girobank, Co-operative and Allied Irish Banks, and building societies such as the Abbey National and the Nationwide.

The great advantage of the automated teller machine is that it gives customers extensive access to basic banking facilities twenty-four hours a day without any particular credit risk for the banks. They open the door to completely new types of account such as the Royal Bank of Scotland's 'Cashline account', designed specifically to be operated through the use of a 'Cashline' card. This type of account is intended for the predominantly 'working class' customer who requires a safe home for his wages pending expenditure and regular cash withdrawals but only limited money transfer facilities. A traditional current account is inappropriate because a chequebook would not be used except for making cash withdrawals over the counter which are, in fact, much more costly to the bank than automated teller machine withdrawals. Where wages are paid into the account direct by credit transfer, this type of customer may well hardly ever enter the branch premises. The Royal Bank of Scotland is able to offer a small rate of credit interest on these 'Cashline accounts'.

Investment services

Deposits

Generally speaking, very few personal customers retain large balances on current account. It is unnecessary and unrewarding for them to do so; the funds should be put to work, if nowhere else at least on a deposit account of some sort. We have already considered the operation of the 'ordinary' deposit and the 'investment' deposit types of account and customers with particularly large sums to invest, especially those who might require access to their funds at short notice, may find that *money market* deposit facilities meet their needs more fully. The banks can advise on appropriate types of deposit and make the necessary arrangements.

Bid deposit accounts

These accounts, which offer interest at rates closely related to money market rates, are designed to attract larger lump-sum deposits; the lower limit for such accounts is usually £10 000. The customer may be required to deposit the funds for a fixed term—anything between one month and two years—in which case the interest rate is fixed for the full period of the loan. Alternatively, the funds may be left on deposit indefinitely, subject to a stated period of notice before the customer may withdraw the funds or before the bank may vary the interest rate. In this latter case, unlike the situation with 'ordinary' deposit accounts, the period of notice will be enforced by the bank. Notice may be set at anything between one day and several months.

The interest rates offered on these accounts are generally quite attractive, unless the bank already has a surplus of funds which it is unable for some reason to lend out. In such a case the bank has no need to offer particularly attractive rates since it will not be seeking to attract further funds! As you are aware, many other financial institutions such as finance houses, merchant banks and leasing companies accept deposits through either the money market or the savings market. Many banks have set up subsidiary companies to operate in these fields and these companies bid for their own deposits independently of their parent banks. Thus, it may be that when a bank's own bid deposit rates may be low the rates offered by its finance company or other subsidiaries could be attractive.

Certificates of deposit

As we discussed in Chapter 10, the high street banks issue sterling certificates of deposit for large sums of money deposited with them for fixed periods of anything of up to five years. The minimum investment is £5000, the maximum being £500 000. The interest rate is fixed at the time the certificate is issued; the longer the period of the deposit, the more attractive the interest rate will be. These certificates are *negotiable bearer documents* and if a holder wishes to recoup his investment before the maturity date it is possible to sell the certificate to a third party. There is an active market in certificates of deposit. Dollar certificates of deposit are also available for customers who have foreign currency available for deposit. In this case the minimum deposit is 25 000 US dollars. Interest rates on dollar certificates are, of course, related to prevailing rates in the United States, rather than to sterling interest rates.

Treasury bills

Some customers invest short-term funds in purchases of Treasury bills which can be arranged through the bank. As you already know from Chapter 2, Treasury bills represent a form of short-term borrowing, falling due for repayment 91 days after issue. They are issued at a *discount* and redeemed at *par*, thereby providing a return to the purchaser. Treasury bill discount rate is one of the basic rates of the money market. The minimum investment is £10 000. If the holder of a Treasury bill wishes to realise his funds before the end of the ninety-one-day period, he can sell it through the discount market. Thus, although the rate of return on Treasury bills is quite low, they represent a very liquid investment which is most suitable for those who may need to lay their hands on the cash value at short notice. The banks charge a commission for dealing in Treasury bills.

Stock Exchange services

We have already considered in Chapter 4 the function of the Stock Exchange as a vehicle for the mobilisation of long-term investment funds. The great advantage of stock exchange investment is that the investor's strategy can be tailored to meet his particular needs taking into account his circumstances. A portfolio of *capital investments* may be structured either for income or for capital growth, or for a mixture of both.

Stock exchange transactions

An investor who wishes to buy or sell stock exchange securities will do so through a 'stockbroker', either a *broker/dealer* or a *market maker*. Generally speaking, personal investors do not approach the brokers direct; a majority of them arrange their dealings using their bank as intermediary, leaving the selection of the broker to the discretion of the bank. The bank is responsible to the customer for the integrity of the broker whom it selects and it will therefore deal only with brokers whom it knows to be good for their engagements. This is to the advantage of the customer and costs him nothing, since the bank is remunerated by receiving a share of the broker's normal commission. Furthermore, the customer is relieved of some of the paperwork and administrative detail of the transaction as this will be handled on his behalf by the bank. The broker also finds the arrangement advantageous as it relieves him of the need to establish the 'bona fides' of the investor. He may assume that any client introduced by the bank is good for the transaction contemplated. The bank will satisfy itself before placing the order that the customer has the funds to pay for the shares he wishes to buy or that he is in possession of the shares which he proposes to sell.

Most of the high street banking groups include at least one broking firm under their umbrella. Deals will usually be channelled in this direction although the customer can specify otherwise.

An interesting development in 1987 was the introduction by Barclays of 'Barclayshare', a broking and investment advice service for the private investor operating through the branches of the bank. For an annual membership fee, customers receive a low cost share transfer service (which makes maximum use of automated settlement systems) plus a monthly magazine, investment advice and valuations.

Safe custody of certificates
Many investors find it convenient to leave the certificates which represent their holdings in safe keeping with the bank. This certainly facilitates bank dealings in the holdings on the customer's behalf and it guards against damage to or loss of the certificates. This latter point is of great importance if the customer has invested in any *bearer securities* which are negotiable and which therefore may be permanently lost if a thief manages to pass them on to a party who takes them for value and in good faith (*see* page 608).

Bearer securities also involve the holder in periodic collection of dividends from the company. These cannot be remitted direct by the company in the way that dividends on registered securities would since the company does not (indeed cannot) maintain a register of bearer shareholders. The usual process is for the bearer to respond to advertisements calling for the collection of a due dividend by clipping a numbered *coupon* from the certificate and sending it up to the company. This process is both tedious and time-consuming and depends on the shareholder spotting the advertisement in the first place. If the bank holds the certificate it will assume the responsibility for collecting the dividends. It is, in fact, much more efficient for the bank to collect the dividends for large numbers of investors at the same time.

Nominee companies

Banks are usually prepared to hold shares and similar items as the *nominees* of their customers, usually through the agency of a separate nominee company. Under such an arrangement the investments are transferred out of the name of the customers and into the name of the bank's nominee company which thereafter receives the dividends on their behalf and deals with any clerical tasks which have to be undertaken. The service is very useful to customers who have very active portfolios as it avoids the need for the investor personally to complete a *stock transfer* form for every sale. The facility is also useful to customers who reside abroad but who wish to retain in this country both their holdings of securities and any income arising out of them. However, there are dangers that this service could be misused by customers wishing to evade tax liabilities on their holdings or otherwise to defeat legislation. For this reason, banks investigate the integrity of customers wishing to use the service.

Investment advice

Duties to the customer

As a general rule, branch bank staff are not allowed to give specific investment advice to customers because of the dangers to the bank should that advice prove to be misguided. In *Woods v. Martins Bank Ltd and another* (1958), it was held that since

Martins Bank had clearly held itself out in its advertising as a source of all types of financial advice, it was therefore responsible for the bad advice about a proposed investment which Mr Woods had received from one of the branch managers. There is little doubt that this decision would extend to all the other banks. It is certainly true that most personal customers look on their bank manager as their chief, often their only, financial adviser, and they would feel understandably aggrieved if any investments recommended to them were to perform poorly.

The standard of care required by the law of an adviser would probably be the same standard of care that the bank would exercise in managing its own investments. Clearly, it is not possible for every branch manager to be an expert on investment or to have access to all the sources of information available to the bank's own investment analysts. The manager's advice should therefore be restricted to more general comments on the principles of investment: the advantages and disadvantages of particular types of investment; the requirements of the customer's situation; the principles of portfolio construction and so on. If the customer requires more specific advice, on whether to invest in particular companies for instance, he should be referred to an expert adviser.

Introduction to brokers

A readily available source of advice is to be found in the services of stockbroking firms. It is, of course, part of a stockbroker's business to advise on portfolio planning and revision and to recommend particular investments. Most branch banks will have developed a working relationship with a number of broking firms to which customers can be introduced when advice is required. The bank will not be liable for the quality of any advice given, except in so far as the customer is entitled to obtain an introduction to a competent broker; clearly this is not likely to be a problem. The broker will charge the customer a fee and none of this will accrue to the bank. Nevertheless, such introductions do have the merit of cementing the working relationship between the bank and the broker.

As you know, most of the banking groups now include a stockbroking arm and requests for advice will of course be channelled in that direction where possible.

Investment divisions

The bank may also be able to supply investment advice through one of its own specialist divisions. These have been set up to manage both the banks' own portfolios of investments and those of customers. Such investment divisions may be able to provide *ad hoc* advice on particular securities, although the general preference is to take on the overall management of a customer's investments. Clearly, any advice given will be subject to the liabilities to the customer which we have already noted but the specialists employed in these sections of the banks are much better placed to give detailed advice than the average branch manager.

Investment management

Most of the high street banks will take on the management of a customer's portfolio of investments. Usually this is done on a *discretionary* basis which means that the bank has the right to vary the investments held without reference to the customer. Clearly, any sales or purchases of securities will be undertaken in pursuit of an overall strategy dictated by the customer's needs and circumstances. The benefit to the customer of the service is that he obtains professional and expert management of his investments, as well as being freed from the need to monitor and review the performance of his holdings himself. A management fee is charged and you will appreciate from the level of expertise required that this is quite a costly service. Consequently, there is a lower limit below which the return on the portfolio does not justify the costs of management. Most banks limit the service to portfolios valued at more than £25 000.

Planned portfolios

The investment manager's job is to construct a portfolio of investments which match the customer's needs. It may take as its starting point the customer's existing investments but it is often found that many of the holdings must be sold off and the proceeds reinvested in other more suitable items. The customer's needs from the investments are largely determined by personal circumstances: important factors include age, income, tax position, future commitments and so on. The principal choice to be made is whether to invest for income or for capital growth;

most protfolios will attempt to effect some sort of compromise between the two but leaning toward one or other of the extreme ends of the spectrum. The investment management service is used by the relatively wealthy whose interest is usually more in protecting their capital than in supplementing their already adequate incomes. For such individuals capital growth is the more important option, especially in times of high inflation when the monetary value of capital has to grow significantly each year simply to maintain the same level of purchasing power.

Diversification of holdings is the cornerstone of investment practice; an investor should never risk all his funds in one company or even in one sector of the economy. Funds should be spread over a number of different areas so that if one sector suffers a serious reverse, the investor will not lose the whole of his investment income or the whole of the value of his capital.

Managed portfolios

A recent innovation has been the introduction of the so-called 'managed portfolio'. This consists of one master portfolio of investments which are managed as a single unit in pursuit of generalised investment objectives. Customers who wish to participate in such a scheme contribute the amount which they wish to invest and this is used to purchase more of the approved holdings. Customers with existing portfolios may contribute these instead of cash; approved holdings will be maintained while other holdings will be sold off and the proceeds reinvested. This system is cheaper to operate than the 'planned portfolio', consequently it is suitable for the smaller investor. In many ways it resembles the unit trust system with the important difference that the customer actually owns a proportion of the shares in the portfolio and receives notification of his holdings.

Unit trusts

The functions of a unit trust are to collect funds from a number of investors, to pool the subscriptions received and to invest the total in a range of securities, principally stocks and shares of quoted companies. The objective is to obtain a greater, and hence safer, diversification of investments than any one investor could achieve individually. As you know, it is a general principle of investment strategy that the more diverse the portfolio, the less it will be vulnerable to changes in the value or income-generating capacity of any one stock. Unit trusts are, therefore, a vehicle for enabling 'small' investors to participate in stock market investment.

The Department of Trade and Industry has the power to authorise unit trusts and few investors will place funds with an unauthorised trust. Before authorisation is given, the Department will ensure that the trust meets certain criteria concerning its range of investments. Generally the range of investments is limited to government securities and quoted stocks and shares. No more than $7\frac{1}{2}\%$ of the total value of the portfolio may be invested in any one security. The operator of a unit trust fund, known as the 'manager', charges a fee for his services of up to 5% of all new monies subscribed, deducted before the funds are invested, plus an annual service charge of up to $\frac{1}{2}\%$ of the total value of the portfolio, deducted from the dividend income of the fund. Many of the banks have set up their own unit trusts to take advantage of this source of income, being ideally placed to sell units in the trust to appropriate customers through their branch networks. The Department of Trade monitors the fees charged by all fund managers, ensuring that they keep within the prescribed limits.

Unlike a participant in a managed protfolio, a unit trust investor does not personally own a proportion of the portfolio of investments. He receives instead an allotment of an appropriate number of units in the trust, entitling him to receive a proportionate share of the trust's distributions of income. The value of his units is determined by the value of the underlying securities, rising and falling according to market prices. The purchase price of new units (the 'offer price') is calculated on the basis that subscriptions will increase the value of the fund and that therefore new securities must be purchased. Thus, the offer price per unit is based on the lowest price at which the managers could purchase the securities backing any one existing unit.

Advantages to the investor
The chief advantage to the private investor is that a unit trust permits, as we have noted, greater diversification of investment in equities and therefore better risk avoidance than would be

possible with the limited funds available to the individual. Nevertheless, investment in a unit trust does represent chiefly investment in stock market securities and, while this offers the possibility of capital growth, it also bears the risk of capital losses. The danger is minimised, however, by the professional investment management from which the fund will benefit. The investment managers will give daily consideration to the structure of the portfolio, which is much more than the normal private investor could or would do. Because of the size of a trust's portfolio, the costs of management to the individual investor are much lower than the costs of any other form of investment management. The same is true of dealing costs which are porportionally very low because of the volumes of business which a unit trust undertakes on the stock market.

Unit-holders wishing to realise their investment may sell their units back to the fund managers who are obliged to re-purchase them on demand. The price at which they will do this is known as the 'bid price' and is calculated on the basis that underlying investments would have to be sold, although in fact the managers may be able to make the payment out of funds subscribed by new investors. The bid price therefore represents the best price which could be obtained in the stock market for the investments, taking account of any accrued income in the fund but deducting the costs of dealing.

Types of unit trust
There are several hundred unit trusts available to investors, some managed by banks, some by specialist managers. All have their own investment strategies. Any investor should therefore be able to find at least one trust which is following an appropriate strategy. There are three principal decisions which the fund managers have to make in setting their strategy. First, there is the question of which sector or sectors of the economy to invest in; a *general fund* will spread its capital throughout the economy, while a *specialist fund* will concentrate on investing in companies in a limited range of different sectors. Second, there are the alternatives of investing for *capital growth* or for *income* or, indeed, for any point on the spectrum in between. Finally, there is the question of what to do with the income arising from the investments and whether it is to be distributed to the unit-holders or reinvested in further

securities. Many trusts offer both alternatives for the same fund issuing *income units*, which pay the holder a periodic 'dividend' on his holding, and *accumulation units*, from which the holder receives periodic allotments of further units representing re-investment of this income.

Withdrawal funds. These offer the investor a minimum guaranteed rate of return on a lump-sum investment. So far as is possible, this is met out of the income from the portfolio but if in any one year this proves impossible, fund units will be realised to meet the shortfall. This can result in erosion of the capital value of the investment, the danger being particularly great if an unrealistically high rate of return is selected.

Savings plans. These are available to investors who wish to contribute regularly to a unit trust. English law does not permit schemes under which the investor binds himself contractually to pay in a set amount each month, so the investor may vary the amount, or even cancel it, at his discretion. A particular advantage to the investor of making regular payments is what is known as *pound cost averaging*. The cost of units will fluctuate from month to month; when units are cheap, more will be purchased for a particular contribution than when they are dear. Over a period the effect of this will be that the average cost of units actually bought by a regular investor will be lower than the average price of the units over the same period.

Financial planning

Personal representatives

Duties
We have already given some consideration in Chapter 6 to the need for personal representatives who will wind up the estate of a deceased person. If the representatives are appointed under the terms of a *will*, they are called *executors*. If there is no will or if the named executors are unable or unwilling to assume their duties, the Court may appoint *administrators* to assume the responsibility; it is usually an interested party, such as a

member of the family, who applies to be appointed administrator in such cases.

The duties of both types of representative are basically the same, covering a number of different tasks. First, the necessary funeral arrangements must be made, the costs of which have to be paid before any distribution of the estate is permitted. Next, the assets of the estate must be gathered together and valued so that the liability for *inheritance tax* can be assessed. If any tax is due, this must be paid before the Court will authorise the representatives to assume control of the assets of the estate. The debts and other liabilities of the deceased must be satisfied before, finally, the remaining assets may be distributed to the beneficiaries. The distribution of the estate must follow the provisions of the will, if there is one. Sometimes a will creates a trust to which some or all of the assets may be transferred. You will appreciate that the duties of a personal representative can therefore be quite onerous.

When a will is being drawn up, the testator's thoughts of who to name as executor will normally turn to close friends and members of the immediate family. It is not surprising that such private individuals often have serious misgivings about taking on the role. Most people find that looking after their own affairs is quite enough for them and they have neither the time nor the expertise to take on the management of someone else's problems. The question of *expertise* is more important than many people think when drawing up a will; the beneficiaries will expect the estate to be wound up without delay and this involves, among other things, such difficult tasks as liaising with tax authorities and arranging the realisation of assets without unnecessary losses.

Executorship service

As an alternative to the appointment of a private individual, a testator may name a corporate body as executor. The banks have offered just such an executorship service for many years, this being one of the very first ancillary services which they provided. A fee is charged for the work done, calculated on an *ad valorem* basis related to the total value of the estate; the more valuable the estate, the higher the fee charged for administering it. This reflects the fact that, in general, the larger estates are also the more complex. There is a minimum charge, which means that the service is not really suitable for very small or simple estates. The fee is not charged until the bank begins to act as executor, in other words after the death of the testator.

There are significant advantages in the appointment of the bank as executor. A customer knows that he has chosen a safe manager and that the possibility of loss through theft or fraud has been avoided as far as possible. The customer also knows that the bank offers continuity of service, meaning that it will be able and willing to act when the time comes. While a private individual might predecease the testator, the bank's executor and trustee department will remain in existence indefinitely. Turnover of staff introduces a measure of impersonality into the relationship between bank and customer but this is a small price to pay for the benefits of the arrangement.

The staff of the banks' executor and trustee departments are specialists able to bring a significant degree of expertise to their operations. It is advantageous if the department's advice is sought before the will is drawn up so as to ensure that it truly fulfils the wishes of the testator. A poorly framed will can lead to numerous problems at a later stage by failing to make its provisions explicit, possibly even resulting in an intestacy or a partial intestacy. The will must include a standard clause appointing the bank as executor and authorising the payment of the appropriate fee.

Trusteeships

The duties of trustees are quite similar in some ways to those of executors. Both involve the control of someone else's assets. However, while the role of an executor in winding up the estate of a deceased person should normally be of quite short duration, the role of a trustee may continue for many years. It is a trustee's duty to hold and manage on behalf of the beneficiaries the trust assets which were formerly owned by the person creating the trust.

Types of trust

Will trusts. The majority of trusts are created out of the provisions of a will. Although executors do not invariably also become trustees, a significant number of wills contain provisions that result in the existence of *residual assets* after the bequests have been carried out. Such assets have to be managed on behalf of certain beneficiaries of the will who may have the right to receive any income generated by the assets but who do not have personal control of them. The will may provide for the assets concerned to be vested into the names of the beneficiaries at some determinable future date, often, for instance, on the beneficiary reaching the age of majority, or it may provide that the beneficiary shall never come into full ownership of the property. In this latter case, a beneficiary often enjoys the income from the property for the whole of his or her lifetime, with the proviso that on death the assets become the property of someone else. Some trusts are set up to run on for many generations.

The principal purpose for setting up such a trust is usually the need to protect and preserve the capital assets, either for the use of future generations or until the beneficiary is considered capable of taking over their management. It is for this latter reason that trusts have often been set up where the beneficiary is a minor or, happily less commonly these days, female.

Inter vivos settlements. A trust may be created which becomes effective while the settler is still alive, an *inter vivos* settlement. Again the objective is usually one of protection, affording some comfort to the settler's dependents in case of the death, bankruptcy or other incapacity of their provider. A principal consideration of such trusts is *tax effectiveness*, the trust being set up to provide the minimum liability for inheritance tax and other forms of taxation. *Marriage settlements* used to be a commonplace example of this type of trust, property brought into the marriage being appropriated to either the 'husband's fund' or the 'wife's fund'. Changes in society have made this latter type of settlement largely obsolete and very few are now created.

Discretionary trusts. The standard form of trust these days is the discretionary trust. This gives the trustee wide powers to deal with the assets of the trust. This is in direct contrast to the older *ministerial trust* which allowed the trustee very little latitude to exercise his discretion. By the terms of the Trustee Investments Act of 1961, a trustee dealing with securities under a discretionary trust has the power to invest up to half of the assets in stock market securities consisting of ordinary shares and other equities. The remainder of the portfolio must be invested in a narrower range of investments comprising chiefly fixed-interest securities such as government stocks. A trustee in such a case is expected to show a high degree of professionalism in managing the portfolio and you will appreciate that a private individual may well feel that such a task is too difficult for him.

Banks as trustees

Banks are ideally placed to act as trustees as they have the resources and the expertise to bring to the task a professionalism which few could match. The benefits of naming the bank as trustee are very much the same as those accruing from naming it as executor, the principal ones being professionalism and continuity of service. In many banks the executors' department and the trustee department have grown up together, the activities of the one complementing those of the other. The later development of an investment management service often took place under the aegis of the trustee department, where significant investment expertise had been built up.

The bank will charge a fee for the management of the trust. As neither legislation nor common law gives a trustee the implied power to charge for his services, provision to charge an appropriate fee must be made in the *trust deed*. The scale of fees will relate the annual service charge to the overall value of the assets, subject to a minimum charge. Generally speaking, the *target market* for this service is the larger trust with significant assets and substantial income; the costs of professional management outweigh the benefits for small trusts. It should be remembered that most trusts today are set up by the comparatively wealthy and that therefore 'small' trusts are rare. The operation of a trustee service is often seen as an important factor in attracting and keeping the general banking business of the wealthy.

Taxation advice

The UK's tax system is complex and each individual is subject to several different taxes on all sources of income as well as on spending. Furthermore, successive governments make constant changes to both levels and methods of taxation. It is somewhat surprising, therefore, that the banks' tax advisory services are not better known and better utilised than they are. In most cases these advisory services grew out of the banks' executor and trustee work, which also requires an in-depth knowledge of the country's taxation systems.

Tax advisers generally, including the banks, prefer to handle their clients' affairs on a long-term basis, taking over the whole of the workload, including such items as the completion of a client's tax returns, ensuring that the client takes advantage of any allowances and concessions, negotiating with the tax authorities and so on. This is known as the *tax agency* service and in the long run it provides the client with a much more cost-effective service than *ad hoc advice* on specific problems as they arise, although such a service is also available. *Tax planning* is an important part of the tax agency service: advising the customer how best to structure his affairs so as to incur the least liability for taxes of all types.

There is again a link with the executor and trustee services in so far as *estate planning* is concerned. This involves assisting the customer to manage the inheritance of his estate so that as little as possible is absorbed by inheritance tax. This may involve the institution of *inter vivos* trusts and settlements. In this respect the banks have an advantage over other potential advisers, such as accountants and financial consultants, since they have on hand a volume of detailed knowledge about the customer's affairs gained from the day-to-day operation of the customer's accounts.

There is, of course, a fee for this service and while it may seem like adding insult to injury to have to pay this fee as well as a tax bill, the customer will normally gain significantly from the transaction. Primarily there is the advantage of being relieved from the need to personally vet your own tax affairs and deal with the tax man. The customer has the peace of mind of knowing that the tax bill is kept to a minimum and, in some cases, the tax savings made can be more than enough to cover the cost of the service. The target market for the service consists of the moderately wealthy and the self-employed, whose financial affairs are complex enough to warrant specialist advice. There are significant opportunities to 'cross-sell' other appropriate bank services to those who might make use of the tax advisory facility. The average salary earner whose principal tax liabilities are taken care of by PAYE contributions is unlikely to benefit from the service.

Insurance broking

The work of an insurance broker is to arrange on behalf of his client a contract of insurance or assurance (the more correct term for life 'insurance') which most effectively covers the risks which the customer wishes to secure. The broker's income comes from the commission paid by the insurer out of the profits which will accrue from the policy. There is no direct cost to the customer over and above the normal premiums payable on the policy. A good insurance broker will place the business with a reputable insurer; usually this will be an insurance company, although a Lloyds underwriter may sometimes be used in special cases. Due regard must be given to the relative costs of different types of cover, the comprehensiveness of the cover and the prospects for changing the terms of the policy if the customer's circumstances change.

The banks have long been a source of insurance advice, arising partly out of their overall role as general financial advisers to their customers. Today they have insurance consultancies staffed by insurance specialists capable of dealing with all types of insurance business. By and large the banks do not write insurance policies themselves, although they have entered into arrangements with particular insurance companies to provide policies for issue solely through the branches in respect of certain standard risks. These include 'home insurance' policies and 'travel insurance' packages.

Types of policy

Life assurance. We have already considered the *life assurance* market in Chapter 4. Life policies fall into one of three broad categories: *endowment policies*, on which the benefit is payable on the survival of the life assured to a stated date or on previous death; *whole life policies*, which mature only on the death of the life assured whenever that may occur; and *temporary policies* (term assurance), which pay out on the death of the life assured only if it occurs prior to a certain date, paying nothing if the life assured lives beyond that date. *Mortgage protection policies* are a specialised form of the temporary policy which provide a reducing amount of cover linked to the amount outstanding on a house mortgage. They are designed to ensure that the mortgage can be paid off if the householder should die before the full term of the mortgage has run out. The banks often insist on adequate life assurance as a condition of granting a loan to a personal customer.

Household insurance policies. These cover the contents of the policyholder's home against loss or damage resulting from theft, fire or similar hazards. In the case of an owner-occupier, the policy may also cover the fabric of the house against damage or destruction or a separate policy may be set up for this purpose. This type of policy may often be extended to cover other risks such as damage to personal possessions away from the home, or personal liability to third parties, such as a falling roof tile which strikes and injures a passerby; again, separate policies may be arranged to cover these risks.

Motor insurance. This is a legal requirement for any motor vehicle in the UK. The minimum insurance allowed is *third-party cover* which insures the vehicle owner against the claims of any third parties whose vehicles have been damaged or who have been injured by his car in an accident. Greater cover can be acquired at greater cost. *Comprehensive cover* insures against all risks of motoring, including the costs of repairing damage to the policyholder's own car following an accident for which he or she was responsible.

Target market
The above types of policy are not an exhaustive list of the standard policies which are available. Moreover, where there is no standard policy, insurers may be prepared to write a special policy. Basically there is no risk which cannot be insured against at a price. The total market for insurance is therefore no less than the whole population of the country, since we all suffer from some levels of risk in our daily lives, and it is no exaggeration to say that most of us are underinsured.

The chief emphasis of the bank's broking services has been towards life assurance. This is understandable since life policies relate quite closely to the more traditional bank services of lending and investment advice. However, the banks claim with some justification that there is no insurable risk which their broking subsidiaries cannot place. As well as personal insurance, much commercial business is undertaken, including employer liability insurance, factory and shop insurance, credit insurance and so on.

Travel services

For many years banks have provided services to travellers, both in the UK and overseas. These services have principally been cash withdrawal or similar facilities, giving the traveller access to money *en route* without the risks which would be incurred by taking all the required funds in cash.

Travellers cheques

Travellers cheques are the most widely known service to travellers. They can be exchanged for cash or used directly to pay for goods and services throughout the world. A travellers cheque comprises a promise by a bank or similar reputable organisation to pay a stated sum of money to anyone taking it from the person to whom it was issued, provided that certain conditions are met. The principal condition is that the person presenting the cheque should *countersign* it in the presence of the benefici ary. The cheque will already bear one example of the signature, having been signed at the time of issue and the beneficiary must ensure that the two examples of the signature correspond with each other.

Issuing travellers cheques

Travellers cheques are available from all the banks. Until recently many banks issued their own travellers cheques. Most, however, have now concluded arrangements to issue the cheques of one of the major international travellers cheque companies. The principal companies are American Express, issued under the aegis of 'Travellers Cheque Associates' by Lloyds, National Westminster and the Royal Bank of Scotland among the British banks; Thomas Cook issued by the Midland; and Visa issued by Barclays. Citibank cheques are issued by the Co-operative Bank.

These internationally recognised cheques have the advantage of greater worldwide acceptability; the customer is unlikely to find that travellers cheques will be refused anywhere in the world.

Travellers cheques are available denominated in either sterling or other world currencies. It can often be an advantage to take cheques in the currency of the country to be visited since these will be exchanged at *face value*, freeing the traveller from worries over fluctuations in the exchange rate between the currency concerned and sterling. Travellers cheques are sold to the customer at their face value at the time of issue. Currency cheques are of course sold for the sterling equivalent of their face value, calculated at prevailing exchange rates. Unused cheques will be repurchased by the issuing bank, also at face value, although the exchange rate used for converting currency cheques may not be the same rate at which they were issued. A commission charge is levied at the time the cheques are issued, generally calculated at 1 per cent of the face value. Cheques are available in several denominations so that issues are possible to any specific amount requested by the customer. Sterling travellers cheques, for instance, are usually available in denominations of £5, £10, £20, £50, and £100.

Using travellers cheques
When customers collect travellers cheques from the bank they will be required to sign them all once. A second signature has to be added when a cheque is used. This is a security precaution designed to protect the parties if the cheques are lost or stolen. Anyone attempting to misuse such cheques would have to reproduce the specimen signature in the presence of the person to whom he or she was attempting to negotiate the cheque. Provided that the beneficiary is vigilant this should be very difficult to do. Customers can obtain *full refunds* on all cheques lost or stolen, provided that they were properly signed at the time of issue. A major advantage of using the cheques of the international travellers cheque groups is that these companies maintain a worldwide network of representative offices from which an on the spot refund or replacement may be obtainable.

Travellers cheques may be used in payment for goods or services, or they may be exchanged for cash at banks, *bureaux de change* and even in many hotels. A commission charge is levied when they are encashed which is, of course, additional to the issuing commission. Cheques in the currency of the country visited will generally be accepted at face value, while cheques in other currencies will be converted. The exchange rates offered by the banks and *bureaux de change* will usually be competitive, reflecting the current value of the currency concerned. Exchange rates offered by shops, restaurants and hotels, on the other hand, are sometimes less so, incorporating an extra profit element in return for handling the cheque.

Cheque encashment facilities

Eurocheques
We have already mentioned that customers holding cheque cards may cash personal cheques at branches of participating banks in the UK. A Eurocheque card enables a customer to cash cheques at branches of participating banks throughout Europe. The advantage of cashing cheques over using travellers cheques is that the customer does not have to pay out in advance the value of the cheques to be used; the cheques are debited to the account only when they are remitted to the branch. Some 15 000 banks with in all 190 000 branches participate in the Euro-cheque scheme. They cover thirty-nine countries throughout Europe and the Mediterranean area and can be identified by the red and blue 'EC' symbol which they display in their windows and at the counter. The Eurocheque encashment card issued to UK customers can be used in any of these branches except the ones in the UK, where the normal cheque card can be used.

Eurocheque cards are used with special *uniform Eurocheques*. The system's great advantage is its resistance to fraud; the card is extremely resistant to alteration and the cheques are issued in only small batches and are difficult to forge. The cards are renewable every two years and guarantee cheques up to the equivalent of £100 each. Cheques are drawn in the local currency when they are used. There is no limit on the number of cheques which may be encashed in any one day but the special uniform cheques must be used. They may be used either in the UK or abroad.

There is a charge of £7.00 for the issue of each card. The cheques are issued free and in small numbers. Cheques are ultimately debited to the customer's account like ordinary personal cheques. A commission charge is levied on the account for each cheque debited, including a 1.6% fee for the encashing bank. No charge is levied at the time that the cheque is cashed. Uniform Eurocheques may also be used to buy goods or services from retailers who display the 'EC' symbol, being made out for the exact amount due, up to £100 per cheque.

Credit opened facilities

The credit opened facility enables cheque encashment facilities to be offered to current account customers who are not in possession of a cheque card, a service which the facility predates by some considerable period. It also enables customers to effect encashments which exceed the cheque card limit. The operation of the system is quite straightforward: a customer requests his bank to write to a bank at his destination authorising the encashment of cheques up to a specified limit. The limit may be expressed as the total amount which may be encashed over a given period or as a maximum per cheque. The encashing bank may be in the UK or abroad. If the former, the authorising branch will whenever possible nominate another branch of the same bank or of an associate bank. Where no such bank is conveniently located, instructions will be accepted by a branch of any of the commercial banks, provided that they are confirmed by both banks' head offices. Similar provisions exist for arranging encashment facilities in other countries.

Each bank has its own standard 'credit opened' form on which details of the arrangement are recorded and communicated to the encashing branch. These details include such items as the limit on encashments, the expiry date of the facility and the signing arrangements on the account: with a joint account for instance it is important to state whether either party may sign alone on the account or whether both have to sign. Specimens of the signatures of all parties to the account will, of course, be added to the form. Once the facility has been established, the customer may draw cash using the normal chequebook. The encashing branch knows that cheques will not be dishonoured provided that they conform to the terms of the arrangement.

Letter of credit

Although somewhat outdated, the letter of credit is still occasionally seen, usually issued on behalf of business customers to a company representative going abroad on business. It consists of a written promise by the bank guaranteeing that up to the limit of the credit any money paid to the holder will be repaid in full. To obtain cash, the holder presents the letter of credit to any of the issuing bank's correspondents throughout the world. The amount of any drawing is marked on the credit, thereby reducing the limit for future drawings. The paying bank reclaims the funds given out from the issuing bank, which charges the sum paid to the account of the party at whose request the letter of credit was issued. The letter of credit still has its uses from time to time, being particularly useful to the business traveller who is going away for a long period, especially on journeys outside Europe, and who knows neither the length of the journey nor the expenses likely to be incurred. Even so, these needs could be equally well filled with the use of an internationally accepted credit card or charge card.

Foreign currency

Although it is safer to take travellers cheques or similar items for the bulk of funds, it is usual also to take some small amounts of the currencies of the countries to be visited. The banks can supply customers with any currency which is obtainable in the UK. Although some branches maintain a *foreign till* containing small amounts of the major currencies, many small branches have to order all their customers' requirements from a central department, as do all branches where an uncommon currency is required. Consequently, the banks prefer customers to give at least one week's notice of their currency needs. The banks sell foreign currencies at competitive exchange rates and may charge a small commission fee for the service. Their main competitors are the travel agents, especially where holiday travel is concerned. Of course, the travel agents have to obtain their bulk supplies of currency from somewhere—usually the banks!

If the traveller brings back some of the currency of the country visited, this can usually be sold to the bank. This service is also available to visitors to the UK who wish to use their own currency to buy sterling. The banks prefer to buy only foreign notes and will not handle foreign coin. Many countries restrict the amount of their currency which can be taken out of the country; the banks can advise the traveller on this aspect before the journey is undertaken. Some countries completely forbid the export of their currency, in which case there will be no market in the UK for any currency which the traveller might inadvertently bring back. For the same reason the banks will be unable to supply any of these currencies to travellers proposing to go to countries which impose such a prohibition.

Travel insurance

It is advisable for all travellers to foreign countries to take out adequate travel insurance before starting their journey. Most banks are able to offer a standard package of travel insurance which, for quite a low premium, insures the customer against the principal risks of travel. The main risk relates to the potential need for medical attention: few countries provide automatic access for foreigners to a 'free' emergency medical care system in the way that the UK's National Health Service does. Consequently, it can be very expensive to fall ill or to be involved in an accident while abroad; hospitalisation is especially costly. Travel insurance provides reimbursement for such costs, although there may be a limit on the maximum amount recoverable under the policy. EEC countries have reciprocal arrangements with the National Health Service, although it can still be worth while to take out insurance because the levels of care provided under these schemes can be quite low. Furthermore, travel insurance provides other valuable benefits.

Falling ill abroad may result in other costs to the traveller: revised travel arrangements may prove expensive, a relative may have to travel out and, in the worst case, the traveller's body may have to be transported home. These are not pleasant things to contemplate but they are much less pleasant if the money is not there to pay for them. Illness at home just before the departure date may result in the need to cancel the proposed journey, as may other problems such as a call to serve on a jury panel. Usually in such cases the travel company will require the traveller to forefeit a proportion of the cost of the journey and the closer to the departure date that the cancellation is made the greater the proportion required. Finally, there are the risks of lost luggage and theft of personal possessions. Cover against all these risks can be obtained by taking out adequate travel insurance.

Most of the banks' standard travel insurance packages are designed for the holiday traveller, although similar facilities are available for business travellers. The premiums payable on these policies vary according to the length of time for which the customer plans to be away and the part of the world which is to be visited. The principal competitors for the provision of this service are the travel companies and the travel agents who often arrange cover at the time the journey arrangements are made for the traveller.

Summary

1 There are three 'traditional' bank services: (a) taking deposits; (b) money transfer; (c) making advances.

2 In recent years, ancillary services have proliferated, encouraging customers to see banks as 'one-stop' financial supermarkets.

3 The benefits of ancillary services must match customers' needs.

4 Promotion of bank services takes place through: (a) national advertising; (b) in-branch promotions.

5 The principal types of account maintained by personal customers are: (a) current accounts; (b) deposit accounts; (c) loan accounts, including personal loans and house purchase loans; (d) budget accounts.

6 Cheque cards guarantee payment of cheques up to £50. Their use has promoted the greater acceptability of payment by cheque.

7 Credit cards can be used to pay for goods or services and they offer a revolving credit facility. Charge cards are similar but have no revolving credit facility.

8 Automated teller machines (ATMs) effectively place a bank computer terminal at the customer's disposal, offering potential access to a wide range of account services.

9 Banks offer a full range of investment management and Stock Exchange services. Some banks operate their own unit trusts.

10 Executorship and trustee services offer the advantages of professional management of trust assets and continuity of service.

11 Banks can offer insurance services through their broking subsidiaries which deal with all types of insurance needs.

12 Travellers cheques can be used to buy goods and services throughout the world. Refund provisions protect the user against loss or theft of his cheques.

13 The Eurocheque scheme permits customers to cash cheques in participating banks throughout Europe and surrounding countries.

Self-assessment questions

1   Define: (a) revolving credit; (b) travel insurance; (c) Eurocheque encashment cards; (d) mortgage protection policies; (e) executorship.

2   List the ways in which funds may be made available to travellers abroad.

3   List the conditions which must be observed by someone taking a cheque under the cheque card scheme.

4   Describe the benefits of appointing the bank as executor.

5   True or false?

(a) Credit cards are unsuitable for raising long-term loans.

(b) Unit trusts are aimed at the wealthy who wish to invest in the stock market.

(c) Banks are unable to advise on insurance matters.

(d) 'Gold cards' are a special form of credit card offering increased access to borrowing facilities.

(e) Travellers in Europe no longer need to take out travel insurance.

6   Explain why some customers fear that credit cards encourage over-spending.

7   Analyse the reasons that have induced the banks to offer a widened range of ancillary services.

8   What would happen if the banks terminated their reciprocal cash withdrawal facilities? Would any particular bank or banks find such a course of action unduly detrimental?

Asssignments

1   Memorandum to: Student
    From: Manager
    Subject: Customer Correspondence

Please draft a reply to the attached letter received in the post today. I am very busy interviewing applicants for loans and I don't have the time to do it myself. The Joneses have about £10 000 on deposit so I would like you to give this priority attention!

---

17 Jermyn Road

Newtown

Dear Sir

In two weeks time my wife and I are going to visit our daughter who lives in Germany. We are driving over and have booked our ferry crossing but have done nothing else yet. We shall probably be staying out 6 weeks and we want to take £500 with us, although we may need more money towards the end of our holiday.

Will you please let me know what services you recommend for making the money available. If there are other services you think we might need, let me know at the same time. Incidentally, my golf club subscription and some other bills will fall due while we are away. Can you suggest anything to help us deal with them?

Yours sincerely

James Jones

---

2   Obtain details of your own bank's 'budget account' scheme. Prepare a presentation on the benefits of using such accounts for the regulation of personal finances. Use as examples a calculation of how such accounts would work for (a) yourself, and (b) a married couple with two teenage children and a joint income of £20 000 a year after tax. What expenses do you think such customers would have?

12   Business services

Chapter objectives

After studying this chapter you should be able to:
- describe the range of business services available to bank customers and state their attributes;
- relate the attributes of these services to the needs of specific business customers;
- evaluate the methods adopted by the banks for marketing their business services.

Introduction

Many of the banking services used by personal customers are, of course, also used by businesses. There are, however, a number of facilities which are designed specifically to meet the needs of business customers and which are not generally used by personal customers. It is to these latter services that we turn our attention in this chapter. You should nevertheless be aware before we start that the distinction between business customers and personal customers is an arbitrary and rather unreal distinction and that, in the final analysis, customers are customers.

Finance for business

The banks are in the business of providing finance, helping customers to purchase assets and iron out short-term discrepancies between income and expenditure. Much of this finance is provided through the traditional banking activities of granting loans and overdrafts. So far as the business customer is concerned, however, the banks can provide access to a number of alternative methods of meeting a finance requirement whether for working capital or for acquiring fixed assets.

Factoring

Some businesses operate principally on a cash basis. Supermarkets, for instance, usually allow their customers to take away their week's groceries only after they have paid for them. Most non-retail businesses do not operate on this basis. Instead, they supply their goods or services *on credit*. Credit sales necessitate an accounting system to produce invoices showing customers how much they owe and when they have to pay. Someone has to monitor the payments received and send out reminders to those who do not pay up on time. More fundamentally, someone should be vetting all new customers to see whether they should be allowed credit and, if so, how much. Existing customers too should periodically be reassessed, good payers being granted more extensive credit facilities, poor payers having their limits reduced. All these activities can be grouped together under the heading of *credit control*.

Credit control is looked on as a necessary evil by most small and medium-sized businesses. They would prefer to forget all about it if they could. Using a *factoring service* makes this possible: the factoring company takes over the management of the trade debts of the business, releasing it from all responsibility in this area. The factoring company becomes, in effect, the customer's accounting department and as well as dealing with the sales ledger and invoicing functions will undertake all the work involved in credit control and debt collection. A service charge is made, usually of between 1 and 2 per cent of the annual turnover of the business and at that level it is often cheaper to the business than operating its own accounts department. There are a number of major specialist factoring companies operating in the UK, many of them being controlled directly or indirectly by the banks. All the commercial banks therefore have an interest in, or a relationship with, a factoring organisation and can put their customers in contact with a factor.

The advantage of using a factoring company is the *expertise* which it can bring to the credit control process. Under a normal factoring arrangement, the factor will vet all applications for credit and the decision whether to grant credit to a particular customer, and to what extent, will rest with him. By undertaking the same function for a number of concerns, the factor is able to build up a comprehensive knowledge of the credit-worthiness of UK traders. Combined with effective debt collection techniques and access to large-scale sources of financial information, this means that businesses whose affairs are handled by a factoring company have a much improved debt collection record. At a small extra charge the factoring company will usually offer a *complete credit protection service*, effectively guaranteeing the client payment of all debts due. If the buyers do not pay, the factor will.

Factor finance. The fullest factoring service available is factor finance. Under this arrangement the factor will agree to purchase the book debts from the client, paying him a proportion of their face value immediately, usually up to 80 per cent, and the remainder when the debt is collected. This improves the trader's liquidity position as funds previously tied up in debtors, or at least a proportion of them, are released as cash immediately. Increasing use is being made of this facility as an alternative to a bank overdraft as a source of working capital finance.

Factor finance is similar in operation to *invoice discounting* which has been available for many years in the UK. Under this a trader can sell an invoice or a number of invoices at a discount to a third party who then collects the funds on his own account. The major difference is that under an invoice discounting arrangement the party buying the invoice is not also in control of the trader's accounting system, whereas a factor is.

Interest is charged by the factor on the amount advanced until payment is obtained from the debtor. This is additional to the commission charge for providing the parallel debt administration service. If the funds due cannot be recovered from the debtor, the factor providing the finance will normally assume responsibility for the debt and will not reclaim from the customer any money advanced against the debt. This is known as 'without recourse' factoring. On occasions the factor may reserve the right to reclaim any amounts advanced on debts which prove to be impossible to collect. 'With recourse' factoring of this nature is not common but can occur either when the debt concerned is one which the factor knows to be a bad risk and which was entered into despite his advice, or when the customer wishes to raise finance in excess of an agreed level.

Leasing

Many businesses lease at least some of their capital assets. Leasing is an arrangement whereby one party obtains on a long-term basis the use of a capital asset which belongs to another party. The lessee pays a regular rental to the lessor but never becomes the owner of the asset. The terms of the leasing agreement vary according to the nature of the assets concerned and the parties involved but, in essence, there are only two basic types of agreement which may be encountered: operating and finance.

Operating leases

These are usually offered by the supplier of the assets which are to be leased. The lessor may be the manufacturer, the agent, the retailer or any other party. The lessor not only supplies the goods but also undertakes to service and repair them. Lessees will often prefer this arrangement to ownership for assets which are highly sophisticated or technically complicated as they are relieved from the responsibility for arranging a satisfactory servicing schedule or providing for the obsolescence of the equipment. For these reasons, operating leases are very common for items such as photocopiers, word processors and computers. (Many people rent their television sets. This is much the same arrangement undertaken for much the same reasons.)

The company which is acting as lessor is, of course, the owner of the assets. When new assets are acquired for leasing purposes their cost can be offset against the lessor's tax liability under the UK's system of capital allowances which applies to all business assets except motor cars. A business offsets its capital allowances against its annual profits and tax is calculated on the net amount remaining. Any capital allowance which is unutilised, perhaps because the business is not making a profit, can be carried forward to subsequent years. The lessor will allow for any tax saving available to him when calculating the rental to be charged. The banks are not involved as principals in this type of leasing but they are involved in finance leasing.

Finance leases

Finance leases have developed as a method of providing finance for the supply of fixed assets to businesses. They provide an alternative to more traditional loan schemes. Instead of lending a business the funds necessary to purchase an asset, the leasing company buys the asset in its own name and the leases it to the user. The principal distinction from the operating lease is that the lessor's chief interest is in providing the finance rather than in supplying the asset. The banks became involved in finance leasing because the capital allowances available in respect of the assets leased out enabled them to reduce their tax bills. This was especially useful in the case of a lessee who would not have been eligible to utilise the allowances himself because he already had a low liability for taxation. In recent years certain restrictions have been placed on the availability of capital allowances to a lessor if the user of the assets would have been ineligible to claim them if he had been the owner of the goods.

Leasing is a very acceptable way of financing the acquisition of capital assets since it does not absorb any of the user's own liquid assets, leaving working capital available to finance sales. This can be very important because new assets often lead to a growth in the potential volume of business, this needing in turn more working capital. The lessee is freed from having to worry about depreciation of the assets or about making provision for their replacement when they wear out. The rental payments will be set at the outset, helping with the forward planning of the cash budgets of the business. When setting the rental the lessor will include in the calculations an allowance for repayment of the capital cost of the equipment within its expected useful life, plus the interest costs on his capital outlay over that period, less, of course, the value of any tax savings. Most leasing agreements allow for a substantial reduction in the rental after the 'repayment' period is over, usually to a nominal amount.

A significant advantage of leasing over lending is that the lessor does not have to check the client's financial stability in such detail as a lending bank although, of course, the lessee's ability to pay the rental must be checked. If the lessee goes out of business, the assets concerned can be removed by the lessor, who is the owner of course, for sale or lease elsewhere. The lessor will not therefore require any supporting security before granting the facility. The only significant danger is the possible discrepancy between the resale second-hand value of the recovered assets and the amount of any outstanding capital cost. This can be quite substantial in the early years of a lease. As you will appreciate, the market value of most capital assets declines most rapidly in the early part of their lives. Motor cars are a prime example of this. For this reason, the repayment period of the lease will be kept as short as is reasonably practicable.

Merchant banking

We looked at the merchant banks in Chapter 2. You will recall that there is no simple definition of this type of organisation, although there are a number of specialist fields to which most of them confine their activities. The commercial banks have moved into several of these areas so as to be able to offer merchant banking facilities to their customers, usually through the medium of subsidiary companies. Like the merchant banks proper, no one commercial bank's merchant banking arm offers the same mix of services but we can pick out a number of the more important ones.

Acceptance facilities
Historically the first service to be offered by the merchant banks, acceptance facilities were originally a means of enabling little-known British importers to enter the world market place. The scheme was later extended and turned around to allow the merchant banks to accept bills on behalf of foreign importers drawn on them by British exporters. The final development was for the merchant banks to accept bills drawn on them in connection with inland trade. These services are still available, both through the accepting houses and the banks' merchant banking arms. An acceptor of such bills will of course expect to be provided with funds to meet the bill before it falls due and will charge a commission for putting his name to the document. Even so, the use of this method of obtaining trading finance can be one of the cheapest means available.

Medium-term lending
In the mid 1960s the clearing banks were under a number of restrictions which prevented them from offering higher interest rates in competing for deposits. To circumvent these restrictions, a number of banks set up subsidiary companies, not bound by the constraints, to bid for larger deposits. These subsidiary

companies also began to operate within the growing Euro-currency markets. They began to attract very larger deposits, often placed with them for lengthy fixed terms, and from that point it was only a short step for them to start lending these funds on a medium or long-term basis to commercial customers. This was a service which had not previously been available from the clearing banks. The banks have since been freed from constraints on their deposits and in some cases the business of these subsidiary companies has been absorbed by the parent bank. In other cases, however, the subsidiaries have been kept in existence to form the basis of a separate merchant bank under the banking group's overall umbrella.

Issuing house services

One of the first merchant banking functions taken on by the clearing banks was that of acting as an issuing house. An issuing house is concerned with *raising capital* for businesses by issuing stock or shares in the company through the investment market. This task may be performed either for a private company seeking to 'go public', or for an existing quoted company wishing to raise further finance.

New issues. There is a steady flow of private companies seeking to 'go public' in order to gain access to the capital needed to finance large-scale expansion. The role of the issuing house in bringing the new company to the market is vital, its first task being to ensure that the company is one which merits a public quotation. A company hoping for a quotation must publish adequate information for the public to decide whether it has good prospects for future success. The issuing house will participate in the preparation and presentation of this material and advise on the most appropriate method of bringing the shares to the market (see Chapter 4), the most common methods being an *offer for sale* or an *issue by tender*. Smaller issues may be the subject of a *placing* or an *introduction*. The issuing house will arrange for the issue to be *underwritten* to ensure that the company disposes of all the shares, thereby raising the required capital. Much time and effort will go into calculating an appropriate issue price so that the issue will be fully subscribed but without being heavily oversubscribed.

Rights issues. When an existing public company wishes to raise further finance, it may decide to do so by offering new shares in the company to the existing shareholders on a proportional basis to their existing holdings. The issuing house would deal with the rights issue, as this is called, and again much care would be employed in calculating the price at which the new shares should be offered. If shareholders wish to take up the new shares they must subscribe the required price. If they do not, they will usually be able to sell their 'rights' to the shares through a stockbroker.

Equity participation

One of the distinguishing features of the long-established merchant banks was their *entrepreneurial outlook*. Investment would be made directly in new ventures seeking development capital and a share taken in the equity of the business, thereby affording the merchant bank the opportunity to participate both in the management of the enterprise and in the profits. Although the commercial banks have never seen the provision of risk capital as one of their traditional activities, a number of them have now set up subsidiaries which provide such equity financing. The principal problem experienced is not in finding worthy applicants to support in this way but in finding businesses whose proprietors are prepared to surrender a proportion of the ownership of the undertaking. There seems to be little doubt, however, that this aspect of the banks' 'merchant banking' activities will continue to develop and become a much more important part of their business in the future.

International business

All of the major commercial banks offer a range of international services, some of which are appropriate to both personal and business customers, such as the travel facilities which were discussed in the previous chapter, and some of which are directed specifically at the business customer only. The banks have built up specialist *international sections* which have great expertise in the specific services associated with international trade and which have made a major contribution to the growth of the UK as a trading nation. In some cases, these international sections are constituted as *divisions* of the operating banks, in others they have been set up as subsidiary companies. In either case, domestic branch banking staff have an important role to play in liaising between branch customers and the bank's international section.

Collection of payment for exports

As a nation, the UK makes its living from international trade. We cannot meet all our needs from our own internal resources, especially those for food and raw materials, and we have to buy what we lack from abroad. We must earn enough in the world marketplace by selling goods and services to other countries to finance the purchases which we make. It follows, therefore, that *exporting* is vital. This has been recognised by successive governments which have encouraged both businesses to enter the export markets and banks to provide financial and other assistance to exporters. In the past, Bank of England *qualitative directives* have sought to channel loan funds in the direction of exporting businesses.

A major concern of exporters is to find a secure but simple method of ensuring that they obtain payment for goods shipped to buyers in foreign countries. The difficulties are similar to those inherent in inland trade but are magnified by the distance between buyer and seller. The principal difficulty is that of *control* of the goods and payment for them. If exporters allow importers to obtain control of the goods before they have been paid for, they are taking the risk that the goods may not be recoverable at a later date if payment is not forthcoming. With inland trade they at least have the option of calling personally on the buyer and asking for their goods back. In export trade, much depends on how the *documentation* relating to the shipment is dealt with.

Documents of foreign trade

For every shipment of goods from the UK, the exporter will assemble a set of shipping documents, some of which will always be present, some of which will be required only when trading with certain countries or when certain terms of trade apply. The banks can offer advice on the preparation of documents to customers who are exporting for the first time or who have not traded with a particular country before.

Commercial invoices. These will always form part of a set of shipping documents. They set out the details of the transaction, indicating who is selling what to whom, how the goods have been shipped, what the price is and when payment is due. The *terms of trade* on which the shipment is made will also be stated; the three most common arrangements for such contracts are 'free on board' (FOB), 'cost and freight' (C&F) and 'cost, insurance and freight' (CIF). Under an FOB contract the quoted invoice price of the goods incorporates only the cost of the goods inclusive of the seller's profit margin and the cost of transportation to the point of departure from the UK; all other costs of shipment must be met by the buyer. A C&F contract covers the same costs as the FOB contract plus the cost of shipment to the point of entry into the importer's country. Under a CIF arrangement, the exporter will also have arranged insurance on the goods in respect of the perils of loss or damage while in transit to the country of importation. The cost of the insurance is added on to the purchase price as shown in the invoice.

A bill of exchange. This may be drawn on the importer by the exporter ordering the importer (the drawee) to pay the agreed price for the goods on the appropriate due date. It is very common in international trade for the exporter to grant the importer a period of credit before payment has to be made for the goods; in such cases a *term bill* of exchange will almost invariably be drawn up. A term bill of exchange falls due for payment at a fixed or determinable future date, often in practice being payable a stated number of days 'after sight'. Thus, a bill payable at '180 days after sight' becomes due approximately six months after it is first presented to the importer (the drawee) on whom it is drawn. If the drawee wishes to *accept* the bill of exchange he will write his acceptance on the bill and sign it. By doing so the importer enters into a binding contract to pay the face amount of the bill on the due date. If he does not pay up at the appropriate time the drawer (the exporter) may sue on the strength of the acceptance. Even when the exporter is not granted a credit period a bill of exchange is often included with the shipping documents. In such cases the bill will be drawn simply *at sight*, that is a bill falling due for payment as soon as it is presented to the drawee.

If the importer refuses payment, the bill may be *protested* on the drawer's behalf. This the first step in taking legal proceedings for the recovery of the money represented by the bill, being intended to provide the courts with adequate evidence that the bill was presented for payment which was refused. It involves the employment of a *notary public* who presents the bill for payment and records any reason given for refusal. The same process is used if a term bill remains unpaid on the due date.

Insurance documentation. This, in the form of either a policy or a certificate of insurance, will be provided with the documents only if the exporter is trading on a CIF basis. If the terms of trade are FOB or C&F shipments, the responsibility for insuring the goods while in transit falls on the purchaser. You will appreciate that goods being moved between countries are subject to significant risks of loss or damage and it is therefore vital that one party to the transaction takes out adequate insurance cover. Where insurance is to be effected by the exporter it is common for it to be evidenced by the production of *insurance certificates* drawn up by the exporter on blank forms provided by the insurance company in connection with an *open cover* policy. Under this arrangement, an exporter who is dealing with many importers throughout the world may arrange a blanket policy covering all shipments abroad up to a stated total value. The exporter informs the insurance company of the details and value of each shipment made and draws up the certificate for inclusion with the shipping documents.

Bills of lading. These are issued by a shipping company in respect of goods received for shipment abroad by an oceangoing vessel. Most goods exported from the UK still go by sea despite the growth of the air-freight business. The bills of lading set out the details of the transport arrangements, specifying where the goods will be offloaded, the name of the carrying vessel, whether freight charges have been paid and so on. More importantly, they also act as *documents of title* to the goods as the shipping company will not give up the goods without production of at least one of the original bills of lading issued when the goods were taken on board. Bills of lading are issued in sets, usually of two or three original copies; when one of a set has been used to obtain delivery of the goods in the country of import, the rest become void.

Bills of lading may be made out specifying the name of a particular consignee, or they may be made out to 'order'. In the case of *consignee* bills of lading, the shipping company will deliver only to the named consignee or on his orders, and then only if he can produce one of the original set of bills. In the case of *order* bills of lading, delivery is made on the orders of the exporter. In either case if delivery is to be made to a third party, the bill of lading must be *indorsed* by either the shipper or the consignee as appropriate. A bill of lading indorsed in blank becomes a bearer document and the shipping company will deliver the goods to any party in possession of any one original bill which is so indorsed.

Other documents which may be produced may include alternative shipping documents such as *air waybills* or *parcel post receipts*, in the case of goods not sent by sea, or *forwarder's receipts* in the case of goods shipped in containers. These are not documents of title to the goods, the carrier in either case delivering only to the named consignee. Different types of invoice such as the *consular invoice* or the *certified invoice* may be called for when trading with certain countries, as may documents such as *health* or *sanitary certificates* and *certificates of origin*. The buyer of the goods may call for other specialist documents such as *packing lists* or *inspection certificates*.

Open account trading

Having shipped the goods and assembled the relevant documentation, the exporter will then wish to obtain payment from the importer against release of the documents. There are a number of ways in which this can be accomplished, the simplest of which is known as open account trading. Under this arrangement the exporter simply sends the shipping documents to the importer on the understanding that payment will be made when it falls due, as specified in the invoice. The exporter's bank will have little direct involvement in such a transaction, being required only to process a payment from abroad for the customer's account when the importer makes the necessary remittance. The payment may be made in any one of a number of forms, the most usual being either an international funds transfer, a foreign draft issued by the importer's bank or a cheque drawn on the importer's own account. In the last case the exporter's bank may either decide to *negotiate* the cheque and credit the customer with the proceeds immediately or it may prefer to *collect* the cheque on the customer's behalf crediting the account only when proceeds are received from abroad. (*See* generally Chapter 7.)

The danger to the exporter in open account trading is that by surrendering the shipping documents to the importer, control of the goods is lost before they have been paid for. If the importer does not make payment on the due date, recovery of the goods would prove extremely difficult to accomplish, if not impossible. For this reason, open account trading is usually engaged in only between long-standing trading partners who know they can trust each other to supply goods of the right quality or to pay up on time. It is not recommended as a settlement method in a new trading relationship.

Documentary collections
The exporter can obtain greater security of payment by employing the services of a third party in the importer's country who will hand the shipping documents to the importer against payment of the amount due or, if a credit period has been allowed, against acceptance of a bill of exchange. Using such a system the exporter does not lose possession of the title documents, and therefore of the goods, until payment or legally actionable evidence of a debt falling due on a specific future date has been received. The principal problem for the exporter is to find a trustworthy party who will act on his behalf in the importer's country. This is where the banks come in. If the exporter takes the documents to his bank, the bank can send them to an *agent bank* in the country concerned to be handed to the importer against payment or acceptance of a bill of exchange. This is known as the *documentary collection* system because the bank is collecting payment against delivery of the shipping documents.

A *collection letter* must be given to the bank with the documents, setting out how the exporter wishes the transaction to be handled. It must deal with such items as what to do with the documents, and the goods, if the importer refuses the transaction. For instance, is non-payment to be protested? Are the goods to be warehoused pending further instructions? Is there a local agent who can be informed if any difficulties are encountered? These instructions will be passed on by the exporter's bank to the agent bank in the importer's country. When payment is ultimately obtained, the agent bank will remit the funds to the exporter's bank for credit to the exporter's account. Both banks will levy a charge for their services, and will add to this the amount of any extra expenses which they have incurred.

If payment or acceptance of a bill of exchange cannot be obtained from the importer, the exporter should still be in control of the goods provided that the documents have been correctly drawn up and correctly handled. The exporter can therefore attempt to recoup the cost of the goods by selling them to someone else in the country of import or by shipping them on to another country where a buyer may be found. If no alternative purchaser can be found in the short term, the goods may be brought back to the UK pending their sale elsewhere. This latter course of action is costly and may prove fruitless if no other buyer is found. This sometimes happens, especially if the goods have been made to special order. Goods are sometimes auctioned off on the dockside in the country of import if the exporter decides to cut his losses and realise what money he can without further ado.

Documentary credits

As you have seen, an exporter can protect himself to some extent against the dangers of non-payment by the use of the documentary collection system but there are still some dangers. If he wants a greater degree of protection he may ask the importer to arrange for the issue of a *letter of credit* in his favour. A letter of credit is issued by the importer's bank and constitutes a promise by the bank that it will pay up to a specified sum of money to the exporter on presentation of certain specified shipping documents relating to goods supplied to the importer. It affords the exporter greater protection because reliance is placed on the more trustworthy promise of payment given by the bank, rather than the promise of the importer. The importer is also protected because his bank will insist on the delivery of the correct documents before it will release payment, thereby ensuring shipment of the correct goods.

The issuing bank acting on behalf of the importer is entering into a real commitment when giving out the letter of credit; it must pay against the specified documents irrespective of whether it can recover the funds from the importer although, if it cannot do so, it will retain control of the documents and may look, therefore, to the goods as a potential source of repayment. (*See* also page 439.) The details of a letter of credit are usually sent to the issuing bank's correspondent bank in the exporter's country to be passed on to the exporter. The correspondent bank is known as the *advising bank*; it may or may not be the bank at which the exporter's accounts are maintained. The advising bank may *confirm* the letter of credit, adding its own promise that payment will be made if the correct documents are presented, or it may simply *advise* the credit, certifying it to be genuine but adding no promise of its own.

Preparation of documents by the exporter must conform to all the terms and conditions specified in the letter of credit. If six copies of the invoice are called for, six must be supplied and so on. If there are any discrepancies in the documents produced, the guarantee of payment is lost and the documents may be rejected by the issuing and advising banks. Quite often documents are refused for simple basic errors which could be corrected. A large proportion of all sets of documents rejected suffer from one, or both, of the two commonest discrepancies: late shipment, that is, goods dispatched after the last acceptable date as specified in the letter of credit; and late presentation, that is documents sent to the bank after the expiry date of the letter of credit. Thus, it is important that on receipt of a letter of credit the exporter checks it to ensure that all the conditions can be met; if they cannot, an amendment should be sought and the importer contacted immediately.

Presentation of documents can be made direct to the advising bank but most exporters prefer to take the documents to their own bank for onward transmission to the advising bank. There are two reasons for this. First, the exporter's bank will *check the documents* against the terms of the letter of credit and ensure that there are no discrepancies. Remember that any deviation from the terms of the credit, however slight, will result in loss of the bank's guarantee of payment. If any errors are discovered, they will be corrected so far as is possible before the documents are presented to the advising bank. If errors are found which cannot be corrected, say, for example, the goods have been shipped from a port other than the one specified in the credit, the exporter's bank assumes its second possible role in the transaction, *attempting to obtain payment* in spite of the discrepancy. If the discrepancy is not too great, the advising bank may be prepared to arrange payment *under indemnity*, which means that payment is made to the exporter's bank on the understanding that the funds can be reclaimed if the importer refuses the documents when they reach him. The exporter's bank gives the advising bank an *indemnity* to this effect and takes a *counter-indemnity* from its customer, authorising it to debit his account with any sums which have to be refunded.

The documentary credit system is much more secure so far as the exporter is concerned and this is a great advantage. Its chief disadvantage is cost. Because at least two, and sometimes three, banks are involved charges are quite high. Furthermore, the issuing bank, as you have seen, is taking a certain risk when it issues a letter of credit and the commission which it charges is therefore higher than the commission for handling a comparable documentary collection. Letters of credit are, however, very popular with exporters who are starting to trade with an importer whom they do not know.

Finance for exports

We have already mentioned that it is common for an exporter to grant a period of credit to a buyer abroad. Indeed, *credit terms* are often an important factor in gaining an order in the international market place, and credit is often granted over longer periods than would be considered normal for domestic trade. As a result the exporter may need finance to bridge the period between the goods and services being supplied and payment being received. Many exporters cover such finance requirements through the use of ordinary loan and overdraft facilities. There are also a number of specialised facilities.

Discounting bills

As we have seen, a common method of settlement in international trade is the *documentary collection*. This uses the term bill of exchange to regulate payment for goods supplied on credit, the documents of title to the goods being delivered to the importer against acceptance of the bill. The accepted bill may then be returned to the exporter for presentation on the due date, or it may be held by the correspondent bank until payment is due. The banks follow the exporter's instructions in this regard. If the bill is returned to the exporter, he may be able to *discount* it with his bank. This involves selling the bill to the bank at slightly less than its face value—in other words at a discount. The bank credits the customer's account with the agreed sum immediately and then collects the full proceeds of the bill on the due date, taking its profit from the difference between the amount paid for the bill and the amount realised. The discount deducted from the face value of the bill will reflect both prevailing interest rates and the length of time that the bank will have to wait to recover its money from the acceptor of the bill. If the bill goes unpaid on the due date, the bank reserves the *right of recourse* against the exporter and can return the dishonoured bill to him, debiting his account with the cost.

It is worth noting that a certain amount of inland trade is regulated through the medium of bills of exchange and accepted inland bills can be discounted in just the same way. When discounting inland bills the bank will look for 'two good names' to each bill. This means that it will check that both the drawer of the bill and the acceptor of the bill appear to be good for the money. With foreign bills it is more difficult to ensure that the acceptor of the bill is good, so greater importance is placed on the creditworthiness of the exporter.

Negotiation of foreign bills. This is very similar to the discounting facility except that the bank buys the bills, and the supporting documents, from the exporter before they are sent out to the correspondent bank for acceptance by the importer. Until a bill is accepted, the bank's 'security' for repayment consists of the shipping documents which are in its control and its right of recourse against the exporter. After acceptance it relies on payment by the acceptor or, if that is not forthcoming, recourse to the exporter. It is possible to negotiate sight collections as well as term collections. It is unusual to negotiate or to discount bills which have a credit period exceeding six months and, although the status of the importer is not the prime consideration, a bank would not deal in bills drawn on an importer who was known not to be good for the amount.

Acceptance credits

This type of facility is often provided for exporters through the merchant banks or accepting houses. It is also available from the commercial banks through their merchant banking subsidiaries. As you already know, the procedure for raising finance through an *acceptance facility* requires the borrower to draw a term bill of exchange on the accepting house for the amount which is needed. The bill is accepted by the accepting house payable at some specified date in the future and is returned to the drawer who can then discount it with his bank or on the discount market. A *fine rate* of discount can usually be obtained because of the good name of the acceptor. The borrower must provide the accepting house with the funds necessary to meet the bill when it falls due, this being required just before the maturity date. The facility can be used to finance both inland and foreign trade.

Where the customer is an exporter, the acceptance facility is often related to the processing of a documentary collection. The exporter prepares the shipping documents in the usual way and hands them to his bank for collection. He then draws a bill of exchange in his own favour on the bank or on its accepting house for an agreed proportion of the value of the documentary collection. This bill falls due for payment slightly later than the bill drawn on the importer under the documentary collection. Once the bill drawn on the bank has been accepted, it may be discounted on the discount market providing an immediate source of finance for the exporter. When the proceeds of the documentary collection are received from abroad, a proportion will be retained by the bank to meet the amount due under its own acceptance which will be maturing in the near future, the balance being paid over to the exporter.

Export Credits Guarantee Department (ECGD)

The Export Credits Guarantee Department is a government-backed body set up originally to provide credit insurance for exporters with the intention of making exporting no more risky than inland trade. The risks which are covered by the policies which the ECGD issues are those which are unique to international trade, including war, civil disorder in the importing country and imposition of exchange control restrictions. Protection is also given against the insolvency of the buyer, provided that the exporter did not know before the goods were shipped that the importer would not be able to pay. Policies may be either 'specific' or 'comprehensive'. A specific policy covers a single overseas contract, usually relating to a large long-term capital project. Comprehensive policies are designed for the more general trader who supplies a standard range of goods to a number of buyers throughout the world.

As a development of its insurance business, the ECGD is prepared to grant *guarantees* to banks to cover advances made to exporters in respect of projects covered by an ECGD specific policy.

These *ECGD Specific Banker's Guarantees* are therefore available to help the banks finance specific large contracts, usually for the supply of capital items such as medium to heavy industrial equipment or major construction projects. In this sort of business, credit terms of two to five years are normal and loans are therefore granted on a medium-term basis, being repayable over a similar period. Longer credit periods can be considered in appropriate cases. For very large projects where the buyer is often a national government, it may be decided that the money be lent to the purchaser of the goods so that immediate payment can be made to the supplier. This is known as *buyer credit* and special ECGD guarantee facilities are available to cover such advances.

Export credit schemes. Many banks offer special export credit schemes for general exporters who have ECGD cover. The details will vary from bank to bank but typically the exporter will be able to borrow up to 100% of the insured value of each shipment. Repayment of each borrowing will be made out of the proceeds received from the buyer abroad and if payment is not forthcoming the amount will be claimed under the ECGD policy. Thus, there should be no recourse to the exporter. Interest is charged at an attractive rate, often around 1½% over the bank's normal sterling base rate. Arrangements can be made to accommodate customers who invoice their buyers in foreign currencies.

Export factoring

We have already discussed the benefits of *factoring facilities* in respect of inland trade; these also accrue when factoring is undertaken of sums due from debtors overseas. Before the export factoring operation begins, the factoring company will undertake its usual investigations into the creditworthiness of the exporter's customers, setting credit limits for each one. The factor will then take over the sales ledger side of the exporter's business, sending out the invoices and collecting payment on the due dates. This relieves the exporter from a great deal of clerical effort, especially where trading is done on an open account basis. The factor also takes charge of the credit control aspect of the business, bringing to bear a level of expertise much greater than that of the individual exporter. This automatically provides a measure of *credit insurance* giving an alternative to the ECGD insurance facilities. In fact, under most export factoring arrangements the factor assumes liability for any bad debts created.

Factoring finance can also be made available if the exporter needs to raise money to finance sales. As we have seen, the normal credit periods of international trade make such a requirement more likely. The factoring company will normally be prepared to advance funds to the exporter as soon as a shipment is made. Usually advances are limited to a maximum of 80 per cent of the value of the goods, the balance of the amount due being paid over when the factor has collected the debt.

Services to importers

Documentary letters of credit

As we have already said, an exporter may request the issue of a letter of credit in his favour before he will trade with an importer whom he does not know. The importer will then have to go to his bank to apply for the credit to be issued. You will realise that from the bank's viewpoint a letter of credit involves a very real credit risk. Once the credit has been issued the bank must pay out under it if the stipulated documents are produced, whether or not it is then in a position to debit the customer's account. Thus, before agreeing to the request, the importer's bank will have to check whether its customer is good for the money. Of course, there may be other previously issued letters of credit still outstanding and these will have to be taken into account, as will any other liabilities of the customer to the bank. If there are any doubts about the creditworthiness of the customer, the bank can request the deposit of adequate security before the credit is issued. In some cases deposit of full *cash cover* may be required, although this is exceptional. If the importer is unable to meet the bank's criteria, the bank can refuse to issue the credit.

The international code of practice concerning the issue of documentary letters of credit is known as the *Uniform Customs and Practice for Documentary Credit*. This recognises two types of documentary credit: revocable credits and irrevocable credits. A *revocable credit* may be amended, altered, or even cancelled by the importer or the issuing bank without the exporter's permission at any time up until the documents are actually presented under it. An *irrevocable credit*, once it has been issued, may not be altered in any way without the consent of the beneficiary: it is absolutely binding on the importer's bank. As you can appreciate, a revocable credit offers little real protection to the exporter and an exporter will normally specify that an irrevocable credit must be issued.

If the exporter is happy to rely on the promise of the importer's bank to pay if the correct documents are produced, an *advised* letter of credit will be acceptable; this involves no engagement on the part of the advising bank, other than its warranty that the credit is genuine. If, as is often the case, the exporter is not familiar with the importer's bank and is unsure whether it is good for its undertakings, he can request the supply of a *confirmed* letter of credit. Under this arrangement the advising bank in the exporter's country will add its own promise to pay out against a satisfactory set of documents. A confirmed letter of credit costs more because of the greater involvement of the advising bank.

Documents to be supplied under the letter of credit will be specified by the importer. The bank can advise on what documents would normally be required for imports into the UK if the customer is new to the import business. Adequate shipping documents must be requested and the bank will normally require them to be drawn up in such a way that the bank could get hold of the goods themselves if necessary. If the goods are coming by sea, for example, the letter of credit may specify the supply of blank indorsed 'order' bills of lading or even bills of lading showing the bank as consignee. Remember that if all else fails, the bank will be looking to the sale of the goods to get its money back. For the same reason, insurance of the goods is important to the bank. If the contract with the exporter is on a CIF basis, the letter of credit will call for supply of an adequate marine insurance policy or certificate, usually for the invoice value plus at least 10% to allow for incidental expenses. If the contract is on FOB or C&F terms, the importer will be arranging the insurance and the bank may call for evidence that this has been effected.

Presentation of documents by the exporter will normally occur shortly after the goods are dispatched. Indeed, the letter of credit may well stipulate a maximum period that may elapse after dispatch before the documents are presented. If the documents are in order, the issuing bank must pay the exporter under the terms of the letter of credit. The documents are then passed on to the importer, provided that the bank is happy that it will be able to recover the money. If it is not happy with the importer's ability to pay, the bank must decide whether to retain control of the documents and thus of the goods. If the documents are not in order, the bank is released from its obligations to pay, although before sending the documents back the bank will usually check to see whether the importer is prepared to accept them despite any discrepancies.

Produce advances

Produce advances are advances made against the security of goods or produce belonging to, or to be bought by, the borrower. Although usually associated with importers, produce advances could be granted to any trader in goods which would form an acceptable security. The goods will be charged to the bank under a *letter of pledge* and the bank will assume control of the goods either by having them warehoused in its name, or by holding the *documents of title*. Clearly, a bank will only enter into this type of arrangement in respect of readily saleable goods which have a stable value. Perishable items or goods made to special order are not, therefore, suitable as the basis of a produce advance. Standard items such as tinned foods or engineering components are the ideal types of goods around which to base a produce advance.

At the time the advance is to be made, the goods may already be in the possession of the borrower or, if the customer is an importer, they may be in transit to the UK. Before the advance is made, the bank must ensure that it has control of the goods themselves or of the documents of title. In the case of an importer, of course, the advance is usually made to obtain the release of documents presented by the exporter under a documentary letter of credit or as a documentary collection. In such a situation the bank would simply retain the title documents, that is the bills of lading, instead of passing them on to the customer, although once the goods have arrived in the UK the documents may be passed on to the customer so that he can arrange for the goods to be warehoused in the bank's name. Produce advances are, in fact, often associated with the issue of a letter of credit at the request of the importer.

Repayment of the advance will come from sales of the goods. As sales are made, an appropriate proportion of the goods will be released to the customer for delivery to the purchasers. Before being allowed to handle the goods, the customer will be required to sign a *trust receipt* promising that all money received from the purchasers will be paid into the bank in reduction of the advance. For ease of control, the advance will be made on a separate *loan account*, the outstanding balance of which should always reflect the value of the goods remaining unsold.

Foreign exchange services

The world marketplace is changing, and one of the major changes concerns the currencies in which international trade is settled. There was a time when sterling was the major world currency, being used as the yardstick against which the values of other currencies could be measured. British traders, both importers and exporters, could expect to negotiate with their counterparts abroad on the basis of prices denominated in sterling. An importer would eventually pay in sterling for the goods bought; an exporter would receive sterling from the buyer abroad. The greater advantage to the British trader was that he knew the domestic price of the goods and therefore he knew his anticipated profit margin. World markets are no longer dominated to the same extent by a few major trading nations, and traders in other countries are not so ready to deal in the currencies of those major nations. Thus, although sterling remains an important world currency and UK traders still do much of their foreign business in sterling, much business is also done in foreign currencies. An exporter may find that to secure an order from a buyer in the United States, for example, he will have to quote a price in US dollars. Similarly, an importer wishing to purchase goods from Sweden could find that the seller would insist on receiving payment in Swedish kroner.

There is no great difficulty in *processing* currency payments. As you have seen, the banks can remit payments abroad in any currency and can exchange their customers' currency receipts for sterling. All the commercial banks deal regularly in the foreign exchange markets and can offer their customers current competitive *exchange rates* for converting foreign currency into sterling and vice versa. The problem for the customer is the volatility of exchange rates, with the *exchange risk* that it entails. The rate of exchange between sterling and any foreign currency is variable, fluctuating in response to relative changes of supply and demand between the two currencies. The rates therefore change constantly, not only from day to day but even many times during each day; over a period the relative values of the two currencies can change quite significantly.

Consider the importer wishing to buy goods from Sweden who has been quoted a price in Swedish kroner. He can find out how much the kroner amount would come to if converted from sterling at today's exchange rates and this will give an indication of the sterling price at which the goods must be on-sold in the UK in order to make a profit. However, it may be some months before the goods are actually received and payment might not be due until some time after that. In the intervening period, the sterling:kroner exchange rate could vary considerably. This does not matter to the Swedish exporter who will receive the agreed amount of his own currency whatever happens to the exchange rates but it does matter to the UK importer. If kroner become dearer, that is the bank supplies less kroner for each £1 sterling, the importer will find that he is paying a lot more in sterling than he expected and this may reduce or even completely absorb his anticipated profit margin. Of course the reverse could happen; if kroner become cheaper, the sterling cost of the goods will be less than originally anticipated. The problem is the *uncertainty*. The importer will not wish to enter into the transaction if he cannot tell whether he will make a profit or a loss.

Similar problems beset a UK exporter who is having to invoice abroad in foreign currencies. His costs of production are met in sterling but his income is in foreign currency. Conversion of these currency receipts at prevailing *spot rates* of exchange may not realise enough sterling to cover those costs if rates have moved against him since the order was obtained. How can these uncertainties be guarded against?

Forward exchange contracts

We have been assuming so far that the UK trader will fix the exchange rate with the bank only at the time that a currency payment is made or received. In such a situation, the bank will apply the exchange rate prevailing at that particular time. This is known as the *spot rate*. The customer does, however, have the opportunity of arranging the exchange rate in advance. Thus, for example, an importer who contracts to make a payment of Swiss francs 50,000 in three months' time can arrange immediately the rate at which the bank will supply the francs when the payment is made. This is known as a *forward rate* of exchange.

The forward exchange rate will normally differ from the spot rate. If the forward rate quoted makes the currency cheaper than it would be at current spot rates, the currency is said to be at a *discount*; if the forward rate makes the currency dearer, it is at a *premium*. Entering into a forward contract to fix the exchange rate in advance does not guarantee a 'better' rate than would be obtained if the customer were to wait until the payment was due and then dealing spot for the currency, but it does take away the uncertainty of not knowing what the rate would be. No-one can predict what the spot exchange rate will be for a particular currency in one month's, three months' or six months' time; it may have fluctuated either up or down. Remember that a change in value which is good for an importer is bad for an exporter and vice versa. If a currency becomes dearer, an exporter's goods realise more sterling but an importer has to pay more for goods priced in that currency.

A fixed forward contract is one in which all details of the arrangement are settled between the customer and the bank at the outset. The bank agrees to buy from, or sell to, the customer a *fixed* amount of a *specified* currency at a *fixed* exchange rate on a *fixed* date in the future. The date on which the contract matures can be any time in the future but most contracts are set up for periods of between one and six months. On the maturity date the contract must be completed: the agreed currency amount must be supplied either by or to the bank depending on the arrangement. Occasionally problems arise if customers find that on the due date they have not yet received currency which they have contracted to sell to the bank or they no longer need the currency which they have agreed to purchase. In such circumstances, the contract must be *closed out* by a reversing transaction undertaken at spot rates. Thus, if a customer cannot provide the currency which he has contracted to sell to the bank, he must arrange to buy the currency on the foreign exchange market. If the spot rate and the contracted forward rate differ markedly, this could result in the customer suffering a significant loss on the transaction.

An *option forward contract* can sometimes be useful in avoiding these problems. Under this arrangement, everything about the contract is fixed as before—in other words the currency, the amount and the exchange rate—except for the maturity date. The customer is given the *option* of completing the contract on any day of his choice within a specified period, usually of a month but sometimes longer. If the option has not been exercised by the end of that period, the contract must be closed out on the final day. This type of contract is useful, for example, to an exporter who knows he is going to receive a currency amount in, say, three months but cannot be certain as to the exact day. An option forward contract can be arranged to sell the currency to the bank during a period of a month centred on the approximate date that receipt is expected.

Currency option contracts

Currency option contracts are quite different from option forward contracts which, as you have seen, are binding agreements to buy or sell an agreed amount of currency at a variable future date.

In a currency option contract, the customer buys the right to take up a deal for a particular amount of currency at a fixed rate at a future date. There is, however, no obligation to take the contract up at all; when the due date comes, the customer can simply let the option lapse. By using this type of contract, customers can protect themselves against adverse rate changes but can still benefit from favourable ones. The snag is that a unreturnable fee is paid when the contract is set up. The amount of the fee varies according to the currency and the length of the option period.

Foreign currency accounts

Customers who deal regularly in particular currencies may find it useful to open a foreign currency account as an alternative to the use of forward contracts. Banks will maintain accounts in all the major foreign currencies. An exporter, for instance, receiving regular payments in Deutschmarks may arrange a special Deutschmark account to which payments can be credited. Periodic transfers from this account to the normal sterling account can be effected when the Deutschmark:sterling exchange rate is favourable to him. This has the added advantage of avoiding the commission costs of entering into numerous separate smaller foreign exchange deals with the bank.

Currency loans can be arranged for customers who need finance. The currency borrowed is converted immediately into sterling at current exchange rates and credited to the customer's sterling account. When currency payments are received from foreign buyers, these amounts are used to repay the currency loan. A possible advantage of this arrangement is that the interest rate on a currency loan reflects the interest rates prevailing in the country of the currency. Thus, French franc loans attract French interest rates, Deutschmark loans attract German interest rates and so on: these rates may be lower or higher than UK rates. Currency loans should not be taken by traders who do not have regular receipts of the currency because of the *exchange risk* attaching to the repayments of capital.

Merchanting

Many bank customers deal on the international markets as *merchants*, buying goods from one country and selling them to another country, making their profits from the difference between the buying and selling prices. In many respects they combine the activities of both importers and exporters, receiving shipping documents from sellers abroad and sending out documentary collections drawn on buyers abroad. Usually, however, the merchant will arrange for the goods to be shipped direct from the country of export to the country of import without them entering his own country.

If a merchant can obtain a documentary letter of credit from the buyer of the goods in which he is dealing, he may request that his own bank issues a *back-to-back letter of credit* in favour of the supplier from whom he is obtaining the goods. This latter credit will be for a lesser amount than the one obtained by the merchant, known as the *prime credit*, because he is paying less for the goods than he is charging for them. This back-to-back credit will call for the same shipping documents as the prime credit but will expire earlier so as to allow the merchant time to get the documents in from the seller and send them out again to the buyer before the prime credit expires! Provided that the prime credit is issued by a reputable bank, the bank acting for the merchant can issue the back-to-back credit with safety, knowing that funds will be available when the documents are presented by the merchant under the prime credit.

Many merchants finance their dealings through foreign *currency accounts* and *currency loans*. This practice began when the UK had a strict system of exchange control and sterling could not be used to pay for goods which were to be sold to another country. Merchants had to pay for the goods either out of the proceeds of sale or by borrowing abroad and repaying the loan out of the proceeds of sale. Merchants have continued to follow this latter course in many cases, principally because of the advantages of using currency accounts.

Business support services

Credit information services

Status enquiries
It has long been the practice of banks to give brief reports on the respectability and standing of their customers in response to requests received from other banks and similar institutions. You might think that replying to such enquiries would consti-tute a breach of the bank's duty to maintain secrecy regarding a customer's affairs. In fact, the practice is of such long standing that it is generally held that opening a bank account gives *implied consent* for replies to be given to such enquiries. As you know, the customer's consent to disclosure of information over-rides the bank's general duty of secrecy. The customer may

specifically revoke the implied permission to answer such enquiries and the bank would be bound by this. In practice, however, it would be very difficult to make sure that no enquiries were answered on just one or two customers' accounts and the bank would probably simply decline to operate an account on such terms.

Banks make status enquiries on behalf of customers who are proposing to trade with the person or firm that is the object of the enquiry. The banks will not ask for reports which they consider frivolous or unnecessary as these might bring the service into disrepute. Customers must show adequate reasons for wanting the information. The customer requesting the enquiry must, of course, first ascertain where the bank account of the subject of the report is maintained. Enquiries can be made through the bank's overseas agency network if the subject of the enquiry is based abroad.

Each bank has its own standard form of enquiry letter and, to help the replying bank give a valid opinion on the status of its customer, the enquiry will indicate the nature and extent of the commitment which is being contemplated. Thus, for instance, an enquiry might ask for the replying bank's opinion as to its customer's trustworthiness in the way of business 'to the extent of £2000 at any one time'. This probably means that the enquirer is being asked to supply goods on credit up to a maximum value of £2000. Clearly, the replying bank's answer might be different if the enquiry was for £200 000, so the way the enquiry is phrased is obviously very important. When the reply to the enquiry is received by the bank, it will be passed on to the customer without comment. Although, as you will see later, the reports given in reply to these enquiries are very tactfully worded, they will generally give a clear indication of whether the subject is considered a 'good risk' by his own bank.

Sometimes a bank may make an enquiry on its own behalf concerning the status of a customer of another bank, for example, when a non-customer is proposing to give a guarantee for the borrowing of an account holder. The bank will enquire of the bankers to the proposed guarantor as to his trustworthiness to the extent of the guarantee. The enquiry will specify the amount of the guarantee and will make it quite clear that the enquiry is 'as guarantor' or even, if appropriate, 'as guarantor jointly and severally with others'. The more that the replying bank knows about the proposed transaction, the better able it is to give a well-balanced reply.

When giving a status report, the bank has a *duty to reply honestly* and to the best of its knowledge of the customer's affairs. It cannot, however, be required to search out fresh information about the customer but care must be taken neither to damage the customer's reputation unfairly nor to give the enquirer too favourable an impression. This important *duty of care* was established in *Hedley Byrne and Company Ltd.* v. *Heller Partners Ltd.* (1963), and it arises when it is foreseeable that the person to whom a statement is made will rely on it. The plaintiffs were advertising agents who contemplated placing substantial orders for a company, Easipower Limited, on terms which would make them personally liable for the cost. They therefore arranged for status enquiries to be made through their bankers on Easipower Limited, which company kept its account with Heller Partners, the defendant merchant bank. Satisfactory, but negligent, replies were received in reliance upon which advertising space was booked. The plaintiffs lost over £17 000 when Easipower went into liquidation. Unfortunately for the plaintiffs, the reference given contained an *express disclaimer* of any responsibility and for this reason the House of Lords held that they were not liable. However, the House stressed that but for the disclaimer they would have been liable.

So, it would appear that a preprinted disclaimer on a status enquiry form means that, at law, a bank can reply negligently to such an enquiry without incurring any liability, the recipient having only the bank's reputation to rely on. For some years this was indeed so but the position was probably changed by the Unfair Contract Terms Act 1977. This Act nullifies certain exclusion and limitation of liability clauses and notices entirely and subjects others, including such a disclaimer, to a *test of reasonableness*. Thus, if a bank sought to rely on its standard preprinted disclaimer when a negligent or reckless reply to a status enquiry had been given which caused the recipient financial loss, the disclaimer could now be challenged under the Act as being unreasonable in the circumstances. You must appreciate, however, that there is a distinction between a negligent opinion and a carefully considered opinion which turns out to be wrong.

Specific information about the customer and the account, such as the balance or the address, will not be disclosed in reply to an enquiry, and generally a number of 'standard' phrases are used to convey the opinion without giving too many particulars. These phrases range from 'respectable and trustworthy; should prove good for your figures and purpose' down to 'we cannot speak for your figures'. In intermediate cases where the bank has some reservations about the amount but is satisfied with the customer's integrity, the reply given might be something like, 'respectable and trustworthy. While your figure is higher than we are accustomed to see, we would not expect him to enter into any commitment he could not see his way to fulfil'.

Replies to status enquiries will never be sent by the replying bank direct to the enquirer; the information will always be routed via the bank through which the enquiry has been made. Each bank maintains a list of organisations to which replies can be given comprising banks, including a large number of foreign banks with offices in the UK, accepting houses, discount houses and a small number of enquiry agencies. A bank will not normally inform its customer that an enquiry has been made on him, nor is it required to tell him the nature of the reply given. The banks are not subject to the provision of s.145(8) of the Consumer Credit Act 1974 which requires all credit reference agencies to disclose to the subject of an enquiry, on request, the content of any opinions given. All bank status reports refer to the fact that the replying bank is not classed as a credit reference agency.

Intelligence reports

A customer intending to enter a new market may ask his bank to prepare an intelligence report on that market to help him assess whether it offers adequate potential for business growth and whether it is safe to grant credit in the market and, if so, to what extent. Usually such requests are made in respect of overseas markets. In producing its report, the bank would have to take into account the general economic status of the region, anticipated future demand for the product, the impact of local and foreign competition and so on. A number of the banks maintain economic research offices to look into such questions both in pursuit of bank planning objectives and on behalf of customers. These offices are capable of combining their own research into published data with information gleaned from the bank's worldwide network of correspondent relationships. You will appreciate that the services of these sections are highly specialised and therefore quite costly when put at the disposal of customers.

Bond support

Banks are often requested to issue indemnities and guarantees on behalf of their business customers. When such liabilities are entered into, the bank will first wish to reassure itself that it is unlikely to have to make any payments except in the most unforeseen circumstances. To cover itself if payments do have to be made, the bank will always take a corresponding *counter-indemnity* so that the appropriate sum can be reclaimed from the customer. The counter-indemnity will, of course, only be as valuable as the customer's ability to make refunds.

Performance guarantees
When capital projects are put out for tender, suppliers who wish to quote for the contract will normally be required to arrange for a satisfactory *tender guarantee*, or *bid bond*, to be issued in favour of the party who will be contracting for the work to be done. The aim of this type of guarantee is to protect the buyer against loss if the contract is awarded to a supplier who cannot or will not thereafter start work despite having put in a bid. If this were to happen, the buyer could suffer financial loss both because of the added costs of arranging for a second submission of tenders and because of losses or price rises resulting from the delay. Tender guarantees are commonly issued for a set percentage of the value of the contract. They are especially common when bids are being submitted for large-scale projects in foreign countries.

Performance bonds provide a similar type of safeguard against the risks of a supplier finding himself unable to complete the contract at some time after having started work. This can be very costly to the buyer because of the extremely lengthy delays which it may cause and because any other supplier would quite probably have to begin again from the beginning, being unable to utilise any of the work done or the items supplied by the original seller. If any stage payments have been made to the original supplier these amounts will probably be irrecoverable, adding to the losses.

Performance bonds are relatively new creatures in banking. Under them the guarantees given by the bank are *unqualified*. For example, any demand by the buyer is usually deemed to be conclusive proof that the money is due under the bond. In fact, in some export contracts the bonds have been treated by the buyer as a kind of discount on the contract price and enforced without any apparent justification. Consequently, the counter-indemnities taken from customers are similarly unqualified. Of greatest legal significance, perhaps, is that the seller (the bank's customer) is unable to prevent the bank paying under the bond even where there is a legal dispute pending between himself and the buyer. Similarly, the seller is unable to prevent the buyer from enforcing the bond. The bank has, in effect, opened a confirmed irrecovable letter of credit. Preventing payment of the bond, however, would allow a person to interfere with a contract to which he is not a party and would also interfere with an established mechanism of international trade.

Road bonds have to be arranged by speculative builders as a condition of being granted planning permission to build housing estates on plots of land which they have acquired. These bonds are in favour of the local authority and are designed to ensure that enough money will be available to make up the service roads to an acceptable standard even if the builder were to go out of business.

The amounts which the bank may be called on to pay under all these types of guarantees can be substantial. Before entering into them, therefore, the bank will wish to be entirely satisfied that the customer has the expertise and the resources to complete the contract. If necessary, security may be taken to ensure that the bank will not incur losses if payments have to be made.

Indemnities

Banks are asked to issue indemnities for both business and personal customers for a wide variety of reasons. We have already mentioned that indemnities are often called for to enable exporters to obtain payment under letters of credit despite discrepancies in the documents and that is a typical example. Other common situations include assisting importers to obtain delivery of goods from a shipping company before bills of lading have been received and helping personal customers to obtain duplicate copies of lost share certificates or life policies. In each case, the bank will consider the integrity of the customer and the value of the counter-indemnity before issuing the required document.

Summary

1. Factoring services provide debt administration systems for businesses and can be used to provide finance.

2 Leasing can be a cost effective method of acquiring capital assets.

3 Through their merchant banking subsidiaries the banks can provide: (a) acceptance facilities; (b) medium-term lending; (c) issuing house services to raise permanent or long-term capital.

4 Foreign trade can be conducted on various terms: (a) open account; (b) documentary collection; (c) documentary credits.

5 Specialist export financing schemes are available, including: (a) discounting bills; (b) acceptance credits; (c) export factoring.

6 Produce advances provide finance for importers against the security of the goods which they are bringing into the country.

7 Customers trading abroad in foreign currencies may protect themselves against the exchange risk by arranging: (a) a forward contract to fix the exchange rate in advance; (b) a foreign currency account for the processing of regular currency transactions; (c) a currency loan to be repaid out of future receipts of currency.

8 Status enquiries can be made to establish the creditworthiness of people with whom a customer intends to start trading. Such enquiries are also answered on customers' accounts.

9 Customers entering into large or long-term contracts may require bond support in the form of: (a) tender guarantees (bid bonds); (b) performance bonds; (c) road bonds (for speculative builders).

Self-assessment questions

1 Define (a) documentary letter of credit; (b) forward contracts; (c) merchanting; (d) bid bonds; (e) finance leases.

2 List the credit information services available to bank customers.

3 List the steps involved in the issue of a documentary letter of credit.

4 True or false?

(a) The advising bank guarantees payment of the documentary letter of credit which it passes on.

(b) The ECGD is a government-backed body which provides credit insurance for exporters.

(c) Under an option forward contract, the customer is at liberty to cancel the arrangement whenever he chooses.

(d) Leasing is especially attractive to businesses which make only moderate profits.

(e) Customers can instruct the bank not to reply to status enquiries made on them.

5 Explain why currency bonds are unsuitable for UK domestic traders who have no dealings with foreign countries.

6 Set out the advantages of leasing capital assets for the small to medium-sized business.

7 Advise an importer on the pros and cons of agreeing to trade on documentary credit terms with a supplier in the United States.

Assignments

1 Memorandum from: Manager
  To: Student
  Subject: Services to exporters

As you know, I am going to visit the Acme Washer and Bolt Co. next week. After a 75-year history of trading in the UK (and 15 years with us!) they are planning to enter the export market and they would like me to to tell them about the pitfalls. I am sure that this sort of request will recur in the future, so I would like you to prepare a brief that we can use when talking to all exporters. I would like you to pay particular attention to two aspects:

1 The particular problems that an exporter faces, from obtaining the order through to obtaining payment.
2 The bank services that go towards providing a solution for those problems.

It might be a good idea to draw up a flow chart to show the steps an exporter has to take with a key showing the services we offer at each step.
2 You have been transferred to a medium-sized branch of the bank (15 staff) on the outskirts of one of the major cities of the UK. In the catchment area of the branch can be found a full cross-section of businesses ranging from small corner shops to major manufacturing companies.

Your new manager tells you that he feels that the branch is too dependent on its personal customer base and that he wishes to attract more business customers. As a newcomer to the area he would like you to select one section of the local business community and prepare a report setting out which of the bank's services would be most useful to it and indicating how you would go about promoting those services. You may select any type of business as your principal target.

13 Lending

Chapter objectives

After studying this chapter you should be able to:
* state the general principles governing bank lending;
* outline the impact of the Consumer Credit Act 1974 on bank lending;
* list the various forms of bank lending and identify their suitability for the purposes of different borrowers;
* outline the special features of contractual capacity that a banker needs to consider when lending to different types of customers;
* explain the circumstances in which security may be required;
* identify the various types of security which may be accepted and list their attributes.

Of the traditional activities pursued by the commercial banks, lending is the one which has always been the principal profit earner and so it remains today despite the growth of ancillary services. Sanctioning advances absorbs a large proportion of the efforts of all branch managers and their staff, not to mention the work done by staff in supporting departments in regional or head offices.

The principles of lending

Lending money is easy; it is in ensuring that loans are repaid that skill is required! When asked to make a loan, the first concern of a bank will be to extract as much information as possible about the proposition so as to be able to assess the probability of repayment. Some loans will become bad debts and cannot be recovered but this should never happen as the result of a risk which could have been foreseen from the outset. In coming to a decision you must check how well the proposition measures up to a number of criteria. Some of the questions to be asked are vital, others less so, but all help the lending officer to obtain an overall view of the proposals. In one sense these criteria can be looked on as a series of hurdles which would-be borrowers must clear; if they fail to completely satisfy the bank on one of the important principles then the application will probably not be pursued all the way through the rest of the decision-making process. On the other hand, it has to be recognised that few proposals for advance are perfectly satisfactory in all respects. In most cases the banker must use skill, judgment and experience in balancing the good points and the bad points of the proposition to judge the probability of the outcome.

Purpose

The first question is, 'What is the advance required for?' Prudence dictates that advances should be made for purposes which fall within those categories usually associated with bank advances. The purpose of the advance will usually give a strong indication of the *level of risk* which is involved; some purposes are quite simply known to be less likely to generate repayment than others. Thus, for instance, you would not normally grant loans for speculative deals where repayment is dependent on the success of the speculation. In the case of advances to businesses, the bank will take into account the fact that different trades have different rates of failure and a more cautious attitude will be adopted towards those with a high failure rate.

The purpose of the advance may also require particular legal provisions to be considered. Clearly a bank would not wish to advance money to finance an illegal or fraudulent project, although happily requests for such finance are rare. More importantly, you must ensure that it does not fall foul of any of the more technical provisions of the law. For instance, when lending to a limited company you must check that the purpose of the advance falls within the scope of the company's stated objectives. If a private individual is borrowing for the purchase of a consumer durable, such as a car, television set, washing machine, etc., the proposition must fall in line with current government directives on consumer credit; there may be regulations in force which stipulate a minimum deposit to be provided by the borrower or which set a maximum repayment period.

Finally, the reason for which the loan is required will often indicate the most appropriate method by which funds may be advanced. As we have seen, all the commercial banks now offer an array of differing loan schemes and most of them consist of variations on the themes of loan accounts and overdrafts. Loan account facilities are generally more appropriate to finance capital purchases over a fixed term while overdraft facilities are best suited to finance cash flow problems where expenditure exceeds income in the short term. It is, of course, not bank practice to finance customers to live permanently beyond their means, although many seem to wish that it were!

Amount

Next you must check the amount that the customer requires and whether he has correctly assessed his requirements. It is important to calculate at the outset the *maximum advance* required as you do not wish to be faced with a request for increased facilities in a crisis situation at a later date. The danger is that in such a situation you will have to choose between the two equally unpalatable alternatives of lending the customer more in total than you think safe or, by refusing further credit, losing the funds which have already been advanced. You therefore need to complete your own careful analysis of a customer's requirements by checking the application for the advance and ensuring that all contingencies have been taken into account. For example, applicants requiring bridging loans to help them move house may not have allowed for all the various items of expenditure such as agent's fees, solicitor's fees and removal expenses.

Where an overdraft facility is requested, especially in the case of a working capital advance for a business customer, a cash flow forecast can be useful to estimate the maximum amount of the overdraft. A *cash flow forecast* is simply an analysis of the customer's estimated income and expenditure each month, projected forward as far as is possible or necessary. If expenditure exceeds income in any one month, the overdraft will increase; if income exceeds expenditure it will decrease. The value of the exercise is that it often discloses basic miscalculations in customers' estimates of their requirements.

Many customers, when working out the amount they need to borrow to complete a particular transaction, often base their calculations on the most optimistic possible estimates of sums to be spent and received. A customer seeking a personal loan to fund the purchase of a new car, for example, will often hope for a much higher trade-in value for his existing vehicle than he will actually get, at the same time, perhaps, deducting from the cost of the new car an unrealistically high discount. This results in the loan requirement being understated of course, and the customer may well pass this estimate on to the bank in the belief that the lower the figure he asks for, the higher his chances of success will be. The danger to the bank is that an understated loan requirement will paint a false picture of the borrower's ability to repay. The reverse of this situation is also sometimes found; the customer asks for a larger loan than he needs, on the grounds that if he is turned down he can negotiate at a lower figure.

When the question of amount is being considered, it is important for you to relate the amount that the bank is being asked for to the amount which the customer is contributing to the venture. It would not be normal for a bank to lend 100% of the sum required. While a fifty-fifty split is probably the ideal, the bank's stake in the project will usually represent more than half of the funds required. For consumer finance, for instance, banks will normally lend between two-thirds to three-quarters of the cost of the item to be purchased. Lending to businesses is more complicated but a comparison will often be made between the stake which the bank is being asked to take in the business by way of advances and the stake which the proprietor has, taking into account all the concern's assets and liabilities.

Repayment

The source of repayment must always be clarified before the advance is taken. Generally this will come either out of income or from realisation of capital assets. Your objective will be to check that the proposals for repayment are feasible in the circumstances of the particular case.

Repayment out of income
In the case of a private individual, income will usually be provided by wages or a salary and you should see some evidence

of the average amount. When the salary can be paid direct into a bank account, and this is not already being done, it should be arranged. The income of a business consists of its profits and the evidence of the levels being generated is to be found in its profit and loss account. If it is expected that profits will rise as a result of the project for which the loan is required, this may be allowed for, although you must beware of over-optimistic profit forecasts.

The *source* and *reliability* of income are other aspects to consider. For example, a business customer relying heavily on one connection or contract is clearly a higher risk than one who has a good spread of trade in a regular market. The individual in receipt of a regular salary from a reputable employer is a more attractive proposition than the freelance worker who cannot produce positive evidence of future income for a definite period. *Levels of expenditure* must, of course, be offset against income in order to find the net amount available to fund repayment. If further expenditure is planned during the period of the loan, or indeed results from it, the ability to repay may be affected. In this connection the payment of interest charges on the loan must not be overlooked.

Repayment out of capital realisation

Instead of regular repayment out of income, loans are sometimes granted with the intention that they will be repaid in a single lump sum out of funds resulting from a capital realisation. A typical example is the 'bridging' type of advance granted to enable a customer to purchase a new asset pending the sale of an existing possession; repayment of the loan comes from the proceeds of the sale. The bridging loan is most often granted to house-owners who are moving house and who wish to complete the purchase of the new property before the old house has been sold.

Your chief concerns will be to satisfy yourself that adequate capital will be realised to effect repayment and to ensure that funds will be paid in to the bank and not diverted elsewhere. If there are any doubts as to the adequacy of the amount which is to be received, it may be possible to agree to the advance if the customer can show that any residual borrowing could be repaid out of income over a period. Generally, however, the amount of any loan will be closely related to the amount which is anticipated, preferably allowing a margin for error. The customer must find from his own resources the amount of any shortfall between the cost of the item to be purchased and the maximum amount of the loan.

Similar considerations will apply to any other proposals for lump-sum repayment; these may include such items as the proceeds of sale of stocks and shares, bequests from the estate or a deceased person, or anticipated payments for damages or compensation resulting from a law suit. In all these cases there is a substantial risk that the borrower may realise very much less than he anticipates, or even nothing at all, and they must be treated with due care.

Term

How long is the advance required for? Although this will depend to a large degree on the proposals for repayment, it is important because the longer the loan is outstanding the more chance there is of something unforeseen happening to prevent the customer from adhering to the agreed schedule.

The funds which banks lend are taken in as deposits from other customers and although these are repayable at short notice the total funds available for lending do not fluctuate greatly. Consequently, medium and long-term loans are now granted besides the traditional short-term loans (usually up to three years). Medium-term loans can be arranged for business customers for periods up to five to seven years. Loans to personal customers for home improvements and house purchase may be scheduled for repayment over ten to twenty years. Requests for overdraft facilities may be agreed on a twelve-month basis with no specific repayment schedule but with a view to regular review. In these situations you must always satisfy yourself that the customer has sufficient income or surplus assets to effect repayment quickly if required.

Security

Once the proposition and its likely success has been assessed you then move on to consider what assets the customer can lodge as security for the advance. It must be stressed that loans should be made only against the proposition as supported by the security and not against the security alone. If the proposition does not seem viable *in its own right* then it is quite wrong to lend against good security knowing that it will almost certainly have to be relied on as the source of repayment. In other words, you should have decided that you want to make the loan before you even look at the availability of security.

Why then is security taken at all? If the proposition is particularly strong or if the advance is made under a scheme which the bank has decided may be operated without security, then it might not be taken. Most advances, however, are secured and the security is taken quite simply as an *insurance* against unforeseen and unforeseeable circumstances. All advances carry some measure of risk and while the risk can be minimised by careful consideration it can never be eliminated altogether.

The types of asset which a bank will commonly accept as security include life assurance policies, stocks and shares and deeds of houses and other properties. The qualities of a good security item are that it should have a value which is both stable and easy to check, that its deposit with the bank should not involve too many complicated and costly procedures and that it should command a ready market and be easy to realise if it has to be relied upon when all other sources of repayment have failed.

Other considerations

Having reached this point, you will have a good idea of whether the advance will be granted, but there are a few further points which should be considered. While perhaps less fundamental than the previous questions, these can nevertheless be important, especially where the request is a marginal one on which it is hard to reach a decision.

Character

The standing and integrity of the customer are important. No lending, however safe it may appear from the point of view of security, would be made to a customer who is unreliable and unlikely to adhere to the terms of any advance granted. A point to be remembered is that there can be a difference between what a borrower can afford 'on paper' to repay and what he will manage in practice to repay. The customer of integrity will make every effort to repay while the less reliable customer will probably keep to the repayment schedule while he is in funds, but will place the bank low on his order of priorities if money runs short.

The stability of the personal life of the borrower speaks volumes to the banker. The 'ideal' borrower is an individual who has lived in the same house for a number of years, who has changed employment only infrequently and who is married, probably with a family; lifestyle with such an investment of stability and order is evidence that the customer is unlikely to voluntarily default on commitments. It should not be assumed, however, that borrowers who do not fit this pattern will be automatically rejected. It is obviously much easier to assess this aspect of lending in respect of a customer who has been with the bank for some years. It is much more difficult, becoming a case of judgment and experience, to assess the character of a new or relatively new customer. Assistance in this direction may be obtained by making sure that normal references are taken up and by making use of credit reference agencies.

Past record

If the customer has borrowed in the past, kept to the arrangements and repaid satisfactorily, then this is a plus factor and would influence the assessment of the proposal. By the same token, evidence in the past of recalcitrance in repayment or lack of co-operation on the customer's part will count against him. Even if the customer has never borrowed from the bank before there may be evidence in the conduct of his account showing his ability, or otherwise, to repay a loan. The customer may for instance have made regular transfers to a deposit account which show that he has surplus income which could, instead, be used to reduce an advance.

Assets and liabilities

It is helpful to obtain a total picture of the customer's financial substance taking into account all assets and liabilities, not just those directly affected by the proposal. With a personal customer, it is much safer to lend to someone who has assets such as his own house and, perhaps, some investments, rather than to an applicant who has no property of his own and who starts off by relying almost totally on borrowed funds. With a business account this information is normally obtained by acquiring as up-to-date a balance sheet as possible and analysing the nature and make-up of the assets shown.

Any liabilities must of course be taken into consideration. For example, if a house or factory is owned, is it subject to a mortgage and, if so, for how much? Any such encumbrances may affect the customer's ability to repay and would also reduce the value of the assets available should bankruptcy or liquidation subsequently occur.

Reward

Finally we come to the question of the reward to the bank from the proposed advance. This is, of course, the *commercial objective* in making the loan. The calculable return may come from two sources: interest charges and commitment fees. In addition, there may be less tangible rewards if the borrower has close connections with other important customers or potential customers with whom the bank wishes to establish and maintain good relationships.

The reward must be commensurate with the risk. It is partly for this reason that banks will not usually lend 100 per cent of the funds required for a particular project, especially in the case of business ventures, however profitable the venture may appear for the customer. It would hardly be good business for the bank to take on the whole of the financial risk in return for the comparatively small reward which it can expect from interest and other charges while the customer collects the lion's share of any profits which are made.

Interest will invariably be levied on any loans granted. It is usually charged at an agreed percentage above the bank's base rate and will fluctuate with it. The additional percentage charged will depend largely on the level of risk which the bank sees in the proposition. Large commercial concerns, which often also provide the bank with a high commission income, may be able to borrow at between 2 to 2½% over base rate; secured loans to personal customers and to smaller businesses may be charged at around 3% over base; unsecured loans will attract rates of 4% or more above base rate. With certain formalised loan schemes, such as personal loans, interest is charged at a set tariff common throughout the bank and which the branch will have no authority to vary. Interest on such loans is often quoted as a 'flat rate' which does not refer specifically to base rate and which does not fluctuate during the life of the loan, having been fixed at the outset. From time to time the bank will adjust the rate of interest applicable to new loans to take account of changes to base rate.

Commitment fees are becoming more common, being most often levied in the case of substantial loans granted for short periods where the interest alone would not repay the costs of setting the loan up. The commitment fee is a once-only charge, levied when the loan is taken; it may be calculated as a percentage of the maximum advance—1 to 5% is the normal range—or simply as a flat fee for a particular type of loan.

Banks and the Consumer Credit Act 1974

Introduction

The scope of the Act is very wide. It affects *all businesses* that collectively make up the credit industry in providing credit facilities up to £15 000 to private individuals, sole traders, part-nerships and other unincorporated bodies such as societies and associations. Thus, it affects hire purchase and rental com-panies, moneylenders and pawnbrokers, and a host of professional people besides all banks. In addition, it also regulates ancillary businesses such as credit and mortgage brokers, debt collectors, debt adjusters and counsellors and credit reference agencies.

Clearly, it is neither appropriate nor possible for us to look at the total effect of the Act in this book and we concentrate on its effects on the business of banking. Indeed, we have mentioned the Act before in the text but we have chosen to deal with it comprehensively at this point rather than give it a frag-mented coverage.

Purpose of the Act

The main purpose of the Act is to provide an effective means of *controlling* virtually the whole range of consumer credit trans-actions by regulating the contract between lender and borrower. For example, the agreement *must* include terms relating to the amount of credit, the credit limit, the rate of interest and the repayments. If such *prescribed terms* are not included, the agreement is *wholly unenforceable*. Remember, however, that the Act does *not* regulate the provision of credit to registered companies and other corporate bodies *nor* credit in excess of £15 000 to anyone.

Provisions of the Act

Licensing
All businesses that provide credit, lend money or hire out goods within the Act's provisions, or engage in ancillary credit activities must be licensed. Licences are issued by the Office of Fair Trading and it is a criminal offence to engage unlicensed in such activities. It follows that you must ensure that any customers who are involved in the consumer credit industry are properly licensed before making an advance to them. For example, advances secured by charges over rental or hire purchase agreements would be put at risk if they were not.

Advertising
The Act imposes restrictions on the *mode of advertising* for credit and gives potential borrowers the right to ask for quotations as to the *true cost* of credit available. This enables them to shop around with confidence to get the best terms to suit their requirements. (On several occasions in the text we mention the difference between the apparent and true rate of interest on a loan depending on its method of calculation.) Remember, of course, that while banks compete with each other there is, in practice, very little difference between the terms which they offer borrowers.

Canvassing
In so far as a banker is concerned, there are two categories of business covered by *canvassing prohibitions*. These are: (a) almost any type of advance and further advance, including credit cards, that separately do not exceed £15 000; and (b) certain brokerage arrangements, debt adjusting and debt counselling.

The prohibitions make it a criminal offence to canvass either type of business when not on trade premises. But what amounts to canvassing, so you can be sure not to be guilty of it? Essentially, it is deliberately attempting to persuade an individual to enter into an agreement for credit facilities and/or to accept an ancillary credit service by making oral representations to the individual when not previously requested to do so and where the visit is made in order to persuade the individual to enter into such an agreement. (The canvassing of *overdrafts for existing customers* is permitted.)

Branches and other bank offices are clearly *trade premises* but problems can arise with the premises of a customer or prospective customer. For example, factories and offices are *not* the trade premises of the employees working in them and the office of a managing director of a limited company would not be trade premises in relation to his personal business. Canvassing of a private customer must not take place off bank premises without a prior invitation.

Remember that the restrictions do *not apply* where the customer or prospective customer is a limited company or other corporate body, nor where the credit facility under discussion exceeds £15 000. Again, restrictions do not apply to telephone conversations, letters, circulars and leaflets (other than to *minors*), where the customer or prospective customer initiates the discussion about credit facilities and to speaking engagements to talk about bank services, provided references to credit facilities and ancillary services remain general.

Particularly restrictions apply to canvassing *minors*. It is an offence to send a circular or any document to a minor which invites the minor to borrow money or use other credit facilities, including credit cards, or to apply for information or advice on obtaining credit or credit services.

It is also an offence under the Act to send a credit token, for example a credit card, to anybody unless requested in writing by that person to do so. Cash dispenser cards and cheque cards are not credit tokens because they give no automatic entitlement to credit.

Regulated agreements

The Act prescribes the form and content of certain credit agreements and provides that copies must be supplied to the prospective borrower. These are known as *regulated agreements*. Loans, overdrafts and credit card facilities are all regulated agreements. One important point is that a *running-account* credit facility, for example, an overdraft or a budget account in a shop, will still qualify as a regulated consumer credit agreement if the borrower cannot draw more than £15 000 at any one time, or if the interest rate increases above a given figure not exceeding £15 000, or if at the time of the agreement it was unlikely that borrowing would exceed £15 000, for example, short-term finance to acquire trading stock. While both are regulated agreements, note that a loan, i.e. fixed sum credit, requires a signed written agreement in the prescribed form, but an overdraft, i.e. a running-account credit facility, does not.

A regulated agreement involving a bank can be *cancelled* within five days after receiving a second copy of the signed agreement in the post if two conditions are satisfied: (a) verbal representations were made by or on behalf of the bank in the borrower's presence; and (b) the agreement was not signed by the borrower at the bank's premises or the trade premises of any other party involved in the overall arrangement. In fact, banks normally regard any agreement not signed on bank premises as cancellable. Note that an agreement which is secured by a mortgage over land, a bridging loan to purchase land and an overdraft are not cancellable. The problem of cancellation is avoided entirely by simply ensuring that the customer signs the agreement at the bank. In the case of an agreement secured on land, however, the Act allows a customer to *withdraw* from the agreement before it is ever (legally) entered into. A *consideration period* of at least 14 days is given during which period the bank cannot approach the customer about the proposed loan.

Failure to comply with the Act's regulations renders the agreement unenforceable without a court order. The court can vary or impose terms or suspend the agreement. These powers extend to any securities taken in connection with the loan.

An *exempt agreement* is one which is not regulated by the majority of the provisions of the Act. Such agreements important to a lending banker are mortgage loans, advances at a low rate of interest, although these are uncommon, and advances to finance the export of goods or services.

Debtor-creditor-supplier agreements
Provided a link exists between a lender and the supplier of goods

or services to an individual, the lender will be *jointly and severally liable* with supplier for any *misrepresentation* or *breach of contract* by the latter. In relation to banks, such an agreement must involve an arrangement between the bank and a supplier whereby the bank is prepared to consider providing finance to enable a prospective purchaser to buy goods and/or services from the supplier. Such an arrangement may be quite loose, for example, a debtor-creditor-supplier agreement might be held to exist if the bank's advertising materials are displayed in the supplier's premises or if the bank encourages the supplier to send customers to its branches.

The supplier in a debtor-creditor-supplier agreement may act as a credit broker and he must be licensed if the bank's advances are not to be jeopardised.

Charge for credit

The total charge must include not only the *interest payments* but also *all other charges* payable under the agreement or transactions made in connection with it, for example, the costs of a security arrangement.

The total charge is converted into a rate of total charge for credit—the annual percentage rate of charge or APR—on the basis of annual compounding. Technically, it is found by equating the sum of the present values of all advances to the present value of all repayments. The calculation is primarily required for quotations and advertising and it enables a prospective lender to make objective comparisons among different credit facilities and different financial institutions.

Both bankers and lawyers consider the Consumer Credit Act to be a highly technical piece of legislation; very few would claim to be completely conversant with it. Because of this, banks have adopted a centralised approach to implementing its provisions. Branches follow procedures determined by specialists at head offices, there is no room for local interpretation, and in this way are able to comply with the Act without problems. Fortunately, few customers ever ask for explanations of the Act's regulations—they are solely concerned with whether or not they are going to be given credit and how much it is going to cost them! So, view the Act mainly as background to current banking practice.

Types of advance

Overdraft

The overdraft is the archetypal bank advance. It is available from hardly any other source and it is the facility which first springs to mind when bank borrowing is contemplated. It depends for its operation on the use of a current account. In the absence of any special arrangement a customer clearly should not draw cheques for more than he has in his account; if he does so, the bank may return them unpaid. If, however, an overdraft facility is arranged, the bank will allow its customer to over-draw the account beyond the credit balance up to an agreed limit.

The overdraft facility enables a customer to overcome short-term cash-flow problems. It allows debts to be paid as they fall due during a period in which outgoings temporarily exceed income. In the case of a business customer, it is often called a 'working capital' facility. The essence of the arrangement is its *temporary nature*. If a customer's expenditure continually exceeds income, an overdraft is not the answer. A bank would be unwise to agree to lend in such a case as the amount borrowed would simply increase each month with no prospect of repayment. The customer must be encouraged instead to balance his budget by rearranging his finances and reducing his expenses. Overdrafts are not really suitable for the financing of capital expenditure such as the purchase of cars or property. This type of proposal is better funded through the use of loan account schemes which have more formal repayment schedules.

The overdraft *limit* will be related to need but must not be greater than the amount which the bank considers recoverable. The danger is that the customer will underestimate the amount needed to meet outgoings. For this reason, as we said earlier, the bank will often ask for a cash flow forecast or a cash budget to be prepared showing all the anticipated inflows and outflows of funds during the period for which the overdraft is required. In practice, cash budgets rarely prove to be completely correct but they can give a general indication of the maximum amount which needs to be borrowed.

The balance of the account will fluctuate like the balance of any current account, probably swinging from debit to credit and back again in response to payments into and out of the account. The bank will not wish to see signs that the borrowing on the account is becoming long term, resulting in longer periods in debit with shorter and smaller swings into credit. If this process continues, the account may eventually show a permanent debit balance, never returning into credit. This is known as 'hard-core' borrowing and shows that expenditure is permanently in excess of income.

The periodic return to credit of a properly 'swinging' overdraft account is not a sign that the borrowing has been repaid; subsequent expenditure will return the account to debit again. Sometimes, especially in the case of overdrafts granted to personal customers, the arrangement will be for the limit on the account to be reduced by a proportion each month until eventually it is extinguished altogether. *Payments into the account* must therefore exceed the payments out by at least the amount of the agreed reduction, thereby ensuring the repayment of the advance. Often no regular reduction of the limit is sought; this is generally the case with working capital advances. In such cases, the bank will be more concerned to see that the customer is solvent and could repay the advance out of capital if the business were to be wound up.

The *term* of an overdraft facility can vary from a few months to a period of years. Many of these advances continue to run for many years, although the bank will review the position at least every twelve months and more frequently if there are any doubts about the financial stability of the customer. The arrangement will not be renewed if there are signs that the customer is becoming insolvent.

Interest is calculated daily on the overdrawn balance. It is therefore among the *cheapest* of all forms of borrowing since the customer pays interest only on money he has borrowed and used; he will not be paying interest on funds 'borrowed' only for them to lie idle on another account. The overdraft is also very simple in operation and the customer needs only to continue using his current account as he did before. The only significant disadvantage is that the account does not reflect clearly the maximum potential liability to the bank in the same way that a loan account does. If the customer does not take into consideration all his forthcoming commitments, he may overestimate the funds available to him and may overspend beyond his limit. This is especially true if a reducing limit has been marked on the account.

Loan accounts

The other traditional method of lending is the loan account. It differs quite significantly in operation from the overdraft. When a loan facility is granted, a separate loan account will be opened in the customer's name. The full amount of the loan is then debited to this account and the funds credited to the current account.

Loans are usually granted for *capital purchases*, such as vehicles, machines, premises, etc; or to complete specific projects, such as buying a business, renovating a factory and so on. Their most common use is in the financing of business customers, although loan accounts are sometimes set up for personal customers whose needs are not covered by the more specialised personal loan services that are available.

There are no hard and fast rules about *amounts* but it would be unusual for a bank to lend 100% of the funds required by the customer. Prudence requires that the customer should contribute something to the project, if only to furnish evidence that he has adequate resources to ensure repayment.

Repayment of a loan is effected through a series of equal instalments credited direct to the loan account, usually at monthly intervals. Interest on the loan is normally charged separately to the customer's current account, although sometimes it may be applied to the loan account itself. In the latter case, the repayment amount must be adjusted to allow for the interest. This calculation is less simple than might be imagined since the amount of interest charged will vary throughout the period of the loan. This is because it is calculated on the actual balance outstanding and this is being continually reduced.

The *periods* for which loans are granted vary with the circumstances of the case. Loans for the purchase of capital assets are not given for longer periods than the expected useful life of the asset. The banks have traditionally viewed themselves primarily as short-term lenders but in recent years, however, they have been increasingly willing to grant medium-term and even long-term loans, mainly in respect of capital projects for business customers.

Interest on a loan account will be charged at regular intervals, usually quarterly. The amount charged is calculated on the outstanding balance on the account and no allowance or set-off is given for any balance standing to the customer's credit on his current account. Interest is charged at an agreed percentage over base rate, except in the case of medium and long-term loans where the interest rate is sometimes linked to the London Inter-Bank Offered Rate (LIBOR).

The principal advantage of the loan account as compared to the overdraft is the greater ease of control which it offers. Both bank and customer can tell how much is outstanding and whether payments are up to date or not.

Personal loans

Personal loans are a modern variant of the traditional loan account. As the name suggests, they are intended to provide finance for the private individual, both customers and non-customers. However, an applicant will usually be expected to maintain a bank account somewhere so as to facilitate the regular repayments normally effected by direct debit or standing order. Granting a loan to a non-customer can be a useful first step to obtaining all that person's banking business.

The purpose of the scheme is to finance personal expenditure, most commonly on consumer durables such as cars, televisions and furniture. However, any personal project may be used as the basis of an application and loans are often made to assist with the cost of weddings and holidays. Experience shows that for some of these purposes repayment can be less assured than for spending on durables; nevertheless, if given careful consideration, they can provide the basis for a very successful advance— in other words, you will get your money back.

Most banks operate separate *home improvement loan schemes.* These are really personal loans with slightly different terms, designed specifically to provide finance for furnishing, renovating or extending customers' homes.

Most personal loan schemes restrict the amount which can be borrowed. Between £500 and £5000 are the usual limits, although home improvement loans permit borrowing to a higher level, usually £10 000. If there are any government regulations in force which restrict the provision of consumer finance, the bank will be bound by them in the same way that a hire purchase finance company would be. (At the moment there are no such restrictions, the government having rescinded all existing controls in 1982.) In any event, the bank will wish to see the customer make a significant contribution towards the total funds required as evidence of ability to repay. Between a quarter to a third of the total cost would normally be acceptable as the customer's contribution.

It is in the practicalities of *repayment* that personal loans show a significant difference from other forms of loan account. The borrower is again required to make a series of regular equal payments into the account, usually on a monthly basis. Each payment combines capital repayment and interest, and the latter is applied to the loan account itself. Interest is calculated at a flat rate percentage on the original amount of the loan multiplied by the number of years that it will take before the loan is repaid. If the interest were to be expressed as a true rate calculated on the reducing balance of the loan, the percentage figure quoted would be a much higher one than the flat rate. This can be misleading to an inexperienced borrower, which is why the Consumer Credit Act 1974 requires the lender to inform the borrower of the true rate as well as the flat rate so as to enable fair comparison to be made with the cost of other forms of borrowing.

The rate of interest applied to a particular personal loan is fixed at the outset according to the bank's published rates and the customer knows from the start the total amount that the loan will cost. For example, a customer who borrows £3000 over two years at a time when the flat rate of interest is $9\frac{1}{2}\%$ will have to repay £3570 in all. The interest of £570 is calculated by taking $9\frac{1}{2}\%$ of £3000 and then multiplying the result by two for the term of years of the loan. The interest charged represents a true annual rate of 18.7% if calculated on the reducing balance.

The normal term for a personal loan will be from six months to three years, although home improvement loans for larger amounts may be granted for up to ten years. Common sense and hire purchase restrictions, where appropriate, will apply and will restrict the loan to shorter rather than longer periods.

The main attraction of the personal loan to the customer is that its cost is generally lower than that of similar facilities provided through other agencies such as hire purchase companies. The agreement form which the customer signs when applying for the loan will incorporate a *penalty clause* which operates if the customer wishes to repay the loan before the full term has expired. It will stipulate that the customer must pay as part of the final redemption figure a proportion of the interest which would have been payable if the loan had run on to its full term. This compensates the bank for the loss of expected interest on the unexpired period.

Banks are somewhat more stringent than other lenders in vetting applications for loans and borrowers are therefore more likely to be turned down. This attitude of the banks is partly because a personal loan does not confer on the lender any rights over the articles purchased with the funds. In this it is unlike hire purchase finance which gives the lender rights to repossess the goods if repayment is not made. Furthermore, personal loans are usually granted without supporting security, except in the case of home improvement loans for which a mortgage, usually a second mortgage, over the borrower's home may be called for. Supporting security is usually not taken because the time and expense which would be involved is not justified by the low risk of non-payment.

Budget accounts

A comparatively recent innovation is the 'budget' or 'personal credit' account which is directed at the *personal customer*. The customer agrees to pay a fixed sum each month by standing order into a separate budget account, out of which regular bills are paid using a special cheque book. The account is marked automatically with a borrowing limit which is related directly to the amount of the monthly payment into the account; the more the customer agrees to contribute, the more he will be allowed to borrow. In a sense the budget account is a formalised version of the overdraft. Its *purpose* is to allow the customer to borrow to even out the ups and downs of income and outgoings without referring to the bank manager every time he wishes to arrange an overdraft.

The budget account is automatically marked with a *borrowing limit* which is a multiple, usually thirty times, of the amount of the monthly contribution. Thus, a customer paying £100 per month into his budget account may be able to borrow up to £3000 on the account without further formality. When the budget account is set up, the customer will be asked to complete a 'budget planner' which sets out the payments which it is anticipated will be made through the account in the coming year; the *monthly contribution* (repayments) must of course be at least one-twelfth of the total. Thus, if the payments work out as planned, the advances will be self-liquidating over the full year. However, in practice the position is more complicated as the customer can use the account to pay for unbudgeted items such as an unexpected car repair bill or the cost of new furniture purchased in a 'sale', provided the overall limit on the account is not exceeded. The facility is *renewable every twelve months*, at which time the customer is expected to reassess his outgoings. Any shortfall in the previous year's contributions and changes in the current year's outgoings must be allowed for by adjusting, if necessary, the monthly payments.

Interest is charged quarterly at a percentage above base rate on the amount of any overdrawn balance. The additional percentage is the same for all customers and is not individually negotiated. If the account is in credit, the bank will pay the customer credit interest at a fixed, but admittedly not a very high, rate. *Commission* is charged on the transactions passing through the account.

The account provides a form of *revolving credit* which is available to the customer at all times. The pattern of transactions on the account is almost entirely in his control: he can overdraw up to the maximum amount right from the start or he can use the borrowing facility more sparingly, taking advantage of it only when he needs it.

Home loans

In 1981 the UK banks began to offer house purchase loan facilities. Although the details of these facilities vary between banks, the general principles are very similar. The schemes are comparable with those offered by building societies with which they are in competition. The demand for these loans has been so great that the banks soon began to experience difficulty in making available sufficient funds to cover all the borrowing that they would have been prepared to sanction. As a result, the availability of these loans to customers has been reduced.

The purpose of these loans is to provide finance for the purchase of domestic property for owner occupation. Commercial and investment properties are excluded, although second homes may be eligible for finance. Houses are the most common type of property for which loans are made.

The bank will require a professional valuation and survey to be made of the property to ensure that it is structurally sound and saleable. It is not usual to advance the whole of the cost of the property and banks usually limit lending to a maximum of 95% of either the cost of the property or of the value placed on it by the surveyor, whichever of the two is the lower. If there is any doubt about the ease with which the property could be resold, either because of the design or condition of the building or because of local market conditions, the proportion advanced may be reduced.

Repayment will normally be made out of the borrower's income. To ensure that this is feasible, the maximum amount of the loan will be limited to two-and-a-half times gross annual income. In the case of a married couple, this calculation is based on the income of the principal earner of the two. If the remaining party is also in employment, their annual income is added to the total without being multiplied.

Under the capital repayment *method*, the borrower makes equal monthly payments to the loan account to cover interest and a measure of repayment of the capital sum borrowed. In the early years, the greater proportion of each payment will be absorbed in servicing the interest charge but, as time goes by, the capital sum will gradually be repaid, thereby reducing the interest due and allowing an increasing proportion of each payment to be applied in reduction of the loan. Under the *endowment repayment method* the capital sum of the loan is not reduced at all during the agreed term of the advance. Instead, the whole amount is paid off in one lump sum at the end of the term out of the proceeds of an endowment assurance policy taken out on the life of the borrower specifically for this purpose. The policy will become payable on the date agreed for repayment of the loan or on the previous death of the borrower. Interest will, of course, be charged on the loan account and regular payments will be required from the borrower to cover this. Home loans are usually granted for a *maximum term* of 25 years or until the date of the borrower's retirement from work, whichever is the shorter period.

Interest is charged on these accounts at a special home loan rate which is not directly related to base rate but which will vary from time to time according to general changes in the level of interest rates. Interest paid by the borrower may be eligible for tax relief. The bank will require a *first legal mortgage* over the property concerned and will wish to see that it is properly *insured* against fire risks. *Assurance cover* will be required on the customer's life. If the loan has been granted on the endowment repayment method, this aspect is automatically covered; if the loan is on a capital repayment basis, a special mortgage protection policy can be set up. This assures the customer's life for the balance outstanding on the loan at any particular time. It is a very cheap form of assurance, but neither the customer himself nor his estate will ever receive a lump sum out of the policy. If the customer dies before the morgage is paid off, the proceeds will all go to the bank. If he survives, the policy will pay nothing.

Types of borrower

The general principles of lending and the various types of advances we have considered so far must, in practice, be related to each individual application. While many applications for loans are similar to each other, in the last analysis each calls for an individual decision to be made. However, borrowers can be classified in so far as particular legal considerations, mainly variations in contractual capacity, apply to particular groups. These, therefore, provide another, and often more rigid, set of guides for your decision.

Minors

As you already know, minors have only limited contractual capacity (*see* Chapter 6). In particular, any contract of loan to a minor is unenforceable and can be repudiated during minority, although the minor can ratify the loan after reaching majority.

Nevertheless, minors are sometimes allowed to overdraw their accounts although there should always be a good reason for this, for example, in order to complete a course of study, and in the hope that the loan will promote loyalty to the bank. (Impecunious student customers of today should become the worthwhile, that is profitable, customers of the future.) Indeed, the Minor's Contracts Act 1987 enables a bank to protect its position. The Act specifically provides that a guarantee of a loan to a minor is enforceable notwithstanding the unenforceability of the loan or its repudiation by the minor. Thus, for example, a parent can personally guarantee a son or daughter's borrowing, supporting the guarantee with additional security if required.

Personal representatives

Personal representatives are known as executors where they are appointed by a will, and as administrators where they are appointed by the court. They may wish to borrow from you for one of three reasons: (a) to facilitate the administration of the estate; (b) to continue the deceased's personal business; or (c) to pay inheritance tax.

One important function in the administration of the deceased's estate is the payment of debts. It may happen that the liquid assets available are insufficient to pay these and a loan may be sought until the other assets can be realised. In all cases a personal representative has power to borrow but you must check to make sure an executor is not prohibited from doing so by the terms of the will. The personal representatives must specifically accept *joint and several liability* on the loan otherwise their liability would be joint. By virtue of joint and several liability they incur personal liability on the loan but they are entitled to be *indemnified* out of the estate and, more importantly to you as bankers, the bank is *subrogated* to their position for the moneys it has advanced. (Subrogation is taking the place and assuming the rights of a creditor against his debtor, often explained by the phrase 'standing in the shoes off'.) If the ·bank requires *security* for the advance, specific estate assets can be charged and/or the personal representatives can charge their own personal security.

The extent of the personal representatives' borrowing powers to continue the deceased's personal business depends on whether or not express authority to continue the business is contained in the will. If it is not, or there is no will at all, authority is limited to borrowing which is necessary to sell or wind up the business and they commit a breach of trust if they continue the business beyond a reasonable time.

Inheritance tax, basically a tax on the value of the estate left by the deceased, may have to be paid before probate or letters of administration are granted. The personal representatives may seek a loan to pay this. Before granting it, a bank must be satisfied that there are sufficient liquid assets, such as cash and life policies, to ensure that the loan is quickly repaid once the personal representatives have authority to deal with the estate. The account mandate will include an undertaking to repay the loan or overdraft immediately assets are realised. Any assets of the deceased already held do not become security for the advance unless they are recharged by the personal representatives.

Trustees

A trustee has legal title to the trust property but must administer the property for the benefit of the beneficiaries. Trustees will seldom need to borrow and they have *no implied power* to do so. Thus, they must be given express authority by the trust deed. Furthermore, trust property can only be charged as security if this is also expressly authorised, and only for trust borrowing.

Trustees must accept *joint and several liability* for the borrowing. This enables a bank to set off a credit balance on a trustee's personal account against a debit balance on a trust account.

Home buyers

Earlier in the chapter we said that banks frequently grant bridging loans, or bridge-over advances as they are also called, to houseowners who are moving house and who wish or need to complete the purchase of their new home before the sale of their existing one is complete. The loan is repaid out of the proceeds of the sale when completed and/or a mortgage advance, usually from a building society. What 'legal' considerations apply here, assuming, of course, that the loan requested is satisfactory on more general banking criteria?

Generally speaking, such an advance will not be granted unless a *binding contract* for the sale of the customer's property exists. This contract does not transfer the title to the property but does bind the purchaser to complete the purchase. In other words, on the contractual completion date he or she must pay the balance of the purchase price. Thus, you are virtually certain that money will be available for repayment. In addition, if the purchase is to be financed by a mortgage loan from a building society, the agreement to grant the mortgage should be verified by the society or its solicitor. Because you will need to rely on his undertakings and deal with him closely, the status and integrity of the customer's solicitor must be checked with his bankers, unless he is already known to you.

Substantial sums of money are often involved in bridging loans and security should be provided. The security would normally be a deposit of the deeds or land certificate to the customer's existing property, thereby creating an equitable charge over them. This security would support the usual solicitor's undertaking to make repayment from the proceeds of the sale.

Sometimes a bridging loan is granted when no contract has been signed. The loan is then open ended. The security here is the property to be purchased and once the purchase is completed the customer will almost invariably be asked to execute either a legal or equitable mortgage over it in the bank's favour. Perhaps, above all, whether or not such a loan is granted depends on the more general considerations we discussed earlier in the chapter. For example, the customer must be a valued and undoubted one, he must have sufficient financial means to meet all the commitments resulting and there must be an adequate margin in relation to the realistic selling price of the existing property, which must also be readily sellable.

One final point, if there are two or more people buying the property jointly, such as husband and wife, the general principles applicable to joint accounts apply. In particular, joint and several liability must be accepted.

Sole traders

A sole trader has no special position at law. He has the same contractual capacity, legal rights and duties as any other adult. Thus, should an overdraft or loan be requested by a sole trader the general considerations relating to the financial soundness of his business, the acceptability of the proposed loan and the provision of security apply. It is essentially a decision based upon commercial and not legal considerations.

Partnerships

A partnership has no separate legal existence distinct from its members; at law it is merely a collection of individuals who carry on business together with the objective of making a profit. We have seen that this is reflected in the procedure followed when opening a partnership account.

A partner in a *trading partnership* has implied authority to borrow money for use in the firm's business, and to charge the firm's assets to secure such borrowing. The mandate will, however, usually contain the express undertaking of all the partners to be liable for any advance made to the firm. Express power must be given to partners in a *non-trading partnership* to borrow money or to give securities on behalf of the firm. It is, in fact, usual for a bank to insist on all the partners executing the necessary documents where the firm's property is pledged or mortgaged as security for an advance whatever the type of partnership involved. The partners will have admitted *joint and several liability* in the mandate and this puts the bank in a very strong position should any loan or overdraft to the firm not be repaid as scheduled.

Limited companies

A limited company is a corporation and its contractual capacity is governed by the *objects clause* in its memorandum of association. Any agreement entered into which is not sanctioned by it is *ultra vires* and void. *Introductions Ltd. v. National Provincial Bank Ltd.* (1970) showed that borrowing is *not* an independent activity, even if the memorandum states it as an

independent object. A company's borrowing powers must therefore be exercised only in connection with purposes within its
objects clause. Thus, before the more general considerations, you
have to ensure that the purpose of the proposed loan or overdraft
is *intra vires* the company and ascertain whether or not the
objects clause deals specifically with the borrowing of money.
The memorandum of association must therefore be referred to.
A trading company does, in fact, have implied power to borrow
and to give security for its debts, for example, by mortgage of
its assets but a non-trading company only has such powers if
expressly given in its memorandum.

It is usual for borrowing powers to be vested in the directors
but occasionally borrowing must be sanctioned by the company
in general meeting. The borrowing powers of the company are
seldom limited by its memorandum but a company's articles of
association frequently limit those of its directors.

Directors' borrowing powers

In addition to any specific limit contained in the company's
articles, the power of directors to borrow money is limited in two
other ways. First, the rules of the Stock Exchange require that
there be a reasonable limit (often liberally interpreted) on the
borrowing powers of directors of quoted public companies.
Second, if the company adopted Table A of the Companies Act
1948 (which continues to apply to companies registered under
that Act) as its articles (Table A was a model set of articles and
was usually adopted, often with modifications), Article 79 limits
the borrowing powers of the directors to the nominal amount of
the company's issued share capital, unless the consent of the
company in general meeting is obtained. The Article included
the value of securities given by a company to cover its own debts
or the debts or liabilities of third parties, for instance a
guarantee; but excluded temporary loans from its bankers in the
ordinary course of business. No certain meaning can be given
to the words 'temporary loan', although it would almost
certainly include an overdraft facility granted to accommodate
variations in cash flow, and this exception should only be relied
upon where the temporary nature of a particular loan is very
clear indeed. Table A of the Companies Act 1985 does not
contain a similar limitation.

Ultra vires borrowing

It is to be hoped you will never find yourself in the serious position of having made an *ultra vires* loan to a company. However, it is useful for you to know, in outline, the remedies available should repayment of such a loan be unforthcoming. Much depends on whether the loan was *ultra vires* the company itself or merely *ultra vires* the directors—in other words, they exceeded their authority. In either case, legal action must always be the last resort. It is expensive, time-consuming and often leads to bad publicity. If at all possible the problem should be resolved without it, for example, by voluntary repayment of the loan in return for a new and *intra vires* loan properly secured.

A loan which is *ultra vires* the company is *void*, as is any charge over company assets taken to cover the advance. Ratification of it is not possible. In addition, as you have already seen, a banker would not be able to take advantage of the protection afforded by s.35 of the Companies Act 1985. Note, however, that any security taken from a *third party*, such as a director of the company, is enforceable if, as is usual, the charge agreement or guarantee includes an *indemnity clause* for this enables the security to be enforced even if the loan is void. In other words, the enforceability of the security is quite independent of the validity of the loan.

So what remedies are available? First, a banker is *subrogated* to the rights of the company's creditors to the extent that they have been paid off with the loan. Second, he can sue for an *injunction* to restrain the company from parting with the money. Third, he can obtain a *tracing order* to recover any identifiable property purchased with the money. Fourth, he can sue the directors for *damages* for breach of *warranty of authority*. This is a rule of agency which renders a person liable for any financial loss he causes by professing to have authority which he has not. It makes no difference that the person acted in good faith. This remedy is unlikely to be useful if the loan was for a large sum but it might be very effective in the case of a small loan to a private company. It is not available if the bank knew that the directors were exceeding their borrowing powers.

A bank's position is not so dire where the loan is only *ultra vires* the directors, even though the protection of s.35 is again not available. In addition to the four remedies we have explained above, the company can be asked to either *ratify* the transaction at a general meeting or to *alter the articles retrospectively* at a general meeting to increase or to abolish the limit on its directors' borrowing powers.

Apart from this, you may be able to rely upon the decision in *Royal British Bank* v. *Turquand* (1856) (the *Rule in Turquand's Case*). The *Rule* states that a person dealing with a company is taken to know the contents of its memorandum and articles and he must ensure that any proposed transaction is consistent with them. However, he may *assume* that the company has properly completed any internal formalities which may be required before the transaction can be entered into by the company. The facts of the case were that the plaintiff bank lent money to a company of which the defendant was manager. The company had power to borrow provided that the borrowing was authorised by a resolution passed by a general meeting of the company. No such resolution was passed. The company was held to be bound by the loan. It was consistent with the company's powers and the bank was entitled to assume that the required resolution had been passed. Because of s.35, the importance of the *Rule* is greatly reduced but it remains important to banks because they almost certainly can never claim the section's protection. The *Rule* would apply, for example, where the loan was authorised at an inquorate, or otherwise improperly conducted, board meeting.

Security

Why security is taken

Earlier in this chapter we mentioned briefly the nature, purpose and usual types of security taken by a bank. This is a most important subject and we must therefore cover it in depth now.

The *purpose* of taking security for an advance is to acquire some right over and above the basic contractual right to sue the customer if repayment according to the terms of the loan is not made. You would take it if you considered that the customer's mere personal obligation to repay was insufficient to ensure full repayment. This is where the general principles of lending that we have discussed must be applied. However, we can generally say that without the safety net of sound security, lending becomes a very speculative activity and could only be carried on, if at all, by charging interest rates which would be prohibitive to normal commercial and personal requirements.

The most common type of security is for some *specific property* of the customer to be set aside as an asset that you can sell to satisfy yourself out of the proceeds if the repayment is not made. Discussion of this type of security arrangement will take up most of this section but we must not forget the importance of *guarantees*. This security does not involve the bank acquiring rights over a specific asset but, instead, a supporting personal contractual obligation from a third party to repay the advance if the customer does not. In practice, however, the guarantor is often asked to deposit tangible security or to maintain a minimum balance in a deposit account to support the personal undertaking.

Remember, however, that any security taken must only be regarded as a last line of defence; the decision whether or not to lend must always be taken on the merits of the application itself and not on the desirability of the security. This only becomes relevant once the initial proposition is found to be acceptable. Nevertheless, the provision of suitable security can be a major item in negotiations for an advance. Indeed, customers frequently do not fully appreciate its importance, even the basic reason why it is taken and, in particular, the full ramifications of having given it. This last aspect is a central theme of this section.

So far we have talked in general terms about the purpose of taking security but we can be more precise about the *reasons*. First, should the customer become insolvent, the bank avoids the *full consequences of his bankruptcy* (if an individual or a partnership) or *liquidation* (if a limited company). Provided suitable securities have been taken the whole debt can be recovered by their realisation, with any surplus being paid over to augment the assets available to other creditors. If the advance was unsecured, the bank would only be able to prove for the amount owed in competition with the other unsecured creditors receiving, perhaps, just a very small percentage (so many pence in the pound) of the debt after the total assets available for distribution have been divided by the total liabilities.

The second reason concerns not the customer's capacity to repay but his willingness. It is neither good banking practice nor kindness to your customer to allow him to think of the bank as an easy source of money, to be repaid when *he* wants to repay. More importantly, it is fundamentally important that bank advances should be 'turning-over' continually; a bank is essentially a provider of short-term credit. Thus, while it is virtually inconceivable that a UK bank would ever find itself in this position, delay in repayment of a substantial loan could damage its cash-flow position. Taking suitable security avoids this possible problem—it can be sold to effect repayment—and also avoids the expense and general hassle involved in litigation.

Types of security arrangement

Besides classifying and discussing securities by physical type, such as land, life policies, etc., we can classify them according to the nature of the arrangement created and then go on to give some specific definitions. These, as you will see, are to some extent independent of the nature of the actual property taken as security.

Whole ownership
The customer (the debtor) can transfer the whole ownership of the property to the bank (the creditor) under a contract in which the bank agrees to retransfer it to the customer if the debt is repaid on the due date. A legal mortgage of shares and an assignment of a life policy take this form.

Possession
The customer can give the bank mere possession, not ownership, of the property. Clearly this stops the customer disposing of it but it does not directly assist the bank unless it also acquires the right to sell it. Pledges and liens (*see* below) take this form.

Documents of title
Documents of title, such as title deeds to land or share certificates, can be deposited by the customer with the bank. The property represented by them cannot be dealt with without such documents and therefore the deposit provides the customer with a strong inducement to make repayment. In addition, a bank

will normally give itself direct rights against the property, primarily the right to sell the property if repayment is not made.

Rights over property

Without giving any rights of ownership, possession or documents of title, the customer may give the bank certain rights over property. The right to apply to the court for an order for sale if the loan is not repaid is the essence of this type of security. Such a transaction is known as a *charge* (*see* below).

We must cover two other security arrangements. The first, a floating charge, is peculiar to companies and the second, a guarantee, involves a personal obligation and not rights over specific property.

Floating charge

A floating charge is an equitable charge which covers the fluctuating assets of a company, such as its stocks, without attaching to specific assets until crystallisation, i.e. until it becomes *fixed*. Crystallisation occurs (a) whenever the company commits any breach of the charge agreement, such as failure to pay interest or failure to repay the capital sum, and the bank takes steps to crystallise the charge, for example, by appointing a receiver; (b) automatically when the company is wound up or ceases business. Until crystallisation, a floating charge allows the company to freely dispose of the assets covered by the charge, their place being taken by others acquired in the general course of business.

Guarantee

A guarantee is 'A promise to answer for the debt, default or miscarriage of another' if that other person fails to meet his obligation(s): Statute of Frauds 1677, s.4. The rather formal language of this old statute means that the guarantor undertakes to make a payment if someone else, who should make it, does not. At this point it is useful to distinguish a guarantee from an indemnity, which we have mentioned several times before. Under a guarantee, *the guarantor* incurs only *secondary liability*; under an indemnity, the *indemnifier* incurs *primary liability*. For example, if when Mr Smith asks you for a loan, Ms Brown says 'Lend him the money he wants, if he doesn't pay you back, I will', Ms Brown is offering to guarantee the loan and would incur only secondary liability. If, however, Ms Brown says, 'Lend him the money, I will see that you are repaid', she has offered to indemnify the bank and would incur primary liability. It is, of course, a question of construction should a dispute arise as to the nature of the undertaking, although banks' standard form guarantees avoid this problem arising. The distinction between a gurantee and an indemnity is of practical importance in so far as a guarantee must be supported by written evidence to be enforceable in court while an indemnity need not.

As you have already seen, an *ultra vires* clause will be included whenever there is doubt about the enforceability of the guarantee, for instance, when the customer is a minor. Under such a clause, the guarantor undertakes to accept primary liability as principal debtor for any sums which cannot be recovered from the customer by reason of any legal limitation, disability or incapacity. The contract thereby becomes an indemnity as well as a guarantee.

It is also possible for a person to specifically charge an asset, such as a house, to secure another's borrowing. In effect, this *amounts* to a guarantee but it cuts out the actual contract of guarantee.

Definitions

Having explained the different legal arrangements that are possible when security is taken, we can now define the most common security transactions entered into by banks.

Mortgage

A mortgage is *the creation or transfer of a legal or equitable interest in property* as security for the payment of a debt or the discharge of some other obligation. The transfer will include a provision for redemption, i.e. that on repayment or discharge of the obligation it will become void or the interest reconveyed. Possession of the property remains with the *mortgagor* (the borrower/customer), while the *mortgagee* (the lender/bank) obtains some or all of the rights of ownership, or the right to obtain ownership if the borrower defaults in repayment. In other words, if repayment is not made, the bank (or other lender) can take action against the property, directly or indirectly depending on the type of mortgage, to recover what is owed.

The term 'mortgage' is used very loosely. For example, legally a customer *gives* a mortgage to the bank and does not get one from the bank; it is also frequently taken to mean the money lent. Also remember that legal mortgages of *land* are almost invariably created by *legal charge* under the Law of Property Act 1925 and not since 1925 by creating a lease. The legal charge does *not* give the mortgagee an estate in the land mortgaged as a lease would but does confer the same protection, powers and remedies. (*See* further, Chapter 15.)

Land is the form of property most usually mortgaged but choses in action, such as life assurance policies, can be mortgaged by assignment and goods by a conditional bill of sale, both subject to a condition that on repayment the property will be reassigned to the mortgagor. A mortgage of goods is rare.

A mortgage may be either legal or equitable. A *legal mortgage* creates rights against the property itself whereas *an equitable mortgage* creates only personal rights against the mortgagor. A legal mortgagee is therefore in a stronger position than an equitable mortgagee and, in fact, the wider and more effective range of remedies available to the former is today the most important practical distinction between the two types. (Legal and equitable mortgages are discussed later.)

Pledge

A pledge is a *deposit of goods*, or documents of title to them, or *negotiable instruments* with a lender as security for a debt. It differs from a mortgage in that the lender obtains possession of the property while the borrower retains ownership.

Hypothecation

Hypothecation is a legal transaction by which *goods* are made available as security. It differs from a pledge and a mortgage in that neither ownership nor possession of the goods passes to the lender. The security is granted by means of a *letter of hypothecation*, sometimes called a letter of lien.

Since neither ownership nor possession is transferred under hypothecation, it is possible to take security over goods where a pledge would be impossible. For example, where goods are temporarily in a third party's custody, for example, in transit, or where they are bulky and stored in the customer's warehouse. Clearly, since the customer retains both ownership and possession of the goods, there is always the possibility that he may fraudulently deal with them and thereby deprive a bank of its security.

Lien
A lien is a right to *retain property* belonging to another until a debt is paid by that person. It differs from a mortgage, pledge or hypothecation in that it arises by operation of law from certain situations. For example, a garage would be entitled to a lien over its customer's car until a bill for repairs was paid. Mortgages, pledges and hypothecation are all the result of express agreements between borrowers and lenders.

A lien may be either particular or general. A *particular lien* gives the right to retain possession only to secure payment of money owing in respect of the particular property over which the lien is exercised. A *general lien* gives the right to retain possession until the total amount outstanding is repaid.

Normally, a lien only confers the right to retain possession of property but by mercantile custom a *banker's lien* is a general lien which confers the valuable right of sale and recoupment. You can exercise such a lien over any of your customer's documents in your possession other than those deposited with you for safe custody. In practice, this means that the lien can be exercised over bills of exchange, cheques and promissory notes paid in to be collected and credited to the customer's account. Other documents, such as life policies and share certificates, are likely to be held under a specific agreement—either for safe custody or as security—and therefore a lien cannot arise over them.

In Chapter 6 we saw that banks offer *safe custody* facilities to their customers and that such facilities give rise to a contract of bailment. We must emphasise that a bailment agreement is wholly inconsistent with a lien which can therefore never arise over articles held in safe custody.

Charge
A charge is usually regarded as a type of mortgage. However, a mortgage conveys an interest in the property mortgaged subject to a right of redemption whereas a charge merely gives

certain rights over the property charged as security, for example the right to ask the court for an order for sale of the property. (NB A *legal charge* under the Law of Property Act 1925 does create an interest in land and to avoid confusion is better considered in practice as a mortgage and not as a charge.)

Basic principles of taking security

Your customer has applied to you for a loan and the proposition is acceptable for lending purposes. The question of security now arises; what qualities will you be looking for in the security offered?

(a) Its *value*: clearly this must be at least equal to the amount to be advanced but it is prudent to ensure that there is a sufficient margin. This consideration is particularly relevant where the property offered can fluctuate in value as, for example, is the case with shares. In addition, it must be possible to fairly accurately determine the value. A life policy, for example, is easily valued, by referring to the company which issued the policy or, in some cases, to a table in a schedule to the policy itself. However, the value for security purposes of shares in a private company can only be determined by an analysis of the company's annual financial statements.

(b) Checking the *customer's title to* and *charging* the property as security: the easier this is the better it is from your point of view. While administrative and legal costs are usually passed on to the customer, possible problems in verifying title and charging the security clearly detract from its desirability as security. An equitable mortgage over land or other property can be obtained by nothing more than the deposit of documents of title but a legal mortgage of land, particularly if it is unregistered land, involves an often relatively lengthy investigation of the customer's title.

(c) Closely connected with the previous consideration is the ease with which your interest in the security can be *protected* and the effectiveness of that protection. A mortgagee's interest in land, for example, can be protected absolutely but the process of protection is somewhat involved and time-consuming. On the other hand, a mortgage over shares can be both easily and effectively protected by registering the bank or its nominee company—banks have set up their own companies specifically to hold customer securities—as holder of the shares in the company's books. Yet again, a legal mortgage of a life policy gives you easy and absolute protection of your interest but does not prevent your customer invalidating the policy, for example, by killing himself hang-gliding or, under a few policies, committing suicide.

(d) Of the essence from a commercial point of view is the ease with which the security can be *sold* or otherwise *realised*. Banks, as we have stressed, are predominantly in the short-term loan business and it is commercial nonsense to lend over a two-year term and then have to rely on a security which takes three years to realise. While it is not possible to foresee all market trends we can say generally that land is less easily realisable than most other forms of security. Nevertheless, land has always been in the long term, and almost certainly will continue to be, the soundest security available. Again, property covered by a legal mortgage is always more easily realisable than that covered by an equitable mortgage. The latter only gives personal rights against the customer and if the customer does not agree to the sale a court order will be required.

Another consideration to bear in mind, although it does not really warrant being termed a 'principle', is that it is often better to take security for a loan to Ms X from Mr Y or Ms Z and not from Ms X herself. Technically, this is known as taking a *third party* security. The advantage of doing this is that it gives you two bites at the cherry, so to speak. If your customer will not pay, you are able to sue her for the debt, possibly threatening bankruptcy or liquidation proceedings against her; if she cannot pay, that is, she becomes insolvent, you are able to prove in her bankruptcy (or liquidation) for the debt and receive whatever dividend is ultimately paid. What is important is that this action will in no way affect your rights against the security taken from the third party. You are therefore able to recoup the moneys from two sources, independently or in combination. There is one practical problem however, the third party probably never believes for one minute that his security will be relied upon and may react somewhat unfavourably when it is!

You will see, as we discuss types of property as security below, that each has its advantages and disadvantages and, in practice, the principles and considerations we have outlined above must be applied realistically and individually for each loan or overdraft application. You may not be able to take what you would consider to be the ideal security in the circumstances but you are in business and, providing the proposition is acceptable, you need to lend to your customers in order to make your profits. Remember too, that you should only have to rely on security if the original decision to lend was a bad one or if unforeseen circumstances arise. Furthermore, at least the direct costs involved in taking the security can be passed on to the customer. Bear in mind these general principles as we deal specifically with types of property used as security.

Types of security

In Chapter 15 we discuss the procedures by which various types of security are actually effected. In this section we are going to look at the attributes of the main types of security for bank advances in terms of their advantages and disadvantages for this purpose.

Land

Advantages

(a) A mortgage of land has one overriding advantage: *land never completely loses its value*. Indeed, a first legal mortgage of freehold land is the surest security that a bank can take.

(b) Land has historically always *appreciated in value*.

Disadvantages

(a) Land is sometimes *difficult to value* for security purposes; for example, where the value depends heavily on planning consent, the possibility of this lapsing must be considered.

(b) Greater *difficulty and formality* attach to a mortgage of land than to other forms of security.

(c) Land is *not an easily realisable security*. In addition, realisation of the security could possibly lead to bad publicity, although a bank would never sell mortgaged property, particularly a dwelling house, unless all other practical possibilities for repayment had been explored without success.

(d) A *second mortgagee* is subject to the rights of the first mortgagee.

(e) An equitable mortgagee must seek the *court's sanction* in any action for realisation of the security.

Stocks and shares

Advantages

(a) The customer's *title* to the securities can easily be established.

(b) The *current value* of quoted stocks and shares can be ascertained easily and fairly precisely.

(c) The security can be taken with *little difficulty*, formality or expense.

(d) A legal mortgage can *easily and effectively be protected* by registering the mortgagee as holder of the shares in the books of the company.

(e) Long-term *stability in value*, despite periodical setbacks; a mixed portfolio of shares as security enhances this advantage.

(f) The security can *easily be realised* by selling on a stock exchange if a legal mortgage is held or a blank transfer with an equitable mortgage.

(g) *Release* of the security is easy.

(h) *Bearer securities* have additional advantages. In particular: (i) as negotiable instruments, title to them passes by mere delivery and a pledgee acquires a perfect title despite any defect in or even non-existence of the pledgor's title; (ii) the pledge requires no formalities; (iii) the securities can be sold without reference to the pledgor or to the court.

Disadvantages

Certain disadvantages attach to certain types of stocks and shares and there is one general disadvantage:

(a) Fluctuations in *market value*; at best a forced sale in a depressed market would be to your customer's disadvantage and at worst would realise insufficient funds to repay the advance.

(b) Shares are still sometimes issued *partly paid* and these are occasionally encountered as security. When a call is made for the balance due on the shares, they are forfeited if the call is not paid. If held as security the bank may have to pay the call for its customer in order to retain its security. If a legal mortgage was taken over them, the bank, as their registered holder, is directly liable to pay. In addition, such shares are less marketable than fully paid-up shares.

(c) *Unquoted shares*; these are normally associated with private companies but unquoted shares in public companies may sometimes be offered as security. They are both difficult to value and to realise. Under the terms of the company's articles, the shares may first have to be offered to existing company members who can to some extent, therefore, fix the selling price. Thus, the true value of the shares may not be realised and a mortgage of such shares is often considered as little more than evidence of a customer's means.

(d) Shares in *private companies*; in addition to being difficult to value because they are unquoted, the company's articles of association will often affect their value as security. The articles may prevent their use as security altogether, prevent another registered company, that is, the bank's nominee company holding them—only an equitable mortgage is possible in such a case—and/or restrict their transfer thereby affecting their realisability.

Life policies

Advantages

(a) The *value* of a life policy can be easily determined, most do not fluctuate with market forces and most steadily increase in value.

(b) *Title* to the policy can be easily checked.

(c) *Realisation* of the security by a legal mortgagee is quick and simple.

Disadvantages

(a) The mortgagor's *possible inability to pay the premiums*. If this happens the bank is put in the position of having to pay them in order to keep the policy alive if the advance has been allowed to exceed the current surrender value of the policy.

(b) Some life policies are linked to unit trust investments and these can and do *fluctuate in value* in line with the general level of stock market investment. Thus, their surrender values can be reduced if stock market values are particularly depressed.

(c) Possible *invalidation of the policy*, and hence the loss of the security through (i) the customer's breach of the *uberrima fides* obligation, or of the conditions in the policy. An insurance contract is one of *uberrimae fidei* (of the utmost good faith) and both the proposer and the insurer are under a duty to disclose all material facts, for example, facts which would influence the judgment of a prudent insurer in fixing the premium or in deciding whether or not to accept the proposal. Failure by one party to do so makes the contract voidable at the option of the other. This rule applies however innocent the failure to disclose may be. In practice, it is the proposer who is most affected by the rule since he alone is in a position to know all the facts which might influence his insurer. An example of the rule working in the other direction would be where the insurer fails to disclose knowledge of previous dubious conduct by the broker with whom the proposer has dealt.

A life policy is likely to include an exclusion of cover if the policy holder indulges in inherently dangerous activities (hence our reference to hang-gliding earlier on), and death during such an activity renders the policy valueless to both the policy holder and the bank.

Guarantees

Advantages

(a) A guarantee is very *simple to take*: no registration is involved and no complications concerning proof of title arise.

(b) A guarantee can *easily and immediately be enforced* by court action.

(c) Since several parties can guarantee a loan, it is a useful security where a customer is unable to provide security but offers a viable business loan proposition.

Disadvantages

(a) Unless supported by a cash deposit or other security, a guarantee is always of an *uncertain value* as a security; a guarantor's financial position can change very quickly. You should only accept an unsupported guarantee after careful investigation into the proposed guarantor's financial standing.

(b) Court action may be necessary to *realise* the security, and a technicality may possibly defeat the bank's claim. For example, special rules apply to guarantees taken from partnerships and companies, although a defeat of the bank's claim would almost certainly be the result of carelessness when taking the security.

(c) Many bankers hold the view that a guarantee is the easiest security to take but the hardest to enforce in so far as liability to pay on a guarantee will often be contested.

Debentures

Debentures are documents issued by a company acknowledging a loan and any charge securing it. Only companies can issue debentures and by them they raise much of their finance.

Debentures are of four main types.

(a) *Secured and unsecured*: the former grants a mortgage or charge over the property of the company; the latter is given without security, it merely acknowledges the debt.

(b) *Single or series*: a single debenture is issued to cover a single debt, for example to a bank to secure an overdraft. More usually debentures are issued in series to several or many holders as a way of raising money. These rank *pari passu* (equally) among themselves.

(c) *Registered or bearer*: most debentures are registered in the names of the various holders in the same way as shares; their transfer is similarly registered. Bearer debentures are negotiable instruments transferable by delivery. They are not registered but Treasury consent is required for their issue.

(d) *Perpetual or redeemable*: the former are only repaid when the company is wound up, the latter are repayable on or before a specified date. Debentures are peculiar to companies, as is the *floating charge* normally contained in a debenture. It is for that reason we mention them here.

Fixed charges

A fixed charge in a debenture, that is, a legal or equitable mortgage of specific property, usually the company's premises, has the same general advantages and disadvantages as any charge over that particular type of property. In comparison with a floating charge it is to the *bank's advantage* in that specific property is always available as security for the advance, but to its disadvantage in that the property charged may depreciate in value. To a company, the disadvantage of a fixed charge is that it cannot dispose of the property without the bank's consent.

Floating charges

A floating charge is an equitable charge over the fluctuating assets of the company, for example its stock, which does not attach to any specific assets until it becomes fixed (crystallises). Until this happens, the company can freely dispose of its assets; clearly an advantage to the company. A bank obtains the benefit of a range of assets as security under such a charge but the *disadvantages* of a floating charge are such that you should not take one by itself unless no other security can be offered. It is beyond the scope of this book to look in any detail at the defects of a floating charge because they involve fairly difficult points of law. However, we will outline the main disadvantages.

(a) There is a danger that the *assets of the company may be run down.* Since a company can freely dispose of the assets charged, your position depends to a certain extent upon the conduct of the company. It could, for example, realise the assets to repay other creditors. You should therefore ensure that the assets charged are maintained at a satisfactory level, although this is still no protection against a sudden depletion of the assets or a sudden and unforeseen fall in their value.

(b) A *subsequent fixed charge on the assets may take priority* over existing floating charges.

(c) The rights of a holder of a floating charge are subject to a variety of other *postponements*, principally to the rights of preferential creditors after crystallisation of the charge and to the rights of unpaid suppliers protected by a 'Romalpa clause' in their contract of sale (*see* below). Both of these require a little explanation. In a bankruptcy or liquidation there are certain categories of creditors. As the name suggests, *preferential creditors* are accorded a certain degree of preference. While they rank after creditors secured by a fixed charge, they rank before creditors secured by a floating charge and unsecured creditors. Examples of preferential claims include the Inland Revenue for PAYE income tax due for any one financial year and employees' wages and salaries due for the four months prior to the bankruptcy or liquidation subject to a maximum of £800 for each claimant.

The inclusion of '*Romalpa clauses*' in contracts for the sale of goods is now common. In essence they mean that the supplier retains the title to the goods supplied until payment for them is received. If the buyer subsequently becomes bankrupt or goes into liquidation, the supplier ranks before both preferential creditors and those secured by floating charges. This is fair enough, but it puts a bank offered a floating charge over a company's assets or security in a difficult position. The security may prove illusory but unless the bank is actually told about the arrangement it has no way of knowing about it. A Romalpa clause can, of course, also seriously affect the apparent strength of the company's balance sheet—a factor to be taken into account when the lending decision is being made. (The clause takes its name from the decision in *Aluminium Industrie Vassen BV* v. *Romalpa Aluminium Ltd.* (1976); more generally it is referred to as a retention of title clause.)

Finally, a floating charge will be *invalidated* by s.245 of the Insolvency Act 1986 if the company goes into liquidation within two years (if in favour of a person closely connected with the company) or twelve months (if in favour of any other person) of having created the charge *except* for money paid in consideration for the charge at the time it is taken or subsequently, *unless*, in the latter case only, it is proved that the company was solvent immediately after the charge was created. This is not quite so complicated as it might seem the first time you read it. It has, in fact a simple purpose. It prevents insolvent companies creating floating charges to secure past debts to the prejudice of their other unsecured creditors. This again illustrates the importance of a careful analysis of the company's financial position before the decision to make the advance is made.

Summary

1. The principles of lending are concerned with eliciting adequate information to reach a balanced judgment on a proposed loan.
2 The most important questions to be asked are:
    (a) *purpose*: what is the loan for? (b) *amount*: how much is required? (c) *repayment*: what are the proposals for repayment? (d) *term*: how long will the loan be outstanding? (e) *security*: what is available in case things go wrong?
3 The banker must be satisfied with the customer's integrity

and standing and will be guided by his track record with the bank.

4   The Consumer Credit Act 1974 affects banks and businesses involved in the consumer credit industry. It controls the industry by licensing all providers of consumer credit and by regulations covering advertising, canvassing, the form and content of agreements, the obligations of the lender and the disclosure of the true cost of all charges incurred by the borrower.

5   Overdraft facilities are most appropriate to finance short-term cash-flow problems.

6   Loan facilities are appropriate to financing capital purchases or specific projects.

7   Budget accounts enable personal customers to spread the burden of their annual outgoings evenly throughout the year.

8   Banks offer house purchase loans in competition with the building societies.

9   When lending money, legal rules demand particular care in relation to minors, personal representatives, trustees, home-buyers, partnerships and limited companies.

10 Security is taken to acquire a right over readily sellable assets in case the borrower does not/cannot make repayment according to the terms of the loan.

11 Security arrangements take one of the following basic forms: (a) a transfer of ownership; (b) a transfer of possession; (c) a deposit of documents of title; (d) granting rights over certain property.

In addition, a company can create a floating charge, and a guarantee, a personal obligation, can secure a loan to another person.

12 Definitions:

(a) A mortgage is a creation or transfer of an interest in property as security for a repayment of a loan.

(b) A pledge is a deposit of property, or documents of title to it, with a lender as security for a debt.

(c) A lien is a right to retain property in lieu of repayment.

(d) A charge gives rights over property but not an interest in it.

13 When taking security, you must consider:

(a) its value;

(b) the ease of checking the customer's title and charging the property;

(c) the ease and effectiveness of protection;

(d) the ease with which the security can be realised.

14 Different types of security have different advantages and disadvantages.

Self-assessment questions

1 List the principles of lending.

2 Define: (a) personal loans; (b) overdrafts; (c) commitment fees; (d) security; (e) a mortgage; (f) a floating charge; (g) capital realisation.

3 List the main prohibitions on canvassing in the Consumer Credit Act 1974.

4 What remedies has a bank when it has made a loan to a company which is (a) *ultra vires* the directors; and (b) *ultra vires* the company itself?

5 What is the essential distinction between a legal and an equitable mortgage?

6 True or false?

(a) Banks never lend for longer than five years.

(b) The availability of security is the principal consideration in deciding whether to grant a loan.

(c) Personal loans differ from ordinary loans in the way interest is calculated.

(d) Interest rates on overdrafts are individually negotiated with each borrower.

(e) Budget accounts restrict the customer's choice of how to pay the bills.

7 True or false?

(a) The Consumer Credit Act 1974 can never apply to a credit facility exceeding £15 000.

(b) A surety incurs primary liability under a guarantee.

(c) A lien involves a transfer of ownership in the property involved.

(d) When taking a mortgage from a customer, the bank is the mortgagor.

8 Explain why the bank must be particularly careful to ensure

that a prospective borrower has accurately calculated his finance requirements.

9 What are the major advantages and disadvantages of taking land as security?

10 Explain why bearer securities are ideal as security for an advance.

Assignments

1 In your manager's absence, you have interviewed Jill Barber about the provision of overdraft facilities to help her pay for repairs to her car which was damaged recently on a rainy night when it went into a skid and hit a wall. No other vehicle was involved and no property damage occurred.

Miss Barber is 22 and earns £6000 p.a. gross as a trainee buyer for a national chain of fashionwear shops. She has banked with you for two years since moving into the area to take up her present job and, although she has occasionally taken some small unauthorised overdrafts, her account has caused you no problems. She lives in a flat with two friends of a similar age and she has no relatives in the area.

She needs £400 to complete the repairs and, as she has no savings, she would need to borrow the whole amount. The car was not comprehensively insured. She thinks that she could repay at £20 per month. From an examination of her account, it would seem that at the moment she spends all of her income but she explained that she can make economies and that the promised repayments are well within her ability to pay. She has no security to offer.

Write a report for your manager stating whether you would grant or refuse the loan and setting out the reasons for your decision.

2   Memorandum to: Student
     From: Manager
     Subject: Applications for loans

I have been asked to provide a speaker to address a forthcoming meeting of the Round Table on the subject of 'How to present your case for a loan to your bank manager'. I am very keen to accept this assignment as I am convinced that I could reduce the time I spend with most borrowers by 50% if they knew the sort of information I would need and had prepared some answers.

I would therefore like you to take this one on. Please prepare a draft of your address and let me see it next Monday. I suggest that you concentrate on the *general headings* under which we would look for information, explaining why each one is important.

14 Financial statements

Chapter objectives

After studying this chapter you should be able to:
- analyse and interpret the final accounts and other financial statements of a business;
- evaluate trends shown in financial statements and state their significance to a lending banker;
- calculate and apply elementary accounting ratios;
- extract data relating to the health of a business as a 'going concern';
- identify the significance of data relating to the value of a business as a 'gone concern'.

Introduction to financial statements

All businesses must produce financial statements at periodic intervals, usually once a year, showing how the business has progressed since the last statement was issued. But what are these statements? In essence they consist of just two items: a *balance sheet* and a set of *profit and loss accounts*. The balance sheet sets out the assets and the liabilities of the concern at a given date. The profit and loss accounts summarise the various items of income and expenditure since the last balance sheet was produced and show whether a profit or a loss was made over the period.

The financial statements of a business, often referred to as its 'accounts', represent the principal source of evidence on the general health of the undertaking and its capacity to repay any loans granted to it. Understanding the significance of the information which they contain is a very important skill for the lending banker. Almost certainly you will have covered or be covering financial statements in your other studies but we are going to consider them from a banking perspective. We are assuming that you have a working knowledge of basic accounting techniques and terminology.

Presentation of balance sheets

Horizontal balance sheets

The traditional method of presentation of a balance sheet is the horizontal format in which the information is set out on opposite sides of the page. Liabilities are shown on the left-hand side and assets are shown on the right, as in the simple example given in Table 14.1 below. The two sides must of course balance out to the same total.

You will see that both the assets and the liabilities have been grouped into categories. The assets are divided into two groups: fixed assets and current assets. The *fixed assets* comprise those items which the business will keep in its ownership for a significant length of time, usually for a period of years. They consist of the things which the business must have in order to operate in its chosen field of activity. These might include premises, machinery, vehicles, and so on. The *current assets* consist of the short-term assets of the business which are 'turned over' at frequent intervals. A shop's stock for instance is constantly 'turning over' as goods are sold and replaced by fresh stock bought from the suppliers.

The difference then between fixed assets and current assets is their *liquidity*: the length of time that they are held by the business. The same is true of the liabilities, which are grouped here into three categories: capital, long-term liabilities, and current liabilities. *Capital* is the longest term of the liabilities. It represents the funds which the proprietors have tied up in the

Table 14.1 A simple 'horizontal' balance sheet

Liabilities	£	*Assets*		£
Capital		Fixed assets		
Share capital	10 000	Premises		12 000
Long-term liabilities		Current assets		
Fixed-term loan	5 000	Debtors	1 500	
		Stock	2 000	
Current liabilities		Cash	500	
Creditors	1 000			4 000
	16 000			16 000

business. Items such as trade creditors and bank overdrafts represent money owed by the business for a much shorter period and they therefore form part of the *current liabilities* which make up the more liquid category.

The balance sheet we have shown has been laid out so that both sides show the most liquid categories last. This presentation is sometimes reversed so that the current assets and the current liabilities appear first, at the top of the relative columns.

Linear balance sheets

The alternative linear, or vertical, presentation of balance sheets is now the more popular. This format assists with the interpretation of the information by showing more clearly the *uses* to which a business puts the funds at its disposal and the *sources* from which it derives its finance.

Using the same figures which we used in the traditional double-sided balance sheet, we can recast them into a vertical presentation as shown in Table 14.2 below.

Table 14.2 A simple 'linear' balance sheet

		£
Capital employed		
Capital		
Share capital		10 000
Long-term liabilities		5 000
Fixed-term loan		15 000
Uses of capital		
Fixed assets		
Premises		12 000
Current assets		
Debtors	1 500	
Stock	2 000	
Cash	500	
	4 000	
Less: current liabilities		
Creditors	1 000	
Net current assets		3 000
		15 000

This is a typical example, although other variations are possible. You will see that using this format, the two sides still come to the same total as each other but that the figure which they both add up to is different from that shown on the 'horizontal' balance sheet. This is because the current liabilities have been deducted from the assets ('uses of capital') instead of being added on to the liabilities ('capital employed').

Table 14.3 shows the balance sheets of a typical manufacturing company for the year 19–3. The 'Acme Manufacturing Company Limited' is a private limited company which produces a range of metal fabrications for sale to the engineering industry. Notice that in this case the medium and long-term liabilities have been deducted from the assets in a similar fashion to the current liabilities.

Balance sheets: assets

We are now going to look at the different components of a balance sheet; refer to Table 14.3 as you read through the text below. The assets section shows how a business utilises the funds at its disposal. As we have seen, details are given under two principal headings: fixed assets and current assets.

Fixed assets
Fixed assets represent the *long-term investment* of the business in the means of carrying on its chosen trade.

Tangible fixed assets. The bulk of the fixed assets of the Acme Manufacturing Company, like those of most companies, are tangible fixed assets. These include land, machinery, fixtures and fittings, and vehicles. When first purchased, these items will appear in the balance sheet at their cost price. Over the years, however, this value will not be maintained: machinery, vehicles and similar items all wear out and depreciate in value until eventually they have no value at all. Provision has to be made for writing down their balance sheet values by deducting an appropriate sum for depreciation each year.

On the other hand, land and buildings, except for land held on short leases, may appreciate in value, reflecting the normal upward trend of property values in general. The same can be true of other assets if they are not subject to wear and tear.

Table 14.3 Balance sheet of the Acme Manufacturing Company Ltd.

The Acme Manufacturing Company Limited
69 Orrell Street, Wetherfield, Greater Manchester

Balance Sheet As at: 31 December 19–3

Fixed assets		£
Freehold land		34 000
Plant, machinery, fixtures, and		
fittings (less depreciation)		72 200
Vehicles (less depreciation)		20 800
Goodwill		5 000
		132 000
Current assets		
Cash	7 700	
Debtors	124 600	
Stock of raw materials	27 300	
Stock of finished goods	41 800	
Work in progress	30 800	
	232 200	
Current liabilities		
Creditors	77 500	
Hire purchase	23 300	
Current taxation	6 000	
Current dividends	4 000	
Bank borrowing	25 300	
	136 100	
Net current assets		96 100
Medium and long-term liabilities		
Loans over five years		60 200
		£167 900
Financed by		
Capital		15 000
Profit and loss account		152 900
		£167 900

While such assets may be periodically revalued and brought up to show their true values in the balance sheet, it is not normal practice to do so every year. A significant 'hidden reserve' of value can be created if an appreciating asset is not revalued for a number of years.

The lending banker will usually wish to compare the 'book values' of the fixed assets with their estimated 'market values'. If proper depreciation and revaluation calculations have been made there should not be too wide a difference between the two valuations.

Intangible assets. These may also be shown as part of the fixed assets, although sometimes they are shown on the balance sheet as a separate category. From a practical viewpoint these are assets which have a 'book value' but which would be difficult or impossible to realise on a liquidation. They include such items as fictitious assets, goodwill, and patents and trademarks. The first of these—*fictitious assets*—include formation expenses, such as discounts on the issue of shares in a new limited company, and negative balances on the profit and loss account representing accumulated losses resulting from unprofitable trading. They represent money which has been spent and which therefore has to be shown somewhere on the balance sheet. It is obvious that these items could not be sold if the business were to be liquidated; they would have to be written off. They have no value.

In respect of a business which has been purchased as a going concern, there will often be an item for *goodwill* in the balance sheet. This represents the sum which has been paid for the trade and custom of the business over and above the value of its assets. Arithmetically, therefore, it is simply the difference between the total price paid for a business and the 'book value' of the assets at the time of purchase. The more profitable a business is, the higher the value the vendor will place on the goodwill. It is considered good practice for successful concerns to 'write off' the goodwill over a period of years by transfers out of retained profits. However, this is often not done, and the same amount for goodwill appears on the balance sheets of successive years, its value of course being progressively reduced by inflation. You must remember that the goodwill figure represents what was paid for the business when it was bought. It does not necessarily bear any relation to what could be obtained if the business were to be sold now and a bank therefore often disregards the book value given.

Patents and trade marks are also treated as intangible assets when they appear in the balance sheet. Clearly the sole right to use a well-known trademark or to produce goods to a patented design is an asset to a business. The cost of acquiring such rights can be shown as such in the balance sheet. However, these items continue to have real value only while the business is trading profitably. How much could we expect to realise by selling either the right to use a patented process which cannot be operated at a profit or the right to use a trade mark which has been associated with unsaleable goods?

Because of the question marks that there must always be about the sale value of intangible assets, the lending bank usually prefers to exclude them from its calculations when looking at the valuation of a business. If these items are therefore deducted from the assets side of the balance sheet, a similar deduction has to be made from the other side. As we shall see, this is done by reducing the amount shown for the capital value of the business to the proprietors.

Current assets

The current assets are very important to the bank as, when looked at together with the current liabilities, they indicate the *level of liquidity* which the business has in its day-to-day trading. Put at its simplest, the principle is that if current assets exceed current liabilities, the business is liquid and should be able to meet its debts as they fall due. If current liabilities exceed current assets, it is illiquid and may have difficulty finding readily realisable funds to pay its debts promptly.

Liquidity problems have caused the failure of many otherwise apparently successful businesses. The importance of maintaining an adequate level of liquidity is often underestimated and too much finance is frequently invested in fixed assets at the expense of the current assets. By way of illustration, consider that if £100 000 of a company's funds are spent buying a new machine, none of that money will be available to pay a £500 fuel bill. If no other liquid funds are available, then the supplier of the fuel may seek to put the company into liquidation to get his money. The current assets include the following:

Cash. This figure includes both cash and credit bank balances. If the balance sheet shows a very large sum under this heading, the bank may wish to enquire whether it has been built up for a specific purpose. Generally a well-managed business will keep its cash holdings at the minimum level consistent with the need for liquidity, as idle funds earn no profits.

Investments. These may appear at cost price or at current market value. It is important for you to know which method of valuation has been used if it is decided to calculate the 'break-up' value of the business if it were to be liquidated.

Debtors. This figure represents money owed to the business by customers who have purchased goods or services on credit. The make-up of this item should be examined to ensure that it is spread over a number of different purchasers. A business is very vulnerable if it is owed large sums of money by one or two major customers: if the customers cannot pay, the business may fail. The bank will wish to check that the system for collecting debts due is satisfactory and that there is adequate control of the granting of credit. This is important in keeping the incidence of bad debts to a low level.

Stock and work in progress. From your point of view, it is preferable if these figures are shown separately as you may wish to give them close consideration. The method of valuation should be known as this has a significant bearing on the reliability of the figures. There is always the danger that a greater or lesser proportion of the stock shown is unsaleable and this must be checked.

Balance sheets: liabilities

As with the assets, the liabilities can be conveniently grouped together under various headings. There are three principal categories: capital, medium and long-term liabilities and current liabilities.

Capital and reserves
This section of the balance sheet shows the 'book value' of the business to its proprietors. If it were liquidated and all the

assets disposed of at their balance sheet values, this section shows how much would remain to be paid over to the proprietors after all liabilities to outside parties had been satisfied. It consists of a number of items as follows:

Capital. In the case of a sole proprietor or a partnership, this will be the amount of cash staked in the business by the proprietors. The figure is adjusted each year to allow for profits left in the business or for losses incurred, after taking account of the proprietor's drawings. In the case of a limited company this heading will reflect the nominal value of the issued share capital, that is the aggregate face value of the total number of shares actually issued by the company. This must not be confused with the 'authorised capital' which is the maximum number of shares which the company's constitution would permit it to issue; they may not all have been issued. Neither does the nominal value of the 'issued share capital' as shown on the balance sheet have any direct comparability with the market value of the shares. The market value is important to the shareholders when they wish to dispose of their holdings but not to the company.

Profit and loss account. Unlike sole proprietorships and partnerships, a limited company does not simply adjust the amount shown on its balance sheet for capital in order to reflect undistributed profits. Instead, the final balance of its accumulated profit and loss account, if in credit, is shown as a separate item after the summary of share capital. The value of the retained profits still belongs to the shareholders and would accrue to them in the event of a liquidation at balance sheet values.

Reserves. These may consist of capital reserves or revenue reserves, although businesses are no longer required to specify the two categories separately. Capital reserves arise when there is some adjustment of capital assets such as the revaluation of business premises. To keep the balance sheet in balance, the amount of the revaluation must appear on both sides. Revenue reserves are created by transfers from the profit and loss account when retained profits are set aside to finance future developments or expansion. You must not think that reserves represent free funds available to the business for spending or distribution at will. The reserves are 'balanced' on the assets 'side' of the balance sheet and it is there that any surplus cash will be shown.

Reserves can also be created to cover contingent or specific liabilities such as the need to replace machinery when it reaches the end of its useful life, or an agreed commitment to pay the shareholders a dividend out of the previous year's profits. These types of reserve are not capital items since they do not represent proprietors' funds retained in the business. As a result, they are shown elsewhere on the balance sheet. 'Asset reserves' are normally shown as a reduction to the value of the appropriate asset. 'Liability provisions' are usually shown as a current liability, or sometimes as a medium-term liability if the payment does not fall due for some considerable time.

Medium and long-term liabilities

The liabilities which appear in this section are those of a long-term nature, such as mortgages, loan stocks and debentures. They are often referred to as 'loan capital'. You will require information as to the terms of repayment of any such item appearing on the balance sheet of a potential borrower, together with details of any assets charged to secure the liability. A secured creditor has the right to remove from a liquidation the assets charged to him. This is of course advantageous to him as it increases the probability of his obtaining repayment in full. It is disadvantageous to the ordinary creditors as losses resulting from a shortfall between the liabilities of the business and the remaining assets will bear more heavily on them.

In the vertical format balance sheet, the medium and long-term liabilities may be shown either as an addition to the 'liabilities' (the sources of capital employed), or as a reduction to the 'assets' (the uses of capital). Looking at Table 14.3, you will see that the latter treatment has been adopted for the Acme Manufacturing Company.

Current liabilities

The current liabilities are those liabilities which are due or which may fall due within a short time. They show the extent to which the business is committed within the near future. As we have said, the relationship of the current assets to the current liabilities determines the liquidity of the business.

Creditors. This item represents funds due for supplies purchased on credit terms. You will wish to know the main items which go to make up the figure shown and whether the total is spread over many creditors or whether it is largely owed to a small number of suppliers.

The creditors' figure may be compared with the amount shown for debtors. As a general rule, a business should not owe more to its creditors than is owed to it by its debtors. There are, however, exceptions to this and much depends on the nature of the business. A supermarket, for instance, makes most of its sales on a cash basis and therefore has no large sums due to it from debtors; conversely, its supplies will almost certainly be obtained on credit terms.

Hire purchase. Any hire purchase commitments are treated as current liabilities although the full amount is unlikely to be due in one amount. This can sometimes distort the apparent liquidity position in businesses which are heavily dependent on hire purchase finance, such as haulage contractors who commonly finance the purchase of vehicles in this way. In a liquidation, the impact of hire purchase debt can be important as the unsatisfied hire purchase creditors will normally have the right to remove from the liquidation the assets which they have financed, thereby reducing the funds available to the ordinary unsecured creditors.

Loans. In this section details will be given of loans obtained from outside sources including, of course, bank loans and overdrafts. Loans from the proprietors of the business will also be included. A sole trader would not normally make a loan to his own business; any additional funds put in would become part of his capital. It is not uncommon, however, to see loans by a partner or by a director to their respective businesses. Such loans often represent undrawn remuneration which is simply left in the business.

In the case of limited companies, you would often require the directors to sign an agreement promising not to withdraw their loan money from the company until any bank advances have been repaid in full. Where you do this, the bank may be prepared to look on the directors' loans as forming part of the capital rather than as part of the current liabilities.

Taxation and dividends. If provisions have been made for taxation due on the previous year's profits or for a dividend to be paid to the shareholders of a limited company, this is where the amount will be shown. When payment actually falls due, the required cash will, of course, have to be found out of the current assets.

Final accounts

The other main component of the annual financial statement consists of the various 'final accounts'. In essence these are a *summary of the income and outgoings* of the business since the last financial statement showing whether a profit has been made and, if so, what has been done with it.

The manufacturing account
For a manufacturing concern, the first stage is compiling the manufacturing account. This details all the expenditure specifically associated with the cost of production and this includes the cost of the raw materials used, the wages of the production workers, power for heating and lighting the factory and so on. The final total of the account therefore represents the total cost to the business of goods manufactured in the year.

Table 14.4 shows the manufacturing account for the Acme Manufacturing Company for the year ending 31 December 19–3. Study this now. You will see that in order to show accurately the cost of materials used, the stock of raw materials and the work in progress at the start of the year are added in to the calculation, the raw materials and work in progress at the end of the year being deducted.

The trading account
The trading account shows the *gross trading profit* earned by the business. Gross profit is basically no more than the difference between the total income from sales to customers and the cost of buying the items sold. For a manufacturing business the cost of goods sold is derived from the manufacturing account. For a

Table 14.4 Manufacturing Account of the Acme Manufacturing Company Ltd. 31/12/19–3

	£	£
Purchases	288 600	
Stock of raw materials 1 Jan	24 900	
Work in progress 1 Jan	29 200	
	342 700	
Less:		
Stock of raw materials 31 Dec	27 300	
Work in progress 31 Dec	30 800	
		284 600
Factory wages	106 000	
Depreciation of machines	6 700	
Heating and lighting	5 900	
Factory rates	10 500	
Sundry factory expenses	6 100	
		135 200
Cost of manufactured goods		419 800

trading business, it is simply the total cost of goods bought from suppliers during the year.

Table 14.5 shows the trading account for 19–3 for the Acme Manufacturing Company. Study this now and you will see that to show more accurately the cost of goods sold, the stock of

Table 14.5 Trading Account of the Acme Manufacturing Company Ltd. 31/12/19–3

	£	£
Sales		569 900
Deduct cost of goods sold:		
Stock of finished goods 1 Jan	38 100	
Cost of manufactured goods	419 800	
	457 900	
Less:		
Stock of finished goods 31 Dec	41 800	
		416 100
Gross trading profit		153 800

finished goods at the start of the year has been added in to the calculation and the closing stock has been deducted.

Profit and loss account

The profit and loss account shows the *new profit* generated by a business after payment of its overhead expenses—such as rates, depreciation, heating and lighting and so on—except for the overheads attributable to the costs of manufacture which have already been dealt with. The profit and loss account also includes any income which has not come from the ordinary course of business, such as profits on the sale of a fixed asset.

For a manufacturing or a trading concern, this account takes as its starting point the gross profit which is carried down from the trading account. For a non-trading business which sells its services rather than goods, such as a firm of solicitors, the profit and loss account is the first of the final accounts and takes as its starting point the income which the business has received during the year by way of clients' fees. Table 14.6 shows the profit and loss account of the Acme Manufacturing Company for 19–3. Study this carefully now.

The net profit (sometimes called the pretax profit) is very important to the lending bank. It represents the *surplus income*

Table 14.6 Profit and loss account of the Acme Manufacturing Company Ltd. 31/12/19–3

	£
Gross trading profit	153 800
Deduct overhead expenses:	
Directors' remuneration	25 000
Staff salaries	42 500
Interest and bank charges	12 800
Depreciation: vehicles	4 800
furniture	2 200
Travel expenses	10 300
Office rates	6 100
Heating and lighting	6 400
Sundry office expenses	16 800
	126 900
Net profit before tax	26 900

generated by the business and is the principal indicator of its ability to repay any loans granted to it.

The profit and loss appropriation account

As its name suggests, this account is produced to show how net profits (or losses) are dealt with. It is often incorporated into the profit and loss account rather than being shown as a separate item. It details the amounts allocated for taxation, dividends and transfers to reserves. The final balance is applied to the capital accounts of the proprietors in the case of a sole trader or a partnership, or to the profit and loss balance brought forward from previous years in the case of a limited company.

Table 14.7 Profit and loss appropriation account of the Acme Manufacturing Company Ltd (year ending 31.12.19–3)

		£
Net profit before tax		26 900
Deduct appropriations:		
Taxation	6 000	
Proposed dividend	4 000	
Retained profits		10 000
		16 900

Using financial statements

Introduction

The figures which go to make up a financial statement are not absolutes and cannot therefore be treated in isolation either from one another or from reality in general. For example, to know that according to his balance sheet a trader owes his suppliers £20 000 tells us nothing useful. What we need to know is whether that amount is reasonable when compared with the volume of business done and whether it is normal for that particular type of trade.

Table 14.8 Financial statements of the Acme Manufacturing Company Limited over three years

The Acme Manufacturing Company Limited
9 Orrell Street, Wetherfield, Greater Manchester

Balance sheet as at:	31 December 19–1		31 December 19–2		31 December 19–3	
Fixed assets	£	£	£	£	£	£
Freehold land		34 000		34 000		34 000
Plant, machinery, fixtures and fittings (*less* depreciation)		82 400		74 800		72 200
Vehicles (*less* depreciation)		19 800		20 300		20 800
Goodwill		5 000		5 000		5 000
		141 200		134 100		132 000
Current assets						
Cash	5 300		6 000		7 700	
Debtors	94 800		104 300		124 600	
Stock of raw materials	20 300		24 900		27 300	
Stock of finished goods	34 900		38 100		41 800	
Work in progress	26 700		29 200		30 800	
	182 000		202 500		232 200	
Current liabilities						
Creditors	64 200		64 900		77 500	
Hire purchase	15 300		20 500		23 300	
Current taxation	6 900		8 100		6 000	
Current dividends	6 000		6 000		4 000	
Bank borrowing	19 700		21 800		25 300	
	112 100		121 300		136 100	
Net current assets		69 900		81 200		96 100
Medium and long-term liabilities						
Loans over five years		68 200		64 300		60 200
		142 900		151 000		167 900
Financed by						
Capital		15 000		15 000		15 000
Profit and loss account		127 900		136 000		152 900
		142 900		151 000		167 900
Manufacturing account						
Purchases	239 200		258 900		288 600	
Stock of raw materials 1 Jan	20 200		20 300		24 900	
Work in progress 1 Jan	25 700		26 700		29 200	
	285 100		305 900		342 700	
Less:						
Stock of raw materials 31 Dec	20 300		24 900		27 300	
Work in progress 31 Dec	26 700		29 200		30 800	
		238 100		251 800		284 600

Factory wages	80 200		99 600		106 000
Depreciation of machines	6 100		6 300		6 700
Heating and lighting	3 700		5 300		5 900
Factory rates	8 800		9 800		10 500
Sundry factory expenses	4 400		4 600		6 100
		103 200		125 600	135 200
Cost of manufactured goods		341 300		377 400	419 800

Trading account

Sales		442 300		499 100	569 900
Deduct cost of goods sold:					
Stock of finished goods 1 Jan	33 700		34 900		38 100
Cost of manufactured goods	341 300		377 400		419 800
	375 000		412 300		457 900
Less:					
Stock of finished goods 31 Dec	34 900		38 100		41 800
		340 100		374 200	416 100
Gross trading profit		102 200		124 900	153 800

Profit and loss account

Gross trading profit		102 200		124 900	153 800
Deduct overhead expenses:					
Directors' remuneration	15 000		20 000		25 000
Staff salaries	29 700		34 600		42 500
Interest and bank charges	9 800		10 800		12 800
Depreciation: vehicles	2 200		3 200		4 800
: furniture	1 300		1 200		2 200
Travel expenses	6 900		8 400		10 300
Office rates	4 200		5 100		6 100
Heating and lighting	4 300		4 500		6 400
Sundry office expenses	10 600		14 900		16 800
		84 000		102 700	126 900
Net profit before tax		18 200		22 200	26 900

Profit and loss appropriation account

Net profit before tax		18 200		22 200	26 900
Deduct appropriations:					
Taxation	6 900		8 100		6 000
Proposed dividend	6 000		6 000		4 000
		12 900		14 100	10 000
Retained profits		5 300		8 100	16 900

The interpretation and use of financial statements constitute an exercise in common sense combined with the use of a few simple techniques and formulae. The extraction of percentages, ratios and so on from a set of accounts will not of itself show whether a business will succeed or fail. Having made your calculations, you must relate them to your overall knowledge of the concern and its proprietors and to the state of trade in general. These factors together should indicate the direction in which the business is moving. Once again, we are going to look from a banker's perspective at information and techniques with which you should already be familiar.

Annual accounts are both *historic and static*. They show the financial state of a business as it was on one particular day at some time in the past. Given the time taken to produce the annual balance sheet, that day is often at least twelve months in the past. Nothing in commerce is static. Businesses come and go; trades flourish and die. In order to assess the health of a particular business, therefore, we need to know more than just its present position. We need to be able to measure that position against the yardstick of *past performance*.

For instance, while it may be encouraging to know that a shop made £10 000 profit last year, it would be infinitely more useful if we also knew that it had made £7000 the year before and only £5000 the year before that. We would conclude that it was a well-managed shop whose proprietors were trading with increasing success each year. If, on the other hand, we found that profits from the shop over the same three-year period had declined from £20 000 to £16 000 and then to the present £10 000, we would draw an altogether different conclusion. In either case, the important indicator is the *trend* shown in the figures, not the figures themselves as absolutes. This is why the lending banker always prefers to compare a series of balance sheets rather than to look at just the most recent one. At least three consecutive years' figures are needed to provide a basis for meaningful comparisons.

We have already in the course of this chapter given details of one year's accounts of the Acme Manufacturing Company Limited. They are shown again on the previous two pages (Table 14.8) in their entirety, together with the figures for the two preceding years for comparison purposes.

Interpretation of accounts

Taking the bare figures provided by the annual accounts of a business, we can isolate a number of important factors for closer examination.

Net worth

Net worth is the measure of whether, on balance sheet values, there is a buffer between the creditors and the loss of their money if the business were to be liquidated. This is the amount which would be left for the proprietors after all the liabilities to third parties had been satisfied if the business were to be wound up assuming, of course, that balance sheet values were realised for the tangible assets. There are two stages in calculating the net worth. First we must establish the *net assets* position of the business by deducting from the total assets figure all the liabilities other than liabilities to the proprietors. In the case of a limited company, this figure will correspond to the 'equity capital'. This is made up of the issued capital, plus reserves, and plus or minus any accumulated profits or losses. You will see that in the case of Acme Manufacturing the layout of the balance sheet is such that the 'net assets' or 'equity capital' figure is readily apparent without further calculation. From the 'net assets' figure we now further deduct the value of any intangible assets, such as goodwill, which may be shown in the balance sheet. On a liquidation, it would be unusual for these items to realise their book values, if they realise anything at all. The figure thereby produced represents the net worth of the business.

Banks often refer to the net worth as the 'proprietors' stake' in the business. As banks are normally unwilling to have more at stake in a business than its proprietors, it is unusual for lending to total more than the net worth. Perhaps more importantly, the net worth is a valuable measure of the safety of creditors' funds because it shows the amount by which realisable assets exceed liabilities to outside parties. If the assets failed to realise their balance sheet values in a liquidation, this is the amount by which they could fall short without the creditors losing money.

In the case of Acme Manufacturing, the only item which must be deducted from net assets is the amount shown for goodwill;

this has remained constant at £5000 throughout. The net worth of the company therefore shows an encouraging steady growth from £137 900 in 19–1, through £146 000 to £169 900 in 19–3.

Working capital

The day-to-day running of a business requires finance: debts, stock and work in progress, along with the other current liabilities must be paid for at some time. By and large it is therefore important that most businesses maintain an adequate level of liquidity so that current debts can be paid as they fall due. We have already noted, however, that some types of business survive long, or even permanent, periods of illiquidity quite well.

The *liquidity* of a business can be measured quite simply by deducting the balance sheet total for current liabilities from the current assets. The greater the surplus, the greater is the liquidity, although it is important always to view the current surplus or deficiency in relation to the total levels of the current assets and the current liabilities. You should note also that apparent liquidity levels can be distorted by, for example, large holdings of unsaleable stock. It is again important to check back to previous years to establish whether the level of liquidity is rising or falling. If there have been any significant changes, the reason must be established. A fall in liquidity, for instance, may be caused by a number of factors, such as investment in fixed assets without sufficient capital backing or the onset of overtrading. (Overtrading is where a business expands the scale of its operations far beyond the level which is safe in relation to the amount of its capital backing.)

The liquid surplus of Acme Manufacturing is clearly shown on the balance sheet under the heading 'net current assets'. It shows a healthy surplus which has increased satisfactorily over the three years.

Turnover

The trading account section of the final accounts shows the *total sales* made by the business during the year. This is usually referred to as the 'turnover' of the business and is a useful guide to whether or not the business is expanding.

A decreasing level of turnover in successive years should always be investigated. Indeed the same is true of a static situation; the effects of inflation are such that a static level of turn-over represents in reality a decreasing volume of trade. The ideal would normally be a steadily controlled growth from year to year. A sudden large increase in turnover is normally an indication that an overtrading situation is developing. The dangers of overtrading have already been mentioned; it is particularly damaging if the increase in turnover is not matched by a similar increase in profits.

Accounting ratios

By comparing various figures extracted from a financial state-ment, several ratios and factors can be produced which may further aid our understanding of the financial state of the business.

Current ratio
The current ratio is derived by dividing the current assets figure by the current liabilities figure. You can see that this is another way of expressing the 'working capital' or net current assets of the business which we have already discussed. The value in dealing with the figures in this way is that it helps us to grasp both the level of the liquid surplus or deficiency and its relation-ship to the overall values of the current assets and the current liabilities. This ratio is sometimes called the *working capital ratio*.

If there is a liquid surplus, the ratio will be better than 1:1. For most businesses the ratio should normally work out at between 1½:1 and 2:1, although the true significance of the ratio may not be obvious until it is compared with the results from previous years. A low or falling current ratio may indicate that the business is becoming illiquid, with all the dangers that that implies. A rising current ratio is generally an encouraging sign, although figures which exceed 4 or 5:1 would probably indicate that the business is not making the most profitable use of the funds which are available to it. The *trend* of the current ratio should also be compared with the trend of the turnover; a declining volume of business will often cause the liquidity to rise. This is because the amount owed to creditors reduces with the volume of business while stocks and other current assets remain at the same level. It is not an encouraging state of affairs.

The current ratio of the Acme Manufacturing Company has risen slightly over the three years as follows: 19–1—1.62:1, 19–2—1.67:1, 19–3—1.71:1. At the same time turnover has risen steadily. Taken together, this would seem to indicate that business is growing at a controlled rate without putting any pressure on liquidity levels.

A development of the current ratio, the *acid test ratio*, sometimes called the 'quick' ratio, is designed to show the true liquid position. It compares the liquid assets of the business (cash, debtors and marketable securities) with the total of the current liabilities. Very few businesses will show a ratio of better than 1:1 when this calculation is made. As before, it is the *trend* of the ratio over a period of years which is more instructive than a single year's calculation taken in isolation.

Credit given and credit taken

It is possible to establish from the balance sheet how long a period of credit the business normally takes from its suppliers and how long a period of credit it grants to its customers. The figures produced must be related to the normal practice in the particular area of activity before any conclusions can be drawn. The important question is whether the length of time given or taken to pay bills is greater or longer than the norm for the type of business. Some businesses trade mostly for cash, for example, so you would expect average periods of credit to be short. Others trade almost wholly on credit, with consequent lengthening of average credit periods.

The formulae used divide the total annual sales by the debtors' figure and divide the total annual purchases by the creditors' figure. Sometimes the final accounts which are attached to the balance sheet do not show the annual purchases figure, in which case the annual sales figure can be used; although the accuracy of the result will suffer, informative comparisons can be made with previous years. The result of this calculation represents the number of times that debtors or creditors are 'turned over' during the year. For instance, a business with creditors of £100 000 and annual purchases of £1 200 000 'turns over' its creditors twelve times a year, or once a month.

Thus, we can tell that the average period of credit taken is one month.

The equation can be re-expressed in a slightly different form so as to show more clearly the average length of time before any one debt is paid or collected. The following formulae will show the periods of credit given or taken, expressed in weeks:

$$\frac{\text{Debtors} \times 52}{\text{Annual sales}} = \text{Weeks' credit given}$$

$$\frac{\text{Creditors} \times 52}{\text{Annual purchases}} = \text{Weeks' credit taken}$$

The periods of credit given and taken should broadly speaking be consistent with one another. A business which takes six months' credit from its suppliers but which allows its customers only one month is probably having difficulty paying its debts. This is not conclusive, however, as it could indicate that the business is so healthy that suppliers are prepared to grant longer than average credit terms as a concession to a valued customer, or that the firm has a monopoly of trade in its particular field and can set very stringent terms for its customers!

As with other calculations, the important indicator is the *trend* over a number of years, having regard to the surrounding circumstances. A lengthening period of credit taken commonly denotes cash flow problems caused by financial weakness. Similarly, allowing shorter periods of credit to customers is commonly a sign that the business has a cash flow problem and is having to demand early payment of debts receivable so that it can pay its own creditors.

Using these formulae on figures extracted from the accounts of Acme Manufacturing, we come to following conclusions:

	19–1	19–2	19–3
Credit taken (in weeks)	14	13	14
Credit given (in weeks)	11	11	11

This shows a very stable position. Slightly longer credit is taken than is given, probably indicating that the company has a reputation for being well run and can therefore obtain favourable credit terms from its suppliers.

Stock turnover

It is always useful to calculate how frequently a business 'turns over' its stock. Much will depend on the nature of its trade: a fishmonger should turn his stock over very frequently, while a car spares dealer may hold stock for some considerable time. The *trend* over a period of years is again important. A falling rate of stock turnover is usually a danger signal which may indicate that the stock or some part of it is unsaleable, or that sales in general have fallen without a corresponding reduction in stock levels.

If we divide the annual sales figure by the closing stock figure, we get an approximation of the number of times in the year that stock has turned over. A more accurate figure can be achieved if we base the calculation on the cost of goods sold and on the average stock during the year. If it is not quoted in the annual accounts, the cost of goods sold can be established by deducting the gross profit for the year from the annual sales figure. Average stock is calculated by adding together the opening stock and the closing stock and dividing by two.

It is possible to express this calculation in a slightly different format to show how long on average any one item will remain in stock. The formula is:

$$\frac{\text{Average stock} \times 52}{\text{Cost of goods sold}} = \text{Average number of weeks stock is held}$$

Using this formula to analyse the figures shown in the accounts of Acme Manufacturing, we can establish that the average stock of finished goods represents around five weeks' sales throughout the three-year period. The actual figures are 5.24 weeks, 5.07 weeks, and 4.99 weeks. It is important always to compare like with like; it would be just as valid to base our calculations on the total average stock of both finished goods and raw materials provided that we use the same basis each year. As we said above, it is the *trend* from year to year which is important.

Gross profit : turnover

We have already noted that business profits must be *in proportion* to the volume of trade being done and that if turnover rises, so should profits. An appropriate way to check this is to calculate the percentage which gross profits represent of the annual sales figure. The formula for this is:

$$\frac{\text{Gross profit} \times 100}{\text{Annual sales}}$$

The result of this calculation enables us to check both whether the business is generating profits at a comparable level with similar concerns and how its performance compares with its results in previous years. The danger signs would be excessively low or falling rates of return. The gross profit margin of Acme Manufacturing shows a small but steady growth: 23, 25 and 27%. Normal levels of gross profit differ enormously between different types of business, commonly varying from below 15 to above 50%. A gross margin of 25% for a manufacturing business is probably about right.

Net profit : turnover
The net profit can be compared with sales in the same way as gross profit. The calculation is:

$$\frac{\text{Net profit} \times 100}{\text{Annual sales}}$$

It is normal to utilise the figure given in the accounts for net profit before deduction of taxation and appropriations. The tax provision may relate to events in previous trading years, thereby distorting the picture.

Clearly the net profit margin will be smaller than the gross profit margin and, although it will vary with the type of business, it will rarely exceed 10%. Acme Manufacturing has maintained a net profit margin of just over 4%. This seems quite satisfactory.

Net profit : gross profit
The difference between the net profit and the gross profit margins is determined by the *operating costs* of the business. If the difference between the two is expressed as a percentage of the gross profit, it is possible to monitor the trend over a number of years to check whether cost control is improving or worsening. The formula for the calculation is:

$$\frac{\text{Net profit} \times 100}{\text{Gross profit}}$$

Net profit : proprietor's funds

As a final check on profitability, the net rate of return can be useful to establish whether a business is producing an adequate level of profits from the funds invested in it by the proprietors. The formula to use is:

$$\frac{\text{Net profit} \times 100}{\text{Proprietors' funds}} = \text{Per cent rate of return on capital}$$

For proprietors' funds we can utilise the net worth figure which we mentioned earlier: this represents, in effect, the *proprietors' stake* in the business, including both money put into the business and retained profits. You must remember that this figure is determined to some extent by the balance sheet valuations of the assets of the firm. If assets are overvalued, the proprietors' stake will also be shown at a higher value than it should be. The reverse is true if assets are undervalued. In either case, the rate of return figure will be distorted and this can be misleading if comparisons are made with rates of return on other investments such as bank deposits.

In the case of the Acme Manufacturing Company there is an encouraging increase in the rate of return of capital, from 12.7% in 19–1, through 14.7% in 19–2, to 16% in 19–3.

Turnover : net worth

We have already mentioned the dangers of overtrading, and noted that it arises when a business takes on too much trade on a restricted capital base. If there are fears that such a situation is arising, we can check by comparing the turnover of the business to its net worth and expressing the result as a ratio. If the ratio exceeds 20:1, then it is almost certain that the business has overextended itself. A ratio of 10:1 is at the threshold of the danger area. Again, the trend of the ratio over a period of years is important. Some types of business seem to be able to survive long periods of apparent overtrading without suffering any ill-effects, and you would therefore expect them to show a high but steady 'trading ratio' over a number of years. It is the business which shows an increasing ratio that is becoming vulnerable.

Gearing

Gearing is a term used to describe the relationship between the loan capital and the equity capital used in a business or, in other words, the relationship between borrowed funds and proprietors' funds. (Loan capital embraces all long-term borrowing by the business, including such items as fixed-term loans and mortgages as well as any loan stocks or debentures. The equity capital is best expressed by use of the net worth figure.) A business which has a high proportion of borrowed funds is said to be 'highly geared'; a business with a low proportion of borrowed funds is 'low geared'.

All capital used in a business has its price. Proprietors' funds are put up in the expectation of receiving a share of the profits and in the hope that the value of their investment will grow over the years. Borrowed funds are obtained against the promise of interest payments to the lender. The difference is that interest has to be paid in bad times as well as in good, even when the business is incurring losses; dividends are paid only when adequate profits have been made. It follows that a highly geared business is vulnerable to fluctuations in profits and a prospective lender must bear this in mind. In addition, where capital substantially exceeds the proprietors' stake, the providers of borrowed funds often run an increased risk of not being able to recoup their money in full in a liquidation.

The gearing ratio is always expressed as:

Loan capital:equity capital

The Acme Manufacturing Company is moderately low geared. There is only one medium and long-term liability to take into account, the loan over five years, and comparing this with the net worth of the company gives successive ratios of 1:2, 1:2.2, and 1:2.7.

Financial statements and the lending banker

The valuation of a business

There are two very different ways in which we can approach the assessment of the value of a business from its annual accounts. On the one hand, we can look at it as a going concern, taking account of its dynamic profit generating capacity. On the other hand, we can simply look at the 'break-up' value of the business if its assets were to be sold off singly and the proceeds used to pay off its debts.

The going concern approach

Your first consideration will always be to satisfy yourself that a business to which you have been asked to lend is viable as a going concern. To this end you must apply to its annual accounts the various tests that we have considered above. You will be looking for evidence that the business is well managed, liquid and profitable. You will also look for the general trend in any changes disclosed by examination of a series of balance sheets and project that trend into the future, both to verify the expectations of the continued good health of the business and to satisfy yourself of the validity of any changes proposed by the proprietors.

Consideration of these aspects will tell you whether you should proceed with any proposals for advances to the business. If on balance you feel that the future of the business is doubtful, matters will proceed no further. If, on the other hand, you believe that any proposals put to you show a strong probability of success, you will then usually go on to estimate how much the business would be worth in a liquidation. The objective of this latter exercise is very much the same as the objective of taking security. You do it to ensure that there is a safety margin to protect the bank against losing its money if, contrary to expectations, the business were to fail. You will wish to be sure that if the asset had to be sold off, enough would be realised to pay off the debts of the business.

The gone concern approach

The production of a 'break-up' valuation of a commercial concern consists of no more than an attempt to estimate how much would be left over or, in the worst case, how much the irrecoverable debts would come to if it were to be liquidated as a result of its inability to trade profitably. It involves placing a *realistic valuation*, perhaps even a pessimistic valuation, on the assets rather than relying on their book value as shown in the balance sheet. Some assets may be worth more than their book values; many will be worth less. On a liquidation the value of an asset is neither governed by what was paid for it nor is it directly related to its productive capacity; its value is what somebody can be persuaded to pay for it on a forced sale when prices are always at a minimum.

Land and buildings. These assets are often very difficult to value without professional help, although this may have been done if the business premises have been taken as security. Perhaps the most significant factor is whether the premises were purpose built for one specific trade or whether conversion for other uses would be possible. Retail shops, for instance, usually maintain their value quite well because they can be easily adapted to meet the needs of many different traders. Similarly, engineering workshops can be adapted to produce a variety of goods. A petrol-filling station, on the other hand, can be used for hardly any other purpose and would not therefore maintain its value so well in a forced sale: a prospective purchaser wishing to use the premises to sell petrol would have to take account of the fact that the previous proprietors were unable to make the business pay.

Competition and anticipated demand for the services of the particular type of business will also affect the value of the premises. Using the filling station example again, its value will certainly decline if it is known that a new bypass will soon divert most of the traffic which currently passes the site. Likewise, the value of a grocery store will be affected if a branch of a national chain of supermarkets is opened nearby.

If the value of the buildings is doubtful, what of the site? Would it be possible to demolish the present building and sell the site for development for other purposes? The cost of the demolition would have to be considered of course. Much would depend on the availability of planning permission for the proposed change of use and on the conditions on which the land is held. If the land is leasehold, the lease may well impose restrictions on the uses to which it can be put. This is not so likely to be a problem if the land is freehold.

You will appreciate that there is *no simple formula* for arriving at the valuation of business premises. It is always instructive to know how the balance sheet valuation was arrived at and how recently the calculation was made. Where purpose-built premises are concerned, it is normal to expect that adequate provision has been made for depreciation. It is important to note, however, that good sites are always at a premium and that land usually appreciates in value. If premises are shown in the balance sheet at their purchase price, this may well be an understatement of their true worth. In such cases there is a 'hidden' asset valuation which we must take into account.

Plant and machinery. Items under this heading lose value very quickly. Secondhand prices are low, especially where the equipment is of a specialised nature. Buyers can often be found only for items which are relatively new and in a good state of repair. Even then, prices are depressed by the added costs of dismantling the equipment and transporting it to the buyer's premises. It is usual to find that a business which has been in financial difficulties has not invested in new equipment for some years and, quite probably, it has not maintained its old machinery to first-class standards. For these reasons, the 'breakup' value of these assets will often be no more than their scrap value.

Fixtures and fittings. These items suffer from similar disadvantages to those associated with plant and machinery. Purpose-built fittings do not find a ready market and they can often be sold only for scrap, if at all. Office furniture, such as desks and filing cabinets, is easier to dispose of.

Vehicles. Commercially used vehicles, especially lorries and delivery vans, are heavily used and wear out quickly. Thus, they do not command high resale prices. Clearly, the age and condition of the vehicles in question must be considered in arriving at a valuation but it is always best to err on the side of caution. Where appropriate, the scrap value only may again be used as the basis of the valuation.

Intangible assets. As a general rule, all intangible and fictitious assets shown on the balance sheet can be excluded completely from the 'break-up' valuation.

Cash. This item can be taken into the valuation at its stated level. It is valid to point out, however, that like all current assets cash tends to be depleted when a business gets into difficulties. By the time that the collapse occurs, all cash and credit bank balances have gone, all the saleable stock has been disposed of, outstanding debts have been collected and so on. All this has been done to generate as much cash as possible so as to finance a few weeks' further trading.

Debtors. The question here is whether all the debtors will be able to meet their obligations in full. In the case of a business with an efficient system of credit control, no significant problems should be anticipated and this item can be valued at up to 90% of its balance sheet level. An indication of the effectiveness of credit control can be gleaned by checking the provisions which have had to be made in the past to cover bad debts. The 'spread' of the debtors is important: if most of the money is owed by one or two major clients, there is a greater risk since the insolvency of such a client could mean disaster.

Investment. Valuation will be on the basis of the current market price less a margin to allow for fluctuations in demand. If investments are spread over a range of stocks, the margin to be deducted may be around 15 per cent of total market value. If holdings are concentrated in just one or two stocks, the margin taken will be much greater to allow for the greater danger of loss which results from the lack of diversification.

Stock and work in progress. The balance sheet valuation of stock is normally based on the lower of cost or market value. To arrive at a 'break-up' valuation, you will wish to satisfy yourself that the figure quoted is a genuine reflection of the amount of stock held. Much depends on the integrity of the proprietors from whom the accountants will have obtained the figures used in the balance sheets. The saleability of the stock must also be questioned, bearing in mind that in a liquidation the most easily sold items will have gone by the time that the business is compelled to cease trading. Unless the bank has any specific indications to the contrary, a rough valuation of the stock of finished goods can be arrived at by taking 50% of the balance sheet figure. Raw materials can be valued at a slightly higher level, being easier to dispose of. Work in progress, on the other hand, must be written down to a greater extent since partly finished articles are naturally much more difficult to sell.

Final valuation

Once the assets have been valued, they can be offset against all the liabilities of the business other than liabilities to the proprietors. In a liquidation some liabilities are given preferential treatment over others by law and we must bear this in mind when considering how much the bank would receive in a break-up. Secured creditors who have a fixed charge over certain of the assets of the business have the right to remove those assets from the general liquidation to obtain full repayment of the sums due to them. Any surplus proceeds must be returned for the benefit of other creditors.

Funds realised by the liquidation of the remaining assets will be applied first to paying off the *preferential creditors*. Only those debts which are so designated by the Insolvency Act 1986

Table 14.9 Break-up valuation of Acme Manufacturing as at 31 December 19–3

Fixed assets	£	£	
Freehold land		90 000	Professional valuation made for the bank in 19–2
Plant, machinery, fixtures and fittings		7 000	Scrap value
		5 500	Estimated sale value
Vehicles		nil	
Goodwill		102 500	
Current assets			
Cash	7 700		
Debtors	132 000		90
Raw materials	18 000		66 \ per cent of
Finished goods	21 000		50 / balance sheet
Work in progress	10 000		33 value
	188 700		
Current liabilities	136 100		As balance sheet
Net current assets		52 600	
Medium and long-term liabilities		60 200	As balance sheet
Net tangible assets		94 900	

are classed as preferential. They include unremitted PAYE tax collected from employees, VAT due to the Customs and Excise and unpaid Social Security contributions. Within certain limits, wages due to employees and loans to pay them are also classed as preferential. Currently the limit is set at a maximum of £800 per employee in respect of earnings during the preceding 4 months. Only when the preferential creditors have been paid in full will any funds be allocated to the remaining ordinary creditors. The proprietors of the business do not, of course, receive anything until everyone else has been paid off. It follows that it is unusual for the proprietors to receive anything when a business is liquidated as a result of trading at a loss.

As an illustration of how a 'break-up' valuation is produced, we can revalue the assets of the Acme Manufacturing Company as given in the balance sheet for 19–3 (Table 14.9).

You will see that valued on this basis, Acme Manufacturing continues to show a surplus of assets over liabilities. If the business were to be wound up, there should be at least £94 900 to go to the proprietors.

Effect of the loan on the balance sheet

When considering lending to a business, you must bear in mind the effect that granting the loan would have on the customer's balance sheet. It is always wise to calculate as far as possible what the balance sheet will look like after the loan has been taken. The amount of the loan will, of course, normally be shown as an addition to the current liabilities of the business, although banks do now grant loans for longer, fixed terms. An equivalent corresponding entry will have to be made somewhere else in the balance sheet reflecting the use which is to be made of the funds.

Purchase of fixed assets
The cost of any new plant, machinery, vehicles and so on will be shown in the fixed assets section of the balance sheet. Unless the necessary funds have been borrowed by way of long-term loans, the apparent liquidity position of the business will be upset as current liabilities will have increased while current assets have remained static. Thus, the available working capital is reduced. This can cause problems in itself but these are often made much worse by the fact that purchase of additional fixed

assets usually leads to demands for increased working capital to finance extra current expenditure.

Unless new equipment has been bought simply as a replacement for old and worn-out items, increased turnover can be expected to result from its use. This in turn leads to the need for increased current expenditure. Larger stocks must be held to ensure that increased sales can be effected. If the increased sales are made on the same credit terms as in the past, it follows that there will be a corresponding increase in the debtors' figure. All this puts greater pressure on liquid resources. Indeed, many businesses have found themselves in difficulties through just such a series of events. The lesson to be learned is that *fixed assets should not be financed out of working capital.*

Changes to working capital

Advances for working capital purposes can be utilised in one of two ways: the funds can be applied in reduction of other current liabilities, or they can be used to acquire further current assets. In the first case, the effect on the balance sheet is negligible; one current liability is increased while another reduces. The overall liquidity position remains exactly the same. As a general rule, however, the banks do not find loans for this purpose attractive. In effect, the bank would simply be paying off debts due elsewhere and the question must always be asked as to why this is necessary. Perhaps the business is running into difficulties and cannot pay its debts by any other means. Clearly, if this is so, the bank would prefer that outstanding debts are not converted into bank loans and that any losses fall on the original creditors.

Loans to increase current assets are much more acceptable. As we have seen, they are often associated with proposals to increase sales. While the concern is carrying on a steady volume of business, the working capital requirement should remain broadly stable. Funds will flow through a steady cycle as debtors are converted into cash which is used to pay off creditors from whom raw materials have been purchased. Further raw materials are obtained and processed into finished goods which are then sold, creating debtors and perpetuating the cycle. If turnover is expanded, however, the working capital requirement also expands. It is important to quantify the required increase in working capital to ensure that any proposed increases to bank lending will provide sufficient funds. It is normally found that the finance requirement increases by a much greater factor than the turnover. By way of example, let us assume that Acme Manufacturing intends to increase sales by 50 per cent. In its latest balance sheet the company has the following current assets:

	£
Cash	7 700
Debtors	124 600
Raw materials	27 300
Finished goods	41 800
Work in progress	30 800
	232 200

These are financed by the following current liabilities:

	£	
Creditors	77 500	
Hire purchase	23 300	
Taxation	6 000	
Dividend	4 000	
Bank loans	25 300	
Working capital	96 100	(this is the 'liquid surplus')
	232 200	

As we have seen, when sales are increased, increased current assets will have to be carried. The result may well be something like this:

	£	
Cash	7 700	as before
Debtors	186 900	
Raw materials	40 900	
Finished goods	62 700	50% increase
Work in progress	46 200	
	344 400	

How is this to be financed? Working capital, dividends, taxation and hire purchase loans will, of course, remain the same as before since no further funds are immediately available from these sources. Doubtless suppliers will be prepared to grant further credit to a well-run company such as this, so we may assume a 50% increase in the creditors' figure. Any further funds needed must therefore be provided by borrowing, probably from the bank as follows:

	£
Creditors	116 250
Hire purchase	23 300
Taxation	6 000
Existing bank loan	25 300
Working capital	96 100
New borrowing	73 450
	344 400

Thus, a 50% increase in turnover would require that overdraft facilities be increased from £25 000 to almost £100 000, a factor of four times the existing level. If you were not prepared to extend facilities to this level, severe strain will be placed on liquidity. The business will be able to survive only on a day-to-day basis by pressing debtors for early payment and by deferring payments to creditors for as long as possible. If you were to agree to provide the necessary finance, the liquidity position would be affected in an interesting way. While net current assets could be expected to remain stable at around £96 000, the current ratio would show a marked decline from 1.7:1 to 1.3:1. This results from the dramatic increase to both sides of the equation and is an indication of the pressure which sudden expansion would place on the financial stability of the business. In fact, it is unlikely that a well-managed company like Acme Manufacturing would contemplate quite such a dramatic increase in turnover.

Cash forecasts

There are two separate financial forecasting techniques which the lending banker may utilise when considering an advance. These are the *cash flow forecast* and the *funds flow*. The two techniques are quite distinct from each other and are used for different purposes. The cash flow forecast is the more appropriate when a working capital overdraft facility is contemplated, while the funds flow is more appropriate when financing capital expenditure is the issue.

Enter Month								
Opening Bank Balance Credit/(Debit).........A								
Receipts in month:								
Trade debtors								
Cash receipts								
Other income								
Sale of assets								
Capital subscribed								
Loans receivable								
Total Receipts.........B								
Payments in month:								
Creditors								
Cash payments								
Wages & Salaries								
Heating, power etc.								
Rates								
Advertising								
Transport								
Interest								
Other expenses								
Corp/Income Tax								
VAT (net)								
Dividends								
HP payments								
Loan repayments								
Capital expenditure								
Total payments.........C								
Cash surplus/(shortfall) B−C=D								
Closing Bank Balance Credit/(Debit) A−D=								

Fig. 14.1 A cash flow forecast form

Cash flow forecasts

In discussing working capital advances, we showed how an attempt can be made to quantify the borrowing requirement which results from proposals to expand a business. The calculations which we made represented, of course, only a very rough approximation to the amount which will be needed. A more accurate estimate can be obtained by asking the customer to compile a cash flow forecast. This consists of no more than an analysis, on a month-by-month basis, of all anticipated items of income and expenditure. It takes as its starting point the present bank balance. If in any one month expenditure exceeds income, bank borrowing will increase; if income exceeds expenditure, the overdraft will be reduced. Thus, the forecast will show the levels which bank borrowing can be expected to reach during the period under consideration. Most banks now produce standard cash flow forecast forms, similar to the one shown in Fig. 14.1.

Cash flow forecasts are usually prepared showing projected receipts and payments for at least the next six months and often the next twelve months. It follows that a margin for error must be allowed, especially towards the end of the period. In practice, very few of these forecasts work out entirely as predicted. Nevertheless, careful forecasting should reveal quite clearly the general level of borrowing which will be required to finance any specific proposals. It is important to ensure that all cash inflows and outflows are recorded, including wages, taxes, payments to creditors and so on.

Funds flow

When we are considering a loan to finance a capital project, the amount required will not be in such doubt as in a working capital advance. The cash flow forecast does not therefore have an important role to play. The bank's primary consideration will be the feasibility of the repayment proposals. The basic indicator of whether a business generates adequate income to meet the required repayment schedule is to be found in the net profit which it makes after tax. For greater accuracy, it is possible to add back to this figure the amount of any depreciation which has been deducted from profits. (Depreciation is a bookkeeping entry only and it does not represent an actual flow of cash out of the business.)

A more comprehensive *funds flow forecast* can be constructed to indicate how much will be available in the coming year to fund repayment of a loan account. The formula to use is as follows:

First calculate the funds available to meet outgoings by adding together:

1   Retained profits—as forecast for the coming year.
2   Taxation as calculated on the forecast profits; this sum will not be payable for at least twelve months.
3   Depreciation for the coming year; as we have noted, this is a book entry only and not a cash outflow.

From the total of these three items, the following sums must be deducted:

1   Current taxation—as shown on the latest balance sheet as this *will* have to be paid in the coming year.
2   Interest payable on the proposed loan.

The final total which results from this calculation represents the *disposable funds* which are available to the business to cover both capital repayments on the loan and any other expenditure which is contemplated. If necessary it may be adjusted to allow for any other known changes which will occur to the outgoings of the business.

Summary

1   Every business produces financial statements consisting of balance sheets and profit and loss accounts showing the financial state of the business on a given date.
2   The assets represent how a business has used the funds at its disposal. They can be categorised as:

    (a) fixed assets: including fictitious and intangible assets;
    (b) current assets: which 'turn over' regularly.

3   The liabilities represent the sources of funds used in the business. They can be categorised as:

    (a) capital: including accumulated reserves and profit and loss balances;
    (b) medium-term liabilities;
    (c) current liabilities.

4 The final accounts summarise income and expenditure. They comprise:

(a) the manufacturing account (manufacturing businesses only);

(b) the trading account;

(c) the profit and loss account;

(d) the profit and loss appropriation account.

5 In examining financial statements, the trend is an important indicator of the progress that the business is making.

6 Factors for close examination include:

(a) net worth: surplus of assets over liabilities;

(b) working capital: surplus of current assets over current liabilities;

(c) turnover: the value of business done each year.

7 Ratios aid comparison from year to year. Principal ratios include:

(a) current ratio;

(b) acid test ratio ('quick' ratio);

(c) credit given and credit taken;

(d) rate of stock turnover;

(e) turnover:net worth.

8 Businesses may be valued as a going concern or as a gone concern. The gone concern approach considers the break-up value of the business if it had to be liquidated.

9 The way in which a proposed loan will affect the balance sheet should always be considered.

10 Forecasting future finance requirements can be aided by the use of:

(a) cash flow forecasts: to show the maximum level of future overdrafts;

(b) funds flow forecasts: to demonstrate the feasibility of capital repayments.

Self-assessment questions

1 Define (a) current assets; (b) goodwill; (c) reserves; (d) working capital; (e) stock turnover; (f) the 'gone concern' approach.

2 Describe the method of constructing a cash flow forecast.

3 List the accounting ratios which you can utilise in analysing a customer's balance sheet.

4 True or false?

(a) The trend of figures shown in a series of balance sheets is more important than the figures for any one year.

(b) A banker should always look at a balance sheet on both a 'going concern' and a 'gone concern' basis.

(c) Overtrading is a sign of healthy expansion of the volume of business done.

(d) It is a discouraging sign if the length of credit taken exceeds the length of credit given.

(e) Calculating the net worth of a business shows its day-to-day liquidity, that is whether or not it can pay its debts as they fall due.

5 Describe the method of calculation and state the value of the current ratio.

6 Analyse the reasons why a bank will always calculate the rate of stock turnover from any balance sheet produced by a borrowing customer. Explain why this calculation can sometimes be misleading.

7 Analysis of a customer's most recent balance sheet shows that the period of credit granted has shortened drastically since last year. The customer maintains that this is because he is in a position to dictate terms to his customers. How would you react and what further checks would you make?

Assignments

1 Obtain the up-to-date balance sheet of a public limited company engaged in manufacturing. This will show figures for at least the current year and the previous year.

Analyse these accounts using the techniques and ratios discussed in this chapter. Write a brief report on the *trends* which you have identified in the figures, explaining what these trends indicate. Give an opinion on the future prospects of the company which you have been examining.

2 You should already be in possession of your own bank's balance sheet. Analyse the figures for at least the last two years using the same techniques as before.

Prepare a report identifying the major differences which you can identify between these accounts and those of the business that you examined in assignment one. Comment on what these differences tell you about the different natures of the two companies.

3 Look at the figures on pages 528–9: Acme Manufacturing Company's profit ratios for the last three years. Produce a calculation from the financial statements given in Table 14.8 confirming that these percentages are correct.

15 Property

Chapter objectives

After studying this chapter you should be able to:
- explain the legal distinction between and classify different types of property;
- outline special factors concerning land ownership;
- identify evidence of ownership for different types of property and the means of checking title;
- describe the appropriate instruments of transfer;
- outline the ways in which different types of property may be taken as security;
- outline the obligations and rights of customer and banker as mortgagor and mortgagee.

Types of property

Introduction: real and personal property

Our legal system classifies property into 'real' and 'personal', the former comprising only freehold interests in land and the latter everything else, including leasehold interests in land. (We explain these terms below.) In fact, freehold and leasehold interests in land are treated in much the same way and it is usual to refer to leaseholds when classifying property as 'chattels real' to distinguish them from 'chattels personal', that is other forms of personal property. Look again at Fig. 8.1 on page 285 and note the categories shown. We will explain some of the terms used.

The word 'chattel' is a linguistic corruption of 'cattle', the ownership of which is still regarded as a measure of wealth in some societies. 'Choses in action' are property which does not physically exist and which consequently cannot be effectively protected by physical means, only by court action. Examples include negotiable instruments, patents, copyrights and the goodwill of a business. You will see later on that apart from land, bankers nearly always take charges over choses in action as security for loans, life policies and shares being obvious examples. 'Chose', by the way, is an old French legal term for 'thing'. 'Choses in possession' are property with a physical existence; such property can therefore be physically possessed and protected, for example this book or your clothes.

The historical background

These somewhat strange-sounding categories are a legacy of the very rigid procedural rules which the common law courts (the Royal Courts) developed early in our legal history. If a man's freehold land was wrongfully taken from him, and this happened quite frequently in a society where might was largely right, he could seek to recover the actual land by bringing a 'real' action in the common law courts. If, however, he was dispossessed of anything else he could not recover the actual property and was only entitled to bring a 'personal' action for money compensation against the person who had taken it. So where do leaseholds fit in? The answer is simple: the concept of the leasehold interest, essentially a commercial creation, developed rather later than the freehold, by which time legal procedure had become so rigid that the 'real' action available to the freeholder could not be adapted to a leaseholder's claim. In time, however, a remedy developed which enabled a leaseholder to recover his land if he had been wrongfully dispossessed.

Already you can see that a knowledge of legal history is extremely helpful in fully understanding our system of property classification. Indeed, the concept of ownership as applied to land is still based on ideas dating back to William the Conqueror and the Normans' own particular brand of feudalism. Fortunately, the present system can be described and explained in general terms without more than a few passing references to the past. Nevertheless, it is a quite remarkable fact that it was not until the Law of Property Act 1925 that our system of land law made any real concessions to the increasingly complex industrial society that it served. Even today, land law may be criticised for being old-fashioned and unnecessarily complex in both principle and practice.

Bankers and personal property

Before we begin to look at ownership and transfer of title to property, we must identify the types of personal property with which we shall be dealing and define the term 'land'; as you will see it has an extensive meaning. Much of the law concerning personal property, its title and transfer, is to do with the sale of goods and is regulated by the Sale of Goods Act 1979. This, however, is of limited relevance to you as a banker since banks will avoid taking goods, for example, valuables, as security unless they must. Therefore, we are going to restrict our discussion to those forms of personal property which are usually taken as security for an advance: stocks and shares, life policies, guarantees and debentures.

It should not have escaped you that all these types of property are choses in action as far as the rights they confer are concerned—you cannot physically enforce your rights under any of them—but the certificates or other documents evidencing or conferring those rights are choses in possession and someone who wrongfully takes or deals with them is committing conversion against their true owners. Remember, we discussed this in Chapter 6 in the context of a bank wrongfully delivering property held in safe custody.

Land defined

At law the term 'land' covers not only the visible surface of the earth but also, in theory, everything above and below the surface and rights over land. When the term is used in Acts of Parliament it is defined by the Interpretation Act 1978 as including 'buildings and other structures, land covered with water, and any estate, interests, servitude or right over land'. (We explain these terms later.) Hence, we can say that land includes minerals, buildings, fixtures in buildings, reasonable rights in the airspace above the surface and rights over another's land such as a right of way.

You should not think of land in purely legal terms. Economists, for example, view land as a *resource*, a space in which to undertake economic activity and are therefore interested in its utility. Lawyers, on the other hand, are primarily concerned with its *ownership*, the transfer of that ownership, *restrictions upon its use* and the *legal obligations* arising from its occupancy. Bankers again have their own perspective. They are primarily interested in land from the point of view of its *suitability as security*. However, if we reflect on this a moment you will see that as a banker you are really interested in both the other perspectives. On the one hand you are concerned to ensure that your interest is legally recognised and protected, on the other you are interested in the commercial value and the ease with which the security can be realised. This concern is really based on the economist's perspective.

Earlier on we used the term 'fixture'; this requires explanation. Fixtures are items which *at law* have become part of the land or building to which they are attached. In deciding whether an object is a fixture, the law looks at the degree to which it is attached to the building (the greater the degree of annexation, the more likely it is to be a fixture) and, more importantly, the purpose of the annexation. If the intention was to permanently improve the building, and not merely to enjoy the object itself, it is a fixture. For example, fitted cupboards in a house and permanent installations in a factory are fixtures, while pictures hung on walls and moveable machinery are not.

Since what is in a building, in industrial and commercial property in particular, can be very valuable, for example machinery, whether or not an item is a fixture or a fitting could affect the value of a bank's security.

Ownership of land

Brief historical background

Since the Norman Conquest in 1066 all land in England has been theoretically owned by the Crown alone and the same has been true of the rest of Great Britain for many centuries. The most that anyone else can own is one of two legal *estates* which now exist: a freehold estate or a leasehold estate, an estate being a measure of a person's interest in a particular piece of land in terms of time. In the feudal days it was held on a certain *tenure*, originally the provision of goods or services of some kind, and later the payment of a sum of money. We still have tenancies and rents of course, but these are very different from the original feudal ideas of tenure which have now almost entirely disappeared. It is important that you remember that a legal estate is an abstract idea, as are interests in land. (This we discuss below.)

As new demands from a changing society were made upon it,

the system of land law was altered and added to but not re-formulated. By the early 20th century it had become completely archaic and as a result was extremely complicated. Change came in 1925; the Property Legislation of that year, consisting of seven statutes, completely reformed the system of land law and conveyancing (the transfer of estates and interests in land). The main aims of this legislation were:

(a) to reduce all remaining feudal tenures to one common form—'common socage'. This may now be regarded as identical to the term 'freehold';

(b) to remove outdated concepts, in particular feudal rights;

(c) to apply the principles of personal property law to real property wherever possible, for example, in relation to the transfer and registration of title to land, the system being based on that used for transfer and registration of shareholdings; and

(d) to simplify conveyancing. This last aim was achieved by reducing the number of possible *legal estates* to two and the number of *legal interests* to five, and by extending the principle of *registration* of title to land and interests in and rights over it. (We cover all these things later in the chapter.)

Legal estates

A fundamental point by way of introduction: a legal estate is an abstract idea and is quite separate from the land itself. It can be bought and sold, transferred by gift or by will, without affecting the actual land itself or the possession of it. This is basic to your concern with land as a banker; the abstract nature of estates and interests enables land to be used as security. A legal mortgage over land, for example, while conferring rights sufficient to ensure its adequacy as security, does not directly, or even indirectly, affect the use of the land or the rights of occupation until and unless the terms of the mortgage are breached, normally by non-payment. Another, and more basic example, is that it is possible to buy the freehold of a large block of flats without in any way affecting the rights of occupation of the many tenants in the flats.

The Law of Property Act 1925 reduced the number of possible legal estates to two.

Freehold land
All land in this country is held on freehold tenure—free as

opposed to unfree in feudal days. For all practical purposes this amounts to absolute ownership. Freeholders may, for example, dispose of their estates to anyone they please. Nevertheless there are important restrictions upon their power to do as they like with their land. The common law prevents them from using their land in a way which would cause an actionable nuisance to their neighbours, and their right to develop land is restricted by the Town and Country Planning Acts. They are also subject to compulsory purchase powers.

Before 1925 there were a variety of freehold estates which the common law recognised but since 1925 only the *fee simple absolute in possession* is recognised as a *legal* estate. (You will see the significance of 'legal' as you progress through this chapter.) This is not to say, however, that the former estates have disappeared as such, but they can now exist only as *equitable interests* in land in conjunction with a trust, an arrangement whereby property is held by one person (a trustee) who must use it for the benefit of another (a beneficiary).

The words used in the term *fee simple absolute in possession* have the following meanings:

Fee: an estate of inheritance, that is, one that may be inherited or which may pass by will.

Simple: the inheritance is not limited to a particular class of the freeholder's heirs, such as males only, or the children of a particular marriage. (An estate where the inheritance was so limited was known as a *fee tail* (*tailé*: cut down); this can now exist only as an equitable entailed interest.)

Absolute: not subject to any conditions, as a *life estate* (now only possible as a *life interest*) would be.

In possession: takes effect immediately, not, for example, from 1 January 2000. The words include not only the right to immediate physical possession but also embrace the immediate right to receive rent and profits where the land is leased and therefore subject to another's right of occupation (*see below*).

Leasehold land

As you have seen, all land in this country is held on freehold tenure but the estate owner may create from his freehold an estate of limited duration: a leasehold. This can be illustrated diagramatically; look at Fig. 15.1. The *freehold* of Whiteacre is

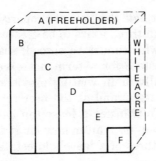

Fig. 15.1 Creation of leases

owned by A. A leases it to B for 99 years (the head lease) for £5000 a year. B in turn leases most of it to C for 90 years at, say, £4500 a year and so on down the chain until a small part is let to F. Alternatively, the *whole* of Whiteacre could be sublet a number of times, often at a profit, leaving F as the last sub-lessee and the present occupier. Yet again, B could transfer (assign) the lease to C who transfers it to D etc. Here there only ever exists the one lease. In all three cases, the right to occupy the land normally reverts back to A (the freeholder) when the (head) lease expires, i.e. at the end of 99 years. The points to note from this are first that leaseholders are usually able to sub-let their land and, second, provided each successive sub-lease is for a shorter period, a number of legal estates can exist at any one time over the same piece of land.

Confusing? Or is it? Your own bank may lease its premises and may possibly sub-lease accommodation in excess of its needs. The lease was invented centuries ago for commercial reasons (land was then virtually the sole source of wealth and money could be raised by selling its use for a given period) and it still fulfils commercial functions. Land as a resource is frequently acquired by buying a lease and high rents in return are a profitable source of income.

Technically a leasehold estate is a *term of years absolute*, and it is the only other legal estate in land which can exist under the provisions of the Law of Property Act 1925. The words *terms of years* include not only leases for a specific number of years but also those for less than a year or from year to year, although short leases are commonly referred to as tenancies. *Absolute* means that the estate is not subject to any conditions.

To create a *legal estate* the Law of Property Act 1925 requires a lease for more than three years to be created by deed: a formal written document which must be signed, sealed and delivered. However, a legal estate for a term not exceeding three years may be created orally or in writing provided it takes effect in possession (immediately) and at the best rent that can reasonably be obtained. To transfer a lease (an assignment) requires a deed to be executed, no matter how short the term assigned.

The essential features of a leasehold estate are:

(a) it gives the right to *exclusive possession*;
(b) it is for a *definite term*, i.e. the start of the term and its duration are fixed or can be determined;
(c) it creates the relationship of landlord and tenant.

The fact that a leasehold is for a limited term is the essential distinction from a freehold estate, for the latter is of unlimited duration.

At common law the land leased reverts back absolutely to the freeholder at the end of the lease. This position can no longer be regarded as acceptable either socially or commercially and a number of statutes now significantly vary this common law position. The Leasehold Reform Act 1967 gives leaseholders of houses, originally let for twenty-one years or more at a low rent and held for at least five years, the right to enforce a sale to them of the freehold on payment of the value of the freehold interest in the site. Alternatively they may ask for a fifty-year extension of the lease. These rights are known as *leasehold enfranchisement*. The Act applies only to houses (not flats) of less than £200 rateable value (£400 in London) as at March 1965.

The Landlord and Tenant Act 1954 protects tenants of flats under long tenancies (21 years or more) at low rents and many other tenancies of both furnished and unfurnished property are protected by the Rent Acts. However, under these Acts the *statutory tenancy* that the tenant is given only protects the tenant's personal right of occupation, a much lesser right than that acquired under the Leasehold Reform Act 1967. Statutory tenants cannot, for example, pass their tenancies on to others, either during their lifetimes or by will.

The Housing Act 1980 covers dwelling houses let to an individual or individuals jointly by local authorities and other listed bodies, such as housing associations, for occupation as dwellings.

Under the Act *secure tenants* have their position protected and acquire various rights, for example, the right to take in lodgers without the landlord's consent and the right to sublet part of a dwelling house with the landlord's permission. Above all, perhaps, a secure (council) tenant of at least three years' standing has the right to acquire the freehold (of the house) or a long lease (of the flat).

A tenant of business premises is given protection by Part II of the Landlord and Tenant Act 1954 as amended by the Law of Property Act 1969. The Act applies to all property occupied by a tenant for the purposes of any trade, profession or employment. The basic aim of the legislation is to allow tenants to conduct their businesses in premises indefinitely, subject to the landlord's legitimate rights when the tenancies expire or a tenant abuses the terms of the tenancy. If a tenant does not wish to give up possession and applies to the court in the proper way, the court is *bound* to grant a new tenancy unless the landlord objects on one of seven grounds specified in the Act, for example, failure to repair the premises or persistent delay in paying rent. A new tenancy granted by the court will be for a maximum of fourteen years but there is no limit on the number of applications that a tenant can make under the Act.

Interests in land

An interest in land is a right to a claim against the land of another less than a claim to actual possession. An estate is a right to the land itself, that is, possession. Interests in land can be either legal or equitable.

Legal interests
These are rights against the land itself—often referred to as rights *in rem*—and are therefore enforceable against all other persons. Thus, whoever acquires the land is bound by any legal interest which exists over it, whether or not he had knowledge of it before the acquisition. Banks must therefore be aware of possible legal interests when a mortgage of land is taken as security because the bank's rights to realise the security will be affected by any existing legal interests.

Since 1925 a legal interest must be held in fee simple absolute in possession or for a term of years absolute. Under the Law of

Property Act 1925 (as amended) there are five types of legal interests:

(a) An *easement, right or privilege* in or over land. This may be a bare right over the land of another (an easement), for example a right of way; or the right to take something of value from the land of another (a profit *à prendre*), such as fishing or shooting rights. Sometimes easements can be quite amusing. For example, in places where houses were built with backyards rather than gardens a right to hang washing over another's land is not uncommon and even, would you believe, a right to use another's outside toilet—a legally enforceable convenience, you may say!

These examples may seem amusing but remember they were, and in some cases still are, very important to the everyday lives of the people involved. Remember, too, that these rights are legally enforceable so even the largest organisation would not build across a right of way without purchasing it from the owner first. Such interests can also be very valuable. For example, fishing and shooting rights can be worth an absolute fortune.

(b) A *rentcharge*. This charges a piece of land, quite independently of any lease or mortgage, with the payment of a periodic sum of money to the owner of the rentcharge. Rent-charges are found only in one or two areas of the country, such as Manchester, and they were created as a way of retaining a perpetual source of income from the land after it was sold for housing development. Under the Rentcharges Act 1977, however, no new rentcharges may be created and existing ones will eventually be extinguished.

(c) A charge by way of a *legal mortgage*. As a banker this is the legal interest with which you are most concerned.

(d) A charge on land which is not created by an instrument but *imposed by law*. Such charges are of little practical importance and you are most unlikely to encounter one as a banker.

(e) A *right of entry* in respect of a legal term of years absolute or annexed to a legal rentcharge. A landlord usually has the right to re-enter if the tenant fails to pay rent or comply with obligations (covenants) in the lease.

Equitable interests

An equitable interest in land originally only gave a right

against the person who granted it (a right *in personam*), but was finally established as being enforceable against anyone except a purchaser who bought the legal estate in good faith for value without notice of the interest. This is important and you should make sure that you have read this point carefully. As you will see, the requirement of 'notice' or, more correctly, the substitution of a system of registration in lieu of notice, is particularly important.

The Property Legislation of 1925 provided that all estates, interests and charges in or over land, both legal and equitable, other than the fee simple absolute in possession, the term of years absolute and the five legal interests listed above, would subsequently take effect as *equitable interests*. For example, a life estate became a life interest, a fee tail became an entailed interest and a future fee simple (that is, one not in possession) became a future interest. All these, as you have read, must now be created behind a *trust*.

There are, however, four important equitable interests which may exist independently of any trust:

(a) A *restrictive covenant*. An agreement whereby one person promises to restrict the use of his land for the benefit of another's adjoining land, for example, an agreement preventing the land from being used for the purposes of trade (quite often the sale of alcohol).

(b) The *equity of redemption*. The right of a mortgagor to redeem the mortgaged property upon payment of the outstanding principal and interest. (This is clearly important to you and we cover it more fully below.)

(c) An *equitable charge*. An interest in land given as security for the payment of a sum of money. The person in whose favour the charge was made is entitled to take legal action for the sale of the land if payment is not made. (Again this is relevant to practical banking and we cover it later on.)

(d) An *estate contract*. A little more technical and of less relevance to banking, this arises where the freeholder or leaseholder contracts to convey the estate to the other party involved, or to create a term of years in the other's favour. Until the actual deed has been executed no legal estate passes but the contract to execute the deed gives rise to an equitable interest which the courts will enforce. An exchange of contracts for the purchase of a house is an example of an estate contract.

Registration and protection of interests
From a banking operations perspective this is more important
to you than a knowledge of the interests themselves because it
fundamentally affects the procedure used when taking a charge
on land as security and the value of that security when charged.

With the considerable number of *legal* estates and interests
existing *before 1925*, the purchaser of land took the risk of there
being an estate or an interest in existence of which he was
completely ignorant at the time of purchase and which would
affect his possession after the purchase. On the other hand, the
position of the holder of an equitable estate or interest was even
worse. His position was secure only if the purchaser had notice
of his estate or interest; his equity (as it was and is known)
would be lost if the legal estate was purchased in good faith and
for value without notice of the equity. (Look back at our definition of an equitable interest.)

After 1925 the position of a purchaser of land was greatly
improved, the number of legal estates and interests had been
reduced. But this in turn meant that many more equitable
interests now existed and the *doctrine of notice* was no longer
adequate protection for them. The Land Charges Act 1925 (now
consolidated with later amendments by the Land Charges Act
1972) established a national state system of registration of many
of the possible interests in land. Since then the old rules on
notice have not applied to *registrable interests*. Thus, a *registrable right is void against a purchaser of the legal estate unless
it is registered*, even if the purchaser had notice of the interest.

A short but important digression at this point. Our discussion
so far has concerned only *unregistered land*; in fact most urban
land in the country is now registered and in due course all will
be. Where title to land is *registered*, such registrable interests
(called *minor interests* under the registration scheme) must be
protected by an entry on the *Charges Register* and not under the
Land Charges Act. The effect is the same, however, and the old
rules on notice similarly do not apply.

The system of registering interests in land applies mainly to
equitable interests for these are the more vulnerable. However,
some important legal interests are also registrable, in particular
a legal mortgage of unregistered land which is not supported by
a deposit of the title deeds with the mortgagee: a *puisne mort-*

gage—pronounced 'puny'. This is a common security taken by banks to secure overdrafts. Normally you would take a deposit of the title deeds as security but with a second, or indeed any subsequent, mortgage the deeds will already be in the possession of the first mortgagee (for example, a building society) and therefore unavailable to you.

On the sale of the land, equitable interests incapable of registration are *overreached*, such as the interest of a life tenant. Overreaching means that a purchaser of the legal estate, even one with notice of the interest, takes free from it. The interest overreached now attaches, and can be enforced against, the proceeds of the sale; it can no longer be enforced against the land itself.

Under the Land Charges Act 1925 there are five registers of registrable interests, the *register of land charges* being the most important. This, in turn, is divided into six classes: A to F. Of these class C is most important to you because under this class are included puisne mortgages and equitable charges, such as an equitable mortgage of a legal estate. In addition to the national registration system, there are registers of local land charges kept at the registering local authority. These record charges acquired by the local authority under statutory authority, such as charges for making up roads or laying drains, and intended compulsory purchase orders.

Registration of title to land

You have probably heard of and might even have seen bundles of deeds which somehow or other prove a person's title to a piece of land. Great mystique attaches to them and they are often attractive and interesting documents. In reality, however, they are an incredibly inefficient way of proving title to anything in an age of electronic databanks. In particular, each time title is transferred there has to be a fresh investigation of the deeds to establish that the transferor's title is good.

Deeds are used to prove title to *unregistered land* and what we have said so far in this chapter relates to unregistered land. However, we did make the point that title to all land in this country will eventually be registered at one of a number of land registries scattered around the country.

The registration system

This is governed by the Land Registration Act 1925, as amended. It deals with the whole title to the land and not just individual transactions. Basically, it replaces the separate investigation of title necessary on every conveyance of unregistered land with a state investigated and guaranteed title. Many charges and incumbrances affecting the land are also shown on the register. However, whether title to land is registered or not, charges acquired by any local authority by statute must still be registered in the Local Land Charges Registers.

It is worth repeating before we move on that if title to land is registered, the system of registering land charges in the Land Charges Register does not apply.

Registered interests

Only the two legal estates can be registered, but restrictions exist on the registration of a lease (*see* below).

Overriding interests

These bind the purchaser or a mortgagee of registered land even though the purchaser has *no notice* of them and they are not mentioned on the register. So what are overriding interests, which appear to run contrary to the whole idea of registering interests?

Overriding interests are those interests which could be discovered from enquiries of the occupier or by an inspection of the land itself and not, if title to the land was unregistered, from the title deeds and documents relating to the land. Examples include:

(a) legal easements and profits *à prendre*;
(b) rights of a person in actual occupation; and
(c) leases for terms of 21 years or less.

Quite simply, their effect means that it is absolutely imperative for any would-be purchaser or mortgagee, a bank for example, to make an actual investigation of the land, through a solicitor perhaps, to ensure that no overriding interest exists.

We can illustrate this by considering the rights of a person in actual occupation. The position can be summarised as follows. If property is vested in the name of *one person only* another person who contributes to the purchase price and who occupies the property has an overriding interest in it. This cannot be overreached (*see* above) on a subsequent sale or mortgage and a possession order will not be granted against such a person: *Williams & Glyn's Bank* v. *Boland* (1980). If property held on trust is vested in *joint names*, then payment of loan or puchase moneys to at least *two trustees* overreaches the interest of the beneficiary(ies) under the trust even though they contributed towards the purchase price and are in actual occupation: *City of London Building Society* v. *Flegg* (1987).

Let us look at these two cases in more detail. In *Williams & Glyn's Bank* v. *Boland* (1980), Mr and Mrs Boland had bought a house with their joint earnings, although it was conveyed to Mr Boland alone and he appeared as the sole registered proprietor at the Land Registry. Mr Boland's company borrowed money from the bank and he gave his personal guarantee as collateral security. Without telling his wife he also mortgaged the house to the bank under a registered charge. The bank made no enquiry of either Mr or Mrs Boland whether the latter had an interest in the house. Subsequently the company ran into difficulties, the bank called upon Mr Boland to pay under his guarantee and when he could not do so it sought possession of the house. The House of Lords held that the bank's action must fail. Mrs Boland's financial contribution to the purchase of the house gave her an interest in land and because she was in actual occupation when the bank took the legal charge from her husband she had an overriding interest under the Land Registration Act 1925, s.70 (1)(*g*).

The decision is important in both family law and land law, and of direct significance to banks. Furthermore, the decision goes far beyond the actual facts. It applies to both registered and unregistered land and not just to matrimonial homes and other dwelling houses. It also protects *any person* with a financial stake in the property who is in actual occupation at the time the mortgage is created (in the case of unregistered land) or registered (in the case of registered land). Lord Wilberforce in the House of Lords expressed its scope in the following words: '. . . a man living with his mistress or . . . a man and a woman, or two persons of the same sex, living in a house in separate or partially shared rooms'. Some wit even suggested at the time that it might cover an adopted cat which came with a legacy which was used to build a sun-room in which the cat lived!

In *City of London Building Society* v. *Flegg* (1987), Mr and Mrs Flegg bought a house with their daughter and son-in-law, the Maxwell-Browns, but the property was conveyed into the sole names of the Maxwell-Browns on an express trust for sale for themselves as joint tenants. The Maxwell-Browns mortgaged the property to the plaintiff and subsequently defaulted on the repayments. The plaintiff commenced proceedings to enforce the mortgage against both the Maxwell-Browns and the Fleggs. The former conceded defeat and the issue was whether the mortgage bound the Fleggs. The House of Lords held that it did and a possession order was granted against them. The crucial distinction with *Boland* was that the property had been vested in joint names.

At the time, the *Boland* decision had alarmed banks because of its apparently wide application; the *Flegg* decision clearly shows that *Boland* is an exception to the general principle that a beneficiary's interest under a trust for sale is overreached on a sale or mortgage of the property. Nevertheless, it gives a clear warning. When you intend to take a charge over land from a sole owner you must identify all occupiers, ascertain their financial stake, if any, in the property and secure their agreement to the owner's mortgage. This agreement usually takes the form of a *deed of postponement* under which these other occupiers declare that the bank's interest in the property as mortgagee shall rank above whatever interest they have in the property.

This, however, is not the end of the story; the position of the occupants could change later and this might affect the bank if it continued to lend, especially on a fluctuating current account. For example, a bachelor business girl mortgages her house to secure a loan to her company, her boyfriend moves in and they open a joint account at the same branch into which they pay a proportion of their salaries to service a prior mortgage on the house to a building society. (Whether they subsequently marry is neither here nor there under *Boland*.) The bank has the clearest possible notice of the boyfriend's interest and therefore the security in relation to subsequent advances would most probably be subject to her interest. A similar situation would arise if husband and wife customers, from whom the bank held a mortgage securing a current account, informed the bank that one of their parents was to live with them and that the house was to be extended at the parent's expense.

Minor interests

These consist of all interests in registered land other than registrable interests and charges, and overriding interests, for example, the rights of creditors when a bankruptcy petition has been presented against the registered proprietor. Broadly speaking, minor interests correspond to those charges registrable under the Land Charges Act 1972 in the case of unregistered land. Minor interests require protection by an entry on the register although even when registered not all such interests bind a purchaser. For example, except in the *Boland* situation, a purchaser takes free from a beneficiary's interest under a trust; this is transferred, as you have seen, to the proceeds of the sale.

The Register

Look at Fig. 15.2 which reproduces a typical register from the Land Registry. You will see that it is divided into three parts.

(a) The *Property Register* describes the land and the estate for which it is held, refers to a map or plan showing the land (also given in Fig. 15.2) and notes any interest held for the benefit of the land, such as easements or restrictive covenants.

(b) The *Proprietorship Register* gives the nature of the title (*see* below) and the name, address and occupation of the registered proprietor. It sets out any restrictions affecting his or her right to deal with the land. In the case of the register reproduced, there are no such restrictions.

(c) The *Charges Register* contains entries relating to rights against the land, such as mortgages and restrictive covenants and notices protecting rights over the land, for example, those of creditors when a bankruptcy petition has been presented against the proprietor or a spouse's right to occupy a house owned by the other spouse. In Fig. 15.2 covenants are referred to and reproduced in the form of a schedule.

Read the Charges Register through in Fig. 15.2. You will see that in addition to the covenants mentioned above, a lease of the property was granted in 1935 and in 1981 Mid Town Bank Limited took an equitable mortgage from the registered proprietors (the joint freeholders) as security for a loan, registering a Notice of Deposit of a Land Certificate to secure its interest.

H.M. LAND REGISTRY

| Edition 3 | opened 1.5.1981 | TITLE NUMBER 00002 | | This register consists of | 2 pages |

A. PROPERTY REGISTER
containing the description of the registered land and the estate comprised in the Title

| COUNTY | DISTRICT |
| BLANKSHIRE | BROXMORE |

The Freehold land shown and edged with red on the plan of the above Title filed at the Registry registered on 12 October 1934 known as 2 Moon Street.

B. PROPRIETORSHIP REGISTER
stating nature of the Title, name, address and description of the proprietor of the land and any entries affecting the right of disposing thereof

TITLE ABSOLUTE

Entry number	Proprietor, etc
1.	ROBERT BROWNING, Sales Representative, and ELIZABETH BARRETT BROWNING, his wife, both of 4 Moon Street, Broxmore, Blankshire, registered on 1 May 1981.

Demand No 8304616 4/82 W & W Ltd 13.4

Register Model III

Any entries struck through are no longer subsisting

Fig. 15.2   A Land Registry register

Page 2   TITLE NUMBER   00002

C. CHARGES REGISTER
containing charges, incumbrances etc adversely affecting the land and registered dealings therewith

Entry number	The date at the beginning of each entry is the date on which the entry was made on this edition of the register	Remarks
1.	1 May 1981-A Conveyance of the land in this title dated 30 September 1934 and made between (1) Mary Brown (Vendor) and (2) Harold Robins (Purchaser) contains the following covenants: "The Purchaser hereby covenants with the Vendor for the benefit of her adjoining land known as 27, 29, 31, 33 and 35 Cabot Road to observe and perform the stipulations and conditions contained in the Schedule hereto. <u>THE SCHEDULE before referred to</u> 1. No building to be erected on the land shall be used other than as a private dwellinghouse. 2. No building to be erected as aforesaid shall be converted into or used as flats, maisonettes or separate tenements or as a boarding house. 3. The garden ground of the premises shall at all times be kept in neat and proper order and condition and shall not be converted to any other use whatsoever. 4. Nothing shall be done or permitted on the premises which may be a nuisance or annoyance to the adjoining houses or to the neighbourhood."	
2.	1 May 1981-LEASE dated 25 July 1935 to Charles Jones for 99 years from 24 June 1935 at the rent of £45.	Lessee's title registered under 00003
3.	1 May 1981-NOTICE of Deposit of Land Certificate with Mid Town Bank Limited of 2 High Street, Broxmore, Blankshire, registered on 1 May 1981.	

Any entries struck through are no longer subsisting

Fig. 15.2 Cont.

H.M. LAND REGISTRY		TITLE NUMBER	
		00002	
ORDNANCE SURVEY PLAN REFERENCE	SF 6205	SECTION C	Scale 1/1250
COUNTY BLANKSHIRE	DISTRICT BROXMORE		© Crown copyright 1974

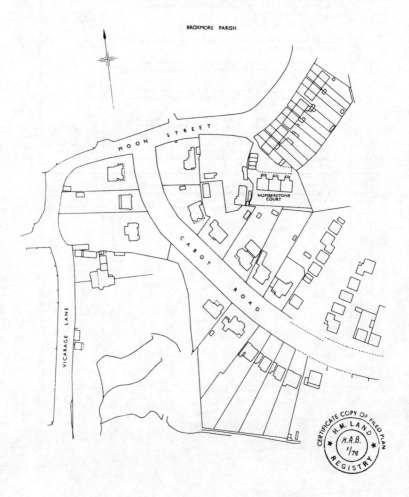

Fig. 15.2 Cont.

Each registered proprietor is given a *land certificate* containing a copy of these entries. This is the document of title which is kept until the land is sold or charged, by deposit of the certificate with a bank for example. Proof of title is, however, the Register itself because the land certificate may become out of date through subsequent entries on the Register.

Registration

This is still not compulsory in all areas of the country. Even in a compulsory registration area, registration is only necessary on a conveyance on sale of a freehold or the creation or assignment on sale of certain leases. In other words, if a property has been owned by the same person for many years, even though it may be situated in a compulsory registration area, the title will not be registered. It will have to be registered, however, as soon as the property is sold. This is what happened in the case of the property referred to in Fig. 15.2. A consequence for you is that for the foreseeable future you have to have an understanding of both registered and unregistered land until, with the passing of time, all property in compulsory registration areas is sold and the remaining areas become subject to compulsory registration and the same process takes place there.

We mentioned the registration of leases a little earlier. Registration of a lease is only compulsory where it is granted for a term of 21 years or more, or, a lease with 21 or more years to run is assigned on sale in a compulsory registration area.

Registered titles

Four types of registered title exist.

(a) *Absolute.* This title is state-guaranteed and subject only to entries on the charges register and overriding interests.

(b) *Qualified.* This title is granted following an application for registration of an absolute title where the title can be established for only a limited period or subject to certain reservations. A qualified title is very rare. It may be converted to title absolute or good leasehold (as appropriate) at any time, and *must* be on an application by the proprietor, provided the registrar is satisfied as to the title.

(c) *Possessory*. This title is not guaranteed prior to its first registration and must therefore be investigated by a prospective purchaser as though the title was unregistered. However, provided the purchaser satisfies the registrar that he is in possession, the registrar must convert a possessory title to absolute title on an application by the proprietor, provided that the registrar is satisfied as to the title or the land has been registered with possessory title for at least twelve years and the registrar is satisfied that the proprietor is in possession.

(d) *Good leasehold*. Obviously, this applies only to leaseholds. It is evidence that the leaseholder's title is good but it does not guarantee title to the freehold from which the lease was granted. A good leasehold title may be upgraded to title absolute at any time and *must* be on an application by the proprietor, provided the registrar is satisfied as to the freehold and any intermediate leasehold title.

Title to property and its transfer

Here we will deal with all the types of property that are commonly taken as security for bankers' advances and which we mentioned at the start of this chapter. Once again, however, much of the text will be devoted to land, both because it is more complicated to prove and transfer title to land than other forms of property, and because land is the best and usually preferred form of security for banks to take. However, we have already said much about the title to land in the previous section (in order to give coherence to our discussion of land) and therefore you will be beginning this section with a good introduction.

Land

The method by which title to land is transferred depends primarily upon whether the title is registered or unregistered. Unfortunately, we have to spend more time on unregistered land, because the methods are more complicated, even though most urban land is now registered. Simplification of the system was, you will remember, the main reason for introducing the system of land registration.

Unregistered land

Freehold. The freehold title to unregistered land is proved by a collection of deeds and documents which together must show a chain of title concluding with that of the vendor. They are known as the *title deeds*.

Transfer of title is effected in two stages. The first stage is the *contract*; this binds vendor and purchaser to complete the transfer. It is usual to use the Law Society's standard contract for sale which contains two closely printed A4 pages of general conditions and a further page of proforma (fill in the missing words type) special conditions which vary the general conditions where necessary. The contract can be bought at any law stationers. The second stage is the *conveyance*, which transfers the legal estate to the purchaser (*see* Fig. 15.3).

A *contract* for the sale of land must be in writing or evidenced by a signed memorandum in writing to be enforceable: Law of Property Act 1925, s.40. In practice the method adopted is usually an 'exchange of contracts'. By the Law of Property Act 1925, s.52(1), the *conveyance* must be by deed.

Under the contract of sale the vendor must produce for the purchaser's inspection an *abstract of title* showing evidence of title going back at least fifteen years to a good root of title. This may be:

(a) a *conveyance* which transferred the legal estate to the vendor;

(b) a *mortgage*; or

(c) an *assent*, a signed document transferring the legal estate in land from the personal representatives of a deceased holder to the person who inherits the land under the will or intestacy.

Following the exchange of contracts, the purchaser (usually his solicitor) examines the deeds, making such enquiries as he or she considers to be necessary. Arrangements are then made for completion, at which the conveyance executed by both parties is handed over with the title deeds (of which the conveyance now forms part) in exchange for the balance of the purchase price, usually in the form of a bank draft.

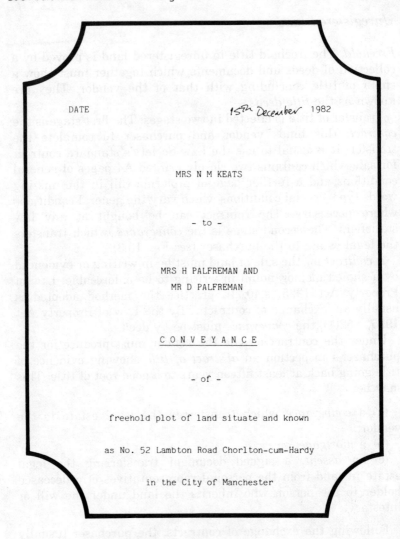

DATE   15ᵗʰ December 1982

MRS N M KEATS

- to -

MRS H PALFREMAN AND
MR D PALFREMAN

C O N V E Y A N C E

- of -

freehold plot of land situate and known

as No. 52 Lambton Road Chorlton-cum-Hardy

in the City of Manchester

Fig. 15.3 A conveyance of unregistered land

THIS CONVEYANCE is made the _fifteenth_ day of _December_ One thousand
nine hundred and eighty two between NORAH MARIAN KEATS of 52 Lambton
Road Chorlton-cum-Hardy in the City of Manchester (hereinafter
called 'the Vendor') of the one part and HELLEN PALFREMAN and DAVID
PALFREMAN of 15 Zetland Road Chorlton-cum-Hardy aforesaid (hereinafter
called 'the Purchasers') of the other part _____

WHEREAS the Vendor is the owner in fee simple in possession of the
property hereinafter described and intended to be hereby conveyed
subject as hereinafter mentioned but otherwise free from incumbrances
at the price of Twenty two thousand pounds (£22,000) _____

NOW THIS DEED WITNESSETH as follows:

1 _____ IN pursuance of the said agreement and in consideration
of the sum of Twenty two thousand pounds now paid by the Purchasers to
the Vendor (the receipt whereof the Vendor hereby acknowledges) the
Vendor as Beneficial Owner hereby conveys unto the Purchasers ALL THAT
plot of land situate in Chorlton-cum-Hardy aforesaid containing in the
whole Four hundred and thirty square yards or thereabouts and more
particularly delineated and described in the plan annexed to the
Conveyance (hereinafter called 'the Conveyance') made the Seventeenth
day of September One thousand nine hundred and twenty five between J.
Lane & Sons Limited of the one part and Jabez Whitehead of the other
part and thereon edged red AND ALSO the dwellinghouse erected thereon
and numbered 52 Lambton Road Chorlton-cum-Hardy aforesaid TOGETHER
with the rights easements and appurtenances thereto belonging and the
rights of way and drainage granted by the Conveyance EXCEPT and
RESERVED like rights of way drainage and otherwise as more
particularly mentioned to be excepted and reserved in and by the
Conveyance AND ALSO EXCEPT and RESERVED as mentioned to be excepted
and reserved in and by a Conveyance made the Twenty fourth day of
November One thousand nine hundred and twenty four between the Right
Honourable Maurice Baron Egerton of Tatton of the first part Montague
Ellis and Robert Henry Grenville Tatton of the second part and the

Fig. 15.3 Cont.

said J. Lane & Sons Limited of the third part and Ernest Lane and
Clifford Lane of the fourth part TO HOLD the same unto the Purchasers
in fee simple as joint tenants in law and equity SUBJECT henceforth to
the payment of the yearly rent charge of Five pounds limited in use
and made payable by and to the observance and performance of the
covenants on the part of the Grantee and the conditions contained or
referred to in the Conveyance_____

2 _____ IT IS HEREBY CERTIFIED that the transaction hereby
effected does not form part of a larger transaction or of a series of
transactions in respect of which the amount or value or the aggregate
amount or value of the consideration exceeds Twenty five thousand
pounds _____

IN WITNESS whereof the parties hereto have hereunto set their hands
and seals the day and year first before written.

SIGNED SEALED and DELIVERED by
the said Norah Marian Keats   *N. M. Keats*
in the presence of:

  B.S. Wordsworth
  Dove Cottage
  Egerton Road
  Chorlton, Manchester
  MANAGER

SIGNED SEALED and DELIVERED by
the said Hellen Palfreman and   *Hellen Palfreman.*
David Palfreman in the presence
of:
           David Palfreman

  Jill Barber

  50 Malvern Road
  Alkrington
  middleton
  Manchester

  Director's Secretary

Fig. 15.3 Cont.

Leasehold. A leaseholder can transfer his legal estate by *assigning* to another person the whole of the remaining term unless prohibited from doing so by the terms of his lease. (An *assignment* is a deed transferring the legal estate in leasehold land. It is similar to the conveyance used to transfer unregistered freehold land.) Subject to the same proviso, a leaseholder may grant a *sub-lease* for a term shorter than that which he himself holds.

Title is also evidenced by a collection of *title deeds*, although the actual lease to be assigned may be the only document. Completion is also similar to completion on sale of freehold land, the lease or an assignment of the original lease being delivered against a bank draft for the balance of the purchase price or payment of the rent. A copy of the lease or the assignment will be placed with the other title deeds.

Registered land

Title to registered land is proved by the registers at the Land Registry. Transfer of a registered title is effected by a short, simple form of registered transfer (*see* Fig. 15.4). This replaces the conveyance or assignment necessary to transfer title to unregistered land.

At completion, the vendor hands to the purchaser the land certificate and a signed registered transfer against payment of the balance of the purchase price. The land certificate and completed transfer are sent to the Land Registry where the new proprietor is entered on the register and on the land certificate. The land certificate is then returned to the new proprietor as evidence of title.

Stocks and shares

Stocks and shares can be classified in two ways: according to the organisation which issued them, for example, a registered company or a local authority (we are not concerned only with shares in companies); or according to the method by which title to them is established and transferred. As a banker you are concerned with both classifications but here it is appropriate for us to adopt the latter.

Under this classification, stocks and shares are classified as registered or bearer securities.

Form 19(JP)
HM Land Registry

Land Registration Acts, 1925 to 1971

Stamp pursuant to section 28 of the Finance Act 1931 to be impressed here.	When the transfer attracts Inland Revenue duty, the stamps should be impressed here before lodging the transfer for registration.

(1) For a transfer to a sole proprietor use printed form 19.

(1) TRANSFER OF WHOLE TO JOINT PROPRIETORS
(Freehold or Leasehold)

(Rules 98 or 115, Land Registration Rules 1925)

County and district (or London borough)

Title number(s)

Property

Date .... 19 ...... In consideration of ....

(2) Strike out if not required.

.... pounds (£ ....) (²)the receipt whereof is hereby acknowledged

(3) In BLOCK LETTERS, enter full name(s), postal address(es) and occupation(s) of the proprietor(s) of the land.

(³)I/We

(4) If desired, or otherwise as the case may be (see rules 76 and 77).

(⁴)as beneficial owner(s) hereby transfer to:

(5) In BLOCK LETTERS, enter full names, postal addresses and occupations of the transferees for entry on the register.

(⁵)

(6) Any special clause should be entered here.

the land comprised in the title above mentioned (⁶) (⁷)

(7) A transfer for charitable uses should follow form 36 (see rules 121 and 122).

(continued overleaf)

Fig. 15.4 A form of registered transfer
(Courtesy: Oyez, The Solicitor's Law Stationery Society plc)

(8) *Delete the inappropriate alternative.*

The transferees declare that the survivor of them(8) $\frac{can}{cannot}$ give a valid receipt for capital money arising on a disposition of the land.

(9) *If a certificate of value for the purposes of the Stamp Act 1891 and amending Acts is not required, this paragraph should be deleted.*

(9)*It is hereby certified that the transaction hereby effected does not form part of a larger transaction or series of transactions in respect of which the amount or value or aggregate amount or value of the consideration exceeds £*

(10) *This transfer must be executed by the transferee(s) as well as the transferor(s).*

(10)Signed, sealed and delivered by the said

_____

in the presence of

Name

Address

Occupation

(Seal)

(10)Signed, sealed and delivered by the said

_____

in the presence of

Name

Address

Occupation

(Seal)

(10)Signed, sealed and delivered by the said

_____

in the presence of

Name

Address

Occupation

(Seal)

(10)Signed, sealed and delivered by the said

_____

in the presence of

Name

Address

Occupation

(Seal)

Fig. 15.4 Cont.

Registered securities

Title. The company or other organisation issuing the securities will maintain a register in which the holder's name and address and the amount of his holding is recorded. The register is the proof of title but the registered holder receives a certificate in his name as *prima facie* evidence of title.

Every company maintains its own register of shareholders and stockholders. The holders of British government stock and national savings securities are registered on either the National Savings Stock Register, and receive a certificate issued by the Director of Savings, or in books kept at the Bank of England and receive a certificate issued by the Bank.

Transfer of title. Legal title is effected by sending the appropriate transfer form signed by the transferor, and sometimes the transferee, and the relevant certificate to the organisation which issued the securities for details of the new ownership to be entered on the register. A new certificate is then issued in favour of the transferee.

The form of transfer used is nearly always the simplified *stock transfer form*. This contains details of the price paid for the shares, the name of the issuing organisation, the number and value of the securities held, details of the transferor and transferee and the former's signature. It is not signed by the transferee. To meet the needs of the Stock Exchange's computerised accounting system, shares in public companies are transferred using the Talisman transfer form. This is a variant of the stock transfer form. The transferee is always SEPON Ltd. In a few cases the transfer must be by *deed* or by a *common form of transfer* signed by both parties. These alternative methods are almost identical except that the latter is not sealed, and even this involves only sticking small, round, red adhesive pieces of paper by the side of the signatures or putting the letters 'L.S.' (*locus sigilli*—the place of the seal) inside a small circle. Units in *unit trusts* can be transferred by any method approved by the trustees but most commonly by a stock transfer form. Usually, however, the holder realises his investment by selling the units back to the managers of the trust. This requires completion of the *form of renunciation* on the back of the certificate.

Some registered securities are not transferrable at all, however, for example, national savings securities and the shares in some building societies. This has obvious implications should they be offered to you as security.

Bearer securities

In Chapter 8 you learnt that the main types of bearer securities are bearer bonds; scrip certificates or letters of allotment; share warrants to bearer and bearer debentures. You also learnt that they are all *negotiable instruments*. This being the case, the person in possession is the holder, (*see* page 304) even if he stole the security, and can transfer a perfect title by mere delivery to a person who takes a transfer in good faith and for value. Clearly, bearer securities are excellent for security purposes.

Remember, the holder of a bearer negotiable instrument may not necessarily be its true owner. While it is reasonable to presume that he is, he may have found or stole the security. Nevertheless, this would not prejudice a bank who took the security in good faith and for value.

Life policies

Title to a life policy is vested in the policy-holder and the policy is evidence of title.

Insurable interest

The policy-holder may or not be the person whose life is assured because it is possible to insure lives other than your own. What is required is an *insurable interest*.

Except where a person insures his or her own or spouse's life, an insurable interest is a *pecuniary* interest, in other words the financial loss which would be suffered by the proposer on the death of the person whose life is insured. For example, a creditor can insure the life of his debtor to the amount of the debt and a guarantor can insure the life of the principal debtor to the amount of the guarantee.

Assigning a life policy

Perhaps you have never considered the idea of *transferring title* to a life policy but this can be done by *assigning* (transferring) the interest, that is, the right to claim under the policy, to a third person. The transferee does not have to have an insurable interest in the life assured. (*Assured* rather than *insured* is the correct term). The ability to assign a life policy is important to a bank not only for the purpose of taking a life policy as security but also because sale of the policy may be a more profitable alternative to surrender if the policy holder wishes, or is compelled, to realise the value of the policy before its maturity. Companies exist which buy life policies as medium to long-term investments.

By the Policies of Assurance Act 1867, s.5, an *assignment* of a life policy must be either by (a) an indorsement on the policy itself; or (b) by a separate document of assignment in the form laid down in the Act.

After a policy has been assigned the assignee may sue, if necessary, for the policy moneys in his own name although this right is subject to two conditions. First, he takes the policy subject to any prior defects in title or personal defences available against the assignor, for example, invalidation of the policy for non-disclosure of material facts—that he was a regular hang-glider pilot for instance. In other words, any defence which would have been available against the policy-holder (the assignor) is available against the assignee. (Compare negotiation: *see* Chapter 16.) Second, notice in writing must be given to the company which issued the policy. This notice is necessary to vest legal title to the policy in the assignee. (Again, compare negotiation.) Sometimes a policy will be assigned a number of times. Where there are second or subsequent assignments, priority of interests between the assignees is determined by the date on which notice of assignment was received by the issuing company.

A life policy will state where notices of assignment are to be given; usually this will be the company's principal place of business. The company is bound by the 1867 Act to give written acknowledgement of the notice if requested in writing to do so by the assignee. A small fee is payable for this although it is often waived.

Guarantees

The question of title to a guarantee or transfer of that title does not really arise. The guarantee itself is proof of the lender's right to enforce payment against the guarantor according to the terms of the guarantee and this right is never in practice transferred. However, bank guarantees are usually expressed to be in favour of the bank, 'its successors and assigns'. This means that if there is any change in the constitution of the bank, or if it merges or is amalgamated with another bank, as Williams and Glyn's was with the Royal Bank of Scotland, for example, the guarantee is not invalidated.

Debentures

You learnt in Chapter 13 that debentures are documents issued by a company acknowledging a loan and any charge securing it. Once again, it is not usual to talk about 'title' to a debenture since the debenture itself is proof of entitlement to the rights it confers. Debentures are transferred, however; a fixed-sum debenture quoted on a stock exchange being transferrable in the same way as stocks and shares. A bearer debenture can be transferred by mere delivery.

Banks' debentures are usually transferrable, but one bank that accepts a transfer of a debenture from another or from any other organisation will seldom rely on the wording of the original debenture. Each bank has its own practices and procedures, albeit similar, and each drafts its own debentures to cover all foreseeable contingencies in conformity with those practices and procedures and its own experience. Thus, it is standard practice to take a new debenture in its own form and have the original debenture discharged.

Taking property as security

In Chapter 13 we covered types of security arrangements, such as depositing documents of title, and defined the meaning of the terms 'mortgage', 'pledge', 'hypothecation', 'lien' and 'charge'. Before you read any further ask yourself whether you can remember their meanings. If you cannot, go back to pages 489–92 and revise, since we will be assuming a good working knowledge of these terms in the text which follows.

Land

You already know that security is taken over land by executing a *mortgage*. You also know from this chapter that this creates an interest in the land mortgaged and that this interest can be legal or equitable. Thus, mortgages of land may be either legal or equitable. (The same is true for most other types of property taken as security.)

A *legal mortgagee* acquires *rights against the property itself* in addition to the personal action available against the mortgagor for the principal and interest due. An *equitable mortgage* gives no rights against the property, only *personal rights* against the borrower, principally a right to share in the proceeds of sale of the property when sold and a right to seek the court's aid in enforcing this right. The wider and more effective remedies given by a legal mortgage are today the main practical distinction between legal and equitable mortgages.

Legal mortgage

A legal mortgage is nearly always effected by a charge by deed expressed to be by way of a legal mortgage. This legal charge was a creation of the Law of Property Act 1925. Before then, and very occasionally today, a mortgage of land was a form of lease.

In the case of *unregistered land*, the mortgage will normally be retained by a bank with the other title deeds. These will have previously been obtained from the prospective borrower. In the case of *registered land*, the mortgage (charge form) must be sent with a duplicate and the land certificate to the Land Registry. The Registrar will retain the land certificate and issue to the bank in its place a charge certificate which includes one sewn-in copy of the mortgage. The legal charge will be entered on the Charges Register. (*See* Fig. 15.5.)

Equitable mortgage

A bank can create an equitable mortgage in one of two ways:

(a) By taking a *deposit of the title deeds or land certificate*. Provided the deposit is intended to be used as security, and is not taken for safe custody, the deposit itself is sufficient to create an equitable mortgage even if a memorandum of deposit is not taken (*see* below).

SECS.

This Legal Charge *made the*   *day of*   *One thousand nine hundred*
and   **Between**

of (whose registered office is at)

(hereinafter called 'the Mortgagor') of the one part and **Training Bank Plc** *(hereinafter called 'the Bank') of the other part*

Witnesseth *as follows:*—

'Base Rate' means the Base Rate of the Bank as stipulated from time to time by notices in branches of the Bank as being the basis upon which interest rates on advances are calculated

1.   **The Mortgagor Hereby Covenants** with the Bank that the Mortgagor will pay to the Bank on demand all moneys and liabilities now or hereafter due from or incurred by the Mortgagor to the Bank on any account whatever whether for the balance then owing from the Mortgagor on any account or accounts of the Mortgagor with the Bank or for cheques notes or bills drawn accepted or endorsed by the Mortgagor or for advances made to the Mortgagor or for the accommodation or benefit of the Mortgagor and whether actually or contingently alone or jointly with another or others and whether as principal or surety for any other person or persons firm or company and in whatever name style or firm or otherwise howsoever including (but without prejudice to the generality of the foregoing) the charges of the Bank's Surveyors and Solicitors in connection with the property and all costs charges and expenses which the Bank may pay or incur in stamping perfecting or enforcing this security and in the negotiation for and preparation and execution of these presents or in obtaining payment or discharge for such moneys or liabilities or any part thereof or in paying any rent rates taxes or outgoings or in insuring repairing maintaining managing or realising the property hereby charged or any part thereof (to the intent that the Bank shall be afforded a full complete and unlimited indemnity in respect thereof notwithstanding any rule of law or equity to the contrary) and whether arising directly or indirectly in respect of this security or of any other security held by the Bank for the same indebtedness and including interest with quarterly rests discount commission and other usual banking charges such interest being computed both before and after any such demand at a rate varying from time to time stipulated by the Bank at any time and from time to time hereafter by notice in writing to the Mortgagor but not at any time of fall below   per cent per annum and in the absence of any stipulation to be

Insert   rates of Interest.

at a rate of   per cent above Base Rate or   per cent per annum whichever shall be the higher and notwithstanding any account intended to be hereby secured may from any cause cease to be carried on as an ordinary banking account and so that interest shall be payable at the rate aforesaid as well after as before any judgment obtained hereunder and that after such demand interest shall be payable at the rate aforesaid on the whole sum due for principal and interest or otherwise at the date of such demand

2.   (i) **For** the purpose of securing such account or accounts the Mortgagor as Beneficial Owner charges by way of Legal Mortgage the premises described in the Schedule hereto together with all fixtures whatsoever now or at any time hereafter affixed or attached to the said premises or to any part thereof other than trade machinery as defined by Section 5 of the Bills of Sale Act 1878 with the payment to the Bank of the principal money liabilities interest and other money hereby covenanted to be paid by the Mortgagor

Only applicable in the case of a charge by a company and to be deleted in any other case.

     (ii) For the consideration aforesaid the Mortgagor as Beneficial Owner hereby assigns unto the Bank **All and Singular** the fixed and moveable plant machinery and fixtures implements and utensils now or hereafter fixed or placed upon or used in and about the said premises respectively described in the Schedule hereto **to hold** the same unto the Bank absolutely **provided always** that if the moneys hereinbefore covenanted to be paid be duly paid according to the foregoing covenant in that behalf the security created by this Charge shall cease and determine.

3.   **Without** prejudice to the generality of the security hereby constituted it is hereby declared that this Charge is made to secure the said account or accounts and further advances by the Bank to the Mortgagor to the intent that it shall constitute a continuing security for all sums which shall on the execution hereof or at any time hereafter be or become owing by the Mortgagor to the Bank in any manner whatsoever.

4.   **The Mortgagor Hereby Covenants** with the Bank that the Mortgagor will at all times during the continuance of this security keep the whole of the said premises in complete repair and insured in an office to be approved by the Bank against loss or damage by fire in the full value thereof (of which the Bank shall be the sole and absolute judge) and will pay all premiums in respect of such insurances within seven days after the same shall have become due and will on demand produce the policies of such insurance and the receipts for every premium payable in respect thereof.

5.   **The Mortgagor Further Covenants** with the Bank that the Mortgagor at all times during the continuance of this security:—

     (i) will observe and perform all restrictive and other covenants and stipulations for the time being affecting the premises hereby charged or the mode of user or the enjoyment of the same or any part thereof

     (ii) will not without the previous consent in writing of the Bank do or suffer to be done on the property hereby charged anything which shall be deemed to be development or a change of use thereof within the meaning of the Town and Country Planning Act 1962 or any Act or Acts for the time being in force amending or re-enacting the same and any orders and regulations for the time being in force thereunder nor do or suffer or omit to be done any act matter or thing whereby any statutory instrument obligation or regulation under the said Act or Acts shall be infringed so as to prejudice the Bank or render the Bank or the premises hereby charged subject to any liability under the said Act or Acts or any of them.

6.   **It is Hereby Declared** that the powers of leasing conferred upon a Mortgagor in possession by Section 99 of the Law of Property Act 1925 and any other powers of leasing vested in the Mortgagor shall not be exercisable without the previous consent in writing of the Bank and that in addition to the powers of leasing conferred on a Mortgagee by such section it shall be lawful for the Bank at any time or times to grant any lease thereof or of any part thereof for any term or terms of years or for any derivative term or terms of years and either in possession or reversion and either with or without taking a premium for the making thereof and at such yearly or other rents and subject to such covenants and conditions and generally upon such terms as the Bank shall in its absolute and uncontrolled discretion think proper.

7.   **It is Hereby Expressly Agreed and Declared** that the power of sale and other powers conferred on a Mortgagee by the Law of Property Act 1925 shall apply to this security but without the restrictions therein contained as to giving notice or otherwise and so that for the purposes of a sale or other exercise of the said powers or any of them the whole of the moneys hereby secured shall be deemed to be due and payable immediately on the execution of these presents and that the restriction on the right of consolidating mortgage securities which is contained in Section 93 of the same Act shall not apply to this security and in any such sale the Bank may sell the fixtures comprised herein either together with the property to which they are affixed or separately and detached therefrom.

Fig. 15.5   A legal charge

8. **It is Also Hereby Declared** that it shall be lawful for the Bank at any time to exercise for and on behalf of the Mortgagor all the powers and provisions conferred on a landlord and a tenant by the Landlord and Tenant Acts 1927 and 1954 (or any statutory modification or extension thereof) in respect of the premises hereby charged but without any obligation to exercise any of such powers and without any liability in respect of powers so exercised **and** the Mortgagor hereby covenants with the Bank that the Mortgagor will as and when received deliver to the Bank all notices served on the Mortgagor in respect of the mortgaged premises under the said Acts **and** the Mortgagor hereby irrevocably appoints the Bank the attorney for the Mortgagor and in the name and on behalf of the Mortgagor or otherwise to sign seal and deliver all notices and documents as it may deem necessary or desirable for carrying out any of the powers vested in the Mortgagor by the said Acts in respect of the premises hereby charged including power to execute any lease or counterpart of any lease to be granted with power to give receipts for any compensation money payable by a landlord and with power for any receiver appointed by the Bank to enter into any arrangements as he or the Bank may consider necessary and with power for the Bank on a sale or other dealing with the said premises to execute an assurance mortgage to itself of any lease granted under the Acts or otherwise or other document vesting the premises or any part thereof in itself or any other person whether for a term of years or otherwise Provided that nothing that shall be done by or on behalf of the Bank hereunder shall render it liable to account as mortgagees in possession.

9. **Nothing** herein contained shall operate so as to merge or otherwise prejudice or affect any bill note guarantee mortgage lien simple contract obligation or other security which the Bank may for the time being have for any money or liabilities due or incurred by the Mortgagor to the Bank or any right or remedy of the Bank thereunder and the Charge hereby created is in addition to any existing Charges (if any) in favour of the Bank and to any other securities held by the Bank.

10. **The Mortgagor** will not without the consent in writing of the Bank create any further mortgage charge or other encumbrance upon the whole or any part or parts of the premises hereby charged.

11. **Any** notice or demand by the Bank hereunder may be served on the Mortgagor personally or by posting the same to the Mortgagor by letter addressed to the Mortgagor at his address herein stated or other the address last known to the Bank and any notice or demand if served by post shall be deemed served at the time when the letter containing the same is put into a Post Office situated within the United Kingdom and in proving such service it shall be sufficient to prove that the letter containing the notice or demand was properly addressed and put into a Post Office. Any such notice or demand or any certificate as to the amount at any times secured hereby shall be conclusive and binding upon the Mortgagor if given under the hand of an officer of the Bank.

Only applicable in the case of a Charge by a Company of registered land and to be deleted in any other case.

12. **The** Mortgagor hereby certifies that the Charge hereby constituted does not contravene any of the provisions of its Memorandum and Articles of Association.

13. **The** expressions 'the Mortgagor' and 'the Bank' where the context admits include their respective Successors in title and/or Assigns and if there are two or more persons as Mortgagors parties to this Deed all covenants herein contained or implied on the part of the Mortgagor shall be deemed to be joint and several covenants on their part.

In Witness whereof the Mortgagor has hereunto set his hand and seal (caused its Common Seal to be hereunto affixed) the day and year first before written.

The Schedule before referred to

Note:—(1) If any registered land is comprised in the security it must be described by reference to the Title Number
(2) If un-registered land insert a short description of the property charged including a reference to the **Conveyance** or Assignment to the Mortgagor.

Description of Property

Fig. 15.5 Cont.

Signed Sealed and Delivered
by the Said

L S

in the presence of:—

*Signature
of Witness:*

Address:

Occupation:

Signed Sealed and Delivered
by the Said

in the presence of:—

L S

*Signature
of Witness:*

Address:

Occupation:

Delete whichever is
appropriate.

The Common Seal *of*
the Mortgagor
was hereunto affixed in the
presence of:—

_____ *Director*

_____ *Secretary*

This Legal Charge
must be stamped
within thirty days
of execution.

Fig. 15.5 Cont.

(b) By taking an *equitable charge*. Such a charge is unusual since it would be unaccompanied by the title deeds but it can be created by any written memorandum (as it is called), no matter how informal, in which the borrower states that his or her property shall be security for the money advanced. As you should remember, the charge creates no actual interest in the property, but the bank can seek the court's sanction for the sale of the property if payment is not made.

Since an equitable mortgage does not convey a legal interest in the property to the mortgagee, the mortgage cannot be enforced without the consent of the court. In other words, an equitable mortgagee cannot sell the property without the court's permission while a legal mortgagee can. It is for this reason that the bank's standard *memorandum of deposit* includes an undertaking to execute a legal mortgage as and when called upon to do so by the bank (*see* Fig. 15.6).

Second mortgages

It is possible for any number of morgages, legal or equitable, to exist at the same time over one piece of land. A bank may be prepared to accept a second mortgage as security for an advance if the value of the property is sufficient to repay both the first mortgage and the proposed second mortgage, i.e. there is sufficient *equity* in the property.

The main disadvantage of a second mortgage is that the first mortgagee may exercise his legal remedies (*see* below) without reference to, and therefore to the possible detriment of, the second mortgagee.

A second legal mortgage is usually created by a legal charge and a second equitable mortgage by a general equitable charge. No deposit of title deeds or land certificate is possible for these will be in the possession of the first mortgagee.

Procedure on taking a bank mortgage

In due course you may be selected by your bank to attend a 'securities course' on which you will learn in detail about the procedure for taking a mortgage over land and other types of property. It is neither appropriate nor possible for us to detail the procedure in a book such as this but we can give you a general idea of the main steps in taking a mortgage. After all, knowing the theory behind something is not much good if you cannot understand how to put it into practice.

MEMORANDUM OF DEPOSIT OF DEEDS BY INDIVIDUALS FOR COMPANIES

To **Training Bank Plc**

1.   **I/We**   of (whose registered office is at)

                                                                                      in consideration of advances
or accommodation howsoever made or given or to be made or given to me/us and/or any other person or persons
firm or company in respect of whom I/we have given or may give you a guarantee by Training Bank
Plc (hereinafter called 'the Bank') have deposited with the Bank the title deeds and other documents specified
in the schedule hereto with intent to create an equitable mortgage upon all the hereditaments and property (real or
personal) mortgage debts and sums of money and/or perpetual yearly rent charges comprised therein or to which
the same or any of them relate in order to secure the payment and discharge on demand of all moneys and liabilities
now or hereafter due from or incurred by me/us to the Bank on any account whatever whether for the balance then
owing from me/us on my/our account or accounts with the Bank or for cheques notes or bills drawn accepted or
endorsed by me/us or for advances made to me/us or for my/our accommodation or benefit and whether actually
or contingently alone or jointly with another or others and whether as principal or surety for any other person or
persons firm or company and in whatever name style or firm or otherwise howsoever including (but without prejudice to
the generality of the foregoing) the charges of the Bank's surveyors and solicitors in connection with the hereditaments
and property and all costs charges and expenses which the Bank may pay or incur in stamping perfecting or enforcing
this security and in the negotiation for and preparation and signing of these presents or in obtaining payment or discharge
for such moneys or liabilities or any part thereof or in paying any rent rates taxes or outgoings or in insuring repairing
maintaining managing or realising the said hereditaments and property or any part thereof and whether arising
directly or indirectly in respect of this security or of any other security held by the Bank for the same indebtedness
and including interest with quarterly rests discount commission and other usual banking charges such interest being
computed both before and after any such demand at a rate varying from time to time stipulated by the Bank at any
time and from time to time hereafter by notice in writing to me/us but not at any time to fall below   per cent
Insert rates of
Interest. per annum and in the absence of any stipulation to be at a rate of   per cent above Bank Rate or   per cent per
annum whichever shall be the higher and notwithstanding any account intended to be hereby secured may from any
cause cease to be carried on as an ordinary banking account and so that interest shall be payable at the rate aforesaid
as well after as before any judgment obtained hereunder and that after such demand interest shall be payable at the
rate aforesaid on the whole sum due for principal and interest or otherwise at the date of such demand And I/we
undertake to pay and discharge all such moneys interest and liabilities as aforesaid on demand.

2.   **Without** prejudice to the generality of the security hereby constituted it is hereby declared that this charge
is made to secure the said account or accounts and further advances by the Bank to me/us to the intent that it shall
constitute a continuing security for all sums which shall on the signing hereof or at any time hereafter be or become
owing by me/us to the Bank in any manner whatsoever.

3.   **I/we** hereby undertake that I/we and all other necessary parties (if any) will on demand at my/our own
cost make and execute to the Bank or as it shall direct a valid legal mortgage or registered charge of or on the said
hereditaments and property or any part thereof and of all my/our estate and interest therein including my/our
vendors lien in the event of any sale or sales in such form and with such provisions and powers of sale leasing
appointing a Receiver or otherwise generally as the Bank or its solicitors may require including the exercise of the
statutory power of sale and other powers without notice and without any such demand as aforesaid.

4.   (i) **The** powers of leasing conferred on mortgagors in possession by section 99 of the Law of Property
Act 1925 and any other powers of leasing vested in me/us shall not apply to this security but shall only be exercisable
with the consent of the Bank in writing.

             (ii) **The** restriction on the right of consolidating mortgage securities which is contained in Section 93 of
the Law of Property Act 1925 shall not apply to this security.

5.   **This** security or any such legal mortgage or changes as aforesaid shall not be discharged or affected by the
Bank giving time or other indulgence to any person or persons firm or company nor shall it prejudice or be prejudiced
by any lien or other security to which the Bank may be at any time entitled but shall be a continuing security
notwithstanding any settlement of account or other matter whatsoever.

6.   **I/We** hereby undertake that during the continuance of this security no person shall be registered as
proprietor of the said hereditaments and property or any part thereof without the Bank's consent in writing.

7.   **I/We** hereby undertake with the Bank that I/we will at all times during the continuance of this security
keep the whole of the buildings and premises in complete repair and insured in an office to be approved by the
Bank against loss or damage by fire in the full value thereof (of which the Bank shall be the sole and absolute
judge) and will pay all premiums in respect of such insurances within seven days after the same shall have become
due and will on demand produce the policies of such insurance and the receipts for every premium payable in
respect thereof.

8.   **I/We** hereby undertake that during the continuance of this security

             (i) **I/We** will observe and perform all restrictive and other covenants and stipulations for the time being
affecting the said hereditaments and property or the mode of user or the enjoyment of the same or any part thereof

             (ii) **I/We** will not without the Bank's consent in writing do or suffer to be done on the said hereditaments
and property anything which will be deemed to be development under Section 12 of the Town and Country Planning
Act 1962 or a change of use thereof within the meaning of the said Act or any Acts for the time being in force
amending or re-enacting the same and any orders and regulations for the time being in force thereunder nor do or
suffer or omit to be done any act matter or thing whereby any statutory instrument obligation or regulation under the
said Act or Acts shall be infringed so as to prejudice the Bank or render the Bank or the said property subject to
any liability under the said Act or Acts.

9.   **Where** this memorandum is signed by more than one party the liability of each of them hereunder shall
be joint and several and every agreement and undertaking on their part shall be construed accordingly A party
hereto being a joint or a joint and several debtor shall not nor shall this security be released or discharged by his
death or by the death release or discharge or the partial release or discharge of any other joint or joint and several
debtor nor by the substitution of any other debtor or security or any change in the constitution of any partnership
of which any party hetero may be a member.

10.   Any notice or demand by the Bank hereunder may be effectually made by parol notice to me or to either
or any one or more of us by any of the Bank's officers or by notice in writing under the hand of any such officer
either served personally on me or on either or any one or more of us or left for or sent by post to me or to either or
any one or more of us at my/our address herein stated or other my/our address last known to the Bank and any
such notice or demand if served by post shall be deemed served at the time when the envelope or wrapper containing
the same is put into a Post Office situated within the United Kingdom and in proving such service it shall be sufficient
to prove that the envelope or wrapper containing the notice or demand was properly addressed and put into a
Post Office Any certificate as to the amount at any time secured hereby shall if given under the hand of an officer
of the Bank be conclusive and binding upon me/us.

11.   **Where** the context so requires or admits references herein to the Bank are to include its successors or
assigns.

Fig. 15.6   Memorandum of deposits

Dated *this*   *day of*   *One*

thousand nine hundred and

The Schedule before referred to

Deeds must be
LISTED   not
described.

Signature: Signature:

(In the case of
a Company the
memorandum
must be under
hand of a direc-
tor or directors
specially autho-
rised to sign and
a certified copy
of the resolution
conferring such
authority must
be handed to
the Bank).

Signature   Signature
   of Witness: of Witness:

Address: Address:

Occupation: Occupation:

This memoran-
dum must be
stamped within
thirty days from
date of execu-
tion.

Fig. 15.6 Cont.

The first step is to *investigate the customer's title* to the land. This may be done by an experienced member of the branch staff or contracted out to a solicitor. A search must be made of:

(a) the Land Charges Register (unregistered land), or the Land Registry Registers (registered land);
(b) the Local Land Charges Register; and
(c) in certain cases, the Registrar of Companies Register of Charges where a company mortgages its land;

to ensure that the proposed security and the customer's title to it are not subject to unacceptable adverse claims.

The decision in *Williams and Glyn's Bank Ltd.* v. *Boland and Another* (1980) highlighted the need to identify all occupiers and secure their agreement to the owner's mortgage in order to avoid an overriding interest prejudicing the right to realise the security and therefore its value.

The next step is to *value the property*. Obviously the value must be sufficient to cover the advance. If a second mortgage is proposed there must be sufficient equity in the property after the first mortgage has been repaid in full. The valuation may be carried out by branch staff or a professional surveyor, particularly when business property is offered as security.

Insurance cover must then be checked and approved. Notice of the bank's interest must be given to the company concerned.

Having completed or checked these things the mortgage is then *executed*. On a mortgage of *unregistered land* the mortgagor must sign the bank's appropriate mortgage forms and acknowledge receipt of the advance in writing. The title deeds to the land, if available, must be deposited with the bank.

On a *mortgage of registered land* the mortgagor must execute the appropriate charge and stamp it. The charge must be registered at the Land Registry.

Lastly, the bank's position as mortgagee must be *protected by registration* where necessary. A mortgage of *unregistered land*, whether legal or equitable, *accompanied* by a deposit of the title deeds cannot be registered. An exception exists where the mortgage is given by a company. In this case, it must be registered in accordance with s.395 of the Companies Act 1985. This is done by lodging the actual instrument of charge accompanied by the appropriate form with the Registrar of Companies within twenty-one days of executing the mortgage.

Any mortgage which is *unaccompanied* by a deposit of the title deeds requires registration as a class C charge at the Land Charges Registry. If legal it is registered as a puisne mortgage, if equitable as a general equitable charge. (Most such mortgages are second mortgages.) If the mortgage is a *floating charge* created by a company, it can only be registered with the Registrar of Companies.

A *legal mortgage of registered land* must be protected by sending to the Land Registry the land certificate, the original charge certificate and a duplicate, an application form and the Land Registry fee. The Registrar will register the charge, retain the duplicate and the cover of the land certificate and return the charge certificate to the bank.

As you have seen, an *equitable mortgage of registered land* is usually created by a deposit of the land certificate with the bank together with a memorandum of deposit. By doing this the bank acquires a lien on the land certificate which takes effect subject to overriding interests, registered interests and any existing entries on the register. The mortgage must be protected by sending a notice of deposit of a land certificate to the Land Registry signed by the mortgagor. The land certificate should also be sent so it can be indorsed with the notice of deposit. After indorsement, it will be returned to the bank. A bank is often prepared to have a legal charge form executed but hold it unregistered to save its customer the Land Registry fees. Such an arrangement creates only an equitable mortgage, however, and must be protected by a notice of deposit of a land certificate. The legal charge can, nevertheless, be registered at any time. This would be done, for example, if the bank thought it might have to rely on the mortgage in the near future.

The mortgagee's (bank's) remedies

Banks are no different from any other types of business organisation in seeking to protect their interests by using the law to their advantage. Theoretically, a customer is free to accept or reject the bank's terms but in practice there is often no alternative to a bank loan when an individual or an organisation wants funds in excess of resources. Clearly the bank has something the customer wants—money—and the bargain, while perfectly proper, is certainly one-sided in terms of the rights given. Even if more customers realised that banks need to lend money to make their profits as much as prospective borrowers need to borrow from them, it still would not enable the average customer to bargain over the terms of a mortgage. Thus, your starting point in this section in that bank mortgages ensure that all possible remedies are available to a bank should its security have to be realised.

Another important preliminary point to make is that the distinction between legal and equitable mortgages really becomes important when remedies need to be enforced. A *legal mortgagee's* rights are superior to those of an equitable mortgagee. This is because an equitable mortgage only gives a right of action against the borrower personally while a legal mortgage gives rights of action against the property mortgaged in addition. Thus, an equitable mortgagee is unable to take action against the property mortgaged without the court's sanction and help. We say that an equitable mortgagee has a right *in personam* (against the person) while a legal mortgagee also has rights *in rem* (against the property).

Legal mortgagee. A legal mortgagee has five remedies. These are cumulative and concurrent. In other words they may be used in any combination at the same time to ensure that the full debt is recovered.

(1) *An action for the debt.* This is a personal action against the borrower to recover the capital sum and any interest owed. It avoids the delay and effort involved in realising the security but it is only suitable where non-payment is the result of unwillingness rather than inability. This remedy is, of course, a general remedy and it is available to an unsecured creditor.

(2) *Sale of the property.* Every mortgage by deed (legal or equitable) confers on the mortgagee the power to sell the mortgaged property. However, as you might expect, this power can only be exercised if one of certain conditions is fulfilled, specifically, under the Law of Property Act 1925, s.103: (a) a demand for repayment has been made and the borrower has been in default for three months; or (b) interest under the mortgage is two or more months in arrears; or (c) the mortgagor has broken some other term of the mortgage. In practice, bank mortgage forms exclude the operation of s.103, and enable the banks to exercise the power of sale immediately a demand for repayment

of capital and/or interest is not met. If the property is *occupied*, fulfilling one of these conditions is still not enough, however. The bank must apply to the court for a possession order followed by an application for eviction if the borrower refuses to do the decent thing and go quietly! To avoid such an unpleasant process, a bank will usually give the borrower every reasonable opportunity to sell voluntarily.

A bank forced to exercise its power of sale is under a duty to take reasonable care to obtain the true value of the property. For example, in *Cuckmere Brick Co. Ltd.* v. *Mutual Finance Ltd.* (1971), the plaintiff company borrowed £50 000 from the defendant, mortgaging a building site with planning permission for 100 flats as security. Subsequently, with the defendant's permission, they obtained alternative planning permission for thirty-three houses. Some five years later the advance was called in and the site advertised for sale without any building having been started. Despite the plaintiff's protest, no mention of the planning permission was made in the advertisements for the property, which was eventually sold for £44 000. The plaintiffs were able to establish that a much higher price would have been obtained for the land if the advertisements had mentioned the planning permission. The defendants were held liable for the difference between the two values.

(3) *Appointment of a receiver.* A bank would appoint a receiver (of rent) (a) where a sale is impractical, for example, if the property is let; or (b) where the property market is depressed and a sale would be unlikely to realise sufficient to repay the advance. The power to appoint a receiver arises when the mortgagee becomes entitled to exercise his power of sale.

The money collected must be applied in the following order:

(a) in payment of outgoings such as rates and taxes;
(b) in payment of interest on prior charges, if any;
(c) in payment of insurances required by law or by the mortgage, and of the receiver's commission;
(d) in payment of interest due to the bank; and
(e) towards repayment of the principal debt due.

(4) *Foreclosure.* This is an extreme remedy and requires the court's consent. Stated simply, foreclosure deprives the mortgagor (borrower) of his equitable right to redeem the mortgaged property (*see* below) and the property becomes the mortgagee's

absolutely. It makes no difference if the value of the property greatly exceeds the debt outstanding.

In most cases, the court will make an order for the sale of the property instead of granting a foreclosure order. Thus, these orders are very rare. An order might be granted, for example, in the unusual event of the mortgagor's disappearance!

(5) *Taking possession of the property.* Originally, a mortgagee could exercise this right even if there has not been a breach of the mortgage! It is usual for the mortgage to provide, however, that this right shall not be exercised unless the mortgagor defaults in repayment. A bank will seldom take possession of mortgaged property because appointing a receiver achieves the same results without the expense and accountability involved in taking possession.

Of these five remedies (1), (2) and (4) are mainly used to recover the principal sum due and put an end to the security, while (3) and (5) are designed primarily to recover the interest due.

Equitable mortgagee. It makes a difference whether the mortgage was merely *in writing* or contained in a *deed*. If the former (under hand, as it is known), the bank (the mortgagee) only has a right (*in personam*) against the borrower (the mortgagor). Thus, a bank holding an equitable mortgage under hand cannot take direct action against the property mortgaged by its customer: it must obtain the court's sanction and aid to realise the security.

A bank's memorandum of deposit or charge form details the remedies available. These will include:

(1) *An action for the money due.*

(2) *An action for specific performance* of the borrower's undertaking to execute a legal mortgage when requested to do so by the bank.

(3) *An action for the sale of the property.*

(4) The right to apply to the court for the *appointment of a receiver.*

(5) *An action for foreclosure.*

(6) If expressly given by the mortgage, a *right to take possession.*

If the mortgage was *by deed* (under seal), the bank, for practical purposes, is in the same position as if a legal mortgage had been executed. This is because an equitable mortgage by deed gives the power of sale and the power to appoint a receiver, the two most useful remedies to a bank.

Redemption of mortgages

A mortgage is redeemed by the mortgagor repaying the advance. Once the mortgagee acknowledges receipt of the money the mortgage automatically terminates.

A mortgagor has a legal (contractual) right to redeem the property on the date stipulated in the mortgage. After this the contractual right to take back the property is lost. A moment's reflection will tell you that if enforced rigidly, this 'legal' right to redeem would be extremely inflexible and potentially unfair. In fact, several centuries ago it was not unknown for mortgagees to hide or generally make themselves unavailable on the contractual redemption date and then take possession of the land *and* bring an action for debt a few days after, on the grounds that the debt had not been repaid according to the terms of the contract—which of course it had not. Quite an amazing state of affairs but, at the time, quite legal and enforced by the courts.

Gradually, however, Equity (the principles of law developed and applied in the old Court of Chancery) began to take the view that a mortgage was given only as a *security* and that it was never intended to transfer land to the mortgagee unless the mortgagor had no reasonable chance of repaying the loan. Thus, Equity allowed a mortgagee to redeem property after the legal redemption was passed provided: (a) reasonable notice was given; and (b) the principal and interest, and the mortgagor's expenses were paid. This became known as the *equity of redemption*. Today, any term of a mortgage which attempts to prevent the borrower eventually redeeming the mortgaged property is void.

In modern mortgages, the contractual date for redemption is usually six months after the execution of the mortgage. Hence, in the vast majority of cases, the mortgagor relies on the equitable right of redemption.

Stocks and shares

Of the two types of stocks and shares (registered and bearer) which we described earlier in this chapter, it is registered stocks and shares, stock exchange securities in particular, that are usually taken as security.

Registered stocks and shares

Legal mortgage. A legal mortgage is effected by transferring legal title to the shares to the bank or, more usually, to its nominee company. In practice, most banks will prefer not to go this far in order to avoid the administrative cost which would follow from being registered as the holder of the shares and therefore receiving all communications from the company to its shareholders. An equitable mortgage, including a blank transfer (*see* below), is usually preferred.

Equitable mortgage. An equitable mortgage is created by merely depositing the share certificates. It is, however, standard practice to take a memorandum of deposit. In addition a bank will often take a *blank transfer* to strengthen its position. This is an incomplete transfer form, usually omitting the transferee's name but bearing details of securities and the mortgagor's signature as transferor. This enables a bank to transfer legal ownership of the securities to its nominee company by inserting its name as transferee (thereby completing the document) and registering the transfer whenever it considers it necessary to do so. Alternatively, the transfer may be completed in favour of a purchaser if the bank exercises its power of sale under the mortgage.

A bank holding an equitable mortgage without a blank transfer would have to obtain a court order for the sale of the securities if its customer was uncooperative.

Realising the securities. Should this be necessary, we again are concerned with the practical effects of the distinction between legal and equitable mortgages. A *legal mortgage* gives a bank the right to sell the securities on default in repayment. The advance is usually repayable on demand. If a blank transfer was taken with an *equitable mortgage*, this may be completed and the shares sold, if not the borrower's consent and cooperation or a court order is required for the sale of the securities.

Bearer securities

The first point to make is that bearer securities are charged by *pledge* and not by mortgage. The second is that bearer securities are negotiable instruments and therefore their deposit alone is sufficient to transfer legal title to them. Provided that the securities are taken in good faith, for value and without notice of any defect in the customer's title, a perfect legal title is obtained.

If you think about it, equitable mortgages of bearer securities do not arise because a legal mortgage is obtained by their mere deposit.

Unit trusts

Trusts give rise to equitable interests in the trust property and therefore the holder of the units only has an equitable interest in them. This, in turn, means that only an *equitable mortgage* of unit trust certificates is possible.

The mortgage can be created in two ways:

(a) by transferring the units into the name of the bank's nominee company and taking a memorandum of deposit, or

(b) by depositing the certificates, which remain in the customer's name, with a memorandum of deposit. The form of renunciation on the back of the certificate may be signed by the mortgagor because this will enable the bank to send the certificates to the managers of the trust and obtain repayment. Alternatively, a blank stock transfer form may be taken which enables a later transfer into the name of the bank's nominee company to be made. Notice of the charge should be sent to the managers who will acknowledge and record it.

Life policies

A *legal mortgage* of a life policy is taken by an *assignment under seal* (by deed) of the mortgagor's rights to the policy moneys. Written notice of the assignment must be given to the issuing company. An *equitable mortgage* is taken by the policy being deposited with the bank, usually supported by a memorandum of deposit which sets out the purpose of the deposit (for security and not for safe custody), the terms of the mortgage and the rights of the bank as mortgagee. Equitable mortgages of life policies are comparatively rare because a legal mortgage is a much better security and is easily effected.

Guarantees

In Chapter 13 you learnt that a guarantee is 'A promise to answer for the debt, default or miscarriage of another', that the guarantor, or surety, incurs secondary liability—'If X doesn't pay you, I will'—and that written evidence of the guarantee must exist if it is to be enforced through court action. You also learnt that a guarantee involves a *personal obligation* and not the acquisition of rights over specific property. We are not, therefore, concerned with, say, legal or equitable mortgages, registration and protection, etc., as we have been so far. Nevertheless, it is usual to take collateral security from the guarantor, for example, a deposit of title deeds or land certificate, to back up the personal undertaking unless there is absolutely no doubt about the guarantor's present and future ability and willingness to pay if called upon to do so. Where collateral security is taken, a bank must protect its position, according to the security taken, in the ways we have described above.

You should not understand from the above that taking a guarantee involves nothing more than obtaining a signature on a standard form. There are procedures to follow and pitfalls to avoid analogous to making searches and valuations in respect of land.

Legal capacity
The first of these steps is to check on the legal capacity of the principal debtor and the proposed guarantor. Regarding the former, you have already seen the potential problems posed by the lack of contractual capacity of clubs and societies and by limited companies acting *ultra vires*. However, provided the proposition satisfies the general lending considerations (*see* Chapter 13), a loan can be safely made supported by a guarantee provided a suitable indemnity clause is included in the guarantee.

In relation to the legal capacity of the guarantor, certain special cases warrant a specific mention. If a bank takes a guarantee from two or more *co-sureties* they must accept *joint and several liability* so that:

(a) if one of them dies the estate remains liable on the guarantee—that surety may, for example, be the one with most money; and

(b) a right of action is gained against each co-surety until repayment in full has been made.

A simple but important rule which must be rigidly adhered to is that a joint guarantee must be signed by *all* the guarantors. If it is not, it is not enforceable against any of them. In *National Provincial Bank* v. *Brackenbury* (1906), for example, three out of four guarantors signed the guarantee and the bank advanced money in anticipation of the remaining signature. The fourth guarantor died without signing. In an action to enforce the guarantee, the failure to obtain the fourth guarantor's signature was held to discharge the liability of the other three.

Should one co-surety repay the whole debt, that surety has a right to compensation from the others in proportion to their respective liabilities under the guarantee.

Partnerships also require special care. A partner has no *implied* authority to give a guarantee in the firm name unless giving guarantees is part of the firm's usual course of business. You must, therefore, ensure than any guarantee given by a partnership is signed by *all* the partners in the firm.

A *registered company* can only give a guarantee if power to do so is given in its memorandum of association. This is, in fact, usually the case. A guarantee by a company must be accompanied by a certified copy of the board's resolution authorising it. To avoid any problems, banks provide draft resolutions for this purpose.

Various statutory restrictions are imposed on a company's power to give a guarantee. For example, the Companies Act 1985 prohibits, with exceptions, a company from giving a guarantee which enables a person to purchase or subscribe for its own shares, or those of its holding company; and from guaranteeing a loan by a third person to one of its directors or a director of its holding company.

Reality of consent

A guarantee is an extremely serious obligation to incur. In the final analysis a surety is inevitably at the mercy of the principal debtor's conduct and the law demands that the surety is in a position to make a free and independent decision whether or not to incur the obligation. Thus, a *misrepresentation of fact* by the creditor, in our case the bank, which misleads the surety will entitle the surety to avoid liability under the guarantee.

More subtle is the problem of *undue influence* which, if proved, again enables the surety to avoid his or her obligations. Undue influence can take many forms but they all have the effect of preventing the person influenced from making a free and independent judgment. In some relationships, for example, solicitor and client, parent and child, a position of dominance is presumed to exist, in others it must be proved by the person seeking to avoid the guarantee. Where the party in the dominant position then victimises the weaker so that a contract between them is clearly to the advantage of the dominant party and to the disadvantage of the weaker party, then the weaker party can set the contract aside in equity (rescind) for undue influence. This is the *ratio* of *National Westminster Bank Ltd* v. *Morgan* (1985), where the House of Lords stressed that inequality between the parties is not enough *by itself* to avoid a contract for undue influence. It must be proved that the stronger party exploited its position to its advantage and the other's disadvantage.

Occasionally a bank may be held to be in a position of dominance over a particular customer. Where this is so and a guarantee is offered by that customer, then the bank owes a very strict duty of care to the customer: *Lloyds Bank Ltd* v. *Bundy* (1975) (*see* Chapter 6). It should be pointed out, however, that this case arose more through bad banking practice than through anything else.

More usually the potential for undue influence arises between the principal debtor and the guarantor. Here the bank could be adversely affected where two conditions are satisfied. First, the dominant party in effect acts as the bank's agent at its request to make the guarantee arrangements. Second, the bank must know of the potential undue influence.

To avoid potential problems of undue influence a bank must

ensure that a prospective guarantor receives independent legal advice before signing the guarantee whenever the bank considers it or the principal debtor is in a position of dominance over the prospective guarantor. A free will clause is consequently often included in the guarantee form to the effect that the surety understands the nature of the document and the liability incurred under it. Such a clause should be witnessed by the guarantor's own solicitor, or a similar professional advisor, who should sign the accompanying 'attestation clause'. This states that the nature of the guarantee and the obligations incurred under it have been explained to the guarantor.

No presumption of undue influence arises between husband and wife, although experience has shown that most problems concerning undue influence and guarantees occur when wives guarantee the borrowing of their husbands. Remember in this context that since the passing of the Sex Discrimination Act 1975, any special treatment of a woman guarantor, such as including a 'free will' clause in her guarantee, must be based upon inability to understand or appreciate the arrangement, and not upon the grounds of sex.

Conceivably, a surety might subsequently maintain that he thought the guarantee that he signed was a completely different document; that he made a *mistake as to its nature*. A surety might maintain, for example, that he thought he was witnessing a conveyance or a will. Unlikely though this might seem, such a plea, known technically as a plea of *non est factum*, could theoretically succeed. However, negligence on the surety's part, for example signing the guarantee without reading it, will defeat the plea.

In practice this possible complication can easily be avoided by ensuring that the guarantee is signed and witnessed at the bank or attested by a solicitor. In addition, this simple precaution would subsequently prevent the guarantor from successfully pleading that his signature had been forged.

Disclosure of information

A guarantee is not a contract *uberrimae fidei* (of the utmost good faith) as, for example, is a contract of insurance. This means that a bank is not under a duty to disclose to the guarantor all the facts known to it that may be relevant. A guarantor must obtain all the information he requires. For example, in *Cooper*

v. *National Provincial Bank* (1945), the bank was held to be under no obligation to disclose to the guarantor of a wife's account that: (a) her husband was an undischarged bankrupt; (b) that he had authority to draw on the account; and (c) that the account had previously been operated in an improper and irregular fashion.

Nevertheless, a bank must obviously not mislead a prospective surety and it must ensure that any information volunteered is complete and true; and that it corrects an entire misunderstanding of the facts on the surety's part.

You will recall from Chapter 6 that a bank owes a duty of secrecy to its customer. A guarantee poses a conflict with this basic rule. Thus, it is either necessary to obtain the customer's authority to disclose relevant information to the prospective surety or to arrange a meeting with both parties to discuss any difficult situation. A surety is not entitled to have or to inspect copies of the principal debtor's account but is entitled to know the extent of the liability under the guarantee. Where the debt does not exceed the guarantee, the surety can be told the amount outstanding. However, unless the loan agreement is regulated by the Consumer Credit Act 1974 (*see* Chapter 13) where the surety is always entitled to know the extent of the liability, the surety should merely be told that the guarantee is being fully relied upon where the debt exceeds the guarantee.

If there is any material change in the principal debtor's circumstances, the bank is under no legal duty to advise the surety of this. Nevertheless, good banking practice normally demands that something should be done in order to avoid the guarantor being unfairly prejudiced by the debtor's action or situation. A meeting with the customer and surety can be arranged and, if need be, pressure exerted on the customer by a threat to demand repayment if his cooperation is not forthcoming.

Debentures

Introduction
In common with guarantees, debentures do not themselves give rise to any rights over property, merely a right *in personam* against the issuing company. They are, remember, documents which merely acknowledge a loan. However, a bank will seldom

take an unsecured debenture and you must take the appropriate steps to register (if applicable) or otherwise protect the interest the bank acquires in the property charged.

A bank will almost invariably take a debenture on its standard terms, securing all moneys owing on any account held by the company at any time. Provided the bank has a free hand and there are no prior charges on the company's property, the debenture would normally be secured by a fixed charge on the goodwill of the business, book debts and any uncalled capital; a fixed first charge by way of legal mortgage on any freehold or leasehold properties, including all fixtures and fixed plant and machinery from time to time in the properties; and a first floating charge on all the other assets of the company. What you might call comprehensive security!

Registration of charges
In addition to any registration required by virtue of the nature of the property charged, the Companies Act 1985, s.395, requires that any charge (among others) to secure an issue of debentures be registered with the Registrar of Companies. This is done by lodging the actual instrument of charge, accompanied by Companies Form 395 giving the prescribed details of the charge, with the Registrar of Companies. It is usual for the bank taking the charge to effect the registration on behalf of the company and claim back from the company the expenses involved.

By s.395, the registration must take place within twenty-one days of the creation of the charge, that is, the date it was actually signed or sealed, not necessarily the date it bears. For example, in *Esberger and Son Ltd.* v. *Capital and Counties Bank* (1913), the bank's charge was set aside because its manager had held a completed but undated memorandum of deposit of title deeds for nine months before dating it and then registering the charge within twenty-one days of having done so.

The importance of making sure that a charge is registered in accordance with s.395 is that an unregistered charge is void against a liquidator or a subsequent registered mortgagee, even though the subsequent mortgagee has notice of the prior unregistered charge. This does not, however, affect the actual loan acknowledged by the debenture, it becomes immediately repayable with the bank's rights being reduced to those of an unsecured creditor. This means that if the company goes into liquidation, the bank's claim is postponed to those of secured creditors and preferential creditors such as the Inland Revenue (for unpaid PAYE) and employees (for unpaid salaries and wages). This must be borne in mind if you are ever asked to hold unregistered a charge from a company.

Remedies of the bank

A bank's debenture will protect its position by specifying in detail the circumstances in which it can intervene to enforce its security. Merely intervening strengthens its position in so far as it *crystallises* any floating charge contained in the debenture, i.e. it fixes on the property at that time covered.

If the bank holds an *unsecured debenture*, two remedies are available; it may:

(a) sue for the principal and interest due; and

(b) petition for the winding-up of the company on the grounds that it is unable to pay its debts.

If it holds a *secured debenture*, it may in addition,

(c) exercise any of the powers conferred by the debenture, such as appoint a receiver, sell the assets charged, or take possession of the assets and carry on the business. A bank's debenture form will contain the power to appoint a receiver on the company's failure to repay. This is the remedy usually chosen by banks.

A short digression: how does a receiver differ from a liquidator? A *receiver* is appointed when the creditors believe that they can recover their money without necessarily closing down the company. A *liquidator* is appointed to wind up the company. Liquidation does, however, often eventually follow the appointment of a receiver.

A bank's debenture will provide that a receiver is the agent of the company in order that the company and not the bank is liable for his acts and remuneration. A receiver is under a duty to the company to use reasonable care to obtain the best possible price when selling the company's assets to make repayment. In *Standard Chartered Bank Ltd.* v. *Walker and Another* (1982), this duty was held to extend to a guarantor of the company's liability under the debenture because a guarantor is liable only to the same extent as the company; the more the overdraft is reduced, the better it is for him.

The facts were that the bank made a loan to a company secured by a debenture which gave the bank a floating charge on the company's assets and power to appoint a receiver. Subsequently, the directors of the company guaranteed the loan. The company's business declined and the bank eventually appointed a receiver, instructing him to realise the assets as soon as possible. He in turn instructed auctioneers to sell the company's machinery. This was expected to realise £90 000. The auction was a disaster, however, and realised only £42 800, since it was held at the wrong time of year and was poorly advertised. This only just covered the costs of the realisation and, after payment of preferential creditors, nothing remained to pay off the bank's overdraft. The bank's action to enforce its guarantee was successfully defeated on the grounds of the incompetent conduct of the auction sale which the bank had authorised indirectly through its instruction to the receiver.

While the case is primarily concerned with the duties of a receiver, the Court of Appeal stated that a bank, despite what its debenture might say, is liable to the company and a guarantor of its indebtedness for the receiver's actions to the extent that it gives the receiver directions or interferes with the receiver's conduct, for example, giving specific instructions regarding a sale.

Summary

1   The primary distinction in property law is between real property (freehold land) and personal property (everything else). This distinction is historical.

2   Bankers are primarily interested in property for its suitability as security for lending. This, however, embraces both legal and economic considerations.

3   The two possible legal estates are (a) the fee simple absolute in possession (freehold); and (b) the term of years absolute (leasehold).

4   Interests in land may be either legal or equitable. An interest does not give a right to possession, only a right to a claim against another's land.

5   The procedure for transferring title to land and protecting interests and security rights against it depends upon whether title to it is registered or unregistered.

6 Stocks and shares can be classified as registered or bearer securities.

7 Transfer of title to a life policy is effected by an assignment of the policy.

8 Security is taken over land by executing a mortgage. This may be legal or equitable; the former gives rights against the property itself in addition to the personal action available against the mortgagor for the moneys due.

9 A legal mortgagee of land's remedies are:
  (a) an action for the debt;
  (b) sale of the property;
  (c) appointment of a receiver;
  (d) foreclosure;
  (e) taking possession of the property.

10 Registered stocks and shares can be taken as security by a legal or equitable mortgage. Bearer securities are charged by pledge.

11 A legal mortgage of a life policy is effected by an assignment by deed, an equitable mortgage by a deposit of the policy.

12 A guarantee is not a contract *uberrimae fidei* but a bank must take care not to mislead the guarantor and to ensure that undue influence has not been used to obtain the guarantee. A guarantor incurs only secondary liability.

13 Any charge to secure an issue of debentures must be registered with the Registrar of Companies within twenty-one days of its creation.

Self-assessment questions

1 Distinguish between real and personal property.

2 What is the essential distinction between a freehold and a leasehold?

3 Distinguish between an estate and an interest in land and between a legal interest and an equitable interest.

4 What is meant by a puisne mortgage?

5 Why are overriding interests in land important to bankers?

6 In what ways will a bank take (a) a legal; and (b) an equitable mortgage over land?

7 Name the remedies of a bank that holds a legal mortgage over land. How do they differ from those acquired under an equitable mortgage?

8 True or false?

(a) A bathroom suite is land within the legal meaning of the term.

(b) 'To X in fee simple from 1990', gives X a legal estate in land.

(c) 'To X absolutely until the death of Elizabeth II', creates a term of years absolute.

(d) Under the Land Charges Act 1972, registration and notice are alternative means of protecting interests in land.

(e) When title to land is registered the only search required when buying or taking a mortgage of land is a search at the Land Registry.

(f) An overriding interest arises whenever anyone can establish actual occupation of the relevant property.

(g) Exchange of contracts for the sale of land gives the purchaser an equitable interest in that land.

(h) A second mortgage of land is possible but a third mortgage is not.

(i) A customer can only redeem a mortgage by repayment according to the terms of the mortgage.

(j) A guarantee by two or more co-sureties is unenforceable unless they all signed at the same time.

9 Explain the nature of a surety's obligation under a guarantee.

10 Explain why banks commonly hold 'blank' transfer forms over registered securities in preference to completing a transfer of title to their nominee company.

11 To what extent is a bank obliged to disclose information about a debtor to the prospective guarantor.

12 In relation to debentures, what is the requirement contained in the Companies Act 1985, s.395?

Assignments

1 *Memorandum*   Date: 1 April 198–
     To: A. Student
     From: Manager
     Re: Attached letter

Please draft a reply for my signature to the attached letter suggesting what action we should take.
DP

1 Holly Bank Road
Alkrington
Manchester
25 March 198–

The Manager
Mantown Bank Plc
High Street
Mantown

Dear Sir,
Six months ago I guaranteed the account of my friend Jane up
to a maximum of £1000 while she was completing her studies.
I think she has begun to gamble in the Casino on George Street.
I would be grateful if you could tell me whether you have had
any of her cheques paid in by the casino and, if so, for how much
and the current overdrawn balance on her account.
Yours faithfully,
Jill Barber (Miss)

PS Can you explain what the following term in the guarantee
means? 'Unless otherwise expressed this Guarantee if given by
more than one guarantor is to be deemed joint and several'.

Does this mean, for example, that someone has guaranteed
her account as well as me?

2   *Memorandum*   Date: 3 April 198–
    To: A student
    From: Manager
    Re: Mortgage procedures

Good work on the letter to Miss Barber, your studies must be
going well! Another job for you.

It's clear many customers are uncertain about what a mortgage really is and, equally, that some staff are not good at
explaining this nor the steps followed in taking the security.

First, I want you to write a couple of simple paragraphs for
the word processor databank explaining (a) the purpose of a
mortgage and the position of the customer under it, and (b) what
rights we have if repayment is not made.

Second, can you draw a flowchart or algorithm showing the
sequence of steps in taking a mortgage. Don't forget to
distinguish between legal and equitable mortgages, and between
registered and unregistered land.

Let me have all this by the end of the week.

Many thanks.

DP

3 (a) Look at Fig.15.2 (Land Registry Register) and answer the following questions:

(i) What is the title number?

(ii) What kind of title do the proprietors hold?

(iii) What charges exist over the property?

(b) Look at Fig. 15.5 (Legal charge) and identify the clauses which have the following effects. (Discuss their significance with your tutor.)

(i) Securing all moneys owed at any time on any account by the mortgagor.

(ii) Making the advance repayable on demand.

(iii) An undertaking to keep the property in good repair and insured against fire.

(iv) Giving the bank power to consolidate mortgages.

(v) Exclusion of s.103 of the Law of Property Act 1925.

16 Bills of exchange: the legal framework

Chapter objectives

After studying this chapter you should be able to:
- define the concept of negotiability and relate it to the use of cheques and other bills of exchange;
- define and distinguish between types of holders of a bill of exchange;
- explain the progress of a bill of exchange from issue to discharge and the rights and liabilities of the parties arising from that progress;
- explain the possible liability of a bank in collecting and paying cheques;
- state and explain the application of a bank's statutory protection in relation to the collection and payment of cheques.

Introduction

In Chapter 8 you had an introduction to negotiable instruments in general and bills of exchange in particular. It would be a good idea to quickly re-read that chapter now since we are going to build upon the knowledge and understanding you should have acquired from it. Some of this chapter will be familiar to you, at the very least some of the terms and their meanings, but we are going to consider bills of exchange, in particular cheques, from a much more legalistic, but nevertheless practical, perspective. You must understand the basic legal framework which governs this central aspect of the business of banking.

Bills of exchange are often viewed as a 'bogey' subject by students. It is true that the subject is fairly technical and is also difficult to simplify without becoming inaccurate. However, it is usually logical and provided that you make sure that you understand each topic before moving onto the next, the pieces of the puzzle will fit together. Stage 2 students usually display a woeful lack of understanding of the subject and this is, unfortunately, sometimes reflected in quite experienced bank staff. Thus, you should make the effort to get to grips with it sooner rather than later.

The legal characteristics of a negotiable instrument

A negotiable instrument has the four following legal characteristics.

(1) *Title* is transferrable by delivery or, in the case of instruments payable to order, by indorsement completed by delivery.

(2) A person taking a transfer of the instrument in good faith and for value (a holder in due course) is unaffected by any defects in the title of prior parties as well as from mere personal defences, such as counterclaims, available among them. Thus, the transferee *can acquire a better title* than that held by the transferor. For example, a person who acquired the instrument by fraud has only a voidable title to it, but a *bona fide* transferee for value from him acquires a perfect title.

(3) The holder *can sue in his own name.*

(4) The holder *need not give notice to prior parties* to establish his title.

The law relating to negotiable instruments developed from the practices of merchants, and these distinctive legal characteristics can all be explained by their commercial origins. For example, a merchant would be unlikely to accept a negotiated bill of exchange instead of cash if he knew that his right to obtain payment of it could always be prejudiced by some defect in the title of a prior party to the bill of which he was completely ignorant. Again, it would be a ludicrous situation if each time a £5 note (a promissory note, remember) changed hands notice and details of the transfer had to be given to the Bank of England!

Types of holder

By the Bills of Exchange Act 1882, s.2, a holder is '. . . the payee or indorsee of a bill or note who is in possession of it, or the bearer thereof'. In Chapter 8 we considered the meaning of this term in some detail and you must understand this before you read further. The holder's role is, as you will see in this chapter, absolutely vital to the legal framework regulating bills of exchange.

Apart from a basic holder we must also understand what is meant by a *holder for value* and, in particular, a *holder in due course.*

Holder for value

A holder for value is a holder of a bill for which value (consideration as it is known in contract law) has at some time been given. The value need *not* have been given by the holder himself.

A holder for value can enforce the bill against all persons who became parties to the bill prior to the value being given. For example, A draws a cheque in favour of B, B indorses it for value in favour of C who gives it as a gift to D. D is a holder for value although he has given no value himself and he can enforce it against A and B. He cannot enforce it against C, however, because he gave no consideration for C's promise to pay.

Unless it can be proved otherwise, any holder is a holder for value but he obtains no better title to the bills than that possessed by his transferor, he does not take free from defects in title of prior parties. Thus, he does not enjoy the full benefit of negotiability.

Holder in due course

Definition
Section 29(1) of the 1882 Act defines a holder in due course as:

. . . a holder who has taken a bill, complete and regular on the face of it, under the following circumstances, namely (a) that he became the holder of it before it was overdue, and without notice that it had been previously dishonoured, if such was the fact; (b) that he took the bill in good faith and for value, and that at the time the bill was negotiated to him he had no notice of any defect in title of the person who negotiated it.

Since the rights of a holder in due course are in many ways what negotiability is all about, it is well worth spending time considering what must be fulfilled for a holder to be a holder in due course.

Requirements

(1) The bill must be *complete and regular* on the face of it, i.e. technically correct. An *incomplete* bill is either undated, or does not state an amount, or lacks a required signature, such as an indorsement. *Irregularity* applies to indorsements and would arise where there is a clear and serious difference between the name of the payee or indorsee and his indorsement. The discrepancy must be such that it raises doubts about the genuineness of the indorsement.

Since an indorsement can account for an irregularity in the bill, this must mean that the face of the bill includes the back! For example, in *Arab Bank* v. *Ross* (1952), the bank held two promissory notes drawn in favour of a firm 'Fathi and Faysal Nabulsy Company'. One partner had discounted them to the bank, indorsing them 'Fathi and Faysal Nabulsy'. It was held that omitting 'Company' from the indorsement made the bill irregular. The bank, therefore, was not a holder in due course of the notes, only a holder for value.

(2) The holder must have taken the bill *before it was overdue*. For example, a bill payable on 30 June is overdue on 1 July and thereafter. A bill payable on demand is overdue when it appears to have been in circulation for an unreasonable length of time. Thus, the holder of a cheque (a bill payable on demand) may find that he is not a holder in due course if he does not present it within a reasonable time of its issue. Although there are no modern decisions on the point, it is generally considered that in the absence of special circumstances a cheque is overdue if it is not presented within ten days of its issue. This does not mean, of course, that the cheque will not be paid, although this would be the case if the cheque is considered to be 'stale'. It is usual for a bank to refuse to pay a cheque which is more than six months old; instead it would be returned marked 'Out of date'.

(3) The holder must have had *no notice* of any previous dishonour. A banker marking a cheque with a reason for dishonour would clearly prevent subsequent parties from becoming holders in due course, although a transfer of such a cheque is unlikely to take place for obvious reasons.

(4) The holder must have taken the bill in *good faith*. Mere negligence is not lack of good faith; the transferee must know or suspect that all is not as it should be concerning the bill.

In *Raphael and Another* v. *Bank of England* (1885), for example, the numbers of some stolen notes were circulated to bankers and exchange dealers, including the plaintiffs, to whom they were likely to be presented. One such note was changed by the plaintiff without consulting the file of notices of lost and stolen notes, he merely asked to see the presenter's passport and obtained his signature and address on the note. On the facts, although he had been negligent, the plaintiff had taken in good faith and was therefore entitled to its value.

(5) The holder *must himself have given value for the bill*; it is not enough that value at some time has been given.

(6) At the time of the bill's negotiation to him, the holder must have *no notice of any defect in title* of the person who negotiated it. Notice means *actual* notice, or knowledge of suspicious circumstances coupled with a deliberate omission to investigate them.

What, however, does 'defective title' mean? By s.29(2) of the Act, the title of the person negotiating the bill is defective if he obtained the bill or acceptance of it by, among other things, fraud, coercion or other unlawful means.

Points to note
Since you are going to be concerned a great deal with holders in due course in any further studies in banking law or practice of banking, we are going to list a number of important points about them. The relevance and importance of some of them may well become more obvious during these further studies.

(1) Every holder is *presumed* to be a holder in due course until fraud or illegality is admitted or proved in the acceptance, issue or negotiation of the bill. The holder must then prove that value in good faith has subsequently been given for the bill.

(2) A person who takes a transfer of a *bearer bill* from a thief can be a holder in due course.

(3) The *payee* of a bill cannot be a holder in due course because the bill is *issued* to him, it is not negotiated.

(4) A person who took an order bill bearing a forged indorsement cannot be a holder and therefore not a holder in due course; he is merely a *wrongful possessor*. This is because a forged signature is entirely inoperative (s.24) and therefore the bill at law has not been indorsed at all. Thus, the person taking

the bill cannot be an indorsee and, remembering the definition of a holder, therefore not a holder.

(5) Section 55(2) of the 1882 Act states that an indorser of a bill is precluded (prevented) from denying to a holder in due course the genuineness and regularity of his signature and all previous indorsements. Now, a moment's reflection will tell us that there is something wrong here. We have just seen that a person taking under a forged indorsement is not a holder and therefore cannot be a holder in due course. And yet s.55(2) clearly implies that a person can be a holder in due course when a bill bears a forged indorsement, otherwise there would be no point in being precluded, or estopped, from denying it. Read the subsection carefully and you will see what we mean. (You will find that in s.54(2) there is a similar position. Here the acceptor is precluded from denying the genuineness of the drawer's signature on the bill.)

From what we have said, it follows that in these circumstances the term 'holder in due course' in s.55(2) must have a special meaning. It in fact means a person who would have been a holder in due course but for the forgery. In short he has the *rights* but not the status of a holder in due course against *certain parties* to the bill. Specifically, when a question of liability arises in this situation, persons signing the bill *after* the forgery are prevented from denying the genuineness of what is actually a forgery and are therefore liable to the person in possession of the bill. Hence estoppel will render the bill valid and enforceable between the parties *subsequent* to the forgery. This means that the ultimate possessor will usually be able to obtain payment from the person who transferred the bill to him and he in turn will be able to claim from the person who negotiated the bill to him and so on. The loss will eventually lie with the person who first took the bill when it bore a forged indorsement unless he or she can trace and recover from the forger. This, of course, is unlikely.

Look at Fig. 16.1. Here the true owner of the bill is C but s.55(2) gives F, in fact a wrongful possessor, the rights of a holder in due course provided the requirements of s.29(1) would have been satisfied if it were not for the break in the chain of negotiation. While D's finding of the bill and forgery of C's signature breaks the chain of negotiation and title, thereby preventing F from enforcing the bill against X, A, B, or C, F can

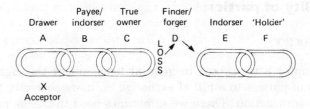

Fig. 16.1 The effect of a forged indorsement and s.55 (2)

enforce the bill against E because s.55(2) precludes E from denying that D's forgery of C's indorsement is genuine. C, still the true owner of the bill, can bring an action in conversion against E or F for the value of the bill or its return and E is most likely to stand the loss. As we shall see later, if C can recover the bill he can still enforce it against X, the acceptor.

Rights of a holder in due course

If you compare the rights of a holder in due course with the legal characteristics of a negotiable instrument, you will see that they are the practical application of those legal concepts and rules. Thus, these rights are the very essence of the concept of negotiability.

(1) He can *sue in his own name* any prior party to the bill.

(2) He can *defeat any defences arising from defects in title or from the dealings between prior parties to the bill.* An example of the former would be where the issue or transfer of the bill was obtained by fraud, making the payee or endorser's title voidable. An example of the latter would be where the cheque was taken in payment for faulty goods, entitling the drawer to a counter-claim against the payee in an action by the latter to enforce payment of the cheque. A holder in due course can therefore acquire a better title to the bill than that held by his transferor.

Remember, however, that crossing a cheque 'not negotiable' prevents a person from becoming a holder in due course if there was any prior defect in title. The title remains permanently defective.

(3) He can *transfer his title* as holder in due course to any person for value or as a gift, provided that that person was not a party to any defect which affected the bill.

Liability of parties

Introduction

In Chapter 8 we talked in general terms about the rights and duties of parties to a bill of exchange or, more correctly, parties to the transaction. There we sometimes used the term 'party' to mean anyone who was in some way connected with the bill. The term does, however, have a stricter meaning at law: a party to a bill of exchange is a person who has *signed it* and thereby incurred liability on it. Thus, it covers the drawer, the acceptor and any indorser. It does not cover anyone connected with the bill who does not sign it, such as the drawee or holder, be the latter the payee (provided he does not indorse it subsequently), the indorsee of an order bill or bearer of a bearer bill.

So, we have three parties liable on the bill. What is the *order of liability? Before acceptance* the drawer is the principal debtor and primarily liable on the bill. If the bill is negotiated, the indorser(s) incurs liability as surety for payment by the drawer. *After acceptance* the acceptor (the drawee) becomes the principal debtor and the drawer and any indorsers become sureties for the acceptor's payment. Thus, the bill can be enforced against the acceptor, drawer and any indorser. Each is liable for its full value and they can be sued individually or in any combination; they are *jointly and severally liable* on the bill.

We must now discuss the liability of each of these three parties. Unfortunately, the law appears a little complicated at first and there is very little alternative to quoting or paraphrasing the actual words of the Bills of Exchange Act 1882. However, this knowledge and understanding is important and if you carefully consider each point as you come to it you should not have too much trouble in understanding it.

The drawer

By s.55(1) the drawer:

(a) *promises* that the bill will be accepted and paid when presented, and that he will compensate any holder or indorser who has had to pay if the bill is dishonoured, provided that the proper procedure for dishonour is followed; and

(b) *cannot deny* to a holder in due course the payee's existence or his capacity to indorse the bill. Hence, if the drawer is called upon by a holder in due course to pay the bill, he cannot escape liability merely because the payee does not exist or has no capacity to indorse.

The acceptor

By s.54(2) the acceptor:

(a) *promises* that he will pay the bill in accordance with his acceptance;

(b) *cannot deny* to a holder in due course the drawer's existence, the genuineness of his signature and his power to draw the bill;

(c) *cannot deny* the drawer's capacity to indorse the bill if it is payable to his order; and

(d) *cannot deny* the existence, or the capacity to indorse, of a third person (the payee) to whom the bill is made payable.

The effect of s.54(2) is, therefore, that the acceptor cannot refuse payment to a holder in due course by proving that the drawer does not exist or that his signature was forged or that he had no capacity or authority to draw the bill, for example, where a clerk draws a bill for his employer and signs on his employer's behalf.

You may possibly have spotted an inconsistency. If the drawer's signature is forged the bill is not a bill at all because it has not been 'signed by the person giving it' as required by s.3(1). This means that there can be no holder and no holder in due course since there is no bill to be the holder of. The solution to the inconsistency is that the possessor (the apparent holder) has the *rights* of a holder in due course against the acceptor although, in reality, he is not even a holder. We mentioned this earlier on in this chapter.

Look at Fig. 16.2. A clerk, say, has forged his employer's signature and no valid bill therefore exists. However, the chain is good between the acceptor (X) and the 'holder' (F) and s.54(2) prevents X from denying that the drawer's signature was genuine. Thus, F can enforce payment against X and, in addition, each indorser is liable as surety for X's payment.

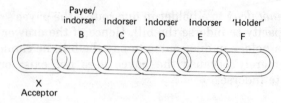

Fig. 16.2 *Forgery of the drawer's signature and s.54(2)*

The acceptor does *not* warrant, however, that an indorsement is either genuine or valid. He can, therefore, set up a forged indorsement against a person seeking to enforce the bill against him. A forged signature on a bill is, as you have seen, entirely without effect and breaks the chain of title from the acceptor to the possessor. Look back to Fig. 16.1 and our comments on it.

An indorser

By s.55(2) an indorser:

(a) *promises* that the bill will be accepted and paid when presented;

(b) *promises to compensate* any party who has had to pay as a result of its dishonour, provided that the proper procedure for dishonour is followed;

(c) *cannot deny* to a holder in due course the genuineness and regularity of the drawer's signature, or of any indorsement prior to his own;

(d) *cannot deny* to a subsequent indorsee that it was a valid bill when he indorsed it, nor that his title to it was good.

A person signing a bill other than as drawer or acceptor incurs the liabilities of an indorser to a holder in due course. Examples would include a director of a company who personally indorses a bill to which his company is a party and a bank which adds its name to enhance its acceptability, such bills being known as 'fine bills'.

Thus, indorsers are responsible to all persons who became parties to the bill after they did. They are also responsible to its holder. Hence, if the drawer's signature proves to be a forgery, the possessor of the 'bill' (remember it would not actually be a bill) has the *rights* of a holder in due course against all indorsers, as well as against the acceptor and, if an indorsement is forged, the same rights against any persons who indorsed the bill subsequent to the forgery.

The progress of a bill of exchange

In this section we trace the progress of a bill from its issue to its discharge, considering all the stages in between. The drawer may issue (put into circulation) the bill before or after it has been accepted by the drawee. The advantage of doing so after acceptance is that the bill will offer greater security to the payee or a subsequent holder who takes it from him in payment. This is because the drawee (now the acceptor) incurs primary liability on the bill by accepting it.

Acceptance

By the Bills of Exchange Act 1882, s.17(1): 'The acceptance of a bill is the signification by the drawee of his assent to the order of the drawer'. The acceptance must be written on the bill and must be signed by the drawee. A signature alone is a sufficient acceptance.

Presentment for acceptance

Presenting a bill for acceptance means exactly what it says: the holder gives or sends the bill to the drawee asking him to sign and thereby accept it. The presentment must be made at a reasonable hour on a business day.

The purpose of presenting for acceptance is first to secure the drawee's liability as a party to the bill, and second to gain an immediate right of recourse (action) against prior parties if acceptance is refused. For these reasons presentment for acceptance is always advisable but under s.39 it is obligatory only where:

(a) the bill is payable so many days after sight (for here acceptance is necessary to fix the date on which the bill becomes payable);

(b) presentment is expressly stipulated; and

(c) the bill is payable somewhere other than at the residence or place of business of the drawee, such as at a bank.

General and qualified acceptance

By s.19, a *general* acceptance is an unqualified assent to the order as drawn, whereas a *qualified* acceptance in some way varies the effect of the bill as drawn.

An acceptance is qualified, for example, if it is a partial acceptance, such as an acceptance to pay only part of the sum specified in the bill; or if it is qualified as to time, such as 'Accepted payable in 60 days' where the bill was drawn payable in 30 days. The important thing to remember is that the holder may treat any qualified acceptance as a *dishonour* of the bill and immediately take action against the drawer and any indorser.

Negotiation

Negotiation takes place when a bill is transferred in such a way as to make the transferee the holder of it. A *bearer bill* is negotiated by delivery; an *order bill* is negotiated by the indorsement of the holder completed by delivery. A bill continues to be negotiable until it has been (a) restrictively indorsed (*see* below); or (b) discharged by payment or otherwise.

Remember the importance of negotiability and its legal characteristics, in particular that a holder in due course is unaffected by any defects in the title of the transferor, that is, he can acquire a better title than that held by the transferor. This is not the case with an *assignment*, from which negotiability developed; here the transferee only acquires the rights the transferor actually had. In the case of a bill, for example, a transferor may have procured it by fraud, in which case his title would be voidable. If he negotiates it, the transferee acquires a perfect title; but if he only assigns it the transferee acquires merely a voidable title. An order bill is assigned and not negotiated when its holder transfers it without indorsing it. Furthermore, an assignee of a bill is unable to sue on it in his own name—he loses another important benefit of negotiability.

Indorsement

An indorsement is the signature of the indorser on the bill, in other words, that of the payee or a subsequent holder.

Essentials

To be a valid indorsement under s.32, it must satisfy certain requirements:

(1) It must be *written* on the back of the bill.

(2) It must be of the *entire bill* and not part.

(3) If there are two or more payees *all must indorse,* unless one is authorised to indorse for the others, such as a partner.

(4) It should *correspond exactly* with the drawing or the previous indorsement; for example, if the payee's name is misspelt, he should indorse it with the same spelling, adding his proper signature if he wishes. Nevertheless, an indorsement which does not correspond exactly with the previous designation on the bill is not invalid, but any *irregularity* will prevent a transferee from becoming a holder in due course. It is also usual banking practice to refuse to pay order bills on which the indorsement does not correspond exactly with the name of the payee or previous indorsee.

Types

If the holder merely signs the bill this is an *indorsement in blank* and the bill becomes payable to bearer. If he adds a direction to pay a particular person, this is a *special indorsement* and the bill becomes payable to, or to the order of, the person specified.

Sometimes a bill bears a *restrictive indorsement.* This prohibits or restricts further negotiation of it. For example, an indorsement 'Pay X only' prohibits negotiation, while an indorsement 'Pay X for the account of Y' entitles X to receive the sum paid to hold as agent for Y; in other words it does not transfer ownership of the bill but merely gives the indorsee authority to deal with it for the specified limited purpose.

Finally, an important practical point: any *conditional* indorsement can be completely ignored and payment is valid whether or not the condition has been fulfilled.

Payment

Presenting for payment

A bill payable *on demand* must be presented for payment to the drawee/acceptor within a reasonable time after its issue to render the drawer liable, and within a reasonable time of indorsement to render the indorser liable. If a bill is not payable on demand, i.e. it is payable at a fixed period *after date*, for example, thirty days after whatever date the bill bears, or *after sight*, for example say, thirty days after it has been presented to the drawee, it must be presented on the stipulated date. 'After sight' means more than merely showing the bill to the drawee— this is not enough to fix the start of whatever period the bill specifies. The drawee's 'sight' of the bill must be provable in a legal way, for example, by the drawee's acceptance of it or by the bill being protested (*see* below).

Fixing the time for payment precisely and clearly is necessary to enable bills to be used and passed from hand to hand as quasi-currency in the business world. Certainty of payment dates is very important when ensuring an adequate cash flow in any business and you have seen how banks endeavour to hold parcels of bills maturing at specific times.

Presentation must be made by the holder or his agent to the payer or his agent at the proper place at a reasonable time on a business day. *Delay* is excused when it is caused by circumstances beyond the holder's control and not by his own fault. When the cause of the delay ceases to operate, the holder or his agent must present the bill as soon as is reasonably possible. Presentation is *excused* and need not be made when (a) it cannot reasonably be made, for example the payer cannot be found; (b) the drawee is a fictitious person; and (c) it has been waived (not insisted upon).

Failure to present a bill in accordance with the Act will discharge the drawer and any indorser. This is a strict provision and it has been held that a delay of only one day is a sufficient failure, as is a presentment on the day before the bill's maturity. The rule is understandable, however, in that rules and the adherence to them are necessary to prevent a system of payment and credit, such as that represented by bills of exchange, from tumbling like a house of cards.

Dishonour by non-payment

A bill is dishonoured by non-payment when it is either duly presented for payment and payment is refused or cannot be obtained; or when presentment is excused and the bill is overdue and unpaid. The bill is *not discharged*; you will see the importance of this later.

An important practical point for you to note is that banks frequently act as agents for the collection of bills and a bank must ensure that it follows the proper procedure to secure acceptance and payment. You must similarly ensure that you take the proper steps if the bill is dishonoured. If you do not, and loss to the customer results, the bank is liable in contract law for that loss. (Dishonour is discussed generally below.)

Payment

Here we must consider three 'types' of payment: payment in due course, payment before maturity, and part payment.

Payment in due course. This is payment at or after the bill's maturity to its holder in good faith and without notice that his title to the bill is defective: s.59(1), Bills of Exchange Act 1882. The importance of payment in due course is that it *discharges* the bill and all parties are released from liability on it.

Look back to Fig. 16.1. What happens if the acceptor (X) pays the bill to F, someone who appears to be its holder but who in fact has no title to it at all? This could happen if the true owner (C) is unaware that the bill has been lost or stolen. If X does in fact pay F, the bill is *not* discharged because payment has not been made to its holder. Furthermore, C can force X to pay again. However, X can recover the sum paid from F who in turn can recover from E who will stand the loss unless he can find D and recover from him. (This position cannot arise with cheques because cheques are not accepted. *See* below for the protection afforded to a bank that pays a person not entitled to a cheque. You will see that payment of a cheque in such circumstances *does* discharge it.)

Payment before maturity. That constitutes a purchase of the bill and the acceptor could theoretically reissue it. The bill is not discharged and except to the acceptor prior parties remain liable on it.

Part payment. If an offer of part payment is made when the bill is presented, the offer may be treated as a dishonour. It may happen that the holder is prepared to take part payment in full discharge from the acceptor. If he does this, he can expressly reserve his rights against the drawer and any indorser who in turn thereby have their own rights against the acceptor preserved.

Time of payment

A bill drawn at so many days after sight must be paid on the *last day* of the time for payment as fixed by the bill. If that day is a non-business day, the bill must be paid on the next business day.

In calculating the date of payment, the day on which time begins to run is excluded from the calculation, and the day of payment is included. Time begins to run on a sight bill from the date of acceptance or, if this is refused, from the date of noting and protest (*see* below). The term month here means calendar month.

Dishonour

What is dishonour?

From your studies so far you will probably remember what constitutes dishonour; if not you could probably work it out. A bill incorporates a promise of payment and clearly 'dishonour' is going to relate to that promise. Thus, a bill of exchange can be dishonoured by *non-acceptance* or by *non-payment*.

Notice of dishonour

You have learnt that a party to a bill of exchange is a person who has signed it, thereby incurring liability on it. The drawer and any indorser stand as sureties for payment by the drawee/acceptor. Since they can normally expect the bill to be accepted and paid, they should certainly be entitled to be informed when their guarantee is going to be enforced against them. Thus, *failure to give notice* of dishonour discharges the drawer and any indorsers from liability on the bill. To this there is one important exception (as always!) and it concerns, as you might expect, a holder in due course. The supremacy of his position is fundamental to the whole concept and practice of negotiability and if he takes the bill after an omission to give notice following dishonour by non-acceptance he is not prejudiced by it. He must, of course, give appropriate notice himself when he is refused acceptance or payment. Nevertheless, the law is not unreasonable, and *delay in giving notice* is excused when it is caused by circumstances beyond his control and for which he is not to blame. Notice must be given as soon as possible after the cause of the delay ceases to operate.

In certain circumstances *notice of dishonour is unnecessary.* The circumstances are a little technical but as a banker it is important that you are aware of the rules if you ever are called upon to give notice of dishonour. Being familiar with these circumstances, so that you can refer to them later, will stand you in good stead.

(a) Notice is dispensed with when after reasonable diligence it *cannot be given*—if, for example, you cannot find the person to whom it is to be given;

(b) when it is expressly or impliedly *waived* by the drawer or any indorser;

(c) as regards notice to the *drawer*:

(i) where the drawer and the drawee are the same person,

(ii) where the drawee is a fictitious person or lacks contractual capacity,

(iii) where the drawee or acceptor was under no obligation to the drawer to accept or pay the bill, such as where a cheque is drawn on an account with insufficient funds to meet it and no overdraft facility exists,

(iv) where the drawer has countermanded payment;

(d) as regards notice to the indorser, where the drawee is a fictitious person or lacks contractual capacity and the indorser was aware of this when he indorsed the bill.

Method of giving notice

Provided that it clearly identifies the bill, notice of dishonour of an *inland bill* can be in any form. A *foreign bill* must be noted and protested when it is dishonoured.

We have already seen that giving notice of dishonour is very important and this is reflected in the very strict time limits which are applied to the giving of notice. Where the parties live in the *same place* (this probably means the same postal district), the notice must be given or sent off to *reach* the other party on the day after the bill's discharge. If the parties live in *different places*, the notice must be *sent off* on the day after the bill's dishonour, provided that there is a convenient post on that day and, if not, by the next convenient post thereafter.

Noting and protest
This is a technical aspect of the legal framework which is both easily explained and justified. It is all to do with the 'certainty' which is so important to the use of bills of exchange. It avoids any argument as to whether a bill has been duly presented for acceptance or payment.

Noting is the formal representation of a dishonoured bill by a *notary public* (an office nearly always held, in this country, by a solicitor) for acceptance or payment. The reply given is noted on the bill. The *protest* takes the form of a formal declaration by the notary certifying the dishonour and containing the relevant facts. This and a copy of the noted bill are then sent to the party from whom payment is sought. In short, noting and protest provide formal evidence of dishonour which will be universally recognised and accepted. It does not, of course, guarantee that payment will be made!

Outside the major cities, particularly outside London, notaries are fairly rare and where the services of one cannot be obtained, a householder in the presence of two witnesses may give a certificate signed by all three certifying the dishonour of the bill. This certificate then operates as if it were a formal protest.

From what we have said above, you will understand that it may well be in the holder's interest to note and protest any dishonoured bill. However, it is only necessary to do so where: (a) a foreign bill is dishonoured; (b) acceptance or payment for honour are sought (*see* below); (c) a bill is dishonoured by an acceptor for honour (*see* below). A bill requiring noting must be noted on the day that it is dishonoured or on the next business day, but the protest, which is an extension of the noting, can be done later. A protest is dispensed with and delay excused under exactly the same terms and conditions as apply to notices of dishonour.

There is also another situation where a bill may be protested. If the acceptor becomes insolvent or suspends payment of debts before the bill matures, the holder may protest the bill *for better security* by a notary engaged for that purpose. The notary first demands better security and then issues the protest if this is refused. Protesting the bill in this way confers no extra right of action on the holder but it does enable the bill to be accepted for honour.

Acceptance and payment for honour

A bill of exchange which has been either protested for dishonour by non-acceptance or protested for better security may be accepted for honour for part or all of the amount by *any person* who is not already a party to it. Let us consider what this means.

What happens if a bill which has been transferred down a chain of holders is dishonoured by non-acceptance or non-payment? You know the answer already; the holder can enforce payment against the person who transferred the bill to him or, indeed, any other party to the bill. The result could be a series of claims, ending with the drawer, which is the reverse of the chain of transfers. This, as you can imagine, would be very inconvenient to all concerned. Remember too that the whole practice of negotiability depends on belief of certain payment and the business reputation of the drawer in particular is going to be badly dented. This is where acceptance and payment for honour comes in.

To avoid the problems outlined above, the drawer or an indorser will sometimes name a person to whom the bill should be presented 'in case of need', that is, if the bill is either not accepted or not paid. The person named is known as a *referee in case of need*.

An *acceptor for honour* (the referee in case of need) is liable to the holder of the bill and to all persons who became parties to it *after* the party for whose honour he accepts. He undertakes to pay the bill provided it is protested following the drawee's failure to pay after a proper presentation to him for payment. If the acceptor for honour does not make payment, the bill must be protested for non-payment by him.

Payment for honour takes place when a person, any person, intervenes and pays a bill after it has been protested for non-payment.

Discharge

This is the last stage in the life of a bill. A bill can be discharged in one of five ways.

By payment in due course
This is defined as payment:

(a) by or on behalf of the drawee or acceptor;
(b) at or after the bill's maturity;
(c) to its holder;
(d) in good faith; and
(e) without notice that his title to the bill is defective.

Each of these requirements is vital and we have considered their meanings before. Most bills (and cheques) are discharged by payment in due course.

Although we shall be considering this point later in this chapter, it is worth noting here that under s.60 of the Bills of Exchange Act 1882, a bank's payment of a cheque which bears a forged or unauthorised indorsement (the presenter cannot therefore be its holder) is deemed to be payment in due course provided the payment was made in good faith and in the ordinary course of business. Such payment *discharges the cheque.*

By merger
Although somewhat unusual, merger takes place when the acceptor is or becomes the holder of the bill in his own right at or after its maturity. Obviously, he cannot enforce payment of the bill against himself.

By renunciation
At, or after the bill's maturity, the holder may absolutely and unconditionally renounce his rights against the acceptor in writing or by giving the bill to him. The holder may similarly renounce his rights against specific prior parties before or after the bill's maturity. Once again, however, the position of a holder in due course is important; he is unaffected by such a renunciation provided he has no notice of it.

By cancellation
To be operative, three conditions must be fulfilled: (a) the cancellation must be made by the holder or his agent; (b) be made intentionally; and (c) be apparent.

It is possible to cancel the whole bill or the signature of one prior party only. The latter cancellation discharges that person's liability *together with* all indorsers who would have had a right of recourse against him.

By material alteration

To be 'material', an alteration must have the effect of changing the operation or business effect of the instrument or the liabilities of the parties. Thus, material alterations include those of: (a) the date; (b) the sum payable; (c) the time of payment; (d) the place of payment; (e) the addition of a place of payment without the acceptor's consent where the bill has been accepted generally.

As a banker, you should remember two points: first, altering the *crossing* on a cheque is a material alteration; and second, a customer owes a duty to his bank to draw cheques with reasonable care in order to avoid fraudulent alterations to them.

The effect of a material alteration is to render the bill *void* against all parties except the one who made, authorised or consented to the alteration, and any party who indorsed the bill after its alteration. However, if the alteration is *not apparent* (and usually this will be the case) a holder in due course may enforce the bill for the original amount as if it had not been altered.

The collecting bank

Introduction

So far in this chapter we have talked about bills of exchange generally and only mentioned cheques and the position of a bank when a specific point needed making. However, since cheques are by far the most common and important type of bill of exchange, and since you are primarily concerned with your own position as a banker under the legal framework, we are going to become more specific in our studies and consider the position of a 'collecting bank' and then that of a 'paying bank'.

Possible liability

Every business has its commercial risks and legal pitfalls. Although banks are expert in protecting their interests, both generally and *vis-à-vis* their customers (to which banks' guarantee forms bear witness), there are certain circumstances where through their own maladministration rather than through operation of law they incur legal liability when collecting, or paying, cheques. In relation to the collection of cheques we must look at two situations.

Liability to its customer

A bank acts as agent when it presents cheques and other bills of exchange for payment on its customer's behalf. If it fails to present an instrument in accordance with the requirements of the Bills of Exchange Act 1882 and established banking practice, it will be liable to its customer for breach of contract.

It would incur similar liability as an agent if it failed to give notice of dishonour in accordance with the Act.

Liability to the cheque's true owner

A bank commits the common law tort of *conversion* against its true owner if it collects a cheque on behalf of a customer who has no title to it. You may say that this is not the bank's fault. This will probably be true but it is *no defence* in an action for conversion to establish that the tort was committed innocently, it is a tort of strict liability. This is partly the justification for the statutory protection we discuss next.

A collecting bank's statutory protection

Banks and the services that they offer are absolutely fundamental to modern commerce and industry. This in itself does not entitle banks to a privileged position before the law; they are merely another group of business organisations subject to the same economic forces and legal rules as any other group. However, so important is their function in the collection and payment of cheques that they must receive reasonable protection against innocently incurring liability to the *true owner* of a cheque if the system is going to function efficiently, or even at all. The relevant protection is given by statute. No other general area of banking business receives similar comprehensive protection.

The Cheques Act 1957, s.4

This section provides that a bank incurs no liability to the true owner of the cheque where its customer had either a defective title or no title at all to it, merely because it received payment of that cheque. The protection applies both when a bank collects as an agent, i.e. for its customer, and when it collects for itself (as holder of the cheque) having already credited the cheque to its customer's account.

As with all the other instances of statutory protection we have discussed, certain *conditions* must be fulfilled for the protection to apply.

(a) The bank must *act for a customer*. As you should recall from Chapter 6, a customer is a person who has entered into a contract with a bank for the opening of an account in his or her name.

(b) It must act *in good faith*. Honesty is required but, as we have seen on several previous occasions, negligence is *not* evidence of bad faith.

(c) And most importantly, the bank must act *without negligence*. Section 4(3) provides that a bank is not to be treated as negligent *purely* because the cheque collected was not indorsed or was irregularly indorsed but in all other cases it must establish that it acted with reasonable care. This is justified quite simply in that s.4 deprives the true owner of the cheque of his common law right to compensation from the bank for conversion.

From your other studies you will probably be aware of the concept and nature of the tort of negligence generally. Here it is in an applied form and the question obviously arises as to what constitutes negligence in relation to the collection of cheques. Before we go on to look at a selection of decisions on the question, the only true way to answer it, we can make a few general observations.

(a) The *standard of care* required is that of an ordinary competent bank.

(b) The criterion for this is *current banking practice*, rather than decisions dating back 50 or more years—times change—although it by no means follows that current banking practice will never itself be held to be negligent.

(c) A bank can plead contributory negligence by the customer under the Law Reform (Contributory Negligence) Act 1945 in an action against it for conversion. A successful plea will reduce the damages awarded.

The defence would be applicable where the owner of cheques carelessly left them lying around, facilitating their fraudulent use, or where carelessly drawn cheques are fraudulently altered. (The *Rule in Macmillan and Arthur* (1918), which we discuss below does not apply to a collecting bank.)

Examples of negligence

In a general book on the business of banking such as this, any discussion of this subject can cover only a selection of cases. The case law is considerable. This is not to say that banks are frequently negligent when collecting cheques, far from it; it is simply that in collecting such vast numbers of cheques each day mistakes are occasionally going to be made. Over the years these mistakes have provided categories, of sorts, into which negligent conduct can be classified. However, what is important is that you, as other bankers before you, learn from these past mistakes using the actual decisions as guides. Because each case is ultimately decided on its own facts, it would be wrong to treat any of the decisions as hard and fast rules but *common themes* have emerged in decisions against banks: *absence of inquiry* where it was reasonably called for or the *unsatisfactory nature of inquiries* which were made.

(1) The classic case of negligence is *failure to make reasonable inquiries* before opening an account. Although taking references is no longer the universal practice, the law is quite clear. References must be asked for and taken up before an account is opened although they are probably not required, as a matter of strict law, where the prospective customer is already known to the bank as a suitable person, or introduced by a person of similar standing. Furthermore, unless the referee is personally known to the bank, for example where he is an existing customer, the authenticity of the reference should be checked, for example, through the referee's own bankers.

The modern leading case on this situation is *Marfani and Co. Ltd* v. *Midland Bank Ltd.* (1968), which shows that while basic inquiries must be made, it is impossible to be categoric concerning their nature and extent. The case concerned a carefully conceived fraud. The office manager of the plaintiff company contrived to make the acquaintance of Mr Akaddas Ali, a respectable restaurateur. He introduced himself as Eliaszade and during the course of the acquaintanceship he aroused Mr Ali's interest by speaking of his intentions to open a restaurant of his own.

Knowing that Mr Marfani was leaving for Pakistan the following day, the fraudulent office manager prepared a cheque on the company's account for £3000 payable to Eliaszade, one of the company's suppliers, and obtained Mr Marfani's signature on it. He opened an account at the Midland Bank with this cheque using the name Eliaszade and as one of his two referees he nominated Mr Ali who already had a good account with the bank. The other referee did not reply, but Mr Ali gave a satisfactory reference whereupon the bank issued a chequebook to the new customer. Over the next two weeks the entire balance was withdrawn from the account, following which the office manager departed for Pakistan—and was never seen again. The company sued the bank for conversion, alleging negligence in opening the account.

The Court of Appeal held that the bank was protected by s.4, following evidence by other bankers that the defendants had acted as reasonable bankers, and the following circumstances were held not to constitute negligence:

(a) Opening an account after only one reference had been received without making further inquiries, the referee who replied was a respected customer and the second referee's failure to reply was satisfactorily explained by the mobility of the ethnic minority community to which he belonged;

(b) Failure to ask the new customer for his passport; and

(c) Clearing the cheque before receiving the reference.

(2) *Failure to obtain the name of its customer's employer or*, in the case of a married customer, the name of the *spouse's employer*. The point in making such enquiries is to avoid being innocently made party to conversion of cheques by your customer. The customer might, for example, steal cheques payable to his employer and hand them in for collection for his own account. Similarly, a spouse's account could be used to collect cheques stolen by the other spouse payable to or drawn

by that spouse's employer. In either case, knowledge of the customer's employment should prevent the fraud.

The case law concerns married women customers but there is absolutely no reason why the same precautions should not be taken when a married man seeks to open an account. Indeed, since the enactment of the Sex Discrimination Act 1975, any apparent discrimination against married women (or, indeed, married men) can no longer be maintained.

Both the situations we have outlined occurred in *Lloyds Bank Ltd.* v. *E. B. Savory and Company* (1932). In the case, two clerks, Perkins and Smith, stole cheques from their employers, Savory and Company. The cheques were payable to various stock brokers or to bearer. They were paid in at City branches of the bank, some by Perkins for the credit of his account at the Wallington branch and some by Smith for the credit of his wife's account at the Redhill branch and, later, at the Weybridge branch. The 'branch credit' system, as it was then called, entailed the branches where the cheques were paid in sending the cheques through the clearing system for collection and passing on credit slips with a form of banker's payment to the account-holding branches. The credit slips bore no details of the items and thus the account-holding branches remained in ignorance of the payees or drawers of the cheques concerned. Even had this information been conveyed it would have been of no use since details of the employers of Smith and Perkins had not been obtained. From what we have said already, you will realise that the bank was liable for conversion because it lost the protection of s.4 by its negligence in failing to obtain details of the employers of the account-holder, or, in the case of Mrs Smith, of her husband.

As interesting and important as the actual decision in this case is, the fact is that it was the direct cause of two important changes in banking practice. First, it became standard practice to ask for details of a customer's employment or the customer's husband's employment and second, full details of cheques had to be recorded on the credit slips used for 'branch credits' so that the division of knowledge between branches, which facilitated the fraud in this case, was avoided in future.

Current practice among banks and even branches would appear to vary. Case law dictates that enquiries are to be made of a married woman customer while the 1975 Act dictates that separate treatment on the grounds of sex alone is unlawful. Often the problem is side-stepped by not asking any married would-be customer for details of his or her spouse and his or her employment. Whether the courts would accept this latter practice as reasonable is uncertain.

The cases above illustrate negligence in opening an account, other instances of negligence (below) involve collecting cheques where the customer has broken his duty of good faith to the drawer or payee of the cheque.

(3) Crediting cheques payable *to a company to the private account of an official of the company*. This applies even where it is a 'one-man company'.

(4) Crediting the *private account of an agent or of an employee* with cheques drawn by him on the *account of his principal or employer*. You have already seen an example of this in *Midland Bank Ltd.* v. *Reckitt* (1933).

(5) Crediting an *agent's private account* with cheques expressly payable to him in his capacity as an *agent*. For example, in *Marquess of Bute* v. *Barclays Bank Ltd.* (1955), the bank was held to have acted negligently in collecting for the private account of an agent three warrants made payable to him because in brackets on the cheques were the words 'for Marquess of Bute'.

A third category of negligence is where cheques are collected without sufficient inquiry where unusual circumstances demand particular care. We give some examples of this below.

(6) Collecting without satisfactory explanation cheques, particularly third party cheques, for *amounts inconsistent with its customer's activities*. For example, in *Nu-Stilo Footwear Ltd.* v. *Lloyds Bank Ltd.* (1956), the plaintiff's company secretary opened an account in an assumed name, giving his real name as referee. The first cheque paid in was drawn in his own favour (under his assumed name) and for a modest sum, but the second cheque was a third party cheque, apparently indorsed to him, for £550 (a lot of money in 1956). While the bank was held not to have been negligent in opening the account, nor in collecting the first cheque, it had been negligent in collecting the second

and subsequent cheques, some of which were also third party cheques, because the amounts were inconsistent with its customer's stated occupation as an agent newly started in business.

(7) Collecting *third party cheques*, that is cheques which have apparently been indorsed to the customer, without sufficient inquiry where the circumstances demand it.

(8) Collecting without sufficient explanation '*Account payee*' *cheques for someone other than the named payee*. As you already know from our coverage of crossings on cheques, the effect of these words is merely to put the bank on inquiry. If its inquiries are reasonably answered, it retains the protection of s.4. (Remember that there is no duty on a bank to make inquiries where it collects for a third party a cheque crossed 'not negotiable'.)

Protection as holder in due course

Introduction
The protection of a collecting bank that we have discussed so far, s.4 of the Cheques Act 1957, is expressly given by the Act, but it will also gain protection as a consequence of establishing itself as the holder in due course of any cheque that it collects.

Section 4 protects a bank when it acts as agent for its customer, merely receiving payment for the customer, or receiving payment for itself after crediting its customer's account. If, however, it gives value (consideration) for the cheque, it will be collecting for itself as holder for value of the cheque and not as an agent. Consequently, it will not be protected by s.4 because this requires it to 'receive payment for a customer'. Nevertheless, establishing itself as holder in due course of a cheque in such circumstances gives a bank an alternative and perfect defence to an action for conversion of the cheque. At law it is the *true owner* of the cheque and you cannot commit conversion of your own property.

The defence afforded by satisfying s.29 of the Bills of Exchange Act 1882 (the section that states the requirements of a holder in due course) has the *advantage* of applying even where the bank may have acted negligently, but it has the *disadvantage* of not being available where it took the cheque under a forged indorsement for this prevents the bank from becoming a holder. As you have seen above, the protection of s.4 of the 1957 Act is not lost in this latter situation.

Quite apart from the defence that it affords, the bank as holder in due course acquires the right to enforce the cheque against all prior parties; s.4 only affords a defence.

Instances of giving value

As we know, to be a holder in due course the holder must *himself* have given value for the cheque; it is not enough that value has at some time been given. Thus, in what circumstances will a bank itself have given value for a cheque which it collects?

(1) Allowing the customer to draw against the cheque *before it has been cleared*. There must, however, be an express or implied contract permitting him to do so.

(2) Where the cheque is paid in *specifically to reduce an existing overdraft*, and not in the ordinary course of business as an overdrawn account.

(3) Where the bank '*buys*' the cheque; for example, where it cashes a cheque drawn by a third party for its customer or where it cashes a cheque drawn on another branch without open credit arrangements.

(4) Where the bank has *a lien on the cheque* it is the holder for value of the cheque to the extent of the sum for which it has a lien. A lien would arise if a cheque sent for payment by a bank acting as agent for its customer is returned unpaid and debiting the account with the amount of the unpaid cheque creates an overdraft.

Indorsement

The Cheques Act 1957, s.2, provides that a bank is to be considered the holder of a cheque payable to order for which it has given value, or over which it has a lien, although the previous holder delivered it to the bank for collection without indorsing it. This provision is necessary because an order bill can only be negotiated by indorsement completed by delivery while the Cheques Act 1957, s.1, removed the need for indorsement of an order cheque paid straight into the payee's account.

Statutory requirements

As you know, a holder in due course is a more complex animal than a holder for value. We have seen what constitutes value, but to be a holder in due course of a cheque received from a customer for collection, a bank must satisfy s.29(1) of the Bills of Exchange Act 1882: *see* above.

The paying bank

Introduction

What of the paying bank's position? To whom may it be liable, in what circumstances and what protection does it enjoy? Once again, you will see that a pragmatic compromise exists between the legitimate rights of the true owner of a cheque and the need to give banks sufficient protection for them to be willing and able to fulfil their functions in relation to cheques.

Termination of authority to pay

As you already know from Chapter 6, a bank owes a contractual duty to pay its customers' cheques but that this authority is terminated in a number of situations. We are now going to study these situations in more detail.

Countermand of payment

This is usually known as 'stopping a cheque'. Certain basic rules apply to an effective countermand:

  (a) it must be *in writing*;
  (b) it must be made by the drawer;
  (c) it must be absolutely *unequivocal*; and
  (d) it must be *communicated* to the *branch on which the cheque was drawn*.

Furthermore, the countermand must give *complete details* of the cheque, in particular: the payee's name, the amount of the cheque and its number. The last is the most important detail and a bank will not incur liability where a countermand gives the wrong number of the cheque and the bank accidentally pays the cheque which the customer intended to stop. One point to remember, a customer cannot stop a cheque which was correctly backed by a cheque card.

An important decision on the countermand of cheques is *Curtice* v. *London City and Midland Bank Ltd.* (1908). Here a telegram countermanding payment of a cheque was delivered after banking hours and left in the bank's letter box. The next day the countermand was accidentally overlooked and was found the following day. By this time the cheque had been paid. It was held that a countermand is not effective unless and until it comes to the *actual attention* of the drawee bank. The countermand in the case was therefore ineffective and the bank was entitled to debit the plaintiff's account with the amount of the cheque. (It is interesting to speculate what the decision would have been if the plaintiff had chosen to base his case on negligence.)

Although we have said that a countermand must be in writing, the obvious reaction of many people who want to stop a cheque is to telephone their instruction to the bank. This entitles you to postpone payment or dishonour of the cheque pending the customer's written confirmation of his initial instruction. If, in the meantime, the cheque is returned, you must indicate that confirmation of countermand is awaited.

Legal bar to payment

This can take two forms: a garnishee order or an injunction. A *garnishee order* is an order of the court which commands a debtor (in this instance the bank) to pay his debt, not to his immediate creditor (in this instance the customer), but to a person who has obtained a final court judgment against the creditor. Therefore, such an order made against a credit balance on a customer's account prevents a bank lawfully paying further cheques drawn on the account.

Since a garnishee order is not made against the judgment debtor himself but against one of his own debtors, such as his bank, it is usually an effective, yet fairly cheap and simple way, of enforcing payment when it is not volunteered. It does, of course, assume that the judgment debtor has not taken the precaution of withdrawing the balance on his account!

An *injunction* is a court order which forbids a person from doing or from continuing to do something. An injunction may be issued to freeze a bank account where, for example, the ownership of certain funds is disputed, the injunction preventing them from being paid away before ownership is determined by the court. In recent years, such injunctions have became known as *Mareva Injunctions* after a 1975 case involving a company of that name.

The legal effect of an injunction is that if the defendant draws a cheque in breach of it he would be guilty of a contempt of court, and if the bank honoured the cheque it would be guilty of aiding and abetting the defendant's contempt. Thus, once a bank has notice of an injunction affecting money (or goods) in its hands it must not allow anyone to dispose of it except with the authority of the court.

Notice of certain events affecting the customer

Notice of the following events terminates a bank's authority to pay:

(a) the customer's *death*;

(b) the customer's *mental disorder*, although the disorder must be such that he is incapable of managing his affairs;

(c) a *bankruptcy petition* against the customer. (A bankruptcy petition is the first step in making a person bankrupt.)

Bankruptcy order or winding-up order

Both orders basically have the effect of bringing to an end the commercial activity of a business organisation, the former applying to sole traders and partnerships, the latter to registered companies. The point to note is that it is the *making* of the order, and not notice of it, which terminates a bank's authority to pay.

Defective title

A bank has no authority to pay its customer's cheque if it *knows* of a *defect in the presenter's title*, for example that he is an undischarged bankrupt, in which case the proceeds might belong to the presenter's trustee in bankruptcy. As you might imagine, it is unusual for a bank to have knowledge of a defect in the presenter's title.

Misapplication of funds

If a bank either *knows* or *should know* that a cheque is a misapplication of funds, it must not pay it. An example would be where an official of a company signs company cheques for the purchase of its own shares contrary to the Companies Act 1985.

The possible liability of a paying bank

Wrongful debit of an account
A bank is liable in damages to its customer if it wrongfully debits his account. It may do so in one of four ways.

(a) By debiting the account after its customer has countermanded payment.

(b) Where it pays a postdated cheque before the proper date for payment. The customer is entitled to stop the cheque before the payment date and an early payment could result in other cheques being dishonoured for apparent lack of funds.

(c) Where its customer's signature on the cheque has been forged for, as you know, a forged signature is completely without legal effect. However, a customer may be estopped from denying the genuineness of the signature, as happened in *Greenwood* v. *Martins Bank Ltd.* (1932). Here the plaintiff's wife held the cheque-book for his account at the defendant bank and over a period of time drew a number of cheques by forging his signature. The plaintiff subsequently discovered this but did not inform the bank. After the wife's death, some eight months later, the plaintiff sought to recover from the bank the amount of the forged cheques. His action was unsuccessful because his inaction after discovering that his wife had been forging his signature prevented him, at law, from denying their genuineness. The bank was entitled to debt his account with the value of the cheques.

(d) A bank is liable if it debits an account with a cheque which has been materially altered without the customer's consent. Usually the alteration would be a fraudulent increase in the amount. A cheque which has been visibly altered is void against all parties to it who have not consented to the alteration but, if the alteration is *not apparent*, a *holder in due course* is entitled to the original amount for which the cheque was drawn. Anybody else presenting the cheque is entitled to nothing.

A bank has little statutory protection if it pays a cheque which has been materially altered, whether or not the alteration is apparent. However, a customer owes a duty to draw cheques with reasonable care to avoid fraudulent alteration of them and his bank may debit his account where his negligence has facilitated the fraud. This is known as the *Rule in London Joint Bank* v. *Macmillan and Arthur* (1918). Here, a partner in the defendant firm signed a cheque payable to the payee or to bearer made out by a clerk for the sum of £2. The amount payable was shown in figures only. The clerk fraudulently altered the figure to read £120, wrote the amount on the cheque and obtained payment from the plaintiff, the firm's bankers. Because of the defendant's negligence, the plaintiff bank was entitled to debit the firm's account with the value of the cheque.

If you reflect on the legal position for a moment, you will see that a bank will seldom be the innocent victim of a fraudulently altered cheque. If a visibly altered cheque is paid without confirmation of the alteration, it has only itself to blame, while most non-apparent alterations will be facilitated by its customer's negligence, thereby enabling the bank to rely on the *Rule in Macmillan and Arthur* (1918).

Wrongful dishonour of a cheque

This is unusual, but if it should happen a bank may possibly incur liability under two heads. First, for *breach of contract* and, second, for *libel*. The first needs no further explanation, the latter does.

As you will probably know from your other studies, libel is a form of *defamation* and the cause of action is based on the statement made lowering the plaintiff in the eyes of right-thinking members of society generally (whoever they might be!), or causing the plaintiff to be shunned and avoided. An action for libel following a wrongful dishonour of a cheque is based on the argument that the words used in stating the reason for dishonour are defamatory. The phrase 'Refer to drawer' is arguably defamatory because it has the generally accepted connotation that the drawer of the cheque has no money in his account and this, it is argued, causes him to be lowered in the estimation of others. This was no doubt the case some years ago when only the wealthy had bank accounts. Alternatively, and perhaps more realistically today, it could carry the connotation that the drawer has been acting dishonestly by using worthless cheques—in so far as he knows that they will be dishonoured—

to obtain goods and services. The problem is neatly avoided by stating a technical reason for dishonour if such is the case.

For breach of contract, a *trader* is entitled to reasonable compensation for injury to his reputation and credit without proof of actual damage. A *non-trader* must generally prove actual damage to be awarded more than nominal damages. By actual damage we mean damage measurable in financial terms. If, however, a cheque is returned to its presenter stating a reason for dishonour which is subsequently held to be libellous, a non-trader's claim would not be limited to nominal damages.

Where such an unfortunate situation does occur, litigation can usually be avoided by the bank admitting its mistake and making a prompt apology to its customer and the presenter of the cheque; the bank is as anxious to keep its customer as the customer is to keep his banking facilities.

Liability to the cheque's true owner

If a bank pays a person who is not the holder (the owner of an order cheque or the possessor of a bearer cheque), it is liable at common law for conversion to the cheque's true owner. However, because a paying bank is seldom in a position to know whether the presenter is the holder of the cheque, it is given limited statutory protection against innocently committing conversion when paying cheques. This protection is discussed in the next section but it is worth emphasising here that it will be lost when the statutory requirements for it are not met.

A paying bank's protection

Payment in due course

Payment in due course discharges all parties to a cheque: s.59, Bills of Exchange Act 1882. As you have seen above, this requires that the bank pays the cheque to its holder in good faith and without notice of any defect in his title.

Forged and unauthorised indorsements

We know that a forged or unauthorised signature is without effect, and therefore a person holding under a forged or un-authorised indorsement cannot be the true owner of the cheque: he is merely a wrongful possessor. However, s.60 of the Bills of

Exchange Act 1882 protects a bank against liability to the holder (the true owner) if it pays a cheque (open or crossed) which bears a forged or unauthorised indorsement provided it pays in good faith and in the ordinary course of business.

For example, A draws a cheque payable to B and B negotiates it to C. D steals the cheque from C, forges C's indorsement on it and transfers the cheque to E. Let us consider the rights and liabilities involved. Look at Fig. 16.3 which represents the situation as a chain.

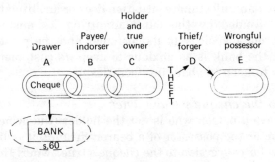

Fig. 16.3 Forgery and unauthorised indorsements and s.60

In this situation C is the holder and the true owner of the cheque, while E is the wrongful possessor. D and E have committed conversion of the cheque against C, as will the bank if it pays it. The bank, however, is protected by s.60 but D and E have no protection (D obviously deserves none) and are liable at common law to C. If E, who has no right to receive payment of course, has to compensate C, he in turn can seek compensation from D, provided he can find him and D proves to have the money to pay. It is a question of which of two innocent parties, C or E, should suffer through the fraud of a third: D.

You will agree that whatever the positions of the other parties involved, a bank will seldom be in a position to know whether an indorsement on a cheque which it is asked to pay is forged— it is almost certain to be the signature of a total stranger—and could not possibly check on an indorsement's authenticity without causing the entire system of paying cheques to collapse. Remember, however, that since only a small percentage of cheques are negotiated, the problems are perhaps more theoretical than real.

The protection of s.60 is not given lightly; it must be earned by a bank. First, payment must be made *in good faith*. Payment of a cheque knowing that an indorsement on it was a forgery would clearly not be a payment in good faith but a *negligent payment* is protected by s.60. Thus, payment in good faith means an *honest* payment. Second, payment must be *in the ordinary course of business*. This means payment according to current banking practice and within normal banking hours. For example, a crossed cheque should be paid only through a bank account and an open cheque cashed over the counter must appear to be properly indorsed. Payment of an open cheque to an 'unusual presenter', for example, to an apparent office junior, particularly if drawn for a substantial amount, would probably not be payment in the ordinary course of business although payment of bills or cheques for large sums over the counter is not in itself outside the ordinary course of business.

An important point to remember is that payment under s.60 is deemed to be payment *in due course*. The cheque is therefore discharged as is the liability of the drawer on it. If the cheque actually or constructively reached the payee before its payment, the drawer will, in addition, be discharged from liability on the consideration for which the cheque was originally given. The drawer is not liable to make a second payment to the payee. Section 60 only applies to cheques, not other bills of exchange, however, and it does not afford protection if the drawer's signature is forged.

The Cheques Act 1957, s.1 (*see* below), has greatly reduced the practical significance of s.60 but it remains important wherever indorsement of a cheque is still necessary. Without s.60's protection, a bank would have to make a second payment to the cheque's true owner (C in Fig. 16.3), having already paid the person presenting it (E), but would not be able to debit the customer's account (A).

Crossed cheques

The main statutory protection when a bank pays a crossed cheque is given by s.80 of the Bills of Exchange Act 1882. This protects a bank against liability to the true owner if it pays a cheque *in good faith, without negligence* and *in accordance with the crossing*. Provided these requirements are fulfilled a bank is placed in the same position under this section as if it had paid the cheque's true owner. It follows that it can debit its customer's account with the amount of the cheque. You should note that the section deals only with crossings and provides *no* protection against other material alterations of a cheque; these render a cheque void.

Once a crossed cheque has actually or constructively reached the payee, under s.80 the *drawer* is also regarded as being in the same position as if the true owner had been paid. He is discharged from liability on the original consideration given for the cheque. In other words, he cannot be made to make a second payment.

In fact, the protection of s.80 has seldom, if ever, been relied upon by a bank. A forged or unauthorised indorsement is by far the most likely defect on a cheque which will involve a bank and s.60 already provides adequate protection where this occurs. In practice, therefore, s.80 virtually duplicates the protection of s.60 while applying only to crossed cheques and requiring a bank to act without negligence. Section 60, as you will remember, requires the bank merely to have acted in good faith, in practice a lower standard of care.

Unindorsed or irregularly indorsed cheques

Under the Cheques Act 1957, s.1(1), a bank which pays a cheque drawn on it which is not indorsed or which is irregularly indorsed is deemed to pay it in due course if it is paid in *good faith* and *in the ordinary course of business*. Thus, if D in Fig. 16.3 opened an account posing as C and obtained payment from A's bank (instead of forging C's endorsement and transferring the cheque on to E), A's bank would have a good statutory defence against an action for conversion brought by C. (C's most profitable course of action would probably be to bring an action against the (collecting) bank at which D opened the account. It would then be up to that bank to successfully plead s.4 of the Cheques Act 1957: *see* above.)

An irregular indorsement must be distinguished from a forged or unauthorised indorsement. An *irregular indorsement* is genuine enough, it merely does not conform to banking practice, while a forged or unauthorised indorsement is one written on the cheque without the holder's authority. Thus, an indorsement on a cheque 'John P Smith' when the cheque was payable to 'John Smith' would be irregular, but an indorsement 'John Smith' in the same situation by Tom Jones who had stolen the cheque would be forged and unauthorised.

Section 1(1) means that if a paying bank fails to obtain an indorsement which it knows to be necessary it cannot rely on the section because it would not be paying in the ordinary course of business. If, however, a cheque is indorsed as required, for example, a negotiated order cheque, but the indorsement proves to be *irregular* it may rely on s.1(1) and, we can add here, if it proved to be *forged or unauthorised* it can, as we have seen, rely on s.60 of the Bills of Exchange Act 1882.

As with the Bills of Exchange Act 1882, s.60, payment under the Cheques Act 1957, s.(1), is deemed to be payment in due course. Therefore, it protects a paying bank from an action for conversion brought by the true owner of the cheque and entitles it to debit its customer's account. The cheque is discharged, and if it actually or constructively reached the payee before being paid, the drawer is discharged from liability on the original consideration given for the cheque.

We have mentioned above that s.1(1) cannot be relied upon if a bank fails to obtain an indorsement which it knows to be necessary. In addition, banks have never fully relied on s.1 of the Act and by a resolution of the Committee of London Clearing Bankers in 1957, the following instruments still require indorsements before payment:

(a) Cheques and other instruments cashed at the counter. (This includes the situation where the customer presents his own cheque for payment. If, however, the 'cheque' is made payable to 'Cash' or to 'Wages' no indorsement is required.)

(b) Order cheques which are to be paid into an account other than that of the original payee, that is, order cheques which have been negotiated.

(c) Bills of exchange other than cheques.

(d) Combined cheques and receipt forms marked 'R'. (Although discouraged by the banks, a few customers still insist on the payee's receipt before payment.)

(e) Promissory notes.

(f) Travellers cheques.

Summary

1 The four legal characteristics of a negotiable instrument are that:

(a) Title is transferrable by delivery or by indorsement completed by delivery.

(b) The transferee can acquire a better title than that held by the transferor.

(c) The holder can sue in his own name.

(d) The holder need not give notice to prior parties to establish his title.

2 To be a holder in due course of a bill, the bill must be:

(a) complete and regular;

(b) not overdue;

(c) taken without notice of any previous dishonour;

(d) taken in good faith;

(e) taken for value provided by the holder;

(f) taken without notice of any defect in the transferor's title.

3 A party to a bill of exchange is a person who signs it and thereby incurs liability on it. The acceptor incurs primary liability and the drawer and any indorser stand surety for his payment.

4 The main possible stages in the progress of a bill are:

(a) issue;

(b) acceptance;

(c) negotiation/indorsement;

(d) payment;

(e) dishonour: by non-acceptance or non-payment;

(f) discharge.

5 A collecting bank may incur liability to its customer for breach of contract and to the cheque's true owner for conversion.

6 A collecting bank's statutory protection is provided by s.4 of the Cheques Act 1957. To benefit from it, a bank must act:

(a) for a customer;

(b) in good faith;

(c) without negligence.

7 Most examples of negligence under s.4 involve a failure to make satisfactory inquiries before collecting a cheque.

8 A collecting bank also receives protection from legal action

by establishing itself as the holder in due course (the owner) of any cheque it collects.

9 A bank's authority to pay a cheque is *terminated* by:

  (a) the customer's countermand;

  (b) legal bar: a garnishee order or an injunction;

  (c) notice of the customer's death, mental disorder or a bankruptcy petition against him;

  (d) a bankruptcy order or winding-up order against the customer;

  (e) knowledge of a defect in the presenter's title;

  (f) knowledge that the cheque is a misapplication of funds.

10 A paying bank incurs liability to its customer for breach of contract if it wrongfully debits his account or wrongfully dishonours a cheque, with the possibility of liability in tort for defamation in the latter case.

11 A paying bank may incur liability in conversion to the true owner of a cheque if it pays a person not entitled to payment.

12 Payment in due course discharges all parties to a cheque.

13 Section 60 of the Bills of Exchange Act 1882 protects a bank which pays a cheque bearing a forged or unauthorised indorsement from legal action by its true owner provided the payment was made in good faith and in the ordinary course of business.

14 Under Section 1 of the Cheques Act 1957, a bank is deemed to have paid in due course an unindorsed or an irregularly indorsed cheque provided it paid it in good faith and in the ordinary course of business.

Self-assessment questions

1 State the legal characteristics of a negotiable instrument.

2 Define the term 'holder'.

3 In what circumstances does the transferee of a bill become a holder in due course of that bill?

4 Explain the reasons for presenting a bill for acceptance.

5 State the essentials of valid indorsement.

6 Explain the meaning of noting and protesting of a bill of exchange.

7 True or false?

  (a) The payee of a bill can never be a holder in due course.

(b) A person taking a bearer bill from a thief can be a holder in due course.

(c) Only a person who has signed a bill incurs liability on it.

(d) The acceptor of a bill is entitled to refuse payment to a holder in due course by proving that the drawer's signature is a forgery.

(e) Altering a crossing on a cheque will discharge it.

(f) In regard to the collection of a cheque, proof that no fault attaches to the bank is a defence against an action for conversion brought by its true owner against the bank.

(g) A cheque crossed 'not negotiable' places a duty on a bank to make enquiries before collecting that cheque.

(h) A telephoned countermand is as effective as a more formal written countermand.

(i) Payment of a cheque under s.60 of the Bills of Exchange Act 1882 is payment in due course.

(j) A bank can *never* debit an account with a cheque on which the drawer's signature is forged.

8 For what reasons should details of the spouse's employment be obtained when opening an account for a married person?

9 Explain why collecting a cheque as holder in due course may offer better protection to a bank than relying on s.4 of the Cheques Act 1957.

10 Explain the relationship between the Bills of Exchange Act 1882, s.60 and the Cheques Act 1957, s.1(1).

Assignments

1 Last week your bank received a postal request from a Mrs Smith for a current account application form. This was duly sent. Yesterday a letter was received from her wanting to know why the form asked for details for her husband's employment. Her letter made it clear that 'It is normal banking practice' would not be suitable as a reply.

Your manager has asked you to deal with the matter and requires you: (a) to write a suitable letter to her explaining tactfully, and in non-technical terms, why banks ask for this information, and (b) to prepare some notes to use in case Mrs Smith decides to seek a face-to-face reply before the letter reaches her.

2   *Jones and Co.* v. *Mantown Bank plc*

The plaintiffs employed a Mr Edwards as their accountant and it was part of his duties to prepare cheques in favour of the plaintiff's suppliers. It was usual practice for him to abbreviate the names of its regular suppliers on these cheques, thus 'Brown, Mills and Co.' would appear as 'Brown'. In preparation for fraud, Edwards opened a deposit account with Mantown Bank plc giving his name as J. A. G. Brown and claiming to be a self-employed business consultant just arrived from Australia.

The bank's regulations required a check of the new depositor's identity and for a note to be made of the name and address of the new customer's employers. A reference was to be taken up if and when a cheque was presented for collection. 'Brown' gave the name of 'Dr' Blake with whom he said he had come over from Australia and in due course Blake provided an excellent reference although he ignored the request to provide the name and address of his bankers.

Once the account was opened Edwards converted cheques totalling £10 000 belonging to his employers all of which were collected through his deposit account. This was easy enough as he made out cheques to 'Brown', leaving a space in front of the name, and once he had obtained his employer's signature he added the initials 'J. A. G.' in front of the surname and paid them into the account he had opened in that name with the defendant bank.

(a) Identify the ways, if any, in which the bank was negligent in handling the opening of the account.

(b) Assuming the bank to have been negligent, identify grounds, if any, on which it can seek to lessen any award of damages.

(c) Familiarise yourself with your own bank's standard procedure for opening current and deposit accounts.

Index

acceptance credits, 56, 118, 437
acceptance facility, 425
accepting house 56
  Accepting Houses Committee, 81
  functions of, 81
  services through banks, 425
Access card, 389
accounting ratios, 526
accounts, types of 380
  budget, 385, 468
  current (*see* current accounts)
  deposit (*see* deposit accounts)
  foreign currency, 446
  high interest, 383
  joint, 237–8
  investment, 383
  loan, 384
  premium, 384
  savings, 383
accumulation units, 162, 402
acid test ratio, 526
administrators, 239, 240, 403
advances
  on bank balance sheet, 108
  illiquidity of, 109
  principles of lending, 110
advances, types of account 470–8
  budget, 475–6
  home loan, 476–8
  loan, 472–3
  overdraft, 470–2
  personal loan, 459, 473–5
advertising of bank services, 378
advised letter of credit, 434
agency, 227–9
  bank accounts, 227–9
  breach of warranty of authority, 228, 484
  estoppel, 228–9
  implied authority, 228
  partnership and, 242–3
  ratification, 228, 229
  rules of, 218–9
  unauthorised borrowing and, 229
aggregate monetary demand (AMD), 333
air waybills, 431
Alumunium Industrie Vdssen BV v. *Romalpa Aluminium Ltd* (1976), 500
annuity, 154
Arab Bank v. *Ross* (1952), 610
articles of association (*see* companies)
assent, 528

assets 508
  current, 506, 511–2, 525, 537, 538
  fictitious, 510
  fixed, 506, 508–10, 537–8
  intangible, 510–1, 534
  net, 523
  reserves, 513–4
  tangible, 508–10
assets of banks
  advances, 108
  Bank of England deposits, 117
  fixed, 111
  liquid, 101, 116
  reserve, 115
assignment, 490, 554, 573, 594, 618
attestation clause, 237, 598
automated teller machines, 275, 392
authorised institution, 39

back to back letter of credit, 447
bailment, 219–20, 491
Baines v. *National Provincial Bank Ltd* (1927), 221
balance sheet, 505
  assets, 508–12
  of a commercial bank, 92
  liabilities, 512–6
  presentation of, 506–8
bank
  advising bank, 434
  bills, 76
  British Overseas Bank, 57
  clearing banks, 48
  Commonwealth bank, 57
  consortium banks, 58
  deposits, 27
  failures of banks, 20, 45
  financial structure of, 88
  foreign bank, 58
  fringe bank, 49
  giro credit, 266
  high street bank, 47
  holder in due course, as, 634–6
  issue department, 63
  issuing bank, 433
  joint stock bank, 20, 45
  licensing of, 59
  merchant bank, 55
  names of, 60
  private bank, 19, 44
  rate, 68
  return, 63

bank (cont'd)
  statements, 232–3
  use of name 216
bank accounts
  budget, 468
  closing, 231–2
  companies, of, 248–9
  joint, 237–8
  mandate, 226, 228, 237, 240, 248
  minors, of, 236
  opening, 225–7
  operating, 227–30
  patnerships, of, 244–5
  personal representatives, of, 239–41
  references, to open, 225–6, 244, 630–2
  set-off on, 239, 240, 245
  trust, of, 241
Bank Charter Act 1833, 46
Bank Charter Act 1844, 21, 47
Bank of England
  bank return, 63
  banking department, 63
  commercial banks' balances with, 117
  development of, 62
  founding of, 21
  functions of, 63
  issue department, 63
  lender of last resort, 70
  nationalisation of, 63
  Quarterly Reviews, 67
  responsibilities of, 61
Bank of England v. *Vagliano Brothers*
      (1891), 291
banker
  agent, as, 621
  card, 386
  Clearing House, 260
  collecting, 627–36
  customer relationship with, 217–22
  defined, 216
  dilemma, 89
  drafts, 279, 293–4
  land and, 549–50
  legal rights and duties, 222–5
  paying, 636–45
Banker Automated Clearing Services
    (BACS), 266
  automated standing orders, 269
  credit payments, 266
  debit transmission, 268
  direct debits, 272
  operation, 266
Bankers' Books Evidence Act 1879, 224
banking
  Banking Department (Bank of England),
    63
  British banking system, 42
  business of, 89, 216
  deposit, 46, 53
  origins of, 42
  practice, rules of, 220–1

  secondary banking crisis, 59
Banking Act 1987, 59, 216
banknotes
  Bank of England notes, 21
  development of, 16
  fractionally backed, 18
  private banks' notes, 19
bankruptcy, 238, 239, 486, 492, 499
  order, 231, 638
  petition, 224, 231, 563, 638
Barclaycard, 389
barter, 3
base rate, 208
'bears', 179
Bechuanaland Exploration Co v. *London
    Trading Bank* (1898), 286
bid bond, 451
bid price, 161
'Big Bang', 175
'big five', 48
'big four', 49
bills of exchange, 287–91, 491
  acceptance, 617–8
  acceptance and payment for honour, 625
  acceptor of, 287, 307, 614, 615–6, 622,
    623
  advantages of, 288
  bearer, 290–1, 305, 611, 618
  definition of, 288–91
  demand, payable on, 290, 619
  discharge, 621, 625–7, 628
  discounting of, 74, 288, 435
  dishonour of, 618, 620–1, 622–5
  drawee, 287, 307, 308, 614, 620, 622
  drawer, 287, 306, 308, 614–5, 616, 617,
    622, 623, 644
  export trade, in, 429
  fine, 76, 616
  first class, 76
  holder of, 221, 287, 304, 305, 307,
    608–9, 614, 617, 618
  holder in due course, 298, 608, 609–13,
    615, 616, 618, 622, 634–6, 639
  holder for value, 609
  indorsee/-or/-ment (*see* indorsement)
  liability on, 614–7
  material alteration of, 627
  negotiation of, 618
  notice of dishonour, 290, 622–4
  noting and protest, 624–5
  order, 304, 618, 635
  overdue, 610
  parties to, 287, 304–8, 614
  payee, 287, 304, 305, 613, 615, 618
  payment in due course, 621, 626, 643
  payment of, 619–22
  presentment for acceptance, 290
  presentment for payment, 290, 293,
    619–20
  referee in case of need, 625
  sight, payable after, 290, 620

Bills of Exchange Act 1882, 220, 224, 614, 628
  s. 2, 216, 304, 608
  s. 3, 288, 291, 296, 615
  s. 17, 617
  s. 19, 618
  s. 24, 611
  s. 29, 609, 611, 634, 636
  s. 32, 619
  s. 39, 617
  s. 54, 612, 615
  s. 55, 612, 614
  s. 59, 621, 641
  s. 60, 220, 293, 626, 642, 643, 644, 645
  s. 73, 293, 294
  s. 78, 297
  s. 80, 643–4
  s. 83, 308
bills of lading, 430
bimetallism, 11
blank transfer, 593, 594
'blue chip' rates, 209
bond support, 451
  indemnities, 452
  performance guarantees, 451
bonus issue, 174
bridging loan, 460, 480–1
British Airways Board v. *Parish* (1979), 249
brokers
  foreign exchange, 367
  money, 349, 351, 355
  stock, 175
building societies 144
  Building Societies Association, 147
  current accounts, 147
  deposit accounts, 145
  savings schemes, 146
  share accounts, 145
  Building Societies Act 1986, 148
bullion bars, 26
'bulls', 178
business development programmes, 376
Business Names Act 1985, 244

call money, 78
capital, 506, 513
  growth, 125
  productivity of, 187
capital items on balance sheet, 506
  capital, 513
  profit and loss account, 513
  reserves, 513–4
capital markets 166
  finance markets, 177
  stock market, 166
cash
  budget, 458, 470
  flow forecast, 458, 542
  ratio, 10
cashflow account, 385

cashless pay, 382
Central Clearing House, 260
certificate of deposit, 310, 359
  discount houses and, 78
  dollar market, 84, 359
  issued by commercial banks, 99
  negotiable, 286, 360
  purchases through banks, 394
  sterling market, 84, 360
certificates of origin, 431
certified invoice, 431
charge, 491–2
  certificate, 580, 588
  crystallisation of, 499, 601
  equitable, 557, 584, 588
  fixed, 498
  floating, 488, 499–500, 588
  legal, 490, 492, 580
  registration of, 600–1
charge card, 391
Charges Register (*see* Land Registry)
cheque, 491
  bearer, 297
  clearing system, 258
  collecting a, 627–36
  countermand (stop) of, 221, 223, 230, 238, 300, 636–7, 639
  crossed, 257, 297, 643–4
  crossings on, 293, 295–9, 627, 644
  definition of, 291–2
  development of, 27
  direct presentation of, 263
  dishonour of, 640–1
  in course of collection, 105
  lien on, 635
  material alteration of, 639–40, 644
  negligence, 630–4
  negotiation of, 292–3
  obtaining payment of, 257
  overdue, 223
  payment by, 294–5
  payment of, 636–45
  post-dated, 255
  stale, 223
  third party, 634
  uncrossed, 297
  unindorsed or irregularly, indorsed, 644–5
  unpaid, 261
  use of, 27, 255
cheque guarantee card, 226, 230, 236, 300–4, 386, 388
Cheques Act 1957
  s. 1, 635, 643, 644–5
  s. 2, 635
  s. 4, 225, 237, 244, 629, 631, 632, 634, 635, 644
choses in action (*see* property)
choses in possession (*see* property)
City of London Building Soc. v. *Flegg* (1987), 561–2

Civil Liability (Contribution) Act 1978, 238, 243
claims for unpaids, 262
classical money market, 71
Clayton's Case (1816), 218, 239, 245
clearing banks, 48
clearing system
  Bankers Automated Clearing Services (BACS), 266
  Central Clearing House, 260
  Clearing House Automated Payments System (CHAPS), 274
  credit clearing, 264
  General Clearing, 258
  Town Clearing, 263
clipping, 11
coinage
  coins, 10
  history of British, 13
  precious metals, 10
  token coins, 12
Coinage Act 1816, 15
collection letter, 432
commercial invoices, 429
commission charges, 381
Commissioners for the National Debt, 65, 139
Committee of London and Scottish Clearing Bankers, 645
commodities futures contracts, 363
common law, 216
companies, 245–9
  articles of association, 247
  bank account of, 248–9
  borrowing by, 247, 482–5
  certificate of incorporation, 248
  directors of, 483
  guarantees and, 596
  limited, 246
  liquidation of, 486, 492, 500
  memorandum of association, 246–7, 482–3
  objects clause, 247, 482
  profit and loss account of, 513
  Registrar of, 246, 248, 587, 600
  trading certificate of, 248
  unauthorised (*ultra vires*) borrowing by, 227, 484–5, 595
  winding up, 224, 231, 638
Companies Act 1862, 47
Companies Act 1948, 483
Companies Act 1985, 224, 229, 246, 247, 249, 483, 484, 587, 596, 600, 639
competition and credit control, 114
composite rate tax, 142
conditional bill of sale, 490
confirmed letter of credit, 434
consortium banks, 59
consular invoice, 431
consumer credit, 457
  banks and, 465–9

regulated agreements, 467–8
Consumr Credit Act 1974, 250, 465–9, 474, 599
rates of interest and, 109
status enquiries and, 450
consumer finance regulations, 344
contract, law of
  general rules of, 217–8
  for the sale of land, 569
contract note, 176
controls on banking industry, 113
  deposits with Banks of England, 117
  liquidity controls, 113
  monetary control provisions, 114, 116
conversion, 219–20, 286, 613, 628, 644
convertability of banknotes, 25
conveyance, 569, 573
Copper v. *National Provincial Bank* (1945), 598
corporation, 246
cost-push inflation, 36
counter-indemnity, 435
coupons (bearer stocks), 397
credit (*see also* consumer credit)
  APR, 467–8
  card, 218, 300, 389
  clearing, 264
  creation, 28
  information services, 447
  insurance, 439
  opened facilities, 414
  transfer, 265
creditors, 486, 515
  preferential, 499, 536–7, 601
  secured, 514, 536, 601
crystallisation (*see* charge)
Cuckmere Brick Co Ltd v. *Mutual Finance Ltd* (1971), 590
currency
  dealers, 363
  exchanges rates, 365
  speculators, 364
current accounts
  attributes, 380
  bank balance sheet and, 97
  building societies, 147
  savings medium, as, 141
current ratio, 525–6
Curtice v. *London City and Midland Bank Ltd* (1908), 230, 637
customer (of a bank)
  bankruptcy order against, 231
  bankruptcy petition against, 231
  death of, 231
  defined, 216–7
  liability to, 628, 639–41
  mental incapacity of, 231
  winding up order against, 231

debasement of coinage, 13
debentures, 286, 498–500, 579, 599–602

debentures (cont'd)
  on balance sheet, 514
  registration of charges in, 600–1
  remedies of holder, 601–2
  transfer of, 579
decimalisation, 15
deeds, 554, 576, 592
  deposit of, 559, 580
  mortgage by, 580
  postponement, of, 562
deferred annuity, 155
deflation
  definition, 36
  monetary policy, as, 333
deposit
  banking, 53
  bonds, 137
  protection scheme, 60
  rate, 209, 382
  receipt, 360
deposit account
  attributes, 382
  bank balance sheet, 98
  building society, 33
  investments and, 393
  savings vehicle, as, 141
depositors' funds, 97
depreciation, 97, 542, 543
direct debit, 272
discount houses, 74
discount market, 74
disinflation, 333
dividend, 516
  warrant, 310–1
doctrine of notice, 558
documentary collection, 432
documentary letter of credit, 433 439
documents of foreign trade, 428
  air waybills, 431
  bill of exchange, 429
  commercial invoice, 429
  insurance documentation, 430
dollar certificate of deposit, 84, 359
domestic credit expansion, 330
double coincidence of wants, 2
Drug Trafficking Offences Act 1986, 224

easement (*see* land)
effective rate of interest, 109
electronic banking, 276
electronic funds transfer, at point of sale
  (EFTPOS), 275
eligible bills, 81
eligible liabilities, 69, 115
encoding of cheques, 258
endowment
  policies, 152, 409
  repayment method, as, 477
Enduring Powers of Attorney Act 1985,
  234
equipment, and bank balance sheet, 112

equity
  capital, 523
  participation, 427
  redemption, of (*see* mortage)
Esberger and Son Ltd v. *Capital and
  Counties Bank* (1913), 600
estate (*see* land)
estate contract (*see* land)
Eurobonds, 84, 359
Eurocheque scheme 413
Eurocurrency
  market, 83, 356
  rates, 207
Eurodollars, 356
exchange
  control, 71
  equalisation account, 71
  rates, 365
  risks, 443
executors, 239, 240, 403
Export Credit Guarantee Dept. (ECGD),
  437
export factoring, 438
external convertability, 356

factoring, 421
  export, 438
farthing, 14
federal reserve banks, 356
fee simple (*see* land)
fiat money, 13, 26
fiduciary issue notes, 19
  control, 24
  development, 19, 23
  monetary policy and, 335
fiduciary relationship, 221
final accounts, 516–9
finance houses market, 82, 360
finance leases, 423
finance markets, 362
financial futures contracts, 369
financial intermediaries, 89
financial statements, 505–43,
  banks and, 531–43
  interpretation of, 519–31
  introduction to, 505–19
fineness of metal, 12
fiscal policy, 332
fixtures (*see* land)
floating debt, 340
foreclosure, 590–1
foreign currency, 417
foreign exchange markets, 362
  forward exchange, 444
  functions of, 362
  nature of, 367
forward exchange contracts, 369
freehold (*see* land)
frequency marking, 388
friendly societies, 156
funding, 70, 340

funds flow, 542–3
funds transfer, 53
fungibility, 7
futures contracts, 369

garnishee order, 231, 637
gearing, 530–1
going concern, 532
goldsmiths, 43
  receipts, 16
gone concern, 532–4
goodwill, 510
government stocks
  characteristics of, 171
  commercial banks and, 107
  discount houses and, 77
  National Savings Stock Register, 140
  purpose of, 65
Greenwood v. Martins Bank Ltd (1932), 639
Gresham's Law, 7
guarantee, 486, 488–9, 497–8, 578–9,
  595–9
guinea, 15

halfpenny, 14
Hedley Byrne & Co Ltd v. Heller Partners
  Ltd (1963), 449
hire purchase
  finance companies, 165
  loans on balance sheet, 515
home buyers, 149, 480–1
home improvement loans, 473
home loans, 476–8
house purchase loan rate, 209
household insurance policies, 410
Housing Act 1980, 554–5
hypothecation, 490–1

immediate annuity, 154
importers, services to, 439
income
  bonds, 137
  circular flow of, 128
  disposable, 123
  flow of national, 127
  units, 162
indemnity, 479, 488
  direct debits, 272
  letter of credit, 435
index linking
  index numbers, 36
  National Savings Certificates, 134
  SAYE contracts, 137
indirect exchange, 3
indorsement, 221, 293, 610, 611, 613, 616,
  618–9, 620, 635
  forged or unauthorised, 612, 616, 626,
    641–3, 644–5
  endorsee, 304–5, 612, 616
  endorser, 306, 307–8, 612, 614, 616–7,
    622

irregular, 619, 629
industrial assurance, 156
Industrial Revolution, 44
Infants Relief Act 1874, 236
inflation
  definition, 35
  demand led, 36
  monetary policy and, 333
inheritance tax, 404, 480
injuction, 231, 484, 637–8
Insolvency Act 1986, 231, 500, 536
institutional investors, 179
insurance
  broking, 409
  export shipments, 430
  travel, 416
  types of policy, 409
intagible assets, 510–1
itelligence reports, 450
inter-company market, 83, 361
inter-vivos settlements, 406
interbank sterling market, 82, 352
interest
  definition of, 184
  flat rate of, 109, 210
  interest bearing eligible liabilities
    (IBELS), 340
  nature of, 184
  notional interest, 98, 381
  pure interest, 190
interest rates, 90
  bank rate, 208
  base rate, 208
  definition of, 90
  deposit rate, 209
  determination of, 190
  differentials between, 191
  domestic rates, 208
  home loan rates, 209
  integrated view of, 201
  London inter-bank offered rate (LIBOR),
    354, 473
  minimum lending rate (MLR), 342
  money market rates, 206
  personal loan rates, 210
  structure of, 202
  true rates, 211, 384
  weapon of monetary control, 341
interests in land, 555–9
  equitable, 552, 556–9
  legal, 555–6
  minor, 558, 563
  overreaching of, 559
  overriding, 560–2, 588
  registrable, 560, 588
  registration and protection of, 558–9
international funds transfer, 277
International Monetary Fund (IMF), 330
international services 427
  collection of payments for exports, 428
  finance for exports, 435

international services (cont'd)
  foreign exchange services, 442
  merchanting, 446
  services to importers, 439
interpretation of accounts, 523–5
Interpretation Act 1978, 549
intrinsic value, 4, 6
Introductions Ltd v. *National Provincial
  Bank Ltd* (1970), 247, 248, 482
investment
  accounts, 383
  advice, 397
  definition, 126
  deposit account, 383
  funds, 185
  management, 399
  relationship with savings, 127
  trust, 163
invoices
  certified, 430
  commercial, 429
  consular, 430
  discounting, 422
irredeemable government stocks, 172
irrevocable letter of credit, 440
issuing house, 426

jobbers, 175
joint liability, 238
joint and several liability, 228–9, 240, 243,
    245, 469, 479, 480, 481, 596, 614
joint stock banks, 20, 45

Kendall v. *Hamilton* (1879), 238

land
  abstract of title to, 569
  defind, 549–50
  easement, 556, 560
  estate contract, 557
  estates in, 550, 551–5
  fixtures, 550
  freehold, 547, 548, 550, 551–2, 569–73
  interest in (*see* interests in land)
  land certificate (*see* Land Certificate)
  leasehold, 490, 547, 548, 550, 552–5, 573
  mortgate of (*see also* mortgage), 580–93
  ownership of, 550–68
  profits à prendre, 556, 560
  registered, 558, 573, 580, 587, 588
  registered title to, 567–8
  registration of title to, 559–68,
  rentcharge, 556
  restrictive covenant, 557, 563
  right of entry, 556
  as security, 494–5
  tenure, 550
  title deeds, 569, 573
  title to, 568–73
  transfer of title to, 568–73
  unregistered, 492, 558, 559, 563,
    569–73, 580, 587

Land Certificate, 563, 567, 573, 580, 588
  deposit of, 580, 584, 588
  notice of deposit of, 563, 588
Land Charges Acts 1925 and 1972, 558,
    559, 563
Land Registration Act 1925, 560, 561
Land Registry, 561, 573, 580, 587
  Charges Register, 558, 560, 563, 580,
    587, 588
  Property Register, 563
  Proprietorship Register, 563
Landlord and Tenant Act 1954, 554, 555
Law of Property Act 1925, 228, 490, 492,
    548, 551, 553, 554, 555, 580
  s. 40, 569
  s. 52, 569
  s. 103, 589
Law of Property Act 1979, 555
Law Reform (Contributory Negligence) Act
    1945, 630
leads and lags, 366
leasehold (*see* land)
Leasehold Reform Act 1967, 554
leaseholds enfranchisement, 554
leasing 423
legal tender, 35
lender of the last resort, 70
lending, principles of, 110, 456–65
lending ratio, 110
letters of administration, 239
letters of credit
  back to back, 447
  circular, 416
  documentary, 433, 439
  prime, 447
liabilities
  capital, 513
  current, 507, 514–6, 525, 537
  liability provisions, 514
  medium and long, 514
  reserves, 512–3
liabilities of banks, 92
  current liabilities, 97
  eligible, 115
  medium and long term, 95
  shareholders funds, 93
libel, 640–1
lien, 222, 491, 588, 635
life policies, 492, 577–8
  assignment of, 577–8
  insurable interest, 577
  legal mortgage of, 493, 494–5
  savings medium, as, 150
  security, as, 496–7
  types of policy, 409
  uberrima fides, 497
Limitation Act 1980, 293
liquidator, 601
liquidity 511
  business, 524
  commercial bank, of, 89
  monetary controls and, 114

liquidity (cont'd)
  preference curve, 200
  preference theory, 197
  prudential control of, 113
  ratios, 338, 525–31
listed securities, 173
'little six', 48
Lloyds Bank v. *Bundy* (1975), 221–2, 597
Lloyds Bank v. *EB Savory and Company*
  (1932), 632
loan accounts
  attributes, 384
  currency loans, 447
  effect on balance sheet, 537–40
  home, 476–8
loan capital 531
  balance sheet, on, 515–6, 531
  banks, of, 95
  company loan stocks, 171
loanable funds theory of interest, 191
local authorities 164
  bills, 351
  deposits, 82
  loans, 164, 352
  market, 82, 349
  stocks, 165
  yearly bonds, 164
local land charges, 587
London inter-bank offered rate (LIBOR),
  354, 473
London International Financial Futures
  Exchange (LIFFE), 369
London Joint Stock Bank Ltd v.
  Macmillan and Arthur (1918), 223,
  630, 640

magnetic characters, 256
mainframe computers, 112
manufacturing account, 516
Marfani and Co Ltd v. *Midland Bank Ltd*
  (1968), 630–1
market makers, 175
marketing financial services, 376
Marquis of Bute v. *Barclays Bank Ltd*
  (1955), 633
marriage settlements, 406
married women, as customers, 236–7
mastercard, 389
maturity transformation, 53, 110
Maxfor SpA v. *Mariani and Goodville Ltd*
  (1979), 249
medium and long term liabilities, 514
memorandum of association (*see*
  companies)
memorandum of deposit, 580, 584, 588,
  593, 595
Mercantile Credit Ltd v. *Garrod* (1962),
  242
merchant banks, 55, 425
merchanting, 446
Metropolitan Police Commissioner v.
  Charles (1976), 303

Midland Bank v. *Reckitt* (1933), 215, 633
milled edges, 13
minimum lending rate (MLR), 68
minors
  bank accounts of, 235–6
  borrowing by, 478–9
  consumer credit and, 467
  contractual capacity of, 478–9
  customers, as, 235–6
  minors' Contracts Act 1987, 236, 479
monetarism, view of inflation, 35
monetary policy, 35
  economic controls, 331
  instruments of policy, 335
  monetary controls, 320
  objectives, 315
money
  aggregates, 33, 321
  attributes of, 5
  banknotes, 16
  changes in value, 35
  coinage, 9
  legal tender, 35
  near money, 33
  need for, 3
  origins of, 2
  today, 27
money markets, 71, 348
  accepting houses, 79
  certificates of deposit, 359
  classical, 74, 348
  discount market, 74, 348
  Eurocurrency market, 83, 356
  finance houses market, 82, 360
  inter-company market, 83, 361
  interbank sterling market, 82, 352
  local authority, 82, 349
  parallel, 74, 81, 348
money supply, 315
  deposits and, 328
  domestic credit expansion and, 330
  interest rates and, 341
  measurement of, 32, 320
  near money, 33
  private sector liquidity, 34
  quantity theory of, 316
moneylenders, 43
Moneylenders Act 1900, 216
Monopolies Commission, 49
moral suasion, 343
mortgage, 561, 563, 569
  defined, 489–90
  equitable, 481, 490, 492, 495, 580–4, 588
  equity of redemption, 557, 592–3
  legal, 478, 490, 492, 494, 551, 556, 580,
    588
  mortgagee, 489, 492, 589, 591, 592, 600
  mortgagor, 489, 591, 592
  protection of, 587–8
  protection policy, 409
  puisne, 558–9, 588
  registered land, of, 587–8

mortgage, (cont'd)
  remedies of a mortgagee, 588–92
  second, 494, 580
  taking a bank, 584–8
  unregistered land, of, 492, 587–8
motor insurance, 410
multiplier effect, 29
mutual institutions, 156

National Debt, 65
National Giro Bank, 54, 143
national insurance contributions, 157
National Provincial Bank v. *Brackenbury*
  (1906), 596
National Savings, 132
  Certificates, 133
  Stock Register, 576
near money, 33
negligence, 219, 298
negotiable instruments (*see also* bills of
    exchange, cheques, promissory notes,
    banknotes, Treasury bills, certificates
    of deposit, dividend warrants, bearer
    securities), 284, 308, 577
  legal characteristics of, 608
  main types, 286
  negotiability, 618, 625
  negotiation, 287, 292–3, 578
net worth, 523–4, 531
new issues, 172, 426
nominee companies, 397
notary public, 430
notes and coins, 15
Nu-Stilo Footwear Ltd v. *Lloyds Bank Ltd*
  (1956), 633

objects clause (*see* companies)
occupational pensions, 159
offer price, 161
offer for sale, 175
Office of Fair Trading, 466
open account trading, 431
open market operations, 68, 336
operating leases, 423
overdrafts, 380, 458
overtrading, 523

packing list, 431
paper money, 15
par value, 167
parallel money market, 74, 81
partnership, 242–5
  accounts of, 244–5
  borrowing by, 482
  guarantees and, 596
  liability of partners, 243
  partners as agents, 242–3
  trading, 243
Partnership Act 1890, 242
payments abroad, 277
pension funds, 157

performance bonds, 451
personal loans, 384, 459
personal pension plans, 159
personal representatives, 239–41, 403
  borrowing by, 479–80
placing, 174
pledge, 490, 495, 594
Policies or Assurance Act 1867,
portfolio planning, 399
power of attorney, 227, 233–4
Power of Attorney Act 1971, 233, 241
premium savings bond, 136
private sector liquidity, 34
probate, 239
produce advances, 441
productivity of capital, 187
profit
  gross, 528–9
  net, 529
  ratios, 528–30
profit and loss account, 505, 513, 518–9
profit and loss appropriation account, 519
profits *à prendre* (*see* land)
promissory note, 308–9, 491, 645
property
  choses in action, 285–6, 291, 547, 549
  choses in possession, 285–6, 548, 549
  real and personal, 547–9
proprietors' stake, 530
Public Sector Borrowing Requirements
  (PSBR), 331
Public Works Loan Board, 350

qualitative controls on bank lending, 343
quantitative controls on bank lending, 343
quantity theory of money, 316
quick ratio, 526

R. v. *Lambie* (1981), 303
R v. *Navvabi* (1986), 303
Raphael and Another v. *Bank of England*
  (1885), 611
ratios, accounting, 525–31
receiver, 590, 601
redemption yield, 187
reflation, 333
Register of Land Charges, 559
Registration of Business Names Act 1916,
  244
regulator, the, 344
remittance of funds, 254
rentcharge (*see* land)
Rentcharges Act 1977, 556
reserves
  balance sheet, on, 513–4
  foreign currency, 26
  gold, 26
restrictive covenant (*see* land)
Retail Prices Index, 36
revocable letter of credit, 440
rights issue, 174, 427

Romalpa Clause, 499
Rose Noble, 15
Royal Mint, 16, 26
run on the bank, 20
running yield, 187

safe custody, 219–20, 239, 396, 491
Sale of Goods Act 1979, 549
savings
  attractions of, 125
  definition of, 122
  media, 124
  motives for, 123
  National Savings, 131
  relationship with investment, 127
  sources of, 130
  uses of, 131
secondary banking, 110
securities
  bearer, 311, 577
  registered, 576–7
Securities and Investment Board, 179
security, 461–2
  arrangements, 487–8
  personal representatives and, 246
  principles of taking, 492–4
  purpose of, 485–7
  reasons for taking, 462
  taking property as, 579–602
  third party, 493
  types of, 494–500
Sepon Ltd, 176, 576
settlement day, 178
Sex Discrimination Act 1975, 236, 237,
  598, 633
shares,
  bearer securities, 495, 577
  deferred, 170
  mortgage of, 495, 593–4
  ordinary, 170
  partly paid, 495
  preference, 169
  private companies, in, 496
  security as, 495–6
  transfer of title to, 576–7
  unquoted, 496
special deposits, 69, 106, 117, 339
special drawing rights (SDRs), 359
specific performance, 591
spot currency, 368
Standard Chartered Bank Ltd v. *Walker
  and Another* (1982), 601
standing order, 234–5, 269
statement of account, 381
status enquiries, 447
Statute of Frauds 1677, 488
sterling certificates of deposit, 360
Stock Exchange, 576
  bank services, 395
  functions, 167
  procedures, 175

stock market, 166
stock transfer form, 176, 576
stock turnover, 528
subrogation, 479, 484
supplementary benefits, 157
supplementary special deposits, 118, 340
SWIFT, 279
Talisman transfer form, 176, 576
tangible assets, 508, 510
target markets, 377
taxation advice, 407
temporary policies, 151, 409
tenant, 555
tender guarantees, 451
tenure (*see* land)
term of years absolute (*see* land)
terms of trade, 429
Theft Act 1968.
token coins, 12
tort, 219
Tournier v. *National Bank of England*
  (1924), 224
tracing order, 484
trade marks, 511
trading accounts 516–8
travel services, 411
travellers cheques, 411, 645
Treasury, 343
treasury bills, 66, 309
  discount houses and, 76
  purchases of, 395
  rate,
trust, 241, 552
  account of, 241
  discretionary, 406
  funds, 241
  ministerial, 406
  will, 405
Trustcard, 389
Trustee Act 1925, 241
Trustee Savings Bank, 51
trustees, 241
  bank as, 407
  borrowing by, 480
turnover, 524–5, 528–9
Turquand's Case (1856), 485

undue influence, 597–8
Unfair Contract Terms Act 1977, 219
unit trusts, 161, 400, 576, 594
United Dominions Trust v. *Kirkwood*
  (1966), 216
United Overseas Bank v. *Jiwani* (1976),
  232
unlisted securities, 173
unpaid cheques, 263

velocity of circulation, 317
Visacard, 144, 1389

whole life policies, 151, 409

wholesale money markets, 349
Williams & Glyn's Bank v. *Barnes* (1980), 222
Williams & Glyn's Bank v. *Boland* (1980), 561–2, 587
with profits policies, 154
withdrawal funds, 403

Woods v. *Martins Bank Ltd* (1959), 397
working capital, 524, 525
  advances, 538
  on balance sheet, 524
  changes to, 538–40
  ratio, 525